1 MONTH OF
FREE
READING

at

www.ForgottenBooks.com

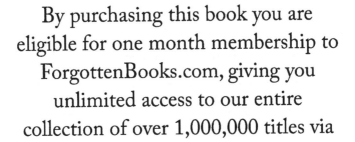

By purchasing this book you are eligible for one month membership to ForgottenBooks.com, giving you unlimited access to our entire collection of over 1,000,000 titles via our web site and mobile apps.

To claim your free month visit:
www.forgottenbooks.com/free149189

ISBN 978-0-365-12897-7
PIBN 10149189

ST. GEORGE AND PLANTAGENET EARL OF LANCASTER.

(*Bodleian Library, Oxford.*)

[*Frontis.*

𝕬 𝕽𝖊𝖈𝖔𝖗𝖉 𝖔𝖋 𝖙𝖍𝖊 𝕻𝖗𝖔𝖌𝖗𝖊𝖘𝖘 𝖔𝖋 𝖙𝖍𝖊 𝕻𝖊𝖔𝖕𝖑𝖊 -

RELIGION, LAWS, LEARNING, ARTS, INDUSTRY, COMMERCE, SCIENCE, LITERATURE AND MANNERS, FROM THE EARLIEST TIMES TO THE PRESENT DAY

EDITED BY

SOMETIME FELLOW OF ST. JOHN'S COLLEGE, OXFORD

AND

SOMETIME FELLOW OF TRINITY COLLEGE, OXFORD

VOLUME II.

A Record of the Progress of the People

In Religion, Laws, Learning, Arts, Industry, Commerce, Science, Literature and Manners, from the Earliest Times to the Present Day

EDITED BY

H. D. TRAILL. D.C.L.

SOMETIME FELLOW OF ST. JOHN'S COLLEGE, OXFORD

AND

MANN, M.A.

SOMETIME FELLOW OF TRINITY COLLEGE, OXFORD

Volume II.

CA   AND COLLANTS. LIMITED

LONDON, PARIS, NEW YORK & MELBOURNE.—MCMII

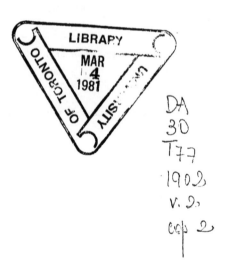
First Edition *June* 1894.
Reprinted October 1894, 1897.
Illustrated Edition, 1902.

CONTENTS.

CHAPTER V.

THE CONSOLIDATION OF THE KINGDOM. 1274-1348.

CHAPTER VI.

THE BLACK DEATH, AND AFTERWARDS. 1348-1399.

CHAPTER VII.

THE CLOSE OF THE MIDDLE AGES. 1399-1485.

CHAPTER VIII.

THE BEGINNINGS OF MODERN ENGLAND. 1485-1509.

NOTES TO ILLUSTRATIONS.

VOLUME II.

—→⊧·⊧←—

the Templars. The story, as told by Camden in his *Britannia*, is that D'Estoreville, the lord of the Castle, having oppressed the hermit St. Robert (whose hermitage still exists not far off), a knight in armour appeared to him in a dream and challenged him to a duel. St. Robert died in 1216.

The original Round Church, built on the model of the Holy Sepulchre at Jerusalem, was completed in 1185, the choir added in 1240. The whole was restored—not conservatively—in 1839-42. The Templars' estate, on the suppression of the Order, was granted by the king to Aymer de Valence. Earl of Pembroke, on whose death it passed to the Hospitallers of St. John, who leased it to the students of common law in 1346. For some centuries it was subjected to a tax, but in 1609 was declared by royal decree the free hereditary property of the Corporations of the Middle and Inner Temple. The church is common to both.

From a kind of cyclopædia of Church teaching, in two volumes, compiled by one Jacob, probably a Benedictine monk. This illustration is appended to the article on " Abuses."

From same MS.; illustrates the article on "Fratres Mendicantes" (begging friars). The lady appears to be giving title-deeds of property to the friar. The author is most unfavourable to the friars, and declares that they do not keep their vows of labour and poverty.

Walter de Stapledon, Bishop of Exeter and founder of Exeter College, Oxford, was murdered by the populace of London in 1326, as an adherent of Edward II. The canopy is restored in part.

The choir and nave probably date from before 1250. the west front before 1270. It is still a parish church as well as a cathedral. It has been well restored.

From an ancient stained glass window on the north side of Long Melford Church, Suffolk, containing the figures of William Haward [Howard], Chief Justice of the Common Pleas in Edward I.'s reign, John Haugh, Judge of the same Court in 1487, and Richard Pycot [Piggot], admitted Serjeant-at-law 1464. Haward is here figured, Pyoot and Haugh will be found at page 649. This glass seems to have been given by one of the Clopton family, to whose ancestors the personages in question were related, and whose monuments are also in the church. They are figured in Dugdale, *Origines Juris*, and in Pulling, *Order of the Coif*, as illustrating the dress of a serjeant-at-law. The illustration is from a photograph taken by the kind permission of the Rev. Sir W. Hyde Parker, of Long Melford, from drawings in his possession.

The tomb of John de Stonore, Chief Justice of the Common Pleas, who died in 1354; Dorchester Church, Oxfordshire.

For this and the next two illustrations *see* above, note on p. 39.

and a towel : the inscription, restored in part conjecturally, seems
to refer to the combined effect on the injury of prayer, bloodletting,
and medicine. In the third, a woman with her leg bare is about
to kneel at the tomb. The inscription, conjecturally restored, is
of the same tenor as the preceding. In the fourth, a man half
dressed is receiving clothes from another, conjectured to be Godwin
of Boxgrove, who gave away his clothes to set an example of
voluntary poverty. *Cf. Notes on the Painted Glass in Canterbury
Cathedral*, with a Preface by Dean Farrar. The illustration is
from a photograph taken by the Rev. T. Field, D.D., Warden of
Radley College.

h

to a charity at Stogursey, the two outer ones to a neighbouring farm Hedges occur between different sets of banks, but generally parallel to one or other set, probably following the line of some former bank. The banks are carefully preserved, and may not be ploughed up even where several adjacent strips are held by the same owner. According to R. E. Prothero, *Pioneers and Progress of English Farming*, p. 7, the common cultivation seems to have been still carried on in 1879, but according to the two-field, not the three-field, system of farming (*see* our text, p. 136). For the photograph and description the Editor is indebted to Miss E. M. Leonard.

Queen Mary's Psalter (*see* note to Vol. I., p. 543), primarily representing Ruth and Boaz.

From a Psalter of the late thirteenth or early fourteenth century, illustrated by Norman artists. The sower illustrates the occupation proper to September.

The inscription contains the name of York, and the word CUSTUME.

See above. note on p. 139.

Probably erected originally in the thirteenth century as the town hall of Yarmouth; subsequently a prison and the scene of the labours of Sarah Martin, one of Mrs. Fry's followers in modern prison visiting, *c.* 1819–1832; now a Free Library.

Carvings (from a destroyed church ?) in the Archæological Museum. Cambridge ; fourteenth century.

Built about 1274, at the cost of the citizens of Norwich, as part of the reparation they were required to make for attacking and plundering the monastery during a quarrel in 1272 as to their rights over Tombland, a cemetery (then disused) just outside the gate, and still preserving its ancient name. The upper part, which was reconstructed early in the nineteenth century, replaces a chapel of St. Ethelbert, King of East Anglia, who was killed near Hereford by command of Offa of Mercia, and whose shrine existed in Hereford Cathedral.

On the lower margin of a page of Geoffrey of Monmouth's *History of the Kings of Britain.*

See above. note on p. 154.

Hardyng's Chronicle, after mentioning the plague in 1361, says:
"In that same year was on Saint Maury's Day
The grete wind and earthquake mervelous."
Mr. Wilson ascribes the inscription to the parish priest of Ashwell.
Most of these at that time seem to have been monks of Westminster.
and the Abbot and twenty-six of the brethren died of the plague.
A slightly different and less satisfactory explanation will be found
in Cussans, *History of Herefordshire.*

This inscription, the translation of which (printed underneath
it) is that given by Dr. O'Donovan in the introduction to the
Senchus Mor, the great collection of ancient Irish laws, attributed
to St. Patrick and eight other authors, about the year 460. gives
vivid idea of the impression produced in Ireland by the Black Death.
This is even more vividly presented by the conclusion of another
contemporary account, that of the friar of Kilkenny (John Clyn),
mentioned in the text (p. 185). Writing as one "among the dead
and waiting for death," he says that he has left parchment for
the continuation of his annals, "if any of the human race survive."
He seems to have lived, however, till 1349. Hugh MacEagan's
prayer was answered, for the *Annals of the Four Masters* mention
his death in 1359. and describe him as "the choicest of all the
Brehons of Ireland" (*cf.* Introduction to the edition of the *Senchus
Mor*, brought out by the Commissioners for Publishing the Ancient
Laws of Ireland, Vol. I., p. 34).

The full text is in the *Statutes of the Realm*, Vol. I., p. 307.

Ascribed to his reign in Birch, *Index of Seals in the British
Museum*. The inscription mentions Lincoln.

From reproductions of fresco paintings found in 1800 behind
panelling in St. Stephen's Chapel. Westminster (used as the House
of Commons and burnt down in 1834). Copies were taken and
the pictures walled up again. There are also figures of Edward III.'s
sons and daughters, of whom Isabella alone is shown here. The
inclusion of Edward's youngest son, Thomas of Woodstock, born
1355, shows that the painting was later than that date. The figures
were directed to the high altar, and scenes from the early chapters
of St. Matthew were represented above them.

The first chapter of the Proverbs ("paraboles") of Solomon.

"There he lies, as he had directed, in full armour. his head resting on his helmet, his feet with the likeness of 'the spurs he won'
at Cressy, his hands joined as in that last prayer which he had
offered up on his deathbed. There you can see his fine face, with
the Plantagenet features, the flat cheeks, and the well-chiselled
nose, to be traced, perhaps, in the effigy of his father in Westminster
Abbey, and his grandfather in Gloucester Cathedral. . . High above
are suspended the brazen gauntlets. the helmet. with what was
once its gilded leopard-crest, and the wooden shield : the velvet
coat also, embroidered with the arms of France and England. now
tattered and colourless, but then blazing with blue and scarlet.

in England early in the fifteenth century.   As is often the case
in MSS., the armour is of an earlier type.

See below on p. 247 (No. I. fig. 1).   The exigencies of space in the
MS. have so contracted the height of the drawing, which is on the
lower margin of a page of the MS., that the machine as depicted
would be unworkable.

According to Prof. Oman, the springald was a modification of the
original balista or catapult, working by tension, which came to
the front again in the thirteenth century and was largely used by
the Emperor Frederick II. in his Italian wars.   "About the end of
the century it receives the new name of springal (espringale).
and is found mounted on wheels and used in battle as a sort of
light movable artillery.   It was nothing more than a large arbalest
(or crossbow) whose cord was pulled back by winches."   Oman,
History of the Art of War (Middle Ages), p. 545.   For the MS. *see*
below on p. 247 (the first).

From a magnificently illuminated fifteenth-century MS. of the
St. Albans' Chronicle at Lambeth Library.   The armour and
costumes are of that period.   The MS. contains the autographs of
John, Lord Lumley and Henry Fitzalan, Lord Arundel, the former
of whom had obtained the collection of MSS. made by the latter
when the monasteries were dissolved.   At his death it was secured
for the Royal library by Henry, Prince of Wales. son of James I.
Kershaw, *Catalogue of the MSS. at Lambeth*, p. 58 *seq.*

From the "Millimete MS.,' Christ Church, Oxford: a very beautiful illustrated MS. treatise on the dignities and functions of a
king, written by Walter de Millimete, an ecclesiastic, and presented
by him to Edward III., probably on his accession. as it is dated
1326.   It is noticeable that the missile represented is a bolt, not a
ball. a circumstance which brings the cannon into close relation
with the balista, particularly as a crossbow firing the same kind
of arrow-bolt is shown in the same MS.   For this information
the Editor is indebted to Mr. T. A. Archer.

The first is from MS. Canonici Misc. 378: a fifteenth-century
MS., one of those collected by the Venetian Canonici. who died
in 1805, and acquired by the Bodleian.   The second is from the
travels of Marco Polo, in MS. Bodl. 264.   This MS. contains (1) the
Romance of Alexander, and associated romances, in old French
verse; (2) the fragment of an Alexander-romance in English
alliterative verse; (3) the travels of Marco Polo in French.   A
note in a fifteenth-century hand at the end says that the MS. was
bought in London on New Year's Day. 1466, by Richart de Wideuielle,
i.e. Earl Rivers, father-in-law of Edward IV.   The writing of
Part I. was ended December 18th, 1338; its illumination was finished
April 18th. 1344, by Jehan de Grise. who was a Fleming, and almost
certainly lived at Bruges.   Parts II. and III. were written in the
first half of the fifteenth century, apparently by a single hand.
Part II. is in West Midland dialect.   For this information the Editor
is indebted to Mr. E. W. B. Nicholson, Bodley's Librarian.

and armed only with a huge axe, entered the hall, and offered to let any man deal him a stroke with the axe on condition that he might return the blow. Sire Gawain accepted the challenge on King Arthur's behalf, and cut off the head of the stranger, who thereupon held it up and charged Gawain to meet him a year hence at "the Green Chapel." He then rode off, and the knights went on with their feast, conversing much over the marvel. On All Hallows Day of the succeeding year, Sire Gawain started to seek the Green Chapel, which was in the peninsula of Wirral, in Cheshire, where few good men lived. On his way he found splendid entertainment at a magnificent castle, where the lady made love to him while her husband was at the chase. Twice he resisted her, the third time he accepted her girdle as a love-token. Then he went to his encounter at the Green Chapel. The Green Knight's axe, however, severed only his skin, inasmuch as he had twice resisted temptation and yielded only so far as to accept a love-token. His antagonist then explained to him that the whole adventure was a device of the fairy Morgana, Arthur's half-sister, to warn Queen Guinevere. The poem, which exists only in this MS., was edited by Sir F. Madden for the Bannatyne Club in 1830, and by Mr. E. E. Morris for the Early English Text Society in 1864, from whose Introduction the above version is condensed.

The child is, of course, in heaven, and describes some of its splendours to her father, who afterwards recognises her as one of the virgins in a 'procession in honour of the Lamb. This romance, together with "Cleanness" (Chastity) and "Patience" (*see* text), all three from the same unique MS., has been edited by Dr. Richard Morris for the Early English Text Society, 1864.

According to Skeat (*Chaucer's Works*, Vol. I., p. 59), "probably the only one which can be accepted as authentic." He quotes Sir Harris Nicolas's description : "The figure, which is half-length, has a background of green tapestry. He is represented with grey hair and beard, which is biforked ; he wears a dark-coloured dress and hood : his right hand is extended, and in his left he holds a string of beads. From his vest a black case is suspended, which appears to contain a knife, or possibly a 'penner' or pencase. . . . Evident marks of advanced age appear on the countenance." The general opinion seems to be that the case contains a penknife, "useful for making erasures" (Skeat). As Occleve "had this portrait made," as stated in the accompanying text, it has the best claim to be considered authentic. Others mentioned by Skeat are : Chaucer on horseback, as one of the pilgrims, in the Ellesmere MS. (*see* on p. 291), and later ones, not authentic, in MS. Sloane 5141, and on wood in the Bodleian. There is also one in the National Portrait Gallery. For two others, *see* p. 287 and note.

From MS. 686, Bodleian Library, Oxford ; described by Skeat (No. 14) as "a neat MS. with illuminations," of the A type, of which the Ellesmere text is the best example. The portrait of Chaucer, compared with the others extant, may indicate that the likeness was traditional. A portrait in a similar position exists in MS. Lansdowne 851.

From the famous Ellesmere MS., which belonged to the Duke of

Bridgewater, of canal fame, and is now in the possession of the Earl of Ellesmere. The figures are the work of two artists, one of whom places them on a base. His drawing is the less satisfactory, according to Mr. W. A. Hooper, who copied the figures for the Six-text edition published by the Chaucer Society. The MS., on vellum, of the fifteenth century, is regarded by Dr. Furnivall and Mr. Skeat as the best of the known MSS. of the Tales.

From a MS. of the fifteenth century, containing the books from the Proverbs to the Apocalypse inclusive, with a calendar of the Gospels and Epistles after the Sarum use. It belonged to Humphrey, Duke of Gloucester.

The earliest portrait of the reformer to which a date can be assigned is an engraving in Bale, *Illustrium Majoris Britanniae Scriptorium Summarium*, 1548. The figure has his hand on a Bible which rests on a balustrade, and this and the background are Renaissance in character. The next, attributed to Antonio Moro, is at Wycliffe-ou-Tees Rectory, and was probably painted before 1554. The portrait given, by the kind permission of the Earl of Denbigh, is on panel, and certainly of considerable antiquity. Copies exist at Balliol College, Oxford, and at Lutterworth Rectory, and it may be regarded as the least unauthentic. Another, more conventional in treatment, is at Knole ; while a fifth, the most graphic of all, is at King's College, Cambridge. It is not at present regarded by the College as certainly a representation of Wycliffe, but it was engraved as such by Faber in 1715. He painted several portraits of founders of colleges, and perhaps this also ; and his plate, retouched by Houston, was published in a series of portraits of Reformers in 1759. The late Mr. L. Sergeant detected in it a likeness to Bale's portrait, and thought the latter might have been based on a sketch discovered by Bale (a great collector of MSS.) in his researches. *See* his *Life of Wycliffe*, p. 305.

The name of the translator will be noticed.

The MS. of the *Wyket*, the most famous of his tracts, is lost. The page given is from MS. Harl. 2385, a collection of tracts, many of them deliberately mutilated. The *De Dominio Divino* exists in MS. at Trinity College, Dublin. Other MSS. of Wycliffe's works are in the Douce collection at the Bodleian.

Miniatures from a Douce MS. of the latest version, or " C-text," of Piers the Plowman, dating from the fifteenth century. That of Pride seems to be meant for a portrait of Purnele Proud-herte, who represents that deadly sin in the text ; but Langland himself regarded her as a female. The other illustrates a quotation of Solomon's words, " He who spareth the rod, hateth his son."

In the quatrain above, which is in Latin elegiac verse, the poet declares that he shoots his arrows at the world, but the just remain unharmed by them ; and he exhorts mankind to search their own hearts accordingly.

a century later; the Halles were erected during the same period. but altered in the sixteenth century. Part of the building was originally intended for a cloth-market.

That of Lincoln represents the Virgin crowned, carrying the Holy Child, and standing on a woolsack; that of Southampton, which may possibly belong to the thirteenth century, a leopard's face in a rosette, with small roses and fleurs de lis; that of Boston, St. Botolph, the patron saint of the town, standing behind a wool-pack, with his pastoral staff and book.

Built by Sir Thomas Erpingham (who fought at Agincourt), possibly as a thankoffering; the arms of both his wives appear upon it, and the date is thus fixed as subsequent to 1411. The seated figures on the buttresses represent ecclesiastics; the kneeling figure under the canopy above is that of Sir Thomas himself.

According to tradition, this cup was presented to the town by King John, but the costume of the figures belongs to the succeeding century, and it has been conjectured to be the gift of King John of France during his captivity; he may have accompanied King Edward III. and Queen Philippa on one of their progresses— possibly that commemorated by the illustration on p. 347, during which he was entertained. *Cf.* Cripps, *Old English Plate*, p. 300. It holds half a pint and weighs 73 ounces, and is 15 inches high; it has a cover, and is enriched with enamels. It is described by Cripps as "the most remarkable specimen of the goldsmiths' work of its period."

In 1373 Bristol was made a county by itself, and this sword, some of the ornamentation of which is of the fourteenth century, may have been given by Edward III. at the time.

This horn was presented by John Goldcorne to the Guild of Corpus Christi at Cambridge about the year 1347, and eventually passed to Corpus Christi College, which was founded by that Guild and the Guild of the Virgin in 1352. The horn is that of a buffalo; part of the mounting is of Elizabeth's reign. It is 24½ inches long and 4½ inches wide at the lip. *Cf.* Atkinson and Bowes, *Catalogue of the Loan Exhibition of Plate in the Fitzwilliam Museum.*

From the lower borders of brasses in St. Margaret's Church. Lynn, Norfolk, in memory of Adam de Walsoken. 1349, and Robert Braunche and his wives, 1374. The upper one resembles in its character the illustrations of the famous MS. of the Decretals, Royal 10 E. iv., from which our illustrations of the Legend of Theophilus and others have been taken (Birch and Jenner, *Index to Illustrated MSS. in the British Museum*, Introduction). The lower one may possibly represent the feast at which King John of France was present (*see* on p. 346). The two have been described by the well-known antiquary. Mr. Walter Rye. as "the two finest memorial brasses in England." Our illustrations are taken from the Hutchison

organ. sometimes made to fold up to the size of a large Bible. A single regal (like that shown), with the player, is represented in a stone carving in Beverley Minster, a doub e regal in Melrose Cathedral; an example with peculiar keys is in a painting by Melazzo da Forli in the National Gallery (Engel, *op. cit.*). The term was also applied to an " instrument of percussion with sonorous slabs of wood." The jugglers, two of whom appear to be monkeys. are from the Tenison Psalter of the fourteenth century. For the other MSS. *see* notes on p. 247. and Vol. I., p. 642.

THE MINSTRELS' GALLERY, EXETER CATHEDRAL 364

The instruments are identified by Mr. Carl Engel (*op. cit*) as : 1, Cittern ; 2, Bagpipe ; 3, Clarion, a small. shrill trumpet ; 4, Rebec ; 5, Psaltery ; 6, Syrinx ; 7, Sackbut ; 8, Regals ; 9, Gittern, a small guitar strung with catgut ; 10. Shalm, a pipe with a reed in the mouth-hole ; 11, Timbrel, like a modern tambourine with a double row of gingles ; 12, Cymbals.

DAUGHTER OF HERODIAS DANCING 366

" Queen Mary's Psalter " : *see* note on Vol. I., p. 543. A still more startling representation of the same scene exists in a Flemish MS. of a work on the interpretation of Scripture (MS. Harl., 1527).

" LONG HOURS OF IDLENESS HAD TO BE FILLED SOMEHOW " . 367

From the great MS. of the Alexander Romance in the Bodleian (*see ante* on p. 247).

PRIEST (WITH PARDON), BEGGAR, PALMER AND HERMIT . . . 371

Three of these are from the MS. of Piers Plowman. referred to in the note on p. 309. The first is the travelling priest who takes Piers' pardon and reads it to him. - .

CHAPEL AT HOUGHTON, NORFOLK, ON THE ROAD TO WALSINGHAM . 375

Fourteenth century : now restored under Roman Catholic auspices. There is a local tradition that the pilgrims used to take off their shoes here and perform the rest of the journey (a mile) to the shrine barefoot.

PILGRIMS' SIGNS, FROM THE GUILDHALL MUSEUM 377

St. Thomas Becket is represented on the extreme left on horseback and in the brooch in the centre. The ampulla or little flask may be from Rheims, but miracle-working water was often brought away from shrines (as to-day from Bari). The cockle-shell is from S. Jago di Compostella. To this day, children in London streets build little houses of oyster-shells, and ask the passer-by to "remember the grotto" with a small coin—a survival of the medieval practice of pilgrimage to the Spanish shrine. *Cf.* Chambers, *Book of Days,* I., p. 334, and on the subject generally, Wright, *Archæological Album ; Archæologia*, XXXVIII., 128 *seq.*, *Journal of Brit. Archæol. Assoc.*, I ; and Roach. *Collectanea Antiqua.*

BOYS' WHIPPING TOPS 380
For the MS. *see* note on p. 247.

SEAL OF HENRY IV. 383

The shields of arms in the panels of the plinth on the obverse are those of the Duchy of Cornwall. Wales, and Chester. The saints in the niches are St. George and St. Edmund, St. Michael, and St. Edward the Confessor, the latter with a palm-branch.

his intention is to write an abridgment of the Great Chronicle [of John of Fordun], adding events of his own time, "together with some other wonderful doings which I who write have known, seen, and heard out of this country ; as also about a certain marvellous maid who brought about the recovery of the Kingdom of France out of the hands of the tyrant Henry King of England, and whom I saw and knew, and in whose company I was; I was present during her endeavours for the said recovery up to her life's end." The chapter in which the .fulfilment of this promise is begun is interrupted, probably by the author's death. The work exists in several MSS., and has been edited by Mr. Felix J. H. Skene in the *Historians of Scotland* series. From his edition the above particulars are derived, but he is in error in stating that the passage given is not in the Bodleian MS. The passage is of interest, in view of the repeated attempts of French critics to destroy and reconstruct the received story of the Maid of Orleans. Pluscarden Priory is not far from Elgin in Scotland.

This was part of the castle built by Philip Augustus in 1205 ; the Maid was examined here during her trial. The tower, which had become part of an Ursuline convent, was purchased by subscription about forty years ago and presented to the town of Rouen.

His fourth seal, used in 1425. Its counterseal is dated at Paris.

From a MS. of the Chroniques d'Angleterre, executed in France late in the fifteenth century.

Cardinal Beaufort re-founded and enlarged St. Cross Hospital.

That on the left is the tomb of William, "the Fox," beheaded off Dover (p. 418); the others are those of his son and grandson.

A castle has existed here since the middle of the sixth century, when it was built by Ida, King of Northumbria. It was besieged by Penda, King of Mercia ; demolished by the Danes ; besieged by and surrendered to William Rufus ; and taken by Margaret of Anjou in 1463. The keep is Norman.

Built by Robert de Montgomery under William the Conqueror ; besieged by Stephen ; held by Richard, Duke of York, in the Wars of the Roses. and taken by Henry VI. It was the residence of the young King Edward V. for some time, till removed to the Tower by Richard III., and afterwards of Prince Arthur, son of Henry VII., and first husband of Katherine of Aragon. It was held for the king and surrendered to the Parliamentary forces in the Civil Wars.

An indenture of August 15th, 1470, between William Paston and Thomas Vyall, master painter, of Norwich, who, being unable to get paid for his work at the monastery of Whitefriars (probably at Norwich), borrowed money from Paston on the security of some coral beads and plate. Gairdner's ed., IV., p. 408. This document is preserved with a number of the original letters in the British Museum. Its jagged edge illustrates the meaning of the word "indenture": *i.e.* it had doubtless a counterpart which fitted its edge and was held by Vigall as a memorandum. The well-known collection of Paston Letters was first printed by Mr. John Fenn. of East Dereham, in Norfolk, in 1787-1789, and by his nephew in 1823. The originals can be traced to the last of the Pastons, the second Earl of Yarmouth, who died in 1732. Those contained in the first two vols. were presented to the king, and are lost; of those in the third and fourth vol. only one is extant; those of the fifth were discovered in 1866, but single Paston letters exist. The disappearance of the originals, however, had caused doubt to be thrown on the authenticity of the collection. which was dispelled by Mr. Gairdner's Introduction to his edition of 1872 (which see).

From a fifteenth century MS., "The Dictes and Sayings of the Philosophers," at Lambeth. Earl Rivers, the translator, dressed in a surcoat bearing the family arms, is represented as introducing a priest, who presents a copy of the work to Edward IV., who is accompanied by the Queen and their son, afterwards Edward V., with their Court. This is the only known contemporary representation of Edward V. Kershaw, *Art Treasures of the Lambeth Library*, p. 38.

From a MS. in the University Library at Ghent, apparently an illuminated copy of a report to Charles the Bold, Duke of Burgundy, on Edward IV.'s final expedition from Zeeland in 1471. Charles the Bold had advised and aided the attempt. A letter accompanies it from Edward IV. to the inhabitants of Bruges, announcing his success, and thanking them for their hospitality. It is fully described in *Archæologia*, Vol. XXI. (1821), where drawings from it are given. Our illustrations are, of course, photographed directly from the MS.

By an unknown artist: presented to the National Portrait Gallery in 1862 by Mr. J. G. Craig, of Edinburgh.

Drawn on the margin of the Chronicon Roffense, or Rochester Chronicle, a history of the world to 1377, by a monk of Rochester; adjoining the passage relating to the measures taken against highway robbery.

From a late fifteenth century French MS. of the Chroniques d'Angleterre; representing the siege of Ribodane in Galicia by the Duke of Lancaster.

From a MS. of about 1450 of a French translation of Valerius Maximus' anecdotes from Roman history; primarily representing the fight of the Horatii and Curiatii. Its interest for our purpose lies in the maces and hammers represented (*see* text), which had been introduced in view of the increasing strength of armour.

Above, on the left. is a horseman's hammer; next are two maces; then a "spit," the hook of which would serve to catch a horse's bridle: next, a bill; finally, a halberd. In the lower row, two halberds, two "morris pikes," a mace, an axe, and a hammer (useful for smashing plate armour or felling a horse). The halberds and morris pikes are later than the rest, probably Tudor.

The cammail disappears, according to the Addington collection, about 1410; after that date the armour grows steadily heavier.

"Here shows how Philip Duke of Burgundy besieged Calais, and Humphry Duke of Gloucester, Richard Earl of Warwick, and Humphrey Earl of Stafford, with a great multitude, went over the sea and followed the Duke, he ever fleeing before them." From the *Life of the Earl of Warwick*, by John Rous, to which this is an illustration.

In the Côtentin, between Cherbourg and Coutances; now part of a hospital. The late Prof. E. A. Freeman (*Sketches of Travel in Normandy and Maine*) describes it as having the air of a Norman keep of the eleventh or twelfth century, but remarks that the details are later, and that it is said to have been built by Sir John Chandos under Edward III. "Did .he recast every detail of an earlier keep, or choose to build in the old fashion?"

From the well-known Harleian MS. of Froissart in the British Museum; showing primarily "the siege of the strong town in Africa" (*Chron.* IV. c. 39), and interesting for the hooped cannon.

From a French MS. of the *Chroniques de St. Denis.*

From the Roll of the Earls of Warwick, by John Rous, which exists in two versions: the earlier, which is said to be Yorkist in tone, belongs to the Duke of Manchester; the later, which is Lancastrian, was written after the accession of Henry VII. to gain his favour. *Cf.* the article on Rous in *Dict. Nat. Biog.* The earlier version (of which imperfect MS. copies exist in the British Museum and the Bodleian) was reproduced in facsimile by W. Courthope in 1845; the drawing given is from the later version, now at the Heralds' College. On the shield Warwick bears the arms of Montague quartered with Monthermer, his mother's coat: at his feet are the Neville Dun Bull and the Montague Green Eagle. The great shield below has Montague in the first quarter and Neville below it, with the eldest son's label superimposed. Quarterings are also shown of Despencer, Beauchamp, Balliol, Ufford, and other families.

From a MS. of a French translation of Quintus Curtius's *Life*

the Greek writer known as the Pseudo-Callisthenes, who wrote at Alexandria about 200 A.D.; the superb MS., containing various romances in French, was executed in France to the order of John Talbot, Earl of Shrewsbury, and presented by him to Margaret of Anjou on her marriage, in order, as he said, that she might not forget her native tongue. The men with heads beneath their shoulders whom Alexander met in the furthest East are mentioned by Greek writers and by Sir John Mandeville, and the belief in them is not quite extinct by Shakespeare's time. The medieval romances of Alexander are said to be derived from an abridgment of the Latin translation of Julius Valerius before 340 A.D. Ward, *Catalogue of MS. Romances in British Museum*, I., p. 106.

A THIRTEENTH CENTURY MAP OF THE WORLD 485

From a Latin Psalter, executed in England between 1250 and 1300. Above, the Saviour, as Lord of the World, with two angels. Jerusalem is in the centre, and on the back are the names of the chief kingdoms and cities of Europe, Asia, and Africa.

THE "MAPPA MUNDI," HEREFORD CATHEDRAL 488

SECTION FROM A FACSIMILE OF THE HEREFORD "MAPPA MUNDI" . 489

This map, now in the Chapter House Library at Hereford, was discovered about 1765 under the floor of Bishop Audley's chapel in the cathedral. It is on vellum, glued to an oak frame. the total height being nearly 6 ft. Above, the Last Judgment; at the top or east of the map, Paradise; Jerusalem in the centre. Babylon. Rome. and Troy are also shown; as also the Cretan Labyrinth, the Pillars of Hercules, Scylla and Charybdis. and Lot's Wife. Abraham is shown in Chaldæa, Moses on Mount Sinai, St. Anthony in the Ethiopian Desert, St. Augustine at Hippo, in North Africa. The British Isles are in the lower left-hand part of the map, and Hereford Cathedral is marked. There are various descriptive notes and drawings of animals. In the lower corner, to the spectator's left, is the Emperor Augustus sending out three learned men (according to a common medieval tradition, which, however, usually names four) to survey the world and report its extent and resources to the Senate, in view of the "taxing" of Luke ii. 1. In the other corner is the author himself, Richard of Holdingham and Lafford (Sleaford, in Lincolnshire) with horse, hounds, and page, and some Norman-French verses describing him. The date is usually given as late thirteenth century, but was fixed by M. d'Avezac at 1314 from internal evidence. His paper on it is translated in the *Gentleman's Magazine*, 1863; there is a good popular description in Murray's *Handbook to Hereford Cathedral*. Both have been freely used in this note.

SECTION FROM THE LAURENTIAN MAP 490

The original is in the Medicean Library at Florence; a facsimile, from which this illustration is reproduced, is in the British Museum. The map is described by Mr. C. Raymond Beazley in another work (*Henry the Navigator*, p. 13) as "the most remarkable of all the Portolani of the fourteenth century, as giving a view of the world, and especially Africa. which is far nearer the actual truth than could be expected."

TOWERS OF THE FIFTEENTH CENTURY (*see* text, pp. 491–492) . . 493

TRACERIED ROOFS OF THE FIFTEENTH CENTURY 495

pages are appropriated to each month, the days being contained
in the first line.   Nov. 1, All Saints, is indicated by the face of
Christ surrounded by other faces ; Nov. 2, All Souls, by faces in a
frame ; Nov. 6, St. Leonard's day, by fetters (he was the patron of
prisoners) ; Nov. 10, the day of SS. Trypho and Respicius, beheaded
under Diocletian, by the axe ; Nov. 11, St. Martin of Tours, by a
bishop's head, and so on.   The "Sunday letters" will be seen below,
but no explanation has, apparently, been attempted of the other
lines of figures, or of the pages appended to the almanack, which
is English and dates from 1412.   Some of these pages appear to
give useful information, as in a modern almanack : *e.g.* one bears
on brewing, another contains a diagram of the times of bleeding
(*cf.* p. 111 of this Vol.), but they are mostly unintelligible.

The church, dedicated to the Trinity, was built in the latter
half of the fifteenth century, and restored in 1851–1869.   It
contains an astonishing number of monuments (*cf. ante.* p. 46),
many of them to connections of the Clopton family : and many
more were destroyed during the Reformation and Civil War periods.

Built about 1450 by Sir John Fastolfe, who served at Agincourt
and was in command at the "Battle of the Herrings."   After his
death its possession was disputed between the Paston family and
the Duke of Norfolk, and the former, who received it after a
temporary dispossession. lived here till the end of the sixteenth
century.   It was one of the first buildings built of brick when
the use of that material was revived.   The tower is 100 ft. high.
For a list of the occasional examples of the use of brick between
the Roman period and the revival, *see Archæologia Cantiana*, Vol. X.

From a Flemish fifteenth century MS. ; one of those collected
by the Italian Canonici, and purchased early in the nineteenth
century by the Bodleian : *cf.* note on p. 247.

A rebus on the name of William Carpenter, a benefactor of St.
Alban's Abbey.   From the late fifteenth century MS. record of abbots
and benefactions to the Abbey, from which an illustration has been
given at p. 557 of Vol. I.

From a MS. of Lydgate's Life of St. Edmund, of about the middle
of the fifteenth century ; representing the building of Hunstanton
by the king.

From the famous "Bedford Missal " a note on which will come
more conveniently at p. 681.   This illustration primarily represents
the Tower of Babel.

John Taylour and wife, 1490 : his business is indicated by the
woolsack and sheep.

The ornamentation has been interpreted as a date, 1406, and

also as a symbol of the Trinity ! The plate formed the back of a fireplace, and is believed to be the earliest English fireback extant. It was no doubt made in Sussex. Starkie Gardiner, in *Archæologia*, Vol. LVI.

From a French fifteenth century MS. of Boccaccio's work on Famous Women. The lady is Minerva, who is described in the work as the inventress of armour.

From a late fifteenth century Flemish MS. of Ovid's Metamorphoses.

From a late fifteenth century Flemish MS. of illustrations in grisaille of the travels of Sir John Mandeville. The illustration refers to the "Fosse of Mynon," near the city of Acon (Acre, in Palestine), 100 cubits in circumference, and full of bright gravel, which is fetched from long distances and exported to make glass. *Cf.* Mandeville's Travels, Chap. IV. Doubtless the artist found his model at home.

The clock turret is, of course, modern ; the body of the building was completed in 1413. It is composed of smooth black flints.

The name is a corruption of "in magna crofta," *i.e.* in the large field attached to the castle. The church, sometimes described as the finest parish church in England, was building from 1430 to 1455, and was well restored in 1860.

Cley is chiefly Perpendicular ; one of its chapels is adorned with double-headed eagles, conjectured to refer to a guild of German merchants once established here. Worstead was chiefly built during the latter half of the fourteenth century ; the town was one of the earliest of the Flemish settlements. St. Margaret's, Lynn, possibly dates in part from the early years of the twelfth century, but is chiefly of the latter half of the fourteenth, as is its daughter church St. Nicholas', Lynn.

Such houses are depicted in the miniatures of donors of houses in the town of St. Albans to the Abbey, shown in the MS. referred to in the note on p. 543.

Originally attached to a lazar house founded in the reign of Stephen by Adeliza. Abbess of Barking, and refounded by Queen Elizabeth in 1572. The present building was erected in the fifteenth century, but lengthened and enlarged in 1889. Its earlier state is shown in Wilkinson, *Londina Illustrata.*

Portrait of Richard II., from a fifteenth century MS. detailing the ceremonial observed at his coronation.

is Flemish, but the borders contain a *red* rose (a difficulty in the way of the later date) ; the design of the crown is English, and the architectural decoration of the tapestry indicates that it was made for this hall. *Cf. Archæologia*, Vol. XXXVI., papers by G. Scharf and J. G. Nichols ; Sharp, *Memorials of Coventry*, 1818.

THE CHAPERON OR HOOD 584

A woman churning interrupted by tramps : from a French fifteenth century MS. of Romances.

HEADGEAR UNDER HENRY VI. (*see* on p. 545) 585

BRASSES ILLUSTRATING WOMEN'S DRESS, FOURTEENTH AND FIFTEENTH CENTURIES 587, 589

That of Lady de Creke (whose husband is shown at p. 55) is noticeable for its wimple or throat-piece. The headdress, it will be noticed, seems to develop till about 1420, then to contract, and then to become extravagant again. But we must not suppose that brasses from all parts of England necessarily indicate uniform changes of fashion. The brass from Minehead is of an unknown lady. Tower headdresses seem to be less frequent on brasses than in MSS., and in England than in France. The brass of Eleanor Corp (of which one shoulder has here been restored) seems to be the only one of a young girl : it is noticeable for the fashion of the headdress and the *côte hardie* with its many buttons.

A GENTLEMAN AT HIS TOILET, FOURTEENTH CENTURY . . . 591

From Queen Mary's Psalter ; *cf.* note on Vol. I., p. 543.

LADIES' CLOAKS, EARLY FIFTEENTH CENTURY 593

From a Book of Hours, executed in England in the early fifteenth century Several other examples in the British Museum of about this time suggest that the ladies represented praying may be members of the family for whose use the book was made.

SLASHED AND PUFFED SLEEVES, UNDER HENRY VI. 595

For the MS. *see* note on p. 545. Primarily, of course, representing King Edmund.

LEATHER SHOE OF MEDIEVAL TYPE 597

LADIES IN MOURNING, TEMP. HENRY VI. *See* note on p. 581 . . 599

HENRY VII. 601

From a MS. of the Book of Hunting, or Master of the Game, executed for him.

HENRY VII.'S CHAPEL, WESTMINSTER ABBEY 603

According to Dean Stanley "the most signal example of the contrast between the king's closeness in life and his magnificence in the structures he left to posterity." It was dedicated to the Virgin, and was a chantry chapel containing his tomb, which is shown on p. 678. Originally it was intended to receive the body of Henry VI., whose canonisation the Pope had promised. but this purpose was quietly dropped. Stanley, *Memorials of Westminster Abbey*, pp. 138, 139.

SEAL OF HENRY VII. FOR FRENCH AFFAIRS 606

PAPAL PROCLAMATION RECOGNISING HENRY VII. AS KING . 608, 609

Probably (according to the British Museum Catalogue) an addition to a broadside or other official document issued when Perkin Warbeck landed in Cornwall in 1497. It recounts the confirmation of Henry

These four illuminations appear to be taken from a MS. abridgment of English law of the time of Henry VI., of which nothing else
remains but part of the table of contents. They were long preserved
at Whaddon Hall, Bucks, but were purchased by Mr. Justice Darling
and presented by him to the Honourable Society of the Inner Temple
in 1894. On the bench of the Court of Chancery are seated the
Chancellor, the Master of the Rolls (probably), and four Masters in
Chancery; below are the Registrars and other officials; the one on
the spectator's right, seated at the table, is attaching the Great Seal
to a document; before him lie writs, with pendent labels (used till a
recent period for Chancery writs); at the bar are three serjeants-at-
law and two "apprentices" or barristers; below are two others, with
three solicitors behind. The shields bear the arms respectively of
Edward the Confessor, France and England quarterly, and England
alone. In the Court of King's Bench are five judges; below, the
King's Coroner and Attorney, and the Masters of Court; on the table
stand two ushers, one of whom is swearing-in the jury. At the bar is
a prisoner in custody of a tipstaff, a serjeant-at-law standing on each
side; in the foreground, other prisoners. In the Court of Common
Pleas are seven judges (the usual number during part of the reigns
of Henry VI. and Edward IV.); below is a defendant in charge of
a tipstaff. No jury is visible. In the Court of Exchequer there is
one Baron, with four assessors; two of the clerks are counting gold
coin; in the foreground, a place of temporary detention for defaulters,
and treasure chests. The chequered cloth which gave its name to
the Court is not shown, but the explanation offered is that it was

xliv

NOTES TO ILLUSTRATIONS.

PAGE

used only in making up the accounts (counters representing various
sums being put in the squares to facilitate the addition), and that
the "receipt," not the "account," is here shown. The illuminations
seem to have been "touched up," and the grotesqueness of the jury
and prisoners is due to the later hand. The particoloured robes of
the serjeants are explained as "liveries," given to them, with retaining fees, by clients of high rank. *See* G. R. Corner in *Archæologia*,
Vol. XXXIX., from which the above description is condensed.

SOLDIERS AND CIVILIANS (for MS. *see* on p. 581) 663

A SCENE IN CAMP 665

These two illustrations are from Lydgate's tale of the siege of
Thebes. The first is entitled "How that none of the citie of Thebes
would undertake to go a message to King Adrastus " (the besieger);
in the second, the heir of Lycargus, one of the besieging kings, has
been slain by a serpent, and the warriors plead for the life of
Isophile, in whose charge the child had been left. The mitred
figure is Amphiaraus, whose powers as a soothsayer earn him the
title, from Lydgate, of "Amphiorax the Bishop."

ARMOUR OF A KNIGHT UNDER HENRY VII. 666

THE BROCAS HEAUME. 667

A tilting helmet of the time of Henry VII., formerly in the Brocas
Collection.

WARSHIPS ENTERING A RIVER. 668

From a late fifteenth century Flemish MS. of *Le Trésor des
Histoires.*

FLEET ATTACKING A FORTIFIED TOWN 669

From the Romance of the Three Kings' Sons. The drawing in
the MS., executed in England late in the fifteenth century, is thought
by the authors of the Class Catalogue of MSS. in the British Museum
to have been copied from a French MS. of an earlier period.

THE *HARRY GRÂCE À DIEU* 670

Reproduced from the illustration in Laird Clowes's *History of the
Royal Navy*, by permission of Messrs. Sampson Low, Marston and Co.

SHIPS OF COLUMBUS, AS REPRODUCED FOR HIS QUINGENTENARY . . 671

These ships were rebuilt according to the contemporary descriptions
for the five-hundredth anniversary of the discovery of America. They
were taken to the celebration at Huelva and afterwards to the
Chicago Exhibition, where the photograph here reproduced was
taken.

RIB OF A WHALE FROM NEWFOUNDLAND . . . . . 673.

St. Mary Redcliff Church, Bristol. Asserted by local tradition to
be a rib of the Dun Cow slain by Guy, Earl of Warwick. Probably
a relic of the early whaling expeditions mentioned on p. 675.

WINDOW IN FAIRFORD CHURCH, GLOUCESTERSHIRE (*see* text) . . 676

TOMB OF HENRY VII., WESTMINSTER ABBEY 678

FRIAR JOHN SIFERWAS PRESENTING HIS BOOK TO LORD LOVELL . 680

From a fragment of the Gospels, illuminated by the Friar for Lord
Lovell, who died in 1408.

d

St Michael Weighing a Saint against a Devil . . . .

These frescoes were discovered in South Leigh Church, near Witney, Oxfordshire, in 1872 : they are of the fifteenth century, and have been carefully restored. The Resurrection, Last Judgment, and Gates of Heaven adorn the chancel. In this design (on the south wall of the nave) the Church looks on, serene in the certainty of victory, while the devil in the scale summons his fellows to turn the balance in his favour, but without avail.

St. Anthony in the Desert . . . .

St. Athanasius, in his life of the saint, in the Bollandist *Acta Sanctorum* (Jan. 17), sec. 676–8, tells how St. Anthony retired into the desert; the brethren insisted on bringing him food; but to save them trouble he irrigated land, provided for himself, and even grew vegetables for the refreshment of his visitors. When beasts, attracted by the water, devoured his crops, he captured one, and thus secured the attention of the rest : then he said to them, "Why harm ye me, who have not harmed you? Depart, and in .the name of the Lord come not back." And they never came near him again.

An Interpretation of the Parable of the Sower . . .

From a treatise, entitled "Speculum Virginum" (the Mirror of Virgins). The MS. was written in Germany in the twelfth century. The "virgins" at the top are unspecified; the widows are—above, Judith and Anna; below, Deborah and the widow who cast two mites into the treasury (Mark xii. 42); the married couples, for whom the seed brings forth only thirtyfold, are Zacharias (Luke i.) and his wife, Lot and his wife, Job (?) and his wife, Noah and his wife (a pleasant contrast to the view taken in the Miracle Plays). The sentence above, literally translated, is, "I accept any consolation for my pilgrimage and trouble from [another] pilgrim." Messrs. Birch and Jenner, in their Index to Illustrated MSS. in the British Museum, refer to Chaucer's "Parson's Tale," and the Latin life of St. Martial (printed in the *British Archæological Journal*, 1872, Vol. XXVIII., p. 384), in both of which there is a similar, though less definite, distinction of three grades of chastity.

The Siege of the Castell d'Amour . . . . . .

Fully described by Mr. John Rokewode Gage in *Vetusta Monumenta*, Vol. VI. He compares the sieges of the Château de Bel-Accueil in the *Roman de la Rose*, and the Château de Joyeuse Garde in the Romance of Lancelot du Lac, though in neither case is the shower of roses introduced. He states, however, that, "according to the Italian historians," a similar tournament was actually held at Treviso in 1214, when a castle covered with tapestry was defended by 200 ladies and besieged by 200 young knights, the only missiles allowed being flowers, fruits, and bon-bons. The subject seems to have been a favourite one with artists, and an ivory carving representing it is in the Mayer Museum, Liverpool.

From a genealogical roll of the kings of England, ending with Henry III. and executed late in the thirteenth century. The rats are the old black variety, nearly exterminated by the "Hanover" or "Norway" rat in the seventeenth and eighteenth centuries, and now surviving only in a few remote places, such as Lundy and Sark.

CONTRIBUTORS TO THIS VOLUME.

BEAZLEY, CHARLES RAYMOND, M.A., F.R.G.S., Fellow of Merton College, Oxford; Author of *The Dawn of Modern Geography; Henry the Navigator* (Heroes of the Nations Series) ; *John and Sebastian Cabot; James I. of Aragon.*

BLAKISTON, Rev. H. E. D., M.A., Fellow and Tutor of Trinity College, Oxford ; Author of *Trinity College* (College Histories Series).

CLOWES, W. LAIRD, Fellow of King's College, London; Gold Medallist, U.S. Naval Institute ; Editor and Principal Author of *The Royal Navy : A History ;* and of *A Naval Pocket Book.*

CORBETT, W. J., M.A., Fellow of King's College, Cambridge.

CREIGHTON, C., M.A., M.D.; Author of *A History of Epidemics in Britain.*

DUFF, E. GORDON, M.A., Oxon., sometime Librarian of the John Rylands Library, Manchester, and Sandars Reader in Bibliography in the University of Cambridge ; Author of *Early Printed Books; Early English Printing ; The Printers, Stationers and Bookbinders of London,* etc.

EDWARDS, OWEN M., M.A., Fellow of Lincoln College, Oxford ; sometime M.P. for Merionethshire; Lecturer in Modern History at Lincoln, Corpus Christi, and Pembroke Colleges, Oxford.

FLETCHER, C. R. L., M.A., Fellow and Tutor of Magdalen College, Oxford.

HALL, HUBERT, F.S.A., Public Record Office ; Author of a *History of the Customs Revenue,* and Editor of *The Red Book of the Exchequer* (Rolls Series).

HASSALL, ARTHUR, M.A., Student and sometime Censor of Christ Church, Oxford; Author of *Bolingbroke; Louis XIV. ; A Handbook of European History ; A Class Book of English History ; The French People ;* Editor of *Periods of European History,* and author of Period VI. (*The Balance of Power*) ; Joint Editor of and Contributor to *Constitutional Essays ;* Editor of the third edition of Dyer's *Modern Europe,* and of *The Student's France.*

HEATH, H. FRANK, Ph.D. Strasburg ; Registrar of the Academic Council, University of London ; one of the Editors of *The Globe Chaucer.*

HEWINS, W. A. S., M.A., Pembroke College, Oxford ; Director of the London School of Economics ; Tooke Professor of Economic Science and Statistics at King's College, London; Member of the Senate, and Examiner in Political Economy, in the University of London ; Author of *English Trade and Finance in the Seventeenth Century ;* Contributor to the *Dictionary of National Biography* and the *Dictionary of Political Economy.*

CONTRIBUTORS TO THIS VOLUME.

HUGHES, REGINALD, D.C.L. Oxon.

HUTTON, Rev. W. H., M.A., Fellow and Tutor of St. John's College, Oxford; Author of *The Marquess Wellesley; William Laud; Sir Thomas More; The Church of the VI. Century*, etc.

JACOBS, JOSEPH, B.A., sometime Scholar of St. John's College, Cambridge; President of the Jewish Historical Society of England, and Corresponding Member of the Royal Academy of History at Madrid and of the American Jewish Historical Society at Philadelphia; Author of *The Jews of Angevin England; Sources of the History of the Jews of Spain; Jewish Ideals*, etc.

MAITLAND, F. W., LL.D., Hon. D.C.L., Downing Professor of Law in the University of Cambridge; Author of *Domesday Book and Beyond; Township and Borough; Canon Law in England;* Editor of *Pleas of the Crown* (Selden Society); joint Author with Prof. Pollock of *A History of English Law.*

MEDLEY, D. J., M.A., Professor of History in the University of Glasgow; sometime Tutor of Keble College, Oxford; Author of *A Student's Manual of English Constitutional History.*

OMAN. C. W. C., M.A., Fellow of All Souls' College, and Deputy Professor of Modern History in the University of Oxford; Author of *The Art of War in the Middle Ages; Warwick the King-maker; The History of Europe, 476-918*, etc.

POOLE, REGINALD L., M.A., Ph.D., Fellow of Magdalen College and Lecturer in Diplomatic in the University of Oxford; Editor of the *English Historical Review;* Author of *Illustrations of the History of Mediæval Thought.*

ROCKSTRO, W. S. (the late), Author of *A General History of Music; Life of Handel; Life of Mendelssohn*, etc.

SMITH, A. L., M.A., Fellow and Tutor of Balliol College, Oxford.

STEELE, R., F.C.S., Librarian of the Chemical Society; Author of *Mediæval Lore;* Editor of *The Story of Alexander* and of Lydgate's *Secrees of Old Philosoffres* (E.E.T.S.).

SYMES, the Rev. Professor, J. E., M.A., Principal of University College, Nottingham; Author of *A Text Book of Political Economy.*

PREFATORY NOTE.

As the story of English civilisation goes forward, the sources available for its illustration become not only more abundant but more diversified. Miniatures from manuscripts supplement the evidence as to costume and manners afforded by the articles of domestic use or personal ornament, which are almost all we have to depend upon for the periods of the Roman occupation and of the Old-English Kingdoms. But these miniatures themselves gradually become specialised: pictures from romances or from purely secular treatises, now on medicine, now on astrology, now on history or politics, replace the representation of Biblical scenes on which we must chiefly rely for our reconstructions of the dress of the eleventh and twelfth centuries; the marginal drawings of the great Psalters and other service books present to us pictures, which we can hardly distrust, of the occupations and amusements of the daily life of the fourteenth and fifteenth. Monumental brasses afford invaluable evidence as to the gradual strengthening and elaboration of armour to meet the ever-increasing improvements in missile weapons, until its very complexity and weight brought about a reaction. The shipping begins to be revealed to us, not in conventional forms, out of whose scattered details we must reconstruct the veritable images of the sea-going craft of a medieval navy, but in drawings approximately like the originals as a whole. By the end of the fifteenth century even the faces of the actors in the pageant are becoming known to us—known as vividly, in some cases, as the faces of our own contemporaries. Corporation and college plate adds its testimony to the growth of economic prosperity, and the architectural examples, as they multiply, tell the same tale. Moreover, they are now, in an increasing ratio, secular as well as ecclesiastical, and civic or commercial as well as military.

In the present volume abundant use has been made of all these opportunities for illustration, and an effort has been

made to keep to strictly contemporary and English MS.
sources, except where a foreign MS. could be legitimately
drawn upon, as in dealing with Continental warfare or foreign
trade. But before acknowledging our obligations a word must
be said as to the arrangement of the text. From the first
inception of the work the exigencies of space have now and
then compelled departure from the strict chronological limits
assigned to each chapter, and the introduction by a retro-
spective, or less frequently a prospective, treatment, of matter
lying outside them. The history of English law is better
understood, and can be more concisely told, when grouped
into four or five comprehensive sections, than when allowed
to proceed *pari passu* with the political and ecclesiastical
history. The story of early English travel is best treated as
an introduction, and a contrast, to the great outburst of
activity in exploration which marks the sixteenth century;
and the treatment under four separate headings of the
manners and morals of the fourteenth and fifteenth centuries,
which Professor Medley has adopted in the new sections
specially written for this volume of the illustrated edition, will
probably be found to secure a gain in comprehensiveness as
well as to save space.

Our acknowledgments are again due to the owners or
custodians of a very great number of valuable MS. or antiquities for their permission to reproduce them in this volume.
We need scarcely mention again how very greatly we are
indebted to the authorities and staff of the British Museum,
or to Bodley's Librarian. We have also to express our thanks
to the Librarians of Cambridge University, and of Trinity
College, Dublin; to Baron von Hügel, Keeper of the Cambridge University Archæological Museum; to the Librarians of
Lambeth Palace Library, of the Advocates' Library, Edinburgh, of Trinity College and of Corpus Christi College,
Cambridge, and of Balliol College and Oriel Colleges,
and of Christ Church, Oxford; to the heads and governing
bodies of these colleges, and also of Merton, New, and
Queen's Colleges, Oxford; to the Corporation of the City of
London, and the Librarian of the Guildhall Library; to the
Corporations of Bristol and King's Lynn; to the Chapter of
the Royal College of Arms; to the Benchers of the Inner

Temple; to the Librarian of the University Library at Ghent; to Major Boileau, R.A., Secretary of the National Artillery Association, and to the General Officer commanding the Woolwich District, for permission to reproduce exhibits in the Rotunda Museum, Woolwich; to the Curators of Ipswich and Lewes Museums; to the Dean and Chapter of Hereford Cathedral; to the Weld-Blundell Trustees, whose unrestricted permission to use the treasures of the Luttrell Psalter has been availed of even more freely in this volume than in its predecessor; to the Right Rev. the Archbishop of Canterbury for leave to reproduce the portrait of Chichele at Lambeth; to the Right Hon. the Earl of Denbigh and the Right Hon. the Earl of Pembroke for leave to photograph historical portraits in their respective possession; and to the Right Hon. the Earl of Ellesmere and the Librarian at Bridgewater House (Mr. Strachan Holme) for leave to photograph the miniatures of the Canterbury pilgrims from the famous Ellesmere MS.—the first time, we believe, that they have ever been reproduced by photography; to the Right Hon. Lord Fitzhardinge for permission to photograph portions of Berkeley Castle; to the Right Hon. Lord de l'Isle and Dudley for a like permission in respect of Penshurst Place; to the Rev. Sir W. Hyde Parker for leave to reproduce his drawings of the Clopton glass in Long Melford Church, itself inaccessible to the photographer; and to the Rev. Henry Wace, Rector of St. Michael's, Cornhill. In all cases specific acknowledgments will be found under the various illustrations.

In selecting subjects, very valuable assistance has been rendered to the Editor by Miss E. M. Leonard, of Girton College, Cambridge; by Mr. T. D. Atkinson, of Cambridge; by Mr. T. A. Archer, M.A., Oxford; and, in respect of certain portions of the present volume, by Dr. C. Creighton and Dr. Montague James, of Cambridge. Professor Oman has given his valued aid in ensuring the correctness of the representations of warfare and weapons, and Mr. E. W. B. Nicholson has rendered us inestimable assistance in ensuring the correctness of the descriptions of subjects from Bodleian MSS.

February, 1902.   J. S. MANN.

SOCIAL ENGLAND.

CHAPTER· V.

THE CONSOLIDATION OF THE KINGDOM. 1274-1348.

SELDOM in the history of a nation do the twin streams of A. L. SMITH. The Reign of Edward I. political and social progress maintain an equal and uniform rate of speed. Now one, now the other, flows the more rapidly of the two. Trade and industry, arts and manners, may undergo a transformation while the history of politics is a comparative blank; or, conversely, an era of political activity may concur with a season of social and economic repose. The period we are now approaching is one of the latter kind: and even the social historian finds himself compelled to give his first attention to the policy and person of a single statesman-king.

The work awaiting Edward I. was of such variety and such magnitude as to surpass in permanent importance even that effected by Henry II. To reduce Wales, and to deal with Scotland; to settle on an enduring basis the judicial and the military system of England; to transform the old taxes into a new financial scheme; to cope with the eternal problem of Church and State, a problem then nearing an acute stage; to accept the principles of the Charters, and the lessons of the last reign, without hampering the royal power or strengthening the baronage; lastly, to find the true path for the progress of representative institutions, a path that even Montfort had missed: all this needed a strong man, as well as a wise and good one. Edward I., indeed, of all our sovereigns, if not absolutely the foremost, yet stands second only to Henry VIII. in strength of character, to Alfred or to Henry VI. in righteousness; but in practical wisdom, in constructive insight, in justice of conception, second to none.

45

The reduction of Wales was the first need.   The Welsh were a standing menace to England.   They had seized the opportunity of every rising, against John, against the Regency, against Henry III.   Their indomitable animosity necessitated the existence of great districts on the borders, where the Bohuns, Mortimers, and Clares were independent " Lords Marchers," and thought less of justice to the Welsh, or

CORONATION OF EDWARD I.
(Chetham Library, Manchester.)

loyalty to the king, than of thwarting and defeating each other.   The English kings had tried force and friendship, alike in vain.   Llewellyn, Prince of North Wales, had been given a bride of the English royal house, and David, his brother, had been specially favoured by Edward; yet in 1282, both revolted (p. 22).   Edward's vengeance was swift.   In appealing to his people for men and money, he reminded them of the countless treasons of the Welsh; how, like foxes, they had troubled the land; how they slaughtered men, women, and children, burned castles and cottages, and feared neither God nor man.   He invaded Wales; Llewellyn fell; David was solemnly tried and executed as a traitor and conspirator, a blasphemer and a murderer.   Wales was assimilated to England, and English laws were introduced.   The process was slow, but by Tudor times it was complete. The story of the baby prince presented at Carnarvon to the Welsh, as their promised Prince of Wales, who could speak no English, shows that popular tradition rightly referred back to Edward I. the whole credit of the result.

From 1286 to 1289 Edward was in Gascony, securing that Gascony. province, the last fragment of the great Plantagenet dominion in France. In 1293 Philip le Bel, by an unworthy trick, seized the strongholds of the province, and seemed to be designing a raid on English coasts. Edward again appealed to his people in 1295 against the King of France, who, "not content with his former fraud and iniquity," was now gathering a fleet and host "to invade the land and wipe the English name from the earth." At last, by Edward's marriage to Philip's sister Margaret in 1299, an accommodation was arranged.

In the meantime the chief constitutional results of the Legal reign had been produced at home. The Statute of Mortmain Reforms. (1279) checked the absorption of land by the Church, and consequent impoverishment of all landowners; and, therefore, of the Crown, the greatest landowner of all. Other statutes with the same view were that called De Donis [1] (1285), which protected reversionary estates and incidentally established a system of entails, and the Act of 1290, Quia Emptores,[2] which, in attempting to retain the profitable "incidents" of feudal tenure, opened the door to changes which overthrew the very basis of feudalism. Indeed, Edward's general aim has been defined by Bishop Stubbs as the elimination of the principle of tenure from the region of government. Hitherto political right, military power, social privilege, had all been distributed according to the distinctions between classes of tenants; the chief tenants alone made the laws, had armed retainers, and still kept private jurisdictions. Henceforth this was to be altered. The great council of tenants in chief was to be expanded into a representative

[1 "Of Gifts," *sc.*. of land, by will or otherwise.]

[2 The opening words of the statute: "Forasmuch as purchasers" (of lands have heretofore held on tenures detrimental to the chief lord, it is provided by the statute that land may be sold only so as to be held of the chief lord). The aim of the statute was to prevent such a subdivision of fiefs as would deprive the chief lords of their privileges in cases of escheat, wardship, etc.]

Parliament; feudal levies were to become a national army; and feudal franchises were to be merged in royal and national justice.   To effect this a thorough inquiry was made by what warrant in each case such franchises were claimed.   The barons resented an inquiry into their title-deeds as an inter-ference with rights of property.   Earl Warrenne threw down an ancient rusty sword before the justices with the proud words, "See, my masters, here is my warrant."   But this was a piece of acting; he submitted like the rest.   Edward's judicial **Judicial Reforms.** reforms, however, had also a constructive side.   He completed the separation between the three courts, Exchequer, King's Bench, and Common Pleas.   He defined the Assize Circuits, he provided new forms of legal remedy, to meet the growth of legal business, and so laid the foundation for the great Equity jurisdiction in Chancery (p. 49), which has done so much for English social life.   In 1289 he dismissed most of the judges for corruption.   His banishment of the Jews the same year (p. 49) was not from mere bigotry, but also from a determination to enforce the usury laws, to protect the coinage, and to destroy an agency by which the powerful dispossessed the smaller landowners.   His military measures included a strict inspection twice a year of the national militia, arranged in its classes from mailed knight to archer armed with dagger; a strict watch by night in all boroughs, and the duty of "hue and cry" at the sheriff's summons; the clearance of 200 feet on each side of all highways, a precaution against lurking foot-pads.   The old caste distinctions of tenure he regarded as obsolete; all men who had property enough were "distrained to take up knighthood," whether chief tenants or mesne [1] tenants, and whether holding by military service or not. Similarly for his wars, he called on all classes alike to fight for their country, whether on the English coasts, or across Scottish or Welsh borders, or in Gascony or Flanders.   But Edward's greatest title to the reverence of Englishmen is as the real creator of Parliament.   Representative institutions had been advancing throughout the thirteenth century.   John himself had been driven to call an assembly of representatives from every shire.   The ministers had called four knights from every shire in 1254, and Montfort had added to his

[[1] "Mediate," *i.e.* holding of the chief tenants, not directly of the king.]

Parliament of 1265 two burgesses from each of certain boroughs; but it was Edward I. who completed the whole process by successive steps in 1275, 1282, 1290, 1294, and 1295—steps so steadily progressive as to prove he had a deliberate plan, and one which grew under his hands. It was he whose action determined that burgesses should sit with shire knights—a point on which turns the whole history of the House of Commons and its indestructibility. It was he who insisted on the great Estate of the clergy being represented like the barons, and the Commons and all the three

SEAL OF EDWARD I.

Estates meeting at the same time and place. Thus, the Model Parliament of 1295 was the full working out of the maxim of his reign: "That which touches all should be approved by all." At the same time, Edward was steadily reducing the House of Lords to a very manageable number, and emphasising the fact that peerage depended not on tenure, but only on royal writ of summons.

His determination that the clergy should not hold aloof **State and Church.** from national burdens was manifested early in the reign. In 1279 the Oseney monk records with horror that "the clergy are to be treated even as the people are," and they had to pay a similar tax. This and the Mortmain Act were his reply to the aggressive attitude which Archbishop Peckham had just assumed. In 1291 he had, by appeal to the Pope, got a tithe of ecclesiastical property. In 1294 he had openly told the assembled clergy to observe how the barons had, in view of the French war, undertaken both to fight and to pay, so that they who could do no fighting must at least pay. Twice they yielded, and twice a still heavier call was made on them. But at this juncture the Papacy had thrown down the gauntlet to the sovereigns of Christendom. The Bull Clericis Laicos[1] forbade kings to take and churchmen to pay taxes on ecclesiastical property. Edward promptly outlawed the clergy. Unfortunately for the king, the same year, 1297, brought him into violent conflict with his barons. Bohun the Constable and Bigod the Marshal refused to serve in Flanders; "they would neither go nor hang," they answered his threat. The barons assembled in arms, "1,500 knights equipped for war": a force of some thousands in all. Edward had to compromise with the clergy; he would confirm the Charters, and they should make a voluntary gift. Then he sailed for Flanders.

King and Barons.

But in his absence the barons combined again with clergy and people to add seven new articles to the Charters, and Edward had to ratify these at Ghent. The effect of this was to restrict tallage, and such exactions within their old customary limits, and to lay down the principle that not the Crown, but Parliament, should have the whole power of taxation. The long struggle which opens with the Great Charter in 1215 thus closes, at least in one aspect. Principles then laid down were now accepted as final. It only remained to ensure this being acted on. But Edward was not a King John; nor was Winchelsey a Langton; nor did Bohun or Bigod rise to the moral stature of the Marshalls or Montforts. It was only on a narrow technical point that the two earls first opposed the king, and not until the Church and the nation had suffered three years of oppressive taxation. Their constitutional cry comes only as an after-thought; and but for the exceptional concurrence of difficulties that beset Edward, and the arbitrary actions to which this hurried him, they would hardly have succeeded.

There is, in fact, a certain theatrical air of unreality over the whole attitude of the barons to the king in this reign. We are irresistibly reminded of Warrenne's rusty sword and empty vaunt. Their constitutional leadership was indeed over.

[1 The opening words of the general introduction to it.]

and done with, though it takes the nation another century yet to realise this. They are passing from feudal barons into ordinary nobles; becoming courtiers and officials instead of petty princes or leaders of provinces. Of the twelve greatest earldoms, no less than seven before Edward's death had come into the royal house by escheat[1] or marriage alliance.

Throughout Edward's later life the sky had been growing **Scotland.** overcast. With the Scottish war the sun of his fortunes set in cloud and storm. He had hoped that the betrothal of his own son to the young Queen of Scots, 1290, would peacefully unite the two kingdoms. But the same year she died. Many claimants to the throne sprang up. The Scots appealed to Edward to arbitrate. He appointed a meeting at Norham, 1291, and marched thither with a great army. His proceedings from that point it seems impossible for any Scotsman, even at the present day, to judge calmly. Yet there can be no doubt on the one hand that the competitors, and Scots themselves, as well as the public opinion of Christendom, regarded the English kings as having some overlordship over Scotland; that there were enough historical instances of homage done by Scottish kings to seem to support a feudal claim; that southern Scotland was closely akin to northern England, and had but little bond with the Celtic north; and that Edward's award, by which John Baliol, a Yorkshire baron, became King of Scots in 1292, was scrupulously just. On the other hand, Edward certainly pressed his feudal rights to the uttermost, and helped to make Baliol's position untenable; and when the Scots made alliance with France, he attacked them as allies of his enemies, sacked Berwick and Edinburgh, captured and deposed Baliol, and left Scotland under the heavy hand of Earl Warrenne, who had won the victory of Dunbar. His defeat of the Scots at Falkirk, and futile campaigns of 1299, 1300, and 1301, and his overwhelming march from end to end of the land in 1303, followed by the execution of Wallace for treason, murder, and sacrilege, acted as stern lessons to teach the Scots patriotism and union. Scottish nationality was the creation of Edward's tyranny. He did what he deemed his duty; but there are some mistakes which

[1 Reversion to the king as overlord, whether through failure of heirs or forfeiture.]

count almost as crimes. If anything could expiate such, it would be the unshaken heroism with which Edward pursued his purpose. Neither disaster nor mortal disease could turn him aside; ill as he was, he took a solemn vow, 1306, to avenge Robert Bruce's murder of Comyn and assumption of the crown. He died in July, 1307, almost in the act of mounting his horse at the frontier town of Burgh-on-Sands, to march against the rebel Robert Bruce; and men believed that the great king, as if his iron will could defy death itself, had ordered that his bones should be carried in the van of his army till the Scots were utterly subdued. Two years before, he had secured from a new Pope the suspension of Archbishop Winchelsey, whom he could never forgive for supporting the Papal claim to overlordship of Scotland, and whose action as head of the Church in 1297 he had never forgotten. The king skilfully contrived that the indignant repudiation of this claim should proceed from the assembled baronage of England.

The Work of Edward I. Thus when he died a great and manifold work seemed to have been accomplished. He had preserved Gascony, conquered Wales, and (apparently) Scotland. The great days of the baronage were over; the boldest and last of medieval declarations of Church independence had been defeated; he had transformed the Great Council and the system of taxation, and reduced feudalism to harmlessness; he had granted the people's demands without impairing the real power of the Crown, which was never before, or for two hundred years afterwards, so strong as now, when it expressed and summed up the national will. And yet the tragic fate that seemed to mock all the Plantagenets foredoomed to futility much of Edward's most earnest endeavours. It was his aggression that first made Scotland into a nation: he had raised a spirit potent to wreck his own plans. Hardly was he dead before his own son showed how much Scottish independence would owe to the incapacity and neglect of Edward's own posterity. He had forced the clergy into his Parliamentary scheme; but in a few years from his Parliament of 1295 they had slipped out of their representation in Parliament, and taken refuge in their own Houses of Convocation. This same ironical fate brought it about that the "Hammer of the Scots" should till recent years have had his history read through the distorting medium of Scottish sources; and that the king, who had taken for a watchword the motto "Keep faith," should be accused, by an almost inconceivable misreading of the events, of three gross breaches of faith with his subjects.

Has it more of the ludicrous or of the pathetic to read of the high hopes which his contemporaries had of Edward II.? With justice has the reign been made the subject of drama. The characters are strikingly contrasted: the idle, heedless, unworthy king, more to be pitied than

SEAL OF EDWARD II.

wholly condemned ; his dashing, sharp-tongued, pernicious favourite, Piers Gaveston; his brutal, sullen, implacable cousin, Thomas of Lancaster, incapable head of the jealous lords; the somewhat enigmatical figures of the two Despensers, the king's later confidants, and the dark under-plot of the vicious queen and her lover, Mortimer; the roll of murders, ending in the horrible story of Berkeley Castle and the "screams of an agonising king." From the first, Edward II. reversed his father's policy ; he made truce with the Scots, and hurried south to his marriage with Isabella and their coronation ; he recalled Gaveston, and heaped on him extravagant honours; for his sake he quarrelled with his father's old ministers. As early as 1308, a bitter wrath had been kindled against the favourite, and the king had to consent to banish him, only to recall him next year. The Parliament held in 1309 presented an urgent demand for reforms, which the Lords took up, and by 1310 the king's authority was practically superseded

by twenty-one Lords Ordainers. These drew up the Ordinances of 1311, besides again banishing Gaveston, and put
the appointment and the power of war and peace in the
hands of the baronage. When the king declared them
null, the barons rose, and captured and beheaded Gaveston.
After Edward's disgraceful defeat at Bannockburn, 1314, the
Ordainers seized the reins completely. Thomas of Lancaster
was supreme, but was too short-sighted or too traitorous to
do anything. Private wars broke out ; the administration

HEAD OF EDWARD II.
(*From Effigy in Gloucester Cathedral.*)

was almost suspended ; the Scots
ravaged the northern counties.
Robert Bruce, who had recovered
his fortresses almost unopposed, now,
by the capture of Berwick in 1318,
completed his royal title. His
marauders in 1319 took blackmail
as far south as Ripon.

Meanwhile the obscure struggles
of the various factions among the
barons continued, governed by the
merest personal motives. It is typical of the times that the two
Despensers (father and son), who
from 1318 to the end of the reign
took the place left vacant by

**The Des-
pensers.**

Gaveston's death, posed as champions of constitutionalism,
but for purely selfish objects ; while the ferocious hatred felt
for them by the other barons, which expressed itself in
the old constitutional phrases of the Charter epoch, was
really nothing more than jealousy and disappointed greed.
The movement, indeed, arose in that hotbed of ancient
hatred and intrigues, the Welsh marches, and began in a
quarrel over the Gloucester co-heiresses, the Despensers having
secured the lion's share. In 1321 the peers of the land declared sentence of exile against the Despensers ; but Edward
with unexpected promptitude, raised an army, struck down
the Mortimers in the west, and defeated and captured Thomas
of Lancaster at Boroughbridge. The mighty earl, "King
Arthur," as Gaveston had called him, with a double sting
in the allusion, the king's cousin, son of one queen, uncle of

1348]

another, Earl of Lancaster, Leicester, Derby, Lincoln, and Salisbury, lord of many castles and honours, and of many hundred manors, had fallen at one blow. He was tried and condemned, and executed before his own castle of Pontefract. Thus was Gaveston's blood avenged by that of Lancaster; but this stain, in its turn, must be washed away by the down-fall of Edward II. and his grandson, Richard II.; and the

Photo: Graphotone Co
BERKELEY CASTLE: EXTERIOR OF BUILDING IN WHICH EDWARD II. WAS MURDERED.

vindictive spirit thus aroused only drank its fill at last on the fields of Towton and Tewkesbury, or the scaffolds where died the last of the Poles, the Staffords, and the Courtenays under the Tudor axe. Edward was for a time supreme, and he dealt a blow at the Ordinances by declaring such laws must be made by a full Parliament, not by barons alone. This hit exactly the weak point in the Ordainers' conduct: they had tried to govern for the people, but not by the people. They had been blind to the great upgrowth of political consciousness in the nation. They were still at heart with the narrow exclusive baronage of 1258, and ignored the rise of representative Parliament in the interval. But their power to harm, despite Edward's triumph, was not exhausted yet. In 1323 he made ignominious peace with the Scots. In 1325 his queen and younger son, whom he had sent to France on a mission, joined Roger Mortimer, the fugitive rebel, and on September 24th, 1326, they returned " to avenge Lancaster, and punish the Despensers"; the barons, the Londoners, the bishops, the king's own brothers, all joined them. They took Bristol, and hanged the elder Despenser on a gallows fifty feet high, and the younger at Hereford. At the Parliament in January the mob clamoured for the king's deposition; the archbishop preached on the text "*Vox populi, vox Dei.*" The king was made to confess himself unworthy to reign; all renounced allegiance, and his son was proclaimed.

The Accession of Edward III.   On the 21st of September it was announced that Edward was dead in Berkeley Castle: murdered, we cannot doubt, and murdered by connivance at least of the adulterous queen and her paramour. These now ruled the kingdom for nearly four years. It is true Edward III. was crowned king, and that Henry of Lancaster was head of the Council; but it was Mortimer who took to himself all the Despenser estates, with the new title of Earl of March; who, through the queen, absorbed two-thirds of the Crown revenues; whose retinue of one hundred and eighty knights and assumption of the state of a " May-day king " provoked his own son's remonstrances, and persuaded the nation that he aimed at the throne itself. It was to little purpose that they had exchanged Edward and the Despensers for Isabella and Mortimer. The failure of the great host raised in 1328 to repel the Scots, and the inglorious terms of the "Foul Peace" of Northampton, were ascribed to treachery on the part of Mortimer. Still more clearly, in the trap laid for Edmund of Kent, the late king's brother, and his consequent execution, was seen Mortimer's handiwork. Already Henry of Lancaster had vainly tried to effect a rising which should throw off the favourite's yoke; but he had failed, and had to pay dearly for it. Thus when, at the instigation of the Lancastrian party, the young king cleverly entered Nottingham Castle at night by an underground passage, and arrested Mortimer, there went up a general cry of triumph from the whole land. He was tried by the Lords, condemned unheard, and suffered a traitor's cruel death at Smithfield, December, 1330. When his great-grandson married Philippa of Clarence, that destiny which made the Mortimers as it were the fated curse of the Plantagenet house began its final fulfilment. Richard, Duke of York, cousin and supplanter of Henry VI., was the son of the last heiress of the Mortimers ; and the name of this powerful family only died out in the general destruction which involved both royal

Mortimer Executed.

SEAL OF EDWARD III.

branches and the families allied to them. With the fall of Mortimer and the seclusion of Isabella the real reign of Edward III. begins.

In a later age, and even in modern times, that reign has often been looked back upon as a golden age of prosperity and glory. But even such a superficial view must recognise that from the year 1349 the picture of the reign assumes a more sombre colouring. From that year the mistakes of foreign policy, the cruel weight of taxation, Court intrigues and quarrels, political discontent, and ominous mutterings of a great social storm, force themselves into notice. But till then, one who saw, like Froissart, only the bright surface of things, had a stirring tale to tell. Edward had supported the raid of Edward Baliol into Scotland to dispossess the young king, David Bruce. In a few weeks Baliol wore the crown, but for a few weeks only. In 1333, the Scots, advancing to relieve Berwick, suffered the crushing defeat of Halidon Hill. The young King of Scots fled to France. Scotland submitted

The Reign of Edward III.

Scotland.

to Edward, and received Baliol back for a while. But it was too late now to revive Edward I.'s great plan. Stubbornly the Scots fought the English back, and in 1341 David Bruce returned to wear an independent crown. This support given by France to the Scots was, no doubt, the determining cause of the Hundred Years' War with France, which began in 1337 by Edward's claiming the throne in right of his mother, sister of the last king. This claim seems to a modern mind both ridiculous and insincere. But there were other meanings in it besides: to save the great Flemish cities from French control; to assert the newly declared "Lordship of the Seas" against Norman privateers; to strike a blow at the alliance of France with the Papacy, by a counter-alliance with the emperor and the German princes. But despite his array of allies, little was done in the first campaigns save the exploit of the sea-fight off Sluys, the first of England's glorious roll of naval victories. In 1345 the three years' truce was broken; next year was the year of Crecy, almost coincident with the great defeat of the Scots at Neville's Cross and the capture of King David. The taking of Calais, in 1347, led to another truce, which lasted seven years.

The War with France.

Thus these years witnessed a mighty outburst of national energy by land and sea, at home and abroad, in warfare and in commerce. The wars were taken up by national patriotism, were fought with the national weapon, the long-bow, and were won by the national character of the new English army. The men who won Crecy and Poitiers were mostly freeholders, serving at good wages, but also for love of "their natural lords," who led them to battle : combining thus the best points of the feudal levy, the national militia, and the new principle of mercenaries. Compared with the tumultuous feudal host of the French, it was a professional army; compared with their reluctant serfs, it was an army that could well face odds of five to one. This triumph of infantry over heavy cavalry was the death-knell of feudalism. What the English archers did in the fourteenth century, the Swiss pikemen did in the fifteenth, and the Spanish swordsmen in the sixteenth. At last the mailed and mounted knight who had dominated Europe for four centuries was seen to be an anachronism.

Features of the Reign.

It was also during these years that the Commons can first be clearly seen sitting as a separate House of Parliament. It was the king's policy to flatter them into responsibility for the war : in 1338 he declared it "at the urgency of the Commons." But as early as 1340 the bill of war-costs had cooled their military ardour ; they would make a fresh grant only as the price of a statute enacting that no charge or aid should be made henceforth save by Parliament. This Act

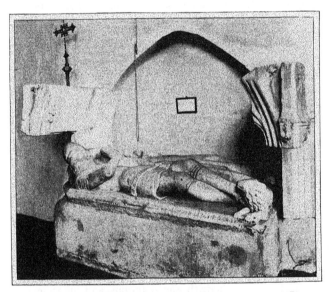

THE EARLIEST REPRESENTATION OF A KNIGHT OF THE GARTER.
(Sir William Fitzwarin, Wantage Church, Berks.)

completed the long series of steps, beginning from the forms used under the Norman kings, by which control over taxation passed from the Crown to the people. Edward's need of money forced him to these and other concessions. The same need obliged him to abandon the siege of Tournai, and brought him into undignified collision with his own ministers. He seems to have suspected them of intercepting funds which ought to have been sent out to him. He returned home suddenly, landed at the Tower at midnight, dismissed chancellor, treasurer, judges, and other officials, and issued a series of violent charges against the two Stratfords. But the Peers stood by the archbishop ; each Estate, Lords, Clergy, and Commons, urged grievances for which the king had to pro. mise redress. He had to bow to the storm which he himself had raised ; but six months later he coolly announced he had " dissembled, as he was justified in doing," and declared void the statutes just passed. This conduct marks the highest point reached by the royal prerogative in the fourteenth century, as the action of the Commons marks their attain. ment of an equal place beside the two other Estates. The re-opening of the war in 1345 led to heavy taxation; in 1347 the Florentine creditors of Edward were bankrupt; in 1348 the Commons refuse to be led into further approval of the war, and their statement of grievances rises to an unexampled tone of bitterness. But all political movements were suddenly stopped by the great plague which reached England in May, 1349. It fell like a -thunderbolt upon national wars, political discontents, and social progress, paralysing them all. For two years Parliament and the Law Courts ceased, the corn rotted ungathered in the fields; and yet it was at this very time that Edward with lavish pomp was founding his Order of the Garter. Nothing could be a bitterer comment on the super. ficial view of this reign.

O. M. EDWARDS. The Struggle for Wales: 613-1284. In the year 613 a great battle was fought beneath the walls of Chester between Ethelfrith, King of Northumbria, and a host of Welsh princes, led by Iago, King of Gwynedd, and Selyf, King of Powys. Ethelfrith was victorious, and his victory was followed by the destruction of Chester, and by an Angle occupation of the plain from which its walls and towers rose. Chester had guarded the plain which divides the mountains of Wales from those of Strathclyde ; upon the strength of its walls depended the existence of the union of the two Welsh regions. In 577 the battle of Deorham gave the Saxons the Severn plain, thereby separating Cornwall from Wales; the battle of Chester separated Wales from Strathclyde, and from 613 Wales has a distinct history of its own. For twenty years and more after the battle of Chester attempts were

made to reunite the two provinces; and the name of Cymry
—"people of the same region"—was adopted by both sections
of the Welsh people during this struggle. Though the national
name survived in both provinces—Cymru and Cumberland—
the reunion of north and west was regarded as hopeless early
in the eighth century.

Welsh political history between 613 and 1284 consists of
two great struggles—the struggle against the English, who
were being gradually welded into one people; and the struggle
of some able Welsh prince for an overlordship over his

Photo: J. Maclardy, Oswestry.
OFFA'S DYKE: NEAR OSWESTRY.

fellow-princes. The geography of Wales is a picture of its
history—its mountains separate it from England, and at the
same time make internal union almost impossible. Both
English king and Welsh prince were engaged in a hopeless
struggle against the mountains.

Between 613 and 1066 three English kingdoms struggled
for the overlordship of England. Northumbria, Mercia, and
Wessex had the supremacy, each in its turn, for a hundred
years; and with each of these, in the day of its power, Wales
had to contend. Ethelfrith of Northumbria separated it from
the north; and the victories of Cadwallon could not break

Wales and
the Old
English
Kingdoms.

46

the power of the Northumbrian, or loose his hold on Chester.
Offa of Mercia narrowed its boundaries on the east, and built
a dyke from the mouth of the Dee to the mouth of the Taff.
But it was during the supremacy of Wessex that the strife
was bitter enough to force all Welshmen to unite against the
Dane, who plundered the western shores, and against the West
Saxon, who was ever trying to subdue the Welsh princes.
Three great princes rose — Roderick the Great, Llywelyn
ap Seisyllt, and Gruffydd [Griffith] ap Llywelyn. Roderick
fell in battle against the English in 877; and the country
swerved back to its old anarchy until Llywelyn ap Seisyllt
arose. The battle of Aber Gwili[1] made him undisputed king
of all Wales. He cleared the country of Dane and Saxon, and
at his death, in 1027, he left Wales in prosperity and peace.
After another interval of disintegration, Gruffydd ap Llywelyn
rebuilt his father's power. The battles of Rhyd y Groes and
Hereford made him not only supreme in Wales, but the terror
of the English borders. He united with Elfgar of Mercia, and
taxed the power of Harold to the utmost extent when Wessex
was at its strongest. The generalship of Harold and the
treachery of the Welsh princes, who were jealous of Gruffydd's
supremacy, destroyed the work of the great Welsh king.
" Gruffydd, who had been invincible," the Welsh chronicler
says, " the head and shield of the Britons, was destroyed by
his own men."

Wales after the Norman Conquest. Harold had not succeeded in uniting England when William
the Conqueror came in 1066, otherwise the Norman Conquest
would not have been possible. It is Harold's policy that explains the ease with which the eastern and southern portions
of Wales were conquered by the Norman adventurers. He
had placed partisans of his own in power—the family of
Bleddyn ap Cynfyn—and these could not hold their own
against the partisans of the great Gruffydd's family without
English help. While this struggle was at its height in Wales,
the Norman barons began to possess the valleys. Hugh of
Avranches was placed in Chester, from the walls of which he
could cast greedy eyes on Welsh land to the west, just as he
had coveted Breton lands from the height of Avranches. At
Rhuddlan, the fierce Robert, half Norman, half Dane, strength-

---

[1] Near Carmarthen.

ened his position as the lord of the Vale of Clwyd, butchering
the Welsh without mercy, slaughtering them like herds of
cattle wherever he came up with them. The wise Roger of
Montgomery obtained the castle and earldom of Shrewsbury,
and his dominion was soon extended over the region of the
Upper Severn and the Vyrnwy. From Hereford, its Norman

PICTON CASTLE, PEMBROKESHIRE.

earls penetrated along the valleys of the Wye and Usk to the
Welsh mountains. The Clares and other families conquered
the pleasant plains of Gwent and Morgannwg,[1] and built castles
along the south coast, and along the west coast as far as
Aberystwyth. About 1081 it seemed as if the whole of Wales
would become Norman.

[1 Welsh names are usually accented on the penultimate syllable —
"Morgánnoog."]

What remained was the wild land guarded by Snowdon, the Berwyn, and Plinlimon. Before this land could be conquered, two great Welsh princes turned back the Norman tide. In 1081 Gruffydd ap Cynan [1] became prince of North Wales, and Rhys ap Tewdwr prince of South Wales. Gruffydd ap Cynan caught Robert of Rhuddlan, and beheaded him. The Normans of Brecon killed Rhys ap Tewdwr [Tudor], but he was succeeded by his son Gruffydd ap Rhys, who was abler and more powerful than his father. Henry I. saw that the march lords could not hold their own, but he died before he could give them any effective help. During the anarchy of the reign of Stephen the Welsh princes became independent; and when Gruffydd ap Cynan and Gruffydd ap Rhys died, in 1137, their place was taken by Owen Gwynedd in North Wales and by Rhys ap Gruffydd in South Wales.

Wales and Henry II.   When Henry II. came to the throne, he saw the dangerous power of the two Welsh princes. He tried to break the power of Owen Gwynedd by detaching his brother Cadwalader from him. He then determined to crush the Welsh princes at one blow; he marched along the eastern slopes of Berwyn, while Owen Gwynedd, Rhys ap Gruffydd, and the minor princes were encamped on the western slopes. The storms and the mountains fought against the English king, and he was forced to leave Wales.

Between the death of Henry II. and the accession of Edward I. the Welsh princes lost their last chance of establishing the independence of their country. Owen Gwynedd died in 1170, and Rhys ap Gruffydd in 1197, and their deaths were followed by the refusal of the princes to obey their successors. The Norman lords found themselves strong enough to renew their encroachments, and the Welsh boundaries again began to recede.

Wales and the English Church.   It was during this time of weakness that an attempt was made to win back the ecclesiastical independence of Wales. Before the end of the twelfth century Wales had been subjected to the archiepiscopal see of Canterbury. This had been done very gradually. When the newly converted English decided at the Synod of Whitby, in 664, to accept Roman rather than British Christianity, the Church of England and

[[1] C in Welsh is hard—"Kinnan."]

the Church of Wales were separated by many important differences—differences which found outward expression in tonsure and the date of Easter (Vol. I., p. 231). In 809 the Welsh Church yielded, and the schism was at an end. The next step was to subject the Welsh sees to Canterbury. In 1107 a Bishop of Llandaff was consecrated at Canterbury; in 1115 a Norman was appointed to the bishopric of St. Davids; and before 1143 the Archbishop of Canterbury had claimed jurisdiction over all Wales. Between 1198 and 1204 Giraldus Cambrensis made a last ineffectual struggle to secure the independence of the Welsh Church by reviving the metro-politanship of St. Davids, which was erroneously supposed to have been once an archbishopric and the metro-politan church of Wales. Giraldus's effort came too soon even for tem-porary success, coming as it did a few years before the rise of the power of Llewellyn the Great. An interest-ing combination it would have been—the greatest organiser Wales has seen, and the gifted writer whose descrip-tions are still in many points vivid descriptions of his people (I. p. 506).

GRIFFITH'S ESCAPE FROM THE TOWER OF LONDON. (MS. Roy. 14 C. vii.)

By 1210 Llywelyn ab Iorwerth—"Llewellyn the Great"—grandson of Owen Gwynedd, had established a supremacy over the parts of Wales that had not been conquered by the Normans. The Wales of Llywelyn included Anglesey and the country to the west of the Snowdon, Berwyn, and Plinlimon ranges. When his position in Wales was secured, he united with the English barons, and his rights were acknowledged by the English king in the Great Charter. When Llywelyn died, in 1240, the castles of Wales were his castles, and the princes of Wales were his vassals. After a short interval of disintegration, another Llywelyn —"Llywelyn ap Gruffydd," or "The Last Llewellyn"—became Prince of all Wales. He pursued his grandfather's policy of first securing his own position in Wales, and then of weakening the power of the English Crown by assisting the English barons. A marriage was arranged between him and Eleanor, the daughter of Simon de Montfort, the leader of the barons. When the barons were defeated by Edward at the battle of Evesham, Llywelyn had to make terms with the English prince. His betrothed wife, Eleanor, had been captured by the English at sea, and he remembered that his father had died in his attempt to escape from an English prison.

Edward I. in Wales. When Edward became King of England, in 1272, he saw that the power of Llywelyn must be crushed, were it only in order to make the English barons obedient. He demanded homage of the Welsh prince, and homage was refused. Edward took advantage of a quarrel between Llywelyn and his brother David; and by 1274 Llywelyn was master of the Snowdon district only. The English administration of the rest of Llywelyn's country caused great discontent, and eventually drove the Welsh to rebellion. David began to fear that the Welsh princes would be utterly destroyed, and returned to his allegiance to Llywelyn. In 1282 Llywelyn and David declared war, and the former hastened to South Wales. The fall of Llywelyn in a skirmish near Builth made the last Welsh struggle for independence a hopeless one. Many of the petty princes took the English side, and the conquest of Wales became an easy matter. David was hunted down and subjected to the terrible penalties of treason; the precious portion of the true cross and the crown of Arthur were carried away. At Rhuddlan—whose ivied towers still stand on the bank of the Clwyd—the Statute of Wales was passed, in 1284. As far as possible the old Welsh law was retained, but the administration became perfectly English. The country was divided into six shires—Carnarvon, Anglesey, Merioneth, Flint, Cardigan, and Carmarthen—and governed in exactly the same way as the English counties. The king's sheriffs took the place of the petty Welsh princes, and the power of Llywelyn was vested in the king's eldest son as Prince of Wales.

By 1284 the subjection of Wales was complete. Archbishop Peckham visited the dioceses; Edward I. passed among the mountains as their lord. The growth of towns was en-

Photo: Chester Vaughan, Acton, W.

RHUDDLAN CASTLE.

couraged, and Wales would perhaps have been eventually assimilated to England, had it not been for the region of great march earldoms that lay between the two countries.

CHARLES RAYMOND BEAZLEY.
The Church and the Crown.
THE history of religion in England, between the accession of Edward I. and the Black Death, is strictly a part of the general story of Christendom. As on the Continent, so in England, this is the age of triumphant Catholicism passing into decline. The thirteenth century, the summer of Latin Christianity, the mid-winter of Islam, unified the civilisation which in the twelfth century seemed moving towards the many-sided and divergent activity of modern life. Abelard's method, and his tendency to free thought, but used in an orthodox sense, reappeared in Aquinas, Albert, and Duns, who used the language and methods of reason to establish orthodoxy. The friars and the inquisitors subdued the heretics and stirred the worldly to a religious revival. The Crusades languished in Palestine; but on one side the Crusading movement extended the religious empire of old Rome to the new, and, on the other, won back from the Moslem all Spain except Granada. The Church of Western Europe lost Byzantium in 1261; but in 1272-4, as Edward of England returned from Acre to London, all the islands and northern coasts of the Mediterranean, except a strip from Malaga to Cadiz, were Catholic lands once more, as in the days of Justinian. The Roman Christendom that had been centralised by Hildebrand was at the height of its power in the era which begins with Innocent III. and closes with Boniface VIII. The Papacy seemed victorious over all its older rivals—over the great Patriarchs, the bishops of Ravenna and Rheims, Cologne and Canterbury, Milan and Compostella; over the emperors, once, like Charles the Great or Henry III., the patrons, and now, after the days of Frederic II., the German instruments of the Apostolic See; even over national Churches, such as the English. A more serious struggle was to come; with the rising monarchies of the Christian Republic, with the towns and Parliaments of the new full-grown nations, France and England.

This contest was provoked by Boniface VIII. In 1274,

under Gregory X., the Pope seemed the friend of all his spiritual children; at the second Council of Lyons in this year even the Greek Church was for a moment reconciled to Rome. On all sides Latin Christendom was expanding; Ice-

A THIRTEENTH CENTURY BISHOP. (MS. Roy. 2 A. xxii.)

land and Greenland had been brought into its federation since the eleventh century; in the thirteenth, Franciscan missionaries preceded Marco Polo across Tartary to China, while Genoese seamen attempted to open up the African coasts and the Sea of Darkness; the Teutonic Knights began to convert

Prussia; the German Hansa started their trading centre at Novgorod (1., p. 651).

But during the life of Edward I. of England this expansion of Christian States came into conflict, on a far larger scale than in the twelfth century, with the Christian Church. His archbishops, Peckham and Winchelsey, struggle against a kingly overlord, as Becket had struggled against Henry II., as the Popes had struggled against the German kings, and were now, with Boniface VIII., struggling against nationalism in general.

All through the earlier part of the thirteenth century, from St. Hugh of Lincoln to Grosseteste, the Church of England[1] had pretty well expressed the mind of the people of England; the clergy, oppressed both by Pope and king, had led the popular movement for responsible, representative government. But now Edward's ideal of a strong island-empire, friendly with Rome but independent of outside power, aimed at pressing religion, with other interests, into common subjection to a national unity expressed in himself. He was resolved to have no divided sovereignty. As far as the clerical estate stood for an "imperium in imperio," his policy was to degrade it. Not only was Rome to be kept at arm's length, and all its claims to homage and fealty and Scottish overlordship rejected, as William the Conqueror had rejected the Papal pretensions of his day; but the hold of the native English Church over land and chattels was to be shaken, its power of aggrandisement to be checked, its spiritual courts subjected to the law of the land.

I. The history of Church and State under Edward I. is chiefly concerned with three legal enactments—the Statute of Mortmain in 1279, the writ Circumspecte Agatis[2] in 1285, and the confirmation of the Charters in 1297. The separate

---

[1] A body completely organised, with a hierarchy minutely regulated. legislating for itself, taxing itself, in its recognised assemblies, judicative and executive, and, though not as a corporation holding common property, yet composed of a great number of persons, each holding property. As an estate of the realm, its clergy acknowledge the headship of the king; as part of the Western Church, that of the Pope (Stubbs, Const. Hist., III., c. 19).

[2 Its opening words, i.e. "Deal circumspectly" (in all matters concerning the jurisdiction and rights in things spiritual of the Bishop of Norwich and his clergy): an order to the Judges of Assize.]

and later battle of Pope and king over Scottish suzerainty, the ruin of the Templars in 1307–12, and the action of the Church under Edward II. and Edward III., either do not properly concern English religion at all, or belong to the purely social part of this section rather than to ecclesiastical politics.

(1) And first of all as to mortmain. Before the Norman **Mortmain.** Conquest a licence from the Crown seems to have been

EDWARD I. CONFIRMING THE CHARTER
OF MARCH 8, 1300. (MS. Claud. D. II.)

expected for alienation into the " dead hand " of a spiritual corporation; but the alarm now felt lest all England should become Church property, enabled Edward, in 1279, to forbid such alienation absolutely. Land so granted was in forfeit to the lord, or, in his default, to the king, and the original law against grants in mortmain was made more stringent in 1285. The clerical resistance seems to have fallen back on legal evasions.

(2) The second of Edward's restraints provoked a more **Ecclesi-** open defiance. Perhaps all churchmen felt satisfied enough **astical** to be conservative on the land question—here they held the **diction.** ground, and were only just withheld from monopoly; but in jurisdiction it was time to make a stand. In spite of Henry II.'s apparent failure, the civil courts had steadily gained on the episcopal. Before the death of Henry III. laymen had in great part replaced churchmen as royal

justices ; now, under Edward I., the Primate admitted the abstract right of the King's Bench to issue prohibitions. The Statute of Westminster the First, in 1275, was construed to direct that clerks charged with felony should not be surrendered to their ordinary till an inquest of the charge had been made; if found guilty, their real and personal estate was to go to the Crown. Ten years later, in answer to a petition of prelates for some relaxation of royal prohibitions, Edward, by his writ Circumspecte Agatis, while seeming to guarantee the actual rights of spiritual jurisdiction, practically evaded the Church's claim in temporal contracts. He did not renounce these contracts, and his judges accordingly claimed them all as the exclusive property of the royal courts. More expressly the king forbade the bishops to infringe his prerogatives by touching cases of breach of contract and rights of patronage.

Taxation of the Church. (3) Thus both in land and jurisdiction the older theocratic tendencies of society found their limit; but the lawyers' third attempt, to tax the clergy at the royal will, was a failure. Edward was apparently resolved to leave to his spirituality only a pre-eminence of money burdens. Not only did he gather representatives of the ordained in a central Parliament with the unordained, but he procured (about 1291) a new and higher valuation of Church property,[1] real and personal, and appointed commissioners for all the monastic, cathedral, and collegiate treasuries. Armed with this fresh knowledge, in 1291, under a Crusading agreement with Pope Nicholas IV., he demanded the tithe of ecclesiastical income, gathered it in for the Holy War, and three years afterwards, in the brief pontificate of the Hermit Celestine V., seized the opportunity to require, in full Parliament at Westminster, one-half of the revenues of the Church. William Montfort, Dean of St. Paul's, sent to remonstrate, fell dead of fright at the king's feet; in the Convocation held within the royal palace, Sir John Havering proclaimed, in Edward's name, "If any oppose the king's will, let him stand up that he may be noted as an enemy of the king's peace." The Primate, Winchelsey, was

---

[1] At £204,143 19s. 2d., without counting the goods of the Bishops of Lincoln and Winchester, and of Christ Church, Canterbury (separately reckoned : Winchester and Lincoln, £3,977 15s. 7d. ; Christ Church, Canterbury, £355 9s. 2d.).

in Rome, and the clergy gave way for the time, awaiting his return. Again the tax was gathered, and next year Edward's cherished design of including the national Church in the national assembly was realised in the Model Parliament of 1295. He had summoned the proctors of the First Estate to York and Northampton in 1283, to London in 1294; now the clerical grants, his main support, were to be an item in the supplies given by the whole nation in one Parliament, in one place, at one time, to the ruler of all estates in the realm.

The clergy, however, soon refused to vote save in their own clerical house and by separate grants. This they ultimately gained; from the middle of the fourteenth century Convocation always sits apart;[1] and the king was obliged to moderate his demands. But now, in 1296, Boniface VIII., by the Bull Clericis Laicos, forbade the clergy to pay taxes of any kind to the laity, and so provoked the crisis of 1297. In full Parliament at Bury St. Edmunds, Winchelsey, on behalf of Convocation, refused to vote any further moneys. Edward, in answer, placed the royal seal on all Church trusts and storehouses; and on the repeated refusal of the Synod at St. Paul's, the Chief Justice formally outlawed the whole body of the clergy, and the barony of the archbishop was seized for the king's use.

Meanwhile the nobles and merchants had likewise broken with Edward; Scotland was rising under Wallace; and the war in Flanders compelled the king's instant departure from England. But he dared not leave his throne and his son amid universal discontent. Winchelsey, who had led the constitutional as well as the clerical cause, was the first to profit by the royal repentance. Edward restored his barony, gave the heir of the kingdom into his charge, and prepared to renew the Charter and respect the liberties of the Church. Like Elizabeth in 1601, he confessed himself misled; it had been in sorrowful reluctance that he had burdened his subjects. The Primate discovered that, though the Pope's Bull forbade

Con-vocation

---

[1] In 1341 the Crown—acquiescing in the rule that clerical tenths (£20,000 on Pope Nicholas's valuation of 1291) should be granted in provincial Convocations—ceased to insist on the attendance of the clerical proctors in Parliament, a custom which in the fifteenth century ceased altogether.

churchmen to obey a royal demand for money, it did not forbid them to volunteer their aid.   The king, who just before embarking for Flanders, had begun the seizure of a third of clerical temporalities and forbidden the excommunication of his tax-collectors, had been foiled by the alliance of Pope and Primate, clergy and nobles, Scotland and France, against his dictatorship ; and, in that alliance, the Church again appeared as the champion of freedom.[1]

After Boniface had fallen, and the Papacy had been moved to Avignon (p. 214), Winchelsey was prosecuted in the Papal Curia, and the old alliance of Pope and king, broken by the Bull Clericis Laicos, was renewed with Clement V., who absolved Edward from his oaths of 1297, and suspended the archbishop. Yet the last years of the reign are not without anti-Papal laws.   Long after the Pope's claims of lordship over Scotland had been repudiated in 1301, the Statute of Carlisle, in 1370, attacked the abuses of foreign patronage, " provisions," " first-fruits," and " Peter's pence."

Edward I. reversed the policy of Henry III. by subjecting the Papal interests to the royal in the national Church.   With this aim, he compelled the renunciation by his clergy of all words in Papal Bulls prejudicial to the Crown's authority, and practically suppressed the elective rights of his cathedral chapters.   The weakness of Edward II. enabled Clement V. to put his nominees into English benefices, as Boniface VIII. had tried to do at York both before and at the time of his jubilee in 1300.   Unlike Archbishop Romanus at that crisis, Edward II. played into the Pope's hands, and his father's policy of a Holy League in which the Pope should serve the king was not restored till the reign of Edward III.   In conclusion, let us take three typical instances of the struggle of the Roman and Royalist parties with the English in the national Church of this time :—

(1) In 1282 Peckham found one Menling, a non-resident prelate of foreign extraction, Bishop of Lichfield, ordered him back to his see, and appointed the Archdeacon of Derby as an English-speaking suffragan, requiring the " Pope's man " to pay him one hundred marks a year and to consult him on all official acts.

[1] As in 1341, when Archbishop Stratford won peers the right of trial by their peers.

(2) In 1333 Archbishop Meopham died of vexation partly caused by innumerable abuses of this sort, all springing from the same cause, the alliance of the Roman and English Courts. The abuses he was powerless to check till the league

TOMB OF ARCHBISHOP PECKHAM.
(Canterbury Cathedral.)

itself was broken up, and so they flourished, as we are told of a certain diocese in 1326 :—

(3) "Out of fifty prebends in the gift of the Bishop of Salisbury, twenty-eight had been 'provided' by the late and the present Pope—not more than three of their holders ever

resided—and, to crown all, eight more were waiting under promise of prebends at their first vacancy."

The
Church
and the
Nation.
II. The social aspect of Church history is the chief interest of these latter years (1297–1348) after the close of the struggle with Edward I. The higher clergy became more and more pliant as they felt their growing dependence on the Crown; the lower, except perhaps the parish priests, were fast losing all the spirit of the last revival of religion. Not a few traces of anti-clerical spirit among gentry and commons appear in the early fourteenth century; it is not simply against Papal interference or monastic overgrowth, it is the beginning of a revolt against clerical influence in politics and society.

Edward I. had found an episcopal regency on his return from Palestine; next year Walter de Merton, Bishop of Rochester, leaves the chancery to Bishop Robert Burnell. Yet episcopal influence decays during the reign; on the board of arbitrators on the Scottish claims nominated by the king in 1296 there are only four bishops. Again, the protests of the Lincoln and Carlisle Parliaments, in 1301 and 1307, against Papal (that is, hierarchical) claims over Scotland and Papal provisions in England remind us of the most independent language of the thirteenth century. Far more notable is the Canterbury riot of May, 1327, against clerical privilege; the Ilchester riot of 1348 against the Bishop of Bath and Wells; the Commons' petition of 1344 against clerical legislation for laymen; the appointment of the first lay Chancellor in 1340; the general and growing reluctance to pay tithes. The suppression of the Templars first foreshadows the general dissolution of monasteries in 1536–39; and the increasing dislike of the friars, and in a measure of all the "religious," warns us of a coming revolt not against abuses of the medieval religion so much as against that religion in itself. Yet in politics, in education, in care of the poor, in general influence, down to the smallest details of life, the Church, even in her decline, still penetrates to every corner of society.

First among the proofs of waning clerical power let us take the scene at Canterbury in Edward III.'s first year. The Prior of Christ Church was summoned to help the bailiff and citizens in sending twelve men-at-arms to Newcastle against Robert Bruce. Lands held in free aluis (frankalmoigne), replied the Prior, could not be held liable to military service.[1] On this, bailiff and citizens held a meeting "in the field by the House of Preaching Friars" and swore to nine articles. First, "To pull down all the tenements in Burgate down to the Mill.' Second, "No one, under penalties imposed by the city, to live in the Prior's Houses." Third, "All rents of 200 marks and upwards to be levied for the city." Fourth, "No one to buy, sell, or exchange drink or victuals with the monastery." Fifth, "All carts and horses from the Christ Church manors carrying victuals or stock for the monastery to be seized and held with their contents." Sixth, "Any monks (even the Prior) coming out of the monastery to be spoiled of goods and clothes and to be attached." Seventh, "To dig a trench at the great gate of the monastery, so that no one should go in or out." Eighth, "To allow no stranger to enter the church, except on oath to offer no gift, even at S. Thomas' Shrine." Ninth, "Each citizen swore that he would have from the same shrine, of the gold rings hung up by pilgrims, one for each finger of each hand." So at Ilchester, in 1348, the Bishop of Bath and Wells was kept prisoner in the church for several hours, and his servants were beaten and wounded in the churchyard by the mob. These quarrels were tided over, but the records remain to illustrate the general rebellion against clerical privilege, and especially the weariness, expressed by Gregory X. in 1274, of the "unbridled multitude" of the religious, and by many thoughtful observers of the pride, avarice, riches, and worldliness of many bishops and monks. They exhibit also the alarm of fourteenth-century provincial councils at the grudging payment of tithes. The clergy, it is ordered, are to take away their tenth sheaf by the same road as the farmer. Sometimes they had been forced to cart on bypaths, not allowed to take any but the last shock left, and that often trampled by cattle. Personal tithes are to be paid out of the profits of trade and labour, even from mines.

But it was in jurisdiction that the "laicising" movement

[1 In theory, the clergy were held to satisfy all obligations by their spiritual work, and were said to hold their land "in free alms."]

47

was strongest. The Church courts were the Church's worst enemy, and their abuses were among the first marks of the attacks of the New Learning—of men like Chaucer and Wycliffe. Matrimonial and testamentary causes, actions for recovery of "spiritual payments" and for "cognisance of vice,"

AN ECCLESIASTICAL COURT. (MS. Add. 15,274.)

and "correction of manners"[1]—these were the subject-matter of the bishops' courts, vaguely limited by the writs of Edward I., and it was against these as touching the laity, in any point, that the Commons petitioned in 1344, "That no motion made

[1] Spiritual payments—tithes and Church fees; moral cases—heresy, slander and usury, as well as adultery, etc.

by the clergy to the injury of the laity might be granted without examination before the king and the lords." The dominance of the prelates in the House of Lords alone prevented an open breach between the Church law and that of the land. But as the protest of 1344 is a sign of the coming end of clerical legislation for the laity, so the Mortmain statute of 1279 and the Carlisle petition against Provisors in 1307 are signs of the future jurisdiction of lay courts over the Church, the system of the Tudor revolution.

Next comes the first faint sign of the official anti-monastic movement on the part of European and Christian States—the first warning of a coming disestablishment of all monasticism.

It was in the autumn of 1307 that Edward II. was urged by Philip of France, and commanded by Clement V., to arrest the Knights Templars within his realm, as had been done in France. At first he wavered; wrote to Portugal, Castille, Sicily, and Aragon (December 4) expressing his doubts, to the Pope (December 10) stating his belief in the faith and morals of the Order; but on December 20 he gave way, arrested all the Templars of England, and examined them minutely on the Papal charges. By the end of 1312 the military monks "of the Temple of God and of Solomon" had been suppressed throughout Christendom, if not "by way of justice," as the Pope said, at any rate "by way of expediency," and the bulk of their estates transferred to their rivals of the Hospital. Were this all, it might pass as a mere piece of statecraft or the natural result of the final loss of Palestine in 1291; but the tales told by English witnesses have a social value as bearing on the national hate of secrecy, of foreign ways, of organisations in any way independent of the community and its rulers. The ruin of the military monks, who affected to disregard English law as subjects of a foreign master, was typical of the approaching fate of the alien priories under Henry V., of the dissolution of all monkery, brought about by much the same causes in 1536-39. "Rome only do ye seek," says Glanvill; "Rome only shall destroy you." "We see you are but half our subjects," ran the sentence of Henry VIII. Now by seven witnesses it was proved against the English Templars that the reception-rite was secret, by three more that the secret could not be discussed among themselves,

The Attack on the Templars.

far less among outsiders; four others swore they were forbidden to confess save to priests of their own Order. Another had heard of dreadful secrets: in Syria they received knights with blasphemy, spitting on the Cross; some worshipped a cat-idol, a brazen head, a calf—others wrote and read that "Christ died, not for our sins, but for His own."

One Robert of Oteringham, a Franciscan, had been at Westerby twenty years before, when the Templars were

A DEFENDER OF THE FAITH.
(*St. Robert's Chapel, Knaresborough.*)

arranging some relics; he had looked through a hole in the wall and seen a blaze. Next day he asked a brother what saint they worshipped; he turned pale: "On thy life, ask no more." Another Templar, one Robert Bayser, had been heard groaning in the fields, "That ever I was born to deny Christ and hold to the Devil!" There was a story of a Templar's little boy, asked by his father if he would join the

Order, answering that he had seen a postulant forced at the sword's point to apostatise. At this the father murdered him. The grandfather of one witness entered the Order in full vigour, and in three days was dead; a certain Walter Savage had likewise disappeared after two years; Adam de Heton

Photo: York & Sons, Notting Hill, W.

TEMPLE CHURCH, LONDON.

knew of a boys' watchword, "Beware of the kisses of the Templars"; William de Berney had heard of one of their secret doctrines, "That man has no more a living soul than a dog." One Roger, rector of Godmersham, had been warned by a brother, Stephen Quenteril, "If you could be Grand Master, yet never join us. We have three vows, known only to God, the Devil, and ourselves." The vicar of Sutton had heard of a priest-Templar forbidden to consecrate in the mass; and a foreigner, one John de Gertia, had heard an old, old story from a woman named "Cacocaca, who lived near St. Giles, in London, hard by some elms," of secret, black and midnight chapters at Dinclee. There they worshipped a black idol with shining eyes and held the foulest orgies. William Bachelor, before he disappeared, had been heard to exclaim, "I have lost my soul in the Temple." Several servants of Templars, caught spying, had been offered death or admission as the only choice, while refractory brethren were sewn in sacks and so drowned. Three deserters from the Order closed the evidence with personal revelations. They had been admitted with blasphemy, apostasy, and un-natural vice; men stood over them with drawn swords and forced them to deny Christ and to confess only the "Great God." The late Grand Preceptor, Brian le Jay, was a traitor to the Crusaders, a scoffer at the faith, a secret Moslem. He "held the least hair in a Saracen's beard worth more than his whole body." The shuddering abhorrence of ordinary Englishmen was felt in the proverbial question and answer, "Are you a Templar? Then, were you in the belfry of Paul's, you would not see more misery than will be yours ere you die."

The Templars Suppressed. On these grounds the proudest and richest among the Orders of religious chivalry was suppressed and ruined; but danger hardly less imminent threatened the preaching and begging friars. As the spiritual Franciscans developed their own principles and became the Fraticelli, they drew upon themselves the hate of Popes and kings, of all established interests; as the lower minds gave up their founder's ideal and sank into Christian fakirs, they seemed to degrade the common, the religious, life as it had never been degraded before. Every reformer like Langland, every man of the world like Chaucer, or reconstructive theorist like Wycliffe, **The Friars in Danger.** came to regard the mendicant Orders as the readiest mark of attack. As early as 1274 Gregory X. had restrained their "un-bridled multitude" to "all the four orders" noted in Piers Plowman. Boniface VIII., in 1301, forbade them to preach in parish churches without leave from the incumbent. Before the death of Henry III. Matthew Paris declared that friars had become more debased in one generation than Benedictine monks in three or four centuries. By the time of the Black Death their fall seemed only a question of time.

The Templars had gone; the friars, even the monks, were going. Of this wider anti-monastic spirit and its spread among all classes under the Edwards there is evidence enough, of which we have noticed some traces, and can only add, in this place, two illustrations: first, in the marked falling-off of religious foundations; second, in the history of Merton, the first Oxford College.

Feeling against the Monks.

MONKS HUNTING AND HAWKING
(MS. Roy. 6 E. vi.).

During the fourteenth century there were only sixty-four new monasteries and friaries, against more than 800 of older date (440 of the twelfth, and 296 of the thirteenth century); and even as early as 1274 Bishop Walter of Rochester, the ex-Chancellor, laid down that the fellows of Merton College, which he had just moved from his Surrey birthplace to the great English University, lost all the benefits of his endowment if they entered any order of religion. He knew how large a proportion, not only of the knights' fees but also of parish livings, had been appropriated to monasteries and chapters by this time; and he knew that, in consequence of this appropriation, a great part of England was not provided with the regular Church

UNDUE INFLUENCE (MS. Roy. 6 E. vii.).

system, but served with substitutes; and that from the overgrowth of the "Regulars" and their abnormal and unnational system had arisen an undergrowth of practical abuses—absentee and pluralist "vicars," the farming of benefices, the new chantry system,[1] the consequent decay of local charities and local interest, all tending to produce a low type of hired mass-priest, in whom there was little of the pastor, the student, or the gentleman.

Like Wykeham, Waynflete, and Wolsey, Merton seems to have aimed at a reformation of religion through education and works of charity, and his method was steadily followed by the wiser churchmen of the later Middle Ages. By the year 1400 there had been founded seventy-eight colleges and one hundred and ninety-two hospitals, and the fifteenth century added sixty schools and charitable foundations, as against no more than eight religious houses, to the roll.

Decline of the Church. In general, however, from the death of Edward II. the social decline of the Church was undeniable—in its relaxing hold upon politics and national life; in the deadness of its monastic orders (there is not one distinguished abbot in this time); in the beginnings of avowed dissent from its creed and system and of over-luxuriance in its architecture; in the decline of its missionary and Crusading spirit, as evidenced by the new plan of "vicarious" pilgrimage; in the growth of superstitious abuses; and in the severance of the clergy from the new spirit in science and letters and faith, foretold in the prophetic work of Roger Bacon, of Chaucer, and of Wycliffe.

The Church and the Masses. But the Black Death marks the beginning of a far more serious severance—of the Church from the people—from the social movements which gather round the Peasant Revolt of 1381. Before this the clergy had not only helped to "enforce the status and affirm the duty" of labour, but had engaged in the same industry and felt the same interests as the mass of the people. Clergy and laity as yet were a "community"; and, however much the union may have been impaired, it was only now beginning to break up. On the other side, the parish priesthood in Chaucer's day, as in the sixteenth century, was the abiding strength of the Church, the permanent and popular section of the hierarchy. And even in the early fourteenth century a movement was beginning towards a real reformation of religion. In education, in

---

[1] One of the earliest chantries seems to be at St. Helen's, Worcester, 1288.

vernacular carols, hymns, and books of devotion, in works of . charity, in readjusted dioceses, and extended parish organisation, the Church was slowly and tentatively adapting means to ends. Retrenchment was half the battle; and with 8,000 parish churches and some 40,000 clergy[1] of all grades and drawn from every class (including monks and friars), with revenues able to bear one-third of the national taxation, with almost a monopoly of learning, except for the bailiff class and a few. lay politicians, poets, and story-tellers, with

EFFIGY OF BISHOP WALTER DE STAPLEDON.
(Exeter Cathedral.)

the sacred Latin still generally understood—for even the political songs are still in a "macaroni" of Latin and English[2] —with all this to work upon, the Church might fairly hope to reform itself, to save all by giving up a part. Oxford and Cambridge Universities, the great training schools for the clergy, were taking more organised shape in the new College

[1] 29,161 about 1340, without mendicants—a number greatly reduced by the Black Death, but making 1 in every 52 of the people over 14 years of age.

[2] For examples of songs in a "macaronic" verse, *cf.* carol of A.D. 1500–30 :—

"Now make us joye in this Festé,   Syng we to hym and say wel
In quo Xtus natus est,   come,
A patre unigenitus   Veni Redemptor Gentium."

foundations (P. 94), the first of which, after Merton College, was that of Bishop Stapledon of Exeter, in 1314. Even more significant is the clergy school of Bishop Sawbridge, founded in Winchester between 1282–1305, and the vigorous attempts to enforce a regular system of catechising by the parish priests between 1270–1370. The provision for lepers, orphans, and destitute poor by hospitals and alms; the rights of " corrody "[1]

LICHFIELD CATHEDRAL.   *Photo: Poulton & Son, London.*

or free maintenance in religious houses, and the use of nunneries as boarding schools for girls; the common-sense permission granted to labourers to work on the Holy Days, so that, on the average, 308 out of the 365 were available; the English versions of the Psalms, Gospels, and Epistles in 1275, in 1320, and (by Richard Rolle of Hampole) in 1349 (p. 128); the new cathedrals and churches of the Decorated style, *e.g.* St. Paul's, London, finished in 1315 by Segrave; St. David's

[1 Corrody or corody (Medieval Latin *corrodium*, provision) was a privilege of founders and benefactors.]

Cathedral and Episcopal Palace, between 1328 and 1347 ; and Lichfield, the best existing type of a fourteenth-century English church—all these things are evidence that the Church, even at this time, and under such a Primate as Reynolds, was still alive.

The avarice of churchmen, the abuses of the Bishops' courts, the constant Papal interference, and the compulsory clerical celibacy leading to concubinage were the chief drawbacks on the Church's usefulness. The higher clergy were, on the whole, pure, and men like Kilwardby, Peckham, and Winchelsey were worthy leaders of English religion; but as the doctrine grew fixed that local or national reformation was heretical without the instance of Rome, men grew tired " both of the evils of the age and their remedies."

On the death of Henry III. there followed some eighteen years which even at this day may seem to us the most brilliant eighteen years in the whole history of English legis ation. At all events, if we are to find a comparable period we must look forward, for five hundred years and more, to the age of the first Reform Bill. Year by year King Edward I. in his Parliaments made laws on a grand scale. His statutes will not be in our eyes very lengthy documents ; but they are drastic, and they are permanent. They deal with all sorts of matters, public and private, but in particular with those elementary parts of the law of property and the law of civil procedure which English legislators have, as a general rule, been well content to leave alone. Just for this reason they are exceedingly permanent ; they become fundamental ; elaborate edifices of gloss and comment are reared upon them. To this day, despite all the reforms of the present century, we have to look to them, and the interpretation which has been set upon them, for some of the most elementary principles of our land law. When all has been said that can be said for the explanation of this unique outburst of legislation, it still remains a marvellous thing.

F. W. MAIT-LAND. Legal Reform under Edward I.

A professional class of English temporal lawyers was just beginning to form itself. We say "of English temporal lawyers," because for more than a century past there had

The Legal Profession.

been "legists" and "decretists"[1] in the land. These legists and decretists constituted a professional class; they held themselves out as willing to plead the causes of those who would pay their fees. They did a large business, for the clergy of the time were extremely litigious. The bishop who was not perennially engaged in interminable disputes with two or three wealthy religious houses was either a very fortunate or a very careless guardian of the rights of his see. And all the roads of ecclesiastical litigation led to Rome. Appeals to the Pope were made at every stage of every cause, and the most famous Italian lawyers were retained as advocates. The King of England, who was often involved in contests about the election of bishops—contests which would sooner or later come before the Roman Curia—kept Italian canonists[2] in his pay. Young Englishmen were sent to Bologna in order that they might learn the law of the Church. The University of Oxford was granting degrees in civil and canon law, the University of Cambridge followed her example. There was no lack of ecclesiastical lawyers; indeed, the wisest and most spiritual of the clergy thought that there were but too many of them, and deplored that theology was neglected in favour of a more lucrative science. And what we might call an ecclesiastical "Bar" had been formed. The canonist who wished to practise in a bishop's court had to satisfy the bishop of his competence, and to take an oath obliging him to practise honestly. The tribunals of the Church knew both the "advocate" (who pleads on behalf of a client) and the "procurator" or "proctor" (who represents his client's person and attends to his cause).

Attorneys and Barristers.   In course of time two groups similar to these grew up round the king's court. We see the "attorney" (who answers to the ecclesiastical proctor) and the "pleader," "narrator," or "countor" (who answers to the ecclesiastical advocate). But the formation of these classes of professional lawyers has not been easy. Ancient law does not readily admit that one man can represent another; in particular, it does not readily admit

[1 Professional exponents of Roman civil and ecclesiastical law respectively, the latter consisting largely of Papal decrees.]

[2 Authorities on ecclesiastical law, which was gradually codified into a body called canon law.]

that one man can represent another in litigation. So long as procedure is extremely formal, so long as all depends on the due utterance of sacramental words, it does not seem fair that you should put an expert in your place to say those words for you. My adversary has, as it were, a legal interest in my ignorance or stupidity. If I cannot bring my charge against him in due form, that charge ought to fail; at all events, he cannot justly be called upon to answer another person, some subtle and circumspect pleader, whom I have hired. Thus the right to appoint an attorney who will represent my person in court, and win or lose my cause for me, appears late in the day. It spreads outwards from the king. From of old the king must be represented by others in his numerous suits. This right of his he can confer upon his subjects—at first as an exceptional favour, and afterwards by a general rule. In Henry III.'s reign this process has gone thus far :—A litigant in the king's court may appoint an attorney to represent him in the particular action in which he is for the time being engaged : he requires no special licence for this ; but if a man wishes to appoint prospectively a general attorney, who will represent him in all actions, the right to do this he must buy from the king, and he will not get it except for some good cause. The attorneys of this age are by no means always professional men of business. Probably every free and lawful man may act as the attorney of another ; indeed, shocking as this may seem to us, we may, not very unfrequently, find a wife appearing in court as her husband's attorney.

The other " branch of the profession ".grows from a different stock. In very old days a litigant is allowed to bring his friends into court, and to take " counsel " with them before he speaks. Early in the twelfth century it is already the peculiar mark of a capital accusation that the accused must answer without " counsel." Then sometimes one of my friends will be allowed, not merely to prompt me, but even to speak for me. It is already seen that the old requirement of extreme verbal accuracy is working injustice. A man ought to have some opportunity of amending a mere slip of the tongue ; and yet old legal principles will not suffer that he should amend the slips of his own tongue. Let another tongue slip for him. Such is the odd compromise between ancient law and modern equity. One great advantage that I gain by putting forward "one of my counsel" to speak for me is that if he blunders—if, for example, he speaks of Roger when he should have spoken of Richard—I shall be able to correct the mistake, for his words will not bind me until I have adopted them. Naturally, however, I choose for this purpose my acutest and most experienced friends. Naturally, also, acute and experienced men are to be found who will gladly be for this purpose my friends or anybody else's friends, if they be paid for their friendliness. As a class of expert pleaders forms itself, the relation between the litigant and those who are "of counsel for him" will be very much changed, but it will not lose all traces of its friendly character. Theoretically one cannot hire another person to plead for one; in other words, counsel cannot sue for his fees.

Seemingly it was in the reign of Henry III. that pleaders seeking for employment began to cluster round the king's court. Some of them the king, the busiest of all litigants, kept in his pay; they were his "serjeants"—that is, servants—at law. Under Edward I. a process, the details of which are

A CHIEF JUSTICE UNDER EDWARD I.
(*By permission of the Rev. Sir W. Hyde Parker.*)

still very obscure, was initiated by the king, which brought
these professional pleaders and the professional attorneys [1]
under the control of the judges, and began to secure a
monopoly of practice to those who had been formally ordained to the ministry of the law.   About the same time
it is that we begin to read of men climbing from the Bar
to the Bench, and about the same time it is that the
judges are ceasing to be ecclesiastics.   If we look back

A CHIEF JUSTICE UNDER EDWARD III.
(The Effigy of Sir John de Stonore, Dorchester, Oxon.)

to Richard L.'s reign we may see, as the highest temporal
court of the realm, a court chiefly composed of ecclesiastics,
presided over by an archbishop, who is also Chief Justiciar;
he will have at his side two or three bishops, two or three
archdeacons, and but two or three laymen.   The greatest
judges even of Henry III.'s reign are ecclesiastics, though by
this time it has become scandalous for a bishop to do much
secular justice.   These judges have deserved their appointments, not by pleading for litigants, but by serving as clerks
in the Court, the Exchequer, the Chancery.   They are pro-

[1 On attorneys, *cf.* Pollock and Maitland, *History of English Law*, I., p. 191.]

fessionally learned in the law of the land, but they have acquired their skill rather as the civil servants of the Crown than as the advocates or advisers of private persons; and if they serve the king well on the Bench, they may hope to retire upon bishoprics, or at all events deaneries. But the Church has been trying to withdraw the clergy from this work in the civil courts. Very curious had been the shifts to which ecclesiastics had been put in order to keep themselves technically free of blood-guiltiness. The accused criminal knew what was going to happen when the ecclesiastical president of the court rose but left his lay associates behind him. Hands that dared not write "and the jurors say that he is guilty, and therefore let him be hanged," would go so far as "and therefore, etc." Lips that dared not say any worse would venture a sufficiently intelligible "Take him away, and let him have a priest." However, the Church has her way. The clerks of the court, the Exchequer, the Chancery, will for a very long time be clerks in holy orders; but before the end of Edward I.'s reign the appointment of an ecclesiastic to be one of the king's justices will be becoming rare. On the whole, we may say that from that time to the present, one remarkable characteristic of our legal system is fixed—all the most important work of the law is done by a very small number of royal justices who have been selected from the body of pleaders practising in the king's courts.

The King's Courts.

Slowly the "curia" of the Norman reigns had been giving birth to various distinct offices and tribunals. In Edward's day there was a "King's Bench" (a court for criminal causes and other "pleas of the Crown"); a "Common Bench" (a court for actions brought by one subject against another); an Exchequer, which both in a judicial and an administrative way collected the king's revenue and enforced his fiscal rights; a Chancery, which was a universal secretarial bureau, doing all the writing that was done in the king's name. These various departments had many adventures to live through before the day would come when they would once more be absorbed into a High Court of Justice. Of some few of those adventures we shall speak in another place, but must here say two or three words about a matter which gave a distinctive shape to the whole body of our law—a shape that it is even

now but slowly losing. Our common law during the later
Middle Ages and far on into modern times is in the main a
commentary on writs issued out of the king's Chancery. To
understand this, we must go back to the twelfth century, to a
time when it would have seemed by no means natural that
ordinary litigation between ordinary men should come into
the king's court. It does not come there without an order
from the king. Your adversary could not summon you to
meet him in that court; the summons must come from the
king. Thus much of the old procedure we still retain in our

ADVOCATE.	JUDGES.	TAKING THE OATH
(MS. Roy. 6 E. vi.)	(MS. Roy. 6 E. vii.)	(MS. Roy. 6 E. vii.)

own time; it will be the King, not your creditor, who will
bid you appear in his High Court. But whereas at the
present day the formal part of the writ will merely bid you
appear in court, and all the information that you will get
about the nature of the claim against you will be conveyed to
you in the plaintiff's own words or those of his legal advisers,
this was not so until very lately. In old times the writ that
was drawn up in the king's Chancery and sealed with his
great seal told the defendant a good many particulars about
the plaintiff's demand. Gradually, as the king began to open
the doors of his court to litigants of all kinds, blank forms
of the various writs that could be issued were accumulated in
the Chancery. We may think of the king as keeping a shop
in which writs were sold. Some of them were to be had at
fixed prices, or, as we should say nowadays, they could be
had as matters of course on the payment of fixed court-fees;

for others special bargains had to be made. Then, in course of time, as our Parliamentary constitution took shape, the invention of new writs became rarer and rarer. Men began to see that if the king in his Chancery could devise new remedies by granting new writs, he had in effect a power of creating new rights and making new laws without the concurrence of the estates of the realm. And so it came to be a settled doctrine that though the old formulas might be modified in immaterial particulars to suit new cases as they arose, no new formula could be introduced except by statute. This change had already taken place in Edward I.'s day. Thenceforward the cycle of writs must be regarded as a closed cycle; no one can bring his cause before the king's courts unless he can bring it within the scope of one of those formulas which the Chancery has in stock and ready for sale. We may argue that if there is no writ there is no remedy, and if there is no remedy there is no wrong; and thus the register of writs in the Chancery becomes the test of rights and the measure of law. Then round each writ a great mass of learning collects itself. He who knows what cases can be brought within each formula knows the law of England. The body of law has a skeleton, and that skeleton is the system of writs. Thus our jurisprudence took an exceedingly rigid and permanent shape; it became a commentary on formulas. It could still grow and assimilate new matter, but it could only do this by a process of interpretation which gradually found new, and not very natural, meanings for old phrases. As we shall see hereafter, this process of interpretation was too slow to keep up with the course of social and economic change, and the Chancery had to come to the relief of the courts of law by making itself a court of equity.

C. W. C. OMAN. The Art of War. EDWARD I. is generally said to have learnt the art of war from Simon de Montfort, and the great earl was no doubt a practised warrior. His victory of Lewes, won with very inferior forces over a gallant enemy, shows that he had much more skill in tactics than his contemporaries. He knew how to keep an army in hand even when part of it was wavering, and had learned to keep a reserve back for the critical

moment and to use it with energy. But Simon was still of
the old school, trusting mainly to the charge of his mailed
horsemen to win him battles, and looking to infantry as a
secondary force. Lewes he won by a cavalry charge; Evesham
was the hopeless endeavour of a gallant band of horsemen to
cut their way through vastly superior forces.

It was not from Simon, then, that King Edward learnt **The**
that judicious combination of the use of archery and cavalry **Longbow.**
which had not been properly utilised since William the
Conqueror first essayed it at Hastings. The device of bringing forward the bowmen under cover of the cavalry, and
using them to break up the enemy's line and make gaps for
the horsemen to enter, is first heard of in the Welsh wars.
We read that it was first used against Llewellyn's host at
Orewin Bridge, and again repeated against Welsh rebels in
1295. "The Welsh," says Nicholas Trivet, "set themselves
fronting the force of the Earl of Warwick with long spears,
standing close together with the butts of their lances planted
in the earth and their points directed upwards. They quite
broke the force of the charges of the English horsemen; but
the earl well provided against them, for placing archers
between his men-at-arms he so galled the spearmen that they
wavered, and then put them to flight by a charge."

Edward's great achievement was the Battle of Falkirk. **The War**
The forty thousand Scots of Wallace's army were nearly all **with the**
spearmen, with a few mounted knights—less than a thousand **Scots.**
in all—and a certain proportion of archers using the short-
bow. Wallace drew his army up in a good position behind a
marsh, in four great masses, and waited to be attacked. The
King of England advanced with his horse in three divisions,
and his archery in the intervals between them. The first
division charged, but got entangled in the marsh and was
driven off. The second division turned the morass, and
chased away the Scottish archers and cavalry, but was
checked by the pikemen, on whom it could make no impression. Edward then halted his horse, brought his archers
to the front, and concentrated their fire on certain points in
the Scottish columns. When they were well riddled, he sent
his knights against the wavering points in the mass, broke
in, and scattered the whole army to the winds with fearful

slaughter. For the next two centuries similar tactics always
proved effective against the Scots, whose horse were seldom
numerous enough to cope on equal terms with the English,
while their archers never learnt to use the long-bow with
effect. Halidon Hill, Neville's Cross, Homildon, and Flodden
were all variations on the same theme. The Scottish pikemen, able to beat off cavalry charges with ease, were helpless
when exposed to the rain of archery, and always suffered
fearfully from the obstinate courage which made them hold
their ground under the shower of arrows till the inevitable
cavalry charge found a weak point in the column, and
when once it was broken into, the whole mass was cut to
pieces.

Changes in Armour. Chain mail had sufficed for two centuries to arm the
feudal horsemen of England. The peaked Norman helmet
with the nasal had long been superseded by a larger helm
covering the whole head, and usually flat at the crown; but
the mail shirt remained as a sufficient protection for the
knight's body. But at the same time that archery commenced to improve, and probably in consequence of that
very improvement, the mail shirt began to be replaced by
heavier and more elaborate armour. Between 1300 and 1350
the general appearance of the knightly panoply changed
completely; over the coat of mail a breast-plate of plate
armour, forming a second protection for the body, was superimposed. Aillettes, or roundels, shielded the shoulders from
downward cuts; arm-pieces and leg-pieces of plate protected
the limbs. Such of the old chain-armour as was retained
was hardly visible, being entirely covered by the extra casing
of plate. The helmet once more became peaked, and was
known as a bassinet, the neck was protected by a light
falling piece of chain-mail, fastened to the bassinet at the
top and to the shoulders at the bottom, and called the
cammail. The superior protection secured by the new armour
was won at the cost of mobility. The knight of 1360 was
far more overweighted and less able to move with rapidity
than the knight of 1260. His forces failed sooner; his
balance both on horse and on foot was less easy to keep. A
generation later, when men still persisted in overloading
themselves with more armour, they became more helpless

Early Plate Armour (MS. Roy. 20 D. i.).

St. George and the Dragon (MS. Add. 23,145).

Fight on Drawbridge of a Castle (MS. Add. 10,293).

Archers (MS. Roy. 16 G. vi.).

WARFARE AND WEAPONS IN THE FOURTEENTH CENTURY.

still; a knight who had been overthrown could not even rise to his feet without his squire's aid, and lay entirely at the mercy of his adversary. Not unfrequently men were stifled by the weight of their armour when they had fallen, and died without having received any mortal wound.

AN ENGLISH KNIGHT OF 1302.
(*Brass of Sir Robert de Bures.*)

The armies which Edward III. and the Black Prince led over to France were not raised on the old principles of the feudal levy and the national militia, nor were they foreign mercenaries engaged purely for pay like the hirelings of John. A new system had now come into use for foreign wars, though the theory of the old universal liability to serve was still maintained for use in time of rebellion, or for border service against Scotland or Wales. The king habitually entered into indentures with his barons and knights, agreeing to take them into his service, not for the short feudal forty days, but for long terms at liberal rates of wages, calculated according to the rank of the contracting party and the number and quality of followers that he brought with him. We have the pay-roll of the army with which Edward III. besieged Calais in 1346 preserved in its entirety, and know the rates of every man whom the king entertained, from his son, the Prince of Wales, down to the meanest

Soldiers' Pay.

light infantry soldier. The prince had one pound a day; thirteen earls and one bishop, six shillings and eightpence each; forty-four barons and knights banneret, four shillings each; 1,040 knights, two shillings each; then came the bulk of the horse, 4,022 esquires and constables, who received a shilling a day. The bulk of the army was composed of archers, 15,480 on foot at threepence a day, 5,104 provided with horses for quick move-

ment (not for fighting) who had double that sum. The rest
of the infantry was composed of 4,474 Welsh pikemen at
twopence a day. Besides these there were some 500 light
horse ("hobbilers") and 300 gunners and engineers. This
gives us an army of 5,600 horse and 25,000 foot. Such an
effort was, however, very unusual: so large and well-equipped
an army was probably never put into the field on any other
occasion. As is well known, Crecy,
Agincourt, and Poitiers were fought
with very much smaller forces.

The troops which Edward III.
habitually raised by contract with
his barons and knights were, of
course, far more expensive than the
old feudal array; and the drain on
the treasury was such, that in spite
of the most liberal grants from
Parliament, supplemented by many
illegal methods of raising money,
the king was always in debt. The
many constitutional advances of the
liberties in England in his day are
all traceable to his incessant need
to bargain with Parliament for more
grants, by ceding some of the more
obnoxious royal privileges.

For service against the domestic
enemies within the four seas—Scots,
Welsh, and native rebels—the three
Edwards had generally recourse, not
to calling out the whole forces of
the shires under the sheriff, as would
have been the case in an earlier
century, but to "commissions of
array," by which mandates were
given to selected persons to press
and put under arms a given number
of men from such and such a

AN ENGLISH KNIGHT OF 1325.
(*Brass of Sir John De Creke.*)

district. As by the assize of arms the men had already been
compelled to furnish themselves with weapons and armour,

the commissioner of array had only to choose and muster his force out of the persons liable to serve. Edward I. regularly paid all bodies of men called out under this system, but his weak and unbusiness-like son, and even Edward III. in his more penniless days, tried to throw the burden on the counties and towns which supplied the men. This was quite unconstitutional, and ere long Edward was compelled by Parliament to promise that all men levied under this system should be paid from the royal exchequer. In 1352 it was even provided that commissions of array should only be issued by the king after he had obtained the common assent and grant of Parliament; and that no man should be constrained to serve outside his own county save in cases of invasion by a foreign foe. At the same time it was enacted that all men chosen to serve in foreign wars should be at the king's wages from the day that they crossed the boundary of their own county.

W. LAIRD CLOWES. The Navy. THE reign of Edward the First was as noteworthy as that of his predecessor for the lawlessness of much of the maritime population of England. In 1293 the riotous behaviour of the crews of a few private ships led to serious, though informal, hostilities between England and France. The dispute was provisionally settled in a manner characteristic of the age. It was arranged that on a given day the fleets of each side should meet at a given spot in mid-Channel and submit the question to the decision of arms. An empty ship was anchored to mark the place for the conflict, and in due course English and French encountered one another, and the latter were badly beaten. Unfortunately the affair did not terminate there, for King Philip took up the quarrel of his subjects, and regular war immediately resulted. A few years later the revival of an ancient feud between the Cinque Ports and Yarmouth led to several very bloody encounters, one of which ended in the burning of above twenty Yarmouth ships, and greatly prejudiced the national cause in which at the time both the Cinque Ports and Yarmouth were assisting the king at Sluys. Significant also of the condition of the coasts are a statute of 1276 that modified the law of wreck, and the fact that for several years the Cinque Ports were in

SINGLE COMBAT, EARLY FOURTEENTH CENTURY. (MS. Roy. 20 D. 1.)

a state of private war with part of Edward's Continental dominions.

Reference has already been made to the granting by an English king of something very much resembling letters of marque. Actual letters of marque were granted in the time of Edward I. A certain Bernard d'Ongressill, a merchant of Bayonne, then an appanage of the English crown, was the owner of a ship, the *St. Mary*, which, bound from Barbary to England, and laden with almonds, raisins, and figs, was driven by stress of weather into Lagos in Portugal. While she was there at anchor some armed Portuguese from Lisbon boarded her, robbed d'Ongressill and his crew, and carried the ship and cargo to their city. The King of Portugal took one-tenth of the spoil and left the rest to the robbers. The merchant, who declared that he was the poorer by £700, prayed Sir John of Brittany, then Lieutenant of Gascony, to grant him letters of marque. A grant was accordingly made, empowering d'Ongressill, his heirs, successors, and descendants for five years "to mark, retain, and appropriate" the people of Portugal, and especially those of Lisbon, and their goods, wheresoever they might be found, until satisfaction should be had. This licence was confirmed by Edward, with the proviso that it should cease when restitution had been made, and that if d'Ongressill took more than he had lost, he should account for the overplus.

Their services obtained from Edward several new charters for the Cinque Ports. One relieved them from paying duty on such wines as they imported; another exempted their ships and rigging from taxation, and gave them other advantages. Their fleet was at this period commanded by one admiral, Gervase Alard, and four captains, with a rector or constable, and a master to each ship. The captains, who seem to have commanded squadrons, received 12d. a day, the masters and rectors or constables 6d., and the sailors 3d., as in previous reigns. The admiral received 2s. The masters also received 20s. for pilotage for the whole coast of Scotland and Ireland. What the sea stores of a ship were in 1290 may be gathered from a list of things purchased for a vessel that was to have been sent to bring the Princess Margaret from Norway—where, however, she prematurely died. The pro-

visions included wine, ale, corn, beef, pork, bacon, stock-fish,
sturgeons, herrings, and lampreys, almonds, rice, beans, peas,
onions, leeks, cheese, nuts, salt, vinegar, mustard, pepper,
cummin - seed, ginger, cinnamon, figs, raisins, saffron, and
gingerbread; and among miscellaneous articles were wax-
torches, tallow candles, cressets,[1] lanterns, napkins, wood, and
biscuit; together with a banner of the king's arms, and a
silken streamer or pennant. All king's ships, it would appear,
flew the royal banner—red, with three golden lions—and
probably also the flag of St. George; and it may well be that
the whip or pennant, as a mark of a king's ship of war in
commission, dates from about this time.

From this period comes to us a very remarkable document, The
which affords weighty evidence that Edward, if not his pre- Dominion
decessors, formally claimed the sovereignty of the Narrow of the Sea.
Seas, and regarded it as indisputable. It is not dated, but it
must have been drawn up between 1303 and 1307, and it
appears to have been the draft of an Anglo-French agreement
or treaty. It begins: "Whereas the Kings of England, by
right of the said kingdom from time to time, whereof there is
no memorial to the contrary, have been in peaceable possession
of the sovereign lordship of the sea of England, and of the
isles within the same, with power of making and establishing
laws, statutes, and prohibitions of arms, and of ships otherwise furnished than merchantmen used to be, and of taking
surety and affording safeguard in all cases where need shall
require, and of ordering all other things necessary for the
maintaining of peace, right, and equity among all manner of
people as well of other dominions as of their own, passing
through the said seas, and the sovereign guard thereof, and
also of taking all manner of cognizance in causes, and of
doing right and justice to high and low," and whereas (to
shorten the phraseology) the Kings of England had been in
the immemorial habit of deputing their powers to their
admirals and masters; and it concludes, *inter alia*, with an
agreement that the King of France shall aid and abet the King
of England in the maintenance of these his rights and powers,
and with what almost amounts to a promise of satisfaction

[1 Lanterns, or rather light-holders, carried in a socket at the end of a pole
or dependent from a chain.]

for an infringement of them by a certain "master of the navy" of the French king, one "Reyner Grimbald," who is better known in history as Grimaldi.

Some space has previously[1] been devoted to a consideration of the claims of the kings of England to the sovereignty of the Narrow Seas. The subject deserves continued attention, for it is impossible to doubt that the maritime jealousy of our monarchs, and the extraordinary pretensions which, even while they were powerless to enforce them, they put forward, had important influences upon the destiny of the race. It has already been shown that the claims in question are very ancient, and that there are grounds—though not absolutely convincing ones—for believing that they were admitted by foreigners in the days of Edward I. In the reign of Edward II. they were indisputably acknowledged. The proof is to be found in the prayer of three Flemish envoys who, in 1320, visited London to obtain redress for outrages which, during a long period, had, as was alleged, been committed by English sailors upon Flemish ships. One of the most flagrant of these outrages had been perpetrated "on the sea of England near Cranden," a place which Nicolas identifies with Crozon, a seaport about eight leagues west of Quimper, in Brittany, near the extremity of the Pointe du Raz; and it is significant that the envoys begged Edward "of his lordship and royal power to cause right to be done and punishment awarded, as he is lord of the sea, and the robbery was committed on the sea within his power as is above said." This recognition by the Flemings carries the more weight from its having been on their part entirely voluntary; and, as Nicolas points out, although it was their interest to fix the responsibility of the outrage upon England, it is not probable that an admission of a great national right would have been spontaneously made in order to attain the object in view, unless the right were regarded as lying beyond all question. By England the admission was clearly accepted as a matter of course: and the officers who conducted the resultant inquiry were ordered to examine into acts committed "by men of England on the sea of England, off the coast of Cranden, within the jurisdiction of the King of England." Cranden itself, it should

[1] *See ante*, Vol. I., p. 456.

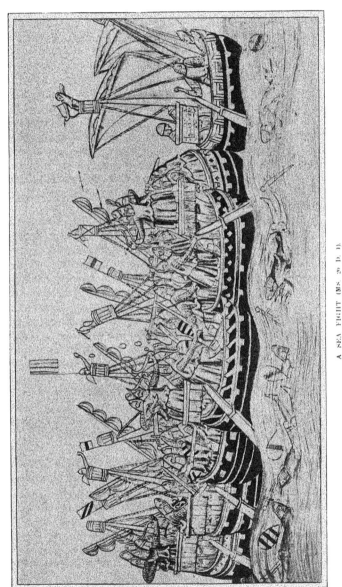

A SEA FIGHT (MS. 20 D. I).

be noted, did not form part of Edward's dominions. It was merely washed by the sea which was Edward's.

The dominion claimed, and thus formally acknowledged, was, however, still much more imaginary than real. The king's peace did not, save in theory, extend to all his own ports, much less to the waters which were out of sight of his coasts; and there was fully as much maritime lawlessness in his reign in the Channel and the North Sea as in the reign of any of his predecessors. In 1316, when the North Sea was, as usual in those days, swarming with pirates, six ships of war under Sir John Sturmy and William Gettour, "captains and admirals," were despatched to defend Berwick against the freebooters; but, instead of proceeding upon that duty, they dropped anchor in various ports along the coast, and plundered the neighbourhood. Ships of Holland, Hainault, and Norway committed repeated acts of aggression with comparative impunity; and the fleet of the Cinque Ports, whenever it was not employed by the king, was engaged in preying upon all sea-borne commerce without distinction of nationality, or in harrying the unfortunate inhabitants of Southampton, Lyme, Weymouth, and Poole. In 1314 complaint was made that a vessel, the *Blessed Mary*, belonging to Fontarabie, near Bayonne, had been driven ashore and plundered by seamen of Winchelsea, Rye, and Romney; and the king ordered an investigation; but in vain. The inhabitants of the Cinque Ports, by force and violence, prevented the inquiry from taking place, and it does not appear that the offenders were ever punished. Indeed, there was in England no power strong enough to oblige these highly favoured sea-rovers to behave themselves.

Maritime Trade. Trade must have suffered terribly. Upon the whole, nevertheless, the maritime commerce of the country increased. It was greatly encouraged by the scarcity which prevailed in England in 1315 and 1316, and which caused the king to hold out special inducements, and to grant advantageous privileges to the merchants of Sicily, Spain, and Genoa. There was also a growing trade by sea with Venice, through which great emporium England at that time, and for many years afterwards, chiefly obtained her spices and other Oriental produce.

In naval architecture several improvements were made at about this period. Two masts became common, and some process akin to the modern method of furling sails was adopted. Elevated stern-stages, or *bellatoria*, and fighting tops on the masts sprang into general use, and the rudder was invented. The stern-stage, or *bellatorium*, which was destined to develop in the course of generations into the poop, was, on account of its elevation, the position assigned to the commander. It therefore contained the principal

A SEA FIGHT (MS. Roy. 10 E. iv.).

banner or ensign, and this, no doubt, is the reason why in all navies the national ensign still flies at the stern of a ship and not in some more conspicuous position. Another *bellatorium* was sometimes erected forward, and there became the origin of the raised forecastle. In the *bellatoria* were stationed the pick of the fighting men, and the apparatus for discharging Greek fire, stones, and other large missiles. The rudder of the early part of the fourteenth century did not materially differ from the rudder of to-day. It was of the same form; it was moved by means of a tiller, and it was affixed by means of pintles and gudgeons;[1] but although, upon its invention, its advantages over the *clavus*, or steering paddle, must at once have been obvious, very few ships, and those only of the largest size, were fitted with it; and for long afterwards the paddle was much more usually met with.

[1 The pintles are the pins on which the rudder turns in the clamps or sockets (gudgeons) affixed to the vessel's stern.]

Sometimes a couple of paddles, one on each quarter, were employed. The sails remained of the same square shape as in earlier times; no fore-and-aft sails were added; and it does not appear that more than one sail at a time was hoisted upon each mast, though there is some slight evidence that larger yards and sails were occasionally used in fine, and smaller ones in foul, weather.

R. HUGHES.
Architecture
and Art.

WINDOW WITH FLOWING TRACERY.
(*Stoke Golding Church, Leicestershire.*)

THE reigns of the first Edward, of his son, and of his grandson, together cover a space of a hundred and five years, and it is habitual to speak of the architecture of the entire period as belonging to the Decorated style. Chronologically this is accurate enough, if we strike off the last sixteen years; but the habitual phrase is unfortunate, as suggesting a breach of architectural continuity, which does not exist in fact. The truth is that the Decorated is not really a style at all. It is simply a rich and highly cultivated variety of that style of Pointed Gothic which goes by the name of Early English. We look, therefore, in vain for anything which we can truly describe as " transitional Early English," parallel to that "transitional Norman" which, a century earlier, bridged the change from Norman to Gothic, or even to that less strongly marked transitional which, a century later, ushered in the victory of the Perpendicular forms. If the nomenclature could be revised, it would be convenient to classify the whole of English Gothic by its window forms, which would give us the lancet style and the traceried styles, including plate tracery and bar tracery, plain and ornamental, the latter being subdivided according as the ornament is added or

Varieties
of Gothic.

constructive. In such a classification the Decorated architecture of the Edwards would be referred exclusively to the last division—the period, that is, of constructively ornamental tracery; and it is in this meaning, and in this meaning only, that we hereafter use the word. This tracery, however, lends itself to further subdivision, according as it is flowing or geometrical. The geometrical is, of course, the older, having been extensively used in Early English times; in Henry's work at Westminster, for instance, where the ornament was not as yet constructive. But the flowing tracery did not by any means destroy the geometric vogue, and inasmuch as we constantly find both kinds of windows side by side in the same building, and with the same mouldings, and of the same age, the distinction is obviously useless for determining the chronological sequence.

WINDOW WITH GEOMETRICAL TRACERY.
(*St. Anselm's Chapel, Canterbury Cathedral.*)

As might be expected from what we have said, the distinguishing characteristics of Decorated work must be looked for rather in details than in general form and outline. We note at once the larger size of the windows, marking the growing search after means to make a fuller display of painted glass. They are invariably divided by mullions, and the tracery, whether composed of circles, trefoils (pointed or natural), or similar regular figures, or running into flowing and irregular lines, is never Perpendicular. The divisions, too, are always cusped, and the cusps [1] are wrought on

"Decorated" Architecture.

[1 Prominences formed by the intersection of the curves of which the tracery is composed.]

49

the actual bar, not merely added on the soffit.[1] The ornaments, such as appear on the capitals of columns, on the bosses or meeting-places of the vaulting groins, on finial[2] and corbel and canopy, are much more numerous and rich than formerly. The carving is less conventional; and, indeed, in the leafage and fruit of oak and vine and maple, fidelity to nature is not infrequently attained at some expense of consistency.

Windows.   Leading examples of early Decorated windows showing geometrical tracery are to be found in the choir of Merton College Chapel, which may be assigned to the penultimate decade of the thirteenth century, being quite twenty years earlier than the sacristy, which the college muniments show to be of 1307. Similar work is to be seen in the windows of the passage to the chapter-house at York, and in some of those in the cathedrals of Exeter and Lichfield. All of these are aggregates of geometrical figures ingeniously put together, and all belong to the first twenty years, or thereabouts, of the reign of Edward I. A little later come the chapter-houses of York and Wells with window forms of the same type, a type which held its own down to the end of the Decorated style. Overlapping hardly describes the contemporaneous growth of geometrical and flowing tracery, for we find the purest flowing forms as early as 1290, as at Stoke Golding, in Leicestershire; while the contract for the famous window in St. Anselm's Chapel at Canterbury, which is the purest geometrical, was not given out till 1336. It is certain too that in the interval between these dates a practice had arisen—though one obtaining chiefly in Yorkshire and the Midlands—of alternating or mixing geometrical with flowing forms, which was followed in the Benedictine abbey at Selby and in St. Mary's Church at Beverley. The most elaborate stone lacework, such as that in the east window of Carlisle, and also the most profusely ornamented mouldings, come a little later, the richest of all belonging to the troubled reign of Edward II. and the earlier years of his son. This work is rarely without the characteristic " ball flower " or the almost equally characteristic "four-leaved flower." These two ornaments are in England (though not in France) the peculiar signs of the Decorated period, belonging to it as the chevron

[¹ The under-surface of the vaulting of the window.   ² Ornaments on a gable.]

belongs to Norman, and the violette to Early English work.
The ball flower is of no great beauty in itself—a sort of half-

WINDOWS WITH BALL-FLOWER ORNAMENT, GLOUCESTER CATHEDRAL.

opened round stone bud, showing a ball in the centre beneath
the pinched but unbroken lip-like corolla. These ornaments,
occasionally connected with a stem, are extensively used in

the external decoration of spires and doorways, and, in spite of their intrinsic ugliness, have a very rich effect. The four-leaved flowers are more elegant, having four petals cut in high relief running from a centre sometimes raised and sometimes sunk. The architects of the early fourteenth century loved literally to smother their window frames with these ornaments; and in the south aisle of the nave of Hereford and at Leominster, in the same county, there are instances where the reticulations are so filled with ball flowers as almost to suggest (of course, in point of mass only) the plate tracery of the previous century. Few of the old patterns of ornament were retained, but, by exception, the crocket survived, though not in its old vigour, and the diaper also; and this last, in the dearth of coverings for wall spaces, flourished exceedingly.

A peculiarity of the Decorated period is the use of the double arched window, the inner arch being frequently very deeply foliated, and separated, by the whole thickness of the wall, from the outer one which carries the lights. This form is noteworthy, because it is never found in Perpendicular times. So, too, of the rose window, which, though less popular here than in France, and rarely given the place of honour in the east or west walls, yet takes with us very beautiful shapes. There are noble examples of these windows at St. Mary's, Cheltenham, at Westminster, and especially in the south transept at Lincoln, where the interlacing stems simulate the freedom of a briar rose, and show how far the builders have travelled since they put up the plate tracery—once a masterpiece—that looks down from the opposite transept. The Jesse window, the central mullion of which forms the trunk of the tree of the genealogy of Christ, is an equally common and characteristic feature of this period. The impression that above all others strikes one in this Decorated work is the passion for richness. The arcades which ornament the walls, the canopies over the tombs, the sedilia, the piscinæ, even such spires and towers as those of Lichfield, seem chiefly valued as vehicles for ornament. The style misses the grave beauty, the reserve, the laborious simplicity, of the Early English.

There is a certain cheapness in this reliance on ornamental

detail which comes out somewhat painfully in the matter of mouldings. One would almost think that the Decorated masons found it too much trouble to cut the deep, shadowy hollows and bold rounds of the earlier men. They favour the easier effects of the flat fillet, with the result that their mouldings are almost invariably few in number and feeble in expression. But the point of most marked inferiority in the style was its treatment of the supporting pillars. These lose their detached shafts; they are still clustered in outline, but the exquisite lightness of such piers as we see at Salisbury is gone. On the other hand, in the matter of vaulting, though they sometimes seem to have had spasms of timidity, the Decorated architects made a considerable advance. In building the chapter-house at York they got rid of

THE JESSE WINDOW, DORCHESTER CHURCH, OXON.

the central pillar, and at Ely they invented a mode of covering the intersection of nave and transept which gave them a central space of the noblest proportions and unrivalled in elegance of design. The octagon at Ely, built by Alan of Walsingham in the last years of Edward II., is unmatched by any similar construction in England. It covers the entire width of nave and transept, and the fluted fans which lead up to the lantern are of surpassing beauty. This feature of largeness comes out again in the nave of York. Like the lantern at Ely, the roof is of wood, but the effect is none the less satisfactory. At York, and still more at Lichfield, we note the tendency of the Decorated architect to enlarge the clerestory at the expense of the triforium; but where, as in the choir bays at Ely (built by the same Alan of Walsingham), the old Early English proportions are preserved, the absolute high-water mark of elegance in proportion, combined with richness of detail, may be said to have been reached.

Tombs.   What may, perhaps, be best termed sepulchral art attained its zenith during this period. Simple slabs with a rudely carved figure upon them seem to have been all that was attempted by the Normans. Wooden canopies adorned with leather were the rule in Early English times. Wood was the material of the beautiful canopy placed over the tomb of Edward III. at Westminster, at the very end of the Decorated period, and of the simple roof which covers the monument of the Black Prince at Canterbury. The figures which were used for decoration were usually of metal—either brass or bronze gilt. Occasionally they were of stone, as in the group of tombs at Westminster, where Aylmer de Valence lies between Edmund Crouchback and his wife Aveline. Aylmer was assassinated when in attendance on the "she-wolf of France" in 1323, and this tomb and its companions are not earlier than the reign of her son. It has a stone canopy, which is something of a rarity, and is well executed, as are the little figures of Aylmer's kinsmen on the base. But of all these monuments that which the monks of Gloucester erected to the memory of Edward of Carnarvon best deserves mention, not only for its intrinsic beauty, but because it became the type which, for two centuries, Gothic sculptors delighted to copy. It is, of course, more or less a wreck that we see now. The subsidiary statues are gone; but, as he lies in a seclusion made by the forest of tapering shafts and pinnacles and niches, decked with the richest ornament of the richest period of Gothic art, one almost ceases to wonder how it was that this weak and worthless creature came to be considered a hero and a saint. At any rate, his tomb is (as, indeed, it has been accounted for five centuries and a half) a model and a masterpiece.

There can be no doubt that considerable skill in the Effigies.

TOMB OF EDWARD II., GLOUCESTER CATHEDRAL.

plastic art had by this time been acquired in England. Not only had materials for the Abbey work of Henry—glass mosaic, porphyry, and alabaster—been brought from abroad by Abbot Ware, but foreign artists and foreign knowledge had come with them. Thirty years later lived William Torel, who seems to have been an accomplished sculptor, and, however foreign in matter of name, he was "a goldsmith and a citizen of London." He certainly cast effigies of Henry and of Eleanor, "the queen of good memory," which have considerable beauty, though of a conventional kind; but a real likeness of Queen Philippa was carved in alabaster by Hawkin of Liège, whose name suggests an English artist trained in the queen's country of Hainault. An Englishman, too, seems to have made the effigies of Queen Eleanor that adorned the crosses erected by Edward in his sad pilgrimage from Nottingham to Westminster. Of these unique memorials to the memory of the wife who, when her husband was stabbed by a poisoned dagger, "sucked forth the poison with her balmy breath," three out of the original fifteen alone remain. These are at Geddington, Waltham, and Northampton; that at the first-named place being the least dilapidated. In form they resemble the famous Schöne Brunnen of Nuremberg, which is a contemporary work. The free copy by Barry at Charing Cross has sufficiently popularised the design, and certainly, in view of the prevailing hideousness of our modern monuments, the sculptor of the nineteenth century did not go far wrong in borrowing from his brother

Portrait Masks. of the thirteenth. The English passion for portraiture doubtless found its best opportunity in modelling the "lively"—that is, lifelike—statues in wood or wax which were laid upon the biers of distinguished persons. Masks from the dead face were frequently taken, and no pains were spared to obtain a good likeness. As the practice dates at least from the twelfth, and persisted as late as the last century, these effigies, had they been preserved, would have formed a series of priceless value, and shed a flood of light, not only on the artistic progress of the country, but in many dark corners of history. Unfortunately, only the more modern and worthless specimens have survived. The effigies of Edward I. and Eleanor, of Edward III. and Philippa, were still to be seen at Westminster as late as the time of Dryden; and Horace Walpole mentions that, though sadly mangled, some, including that of Elizabeth of York (a fifteenth-century work), were still recognisable. The present survivors of this "ragged regiment" are all much later, the oldest being that of Charles II.

But if we can only guess what was the state of the plastic

Comment Noe envioye vn corbeu e vne columbe sauoir mout si il crauonent.
pur de cele le corbeu si ad aoue la teste de vn chiual ou il se arreste. Ele co
loumbe est retorne si apres vne branche en soun bek en signe qil ad aoue tre
e Noe a le entre de la neef: si ate bisoiate ou il seer a la gouernaigle. E il
puable sen fuijer p mi le souniz de la neef: e la colouere bote sa coue par mi le
pertuiz.

THE ARK AFLOAT. (*MS. Roy. 2 B. vii.*)

[To face p. 72.

arts under the three Edwards, we are almost totally in the Painting.
dark as to the progress of the art of painting. The "liberate"
rolls of Henry III.'s reign abound with orders for the painting
or decorating of the oratories and chapels of that devout
king. Nor is it likely that there was any falling-off in the
art during the reign of Henry's more accomplished and more
widely travelled successor. "Trees," no doubt "trees of Jesse"
and the like, are among the objects mentioned, and unquestionably various polychromatic schemes of colour were used.
The figures of saints in wood and stone had been painted and
gilt for generations, but probably this should be treated as
the work of the decorator rather than the artist. Several
traces of foliage and similar ornament on the vaulting of
sepulchral canopies which may be safely attributed to the
reigns of the Edwards, suggest a certain progress in artistic
feeling. So, too, of the fragments of fresco with a figure
subject, recorded as the work of Master Waller, of Durham,
at Westminster, and to be found near the tomb of Eleanor.
Plenty of such work must have existed (*cf.* I., p. 598), but
very little has come down to us. It is bad luck, for a
fragment of the fresco of the coronation and marriage of
Edward I. which Bishop Langton, of Lichfield, ordered to
be painted on the walls of his palace, would have told us
more than all the manuscripts. In fine, though we have
abundant evidence of the advance of the painter's art in
England, for the extent of that advance we must trust to
faith rather than to sight.

The increased application of coloured glass, and the im- Coloured Glass.
provements in its design, are less open to question. The
earliest painted windows, which were probably transitional
Norman, were, no doubt, mere tesselation, which continued
to be applied to the borders of lancets in the first period of
Early English. Something more was attempted in the pre-
Decorated, geometrical forms, when medallions, with figures
rudely designed and dressed in the stiffest of draperies, made
their appearance, together with conventional foliage. The
colours are fine, particularly the ruby and two shades of
blue, and a golden pot-metal yellow. In the Decorated period
there were marked changes in this respect. The blues begin
to fade; a cold emerald colour seems to have been invented,

and also a new yellow of a lemon tint, which was applied to the surface of the glass.   The old deep ruby glass remains the finest colour, and becomes far less uneven than in the Early English time, but even that gradually loses its depth of colour.   The medallions, lately so popular, give way to canopies and figure - subjects.   The abrupt alternation of masses of variegated colour with masses of white glass

PAINTED WINDOW IN "BECKET'S CROWN," CANTERBURY CATHEDRAL.
(From a Photo, by permission of the Warden of Radley College, Abingdon.)

becomes the leading fashion.   There is an increased know-ledge of drawing, particularly in the draperies, and the foliaged ornament becomes — perhaps this is the most characteristic change of all—almost naturalistic, as if copied from the actual leaves of the ivy or the oak.   Something of the same kind is observable in the missal-painting of the time; but the illuminator was not in the van of progress, nor was the scriptorium of the monastery a school where freedom of invention or a knowledge of perspective was highly prized.

PAGE FROM THE ORMESBY PSALTER.
(*Bodleian Library, Oxford.*)

Domestic Architecture.   The differentiation of the castle from the baronial residence made enormous strides under the Edwards.   The moated grange and the castellated manor-house were fast superseding the private castle, while the castle was becoming more and more a great military and governmental fortress.   Everything tended to depress the private building of castles during these reigns; the increased power of the Crown, the spread of subinfeudation, the love of comfort, and the beginnings of luxury.

Photo: T. Jones, Son & Harper, Ludlow.

STOKESAY MANOR HOUSE, SHROPSHIRE.

Now that the king could command a great mercenary army, it was hopeless for an individual to think of standing against him ; while, with the increased security of the greater part of England, the risk of private violence was fast diminishing to zero.   The great castles once more became royal, not only in theory, but in fact ; and though some imposing edifices of the sort were undoubtedly erected by private enterprise, their erection seems generally to point to individual pride and ostentation, rather than to the desire of the owner for safety against all comers.

Castles.   Before a castle could be built, the licence of the Crown was indeed required, but seems to have been given readily enough. Henry granted twenty, Edward I. forty-four, Edward II. sixty, and Edward III. a hundred and eighty of these licences; but a very few of them refer to buildings of the impregnable type, or were castles of the first, or even of the second or third, rank. On the Scottish and Welsh borders a strong house was still needed, and a strong man to keep it; but elsewhere the castle as a residence was an anachronism. Still, the finest castles in Great Britain were erected in this period. They were due to the initiative of Edward I. himself, and their design is alleged, although on insufficient evidence, to have originated with the king. To this design the name of Edwardian has in consequence been given, and is so far justified by the great works begun and planned, if not completed, by him.

The new form of fortification, which superseded both the square Norman keep and the round julliet,[1] was essentially concentric, consisting of two or more rings of defence lying one within the other. First comes the deep ditch or moat, then the outer wall, planted with towers at convenient distances, each pair commanding the curtain wall between them, so that assailants endeavouring to batter in the curtain (which was, of course, the weakest part) were exposed to a cross-fire. Inside there was another fortified wall, the space between the two walls being broken up with cross-divisions, so as to isolate a storming-party which might have breached the outer defence. The keep was dispensed with, its place being taken by an open court, walled and towered at the corners, and having its hall, its chapel, and its living-rooms and offices, built against the walls. Between it and the second line of defence there was sometimes a moat—always some work which had to be carried—and this second ward was usually of sufficient size to accommodate a herd of cattle, driven in when a siege was expected. Sometimes, as at Caerphilly, which was a private fortress, begun in the last years of Henry III., the water formed the chief part both of the first and second line of defence; but, of course, this was not often possible. Occasionally, too, the ground did not permit or require the complete encircling arrangement, as at

The Edwardian Fortress.

[1 Round towers were so called, from a popular belief that Julius Cæsar had built such towers.]

Chepstow and Conway; but the desired result—a series of
defences, each of which had to be successively carried, and
each capable of resisting attack—was obtained none the less.
The gateway which gave admittance to the castle was, of
course, of the highest importance, and was an imposing
structure. It was usually square, flanked by two drum
towers, which commanded the approach, and the connecting
parapet was either machicolated in the common fashion, or a
sort of stone bridge was formed between the towers (remains

HARLECH CASTLE.   *Photo: Chester Vaughan, Acton, W.*

exist at Neath and Pembroke) so as to serve the purpose of
a bretache.[1] In front there was a portcullis, then a door,
and at the back of the gatehouse (in the most perfect form)
a second portcullis and door. In addition, the vaulted roof,
covering the intervening space, was pierced with meurtrières,
or apertures, for convenience in spearing an enemy who had
surprised the warder. Such a fortress, with its inner ward
arranged like a manor-house, was a far more comfortable
building than the old Norman castle to live in, but it required a considerable garrison, and could only be maintained

---

[1] The wooden structure projecting from the wall or tower, so as to enable ‘
the defenders to repel assault, *e.g.* by shooting missiles through holes in its
bottom, traces of which are seen at Coucy and Norham (I. p. 608).

Caerphilly Castle.

Chepstow Castle.

Conway Castle.   *Photo: Clester Vaughan, Acton, W.*

ENGLISH CASTLES IN THE FOURTEENTH CENTURY.

at vast expense. As a defensive work the castle had, in truth, very nearly reached perfection at the very moment when the discovery of gunpowder was about to render its perfection useless. The English castles of this kind in Wales, such as Conway and Carnarvon, Beaumaris and Harlech—not to mention Alnwick and Bamborough, Ludlow and Warwick—form, indeed, a series unmatchable in all Europe, surpassed only by the earlier Coucy in the East of France, and by the later St. Sauveur; and this last example was built, not by a Frenchman, but by John Chandos, the great English captain of Edward III.'s wars.

The Edwardian Dwelling House.   Although in essentials the distinction between the castle and the residence was very marked, the residence retained, throughout the Decorated period, much of the outward semblance of the castle. It continued to be fortified, though its military appearance was frequently quite deceptive, its sole and inadequate means of defence being an easily drained moat. Inside it was usually a courtyard, having the lodgings, the hall, and the stables disposed round the sides, an arrangement which continued in vogue long after castles, as means of defence, had been definitely abandoned. When there was no moat, a tower of refuge was sometimes built near the house, and on the Scottish border the tower was very often the house itself. In the greater part of England, however, there is little doubt that the moated grange was the prevailing fashion, and the contract for such a building at Lapworth has been preserved. We learn from it that the walls were to be very thick, that the outer door was to admit of a drawbridge being fixed to it, that there were to be base chambers with windows and fireplaces, and a principal hall, forty feet long, for strangers and retainers, with small rooms opening out of it. This hall or "sovereign room" was a universal feature, and, with its lofty double windows, is usually taken for the chapel; but, as Mr. Parker points out, the lay apartment can be readily distinguished by the seats in the window-sills. The arrangement of its interior will be described on a later page (p. 166).

Coins.   The reign of Edward III. is, to the numismatist, a great epoch. The reigns of his two predecessors had been barren, although his grandfather's reign is famous as that in which

Photo: Chester Vaughan, Acton, W.

CARNARVON CASTLE.

50

the type of the King of England, as he was to appear on his coins, was fixed for two centuries. It is a boyish, beardless full face, with the hair falling from beneath an open "fleury" crown, in a long curl on each side of the head. It is purely conventional, bearing no trace of a resemblance to any Plantagenet that ever lived; but it did duty for ten kings of that race, and the first of the Tudors—remaining unchanged from the first coinage of Edward I. until the second or third of Henry VII. Then the arched crown appears, together with a genuine likeness, this time in profile, of the Tudor king. When Edward I. got back from the Holy Land, one of his first reforms was directed to the coinage. Clipping was universally prevalent, the Jews being supposed to be the worst offenders, though the statement that vast stores of clippings were found in their houses may be dismissed as being prompted by the hatred which led to their expulsion. At any rate, a vast number of both Jews and Christians, of the lower orders, suffered the cruel death of the coiner, and even a gentleman and a churchman like Guy, Prior of Montacute, was tried, convicted, and heavily fined. Seven years after the king's accession new dies were delivered for pennies, halfpennies, and farthings. Groats were also issued,[1] though it is doubtful if they had much circulation. They were not very beautiful coins; the conventional head on one side, and on the other the cross with pellets, though in some struck at Berwick there is a boar's head in two of the angles. But Edward I., if he punished clippers, was himself guilty of debasing the coinage by reducing the silver in the penny about one per cent. Probably this was not the only depreciation of the coinage, for in Edward II.'s reign the Commons prayed the king that the money should be current at the value it bore in his father's time. The second Edward troubled little about such matters, and his coins, limited to pennies and subdivisions of a penny, are hardly distinguishable from those of his father; but the coinage of his son became famous throughout Europe.

Gold Coins   The seventeenth year of Edward III. is memorable for the new coinage. It was not only a new coinage, but a coinage in gold. Three pieces were struck—florins, half-florins, and

---

[1] "Gros Tournais Englays que valent verayment quatre esterlings."

quarter-florins;—the largest to be current for seventy-two silver pennies—fifty went to the pound troy—the weight to be that of two little florins of Florence. It was a handsome

COINS OF EDWARD III
Groat. Noble. Florin.

coin, and showed the king on his throne between two leopards, the cross on the reverse in a tressure. The half-florin—or one leopard, as it was called in the royal proclamation—showed that beast, crowned, carrying the banner with the arms of France and England quarterly flowing over its shoulders. The quarter bore a helmet on which was a lion passant guardant, crowned. They were handsome coins, but were ill received, merchants declining to accept a fiftieth of a pound of gold as equivalent to six shillings. They were, as we should now say, called in, and no doubt recoined, for they are extremely rare, not more than two or three of these florins being known to exist. Edward was, however, determined to have a current gold coinage, and at the end of 1343, the year (if we reckon from January) which had seen the appearance of the unpopular florins, he effected his purpose. The new issue was of nobles, maille nobles, and ferling[1] nobles; the large coin passing at six shillings and eightpence, thirty-nine and a half going to the pound of gold. The device was entirely new; and the coins, which were extremely beautiful, acquired immediate popularity. Edward is represented standing in his ship, the banner of St. George flying at the mast-head, in his right hand a sword, in his left a shield with the arms of France and England. It is not certain how the device came to be adopted. The notion that it was a claim to the dominion of the seas flattered, and flatters, the national sentiment; but it is probable that the design was intended merely to perpetuate the memory of Edward's success as an admiral, and has reference to the affair at Sluys, on Midsummer Day, 1340, where, under his personal captaincy, the English gained a victory over the French fleet. The popularity of the noble was European, so that there was great difficulty in keeping it in England; and in the two successive coinages which followed, the weight of gold was reduced to one-forty-second of the pound, without materially checking exportation. On all these pieces, up to 1360, Edward appears as, by the grace of God, King of England and France and Lord of Ireland. Afterwards, as a result of the Peace of Bretigny, the style of King of France was dropped, and Lord of Aquitaine inserted in its place in the noble. After that date the claims to France and Aquitaine appear on the pieces of larger denomination, the claim to France only, on the smaller. In his silver coins Edward made little change, but groats and

---

[1] Maille nobles (from *médaille*, *maille*, a coin) were half nobles; ferling (*i.e.* fourthling) were quarter nobles.

half-groats were circulated as well as pennies, half-pence, and farthings.

But the popular feeling was all in favour of the gold coinage, and the Commons presented an article to the king asking him to issue a gold piece smaller than the quarter-noble. Their request received the royal assent; nothing, however, seems to have come of it. In like manner the royal attempt to establish an international circulation, founded on gold, between England, the country of the staple,

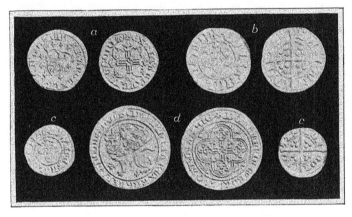

COINS OF EDWARD III.
a Quarter-florin.   *b* Penny.   *c* Half-penny.   *d* Half-florin.

and Flanders, the country of the manufacture of woollens, proved abortive. It is, however, a curious piece of evidence of the antiquity of the idea of a monetary union.

DURING the thirteenth and fourteenth centuries the whole intellectual life of the English nation is derived from, and centres in, the two Universities,[1] which served as places of higher education or *studia generalia* to the regular and secular clergy, and thus to nearly all professional men. The University of Oxford—whose claims to have been founded by King Alfred, St. Neot, and St. Grimbald were based on legal

---

[1] *See ante*, Vol. I., p. 489 *seq.*

**Oxford:
Origin.**

and literary forgeries, and are now known to be as mythical as the stories of Mempric, Brutus the Trojan, and the *Greeks* from *Crick*-lade—was already full-grown when St. Edmund Rich studied and taught there *c.* 1200. Thibaut d'Estampes, Robert Pullein, and the jurist Vacarius of Bologna lectured there between 1100 and 1150; and by 1190 Oxford Masters and Clerks were well known, and foreign students, such as Nicholas the Hungarian, to whom Richard I. granted an exhibition, were attracted. The early studies and customs are similar to those of Paris, and may well have taken shape after a recall of English students thence during Henry II.'s French wars; and Oxford gradually overtopped both Paris and Bologna. The earliest records of Cambridge are said to have been burnt by the townsmen in 1261; its origin may be attributed to a migration from Oxford in 1209. The Oxford students were subject only to the distant authority of their diocesan, the Bishop of Lincoln; Cambridge obeyed the nearer see of Ely; the bishop's commissary, the Chancellor, subsequently became an independent academic official with ecclesiastical powers. The studies, mainly theological and legal, were already supervised by the Faculties when Giraldus Cambrensis visited Oxford in 1187 to give a public reading of his work on the Topography of Ireland. The degrees were in the nature of licences to teach, granted to the aspirant with great care and formality by those already qualified; and the necessary exercises both before and after graduation often took the form of lectures and disputations by which more junior students were instructed. Oxford in the thirteenth century had grown into a corporate society of teachers and scholars with a definite constitution and considerable privileges composed of learned guilds which promoted into their own higher grades candidates who had studied under their direction, by means of degrees, valid at first locally, but afterwards internationally. The full-blown teacher was a Master, Doctor, or Professor, and, when actually teaching, a Regent; the half-developed student, like the apprentice or the aspirant for knighthood, was known as a Bachelor; undergraduates were Grammarians, General Sophists, and Questionists. University buildings there were none till the old Congregation House was built in 1320; previously

business was transacted in the adjacent church of St. Mary,
or in St. Mildred's; lectures and other forms of instruction
were given in large rooms called schools, mostly private or
monastic property.

The masters of Oxford had no great difficulty in dispensing Auto-
with the ordinary ecclesiastical superiors. They got rid of nomy.
the Archdeacon of Oxford in 1346, and of their bishop after
a complicated quarrel in 1368. They were not too polite to

SEAL OF THE UNIVERSITY OF OXFORD.

the Papal legates, though the Popes were the greatest patrons
of universities. To the local abbeys they were fairly courteous. With the Dominicans, who settled in Oxford in 1221,
and the Franciscans, who hurried after them in 1224, the
relations were less harmonious; but the university availed
itself of their excellent lecture-rooms and lecturers ("doing
Austins" was a phrase for certain academical exercises three
centuries after the suppression of the Augustinian friary), and
eventually baffled their pretensions to be admitted to the
theological degrees without the preliminary arts course on
which Oxford education has always been based. With the

Town and Gown. city of Oxford the struggle was more prolonged, but the victory even more decisive. Oxford, situated centrally on a great waterway, had long been a prosperous market-town ; and the citizens, as well as the Jewish quarter, revenged themselves for the loss of their former quiet by practising manifold extortions on the clerks. The latter were always ready to fight, though of the numerous outrages those committed by the townsmen were on a larger scale. In 1209 the students dispersed in disgust; but the Papal legate laid the town under an interdict, and soon forced it to recognise the immunity of the clerks from lay jurisdiction, to pay an annual fine (the first endowment of the university), and to submit to regulations moderating the cost of lodgings and provisions. In 1244 the clerks sacked the Jewry, and the king quieted them by a decree consolidating the special powers of the Chancellor. The murder of a Scots scholar in 1248 gave the university an opportunity of obtaining a fresh charter of privileges which included acts of submission from the townsmen and · Jews. In 1264 occurred the migration to Northampton, whither Cambridge had also retreated ; and only the prompt interference of the king prevented a permanent coalition there. An act of sacrilege by some Jews in 1268 paved the way to their final humiliation. In 1298 the knavery and violence of the townsmen led to a really dangerous riot; and in 1355 occurred the great conflict of St. Scholastica's Day, in which the town, without having received serious provocation, commenced a wholesale massacre, with the assistance of a band of two thousand rustics, " crying Slay and Havoc ! " The clerks prepared to leave Oxford for ever, but the combined forces of the Church and the Crown reduced the town to subjection, and the Chancellor received as compensation an absolute control of the market and an annual act of submission to his authority which lasted into the nineteenth century.

North and South. There were also internal disorders, some arising out of the struggle for precedence between the Faculties, others due to the fact that young men coming from all parts of the country—Northerners and Southerners, Scots, Irish, Welsh, and foreigners—did not leave behind them their local animosities. Hence, of the two officials delegated by the Masters to assist the Chancellor, one was the Northern and the other the Southern Proctor. Festivals of national or patron saints were suppressed, and jousts and tournaments kept at a distance. After the great secession to Stamford (I. p. 615) of the more studious and probably defeated Northerners, the king had to intervene to procure reunion. In 1385 they were still so sensitive that he had to prohibit the application to them of the designation of their allies, the Scotsmen; and till 1827 all candidates for a degree were statutably obliged to swear that they would never lecture at Stamford! Partly for similar reasons, no doubt, the scholars of the earlier colleges were generally selected from particular localities, and such connections survive in some cases. Bloodshed was a usual feature of these disturbances, and a disorderly career at the university often developed into armed brigandage on the king's lieges and was terminated by the dagger or the rope.

The university of Cambridge, occupying a less central and **Cambridge.** more unhealthy situation, and having less powerful protectors, did not compete in popularity or privileges with the older society before the sixteenth century. It was not even formally recognised till it received the licence of Pope John XXII. in 1318. The students were more homogeneous than at Oxford, the religious Orders were less active there, and the number of eminent men produced by it was insignificant during this period. Oxford schools were renowned as a "staple product" at a time when Cambridge was famous only for eels.

The medieval undergraduate students were mainly lads of **Student** humble origin; though many older men, such as the monks or **Life.** friars, shared their studies, and in rank they ranged from the poor scholar, who supported himself during term by the profits of licensed mendicancy or manual labour in the vacations, to the privileged sons of earls and nephews of bishops. At Oxford *c.* 1300 the number was about 3,000; for the estimate made by Archbishop FitzRalph of Armagh before the Consistory at Avignon in 1357, that there had been as many as 30,000 in his day, must be considered rhetorical. They lived in lodging-houses known as halls, where the meals were provided from a common fund and called commons (extra food was battels), while most scholars could rent a small chamber as bedroom and study. One of the inmates, usually a Master, was the principal of the hall, and was responsible for the financial arrangements and for the main-tenance of order ; and the post was not unprofitable. A man-ciple,[1] or steward, catered for the party ; and in most cases some lectures were provided within the hall. From wills and inventories may be estimated the extent of a clerk's posses-sions, which often included musical instruments and lethal weapons, besides a few books, bed-clothes, and some cooking utensils. On " legible," or full reading days, lectures went on from an early hour in the morning to some time after the noon-day dinner ; but there were many non-legible days. Daily attendance at Divine service was a matter of course. All the steps in a man's progress to his degree, especially the process of Determination for the bachelor, and the Inception for the higher degrees, were marked by numerous disputations (a sort of *vivâ voce* examination), attendance at or delivery of lectures, licences, oaths, fees, ceremonies, and entertainments. The shorter vacations were usually, and the long vacation often, spent at Oxford and employed in private studies. A university education commenced at an early age with the acquisition of a working knowledge of Latin, the language of theology, law, and science, in the Schools of Grammar, where the text-books used were Terence and Priscian. To obtain the degree of B.A. required a four years' course of logic, and mastership was not reached till after seven or eight years of the seven arts and three philosophies (grammar, dialectic, rhetoric, music, arithmetic, geometry, and astronomy, with physics, metaphysics, and ethics), while the D.D. seldom attained his position of distinction before the twentieth year from matriculation. During the whole of this period the arts course was a severe one, and the discipline was really testing and the results brilliant. In the next century students of the type of Chaucer's clerks, Hendy Nicholas, John and Alein, and the loafers known as chamberdekyns,[2] were more common. The expenses of an ordinary university career of ten years ranged from £35 to four times that sum ; but no doubt large

[1] The term is still in use at Oxford.

[2] Poor scholars, possibly in minor orders, unattached to any college or hall.

numbers never proceeded to a degree. The more popular of the teaching masters derived an adequate revenue from their pupils' fees, which were paid terminally and known as

Photo : Gillman & Co., Oxford.

THE MOB QUAD, MERTON COLLEGE, OXFORD.

Collections, a word still used for the examination at the end of a term's lectures.

The maintenance of poor clerks was an object which soon Colleges. attracted the attention of the charitably disposed. The earliest attempts at endowment took the form of chests. The Frideswide Chest was the capitalisation by Grosseteste of the fine paid annually by the abbey of Eynsham on behalf of the town of Oxford; and there were several legacies kept in coin in iron boxes, from which small loans were obtainable by the temporarily impecunious on depositing a valuable book, silver cup, or other article, sworn by the university stationer fairly to exceed in value the sum borrowed. Some of these funds showed a profit, probably unintentional, on this pawnbroking business; and before 1500 the total capital in circulation in this way was about 2,000 marks, an enormous sum for the time. The first regular exhibition fund originated in 1243 in a payment to be made by the priory of Bicester under the will of Alan Basset for two chaplains at Oxford. Bishop Kilkenny of Ely left money for a similar purpose to Barnwell Priory near Cambridge, in 1256. In 1249 Master William of Durham left 310 marks to Oxford University for the support of ten to twelve masters; and John Baliol carried out a penitential vow by maintaining a few poor clerks from the north in a sort of almshouse.

Merton College.
But the institution of the collegiate system in England is due to the brilliant administrative genius of Walter de Merton, Lord High Chancellor and Bishop of Rochester, who between 1262 and 1274 elaborated a scheme, by which he had intended to assign certain manors for the support of his eight nephews at the schools, into a complex foundation at Oxford, with statutes known as the Rule of Merton, from which most subsequent codes were more or less copied (I., p. 620). This establishment was an adaptation to the promotion of general learning of the best features of the monastic system, and had already been successfully tried at Paris. The incorporated Scholars or Fellows, described as the House, Hall, or College (*i.e.* corporation) of Scholars of Merton, were soon provided with a magnificent chapel (by the rebuilding of an impropriated parish church), a fine hall and kitchen, and common dormitories, from which corners were partitioned off to serve as private studies or *musaea*. The members were provided with instruction, pocket-money, clothes (then called *livery*), and all other necessaries. They swore to obey the rules of the house, and were obliged to take the usual arts course of logic, philosophy, etc., proceeding usually to the study of theology. A scholar vacated his place if he accepted a

benefice or entered a monastic order. His conduct was reviewed minutely by his fellows at the scrutinies, or chapters, which resembled those of the religious Orders. The government was vested in the seven or eight seniors, at the head of whom was the Warden, who was charged specially with the care of the estates, and received considerable allowances

TOMB OF WALTER DE MERTON, ROCHESTER CATHEDRAL.

for the exercise of hospitality. Other disciplinary, financial, or religious functions were entrusted to Deans, Bursars, and Chaplains. There were also some "poor boys," who were educated to fill vacancies as they occurred among the scholars. Many of the regulations were monastic in character; but there was not the same absolute uniformity of life, and the perpetual vows of poverty, chastity, and obedience were not required.

At Cambridge, Hugh de Balsham, Bishop of Ely, founded Peterhouse, after the Merton rule, though on a less adequate scale, in 1284. In the same year Archbishop Peckham had to visit Merton College severely in order to correct several abuses and violations of the Founder's Statutes. At Oxford four small colleges sprang up at once. The trustees of William of Durham in 1280, and Dervorguilla, widow of John Baliol, in 1282, turned their exhibition funds into incorporated societies, soon to be known as University and Balliol Halls. These endowments were increased by subsequent benefactions, amounting, in the case of Balliol, almost to a refoundation by Sir Philip de Somerville in 1340. Stapledon Hall (afterwards Exeter College) was the work of Walter, Bishop of Exeter, in 1314. Edward II.'s almoner, Adam de Brome, founded in 1324 a more extensive "House of Scholars of St. Mary at Oxford," soon called Oriel College, from some architectural feature in one of the original tenements. The founder himself became the first Provost, and secured the patronage, first of the king, and then of Henry Burghersh, Bishop of Lincoln. The first statutes were modelled on those of Merton, but in 1326 a fresh set was issued which made a degree a necessary qualification for a scholarship. This society was self-governing, like Merton; the other three halls were only partially independent of their trustees as governors. In 1324 a Chancellor of the Exchequer founded at Cambridge a very similar institution, Michael House, now merged in Trinity College. In 1338 Clare Hall absorbed an unsuccessful University Hall of 1326; and in 1337 Edward III. endowed munificently a "King's Hall of Scholars," which was also swallowed by Henry VIII.'s Trinity.

"The Queen's Hall of Oxford" (1340) was the erection of Robert de Eglesfield, chaplain to Queen Philippa. The statutes are very ecclesiastical in tenor, and provide for theological studies, certain religious services, and the elementary education of "poor boys" as well as the usual objects. Some of the institutions are symbolical of the habits of the apostles, and some curious "canting" customs, such as the present of a needle and thread on New Year's Eve (*aiguille et fil* = Eglesfield), still remain. The next Oxford foundation was New

College, in many ways a new departure, in 1379. At Cambridge between 1346 and 1352 the Hall of Valence Marie (now Pembroke) was endowed by the widow of Aymer de Valence, Earl of Pembroke; Gonville Hall (now Gonville and Caius), by Edmund Gonville and his executor, Bishop Bateman of Norwich, who himself founded Trinity Hall for students of civil and canon law; and the "House of Corpus Christi," by a local guild of that name, under the patronage

THE FOUNDER'S HORN, QUEEN'S COLLEGE, OXFORD.

of Henry, the "good Duke" of Lancaster. Several of these establishments were quite humble, and often added to their revenues by letting their spare rooms to strangers, at first elderly, who were known as Perendinants,[1] or as Commoners, since they paid for a place at the common table, to which the college farmers, or artisans, or friars were often invited as guests. The original buildings were mostly heterogeneous and unsystematic. All were intended to shelter that particular class of students in which the founders were interested from the temptations to idleness and vice to which young men living at a distance from their families were exposed in

[1 "Indwellers," boarders.]

medieval towns; and it speaks well for Merton and the "similar halls" that their members, possibly because almost entirely restricted to their college bounds, appear to have taken no part in the great riot of 1355.

The Monasteries and the Collegiate System. The Benedictine monasteries, themselves for many centuries the chief guardians of learning, soon saw the value of this collegiate system. University teachers were generally abler than the local Masters of the Novices who taught in the cloister the "primitive sciences" of grammar, logic, and philosophy; but the Benedictines had no settlement at Oxford or Cambridge; and disliked the association of Regular with Secular clerks in halls or lodgings. In 1283 the abbey of St. Peter at Gloucester secured a benefactor, and their "nursery or mansion-place" for thirteen student-monks was soon enlarged by the addition of distinct hostels there for nearly every large Benedictine house in the South of England. The great northern abbey of Durham began about 1286 a separate Hall, which became very important as Durham College, and was fostered by two Bishops of Durham, Richard de Bury, the greatest book-collector of the Middle Ages, who left his library to the students, and Thomas Hatfield, the great architect, who gave it a permanent endowment for eight monks and eight secular scholars. Both societies were originally supported by levies from the parent abbeys or cells; both perished at the Reformation, though remains of their buildings may be seen incorporated in Worcester and Trinity Colleges. The Benedictines kept an officer, the "Prior of Students," at each university; but at Cambridge there was no Hall till 1428. Oxford was more frequented by the religious Orders; and the Benedictines of Canterbury secured a house of their own, now included in Christ Church, from Archbishop Islip in 1363. The Augustinians and Cistercians, being able to lodge at St. Frideswide's or Rewley, did not move till 1435 and 1437 respectively. The monastic students were comfortably maintained; but they became eminent as administrators and historiographers rather than as philosophers and theologians.

The universities thus afforded an open career to rich and poor clerks alike, and men who showed ability there often

SHRINE OF ST. THOMAS CANTILUPE, HEREFORD CATHEDRAL.

51

Eminent Teachers. rose to the highest places in the kingdom. Among the earlier Oxford teachers were the three canonised bishops Edmund Rich (Canterbury), whose M.A. degree is the earliest recorded; Richard of Wych (Chichester); and Thomas Cantilupe (Hereford), Simon de Montfort's Chancellor and the last English saint; Ralph of Maidstone, Bishop of Hereford, who came with a migration from Paris in 1229; Francesco d'Accorso, invited from Bologna by Edward I. to lecture on Roman law; Bishop Cobham of Worcester, who founded the first university library in 1320, though the books had to be taken away by force from Oriel College in 1337; Archbishop John Stratford, and his brother Robert, Bishop of Chichester, both Chancellors of England; Richard FitzRalph of Armagh, the great opponent of the unscrupulous friars of the fourteenth century; William Shyreswood (died 1349), who wrote the chief text-book on logic; Robert Holcot, one of the most widely famed scholastic expositors of Scripture, who, with Bradwardine, FitzRalph, and others, formed the circle patronised by Richard de Bury; and John Wycliffe (Master of Balliol, 1360), the last Schoolman and the first Reformer. But the most important set of men during this period is the group known as the Oxford Schoolmen, and of these the majority were connected with the Dominican or Franciscan Orders.

The Oxford Schoolmen. The original schoolmen, such as John Scotus Erigena, Roscellinus, Anselm, Peter Lombard, and Abelard, occupied themselves with speculation of a dialectical character in metaphysics and divinity, based on Aristotelian logic filtered through Porphyry and Boëthius (I. p. 486). But this philosophy was completely transformed by the introduction into Western Europe, chiefly through Arabic and Latin versions, of Aristotle's Metaphysics, Physics, Psychology, and Ethics, and by the partly Neo-Platonic, partly Peripatetic writings of Arabian and Jewish philosophers. The new doctrines at first excited alarm, and were censured by a Council of Paris in 1209; but they were soon appropriated by theologians, and modified to suit the dogmas of the Church. The "Irrefragable Doctor," Alexander of Hales, a friar from Gloucestershire, taught at Paris before 1245; Robert Grosseteste, afterwards the famous Bishop of Lincoln, and the staunch protector of the clerks, attracted large crowds to the Franciscan schools at Oxford, built by their first English provincial, Agnello da Pisa. Grosseteste (I., p. 574) was a man of indefatigable energy and independence; he translated Aristotle's Ethics from the Greek, studied Hebrew and physical science, and gave Oxford scholasticism a European reputation. Among his pupils were Roger Bacon, and Adam Marsh, the "Illustrious Doctor," a man of multifarious interests and wide political influence.

Meanwhile, the newer Scholasticism had received more systematic treatment at the hands of Albertus Magnus, the "Universal Doctor" (and reputed magician), in his scheme of rational or philosophised theology, and from his pupil, St. Thomas of Aquino, the "Angelic Doctor," who effected the most perfect accommodation that was possible of the Aristotelian principles to ecclesiastical orthodoxy. The main doctrines of the *Thomists* were the immanence of universals[1] and the demonstrability of the existence of God from the contemplation of the world as His work. Aquinas was a Dominican, as were two other eminent Oxford men, Robert Bacon and Archbishop Kilwardby; his chief disciple in England was the "Profound Doctor," Thomas Bradwardine, a fellow of Merton, designated Archbishop of Canterbury and of great influence as confessor to Edward III. Partly, no doubt, from jealousy this system was soon attacked by the Franciscan teachers, who, moreover, were imbued with the ideas of Averröes and of Neo-Platonism, which St. Thomas rejected dogmatically. They found a leader in John Duns Scotus, the "Subtle Doctor," an Oxford friar from Northumberland, who taught at Oxford, Paris, and Cologne, where he died at an early age in 1308. The Scotists or Dunces (a term afterwards misused), as his followers were called, attached immense value to logic as a science. Their strength lay in negative criticism; and while they demanded a strict faith in all the tenets of the Christian Church and the corresponding philosophical positions, they exercised considerable scepticism as to the arguments by which these were supported. Having destroyed the rational grounds of belief, they left nothing but the unconditional will of God, set over against the voluntary submission of the believer to the

[1 *See ante*, Vol. I., p. 484, on the controversy between Nominalists and Realists.]

authority of the Church, as the basis of a man's religious convictions. The influence of Duns was so great in England that the system of Aquinas never regained popularity; the Franciscans became arrogant, and made themselves unpopular by proselytising from other orders and by enticing mere boys to take vows, against the wishes of their parents. A Franciscan Archbishop of Canterbury, John Peckham, protected them; but they excited a powerful enemy in Archbishop FitzRalph.

Ockham.   The last of the Schoolmen proper, the "Invincible Doctor," William of Ockham (in Surrey), was also an Oxford Franciscan, and a pupil of Duns, to whose doctrines he applied his own principles of criticism. He took a prominent part in the struggle against Pope Clement VI., by whom he was imprisoned at Avignon and excommunicated; and he died at Munich about 1349. In his voluminous political and theological works, he abandoned all attempt to harmonise philosophy and theology; and, denying that any theological doctrine was demonstrated by reason, made even the existence and unity of God solely articles of faith. By renewing the theory called Nominalism—namely, that the particular thing alone has any real existence—he paved the way for the inductive method in the investigation of external nature and psychical phenomena.

Learning.   Though some attempts were made to understand Greek, Hebrew, and Arabic writings, there was during this period nothing resembling the modern study of literature known as classical scholarship. The Schoolmen wrote in a barbarous jargon of Latin, and their arguments are cast in extremely technical and complicated forms derived from the syllogistic method of Aristotle. The great classical authors were, however, preserved in the libraries of the rich monasteries, as at St. Alban's, Glastonbury, York, and Durham. Richard de Bury obtained many manuscripts from Italy early in the fourteenth century; and wrote the "Philobiblon" on the book-collector's pursuits; but collections like his were rare before the time of Duke Humphrey. The monks of Durham College, even before De Bury's bequest, frequently received parcels of books from the fine library of Durham, of which the catalogues are preserved. Ancient or contemporary history

and geography were left mainly to the monkish chroniclers;
the most popular work was the "Polychronicon," or Universal
History of a Chester Benedictine, Ranulph Higden (d. 1364),

PSALTER IN LATIN AND GREEK, FROM RAMSEY ABBEY.
(*Corpus Christi College, Cambridge.*)

which contains an extraordinary farrago of popular delusions,
as well as a vast amount of real information. French was
taught in the schools of grammar as well as English, as the
pupils were required to translate from Latin into either
language.

But of all the philosophers of this period, in which there are traces of interest, though few of advance, in scientific studies, the most encyclopedic was Roger Bacon, who, after devoting twenty years of patient labour and over £2,000 to scientific investigations, committed the mistake of joining the Franciscans at Oxford. He soon learnt that to confront authority with experience, or break away from the useless intricacies of scholastic metaphysics, was an unpardonable offence; and his work was thwarted at every turn till 1266, when the French Pope, Clement IV., heard of his researches and asked for a short account of his results. This was not yet composed; but the Papal mandate, undiscerning as it was, set Bacon free; and in fifteen or eighteen months he produced a comprehensive survey of the whole range of science, as science was then understood. Theology, grammar, mathematics, geography, chronology, music. the correction of the calendar, optics, chemistry, mechanics, and ethics are successively discussed. He intended to note every kind of natural phenomenon in connection with metals, plants, colours, animals, agriculture, and medicine. The whole of his work is marked by an appreciation of the function of applied logic, which it was reserved for his more fortunate namesake, Francis Bacon, to popularise. On many subjects, such as astrology and alchemy, Bacon shared the superstitions of the age in which a Pope wrote a treatise on the transmutation of metals; and in this he may plead excuses which are not available to a seventeenth-century inquirer. But when he insisted on the necessity of experiment in natural science, and of accurate versions in using Greek and Arabic treatises, he did more for the advancement of learning than if he had actually invented gunpowder, clocks, and telescopes, or explained the rainbow. Bacon was reimprisoned by Pope Nicholas IV., but released in 1292; his superiors managed to suppress his writings so effectually that nothing was printed till 1733. His name, with that of his friend, Friar Thomas Bungay, was traditionally associated with the Black Art; the tales told of his talking brazen head, and his moving statues, may be due to his unceasing efforts to obtain accurate geometrical and astronomical instruments, the scarcity of which, and of adequate translations, he often deplores. Robert Bacon.

the influential Dominican, and John Baconthorpe, Provincial of the Carmelites (1329), who was called "the Averröist," from his attempts to reconcile the Arabian philosophy with the arguments of Aquinas, were respectively uncle and nephew of Friar Roger.

Grosseteste before Bacon, and Bradwardine after him, studied physical science and astronomy; and Bradwardine at least, who, as a young man, had been one of Richard de Bury's secretaries, had a first-hand acquaintance with the works of Seneca, Ptolemy, Cyprian, Jerome, Augustine, Isidore, and the early schoolmen, and his treatise "On the Cause of God" is the source of much of English Calvinism. But scientific discovery rose only on the ruins of Scholasticism; and it is not the least surprising of his achievements that the persecuted Oxford friar, even more hopefully than the philosophising Lord Chancellor, marked the destinies of the experimental method, and, with no magic but that of a single-hearted devotion to truth,

"Saw the Vision of the world and all the wonder that would be."

THE special feature of this period is the growth of interest in natural science. No doubt the knowledge of Nature diffused through the community, especially in the form of "old wives' sayings," had always been considerable; but up to this time there existed neither the means of getting information readily, nor of imparting it to any wide circle of learners. It is not that the disposition was wanting; on the contrary, we have a long succession of treatises, beginning in Bede's time, dealing with popular science in the vulgar tongue, and valuable alike philologically and as showing the sciences in demand. But the circulation of these was limited to a few monasteries, and hardly ever reached the outside world. Now, however, new sources of knowledge had been tapped, new centres of study were crowded, and new means of propagation through the length and breadth of the civilised world were in their first outburst of life.

Astronomy and medicine, with their allies astrology, magic, and alchemy, are the first sciences cultivated in any country, and most of the treatises above referred to fall under one of

ROBERT STEELE.

Science and Pseudo-Science.

these heads.   The medicine of the early English folk consisted largely of the knowledge of simples and of charms,
while their astronomy was devoted, as astronomy has been
since the birth of time, to the calculation of the recurring
religious festivals.   Among medieval Christians the system of
fixing these was sufficiently complex.   As is well known, the
movable feasts depend on the date of Easter; and the necessity
of making this an anniversary, and also a lunar festival, of
insuring that it should not fall on the Jewish Passover, and
of avoiding the Quartodeciman[1] heresy, led to its being fixed
for the first Sunday after the fourteenth day of the moon
after the spring equinox.   Up to this period astronomers
had been unable to get a proper length for the solar year,
the equinox was yearly falling earlier than the calendar date,
and the seasons of the year seemed to be falling into confusion.   The priests of Bremen, indeed, on one occasion when
a full moon fell between the true and calendar equinox,
kept Easter a month before the rest of the Christian world
and earned for themselves the name of Pre-menses;[2] but
such heroic remedies were not for all, and one of Bacon's
most pressing appeals to the Pope was for a reformation of
the calendar.

Eastern Influence.   The Eastern world—opened to us, not by the Crusades,
but by the settlements in Sicily, Spain, Tripoli, and Syria,
where Moslem and Christian lived in friendship side by side,
and where the Jew was tolerated by both—had inherited and
added to the scientific traditions of the Greek world, and the
results of Eastern science were now laid open to the West
by translations.   A few translations from the Arabic were
made in the early years of the twelfth century, but the
bulk of them were made in the early part of the thirteenth
century.   The new learning soon altered the character of the
places where it was taught.   Up to this time all learning
had passed through the great monasteries, was received by
monks, was in general limited to monks of one order, and

[1 The keeping of Easter at the time of the Jewish passover, *i.e.* on the
fourteenth day of the month Nisan, whatever day of the week it might be.
The Councils of Nicaea (325) and Antioch (341) ordered the festival to be
kept as described in the text.]

[2 An obvious pun on "Bremenses" (men of Bremen), suggesting the sense
"before the month."]

"THE HIERARCHY OF THE SCIENCES," AS CONCEIVED BY MEDIÆVAL THOUGHT.
Frontispiece to the Berri Bible (MS. Harl. 1585.

was deeply tinged by the channels it passed through. The new matter, coming from Moslem sources through Jewish interpreters, was distinctively secular, and the Universities, just rising into prominence, gave an opportunity for its study. The international character of these bodies, maintained by the acceptance of each other's degrees, led to a fluidity of learning up to then unknown; but while the Universities were, and remained, secular bodies, most of their students and most of their teachers were studying with one object— to become better preachers. The preaching friars, black or grey, Dominican or Franciscan, were still in their early outburst of enthusiasm, ripened by a generation's experience. Owning neither corporate nor private property, they passed from place to place, gathering knowledge and experience, and using it at the will of their superiors, as teachers in the University, or as preachers in the market-place. Just as Anselm, Lanfranc, and Abelard had taught in a monastery to an audience of monks, so Albertus Magnus, Thomas Aquinas, Bartholomew Anglicus, Alexander Hales, Ricardus Rufus, and a host of other friars, taught in the medieval Universities, and were heard by friars and their novices.

We have, then, when forming our mental picture of England at this period, to take into account that in every village of our land, men skilled in the science of their time were using it, as they had been taught it, in illustration of every text they preached on, of every doctrine they taught, and that thus general notions of science were becoming familiar to the mass of the people. That science, however, bore but little relation to our own, and it now becomes our task to show of what nature were the beliefs thus spread among our forefathers.

Astronomy.   Practical astronomy had reached a state of great perfection, considering the imperfect instruments at the command of observers, and tables of over 1,000 fixed stars and planets had been drawn up in the East from an early period. One of these, probably the Persian tables of the eleventh century, fell into the hands of Roger Bacon, who (1267) calls them "Almanachs." Just at this period, too, the celebrated Alphonsine tables were drawn up at Toledo by Jewish astronomers from Arab sources. The English men of science were among the

first in Europe to receive and spread the knowledge of
astronomy, and they speedily came to the forefront.   The
best known of them all is John of Halifax, whose treatise
on astronomy, founded on the Arabic of Alfaragan, exists in

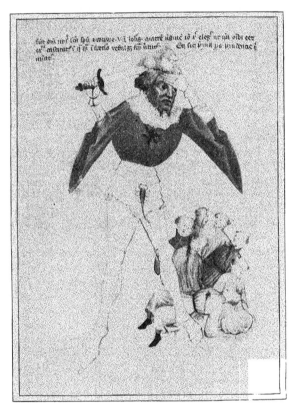

FIGURE OF THE PLANET MARS.
(Trinity College, Cambridge.)

innumerable MSS, and ran through sixty editions in the first
century of printing ; while the works of forty writers, nearly all
Oxford men, remain to attest the fruitfulness of this period.
But the theoretical astronomy of the day was fundamentally

wrong, and had to be proved so by centuries of toil, dragged meanwhile at the heels of every charlatan of later days.

Astrology.   As we all know, people used to suppose that the earth was in the centre of the universe, and that the heavens lay round it in an enormous vault, revolving once every day. The fixed stars scattered over the sky were early gathered into constellations; the most notable of these formed a belt round the heavens called the zodiac, divided into twelve signs or constellations; within this belt the planets have their apparent path. Each sign of the zodiac was supposed to have its peculiar action on Nature, animate or inanimate, and to act on the other signs, and as the lines of force came near the earth or not, their effect on its inhabitants was great or small. At the moment of birth their effect was especially great, the most important being the sign rising in the East, and that vertically overhead. The action of the planets, too, was of equal importance. To study it the heavens were divided into twelve equal portions, starting from a point depending on the position of the sun and moon at the instant of birth. This point was called the horoscope. To each division was assigned a part of the destiny of the child—fortune, marriage, war, death, etc. etc. Each of these houses or divisions was again divided and subdivided, planets were assigned to each subdivision, and if a planet chanced to be at the time in a fortunate subdivision of an appropriate house, the result was an enormous increase of its power. Thus the "Secreta Secretorum"—the most typical medieval book remaining—tells us of the weaver's son who was born when Venus and Mars were in their own degree in the signs of Gemini and Libra, thus promising that he should be wise, courtly, of good counsel, and loved by kings; and who, accordingly rose through the most adverse conditions to be the king's vizier.

Another important office of medieval astrology was to pronounce on the proper time for doing anything, whether it were marriage, a journey, or a war. Thus if one wishes to succeed in war, commence when the house of the moon is vertically overhead, and when Mercury is in a favourable relationship to it. If one wishes to make a journey, arrange that the houses of journeying, and the constellations governing the cities to which one travels are in the ascendant, and the house

which governs the object of one's journey should be directly
beneath the earth.   If one wishes to take medicine or to be
bled, the astrologer again steps in.   You cannot be bled while
the moon is in Taurus or Pisces, nor in the new moon, nor

FIGURE OF THE PLANET MERCURY.
(*Trinity College, Cambridge.*)

if it is in conjunction with another planet in a watery sign,
and you must look out for the position of Mercury and
Saturn.   For scarification a different set of rules prevails.
Medicine is to be taken while the moon is in Libra, Scorpio,
or Pisces, but it will be fatal if Saturn is in conjunction.

It will thus be seen that to start in life as a medieval astrologer required a considerable amount of real astronomical skill, as well as an intimate knowledge of a vast number of rules, most of them arbitrary, or founded on ancient myths; and that in course of time an enormous mass of real observations, taken to check the tables used, would be accumulated. In fact these observations ultimately led to the destruction of the system on which they were based. But it may be asked, What did the Church say to all this? Practically, though with occasional exceptions, it said what an early English translation of the "Secreta Secretorum" says: "He that is a

THE DANGERS OF ASTRONOMY.
(MS. Roy. 6 E· vi.)

perfect student in this science may know and see perils that are to come of wars, pestilences, famine, and other things for which he may ordain remedy (and if thou canst find no remedy, it is good that thou pray heartily to God that He ordain remedy). For whatever evils the planets show in their working, good men may so pray unto God, by orisons, fasting, sacrifice, alms-deed-doing, and penance for their sins, that God will turn, resolve, and revoke all that men fear."

Medicine.

We have just seen how medicine linked itself to astrology; we now turn to its connection with magic and alchemy. Our forefathers brought with them to this land a belief in runes and spells, and when the medical man, at first a stranger, probably a Jew, settled among them, the cures he wrought were set down to the superior efficacy of his charms. A book of counsels to young practitioners (1300) gives curious side-lights on the manners of the time. It seems he was expected from a sight of the patient's urine, to pronounce on the age, sex, and malady, and that usually a preliminary trial of his ability was made by trying to impose upon him with some counterfeit liquid. He was cautioned to use long words that

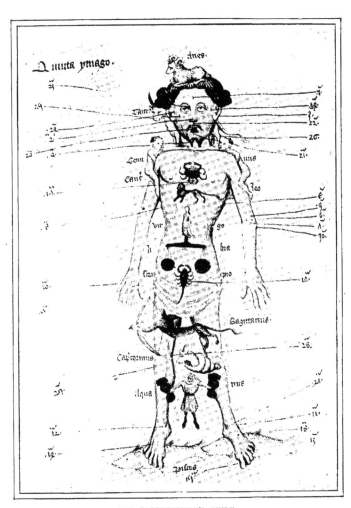

THE PHLEBOTOMIST'S GUIDE.
(*Trinity College, Cambridge.*)

would not be understood, never to visit a patient without doing something new, lest the patient should say "he can do nothing without his book"; and, in short, to sustain a reputation for infallibility at all costs. Such men were not likely to combat popular beliefs, if they did not directly encourage them. Bacon quoted Constantine (the introducer of Arab medicine into Europe) with the express approval of the use of charms. These talismans, said he, are not to be used because they can bring about any change, but because they bring the patient into a better frame of mind.

One often wonders that pretensions so utterly baseless as those of magic were not exploded at once. Several reasons prevented this from being the case. We must remember that this was an era of dawn when wonderful things were expected if one left one's own parish. It was a matter of everyday knowledge that there was a place in Ireland where men could not die, cinnamon was shot from the phœnix's nest with leaden arrows, the Wandering Jew was alive and might visit one some day, and all the dreams of the Arabian Nights were happening somewhere. Learned men like Albert and his pupils were laboriously collecting stories of the properties of animals, plants, and stones, and verifying them. when possible. The science of the age was as destitute of perspective as its art had been, and nothing, however marvellous, was, *prima facie*, impossible to the men of the period.

Magic.
The magic of our forefathers may be gathered from the Penitential of Theodore in the seventh century, where its practices are enumerated and their due penance allotted. Many of them are still common among the peasantry. The laws of Edgar, Athelstan, and Canute forbid it, punishing it as a crime when used as a means of inflicting personal injury on another, much as they would manslaying. A curious trial for witchcraft may be read in the life of Hereward the Wake. The Normans brought into England a new cycle of stories, such as the Melusine legend; and soon the tale spread how Herodias continued her unholy dance in the woods, sometimes confused with Diana, or with a certain Habunda. The progress of the story can be read in Walter Map, John of Salisbury, Matthew Paris, and the "Romance of the Rose." Women from all parts come to join in the revels. Then the

story grew, and the Evil One was present at the gathering, and was adored with obscene rites.   Lastly, men began to whisper of a compact between the necromancer and the fiend, and Black Magic was fully established in the popular imagination.   Now the Church stepped in, and the crime became that of heresy, though in England it was still under the cognisance of the civil courts.   But, side by side with this offspring of popular imagination was the White Magic of the age, largely composed of a knowledge of what may be called sympathetic properties of things—thus chrysolite, being clear and bright, typified wisdom.   Accordingly the wearing of chrysolite brings wisdom.   It is certain that a man who thought he could become wise by putting a piece of chrysolite in his right ear would be very slow to find that the charm was ineffectual.   Other charms may be explained by self-hypnotism, etc., and by the action of drugs and fumes. Others, such as " tying the knot," acted strongly on the mind of the person charmed.   Others again are surrounded by such a network of ritual that failure is almost inevitable, or depend on rare conjunctions of planets.   Lastly we must remember that till the invention of printing, books containing the necessary information rarely were in the hands of any one who desired to practise magic, but that they were invariably regarded as containing proved facts, unnecessary and perhaps unlawful to be repeated, which tended to throw light on the nature of things, and to explain hidden scriptural allusions. · It must be admitted, however, that a class of magical books existed, whose charms relied on direct invocation of the Enemy of mankind, and whose very titles, with one or two exceptions like " De Morte Animæ," have perished. During the fourteenth century an important change took place consequent on the attitude of the Church.   All magic was now considered by it as the result of a diabolical compact expressed or understood.   Such credulity as the Crusade of the Shepherds and the conspiracy of the lepers to poison all the wells of Christendom show, in the popular mind, made the charge of magic (which was now heresy) against the Templars easily believed.   In 1324 we find a woman burnt alive for magic at Kilkenny—the first person burnt for heresy in Ireland ; and several other records of the same date exist, such as John of Nottingham, the necromancer of Coventry, who died in prison before his trial, who made waxen images of the king and the Despensers. When we remember the science of the period, the men by and for whom it was collected, and the uses to which it was put, we cannot be surprised at the unquestioned belief in magic during the period.

Alchemy, too, the speculative and practical science of the day, first makes its appearance in England at this period, brought with medicine from its Eastern home. The earliest works translated from the Arabic were the Koran and a work on alchemy at the middle of the twelfth century. The first names connected with alchemy in England are those of writers on medicine; and the rise of alchemy at all was due to a mistaken analogy from medicine. As metals were considered to be all made of the same matter—sulphur and mercury—the differences between, *e.g.*, lead and silver were put down to a corrupt or diseased sulphur and mercury. This is brought out in the fable of the king and his leprous brothers, told by Dastyn, the English alchemist (*c.* 1200), where the drug that restores them to perfect health is the blood of the king. The common demand from medical practice was a panacea. Accordingly, alchemists sought for a panacea which should expel the corruption from the sulphur and mercury of the imperfect metals, leaving them pure silver or pure gold. Undoubtedly, the writings of Roger Bacon—especially his "Opus Minus"—gave a great impetus to the study of Alchemy. He was, like the other friars, rather a theoretical chemist than a practical one. When Alchemy became practical it was at once recognised that the alchemists could not make natural gold, and they accordingly

THE ERRING PRIEST, THE SORCERER, AND THE FIEND (MS. Roy. 10 E. iv.).

insisted that theirs was better. We can judge of the public feeling on the matter by reading the numerous proclamations against bad money. An old tradition connects our first and most beautiful gold coin with Alchemy. Raymund Lully was an ardent apostle of Christianity among the Moors, but finding they turned a deaf ear to him, he set himself to preach a crusade. Coming to England he found Edward III., who had just come to his power, was willing to aid, but funds were urgently needed—in what good cause are they not? Contrary to use, the preacher was willing to supply them. He asked for a room in St. Katherine's by the Tower, and a supply of lead, mercury, and tin, and in a few days turned out enough gold for an extended campaign. When the king got hold of the money, however, he broke faith with the simple brother, and used the money to fight the French with, imprisoning Lully till he made some more. Of course, this tale is untrue in all particulars—Edward's first gold coinage is in 1343, and Lully died years before Edward came to the throne; but it is certain that alchemy was flourishing in England then. We have a writ dated 1329 for the seizure of Master William de Dalby and John le Rous, who have made silver by the art of "Alkemony." Probably, however, the historical truth underlying this is that some fresh discoveries were made in the art of refining silver from lead, lead-mining being one of the great industries of England then. The warrants of appointment to the Mint mention at this time alchemy as one of the sources of the precious metals. In a very few years the practice of alchemy became so widespread that it grew a public danger, and "the craft of multiplying gold and silver" was declared a felony by statute in 1403.

A SUCCESS FOR THE BLACK ART (MS. Roy. 10 E. iv.).

CHARLES
CREIGHTON.
Medicine
and
Surgery.

THE theoretical medicine and surgery of England in the earliest times were those of the Byzantine writers, whose works, or excerpts from them, had a place in the libraries of monasteries. One or more of the monks, sometimes the abbot, would devote himself to a study of these authors, and so become reputed as a leech. From the writings of Alexander of Tralles or of Paulus of Ægina, the English practitioner of the time would make a collection of receipts, prescriptions, or leechdoms for the various injuries, wounds, and common maladies, substituting the native herbs when foreign drugs were not to be had. The resources of the native herbals were extensive, especially in the way of fomentations, plasters, or other outward applications, and in the form of decoctions; among the more potent herbs used in strong doses were pennyroyal, wormwood, feverfew, male-fern, sage, savine, sedum, betony, marsh-mallow, and costmary. King Alfred is said to have had sent him from the Patriarch of Jerusalem, by the hands of pilgrims returning from the Holy Sepulchre, a supply of Syrian drugs, including scammony, aloes, galbanum, ammoniacum, myrrh, and frankincense. The surgical instrument most used was the lancet in blood-letting. The days and hours for drawing blood, following the changes of the moon, were closely observed (p. 111), and it passed as a maxim that there was no time for phlebotomy so good as the season of Lent, when the evil humours, having gathered during winter, were waxing, in the hollow vessels of the body, just as the sap was stirring in the trees and worts. Many other rules derived from the doctrines of the humours and the qualities (hot or cold, moist or dry) were joined to the several leechdoms or prescriptions, while an august authority was claimed for the whole collection, as in the Anglo-Saxon Herbal of Glastonbury, which was the work of Apuleius Platonicus, handed down from Æsculapius and Chiron the Centaur. A prescription, or regimen, might have a special vogue: Oxa taught one, and Dun taught another, while the immemorial differences of the faculty were reflected in the words appended to a third, that "some teach it." None of the remedies were administered without ceremonial. While the medicine was being compounded, the patient would say twelve times over one of the

Psalms beginning *Miserere mei, Deus*,[1] then several *Paternosters*,
"then drink the dose, and wrap thyself up warm;" or he

A PAGE FROM A HERBARY (MS. Harl. 1585).

would sing the Psalm *Salvum me fac, Deus*,[2] then drink the
draught out of a church bell, the priest finishing the cure
with the prayer over him, *Domine sancte, Pater omnipotens.*

[1] *E.g.* Ps. li.   [2] Ps. xvi.

It was on consecrated ground that remedies had most power —at the shrine of a saint, or after touching the bier of a holy man, or at a holy well.   Mixed with the ceremonial of the Church was a good deal of more or less incongruous heathenism—the traditional folk-lore of the country, in the form of charms, magic, and star-craft. Much of the treatment was, of course, purely domestic, especially in the ailments of children.

A PHYSICIAN CONJURING THE VEGETABLE WORLD
(MS. Harl. 1585).

It is clear from the cases preserved by monkish chronicles that the maladies of the Middle Ages had an unusually large element of hysteria in them, so that a proportionately large element of faith came not amiss in the course of treatment. But the extant leechdoms provided for all the ordinary maladies of our own day, as well as for the usual injuries, wounds, and sores,—for consumptions, cancers, stone, gout, epilepsy, St. Vitus's dance, palsy, lethargy, whooping cough, catarrh, ague, megrim, rheumatism, stiff joints, deformities, dropsies, jaundices, hæmorrhages, fluxes, ruptures, prolapses, worms, and external parasites.   The resources of surgery were comparatively few, and the instruments simple; but, of course, splints and bandages were used, heat was applied by cauteries or by hot bricks, and it was known how to stanch blood, to extract missiles, to reduce dislocations, and to perform the simpler operations of cutting, trepanning, and the like.

The medical and surgical teaching of the Byzantine authors, in English or Latin translations, or even in the original

Greek, remained the groundwork of practice in the English monasteries from the time of Bede to the Norman period. A few of its numerous manuals have survived the ravages of time and the final spoil of the monasteries, and are still to be seen in the libraries of chapter-houses or in other collections. The Byzantine teaching was succeeded by the Arabian, of which the more famous schools were at Salerno (from A.D. 1060) and Montpelier; and the Arabian medical writings in due time found their way to England, and became authoritative

AN OPERATION.
(*Trinity College, Cambridge.*)

until the Reformation. Gilbert de Aquila, who was physician to Hubert Walter, Archbishop of Canterbury, is said to

SURGEON OPERATING ON THE SKULL.
(*Trinity College, Cambridge.*)

have studied at Salerno in the end of the twelfth century. When the archbishop was on his deathbed at one of his manors, on the way to Rochester, suffering from a carbuncle in his back, his physician declared that the disease might have been cured if taken in time; but, from his judgment of the urine, he had now no hope, and advised the prelate to make his peace with God.   The satirist of that age, John of Salisbury, becomes more than ordinarily biting in his references to medicine.   For his sins he was in the doctor's hands oftener than he wished, and he will not exasperate the profession by any original reflections of his own; he contents himself with quoting the sentence of Solomon, that medicine is from the Lord God, and a wise man will not despise it. Greed, he hints, and love of power or authority, are the besetting vices of the physician; and those vices we know to have been common among the clergy in general.   Love of gain grew so upon the monastery leeches that they were led to wander too far afield in attendance upon patients, so that they were at length wholly interdicted from meddling with physic and surgery by a decree of Innocent II., in 1139, and again by a decree of the Council of Tours, in 1163.   By

Jewish Physicians. the canon law, in like manner, no Jew might give medical advice or physic to a Christian.   But those decrees of the Church were easily evaded by the monks and by the Jews

EXTRACTING AN ARROW-HEAD.
(Trinity College, Cambridge.)

equally, probably because they had no competent rivals.
There were Jews practising medicine at every Court of Europe:
in the twelfth century the learned men of that nation were,
indeed, the chief deposi-
taries of the Arabian
medical teaching, which
was then the dominant
authority. One of the
Jewish physicians in
England, a skilful and
humane man, who per-
ished in the massacre of
his countrymen at Lynn
in 1190, seems to have
stood for the Rabbi Ben
Israel in " Ivanhoe."

JEWS AND CHRISTIANS (MS. Roy. 6 E. vi.).

' When we next hear
of physicians in England,
it is in association with the Franciscan friars. Peter, rector of **The Friars in Medi- cine.**
Wimbledon, physician to the queen (of Henry III.), is mentioned
in a letter of Adam de Marsh to Grosseteste as a man of excellent reading and of great probity, by whose hands he wished
his copy of Aristotle's "Ethics" to be returned. Another of
the same period was Reginald de Stokes, of Oxford, "an
honourable man of mature judgment, of advanced learning
and skill in the arts and in medicine, whose knowledge of the
world, circumspect discretion, mature discourse, and humble
devotion made him worthy of trust." The Franciscan missionaries had been hardly a generation in England before they
became identified with learning. The most famous of the order
at Oxford was Roger Bacon (p. 102), who included medicine in
the wide range of his studies. Few of the physicians of that
age, he said, knew astronomy, and so they neglected the better
part of medicine. He applied, also, his chemical knowledge
to the removal of diseases and the lengthening of life; he
knew how to make tinctures and elixirs, among them a
tincture of gold which was good for the renewal of youth.

Roger Bacon was an innovator in medicine, as in other
things, and he suffered for his too great zeal in mundane
research. It is singular to observe the claim he makes, as if

Medicine and Astrology. to conciliate the Church, that astrology had also an application to ethics; but its chief use was in medicine, and by the time that Roger Bacon had been dead a whole century a knowledge of astrology was everywhere admitted to be the qualification of an academical physician and as distinguishing him from a quack. There is nothing to show that John of Gaddesden, the first English writer on medicine (1316), was an educated physician in that sense, although he was a dexterous plagiary. But the physician in Chaucer was grounded in "astronomy," a science which taught him how to choose a remedy suited to the particular case—to the complexion or constitution of the individual, to the season, to the locality or climate—which was a very different thing from merely repeating the generalities of Avicenna. Even in plague itself, which was a practically uniform type of disease at all times and in all countries, it was necessary to resort to astronomy; and it was in the plague that this physician had made his money. Chaucer's physician corresponds exactly to a well-known physician of the time, John of Burgoyne, who passes as Sir John Mandeville. "They that have not dronken of that sweete drynke of astronomye," says Burgoyne, "may putte to these pestilential sores no fit remedies. . . . He that knoweth not the [astrological] cause, it is impossible that he heal the sickness." Chaucer's physician is richly clad, and so is Physic in the other poem of the time, "Piers Plowman"—in a furred hood and a cloak of calabre (squirrel fur), with buttons of gold. The plough-man, however, thought that physic was hardly an honourable calling. "There be more liars than leeches," he cries; "Lord, them amend!" and he looks forward to the time when the English would be so abstemious that Physic, having nothing to do, might sell his expensive costumes and "learn to labour with land, lest livelihood fail."[1] The best-known surgeon of the time was John Ardern, who practised first at Newark and then in London, in the latter part of the fourteenth century. He has left a treatise on the cure of fistulas of all kinds, in one MS. of which he is himself pictured in gorgeous raiment; his instruments also are figured, and he gives the names of his patients, both lay and cleric, with many minute particulars of their sometimes compromising maladies, of the

[1] Text A, Passus vii. 258, *seqq.*

fees they paid him, and of the triumphs of his skill. Shortly after his time, the Barber-Surgeons were incorporated in a guild, both at London and York : and with these corporations the history of surgery enters on a new phase.

BESIDES the popular and Court romances mentioned in the last chapter of Vol. I. there is much of romance, though of course not chivalric, in the religious epic, which, especially in the south, underwent great development in the second half of the thirteenth century. The abbey of Gloucester is the centre of activity for this form of literature, and the greatest variety of theme is noticeable; though little talent in the treatment. The growth of these legends in popular

JOHN ARDERN (MS. Sloane 2002.)

favour was greatly encouraged by the adoption of the French custom of reading the lives of saints in the church on festival days, for which the way had been paved by Aelfric's rhythmical homilies. The metres used were threefold, viz. short rimed couplets, tail - rime (Vol. I., p. 637), and a long-lined measure with a marked caesura in the middle, vacillating between the Alexandrine and the septenar, and generally called the Middle English Alexandrine. The second, originally a lyric measure, was never so popular with the religious poets as with the ballad-mongers, who adopted it about the same time (the end of the thirteenth century) for the chevalresque romance. The rimed couplet, which is the most important of the three, was the verse of the older versions of the "Assumptio Mariae" (*c.* 1250) and other subjects, *e.g.* the apocryphal Gospel of Nicodemas. For

H. FRANK HEATH.

Literature: the Religious Epic.

the lives of saints in the south the Middle English Alexandrine was chiefly used, and when this took the tetrameter form it was often adorned with middle-rime, which gave it the appearance of a strophe with cross-rime.   The legends of St. Margaret (*c.* 1270), St. Catherine, and Mary Magdalen (rather later) were in this long-lined metre; that of Gregory and Mary Magdalene[1] in the same measure with division into short-lined stanzas by means of middle-rime.   In the last quarter of the century these poems were collected into a cycle, consisting of a "Fragment of the Life of Jesus" and the lives of fifty-seven saints, those of England being very well represented.   There was a second edition[2] which increased the total number by half and arranged them in accordance with the ecclesiastical year, while a still later revision (1370–78), made in the same district, included the religious literature of every dialect.   But as time goes on these poems lose more and more of their epic and take on a

Didactic Poetry. purely didactic character.   Stories are taken from all parts of the world, saints of all ages and countries are admitted with equal honour, tales full of tender sentiment are found side by side with others full of the coarsest, vulgarest realism whilst a constant tendency is seen to exaggerate the miracles and to compensate for want of novelty by a sensational colouring.   A striking instance of this is the increasingly important *rôle* which the Devil plays.   The chronicle of Robert of Gloucester stands in close relationship to the literature just discussed, for not only are his verse (Middle English Alexandrine) and style those of the southern cycle, but he made use of these tales, especially the life of St. Thomas à Becket, together with Geoffrey of Monmouth and other trustworthier writers as the sources of his history.   It is a dull and moralising book, which traces the story of England from Brutus (as Layamon had done, with far more poetry, if with rather less learning), first down to 1154, and afterwards to 1270–2 in two continuations.   It was probably finished about 1300.   Robert as a lad had seen the thundery weather in which the battle of Evesham had been fought not thirty miles away, when Simon de Montfort had lost his life and

---

[1] Laud MS. 108, ed. E.E.T.S., 1887.
[2] MS. Harl. 2277, in British Museum.

the barons their leader. When he grew up he became a warm patriot, who looked on the Norman Conquest as a Divine punishment, and on the royal victory at Evesham as a national calamity.

Another "chronicle" written at Gloucester, rather later and even duller than Robert's, carries our history down to 1327 in its second edition.

More evidently didactic than either saints' lives or chronicles

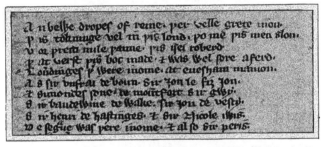

ROBERT OF GLOUCESTER ON THE BATTLE OF EVESHAM (MS. Calig. A. xi.).

are the sermons and religious tracts, many of them in verse, **Sermons** written in numbers in the latter half of this century. No **and Tracts.** work could be more typical of this genre than that of William of Shoreham, a Kentish man, who had been made vicar of Chart-Sutton by Leeds in the first quarter of the fourteenth century. He wrote theological treatises in the verse of the Poema Morale, or even tail-rime, upon the Sacraments, the Commandments, the Seven Deadly Sins, and other subjects, with depth of feeling and some insight, but little poetical power. From the same county, but somewhat later (1340), comes a popular treatise on morals, called "Ayenbyte of Inwyt." [1] The author, Dan Michel, an Austin friar in Canterbury, but born at Northgate, based his work on "Le Somme des Vices et des Vertues" (1279), by Lorrens, a work

---

[1] In modern spelling, "the Again-bite of Inwit," a syllable for syllable translation of the Latin words for "remorse of conscience." The sections dealing with the seven deadly sins and the seven gifts of the Holy Spirit are the basis of the second part of the Parson's Tale. This portion is not by Chaucer.

subsequently much imitated both in prose and verse. In the
north the chief representatives of this kind of writing are a translation of the Psalms in rimed couplets, the favourite northern
measure, written in the second half of the thirteenth century,
the "Cursor Mundi" and Richard Rolle of Hampole's "Pricke

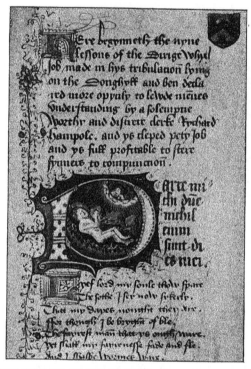

A LESSON FROM JOB, BY RICHARD ROLLE OF HAMPOLE (MS. Douce 322).
(Bodleian Library, Oxford.)

of Conscience." The "Cursor Mundi" is a biblical history of
the world in short rimed couplets[1] down to the finding of
the cross by St. Helena, followed by an account of the Last
Judgment. This idea of bringing together the chief points of

[1] The part dealing with the Passion, however, is in septenars, which
possibly points to a southern source for this portion.

AUTOGRAPH MS. OF THE AYENBYTE OF INWYT (MS. Arundel 57

Bible and Church history under one presentation was the same which underlay the arrangement of the mystery-cycles, that began soon afterwards to come into existence. The extreme zeal which made a hermit of Richard Rolle, who had studied theology at Oxford, is reflected in his "Pricke of Conscience," a work intended to present in liveliest colours the falseness and wickedness of the world, the hideousness of sin, the beauty of virtue. As in title so in treatment and subject it has much in common with the "Ayenbyte of Inwyt," and was written about the same time. Richard wrote many other books, and still more was ascribed to him.

What Richard Rolle was doing for the morals of the north and Dan Michel for those of Kent, that Robert Mannyng of Brunne or Bourne (1260–c. 1342) had already done for the Midlands in his "Handlyng Synne" (written 1303), a book based on an Anglo-Norman original, the "Manuel des Pechiez" of William de Wadington, a Yorkshireman. Like the northern poem, it is in short rimed couplets. In 1338 Robert finished a "History of England," chiefly based on Wace and the chronicle of Peter Langtoft. The first part based on Wace is, like the original, in short rimed couplets, the second part in Alexandrines, also in imitation of the corresponding part of the "Brut d'Engleterre," the conclusion in twelve-lined stanzas of tail-rime.

The Religious Drama. The kind of religious literature, however, which made the widest appeal at this time was undoubtedly that in dramatic form. The origin of the drama and the relation of miracle plays to mysteries, and of both to the lay drama, will be dealt with in a later chapter; here a few words must suffice. The "mystery" was, strictly speaking, a play based upon the Bible Story, the "miracle" dramatised the life of some popular saint; but in England both types were indifferently called miracle plays. And this was probably so because the earliest religious dramas acted in England, such as the "Norman Geoffrey of St. Albans" play of "St. Katherine" (beginning of twelfth century), and those referred to by William Fitzstephen in his "Life of St. Thomas à Becket" (c. 1182), were either "representations of miracles worked by holy Confessors or of sufferings wherein was demonstrated the endurance of martyrs." It was only later that the English religious sense was reconciled to a dramatic treatment of Scripture itself, but the "mystery" became so popular finally that there are no plays extant with subjects so completely out of relation to the Biblical narrative that they can be called "miracles" in the

AN EASTER SEPULCHRE, ILLUSTRATING THE ORIGIN OF THE RELIGIOUS DRAMA.
(*Heckington Church, Lincolnshire.*)

strictest sense. The first dramatic piece in the mother-tongue was a mystery called the "Harrowing of Hell," produced in the north-east Midlands about the middle of the thirteenth century. The action has much in common with the Romance

53

"disputacions," and in less degree with the Old English Dialogues, *e.g.* that between "Solomon and Saturn," for it consists of a word-duel between the risen Christ and Satan at the gate of Hell. The whole, which is in short rimed couplets, shows clearly enough its intimate connection with the church ceremonial at Easter, from which this form of art had sprung five hundred years before. In the same way other mysteries grew up around the Christmas festival. These plays soon became so popular that at the beginning of the fourteenth century we find them collected into cycles beginning with the Creation and concluding with the end of the world, after dealing in turn with the events of the Old Testament and the life of Christ. The several plays of each cycle had become traditionally connected with one or other of the guilds. These combined at the popular festivals of Whitsun, or more usually Corpus Christi (introduced in 1264), and in this way the labour and expense of production were divided. The chief existing cycles are those of Coventry, a complex of heterogeneous plays;[1] of Chester, in existence after 1328; of York (*c.* 1330), of which only five plays and a few fragments of others survive. There is a later York cycle, and a still later collection, that of Widkirk near Wakefield, both of which have these five plays and fragments in common. The metre of all except the earliest plays, which are in short rimed couplets, is a medley of this measure and of various more or less regular stanza forms. Tail-rime is common, especially in the Chester cycle, and frequent in the York cycle is a dignified strophe, consisting of a quatrain of long alliterative lines with cross-rime added, followed by a quatrain of four-accent lines with frequent alliterations (usually three) and rime order *a b b a.* This, like the work of Laurence Minot, shows West Midland influence at work.

To modern readers the Chester plays, as left us by their editor, will doubtless seem in better taste, and their spirit a more fitting one, than those of York. The Towneley plays will bear the test of comparison even less successfully, for their authors were free from the restraining supervision of town-councillors and others. But it was easy for the medieval mind to allow, and even find pleasure in, the

[1] Certainly not those traditionally ascribed to the Franciscans of Coventry.

crudest contrasts. There is a constant juxtaposition of the
strongest realism, the coarsest humour, and an even mystical
idealism, in the art of the Middle Ages, but if we except the
best work of Chaucer, their perfect fusion is never reached,
at any rate in England. The good people of Wakefield, who
witnessed the Shepherds' play, felt no shock in passing from
a scene of the broadest and, as it would have appeared to our
modern sentiment of reverence, the most profane buffoonery,
to the song of the angels proclaiming the birth of the
Saviour. The almost Titanic brutality and blasphemy of Cain,
or the undignified spectacle of Noah knocked down by his
irascible wife, was not felt to be less consistent with the
tender pathos of such a character as the young Isaac in the
Broome play; or with the general fitness of things in a body
of drama, intended to display the deepest mysteries of the
Christian faith, than were the grinning devils on the parapets
of Notre Dame with the rapt saints ranged below them, or
with the imbuing spirit of the House of God. The very refinement of the Chester Whitsun plays, their less vivid
characterisation and larger moralising element, proves them
to be a less perfect mirror of the people's everyday life and
conceptions.

THE first thing to do in order to understand the system of
farming in the thirteenth and fourteenth centuries is to get
a clear idea of the composition of the typical great estate.
This was very different from what we see now, for it consisted
of a number of separate manors, not lying close together, but
scattered up and down all over England, in such a way that
hardly any one adjoined another. For example, in the so-
called Domesday of St. Paul's, or collection of early " extents "
relating to 1222, we read of eleven manors in Essex the property of the canons of the cathedral, no two of which lay
closer together than four miles, while the average distance
between them is over fifteen. Or, to take another example
from one of the earliest Court Rolls that has yet been found:
of eleven manors which in 1246 belonged to the Norman
abbey of Bec, ten were in different counties, stretching from
Dorsetshire to Northamptonshire and Norfolk. Nor were these

W. J.
CORBETT.
Agri-
culture.

estates by any means the most widely scattered, as some,'like those of Merton College, Oxford, stretched from Northumberland to Kent. The result of this was that no one man could ever attempt to supervise a single estate, and that each manor had to be handed over to a separate agent or bailiff, from which the whole system has come to be called bailiff-farming.

Estate Management. In appointing this bailiff, who held the leading place in the village, and who often lived in the manor-house, the greatest care was needed; for he was necessarily for the greater part of the year his own master, and everything depended on his skill and energy. Generally speaking, his duties were those of an overseer; but in this he had assistance, his peculiar province being to keep the accounts, and to see that nothing was bought or sold unnecessarily. In extraordinary matters or cases of great danger he might apply to the lord's head agent or steward for instructions; but this was not always possible, and as a rule a bailiff who could not depend on himself was not thought a profitable servant. The steward's duties, in fact, though they included general superintendence, were rather legal than economic, and most of his time was taken up in journeying from one manor to another in order to hold the more important courts on behalf of his lord. How short his visits to any one manor usually were may be seen from the itinerary of the steward of the abbey of Bec, as set forth in his Court Rolls, who in 1247 between September 17th and October 9th visited six manors in the six counties of Wiltshire, Berkshire, Northamptonshire, Norfolk, Suffolk, and Surrey. Incidentally this also suggests that travelling was not at all difficult at this time, and that the roads as a rule must have been safe, for the stewards took large sums of money with them—an idea which is confirmed by the record we have of an equally rapid tour made in January, 1181, by the dean and two canons of St. Paul's to inspect their estates in Hertfordshire, Essex, and Surrey, when the party, though it was winter, covered over two hundred and thirty miles across country in twenty-two days, and held inquisitions in nineteen manors.

The Manor. The typical manor which the bailiff had to look after consisted of a single village, in which all the land legally

AGRICULTURE, FROM THE LUTTRELL PSALTER.

[To face p. 132.

belonged to the lord, and all the inhabitants had to submit
to his seigniorial jurisdiction.   Not all the land, however,
which was used for tillage was kept by the lord in his own
hands, but only a portion—usually about a third—which was
called his demesne.   The rest of the arable was divided amongst
the villagers, with whom also the lord shared whatever hay
was grown upon the meadows and the grass and acorns to be
found upon the wastes and in the woodlands.   In return for
this the villagers did not pay the lord any money-rent, but
only rendered him various services.   In the case of a freeman

A WATERMILL
(*Luttrell Psalter.*)

these were not very arduous, and no doubt there was always
a tendency to commute them into quit-rent; but in most
manors there were very few freemen, and nearly all the
villagers or tenants were of the unfree or villein class, whose
services were much more burdensome.   Chief among these
services was the duty of cultivating the lord's demesne.   In
fact, in the typical manor theirs was the only labour that was
available for this purpose, and to see that they did it properly
was the chief duty of the bailiff.   Success in this, however,
was by no means easy; for only a customary amount of labour
could be demanded, and even this differed at different seasons
of the year and among the different classes of villeins.   If
for any reason the number of villeins on the manor became
too few, there was no way out of the dilemma, and the land
had to be allowed to go out of cultivation.   As a rule
the services which could be demanded were of two kinds,

distinguished into " week-work " and " boon-work." [1] Of these,
week-work was regular, and consisted of ploughing or reaping
on the demesne or doing some other agricultural service for
the lord for two or three days a week throughout the year,
with most likely something extra during the harvest; while
boon-work, though fixed in amount, was irregular, and consisted
in performing some such service as carting, whenever the lord
might require it. Many villeins had further to render a small
tribute in kind—such as some eggs and two or three capons
on the three great feast-days, or a quarter of seed-wheat once
a year; but in return they often had meals of herrings and
bread and beer provided for them when employed upon the
demesne. All this, to a modern farmer, would seem a clumsy
way of getting labour, and so no doubt it was; nor could it
have worked at all if the bailiff had not been assisted in the
work of superintendence by subordinates who were villeins
themselves, and who were chosen by their fellows as representatives to be responsible for them if they failed in doing
their services. The most important of these were the reeve
or provost and the hayward,[2] both of whom must often have
found the office of making the others work anything but
remunerative; for the court rolls in some cases tell us of
villeins who paid as much as twenty shillings to be excused
from being reeve after having been elected. In the last resort,
too, the villeins as a whole were responsible for each other, so
that the lord could fine the whole township if he failed to
get satisfaction from his officers.

The typical holding of a villein was the " virgate," of about
thirty acres; but some held more, and many much less, while
there was a large class of cottars, or cottagers, who had little
beyond a garden. None of these holdings, however, of whatever size, were cultivated separately, but, great and small alike,
were worked together as one farm in conjunction with the
lord's demesne. Nor was this merely a matter of custom, but
rather the unavoidable result of the very peculiar composition
of these villein-holdings; for just as the typical estate at this
date consisted of scattered manors, so the typical holding

---

[1] The Latin terms were "dies operabiles" and "dies precariae," working
days and casual days.

[2] Called respectively "praepositus" and "messor."

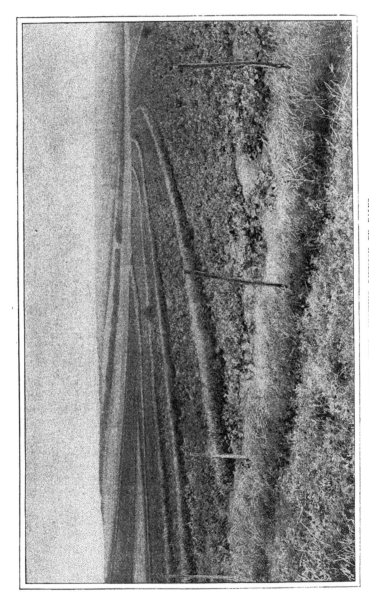

COMMON FIELD, SHOWING DIVISION BY BALKS.

(*From a photograph by Miss E. M. Leonard.*)

consisted, not of a compact block of land, but of a number of acre and half-acre strips scattered up and down the cultivated part of the village, in perhaps as many as sixty different places, and only divided from the equally scattered portions of other holdings by narrow "balks," or strips of unploughed turf. In some cases the lord's demesne may have been kept separate, but this was certainly unusual, and in any case it was cultivated on the same plan and as one with the villeins' holdings.

Tillage.   The methods of tillage in use, according to Walter of Henley, were either the three-field or two-field system, as they have been called, according as the rotation of crops was effected either in three or in two years. The former seems to have been by far the commoner. To carry it out, the whole of the arable land in a village was divided into three great fields, and every year one of these produced wheat, another barley or oats, while the third lay fallow. Put in another way, the three years' course in any particular field would be as follows:—In January of the first year sow with barley; in August reap the barley; from September in the first year to June in the second leave the land fallow; in June plough up the fallow ready for wheat; in the autumn sow with wheat; in August of the third year reap the wheat; in the autumn plough up the land ready for the barley; in January of the fourth year sow again with barley. In most instances this rotation was regularly followed, but occasionally rye might be substituted for wheat. There were also two sorts of barley, the second being called "drageum," while three leguminous plants—viz. beans, peas, and vetches—were generally, but not extensively, cultivated. Crops of hemp and linseed are not unknown in the manorial records.

In preparing for the crop the land was usually ploughed twice; but as the great wooden ploughs were very cumbrous, the soil was not very effectually turned. Oxen, too, in teams of four or eight, were used to pull them, in preference to horses—possibly because, iron being dear, the latter were very expensive to keep shod. Very little manuring was, as a rule, attempted, beyond marling in some localities, and the occasional folding of sheep on the fallows, while the art of drainage was equally backward. After sowing there was no harrowing or rolling, but the corn was sometimes hoed. In reaping, the crop was cut high on the stalk, and this gave a double advantage; for it prevented the wet straw and weeds from being carried, and at the same time left as much stubble as possible behind, either to be cut later for thatching and litter, or to be ploughed in instead of manure. The harvest as a whole usually took about six weeks, and directly it was over the whole stock of the village was turned promiscuously on

GLEANERS AND REAPERS (MS Roy. 2 B. vii.).

to the stubbles. The amount of wheat harvested varied from sixteen bushels an acre on the best lands to four bushels, two bushels being the amount originally sown; but this was only in favourable years. Even so the average is less than a third of what would now be expected; nor did the other kinds of grain do any better. The next operations were the winter ones of threshing and winnowing—the latter being done chiefly by women—after which the grain was not as a rule sold, but carefully stored in the barns or granges, and sometimes in the churches; for even in good years there was not much more produced than would suffice to support the village till the next harvest, and there could never be any certainty that in the next year there would not be a scarcity. When wheat was sold, it fetched about 6s. a quarter, and barley about 4s. 3d.

Live Stock.   The live stock kept consisted chiefly of cattle and sheep, but there were also a few horses, and nearly every villein family had its pig, and lived largely on salt pork. In the summer all these were sent out, under common cowherds, shepherds, and swineherds, to feed in the woods and wastes,

THRESHING.
(*Luttrell Psalter.*)

and ordinarily there was plenty of food : but in winter the majority of the cattle and sheep had to be killed, as there was little hay and no roots to feed them on. The draught-oxen, of course, were preserved, and just enough of all kinds to breed with ; but even these were nearly starved, while in the spring, as there were no hedges, the calves and lambs could get no protection from the weather. In these circum-stances it is not surprising that there were not many attempts to improve the breeds, and that the losses were enormous, on the average as much as 20 per cent. a year. Sheep-keeping, however, in spite of all this, was probably the most profitable part of farming ; for at this time England had a monopoly of the wool trade, and there was a constantly increasing demand for fleeces, which were exported to supply the looms of

Flanders. As the sheep were small, the fleeces were very light, and often under 2 oz.; but what made wool-growing profitable was really the comparatively small amount of labour it required—an advantage which became doubly plain after the Black Death, and led eventually to a partial abandonment of the industry of corn-growing. As to the dairy and poultry departments of farming, it will be sufficient to say that every

FEEDING PIGS.   KILLING A PIG.   SOWING.
                       (MS. Add. 16,075.)

village engaged in them; but that, as the practice of making cheese and butter, and of keeping chickens, ducks, and geese, was universal, these products were always very cheap, and hardly ever sold.

Hitherto we have been describing the typical manor as it appeared to Walter of Henley at the beginning of the thirteenth century, and as in many cases it existed until long after the Black Death. But, as has already been noted (I., p. 640), even in the early years of Henry III. a great change was impending in many manors, and one that became more prominent as the thirteenth century advanced. This was the gradual disappearance of the villein as we have described him,   Rise of Free Labour.

with his obligation of rendering services on the land and of helping to cultivate his lord's demesne, and in his stead the substitution of a free class who worked for wages. One might perhaps have expected that so great a social revolution could be traced to some popular movement in favour of emancipation, and that, as the tone of society became gentler, the lords naturally had a tendency to free their serfs; but of this there is not much evidence. On the contrary, in the eyes of the law the villeins remained serfs, certainly till their great revolt in 1381, and perhaps later; for neither then nor afterwards was there any clear admission of their freedom. Long before

THE GOOSE-HERD.
(*Luttrell Psalter.*)

this, however, the great mass of them must have been free in the eyes of the bailiffs; for they had ceased to be tied to the soil, and the revolt itself, as will be shown later, was only caused by an attempt to re-exact their services, which had become obsolete. The agency that effected this was neither sentiment nor even piety, but the self-interest of the average manorial lord; for, as has already been shown, it can never have been very easy to get the demesne properly cultivated, even when the duty was entrusted to the most energetic of bailiffs. Compulsory labour is proverbially ineffective, even when the labourer can be made to do whatever he is told; while on the manor the villeins could always be setting up the customs, and claiming that they had done all that could be required of them. The very variety of the customs, too, made evasion easy, and by necessitating an inordinate amount of superintendence helped to lessen what small margin of profit there might otherwise have been. At the same time, the expenses of the lords were growing; for the age was one of progress, and civilisation brought greater luxury in its train. The chivalry, too, of the time with its pomp and splendour, the prevalent taste for building, and a somewhat ostentatious charity, all demanded ready money, and this was just what the lords failed to get so long as their rents were only paid in labour. As a consequence, it became customary to commute the services of the more sub-

WOMEN WEEDING THE CORN.
(*Luttrell Psalter.*)

stantial villeins for a money payment. At first this was only done provisionally, and the lord was left at liberty to exact either the money or the services, whichever might be the more convenient, while in any case he could fall back on the latter if the villeins failed to produce the money. Even if he took the money, he was not independent of the villeins, for he still had to find the labour necessary to cultivate his demesne, and this he did by engaging the same villeins as hired labourers. But in this he gained largely, for he now got not only permanent servants who worked better, but servants who could be employed exactly when and as they were required. The villeins, too, gained equally; for they now felt that their work was voluntary, and that it was re- munerative.

The mutual advantages of the new system were indeed so obvious, that its provisional character was certain to disappear as soon as the lords grew confident that the commutation money would be regularly paid. In earlier centuries, when disturbances were common, this could hardly have been attained. This period, however, as already noted (I., p. 641), was a time of peace, and notable in agriculture for the growth of material prosperity; and so it was not long before money-rents were permanently adopted by some lords, and gradually extended to all their tenants and every sort of service. The amount of rent paid varied, of course, with the size of the villein's holding, as had the older services, and to some extent according to the kind of services he had performed; but it was not often that it exceeded ten shillings a year, even for the holder of a virgate, while it was frequently much less. When once the commutation had taken place, and the lord had provided himself with enough labourers to work his demesne, he naturally did not much care whether the remainder stayed upon the manor or not. On the contrary, for a small extra fine he would usually be willing to let them seek employment elsewhere, if they considered it better than culti-vating their holdings; and so in course of time it came about that a great number of villeins took to migratory trades, and became detached from the land and as good as free. Another large body, by accumulating in their own hands the holdings thus vacated, gradually grew into a class of yeomen, well enough off to rival and often to take precedence of the enuine freeholders, and under no necessity of labouring for hire.

Earnings.   The villeins who continued to work on the lord's demesne may be divided into two classes, according as they were employed regularly throughout the year, or only occasionally as extra hands. The regular servants kept on most manors included the ploughmen, the carters and drivers, the herdsmen, and the daye or dairymaid, all of whom worked for about 310 days in the year. For this the better sort were paid about 6s. annually, but this was the least part of their remuneration; for, in addition, each received a regular allowance of grain, varying from a quarter every nine weeks to one every fourteen, according to their employments. Occasional labourers, on the contrary, were paid entirely in money, and usually by the piece—6d. an acre for ploughing, 1d. for hoeing, 2½d. for mowing, and so forth, being ordinary rates. Women, too, were frequently employed, and could earn about 1d. a day. In this way it has been calculated that cultivation cost the lord about £1 an acre, a rate which not only left the labourers well off, but also paid fairly well. The whole system, however, depended on there being plenty of labourers who would accept the ordinary wages, and this ceased to be the case in 1348; for in that year nearly half the labourers in England died, and as the survivors refused to take the old wages the landlords were almost universally ruined, and a new system of farming had to be adopted, known as the stock and land lease. This and the Great Plague, which led to its introduction, will form topics for another chapter.

THE long and peaceful reign of Henry III. was not, as we have seen, in any large sense an age of industrial progress or commercial enterprise. The nation was, indeed, passing through a stage of transition, which was in itself unfavourable to commercial development; and, moreover, the whole system of trade regulation was excessively provincial and archaic. Hitherto its regulation had been, to a great extent, in the hands of local magnates, who vied with the Crown in imposing vexatious restrictions and intolerable burdens on the whole race of merchants; but with the accession of Edward I. a new force comes to the relief of oppressed industry, in the form of commercial legislation enacted " with the council and consent " of the Commons of England. As yet, moreover, apart from royal exactions and local customs, the imperial measures adopted for the regulation of trade had been of the most meagre character—an assize of bread and ale and cloth, which was, to trade, what the historical assizes of the twelfth century were to the land and police systems of the country. Henceforth trade was no longer to be regulated in the sole interests of the great landlords, but in those of the subjects at large; and the latter, having at last found their voices, used them to some effect in Parliament during the succeeding century. The beneficial effects of this centralisation of trade

HUBERT
HALL.
Trade and
Industry.

policy may easily be imagined, and the result is seen in the proceedings of Parliament which have been preserved to us.

This new departure is not, perhaps, altogether surprising, for we have already seen in the case of the towns that the common interests of the mercantile community had inspired a very elaborate and fairly representative system of self-government. The new methods were adopted, and further expedients were devised by the Commons. The pursuit of wealth had become a national and laudable industry, and the conditions under which it could be safely and profitably carried on were henceforth the especial care of the Legislature; and so far from trade being fettered by these enactments, it was really released from many vexatious restrictions in the shape of local usages. This happy result was largely due to the active and enlightened foreign policy of Edward I. and his immediate successors. It is true that this policy was originally a warlike one, and that the king's diplomatic relations with Flanders were neither very patriotic nor very successful at their inception; and we have to deal with the further fact that the commercial policy of each of these kings in turn produced a constitutional crisis of the greatest gravity. In the reign of Edward I., himself a notable founder of new towns, the free cities of Europe reached the zenith of their political power and commercial prosperity, and the intermunicipal system of trade flourished in proportion. Thanks to the personal despotism of Henry III., the Crown had already assumed a nominal control over the foreign intercourse of the country. The carrying trade was, to a great extent, in the hands of the merchants of the Hanse, and the internal trade in those of the Jews and Flemings. All three bodies were strictly controlled and licensed by the Crown, and to these were now added the great commercial houses of Lombardy, such as the Friscobaldi.

Policy of Edward I. The position assumed by Edward I. and his successors in regard to the interests of English commerce is a somewhat remarkable one. In their view the interests of the Crown were identical with those of the nation itself. The Jews were expelled, and the Lombards were patronised in their place. France was to be hemmed in between a dependent English ally in the north, and a flourishing English province to the south; and the whole fiscal arrangement was to be revised in order to harmonise with these conditions. Again, the king looked on the produce of the land, together with the wealth of the Church and of the towns, as available to relieve his necessities, either by means of direct taxation or by assignment to the alien financiers. Edward I. insisted that he was " free to buy and sell like any other," when the Commons remonstrated at his illegal seizures of staple wares by way of purveyance or pre-emption (I., p. 663); and from this time

CUSTOMS SEAL, PROBABLY OF EDWARD II.

onwards, the plan of farming out the revenue collected at the outports to societies of foreign merchants was frequently resorted to. .In fact, the importance of the foreign intercourse of the kingdom had become so great, that it could not safely be allowed to remain under the guidance of the guild-brethren of the free cities, especially when the feudal revenues of the Crown no longer permitted the king " to live of his own," and the control of trade offered an easy means of supplying the deficiency.

Edward II. reaped the fatal consequences of this arbitrary action, and the struggle was renewed and concluded during the first twenty years of the next reign. Henceforth the regulation of foreign intercourse, so far as it might be regarded as a question of diplomacy, was left to the discretion of the king and his council; but the material side of the subject, the protection of native exports, the taxation of foreign imports,

54

and everything connected with what was afterwards known as the " balance of trade," was esteemed a proper subject of consideration for the Commons of England.

It may fairly be suggested that the Edwardian statecraft was intended to secure certain commercial advantages of which English merchants seem to stand in need. The most important of these were, in the first place, a secure and profitable market for English exports : and next, an abundant and unrestricted supply of needful imports. In fact, to sell in the dearest market and buy in the cheapest was beginning to be recognised as an elementary principle of economics ; only that the means taken to effect this desirable end were not of a very enlightened character. Aliens were encouraged to import freely, in order that their lucrative monopoly might be broken, while the conditions imposed were always such as to favour the native retailer. On the other hand, the prerogative and diplomacy of the Crown were actively employed for the regulation of the exchange, for the safeguard of the seas, and for the establish- ment of a Continental market for English staple-wares. The most striking feature in the commercial policy of Edward I. and Edward III. is the supersession of the old intermunicipal arrangements by an imperial policy, enunciated by treaties or by statutes of Parliament. The great cities of England and the Continent still continued a useful correspondence to facilitate the collection or recovery of private debts, but they were not in a position to protect the national interests which they severally represented. Trade had begun to follow the flag. The English Admiralty had been established, and the doctrine of the sovereignty of the sea led to constant collisions betwixt the mariners on both sides of the Channel. Moreover, the old feudal relations with France had been rudely broken, and English merchants stood in special need of the passports or safe-conducts which were plentifully issued from the Chancery during these reigns.

Economic Legisla- tion.

In an earlier period, the regulation of trade by the Crown had taken the form of occasional licences, which implied the advantage of the king's protection to all such as had paid a fine to obtain his " good-will." This patriarchal system doubtless worked well in a state of society in which the peace of an absolute monarch was the only bond of law and order, just

as it is necessary to the present day in certain uncivilised
countries; but the victory of the Crown over the forces of
feudal anarchy, and the recent vindication of the ancient
constitution in the statute of Winchester, and the reorganisation of the machinery of justice, made some further arrangement between the Crown and the merchants imperative.
Although Magna Charta had expressly asserted the common-
law right of merchants at large to freedom of traffic, provided
that the usual regulations were complied with, it was still
found convenient to obtain the good-will of the Crown by
means of fines for charters of liberties or safe-conducts, and
this practice continued in force till long afterwards. The
chief consideration, however, was in respect of the imperial
and local taxation, for which merchants were admittedly liable.
The former species of exaction had usually taken the form of
a tithe of all merchandise, a tenth or a fifteenth collected at
the king's ports; but, in addition to this, there were seigniorial
franchises to be reckoned with, and tolls or dues levied at
fairs, markets, or at the city gates and quays.

The great achievement of the Edwardian commercial ^{The Customs Revenue}
legislation was the consolidation of these arbitrary, uncertain,
and scattered dues in the customs revenue of the Crown.
In the first place, the private branches were, as far as
possible, acquired by the Crown, or strictly curtailed by the
great inquest preserved in the surviving Hundred Rolls. The
first Parliament at Westminster was induced to make a "great
contract" with the Crown, by which the latter abandoned
indefinite prises [1] upon native exports of an earlier period, in
exchange for a fixed scale of custom duties on wool, woolfells,
and leather, which was henceforth known as the Great, or
Ancient Custom; while the old scale of tolls upon wines
imported by natives was likewise ratified as the Prisage.
Before the end of the reign a similar contract was made with
the alien merchants, whereby they obtained equal advantages
with natives by paying an increased duty of 50 per cent.
on wools and leather, together with a fixed tariff for cloths
and wax, a tunnage of two shillings on the cask of wine, and
a poundage on all other exports or imports. The New, or
Petty Custom, as this tariff was called, was at first viewed

[1 Levyings of dues, "takings."]

with considerable jealousy by native merchants, but its success, both as a fiscal and commercial measure was undoubted.

The Customs revenue created by the Statute of Westminster and Charta Mercatoria was successfully administered by a highly organised staff of Custom-house officers. The out-ports of England became now, for the first time, in actuality, " the king's gates." A vigilant coastguard was maintained, the local authorities were overlooked ; and, as a result, the condition of the harbours, quays, and streets was vastly improved. In the same way the Statute of Winchester cleared the roads leading to the great cities of the banditti which formerly infested them ; the Statutes of London secured the good order of the city wards by day and night ; and the persistent complaints of the obstructions and encroachments practised by riparian owners in the great waterways were about to be the subject of practical legislation. By the Statute of Merchants, trade debts were to some extent secured, and a system of registration was permitted—the first step in the direction of a change in the whole composition of feudal society, by admitting the merchant to a place among the landed gentry.

Foreign Trade under Edward III.

The policy of the first Edward was pursued with still greater energy by the third of that name in other directions. It is probable that his intentions were viewed with some distrust by a considerable body of his subjects; but although his policy is in some respects that of a doctrinaire, there can be no question as to the sincerity of his aims or the lasting improvements which he effected. Like his grandfather, Edward III. was bent on the extension of foreign trade, and the many facilities offered for this purpose are the chief feature of his commercial policy. Charters were granted or confirmed to merchants of Gascony, who imported wine, and to other branches of trade. Aliens were expressly protected by the Statute of the Staple, whilst a statutory fare for the passage between Dover and Calais was even fixed in their behalf. In spite of this encouragement by the Crown, we find that the foreign merchants laboured under the same local disabilities as of old, and in particular their sojourn for more than the customary forty days was keenly resented by the

English Commons. We find also that the influx of foreign commodities, coupled with the success of the French war, had a tendency to demoralise English middle-class society, and before the end of the reign rigorous sumptuary laws had become necessary, with the ulterior object probably of protecting native industries. Another experiment of this king was more favourably received—namely, the settlement of Flemish weavers in England under the special protection and patronage of the Crown; but the most important of all his commercial projects was the scheme, long in preparation and finally elaborated in 1353, by which a Staple for English exports was brought under the direct control of the Crown.

TREADING GRAPES (MS. Add. 16,975).

Since the settlement of the Customs Revenue in the reign of Edward I. the importance of the export trade which now flowed through one main channel was very evident to an intelligent sovereign as a means of revenue. The assessment of 1275 was not, however, sufficient to meet the necessities of the Crown in time of war, and as the king's claims to scutage (I., p. 374), aid, and other feudal taxation, were still in hopeless abeyance, the temptation presented by the manipulation of the "sovereign treasure of the kingdom," in the shape of woolsacks and bales of fells and hides, proved too great, even for a well-meaning king. Towards the end of the reign of Edward I. an imposition, known as the Maletolte,[1] of forty shillings had been levied on the sack of wool, and a constitutional crisis was provoked which ended in the confirmation of the charters in 1297, whereby it was clearly understood that in case of necessity the Crown must apply to Parliament

[1 So called as "illegally levied"—in medieval Latin, *male tolta (tollita).*]

for an extraordinary grant. Forty years later this necessity arose during the progress of the great war with France, and henceforth a Parliamentary grant of the subsidy of wools became the mainstay of the annual Budget. This unfailing source of revenue, whether as custom or subsidy, was the security for the financial dealings of the Edwards with Flemish or Lombard capitalists, and it was with a view to its utmost development that the Staple received the close attention of the Crown.

There can be little doubt that if the merchants of the Staple were not a recognised society as early as the thirteenth century, they formed a compact body of traders with distinct objects and interests at that period. At first, however, they exported wool and other staple wares to the great fairs of the Flemish cities without discrimination. For the protection of native interests it was thought desirable in the reign of Edward II. that a fixed Staple should be assigned for the sale of English exports. The monopoly which thus accrued to a single town, like Bruges, was soon found to be unbearable, and in 1353 the Staple was transferred to England, in the expectation, probably, that free competition amongst the foreign merchants who visited the English marts would tend to enhance the price of wool, and so diminish the burden of the indirect taxation in the shape of custom and subsidy, which fell upon the producer. At the same time the prosperity of the English towns, at which the Staple was appointed to be held, would be increased, and the greater volume of foreign imports would tend to lower prices and leave a balance in favour of this country.

By the famous Ordinance of the Staple ten English towns (p. 340) were assigned for the exclusive sale of wool. These were situated within easy reach of the coast, from Newcastle in the north to Bristol in the west, with separate Staples for Wales and Ireland. Each of these towns was linked with a convenient port, and in each a separate Court merchant was established, with a mayor and officers and assessors. Here the wool was weighed and certified, and all disputes were settled, after which it was conveyed to the proper port, and after being tested by the king's officers, the Custom and Subsidy was exacted. No subject might export wool on

pain of life or limb, while every inducement was offered
to aliens to frequent the English marts. The immediate
effect òf this important measure was a great stimulus to the
Staple trade, aliens exporting a greater bulk of wool than
had ever before been recorded. The official restrictions imposed
by the statute were, however, highly inconvenient, and the old

THE TOL-HOUSE, GREAT YARMOUTH.

jealousy of foreign traders, together with a great increase
of smuggling, led to a compromise by which for the next
ten years the Staple was mainly·fixed at the new English
colony of Calais.

In an earlier age the internal regulation of trade was the
peculiar care of the local authorities. The assize of bread and
ale was everywhere observed, and the election of local inspectors

and the presentment of offenders against the assize are familiar details in manorial and municipal records. This close supervision over the quantity and quality of the wares exposed for sale in the villages and towns by local officers was clearly in the interest of the whole community, and it is characteristic of the new *régime* of imperial legislation that almost precisely similar measures were adopted by the Crown for the welfare of the subjects. Royal officers were appointed for the gauge of wines and the aulnage[1] of cloths, and stringent edicts were enforced against such practices as forestalling or engrossing, and all other devices of middlemen to raise the price against the consumer. An attempt was even made to regulate prices, and the great distress which prevailed in the year 1316 was considerably aggravated by this disastrous expedient. But the chief and most legitimate object of attention to the Crown was the currency itself.

The Currency.   Ever since the royal revenue had become payable in specie instead of in kind, the greatest precautions were observed by the Treasurer and his staff to ensure a high standard of purity in the current coinage. The sterling money of England, famous throughout Europe for its purity, was the silver penny which passed from hand to hand by weight as well as by tale, a large proportion of the coins in circulation being further subjected to the yearly assay or Trial of the Pyx[2] at the audit of the sheriff's accounts in the Exchequer. In addition to these precautions, a very strict watch was kept on the operations of the royal moneyers, and a terrible example was made of such as were detected in malpractices. On occasion, the debased currency was called in, and a new coinage was issued, while very substantial improvements were effected in the reign of Henry III. in the establishment of the Exchange and the Mint, always a royal monopoly, but which now became for the first time an official department. Still greater improvements were effected in the first half of the fourteenth century, and treatises on coinage are extant which evince a considerable degree of scientific knowledge. But the great feature in the history of the currency at this period

[1 Measurement and official inspection : from Old French *aulne*, ell.]
[2 The Pyx is the box at the Mint in which specimen coins are deposited. The trial still takes place periodically.]

consists in the long array of ordinances by the king in council for its better regulation, beginning with an ordinance of 1248, and ending with an amended order in the year 1298, which may be regarded as completing the establishment of the Mint and Exchange.[1] The denominations of pounds, shillings, and marks were, of course, purely figures of account, but under Edward III. (p. 82) a double standard of currency, namely, gold and silver, was partially introduced, the former being represented by the well-known Flemish "Nobles" and Italian "Florins," following the experiment of a gold penny or "Royal" in 1248 (I., p. 612). A new evil had, however, begun to be felt since the middle of the previous century from the circulation of base foreign coins, which tended to drive out the good money. At a very early date such coins as besants (or byzants) had been passed by the foreign merchants in England, but now the country was flooded with base money introduced by foreign merchants. To remedy this evil, statutes were passed prohibiting the use of foreign coins, and alien merchants were required to bring with them a certain proportion of actual bullion in payment for their purchases, while the exportation of English bullion was checked as far as possible. Finally, an entirely new coinage of gold and silver was issued in the year 1351.

The progress made by the artisan class during the four-   **Industry.** teenth century is one of the chief causes of the national strength and prosperity during the French wars, and there can be little doubt that this progress was largely due to the careful protection of the Crown and the enlightened legislation of Parliament. The planting of new industries in the reign of Edward III. was no rash experiment, but a continuation of an early and successful policy. There was naturally a certain display of jealousy at the patronage of Flemish weavers by the Crown, just as a similar sentiment prevailed in earlier and down to much later times, but there was a tacit agree-

---

[1] During the whole of this period this establishment was almost entirely recruited from that class of foreign experts whose connection with the coinage of this country is commemorated in the very name of sterling. In addition to their want of skill, the well-to-do London goldsmiths were doubtless unwilling to compete for the meagre pittance offered by the foreign farmers or contractors, and it was more than once found necessary to resort to the expedient of imprisoning native workmen by force, an exercise of authority which was one of the reputed liberties of the Mint.

ment as to the benefits derived from this connection, and the English clothworkers were themselves in a highly favoured position.

FOLDING CLOTH.
(*Archæological Museum, Cambridge.*)

Besides the colonies of Flemish experts in the western and eastern counties, other trades were settled in England, such as the clock-makers, and the elaborate sumptuary laws of the period were probably designed for the encouragement of native manufacturers. In the case of native industries the gold-smiths' trade was entirely reorganised at the end of Edward I.'s reign, and the well-known trademark of the company was, by direction of the Crown, affixed to all silver plate. The remaining trades, however, were still indi-vidually regulated by their governing bodies, although all had bene-fited greatly by the diplomatic and legis-lative activity of the period.

The Guilds.

The towns of Eng-land in the fourteenth century were passing through a period of transition from a general to a special form of self-govern-ment for purposes of trade. By degrees all towns of any import-ance had already

CUTTING CLOTH.
(*Archæological Museum, Cambridge.*)

acquired the privileges that were essential to freedom of trade

—exemption from the sheriff's farm (I., p. 520), from local tolls, and from pleading outside the city; while the right to elect their own officers had given them already a political independence that was only forfeited by their misfortune or default. Before the close of the thirteenth century the whole body of traders had become subject to the jurisdiction of the central governing body, which in one aspect consisted of the mayor and alderman, and in another aspect of the guild merchant. The former body, with the Court of Common Council, exercised a sort of general control over the whole working of municipal trade, and its functions were essentially legal and official. The latter was a democratic body parallel to the Common Council, but with the single mission of regulating the external and internal trade pursued by the guild brethren. This was formed out of the two great classes of merchant-traders and artisans, both of whom were on equal footing, membership of the guild conferring equally the freedom of the borough and the legal status of burgess. It is probable, indeed, that the craftsmen, organised as early as the twelfth century, formed in most towns a majority of the guild brethren, and many foreigners and merchants residing at a distance from the town were honorary members (so to speak) of the guild merchant. In the fourteenth century the latter body ceased to possess sufficient vitality to satisfy the rapid expansion of the industrial interest, and the real supervision of trade fell into the hands of the craft guild. Four distinct forces were thus at work with the common object of regulating trade in the interests of the whole community—the Crown, by legislative or executive process; the municipal body, by virtue of the liberties and free customs conceded by the Crown; the guild merchant, representing the customs of the merchants, and still surviving as an aggregate of craft guilds; and lastly, the individual craft guild, by whom the regulation of trade was now conducted on new and scientific principles.

A typical craft guild in the fourteenth century contained three classes of artisans—masters, journeymen, and apprentices and in spite of certain inequalities and hardships, the interest of all three classes was identical. The internal economy of such a guild had probably not varied much from that of a much earlier period, but the great influx of labour into the *The Craft Guild.*

towns had emphasised the distinction between capital and labour, while it was essential that each craft should be so regulated as to provide employment for all its members. Another peculiarity of each craft was its isolation from surrounding fraternities. Thus the man who made bows must not provide arrows for the same; a cordwainer might not patch shoes nor a cobbler make them. Four separate crafts contributed to the making of a finished saddle and bridle; the joiner made the woodwork, which was decorated by the painter; the saddler supplied the leather, and the lorimer the metal trappings and appointments. Each craft had, as a rule, its own guild court and elective officers, and here all cases arising out of trade disputes or discipline were most conveniently determined. In some cases, indeed, the craftsmen could even claim to be tried by their guild court, rather than by the municipal authorities.

The duties of the guild officers were not confined to hearing cases brought for trial; they were actively engaged in the supervision of the workmanship and dealings of the craftsmen, particularly with a view to prevent frauds and misdemeanours, such as the use of improper weights and measures. In this way a very high standard of work was ensured, all "false" work, and "false" weights and measures and other tricks of trade being infallibly detected by these expert inspectors, and the offenders heavily punished. The importance of these precautions, in an age when skill supplied the place of capital, for procuring a connection in every trade will be obvious, and the Government had already set the example in another direction by a general insistence on fair dealing.

The few essential craft guilds which are enumerated in the Exchequer Rolls of the twelfth century had reached the number of some fifty important "mysteries" in London alone before the close of the fourteenth. The titles of these guilds are sufficient to prove the high degree of civilisation and even of luxury which had been attained in England before the middle of the fourteenth century. Manufactured articles in common use were no longer of necessity imported, and English craftsmen were able to hold their own with foreign artisans, though a number of the finer crafts were not successfully practised in England until the immigration of the Protestant refugees in the sixteenth century.

It should be remembered, however, that the trades were not supported as in the present day by consumers of all

THE ETHELBERT GATE, NORWICH.

classes, but chiefly by the Court and nobility and wealthy burgesses, and that the rural districts had little share in the luxury of the towns.

Side by side with these minute trade regulations, others

Aliens. were framed for the purpose of limiting the operations of foreign merchants to the importation of desired commodities and the export of surplus products. On no account were they to intermeddle with the native trade, either by retailing or by occupying any position of profit or trust. Thus no alien might be an innkeeper, and the outcry against the alien farmers and customers of the Crown was loud and irresistible under the second Edward. Moreover, the duration of their stay was supposed to be limited to forty days, during which period they must pay the "rightful customs" (an increase of fifty per cent. in the case of wool) on coming into the city, whilst sojourning there, on "going forth into the parts of England," on returning thence to the city, and on departing homeward. Besides this, they were bound to sell *all* their wares within the forty days allotted, to prevent them from "enhancing" prices. They were also expected to spend freely during their stay, and to facilitate this good object a host was usually assigned to them. Strict precautions were also taken against "coverture," or a secret agreement by which aliens conducted their trade through the agency of natives. On the other hand, this uncharitable policy could not be carried out in all its rigour, and many concessions were made by the Crown in spite of the jealousy and distrust displayed by an interested class of its subjects. The most important of these concessions were made, however, on behalf of the merchants of Aquitaine and the Calais Staplers as representing the colonial interest of England; and even the Hanse traders ceased to enjoy the same favour as of old. The pursuit of national wealth was beginning to be associated with the growth of national power, and the favoured German traders of the thirteenth century only shared the fate of the Dutch in the seventeenth.

Economic Doctrine. At the end of the thirteenth and beginning of the fourteenth centuries the zenith of medieval prosperity had been reached, and it becomes worth while to consider the nature of the economic doctrines through which this happy result had been attained. Like all other sciences of this period, economic science is a strange mixture of shrewdness and credulity; but there is one feature of it which stands out with great distinctness—the rough, masterful policy by which the immediate interests of the Crown or of the individual, and the fancied interests of the nation, were pursued at the expense of every external interest. We may criticise this policy as we please, but the fact remains that it was successful at the time and for long afterwards. It may be that this is only a question of sentiment, but sentiment was a very powerful economic factor even in those days. English citizens in the fourteenth century insisted on a rigorous exclusion of foreign competition, but they shrank from the

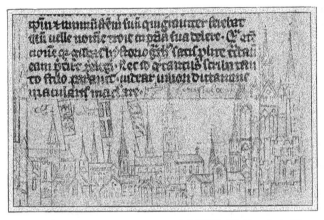

A THIRTEENTH-CENTURY DRAWING OF LONDON (MS. Roy. 13 A. ñi.).

practice of "usury" as a deadly sin. The impression left on our minds is that they understood their own interests too well to be mistaken in this matter. Their distrust of alien competitors was prompted by the instinct of self-preservation, strongly developed, like every other instinct in a rude state of society, and their aversion from "usury" was equally caused by an instinctive desire to provide for the welfare of all alike. No place could be found for capitalists and financiers in their economic theory. This, at least, was the avowed object of the lay and spiritual rulers who desired to follow the traditional policy marked out by the great English kings, while the relations of an unworthy or necessitous sovereign with Jewish mortgagees and Flemish or Lombard farmers of the customs must assuredly have inflamed the passionate prejudices of their subjects.

The whole of the commercial history, and a large part of the constitutional history, of the Middle Ages is inextricably connected with this great problem, which may after all be interpreted in several different ways. In any case the subject is scarcely a profitable one, and we may turn with advantage to more pleasing topics.

Products   The pursuit of art in the several branches of trade in

MASON PREPARING STONE.
(*Archæological Museum, Cambridge.*)

which it played a part — architecture, metal work, embroidery—was alike honourable and successful. There was no scamping of work in any English industry, and the charges brought against English merchants in this and other respects by foreign purchasers may be regarded in the light of professioual recrimination, or of a diplomatic device to secure some commercial advantage. The attention paid to an unequalled coinage, the marvellous precision and elasticity combined of the fiscal arrangements, a vigilant police, improved methods of conveyance, and a noble outlay upon public works—all these things bear witness to the same high purpose of a commercial policy.

and Producers.   But the most healthy symptom of the national life, though not always so regarded in its own day, is the desire to improve upon the sordid surroundings of an imperfect civilisation, which is witnessed in an ever-increasing attention paid by the great middle class to decoration and learning, dress and all the other comforts and adornments which help to make men's lives wise and beautiful. Even the period of depression and

1348]

degradation which set in with the wanton war with France, and which was still further darkened by pestilence and political and social agitation, had its lessons and its compensations. But this harvest was not reaped until after the lapse of more than a hundred years from the close of the period before us, when the idea of a "national economy" begins for the first time to direct the commercial policy of statesmen and legislators.

THE otherwise weak rule of Edward II. was put to an unusual strain by a great famine in 1315–16. Prices for grain had been high for many years before, taxes had been heavy for the Scots wars, Bannockburn had been fought and lost in 1314. When the king lay at St. Albans Abbey, at Lawrencetide, 1315, it was hardly possible to buy bread for himself and his household. The harvest of that year was greatly damaged by rains, and the winter was passed in misery and sickness, the diseases named being fever, dysentery, and "plague of the throat." The dead bodies of the peasantry were found by the roadsides; the dead in cities were buried in trenches, at all hours, canonical or other; the gaols were full of thieves; the people were driven to use horse-flesh, dog-flesh, and (it was whispered) even the flesh of children; and the starving felons in the gaols fell upon the thieves last brought in and tore them to pieces. It is significant of the habits of the English at the time that one of the remedial measures was to restrict the quantity of grain turned to malt instead of bread. According to one annalist, it was not until 1319 that the country came back to abundance; but it was not lasting, for in 1322 the king lost many of his men in Scotland by famine and disease; and such was the pinch in London the same year, that fifty-five persons, children and adults, were crushed to death in a scramble for bread doled out at the Blackfriars. The dole was on the occasion of a rich man's funeral. Whatever the common people suffered, the upper classes were living in luxury, and most of all the monks, who were at no period more splendid in their equipages and households.

C. CREIGH-TON.
Public Health.

55

JOSEPH
JACOBS.
The Expul-
sion of the
Jews.

BEFORE Edward I. became king, he had successfully resisted the attempt of the Jews to obtain the feudal privileges attaching to the possession of the lands they held as pledges. This was violently opposed by the Bishops of the Council, for among the privileges would have been the right of presentation to livings, and to prevent such a sacrilege Jews were forbidden to hold land in any way, or even to receive rent charges. As this was the chief security on which money could be lent, this Statute of 1270 must have considerably restricted the possibilities of Jewish usury. Immediately after his return to England in 1274, Edward went still further, and adopted the heroic measure of forbidding all usury, whether by Jew or Christian. This was in direct response to the rescript of Gregory X. at the Council of Lyons calling upon all Christian princes to do their utmost for the repression of usury. Accordingly Edward I. in 1275 forbade usury to his Jews, and proposed, as an alternative, that they should become merchants or traders, or rent farms, though not for a longer period than ten years. But it was impossible to uproot in this arbitrary way the habits of centuries. Edward would not allow them to be in scot and lot[1] with other citizens of the town in which they dwelt, since they were " talliable (liable to pay dues) to the king as his own serfs and not otherwise." They could not, therefore, become burgesses, and were thus prevented from entering the Guild Merchant, while it was impossible for them to enter any of the craft guilds, since the Church forbade any Christian master having a Jewish apprentice. The natural result of the Statute of 1275 was that the Jews continued their usury in a disguised form, taking their interest in kind and not in money, receiving it as a benevolent " gift," or entering a larger sum upon the deed of loan than they actually handed over to the debtor. The lower classes of the Jews were tempted to resort to still more dishonourable means of gaining a livelihood, that of clipping the coin. Three years after the Statute of 1275 all the Jews of England were seized and imprisoned on this charge, and no less than 293 were hanged and drawn in London. Edward was compelled to revise his policy and to permit usury in a modified

[1 *I.e.*, on an equal footing as regards taxation and rights.]

form, the rate of interest being fixed at about 7 per cent., which was to run for only three years, while the registration of Jewish debts, and, therefore, their legalisation, by the State was again resumed. This might be sufficient to permit the Jews to earn a scanty livelihood, but was utterly inadequate to enable them to amass sums large enough to assist the king. It was from this period that the dependence of the English Treasury on the Italian banking associations began to be remarked. This measure could not, therefore, solve the Jewish question in England. If the Jews were not to be allowed to amass wealth sufficient for them to act as tax-gatherers to the king and bankers to his people, they had no function to play in the national life. If the king had been willing to give up his right of direct tallage upon them so that they might have joined in the commercial life of the English boroughs, they might have become traders and merchants. But, even if the king had been willing to forego his rights, the Church would have rendered any such attempt nugatory by preventing free intercourse between Jew and

A DISESTABLISHED USURER.
(MS. Nero D. ii.)

Christian on pain of excommunication to the latter. The only alternative seemed to lie in the hope of Jews becoming Christians, and that hope by the end of the thirteenth century had become faint indeed. Inducements had been held out to the Jews by the foundation of homes for the converted in Bristol, Oxford, and London, where they would be received and supported for life upon conversion. But only a ridiculous handful had succumbed to this temptation. Every assistance had been given by Edward to the preaching of the Dominican Friars, which was directly and almost mainly applied to the conversion of the Jews, but without result. Indeed, to the Church in its irritation there seemed more danger of Christians being converted to Judaism, and in

1286 Honorius **IV.** addressed a Bull to the Archbishops of Canterbury and York and all their suffragans, complaining of this danger, owing to the close intercourse of Jew and Christian, and calling upon the English Church to do all in its power to prevent such scandal.

There was only one way to prevent it. If the English Jews were not allowed on the one hand to work freely, on the other to mix freely with their fellow-citizens, they must be entirely removed from contact with the English soil by expulsion. Edward, as a faithful son of the Church, recognised the alternative. He was in Gascony when the Bull was issued, and immediately expelled the Jews from Gascony; and on his return to England four years later issued the Decree of Expulsion for all English Jews, numbering 16,000, by All Saints' Day, November 1st, 1290. It was the only logical result of the attitude of the Church towards Jews, or, indeed, towards all heretics in a State professing to be Christian. At the time of their explusion the English Jews had absolutely no means of earning a livelihood in an English State owing to the action of the Romish Church, which branded them as unworthy of any intercourse with Christians.

The medieval history of the Jews of England passes through the same phases as that in other countries throughout Europe—advantageous position at first, afterwards restrictions, then increasing dependence on the king or barons, confiscation, pillage, and, finally, expulsion. While the Church would not permit the entry into a Christian State of any but orthodox Christians, and while the Jew remained true to his faith, there was no logical alternative.

D. J.
MEDLEY.
Home Life
in Medieval
England.

THE two forms of secular dwelling which we associate with the Middle Ages are the castle and the manor house. In the twelfth and thirteenth centuries the former represented the strategical position which in days of imperfect social order it was important permanently to occupy: the protective contrivances of the manor house were of a very flimsy and temporary nature. In either case the internal arrangements were those of a manner of life which was spent largely in the open air. But as the power of the central Government increased at the expense of the great feudal barons, the importance of the castles as means of defence diminished. True, the outward form of thick walls and battlements, gate-house, drawbridge, portcullis and moat was long retained. But the windows gradually ceased to be mere slits in the wall, the embattled form became a means of ornamentation often used where there was no structural need; the gates opened wider than prudence or necessity would dictate; the drawbridge became not only fixed, but a permanent structure of brick and stone; the moat not only stood dry, but ceased to encircle the complete range of buildings; a wall of circumvallation became the real boundary mark. Even more detrimental to the idea of defence were the buildings of all kinds which were gradually erected under this outer wall. For a long time these were mere wooden sheds, and were thus easy both to erect and also, when necessary, to destroy. About the middle of the thirteenth century these scattered buildings were gathered together into one block centring round the hall. Then, in process of time the walls of defence disappeared, and the retention of the castellated form of ornamentation scarcely concealed the difference between the old castle and the manor house. For, meanwhile, a change had also passed over the ancient manor house. For one cause and another, life became less nomadic. Landowners ceased to cultivate their more distant estates, and let them to tenant farmers. Hence the halls on the estates which they kept in their own hands became more permanent abodes, and buildings of stone accumulated round the original hall. Prudence as well as convenience dictated a quadrangular shape. If there was no strategic position to hold, there were the lives and possessions of its family to defend. Thus fortification of some kind became a practical necessity; licences to crenellate were obtained from the Crown, the buildings were surrounded with a moat which should prevent a too sudden incursion, and, but for the absence of a keep, the manor house of the fourteenth century became a small castle.

But in both these cases the old type of life remained unchanged—the life which found its domestic centre in the manorial hall. For, the changes just noted had done nothing to disturb the old form of the manor house. The central hall still stood, flanked on the one side by the cellar and the solar above it; on the other side by the domestic offices. The solar was placed invariably at the same end of the hall as the daïs, and was still generally approached from the court outside, not from the interior of the hall. At the opposite end of the hall would be two doors opening out into the "screens" —the name given to a passage which led from the front into the back court. On the further side of the screens were two doors admitting respectively to the buttery and the pantry, and between them ran a passage to the kitchen beyond.

MAKING TAPESTRY (MS. Add. 20,698).

The doors from the hall to the screens lay under the minstrels' gallery, to which access was often gained from a kind of antechamber placed over the screens themselves.

The interior arrangements of the hall continued much as they had been in previous centuries. In some colleges of the two old universities the fire continued to be lighted on the "reredos" or brazier in the middle of the room up to the beginning of the present century, while in the hall of Westminster School the practice was kept up until as late as 1850. But as early as the fourteenth century there were added fireplaces, either a single one or one on either side of a large hall, and the mantelpiece became a conspicuous

means of ornamentation. Similarly, the recess at the end of the
daïs in which stood the cupboard of plate gradually increased
in magnitude, until by the fifteenth century it had become

THE HALL, PENSHURST PLACE, KENT.
(By kind permission of Lord De l'Isle and Dudley.)

a handsome bay-window, and, without no less than within,
formed one of the most striking features of the buildings.
More generally, the floors were often tiled, but although
carpets were used in other rooms, the hall continued to be

strewn with straw, rushes, or the boughs of trees. On the other hand, in the thirteenth century the walls of the hall had been wainscotted and painted, or merely whitewashed, while tapestry hangings were reserved for the solar, or, at the most, were displayed at the back of the daïs. But in the course of the fourteenth century tapestry became at once more attainable and more prized, and it came to be hung all round the walls of the hall itself. The famous fabrics of Arras gave the most common name to such hangings. They formed the subject of princely gifts; they were moved from one house to another as the family changed its abode; on public occasions they were displayed along the streets and were carried in solemn procession. Moreover, as painted glass became sufficiently common to allow of its use for the windows of houses as well as of churches, the tapestry and the windows of great halls would be so arranged as to harmonise in composition of subjects and in scheme of colours. This was rendered more easy by the fact that for a long time windows, no less than tapestry, were movable. Casements were made to contain the painted glass; and the windows in different houses belonging to the same owner were built or altered to permit of the casements being transferred from one to the other. Nor did the fresco work of previous centuries disappear. Tapestry below, stained glass above, with the space between painted in fresco, the whole schemed to harmonise in subject and colour—the mural decorations of a large medieval hall in the fifteenth century in magnificence could hardly be surpassed by all the resources of modern art.

Food and Drink.   It is very probable that in modern eyes the ornamentation just described would appear tawdry, if not vulgar. And, that elaborateness does not mean refinement will be sufficiently clear from a consideration of the food provided for consumption in wealthy households. The dinner, which still remained the first real meal of the day, consisted, it is true, only of three courses; but each course comprised five or more dishes, and in their composition figured quantities of spices and all manner of rich sauces. Eating and drinking were both very gross. The quantity was great and the quality was strong. Thus in a receipt for hippocras—the " company " drink of the Middle Ages—the brewer is bidden, if preparing it for a lord, to add well-paired ginger, thin sticks of cinnamon, graines of paradise, sugar, and turnesole (heliotrope), while for common people ginger, canel, long pepper, and honey are deemed sufficient. Again, in one year's consumption of the Percy household nearly £26 was expended on spices alone, and the items comprised not only ginger, "graines," mace, cloves, cinnamon, almonds, nutmegs, aniseed, galingale, long pepper, and saffron, but also raisins, prunes, dates, rice, and comfits, which we should not reckon among spices at all. It must be remembered that until the seventeenth century winter roots were practically unknown, so that it was impossible to keep alive more cattle than were necessary for the purpose of

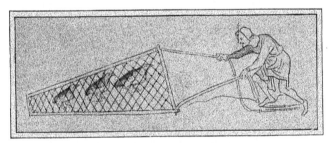

SNARING BIRDS (MS. Roy. 2 B. vii.).

replenishing the stock. Consequently, in the autumn those destined for winter consumption were killed and salted down, and it was on this salt meat that even the greatest in the land lived for half the year. No less serious was the want of green vegetables, which explains the prevalence of scurvy and other skin diseases. The elaborate cookery was an attempt to overcome these disadvantages, and it was only the open-air life and the quantity and violence of the exercise taken by persons in all stations of society that endowed them with digestions sufficiently strong to cope with such unwholesome fare. Fast days and days of abstinence prescribed by the medieval Church brought no relief, except in a change of food. Meat was omitted, but the preparation of fish for the table was as careful a study as that of bird or beast. And, in the scarcity of fresh meat it seems as if the heavens and the earth were scoured, no less than the depths of the waters, in the endeavour to procure edible food. All kinds of fish and fowls and animals, no matter how large or how small, were served up to table, and were esteemed great delicacies, which we should consider too coarse for our palates. Whales, porpoises, and sword-fish at one end of the scale, and minnows at the other end; mallards, ospreys, bustards, herons, cranes, and, of course, peacocks, no less than rooks, magpies, starlings, and even sparrows are all found figuring in medieval bills of fare. Nor did the true epicure disdain a hedgehog or a squirrel prepared with the appropriate sauce. But the great triumph of the culinary art was the "subtilty" with which each course of a banquet was ended. This consisted of an elaborate device in pastry, shaped into all kinds of fantastic forms, and bearing a rhyming motto in English, French, or Latin. Thus at the coronation feast of Henry V.'s Queen Katharine the first course was closed by

A sotyltie called· a pellycau sytiynge on his nest with her byrdes, and an image of Seynt Katheryne holdyng a booke and disputynge with the doctours, holdynge a reason in her right hande, sayinge, *Madame le royne*, and the pellican as an answere, *c'est la signe, Et du roy, pur tenir joy, Et a tout sa gent, Elle mete sa entent.*

The means of quenching the thirst were almost as numerous in the Middle Ages as at the present day. Ale was the common drink, and is not to be confused with beer. The former was made from barley or oaten malt, and must be drunk in a comparatively fresh condition. The addition of hops made it into beer which would keep longer, but which connoisseurs did not consider such a wholesome drink. Hops, however, were not introduced into England until the reign of Henry VIII. Another very common drink was mead, which is described as a compound of ginger, sugar, and honey. Mention is also found of metheglin, a preparation of herbs and honey ; of braggot, a concoction of spices; and of posset, which was hot milk poured on ale or sack and flavoured with sugar, eggs, grated biscuit, and other ingredients. The wines in use were almost as numerous as at the present day, and came not only from Gascony and Spain, but also from Italy, Greece, Cyprus, and the islands of

CATCHING A HARE (MS. Roy. 2 B. vii.).

FISHING (MS. Roy. 2 B. vii.).

HUNTING DEER (MS Roy. 2 B. vii.).

the Archipelago. The most familiar names to modern ears are muscadel and malmsey. The extreme acidity of many of these wines would prevent a large consumption, but they were used extensively in the concoction of drinks described by the terms pyment, clarry, and the favourite hippocras. The two former were preparations with honey; the compounding of hippocras was a matter of the most serious thought, and all the choicest spices went to its making.

Growth of Domesticity.   So far, then, the old form of life remained, elaborated in details, but in spirit the same. The fifteenth century gradually introduces a new type. On the one side the feudal array had practically disappeared, and the feudal courts were attenuated: on the other side the status of the towns was increasing, and a wealthy merchant class was rising to importance. It was perhaps some compensation that the practices of "livery and maintenance" surrounded the great nobleman with a large retinue. But this did not affect the small landowners. At the same time, the change from tillage to pasture was displacing a large part of the rural population, and transformed the lord into little more than a mere rent-receiver. Again, the prevalence of guilds in small country towns is evidence of a wide development of the artisan class, which made it less necessary for manorial lords to keep large bodies of workmen on their domestic establishment. Finally, luxury was growing with the growth of trade, and comfort was preferred to splendour. As a consequence of these changes, life for the country gentleman became more domestic. On the one side he had to find food and accommodation for a smaller number of dependents; on the other side he wanted more accommodation and better food for himself and his own family. The outward mark of this change was the gradual disappearance of the importance of the hall as the centre of social life. Among monastic buildings we distinguish the parlour as a reception-room for business visitors. The first step towards domesticity in private life was the introduction of a similar apartment into the manor house. Here it formed at first a kind of lesser hall where the company for the daïs assembled before dinner, and then it passed into a dining-room where the lord and his friends could enjoy each other's company in a more private and comfortable manner. Unlike

Roasting.

Preparing Dinner.

Dishing up.

AT TABLE.
(*Luttrell Psalter.*)

New Rooms.

the solar, the parlour never served also as a bedroom. But large houses soon passed beyond this simple arrangement. The elimination of the hall was the result of a growing distinction between the dining-room, the sitting-room, and the bedrooms. The parlour of the small manor house became the dining-room of the large mansion; the withdrawing-room took the place of the old solar as the private sitting-room of the family and their distinguished guests. These new rooms were obtained in various ways. The simplest method of all was to turn the cellar into the dining-room, and to appropriate the solar above to the special uses of a withdrawing-room. It did not require a much greater expenditure of labour to partition off the daïs end from the rest of the hall for use as a dining-room. But occasionally the whole character of the old building was changed; a lofty hall was divided horizontally by the insertion of floors, the ground floor serving as the dining-room, with the drawing-room above it, and occasionally a second floor was used as a dormitory for the servants. The lady's bower, or boudoir, and the lord's room were further developments in the direction of individual privacy. But to our ideas the chief test of privacy of life

Bedrooms. would be the provision of separate bedrooms. The appropriation of the solar for the drawing-room was only possible because strangers were now furnished with separate guest-rooms, and the lord and lady had their own bed-chamber.

AN INTERIOR (MS. Canon. Lit. 99).
(*Bodleian Library, Oxford.*)

Even the domestic servants, on ordinary occasions, ceased to sleep in the hall, and, where the hall was cut up into dining-room and drawing-room, provision had, of course, to be made for them elsewhere.   This growth of the desire for privacy had an instructive effect on the furniture of the bedroom.   Instead of several persons occupying one bed, and that bed a mere pallet of straw stretched on a wooden frame, we now read of beds with the most elaborate hangings and coverlets.   The four-poster of our grandparents did not come into use until the sixteenth century.   The canopy, or tester, which preceded it, was fixed to the wall, not to the bed itself; but it was often so extended as to cover the whole bed beneath.   Mattresses were more commonly made of down and feathers, and the elaborateness of the hangings and of the general furniture of the bed may be gathered from the fact that in the fifteenth century they found a prominent place in the bequests of donors both of the wealthy and of the middle class.   A characteristic arrangement of the age should not be omitted.   The valet or maid sleeping in the same room with their master or mistress occupied a truckle or trundle bed which, as the name implies, could be rolled out of the way under the larger bed.   Nor, in noting the movement towards a more refined manner of life, should mention be omitted of the introduction of nightshirts during the fifteenth century.

BAKEHOUSE (MS. Canon. Lit. 99).
(Bodleian Library, Oxford.)

But we have not yet done with the manor house. So far we have dealt only with the changes at one end of the hall. But during the fourteenth century the more sedentary habits of the lords transformed the kitchen and domestic

BERKELEY CASTLE CHAPEL.
(By kind permission of Lord Fitzhardinge)

offices into permanent structures of stone and brick. At first these offices were very numerous, and included such chambers as the *lardarium*, where the meat potted for winter use was stored, and the *salsarium*, which similarly contained the salted provisions, as well as a bakehouse and a brewhouse. But the development of trades did away with the need of most of, or sometimes all, such chambers, while the resulting simplicity of life was perhaps in its turn responsible for the frequent disappearance of the distinction between such universally existing rooms as the pantry, whence the bread was issued, and the buttery, whose official was the dispenser of the drink. The beer and wine were now the exclusive contents of the cellar, and in the place of the extensive wardrobes or store-rooms of a previous age is found the less unwieldy cupboard of modern days.

Two other characteristics are worth noting in the buildings of the fourteenth and fifteenth centuries. The gateways, no longer devoted primarily to defence, became handsome gatehouses, divided off into numerous chambers, often bedrooms. Sometimes they even contained the private chapel. Very often, however, for the chapel a most noteworthy disposition seems to have been made in the main building. The part which contained the *sacrarium*, or chancel, with its altar, was open from floor to roof of the house; the other part, representing the nave, consisted of two floors, separated from the sacrarium by a screen which ran the whole height of the building in front of both floors. The lower floor might form the priest's room or the place of attendance for the household: the upper floor was a sitting-room, or even a bedroom, appropriately furnished and adorned with a fireplace. Thence the lord, his lady, and their friends, no matter what their occupation, could witness the elevation of the host in the chapel below.

Writers have noticed the tendency of the Middle Ages to confound the major and minor morals—to make as much of a breach of etiquette as of a sin against one of the Ten Commandments. This is aptly illustrated in a number of rhyming treatises[1] of the fifteenth century, written for the instruction of the young in the rules of good conduct. Many of them are concerned merely with behaviour at table, and with such important branches of the art of living as cookery and the carving of joints. The precepts of one of these

The Training of Children: Boys.

---

[1] Collected by Mr. F. J. Furnivall in "Manners and Meals in Olden Time," published for the Early English Text Society (No. 32).

56

their modern editor illustrates by reference to a book of directions to footmen, published in the earlier part of the nineteenth century.   Many of these directions are of precisely

BOYS' SCHOOL (MS. Roy. 6 E. vi.)

similar tenor to those found in the fifteenth century treatises.   But, for the present purpose the instructive part of these treatises lies in the fact that they were not, like modern books of etiquette, written by a socially superior class for the information of their inferiors who ministered to their material comforts or whose life was cast among surroundings superior to their birth.   Many of the old treatises in question are concerned with the conduct of the whole of life, and all are written for the young at a period when one of the most important duties of the gently nurtured youths was to wait at their lord's table and minister generally to his material wants.   The triviality of the directions contained in some of these short treatises might incline a modern reader to question their intention; but there is no doubt that they were written in all seriousness, and the rhyming form which they commonly take was meant to aid their retention in the memory at a time when books were rare and all teaching was perforce oral in character.   Thus they present us with the most vivid picture of the standard of refinement reached by the well-to-do classes in the fifteenth century.   The spirit in which the writers set about their work may be gathered from a " Lesson of Wysedome for all maner Chyldryn," in which " Symon," the author, says :

My child, I rede thee be wise and take heed of this rhyme !
Old men in proverb said by old time,
" A child were better to be unborn
Than to be untaught ; "

while two others, in almost identical terms, preface their directions for courteous behaviour by the remark that

All vertus be closyde iu curtasy.

The youth is recommended to get up betimes, to wash himself, and to say his prayers. Directions are sometimes added about the way in which he shall dress himself, and details are even given about blowing his nose, paring his nails, and other operations of the toilet which we should expect our children to learn in the nursery, and which, however necessary, we should consider indelicate, if not positively indecent, to find in a book of precepts for behaviour. The boy is then bidden to salute his parents, and even to kneel and ask their blessing. On his way to school he is to greet the passers-by, not to throw stones at dogs or hogs, or to go birds' nesting. At school he is bidden to stick to his books, and is reminded that learning and industry are the road to preferment in life, while for the laggard and the careless there remains the birch. The unwillingness of the natural boy to learn is humorously illustrated by a short poem, in which the boy laments the necessity of learning in order to become a "clerk." When he is late

BIRCHING A BOY (MS. Roy. 6 E vi.).

My master lokith as he were madde :
"Wher has thou be, thou sory ladde ?"
"Milked dukkis, my moder badde."

The master has heard the kind of excuse before, and the youth, sore in mind and body, vents his impotent rage in characteristic schoolboy imaginings :

I wold my master were an hare,
And all his bokis howndis were,
And I myself a joly huntere :
To blow my horn I wold not spare !
For if he were dede I wold not care.

A great many irreproachable moral precepts are scattered up and down these numerous treatises—be careful what company you keep, don't be a tale-bearer, avoid dicing and such-like dangerous amusements, be courteous and unselfish to everyone. But the larger part of the space which the writers devote to their theme is in most cases taken up with directions for waiting on a lord at table and for one's own behaviour during meals. The demeanour of a squire towards his lord is at all times to be marked by a deferential courtesy of act and speech which modern minds associate with the "good old days." Bow to your lord when you speak to him; kneel on one knee when you offer him anything; don't speak unless he speaks to you, and then answer in as few words as possible. As for the youth's own behaviour, it was evidently thought that directions for his guidance could not be too minute. He was recommended to keep his nails clean lest he should offend his neighbour, not to spit upon the table, nor to pick his teeth with a knife nor to clean them with the tablecloth. The management of the nose seems to have given our authors much cause for thought. Allusions to a pocket handkerchief in the fifteenth century are not quite unknown; but the use of the fingers is generally presumed, and the neophyte is bidden to wipe his hand secretly on his shirt or in his tippet. For a man capable of such social solecisms it would seem to us a small matter that he should put his fingers into his cup, or, before placing his food in his mouth, should dip it piece by piece into the common salt-cellar.

Girls.   These tracts are almost entirely concerned with the conduct of men, especially of young men. But there is one dealing with the gentler sex, of which mention should by no means be omitted. "How the good wife taught her daughter" consists for the most part of sufficiently commonplace senti-ments—accept a good offer when it comes; be true to your husband; look well after your household. There is much sense in the recommendation that if children are naughty the young wife should not nag at them,

> But take a smart rodde and beta them on a rowe,
> Til they crie mercy, and be of their guilt aknowe.

A warning against extravagance is enforced by a forgotten

proverb, "After the wrenne hath veynes men must lete hir blood"; in other words, you must cut your coat according to your cloth. But a flood of light seems to pour in on medieval society from the remark that respectable women don't go to public entertainments, such as a "wrastelinge" or a "schotynge at cok"; while we stand aghast at the direction that if good ale is "on lofte"—that is, to be had—a woman must drink moderately, for if she is often drunk she falls into disgrace. The concluding aphorism that

> Those that ben oft drunken
> Thrift is from them sunken,

is borne out by all the statistics of modern intemperance.

AUTHORITIES.—1274-1348.

GENERAL HISTORY.

Reign of Edward I.—Rishanger's *Chronicle* and Trivet's *Annals;* Matthew of Westminster; the Monastic Annals, especially those of Osney, Dunstable, and Waverley; the full and valuable Chronicle of Walter of Hemingburgh; these, with the Statute Book, the Royal Rolls, and Rymer's *Fœdera*, give a full and picturesque contemporary view of Edward I.'s reign. The Political Songs supply some touches, and the collection of writs in Stubbs's *Select Charters* is invaluable.

Modern Books.—Few, if any, periods of our history have been so grossly misrepresented as this reign. For the Scottish question, Burton's *History of Scotland* may be taken as an impartial book, between Freeman's *Essay* on Edward on the one side, and Robertson's *Scotland under Her Early Kings* on the other. The Church quarrel, the constitutional growth, and the deeper aspects of the time are best seen in Stubbs's *Constitutional History and Early Plantagenets*. For a good general view, *see* Tout's *Edward I.* (Statesmen Series).

Reign of Edward II.—The chief contemporary writers are: John of Trokelowe and St. Albans; the misnamed Monk of Malmesbury; the knight, Sir Thomas de la Moor; the diplomatist, Adam of Murimuth; and the continuator of Hemingburgh; these, and others, are given in the volumes of the Rolls Series on Edward II. Best modern accounts: Stubbs's *Constitutional History* and *Early Plantagenets* (last chapter), supplemented by Burton for Scottish affairs.

Reign of Edward III., 1327-1348.—The Chronicles of Walter of Hemingburgh, Adam of Murimuth, and Robert Avesbury are the primary contemporary authorities, supplemented by a St. Albans Chronicle in the Rolls Series, the Lauercost Annals, and the Chroniques of John le Bel (so largely used by Froissart), and by the somewhat later works of Knyghton and Walsingham. The Rolls of Parliament and the Fœdera Collection give invaluable details. Of modern works the most useful are: Longman, *Life and Times of Edward III.* (for social history and the wars); Bright, *History of England* (for full and accurate facts); Green, *History of the English People* (especially on social and literary subjects): and, above all, Stubbs, *Constitutional History*, Vol. II., which has in most parts, but not in all, superseded the account in Hallam's *Middle Ages*.

Wales.—*Annales Cambriæ; Brut y Tywysogion;* the works of Giraldus Cambrensis (Rolls Series); the *Ecclesiastical History* of Ordericus Vitalis; Royal Letters (Rolls Series); Welsh poems published in *Myfyrian Archæology*. See list for Chap. xi.

Religion.—*Chronicles of Edward I.*, ed. Stubbs, viz.: *London Annals*, Lambeth Continuation of the *Flores Historiarum, Encomium of Edward I.*, *Lives of Edward II.* by the Monk of Malmesbury, a Canon of Bridlington and Sir Thomas de la Moor; Chronicle of Bartholomew Cotton; *Flores Historiarum*, Vol. III.; Chronicle of John de Oxenedes; Peckham's *Register*, 3 vols. (all the above in Rolls Series). Wright, *Political Songs.*(Camden Soc.). *See also* Thorold Rogers, *Six Centuries of Work and Wages;* Stubbs, works cited above, and prefaces to volumes above mentioned. Many interesting examples of Church usages are brought together in Cutts's *Dictionary of the Church of England* and Perry's *History of the Church of England.*

History of Law.—The authorities consist chiefly of (1) Statutes, (2) Reports, (3) Text Books. Of the statutes there are many editions: the fullest is that published by the Record Commission. A series of Reports, known as *Year Books*, begins in the reign of Edward I. and ends in that of Henry VIII., but there are many gaps in the series; those of Edward I.'s reign are printed in the Rolls Series, and some of those of Edward III.'s reign are being edited in the same Series by Mr. Pike. The old printed editions of the other *Year Books* are extremely faulty. When the *Year Books* stop in Henry VIII.'s reign, we begin to get, for the first time, reports which are known by the names of their compilers, *e.g.* those of Dyer; the reports of Plowden and Coke are among the most celebrated. Of the text-books of the later Middle Ages, Littleton's *Tenures* is the only book of any merit; it comes from the 15th century. Coke, in his four *Institutes*, sums up a great part of the law of his own day and of earlier times in a very disorderly fashion. Much historical matter is to be found in Hale's various works and in Blackstone's *Commentaries*, and several portions of English law have in recent times found historians. The best general history is still that compiled by John Reeves.

Warfare.—Froissart, and other chronicles, *passim;* Hewitt, *Ancient Armour* (Oxford, 1860); Clark, *Mediæval Military Architecture* (1886); Oman, *Art of War in the Middle Ages;* Köhler, *Kriegswesen in der Ritterzeit* (Breslau, 1889).

Naval Matters.—See list for Chap. III. Most of the original authorities have been published by the Record Commission. Among modern books Sir Harris Nicolas's *Naval History* and Laird Clowes's *History of the Royal Navy* may be mentioned.

Architecture and Art.—Fergusson, *Gothic Architecture;* Rickman, *Gothic Architecture;* Parker, *Glossary* and *Introduction to Gothic Architecture;* Murray's *Cathedral Handbooks;* Scott, *Mediæval Architecture;* Turner and Parker, *Domestic Architecture of the Middle Ages;* Willis, *Canterbury;* Stanley, *Westminster Abbey;* Eastlake, *Materials for a History of Oil Painting;* Clark, *Mediæval Military Architecture in England;* Winston, *Inquiry into the Difference of Style in Ancient Glass Paintings.*

Coins.—As for Chaps. II. and IV.

Learning and Science.—*The Universities:* Maxwell Lyte, *History of the University of Oxford;* Prof. T. Holland in Oxford Historical Society's *Collectanea, II.;* Anstey's *Munimenta Academica* (Rolls Series); A. G. Little, *Grey Friars in Oxford* (Oxf. Hist. Soc.); Bass Mullinger, *The University of Cambridge to* 1535; Willis and Clark, *Architectural History of the University of Cambridge;* Ingram, *Memorials of Oxford;* Rev. A. Clark, *Colleges of Oxford;* Brewer, *Monumenta Franciscana* and *Opus Tertium*, etc., *of Roger Bacon* (Rolls Series); *Catalogi Veteres Librorum Ecclesiæ Dunelmensis* (Surtees Society); Dict. of Nat. Biog. (art. *Bacon*, etc.). For the *Scholastic Philosophy*, Hauréau, *Histoire de la Philosophie Scholastique;* Ueberweg's or Erdmann's *History of Philosophy;* Poole, *Illustrations of Mediæval Thought.*

Alchemy, Astrology, etc.—Many early treatises in Latin on Alchemy are in the *Theatrum Chemicum* (1689). English tracts in Ashmole, *Theatrum Chemicum Britannicum.* The legal documents on Alchemy are collected in the *Antiquary* of Sept., 1891. None of the early English astrological works have been printed, but Cockayne (*see* below) contains much that survived the Conquest. Wright's *Popular Treatises on Science* shows the important position of Astronomy in medieval Science ; *see also* Bacon, *Opera Inedita* (Brewer).

Medical Science.—*Leechdoms, Wort-cunning, and Starcraft of Early England*, ed. Cockayne (Rolls Series) ; Freind, *History of Physic from the time of Galen to the 16th Century* (2 vols., 1726) ; J. F. South, *Memorials of the Craft of Surgery in England*. *Public Health.*—Creighton, *History of Epidemics in Britain*.

Literature.—Robert of Gloucester's *Chronicle*, ed. W. Aldis Wright (Rolls Series) ; Robert Manning of Brunne, *Story of England*, ed. F. J. Furnivall (Rolls Series) ; *The Harrowing of Hell*, ed. Dr. Eduard Mall (Berlin, 1871) ; *The York Plays*, ed. L. Toulmin Smith (Clarendon Press, 1885) ; *The Townley Mysteries* (Surtees Soc., 1836) ; *Ludus Coventriae*, ed. Halliwell (Shakespeare Soc., 1841) ; T. Wright, *Early Mysteries of the Twelfth and Thirteenth Centuries* (London, 1838) ; A. W. Pollard, *English Miracle Plays ;* V. L. Bates, *The English Religious Drama ;* R. Genée, *Die Engl. Mirakelspiele, etc.* (Berlin, 1878) ; C. A. Hare, *Miracle Plays, etc.*, trans. by A. W. Jackson ; J. L. Vilein, *Gesch. d. Dramas* (Leipzig, 1865-86, Bd. 12) ; A. W. Ward, *History of English Dramatic Literature*, 2 Vols. (1875) ; J. A. Symonds, *Shakespeare's Predecessors and the Drama* (1884) ; Henry Morley, *English Writers*, Vols. IV. and V. ; Bernh. Ten Brink, *Gesch. d. Englischen Litteratur*, Bd. II., i. Hälfte (Berlin, 1889) ; A. Brandl, *Mittelenglische Litteratur*, in Paul's *Grundriss d. Germ. Philologie*, Bd. II., Abth. I., Lief. 6 (Strassburg, 1892).

Agriculture.—Ashley, *Economic History ;* Cunningham, *English Industry and Commerce ;* Thorold Rogers, *Six Centuries of Work and Wages*, and *History of Agriculture and Prices ;* Walter of Henley, ed. Lamond ; *Domesday of St. Paul's*, ed. Hales (Camden Soc., 1858) ; *Custumals of Battle Abbey*, ed. Scargill Bird (Camden Soc., 1867) ; *Fleta*, ed. Selden ; *Hundred Rolls* (Record Commission).

Commerce, etc.—Cunningham, *History of Industry and Commerce ;* Ashley, *Economic History ;* Thorold Rogers, *Agriculture and Prices*, Vols. I., II. ; Hall, *History of the Customs Revenue*, Vols. I., II. ; Madox, *History of the Exchequer ;* Cross, *The Gild Merchant ; Monumenta Gildhallæ* (ed. Riley, Rolls Series) ; Jacobs, *Jews in Angevin England ;* Karl Kunze, *Hanseakten aus England*, 1275-1412 ; Ruding, *Annals of the Coinage*, Vols. I.–III. ; *Report* of the Royal Commission on the Mint (Sessional Papers, 1849) ; *The Red Book of the Exchequer* (Rolls Series).

Home Life.—Turner and Parker, *Domestic Architecture ;* Addy, *Evolution of the English House ;* Wright, *History of Domestic Manners during the Middle Ages ; Quarterly Review*, article on Medieval Cookery, Jan., 1894, and authorities there quoted ; *Manners and Meals in the Olden Time* (including *The Babees Book*), ed. F. J. Furnivall, Early English Text Society.

WRESTLING, TO BE FOLLOWED BY COCK-SHOOTING (MS. Roy. 2 B. vii).

CHAPTER VI.

THE BLACK DEATH, AND AFTERWARDS. 1348–1399.

CHARLES
CREIGH-
TON.
The Black
Death.
THE political history of the latter half of the fourteenth
century is far from unimportant ; but its greatest events
shrink into insignificance in presence of that tremendous
social calamity which changed the whole face of rural England, and, by transforming her agricultural system, gave a new
direction to her industries, left a lasting impress on her laws,
her arts, and her manners, and, in a word, profoundly and
permanently affected the whole future course of her political,
social and economic life.

The Black Death which invaded England in 1348 was
the same disease that was afterwards known as the plague.
From that invasion it had a continuous history in England
down to the Great Plague of London, and was indeed the
grand zymotic disease of the country for more than three
hundred years. It was a peculiarly fatal infection, and, for
the most part, quick in its operation. In later times about one-
half of all that were attacked died, the fatality growing less and
the course of the disease more chronic as an outbreak declined ;
but in the first great invasion it is probable that the deaths
were many more than the recoveries, and it is known that the
victims often died within twenty-four hours of the onset,
and probably in most cases before the end of the third day.
In later times, also, it was nearly always the poorer classes
that died, perhaps because they had not the means of
escaping from the infected spot as their betters did ; but in
the Black Death all classes died—the Archbishop of Canterbury and many wardens of City Companies in London, abbots
and priors of monasteries, with a great part of the monks
and lay brethren, the parish clergy, and the farmers or yeomen
of the manors, as well as the labourers. There was no escaping from the Black Death by flight, unless those escaped who
took to the water in boats, just as many Londoners in the

plague of 1665 passed the dangerous time on board vessels in the Thames. More men than women died, and more in the prime of life or of middle age than aged persons or children.

The one great and appalling symptom was the sudden appearance of risings or botches in the groin, or in the armpit, or in the neck; these were the natural lymph-glands or absorbent glands of those regions, enormously swollen, to the size of a hen's egg or larger, tense and painful, and occupied with a hard or dry substance which yielded not one drop of matter when lanced, and could not be made to break by poulticing. Many cases had also red or livid spots on the breast or back, which were of the worst possible omen, and were known as "God's tokens." Carbuncles were apt to form in the fleshy parts of the trunk and limbs; and there might be still a fourth class of external signs in the form of blains or small boils dispersed over the skin, which had a core as if they had been diminutive carbuncles. In some cases— but it would seem not in all—the skin around these various formations was red, hot, tender, and swollen; thus the thigh would be inflamed if the bubo were in the groin. Whenever the buboes broke or suppurated, as they were most apt to do towards the end of a plague-season, the patient's chances of recovery were greatly increased, while his recovery would be at the same time very slow. These were the external marks of the Black Death and of plague at all times and in all places. But the Black Death had another symptom, which indicated a special degree of malignancy—namely, vomiting or spitting of blood; it is mentioned by only one of our native chroniclers, a friar of Kilkenny, and mentioned by him in such a way as if it had not been a symptom of every case. One other great symptom, common to plague at all times, was the delirium or raving, which was sometimes gentle and sometimes violent, and by no means universal in either degree. As in the other infections which rank with plague in deadliness, Asiatic cholera and yellow fever, the last hours of the patient were often placid and conscious; but there was also a more militant type of symptoms with loud crying from the pain of the dry and tense botches, and delirium, even to the extent of rising from the bed and rushing out of doors.

Symptoms and Character.

The Black Death is first heard of in the Crimea, at the siege of a small Genoese fort on the Straits of Kertch. The fort was a trading place of the Italian merchants engaged in the overland China trade by a northern route which left China close to the Great Wall and had its European terminus on the Volga and the Caspian, the Don and the Euxine. According to the rumour of the time, the Black Death arose in China from the putrefaction of innumerable unburied corpses; and it is known that the natural calamities of China —floods, droughts, and earthquakes, attended by famines and fevers and by an immense loss of life—were frequent throughout a whole generation preceding. It is natural to think of the overland caravan trade, which was then an extensive one, as a means of bringing the infection to Europe. At all events, it is significant that the Black Death is first heard of at one of the fortified posts of the China merchants, within which they had taken refuge with their goods from the depredations of the Tartar hordes. The outbreak of the plague had the effect of raising the siege; the Tartars dispersed all over the regions of the Black Sea and Caspian, and started the infection on its travels eastwards to the Central Asian khanates, as well as to Asia Minor, Syria, and Egypt; while it was brought to Constantinople by ships from the Euxine, and to Genoa by the very ship which rescued the besieged China merchants from the Crimean fort.

These events appear to have happened in the years 1346–47; by 1348 the disease was spread all over the shores of the Mediterranean; and in the beginning of August in that year it landed at Melcombe Regis, in Dorsetshire. Within a fortnight it was in Bristol, and soon after that in Gloucester; by the new year the whole diocese of Bath and Wells was feeling the want of priests to perform the last offices for the plague-stricken. London, in the one direction, was reached about the 1st November, while in its south-western progress the infection had got as far as Bodmin shortly before Christmas. Early in the spring of 1349, the mortality began in Norfolk, and in the course of that summer and autumn it seems to have overtaken all other parts of England, being heard of in the abbey of Meaux, in Holdernesse, in the month of August. Wales, Scotland, and Ireland were all invaded in due course. In Ireland the disease was first seen on the shores of Dublin Bay in August, but whether of 1348 or 1349 is uncertain, and it was in Kilkenny during the Lent following. The chief part of the mortality in

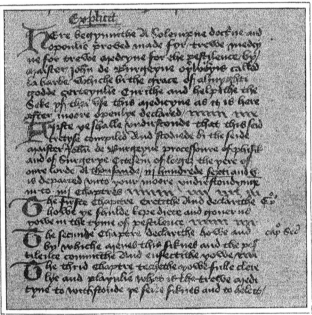

PAGE FROM A TREATISE ON THE PLAGUE (MS. Ashmole, 1444).
(*Bodleian Library, Oxford.*)

Scotland was in the year 1350. In London the epidemic is said to have ceased about Whitsuntide, 1349, and it was certainly on the decline by that time, April having been its worst month, as appears from the number of wills proved. It is said to have come to an end in the city of York in July, and all over England about Michaelmas, 1349; so that it would have lasted about fourteen months from its landing in Dorset, and perhaps from four to six or eight months at any given point of its progress, according to the number of people left alive and susceptible.

Two-thirds of the parish clergy in Norfolk died, and at least one-half in the archdeaconries of Nottingham, the West Riding and the North Riding of Yorkshire; according to the new researches, the rates were similar in all England. In the monasteries, with the remarkable exception of Canterbury, the mortality was even greater than among the parish clergy. In London the highest mortality was over two hundred in a day, which would mean, according to the usual course of plague-epidemics in the capital in later times, a total mortality of some twenty thousand, or nearly one-half of the population. In Bodmin fifteen hundred are said to have died, and in Leicester about eighteen hundred—in both cases about one-half of the estimated population; and these may be taken as fair samples of the towns. In the manor of Winslow one hundred and fifty-three tenants died, and it is reckoned that the proportion of deaths among the small farmers who served on the jury was three-fifths. The eastern counties suffered most, especially the city of Norwich, which was for many years afterwards reduced from being the second city in the kingdom to the sixth place, with a population not more than one-third of what it had been before the Black Death. The whole of England, town and country alike, had probably lost from one-third to one-half of its inhabitants. England was not so populous again until the reign of Elizabeth.

W. J. CORBETT. The Agricultural Revolution.

THE state of the agricultural classes in England during the first half of the fourteenth century, though not, perhaps, quite so prosperous and satisfactory as in the thirteenth, was still, as has been shown, steadily progressive. From the point of view of the peasantry, indeed, there was a very remarkable advance: for it was during this period that the first definite steps were taken towards the extinction of serfdom. In consequence, as we have already seen, by the middle of the reign of Edward III. there had arisen an entirely new and increasingly numerous class of labourers who worked for wages, and who, though not legally free, were for the most part so far their own masters that they sought work wherever they could find it. This great change, which on the Continent was not even initiated till some centuries later, in most countries was not

completed till after the French Revolution. But in England
it had begun so spontaneously, and, up to the period now
before us, progressed so rapidly and smoothly and in such a
variety of localities, that when the year 1348 opened, there
really seemed to be no reason why, in the course of another
few decades, the spirit of liberty should not have obtained a
complete triumph throughout the length and breadth of the
country, and the ancient obligations of the serfs to render
personal services on their lords' demesnes become entirely
obsolete. Even the disastrous period of famine between 1311
and 1321 followed as it undoubtedly was by a decline in the

THE BLACK DEATH: A CONTEMPORARY INSCRIPTION.
(Ashwell Church, Herts.)

number of the working population and a consequent rise in
wages, does not appear to have materially deterred the landowners from continuing to adopt the new wage system in
farming their estates, or to have tempted those who had already
done so to revert to the older system of services when they
found their expenses in wages much greater than they had
originally expected. In fact, at this time all the signs served
to point to continued progress, and there was hardly a cloud
to darken the agricultural outlook unless it were the growing
luxury and ostentation which became a feature in the life of
nearly all classes of the nation in the reign of Edward III.;
while even this seemed to be justified by the constant growth
of commerce and the still more extraordinary successes which
attended our armies in the great French War.

In a moment, however, all this was changed, and before
1349 had run its course all further hope of progress for

some time to come had died away.   For a struggle had been
inaugurated between the labourers and their employers, which
was to last for at least two generations, and which in its earlier
stages even seemed likely to lead to a complete reaction, and
a general reintroduction of the discarded labour services.   In
the end such a retrogression was happily avoided, but for a
time the fate of the labourers undoubtedly hung evenly in the
balance.   That so startling a change could ever have become a
possibility demands an explanation, and the explanation is found
in the Black Death.   The mortality in the towns has been
described in the previous section : and in some country districts
where the evidence has been most fully examined, it can even
be shown that the disease was more virulent and deadly than
in the crowded alleys of the towns.   For example, with regard
to East Anglia, at this time one of the most populous and
prosperous districts in all England, we are told by Dr. Jessopp
that in Hunstanton, a parish of some 2,000 acres, 172 tenants
of the manor all died within eight months, including the parish
priest ; and that of these, seventy-four left no male heirs behind
them, and nineteen others absolutely no blood relations at all
to inherit their holdings.   That in a similar way at Hadeston,
near Norwich, there died fifty-four men and fourteen women
out of a population of less than 400, and that in many cases
their whole families must have perished with them ; for, as the
court rolls show, twenty-four of these holdings escheated to the
lord.   At Heacham, near Hunstanton, a dispute between a
husband and wife about the latter's dower, was in April put
down by the steward of the manor for hearing before himself
and the homage at the next sitting of the court, which would
occur in two months' time ; but when the day came every one
of the wife's witnesses was dead, and the husband also.   These
exact statistics from the court rolls are, however, perhaps hardly
so eloquent as the absolute silence with which these months
of pestilence are passed over in the otherwise unbroken records
of many manors, showing that the courts had ceased to be
held altogether, and that in all probability not only the
steward, but also every one else who was capable of keeping
the rolls, had succumbed.   For when the records do begin
again, it is usually in the scrawling handwriting of a novice,
and in the most informal style.

We may dismiss as an exaggeration Walsingham's assertion that only a tenth part of the people of England remained alive when the fury of the plague abated in 1350; but there is no real danger of our making a mistake if we estimate the total loss in life to the nation from the epidemic at about one-half of the population (p. 188). This is a large but not too liberal figure, for it must be remembered that as usual the pestilence did not come alone, but was attended by its handmaidens dearth and starvation; and these also claimed their victims. For a time, indeed, cultivation became impossible, and the "sheep and cattle strayed through the fields and corn, and there were none left who could drive them." Harvests rotted in the ground, and the fields were left unploughed. The disorganisation of labour in fact was complete, and must be insisted on, for it is only after first grasping the great extent of the mortality of these years, and the extraordinary decrease in the number of men available for labour in the fields that consequently ensued, that we can adequately account for or even understand the subsequent course of agricultural history. When once this has been done, however, all becomes comparatively plain, and it is easy to see what a formidable difficulty the landowners found themselves in as soon as ever Scarcity the panic caused by the Black Death had begun to subside. of Labour For now instead of there being everywhere a fair abundance of labourers who were either willing or who could be made to work, there was everywhere a scarcity. The supply, too, of hired labour which was available to carry on the farming of the country had not only absolutely diminished, but the demand for it on the part of the landowners had also relatively increased. For nearly all landowners must have had large quantities of land thrown upon their hands, owing to their tenants having died without leaving any successors; and this they were now obliged to work for themselves in addition to their old demesne lands proper, or else they must allow it to go out of cultivation and lie idle altogether. Consequently, even supposing that they could still count upon securing enough hands to work what they formerly farmed, they would none the less still be in want of extra hands, in addition to the number that they employed before the plague, in order to work the extra area and thus make up for the loss of the rents and other fees which the disappearance of the tenants had entailed. In a similar way, even those landowners who had held fast to the old methods of farming, and never commuted the labour services of their villeins, now for the first time in many cases were obliged to have recourse to hired labour whether they liked it or not. For many manors were so depopulated and devastated by the plague that there was no longer a tenantry to be found on them either numerous enough or efficient enough to carry on the cultivation of the demesne with their services, and the farming never could have been kept up unless additional labour had been introduced. This, however, could only be secured by paying for it, for not even the most exacting landlord could have dared to increase beyond what was customary the amount of services due from those who survived; while it is very improbable that it would have been of any use at such a season as this to fall back upon their collective responsibility, although, as we have seen, in theory this would no doubt have been possible.

Just at this time, therefore, when the ranks of the hired labourers had been extraordinarily thinned, hired labour became the one thing that all landowners alike were most in need of. In other words, the labourers having become indispensable, found themselves the masters of the situation, and the natural result of course followed. Their demands for wages increased enormously; in some cases they even more than doubled them, and yet they were not satisfied. Especially was this the case, as might be expected, in those employments where the rate of wages formerly paid had been exceedingly low, for now it took a great deal to induce any one to undertake any service that was more than usually exacting or disagreeable. Women, for instance, who before had done a great deal of the inferior kind of work for a penny a day and even less, now invariably demanded twopence, and sometimes even obtained threepence. As the poet, William Langland, who wrote only a few years later than 1350, tells us: "Labourers that have no land to live on but their hands, disdained to live on penny ale or bacon, but demanded fresh flesh or fish, fried or baked, and that hot and hotter for chilling of their maw; and but if they be highly hired, else will they chide and wail the time that they were

["One thousand three hundred and fifty years from the birth of Christ till this night; and this is the second year since the coming of the plague into Ireland. I have written this in the twentieth year of my age. I am Hugh, son of Conor MacEagran, and whosoever reads it let him offer a prayer of mercy for my soul. This is Christmas night, and I place myself under the protection of the King of heaven and earth, beseeching that He will bring me and my friends safe through this plague. Hugh, son of Conor MacEagran, who wrote this in his father's book in the year of the great plague."]

A CRY FROM PLAGUE-STRICKEN IRELAND.

(Trinity College, Dublin: written on the lower margins of two pages of the Senchus Mor.)

made workmen." Of every quarter of wheat harvested, one-eighth had now to be paid over to the workmen as wages, instead of one-twelfth only as before the plague, while a further addition of thirty per cent. on the old rates had to be paid to get it threshed. Very little time had to elapse before such a state of things began to tell heavily on the landowners, and they were soon at their wits' end to know what to do, for one and all found themselves in a dilemma, and had to choose between losing their incomes by letting their fields lie uncultivated, or equally losing by attempting to cultivate them.

The Landlords' View. It could not be expected that any large body of men, when they found themselves in such a predicament, would long be content to submit passively to their evil fortune. The Berkeley, for instance, whose manor of Ham had become so depopulated that he had to hire "as many workfolk as amounted to 1,144 days' work" to gather in his harvest, must soon have lost patience and begun thinking of how things might be quickest restored to their old position. So also must the lord of Great Tew in Essex, whose tenants had once owed him 2,000 days' service in winter and 580 in autumn, for which, however, he had unfortunately accepted a commutation at the rates of a halfpenny and penny respectively. Only a small proportion of these could now in all probability have been paid, while instead, even in winter, he had to give each labourer threepence for doing an equivalent amount of work, and much more in the busier season. It must be remembered, too, that in the eyes of the men of these times the increased demands of the labourers, however natural they may seem to us, must have appeared distinctly immoral. For what else was it but an attempt to take advantage of the necessity of others, an action which all medieval teachers denounced, and which in many cases was even forbidden by legislation? It was very obvious, also, that in another way the new state of things was likely to become a danger to the country, for when the wandering labourer could find no landlord who was willing to pay him exactly what he demanded, he very easily turned into a "sturdy beggar," even if he did not go to greater lengths and take to the woods in the character of Robin Hood. The landlords,

in fact, can have had very little difficulty in convincing themselves that the new state of things was not one which they
could tolerate—was one, indeed, which they could not, consist-
ently with a proper sense of their duty towards their country,
allow to continue ; and so they at once applied to Parliament—-
that is, to themselves under another name—to have it brought
to an end by enacting that both the payment and receipt of
higher than the customary wages should henceforth be illegal.
To them, no doubt, this expedient seemed both the quickest
and the simplest; in reality it was far otherwise, for it marks
the beginning of the long quarrel between the capitalist and
the wage-earner, which in one way or another has ever since
continued to exist.

The most celebrated of the legislative efforts made by the The
landowners in the direction of fixing wages upon what they Statute of Labourers.
considered to be a fair basis is that known as the Statute of
Labourers, which was passed upon the first reassembling of
Parliament after the plague, in 1351 ; but in reality this
enactment was only a second edition of an ordinance which
had been drawn up by the king as early as June 18th, 1349,
when the plague had only just reached its height, and issued
in the form of a proclamation so as to provide a summary
remedy for the grievances under which many of his subjects
were already at that early date beginning to suffer. These,
indeed, are well set out in the preamble, which runs:
" Because a great part of the people, and especially of Workmen and Servants, late died of the pestilence, many, seeing
the necessity of Masters and great scarcity of Servants, will
not serve unless they may receive excessive wages, and some
are rather willing to beg in idleness than by labour to get
their living ;" while the eight chapters which follow are
said to have been ordained in consideration of " the discom-
modity which of the lack especially of Ploughmen and such
labourers may hereafter come." Chief among the remedies
consequently provided were the following: That every man
or woman, bond or free, able in body and within the age of
threescore years, not having his own, whereof he might
live, nor land of his own about which he might occupy himself, and not serving any other, should be bound to serve the
employer who should require him to do so, provided that the

lords of any bondman or landservant should be preferred before others for his services. That such servants should take only the wages which were accustomed to be given in the places where they ought to serve in the twentieth year of the king's reign, that is in 1347, or the year before the plague; and that anyone who should neglect so to serve should be committed to gaol until he found a security. That any reaper, mower, or other workman, who should leave his service, should be imprisoned, and that none, under the like pain, should receive or retain him. That any workman demanding or receiving more than the accustomed wages should be prosecuted in the court of the manor where he was serving, and pay double as a penalty; while any lord promising to give such wages should be fined treble. That contracts for such wages should be unenforceable; and finally, that no one should give anything, even under colour of alms, to valiant beggars, upon pain of imprisonment.

It would appear from the sweeping way in which the above provisions follow one another, that the authors of the ordinance were not much troubled with doubts as to the possibility of effecting what they wanted: but if so, they were soon undeceived. For already in the preamble to the statute of 1351 there is a confession that "it is given the king to understand that the said servants have no regard of the said ordinance, but to their ease and singular covetise[1] do withdraw themselves, unless they have livery and wages to the double or treble of what they were wont to take, to the great damage of the great men." The candour of this last phrase is certainly remarkable; but, nevertheless, there is no necessity for us to believe, as some have done, that the landlords were consciously unjust in trying to prevent the labourers from succeeding in their demands, or acted otherwise than under the honest belief that the introduction of a system of competitive wages, till then unknown in the country, would be merely a source of mischief. For it is not as if they tyrannously attempted to keep down wages at a time when the cost of living and prices generally were rising, without making any effort to allow for such a disturbing influence. On the contrary, they seem to have been fully aware that

[1] *I.e.* for their individual greed.]

ORDINANCE PREPARATORY TO THE STATUTE OF LABOURERS.

(Record Office.)

such a course would have been oppressive. For both in the
ordinance and the statute they inserted clauses which were
also intended to regulate prices. For instance, in the ordinance we read that "butchers, fishmongers, regraters,[1] hostelers,
brewers, bakers, pulters,[2] and all other sellers of all manner
of victuals, shall be bound to sell the same victual for a reasonable price, so that the same sellers have moderate gains and
not excessive; and that if any be convicted of selling in any
other manner, he shall pay the double of the same that he
so received to the party damnified." In the statute they
even went further, and regulated the prices of boots and
shoes. In fact, what ought to be criticised in this legislation
is not its want of justice, nor even its bad policy, but its
obvious futility. To the impartial man of that day it no
doubt seemed fair, and may well have seemed advantageous,
but it is hard to believe that it ever had the least chance of
succeeding. For even the landlords themselves, though they
did not perceive it, must have been at heart its opponents,
as they would have been the very first to object to a reduction
being made in the prices they obtained for the products of their
estates; and without this as a preliminary no permanent
change could be expected, as without it the old rate of wages
was no longer reasonable. It was the failure of Parliament
to see this that had such bad results, and in the course of
the next few years caused a widespread social discontent to
be added to the other misfortunes which had overtaken the
country. Instead of altering their policy and looking out for
modes of relieving the distress when they found that neither
prices nor wages would diminish in obedience to their desires,
the majority of landowners only urged upon the king the
advisability of further increasing the severity of the Statute
of Labourers. The labourers again became tied to the soil, and
were forbidden to travel without letters of authorisation.
Runaway labourers were ordered to be outlawed, and branded
with an " F " for their falsity. Towns which harboured them
were to be fined ten pounds. Even the slightest infraction
of the law was no longer to be punished with a fine, but imprisonment without the option of bail was to be inflicted in
every case. To enforce these laws universally was of course

[1 Sellers of small quantities by retail.]   [2 Poulterers]

impossible, but in many instances the landlords did not flinch from the attempt, while Parliament kept constantly encouraging them and egging them on by repeatedly re-enacting the laws, and adding to the penalties and to the coercive powers of the justices. Every recurrence of the plague, in fact, and every outbreak of dearth or murrain, by renewing the disorganisation of labour, seems to have stirred up the Legislature to fresh activity, whereas by rights these calamities should have shown the Commons that they were running their heads against a brick wall, and that no amount of obstinacy on their side was ever likely to triumph over a stubbornness which in their opponents was born of necessity, and which, sooner than capitulate, would have recourse to rebellion if only sufficiently provoked.

THE years of truce witnessed some important legislation besides the Statute of Labourers. In the three successive years, 1351, 1352, 1353, were passed the Statutes of Provisors, of Treason, and of Præmunire. Each of these was a vindication of national rights as against royal prerogative. Since the older Anglo-Saxon days when a king's life, like a subject's, could be atoned for by a money payment, there had come a great change in men's ideas about royalty. The Church rites of coronation sanctified " the Lord's anointed"; the feudal theory exalted the suzerain in theory as much as it threatened to reduce him practically to impotence ; the lawyers made almost a mystical creature of the king that never dies and can do no wrong, and is the fountain of justice and of honour. Treason became a crime for which mere death was too merciful a punishment, and a crime which seemed likely to become, as it had been in Rome under the dark shadow of Cæsarian tyranny, the complement of every other accusation. Now, at the prayer of the people, high treason was defined to consist in compassing the death or disgrace of any of the royal family, counterfeiting the king's seal or coinage, or slaying the great ministers in the exercise of their duty. Till the Yorkist and Tudor laws developed the iniquitous subtlety of " constructive treasons," the Act of 1352 remained a bulwark of the subject's liberties, and is the basis of the law as it now

A. L. SMITH.
The Political Changes.

The Statute of Treason.

The Statutes of Provisors and Præmunire.

stands. The two Statutes (p. 216 *seq.*) of Provisors and Præmunire dealt with the relation of England to the Papacy. Ever since the defeat of King John in the struggle over the election, in 1206, to the See of Canterbury, the Papacy had been steadily drawing to itself the appointments to English benefices and prelacies. It is strange at first sight to see this usurpation as marked under the strong rule of Edward I. as under the weak rule of Henry III. and Edward II. But the fact was, it was an irresistible temptation to the kings to make collusive arrangements with the Popes for division of the spoils between the Crown and the Papacy. The Pope's interest pointed the same way. "Were the King of England to petition for an ass to be made bishop, we must not refuse him," is a saying attributed to Clement VI. The connivance went on at the expense of the English nation, and still more of the English Church, now filled with "provisors," or persons whom the Pope had intruded into ecclesiastical posts (p. 217). Such men were often foreigners or absentees. It was this system at which the statute of 1351 (p. 217) struck a bold blow. But the very enactment of the first Præmunire Statute[1] (of 1353) proves the failure of the earlier act which it aimed at repeating in a more stringent form, while also forbidding, under pain of forfeiture, the appeals to "any jurisdiction outside the realm." In vain were the acts confirmed, amended, and enlarged, in 1365, 1377, 1390, and 1393. Their repetitions only register their failure. All that was finally effected was to put in the hands of the Crown the weapon of Præmunire, by which the Tudor kings were enabled to beat down the independence of the English Church, and to monopolise the plunder which hitherto had to be shared with the Popes.

The Statute of the Staple.

One other statute, the Statute of the Staple, 1353, also attests the popular influence in legislation. It ordered that wool and hides, tin and lead, should be sold only at certain staple towns, some in England and Wales, some in Ireland, with Calais and Middelburg (p. 340). This was partly to facilitate the levy of customs, partly to secure that inspection of the quality of the articles sold, which did not seem to the medieval mind inconsistent with the trader's own interests.

[1 From the opening words of the writ. "Præmunire facias ("Cause to be forewarned," præmoneri), issued in proceedings under the statute]

But partly, no doubt, it was an assertion of the rights of the Commons in Parliament to control indirect taxation, as their control over direct taxation had been asserted in 1340. To this end it was necessary to step in between the king and the assemblies of merchants, which were so ready, in return for monopoly, to allow his officers to raise the wool custom from the ancient rate of 10s. a sack to that of 30s. or 40s., or even more. If this was to go on, the Commons' "power of the purse" would be an empty phrase. Hence came a battle over this point, decided, in 1362, by the enunciation of the

SEAL OF EDWARD II. FOR CUSTOMS ON WOOL AND HIDES.

principle that no charge should be set on wool but by Parliament. Thus a great danger passed over ; for at one time it had seemed that there would be a fourth Estate, an Estate of merchants.

Amongst other forms of indirect taxation, which under the *The Burden of Taxation.* firm and persistent remonstrances of the Commons were abandoned, at least in principle, were included, first loans (and when a magnificent but impecunious king was the beggar, an abbey or a borough found it hard to refuse); secondly, "commissions of array"—these a statute of 1352 stigmatised as illegal if taken without consent of Parliament, but when a French fleet or Scottish army was descending on the land, the king would not be patient of claims that the militia should serve only in its own county or at the king's wages; thirdly, there was purveyance, the royal right of taking goods and means of conveyance at a low price. The right itself was burdensome enough, but the vast abuse of it made it intolerable. "They seize your cattle and pay with a stick of wood " (a tally).   " At the king's approach, thanks to this accursed prerogative, there is general consternation; men fly to hide their fowls and eggs; I myself shudder for the people's sake "· (it is Archbishop Islip who thus expresses himself). This, too, was somewhat alleviated after the statute against it in 1362.   But all these extortions and all this struggle over various forms of taxation were the logical consequence of the defective fiscal theory of the age.   Since the minority of Henry III. the cry had been more and more heard, " Let the king live of his own."   In the closing years of Edward III. it was the watchword of the reforming party.   It meant that for ordinary years the ordinary revenue, about £65,000 a year, should suffice.   If there arose an extraordinary requirement, if a war called for an extra grant, the king must come to Parliament for it; it was not " his own " to take at will, but the nation's, to grant at discretion.   This was neat and plausible, but it had two fatal flaws in it.   The ordinary revenue did not suffice for ordinary years; and in the extraordinary years Parliament would never pay the whole war-bill, but would " aid " the king with some inadequate contribution.   Hence in all years, ordinary or not, deficits accrue, the king recurs to purveyance. He promises to drop the abuses; but promises what he will not, and indeed cannot, perform.   It was well that the nation should learn the cost of war and glory; it was well that it should not win too easily its victory over the prerogative; it was well that the pressing needs of taxation should summon the third Estate to take the lead of the other two, and that the battle of English liberty should continue to ·be fought on the broad simple ground of bargain between king and people.   In all this lies the constitutional influence of taxation in the fourteenth century; it is regulative, not formative as hitherto.

New Forms of Taxation.   In the fourteenth century the system also and method of taxation underwent a complete revolution.   Under Henry II. it had been a system of taxation by classes; the feudal class paid scutage; the freeholders hidage, or, later, carucage; the villein class, which in theory included the boroughs, paid tallage (Vol. I., p. 672). After 1188, tenths from the clergy were added. But there were grave dangers in this severance of classes; and Edward I. made taxation like everything else, national and uniform. The feudal aids died out, and scutage and carucage with them. These were all land taxes; and the wealth of the country no longer consisted mainly in its lands. Tallage, again, though not strictly illegal after 1297, was felt to be both wasteful and oppressive, and was never taken after 1322. In their place came in the system of "tenths and fifteenths" levied on income and chattels, and the increased Customs fixed at 2s. the tun of wine, and 6d. in the £ on other goods. This "tunnage and poundage" with the ordinary wool Custom of 10s. on the sack, became an annual grant, and produced about two-fifths of the ordinary revenue. The total amount which could be raised with extra taxation in a year of great stress would be as much as £180,000.

In 1355 the French war broke out again, though in 1354, when asked if they would accept a lasting peace, the Commons had shouted "unitedly and all together, 'Yes, Yes.'" The startling victory of Poitiers led to the Peace of Bretigny in 1360, which assigned to England more than half the provinces of France. But the appalling ravages of the Free Companies[1] in France had created in that country a new spirit of union and patriotism. The Black Prince had wasted his resources and ruined his health in the futile Spanish expedition, which replaced Pedro the Cruel for a while on the throne of Castile. In 1373 the Prince came home a broken man, his fair fame stained by the massacre of Limoges, and the fleet coming to his aid defeated by the Spaniards at Rochelle in 1372. The mocking phantom of English dominion had already faded away. Little was left but Bordeaux and Calais. Edward III. himself had already turned aside to other objects. By marrying four sons to the heiresses of the great English families, he had initiated a new domestic policy for the Crown. Like so much that this selfish ruler did, it made a splendid show and lasted his time, but proved the ruin of his posterity. For with the great fiefs he brought into the royal house their unquenchable feuds; and to Edward III.'s policy must be traced back

Poitiers and the Sequel.

Storm Signs at Home.

[1 Bodies of disbanded soldiers—of both nations, but popularly regarded as English—who had lived by brigandage during the years of truce.]

the full disastrousness of the Wars of the Roses. His later reign was clouded by strife and omens of coming storm. His Queen, Philippa, died in 1369; and henceforth his mistress,

Alice Perrers, ruled almost openly at court. The courtiers, attacked the great churchmen, like William of Wykeham, and for a time drove them from office. Above all, the Good Parliament of 1376, besides impeaching the chief courtiers, banishing Alice Perrers, and giving voice to the popular hatred and suspicion against John of Gaunt, brought in what might be called "the Grand Remonstrance"

WIFE AND DAUGHTER OF
EDWARD III.
(*National Portrait Gallery.*)

of the reign, a list of 140 petitions which throw a lurid light on the administration. The old feudal abuses have, it is true, ceased to be formidable; but the old grievances of Magna Charta, of the Mad Parliament in 1258, of the Ordinances in 1311, remain unredressed. New perils have appeared in the sheriffs' power of packing a Parliament, and in the general animosity expressed against the Church for its ill-used wealth, its corrupt tribunals, and its foreign tendencies, and against the Papacy, from which already in 1366 there had been a national revolt, the whole Par- liament repudiating John's act of homage and the annual tribute of a thousand marks.

Constitu- tional Changes.
A new political weapon, and one which was to prove two-edged, has been invented, in impeach- ment. A new constitutional device for solving the great problem of all government, the control of the executive by the legislative, has

EDWARD III. AND ST. GEORGE
(*National Portrait Gallery*)

been discovered, when the Commons appoint ten lords of the reforming party to "enforce" the royal council; the first of a long series of steps destined to lead to cabinet government.

PAGE OF A BIBLE BELONGING TO KING JOHN OF FRANCE.
(Captured at Poitiers: MS. Roy. 10 D. ii.)

Above all, a new force has at last appeared, to take the leader_
ship out of baronial hands. For when John of Gaunt insolently
reversed the Parliament's measures as soon as it was dissolved,
and even packed a new and servile Parliament in the next

The
Reign of
Richard
II.: Rise
of the
Commons,

year, and brought back the timid lords to their wonted time_
serving, the death of Edward III., June 21, 1377, following
closely on that of the Black Prince, introduced a minority, a
political condition which always leads to a compromise. John
of Gaunt was no longer supreme. The Commons in the Parliament of October, 1377, chose again the old Speaker, and returned
triumphantly to their old constitutional positions.

The nation has at last learnt to do without the baronage
as constitutional leaders. Henceforth the political extinction
of the baronage is only a question of time and opportunity.
By thus securing their right to submit royal ministers to
a strict account, the Commons had got a hold upon the
administration. Their share in legislation had been similarly
advancing throughout the century that had elapsed since
they had been convoked by Edward I. for little more than
assent to taxation and presenting of petitions. By a long
struggle with his shifty grandson they had secured that their
petitions should have an answer, that the answers should not
be merely oral but formally recorded and sealed, and that the
answer to each petition should be endorsed on the back thereof.
Only one more step was required to make the petition into a
Bill, and to win for them the initiative in legislation.

and of the
Residuum.

The victories of the Commons, in the Parliamentary sense,
were, after all, the victories only of an aristocratic class. Below
the small group of the county freeholders and the burgesses in
towns came the great mass of the unrepresented, the villeins
and the unprivileged artisans. When those classes began for
the first time to stir and to find expression for themselves—
when in the Peasant Revolt, and the Lollard movement, and
the poem of "Piers Plowman" they began to make themselves
heard, it must have seemed a portent; as Roman augurs fabled
before the Punic War, *bos locutus est*. As early as 1366 (p. 222)
Wycliffe had published his book on "The Lordship of God,"
an attack on the current ecclesiastical theory of the subordination of State to Church. He next appears condemning
the papal usurpations of English benefices. Then he joined with

TOMB OF THE BLACK PRINCE, CANTERBURY CATHEDRAL.

John of Gaunt—strange alliance of a religious enthusiast with a corrupt courtier—to attack the temporal position and wealth of churchmen, and was cited before Courtenay, Bishop of London. The trial was broken up by an outbreak of the Londoners against John of Gaunt. Another trial in 1388 was interrupted by another popular riot against the Papal Bull. From this date Wycliffe, hitherto a reformer, became a revolutionary. He advanced to the very key of the Church position in denying the doctrine of Transubstantiation. He inveighed unsparingly against the standing army of the Church, the monks and the friars. He appealed from the churchmen to the people, and turned from Latin treatises to brief tracts in English. By these and his English version of the Vulgate Bible, and by his order of " poor priests," or travelling preachers (p. 230), he brought the most fundamental problems of medieval thought down to the arena of popular discussion. He is the first of the roll of English prose writers; and his prose (p. 306) has already the best characteristics of English writing—brevity, force, and trenchant humour.

The Lollards.   In 1384 he died. His followers, the Lollards, were at the height of their influence about 1394. The petition they then presented to Parliament condemns not only many Church doctrines and rites, but also war and capital punishment, and trades in luxuries. Wycliffe's successors, his guiding hand removed, had allowed the movement to drift into wild socialism, and it soon became discredited. About 1390 every other man you met was a Lollard, according to Walsingham. But in 1401 Parliament was willing to pass the Act which provided for the burning of heretics. Wycliffe has sometimes been held responsible for the great rising of 1381, called the Peasant Revolt. But there are other causes quite sufficient to account for this.

The Peasant Revolt.   It is sufficient to bear in mind the great strain resulting from the sudden and enormous rise in wages and prices consequent on the Black Death on the one hand, and the increasing stringency of the Statutes of Labourers which strove to force back this irresistible rise on the other hand. As in all revolutions, many other influences co-operated. The disorganising and demoralising influence of the long war, the grievances of townsmen against their feudal lords, and of craftsmen against oppressive guilds, the circulation of doctrines such as those attributed to John Ball, and of watchwords borrowed from "Piers Plowman," must all be taken into account. In Kent, where, according to legal theory, there was no villeinage, the rising was political rather than social. It found its pretext in

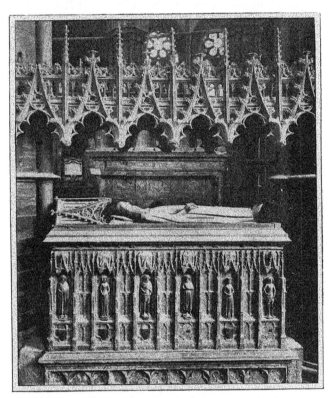

TOMB OF EDWARD III., WESTMINSTER ABBEY.

the hated novelty of poll-taxes; but the poll-tax of 1381 (p. 330) must be regarded rather as the signal than the motive cause of the rising. The remarkable features about it are its almost universal range from Kent to Lancashire, from Norfolk to Devon; its extraordinary evidence of organisation and concert; the panic of the well-to-do classes, and the

precocious wisdom and courage of the young king. When
Walworth, the mayor of London, struck down Wat Tyler at
Smithfield, Richard II., a boy of fifteen, stepped forward to
cry, "I will be your leader," and induced them to return home
by charters of manumission, such as the day before at Mile End
he had promised to the villeins of the eastern counties. These
charters, within three weeks, his advisers made him annul;
and Parliament concurring in this treachery, made political
capital out of the revolt by attributing it to administrative
abuses, to taxation and purveyance, and official embezzlements.
But one, at least, of its effects survived. It undoubtedly
accelerated the transformation of villeinage into copyhold
tenure, and of bailiff farming into a leasehold system (p. 334).

The King's Advisers. The chief personage about the court since the death of
Edward III. had been John of Gaunt; but 1381 had shown
the detestation felt for him throughout the land. He betook
himself in 1386 to Gascony, for another futile attempt to make
good his right to the throne of Castile. To counterbalance the
control exercised by his uncles, Richard II. had relied on Vere,
Earl of Oxford, and Michael de la Pole, Earl of Suffolk. When
the former was created Duke of Ireland, a vehement attack was
made on the two favourites by both Houses of Parliament.
The king's defiant answer that he would not at their will dismiss a single varlet from his kitchen was met by a significant
reminder of the fate of Edward II. This cowed him: he
bowed to the storm. Suffolk was impeached and dismissed.
The king was put under a council to hold the regency for a year.
But as soon as Parliament was dissolved he showed a bold front.
He made a progress through the country to collect adherents;
he appealed to the sheriffs to pack the next Parliament; and he
got from the judges a pronouncement that the commission was
unlawful, and made to himself a party in London. But
"London was mutable as a reed;" the sheriffs told him that the
commonalty were against him; Vere's small army was defeated
at Radcot Bridge; and a formal "appeal" of treason was made
against the king's advisers by five great lords. These "lords
appellant" were Thomas, Duke of Gloucester, the king's
youngest uncle; Henry of Derby, son of John of Gaunt;
Mowbray, Earl of Nottingham; Beauchamp, Earl of Warwick;
and the Earl of Arundel. Under their influence the Merciless

RICHARD II. PRESENTED TO THE VIRGIN: DIPTYCH AT WILTON HOUSE.

(*By permission of the Rt. Hon. the Earl of Pembroke.*)

Richard assumes Authority. Parliament met in February, 1388, and continued for four months at the work which earned it its title. A clean sweep was made of the king's friends. For nearly a year Richard bore the yoke without a sign; but on May 3, 1389, he entered the Council, announced that he was of age enough to govern (he was now twenty-three), and dismissed the "Appellants." But satisfied with the complete success of this sudden stroke, he soon recalled them; and a halcyon period set in: eight years of quiet popular and constitutional government. It was even an interval of peace with France, for the truce made in 1389 was cemented in 1396 by the king's marriage to a French princess. It was also occupied by important legislation: the old statutes against Provisors and against Mortmain were amended, and new Acts passed against "livery and maintenance."[1] John of Gaunt now returned from Gascony, acted the part which he holds in Shakespeare's play, and laboured to keep peace in the royal family. Richard himself, with that singular adaptability of character which Shakespeare has drawn so subtly, was indulging the other side of his nature, his taste for music and books, art and pageantry.

Growth of Absolute Monarchy. But beneath the surface critical changes were going on. The arrogance of Gloucester grew yearly more intolerable; the death of the popular Queen Anne, in 1394, and the legitimation of the Beauforts, children of John of Gaunt by a mistress, broke up the royal family union. The king had completely won over two of the appellants, Henry and Nottingham, and had formed as a counterpoise the group of royalist nobles (the Hollands, Montacute, Scrope, etc.). An accident exploded the mine. A petition appeared from Parliament in 1396 attacking the administration of the household. The king indignantly demanded the author, whose name was Haxey; the Commons, intimidated and apologetic, gave him up. Elated by this victory, and hearing that the three hostile appellant lords—Gloucester, Arundel and Warwick—had met at Arundel to concert their plans, the king struck his blow suddenly, and within three months Arundel had suffered a traitor's death, Gloucester was found dead at Calais, Warwick was banished. The Parliament reversed all the Acts of the Merciless Parliament of 1388; it granted the king the wool subsidy for his

[1 *See* the section on Warfare, Chap. VII.]

life, and it completed his now despotic power by delegating its own authority to a committee of Lords and Commons. The English monarchy had suddenly become an absolute monarchy. It was impossible that such a reversal of the work of three centuries should be permanent. To complete his triumph, Richard had seized the opportunity of a quarrel between the two last of the appellants—Henry of Derby and Mowbray of Nottingham—who had lately been created Dukes of Hereford and of Norfolk respectively. There was to be a public duel

RADCOT BRIDGE.

between them; it had just begun when the king interposed and banished both. On John of Gaunt's death Richard seized the Lancaster estates; Henry returned to claim his inheritance; the king was absent in Ireland. Henry had long been the most popular man in England, and doubtless had an understanding with the great nobles. All deserted to his side, and Richard on his return found all was hopeless, and abdicated September 29, 1399. The contemporary chronicler, the monk of Evesham, sees in Richard's fall the moral that 'he who smites with the sword shall perish by the sword." Like Rehoboam, he had despised the counsel of old men and followed the young to do evil. Henry stood forth in Parliament to assert his right to the vacant throne as " descended in the

Abdication of Richard II.

right line from Henry III.," and as " sent by God to recover his right when the realm was in point to be undone for default of governance."   Thus fell the medieval form of monarchy and its assertion of absolutism, not to be heard again till national needs recalled it to a temporary life under the Tudors, and the Stuarts were misled into a factitious and fatal attempt to revive it, not only in practice, but in the form of a theory as offensive as that of Richard II.   He had said that the laws were in his own mouth and breast, but his deposition closed the long struggle between the constitution set up by Edward I. and the older idea of royal prerogative.   Before the next spring Richard was dead : but Pomfret Castle has kept its secret well, and the manner of his death is still unknown.

R. L. POOLE. Wycliffe and his Work.

THE removal of the Papacy to Avignon in the beginning of the fourteenth century was attended by serious consequences affecting both the material resources and the public prestige of the Holy See.   Avignon lay just without the French border, and the Popes of the " Captivity " (as this term of absence from Rome is called) were all Frenchmen.   Some, indeed, might be, as the result of King Edward III.'s conquests, English subjects ; but their attachment, as their language, was not the less French.   The Papacy became the steady ally of France, and lost to a great extent its proud position of standing as a free and absolute power above all the courts of secular kingdoms.   In England, especially after its armies had overrun and humbled France, a French Pope, identified altogether with French interests, could not be regarded with the same devotion

England and the Papacy.

as of old ; and here, in the country which had been most loyal to the Holy See, the seeds of dissatisfaction grew silently into ill-will, which from time to time broke forth into outspoken complaint, and even into declared opposition.   For England was the harvest-field from which the Papacy reaped its greatest profits.   Now that the Pope was no longer resident in Italy, the income due from his possessions there was levied with greater difficulty and rapidly shrank in amount.   He was more and more dependent on gifts and exactions from the other lands of his obedience.   France, however, by the

MEETING OF HENRY OF LANCASTER AND RICHARD II.

DEPOSITION OF RICHARD II. (MS. Harl. 1319).

second half of the fourteenth century was exhausted by war-fare, Germany had little to spare, and the chief weight of the burthen fell upon England, which had to disburse to the Papal treasury sums largely exceeding its proportional due, were we to reckon only by population, as well as a yearly tribute of one thousand marks (partly levied in Ireland) inherited from the recklessness of King John.

Nor did the country suffer from this direct taxation only, harassing as it was. Dispensations and other privileges were constantly required, and they could only be obtained by those who were willing to pay the charges imposed according to a fixed tariff regulating minutely the cost of each; and appeals to the Papal court not merely involved heavy expense, but they were open to a further objection on the part of English statesmen, since they appeared to them as a dis-paragement of the king's right of jurisdiction. It was not disputed that certain causes might properly be removed to the Pope's cognisance; the complaint was that suits were brought before him the judgment in which might extend to issues properly, it was held, amenable to the civil authority alone. But so much did the spheres of temporal and spiritual jurisdiction overlap, that it was hard to lay down a rule which should exclude the latter class of cases and leave only the right of appeal in those of which the legality was unassailed. For example, in 1358, the Bishop of Ely brought an appeal before the Pope, the sentence in which carried with it the excommunication of some members of the King's Council; but no sooner had the Papal commissioners reached England than they were imprisoned, tried before the judges, and at last put to death. This was a case which might be claimed on either side. And although appeals of a serious character were less numerous than they had been under King Henry III., they were still frequent enough, and often irritating enough —since the Papacy was in close alliance with the French monarchy—to produce constant friction. Hence in 1353 the ordinance of Praemunire (p. 200) was passed "against annullers of judgment in the king's courts" which forbade the prosecution in foreign courts of suits cognisable by the law of England. Thirteen years later a statute was passed which applied the prohibition by name to the Papal court;

and, finally, in 1393 the great statute of Praemunire subjected all persons bringing Bulls or other instruments from Rome to the penalty of forfeiture. The law was highly obnoxious to the Curia, but the Pope was not in a position to enforce its withdrawal. His protests were in vain, and appeals became less numerous. Still the Pope's power of dispensation covered a good many of the causes about which appeals arose; and for the rest, it became usual for him to send judges "delegate" to act as his representatives in England, so that the foreign jurisdiction was not altogether excluded, though it was now exercised on English soil.

The system which perhaps caused more discontent than anything else in the minds of those who wished for the efficient government of the English Church, was that which had come into practice with regard to the bestowal of preferments in it. The Pope was accustomed to make *provision* for the next presentation to a benefice during the lifetime of the incumbent; or he would nominally, for special reasons, *reserve* to himself the right of appointment to a vacant post. He had also the unquestioned prerogative of nominating to bishoprics vacated by translation; and his policy was to translate bishops as often as possible, and so to obtain not only the fees and the firstfruits (or first year's income) of the bishop who was translated, but also those of the prelate who was appointed in his room. The grievance was not merely that the interests of the see or other benefice were likely to be neglected, but also that foreigners were frequently nominated, who were contented with the enjoyment of its revenues without being at the pains even of visiting England. In 1351 the Statute of Provisors prohibited the acceptance of Papal letters of provision, and handed over the patronage of benefices so dealt with to the king. But the law was constantly evaded, and all attempts at setting matters on a more satisfactory footing failed of any real success.

It is necessary to bear these facts in mind in order to understand how it was possible for a movement such as that set on foot by Wycliffe to attain even a transitory success. The Papacy, it was considered, was becoming more and more of a temporal institution, whose action might be criticised like the action of ordinary temporal powers, and was at this time judged with the greater jealousy on account of its association with the politics of France. The fourteenth century, moreover,

Rome and National-ism.
witnessed a remarkable growth of national sentiment in the western States of Europe. The German Electors in 1338 asserted their right to choose a king whose title should need no confirmation by the Pope ; and in the same year when two cardinals were sent into England, obviously in the French interest, to bring about a peace between England and France, the Archbishop of Canterbury himself denounced them from the pulpit. Each nation was resolved to manage its own concerns without interference from without, and the affairs also of the Church in each country were looked upon in the same light. The English Church had always claimed for itself a distinct existence, and it was natural that the centrifugal tendency should be hastened by the present conditions of the Papacy. Nor is it to be forgotten in this connection that the reign of Edward III. was marked by an increased use of the English language in preaching and for the purposes of devotion ; and the more religion presented itself to plain people in an English guise, the more would the Latin ritual of the Church appear as a foreign importation. Thus a national patriotic sentiment might combine with political considerations and with a religious motive in pleading the desirability of resistance to the French dictation and the secular tendencies of Avignon. Of this complex of opinion Wycliffe was the spokesman. The thoughts which were in others' minds, and the views which descended to him by literary tradition, found their expression in his highly trained Latin argument, or his nervous English invective; and if the substance of his ex-position is largely borrowed, the form is still mainly his own. He put what was vague and undefined into a tangible shape, and drew up the case against Rome in clear propositions which could be taken up and fought for by his disciples.

Wycliffe.
John Wycliffe was a Yorkshireman, and doubtless a member of the family which for centuries occupied the manor of Wycliffe-on-Tees. Born about 1320, he made his way to the College which had been founded at Oxford half a century before his birth by his neighbours, the Balliols of Barnard Castle, and in 1360–1361 held the office of Master of that College. He then accepted a living in Lincolnshire, which in

THE PAPAL PALACE, AVIGNON.

1368 he exchanged for one in Buckinghamshire, within an easier distance of Oxford. He appears, indeed, to have been frequently, if not usually, resident in the University from 1363 onwards, and was able by this means to satisfy the conditions required for the degrees of Bachelor and Doctor in Divinity. He took the higher degree sometime before the end of 1373. It is generally believed, also—though the fact is by no means certain—that he is the same person with the John Wycliffe who was made Warden of Canterbury Hall by Archbishop Islip in 1365. This hall had been recently founded by the archbishop for a mixed body of monks and secular clergy-men; but the association of these discordant elements proved unsatisfactory, and Islip, when he appointed Wycliffe, removed the monks and adapted the hall to the normal academic pattern. The next archbishop, Langham, who was himself a Benedictine monk, recognised the injury done to the interests of his Order, and in turn deposed Wycliffe and his Secular colleagues. An appeal to Rome followed, but the representative of the Seculars, for some unknown reason, did not put in an appearance, and judgment naturally went against them. By the Papal decision of 1370, which was confirmed by the king in 1372, Canterbury Hall was left exclusively monastic. Con-sidering that the hall had been originally designed in part expressly for the benefit of the monks of Canterbury, and that the plan of a mixed foundation had notably failed, the decision probably was the fairest one possible in the circumstances; but it is not to be denied that the Seculars had a grievance, and that this grievance may have directed Wycliffe's attention more distinctly to the abuses which he deemed to exist in the Roman Church. This latter inference, however, is not to be pressed too decidedly, since the identity of the warden with the reformer remains unproved and there were certainly two John Wycliffes living at the time.

Wycliffe's academical position stood high. He had not only amassed solid attainments in the school-learning of his day—in which, indeed, he was reputed to be unsurpassed—but he also possessed the gift of teaching and of drawing round him a band of disciples, so that, however far he separ-ated himself from the authorised standard of theological correctness, he enjoyed an unvarying personal popularity at

Oxford, where his following held its ground and called for energetic measures of repression at a time when his doctrines hardly survived in other parts of England. It has been usually supposed that the position he had arrived at with respect to the Papal power was already notorious in 1366; for in this year, when Parliament repudiated the payment of the yearly tribute to the Pope, it was he who was called upon to draw up a statement of the arguments in support of that action. Recent criticism has, however, made it nearly certain that this took place on a later occasion, when the demand was renewed in 1374. The statement, from which we gather that Wycliffe was one of the doctors of theology summoned to Parliament, is of special interest from the light it throws on the course of his opinions on the great question of the relations of the ecclesiastical and civil powers.

In Public Life.

He puts his statement to a large extent in the form of a report of seven speeches made by seven lords in the Council when the discussion as to the tribute was raised. It is possible that the arguments brought forward at such a council may serve as the basis of Wycliffe's paper; but it cannot be seriously doubted that the paper itself—its plan, arrangement and most of its reasoning—is to all intents and purposes Wycliffe's own production; and that the detailed arguments of the lords are his arguments. Thus he makes one lord deny the lawfulness of the Pope's receipt of tribute on the ground that Christ and His apostles held no property, and that the owning of property by the Church was the token of her decline from original purity. This is the doctrine of Evangelical Poverty, which was the watchword of Marsiglio of Padua, and of William of Ockham and the stricter Franciscans, and had animated them in their support of Lewis the Bavarian against Pope John XXII. nearly half a century earlier. Another class of arguments relies on feudal principles. The payment of a tribute involves reciprocal obligations; it is a rendering of a "service" which implies the rendering of service in return. But the Pope, far from helping or protecting this country, aids its enemies: he can therefore have no claim to help from us. Here we have enunciated Wycliffe's leading principle of lordship (*dominium*) as conditioned by service.

The full exposition of these two doctrines—of Evangelical

Poverty and of Lordship—is found in the treatises *On the Lordship of God* and *On Civil* (or human) *Lordship,* the former of which may have been composed some years previously. Lordship and service are necessarily correspondent terms; the one cannot exist without the other. A man cannot have lordship unless there be something upon which he can exercise it. God Himself was not Lord until by creation He had provided objects to be His servants. But God's lordship is distinguished from that of man by the two facts that it holds under its sway all creatures, and all on the same terms of service: for " God rules not mediately through the rule of vassals who serve Him, as other kings hold lordship, since immediately and of Himself He makes, sustains, and governs all that which He possesses, and assists it to perform its works according to other uses which He requires." [1] The principle that all men were equal in the eyes of God—or, as Wycliffe would put it, that all held of Him, and on the same terms of service—was, of course, a commonplace of Christian doctrine. But Wycliffe transferred the conception from the religious to the political sphere. The rank which a man has in the sight of God must determine his rank, consequence, position, all that he has or is, in the sight of men. If by sin he forfeits the former, necessarily also the latter goes with it. In a word, in Wycliffe's formula, *lordship,* spiritual or temporal, *is founded in grace.*

This doctrine is not Wycliffe's own: he took it fully matured from the writings—possibly from the oral teaching— of Richard FitzRalph, who had been a fellow of Balliol College, about the time of Wycliffe's birth, and who is known to have been resident in Oxford at least as late as 1333. He died Archbishop of Armagh in 1360. But FitzRalph had employed his doctrine of lordship as a weapon to assail the Franciscan doctrine of Evangelical Poverty. -To abjure all holding of property was, in his mind, to run counter to the law which governed all the relations of man and man, as of man and God. Wycliffe sought to combine the two doctrines. He would go with FitzRalph so far as the definition of lordship was concerned, but into the further issues which he raised he could not follow him. On these points he stood firm with Ockham and the Franciscans. It was only in the latter

---

[1] *De dominio divino,* i. 5.

stages of his career that he broke away from his friendly
attitude towards the friars; and this he did, not on any
ground of theory, but because the friars were the hearty
advocates of the Papal authority, which he came year by year
more stoutly to resist.

Wycliffe's doctrine of lordship was powerfully affected by
the teaching of St. Augustine as to the nature of sin: "Sin
is nothing, and men, when they sin, become nothing." Evil is
a negation, and those who yield themselves up to it cease to
retain any positive existence. Clearly, then, they can possess
nothing, can hold no lordship. That which they seem to
possess is no real or proper possession at all; it is but the
unjust holding of that which they must one day restore to
the righteous. "From him that hath not shall be taken even
that which he seemeth to have." As thus the wicked hath
nothing, so on the other hand the righteous is lord of all
things. To that which he has not now actually, he has a
potential right; and since every righteous man has this unlimited lordship, it follows necessarily that all goods must be
held in common. Wycliffe's doctrine of community is one of
the most express points in his system, and it is one which,
we can hardly doubt, had more serious practical consequences
than its author intended. Wycliffe, in truth, guarded it by
important reserves as to the nature and value of human
possessions. Civil society, he maintained, originated in sin,
in the lust of acquisition; and civil lordship is only so far
good as it is correlated with natural lordship; in other words,
with the lordship based on the law of the Gospel. Civil
rulers are only justified in so far as they recognise the duty of
"service," that is, of their corresponding obligations towards
their subjects. Still the ideal remains, that no man should
hold separate property, and that all things should be had in
common.

His Communism.

If this was the ideal for all men, plainly it was such in
the first degree for the Church. The Church, Wycliffe urged
with Ockham, should hold no property; endowments were a
hindrance to its proper work. It should be limited to its
strictly spiritual province. The Papacy should revert to its
primitive position of an exclusively spiritual power: "for to
rule temporal possessions after a civil manner, to conquer

His Views of Church Property.

kingdoms and exact tributes, appertain to earthly lordship, not to the Pope; so that if he pass by and set aside the office of spiritual rule, and entangle himself in those other concerns, his work is not only superfluous but also contrary to Holy Scripture."[1]   If then the Church exercised functions which properly belonged to the State, it was the duty of the latter to vindicate its right over its own affairs.   In such a case the State might resume possession of the lands and revenues held by the Church.   But what if the Church should pronounce excommunication against its spoilers?   Excommunication, is the answer, has no effect unless its object be already excommunicated by his sin.   If he sin, he is already beyond the pale of Christian communion; if he have done righteously, no sentence of condemnation can alter his condition of grace. The example illustrates well the clearness with which Wycliffe pushed to its logical conclusion his view that man's position, alike civil and spiritual, was determined solely by his personal relation towards God; only his own act of rebellion against Him could expel him from the Church.   It was his own character, and not his office or rank, nor any declaration made by another against him, that constituted him what he really was.   The Pope himself, if unrighteous, lost his entire right to lordship.   His decree, if contrary to the will of God, had no binding force.   Wycliffe is careful to avoid saying a word against the existing Pope; but his devotion to him, which he expresses in terms of hearty loyalty, is no argument against the necessary right of resisting him if his commands should contravene Holy Scripture.   It is evident that Wycliffe's general line of argument—setting aside his visionary communism, the drift of which was probably not at once perceived—fell in readily with the aims of those nobles who, like John of Gaunt, Duke of Lancaster, desired a large measure of confiscation of Church property.   But for many years he did not pass beyond theory; it was not until the great schism in the Papacy began in 1378 that he came forward as a practical reformer, every day more vehement and uncompromising.   For the present he is no more than the trained Oxford doctor, whose learning the Government might make use of in responsible employment in matters affecting

[1] *De civili dominio,* i. 17.

the Church. In 1374 he was appointed by the Crown to the Rectory of Lutterworth, in the archdeaconry of Leicester, a living which he held for the rest of his life; and a few months later he was sent on a commission to Bruges, in company with the Bishop of St. Davids, and some others of less consequence, to treat with the Pope's

FIGURES ABOVE THE DOOR OF LUTTERWORTH CHURCH.
(Part of a design representing " Les Trois Morts et les Trois Vifs.")

representatives on the vexed question of "provisions." That no permanent settlement was arrived at can hardly excite surprise; but it is possible that, besides the slight and temporary concessions which were then agreed upon, there were certain other articles of more solid value which were not at the time recorded, but were, in fact, laid before Parliament three years later.

Wycliffe's career as a public man had now well begun. The duties of his country benefice did not prevent him from

59

lecturing in theology at Oxford, where a school was forming
itself around him; and from time to time he made his
appearance as a preacher in London, where his opponents
allow his influence to have been powerful and lasting. It
can scarcely be doubted that part of his popularity was
derived from the vigour of his attack upon the endowments
of the Church, and that in this attack he was looked upon
as the instrument of John of Gaunt's anti-clerical party. If
it was desirable to strike at the Duke, it was a simple
course to strike at him through Wycliffe. And so, in
February, 1377, probably in consequence of some sermon
preached in London, he was cited to appear before the
bishops in St. Paul's Church. He obeyed the summons
accompanied by John and the Lord Percy, the Marshal of
England; and the Duke was attended by four friars, doctors of
divinity. The opposition of parties could not be more clearly
marked; but an angry brawl between Wycliffe's supporters
and Bishop Courtenay put a stop to any trial of the charges
the precise nature of which we are left to conjecture.

Wycliffe and the Papacy. Steps had, however, been already taken to bring Wycliffe's
obnoxious opinions before the Pope; and in May, Gregory XI.,
who had just restored the seat of the Papacy to Rome,
executed five bulls reciting eighteen erroneous articles found
in Wycliffe's writings, in which if he persisted he was to be
placed in confinement to await the Pope's sentence. The
articles are substantially accurate quotations from the treatise
Of Civil Lordship, which itself embodied courses of lectures
delivered at Oxford. They turn upon the questions of Church
endowments, and whether the State has power to take them
away; of excommunication, within what limits it may be
lawfully denounced; of the authority of the Holy See, how
far it is conditioned by the personal worthiness of its occupant.
Wycliffe was charged with the errors of Marsiglio of Padua, the
champion of the Imperial contest against Pope John XXII.;
and the charge is, in effect, historically true, although
it is likely that Wycliffe learned them not from Marsiglio
but from his more scholastic fellow-worker, Ockham. The
doctrine of Evangelical Poverty which they had set against
the worldly magnificence of the Avignon Papacy, combined
with FitzRalph's independently worked-out theory of lordship,

Cope.

Pulpit.

Wycliffe Bibles.

Table.

Chair.

MEMORIALS OF WYCLIFFE AT LUTTERWORTH CHURCH.

furnished well-nigh the sum-total of Wycliffe's views as to the nature and conditions of the spiritual power.

Gregory XI.'s bulls were addressed to the king, to the ecclesiastical authorities, and to the University of Oxford. They reached England at an inconvenient moment. Edward III. had died on the 21st June, and the Princess of Wales, who presided over the government on behalf of the young king, appears to have been not less well disposed towards Wycliffe than was John of Gaunt, who was himself excluded from the new council. As soon as Parliament met, Wycliffe was asked to give his opinion as to the right of refusing to allow treasure to pass out of the country even at the Pope's command; and his answer is still preserved. As a matter of precaution, however, he was enjoined to keep silence on the subject. On the question of the Papal condemnation he was far from desiring to keep silence. He drew up a statement of defence on the articles incriminated, which he laid before the House; and though no immediate steps were taken by the government for his protection, it is impossible to read the account of the various proceedings in his case which followed, without being persuaded that, however greatly John of Gaunt had excited public hostility, and to whatever extent a share of this hostility might have been expected to fall upon his ally, Wycliffe at this juncture enjoyed in no small measure the support and confidence of Englishmen.

If the bulls against the popular Oxford teacher were received with slight favour at the Court, still less ready was his University to act upon them; and its reluctance was increased when the Archbishop of Canterbury and the Bishop of London issued a mandate to the Chancellor requiring that Wycliffe's opinions should be examined by the Oxford divines, and that he should himself be sent up for trial in London. The University thought for a moment of standing upon its privileges and refusing to receive the bull at all. It finally decided to order Wycliffe to keep within the walls of Black Hall, where he resided, while the question of his opinions was being examined. The report was substantially in his favour; his views, it affirmed, were correct, though expressed in terms liable to be misunderstood: so little inclined was the University to take up charges brought from without against one of its members.

Early in 1378 Wycliffe went to be heard in person before the bishops at Lambeth Palace; but the Princess of Wales anticipated the issue by sending a messenger the day before, commanding them not to deliver sentence, and when Wycliffe actually appeared with a written defence expressed in some respects in more guarded language than he had hitherto used, there appeared also in his support a body of London citizens, with the rabble at their heels. It was impossible to proceed, and the bishops could do no more than proffer a mild request that Wycliffe would avoid discussing the obnoxious propositions. Thus Wycliffe was rescued by the London mob thirsting, as it seems, for the plunder of the Church. He was now looked upon no longer as the mere adherent of the hated Duke of Lancaster, but as the champion of the national rights of the Church in opposition to the encroachments, as they were deemed, of the Papacy.

Still, Wycliffe had not at all abandoned his support of John of Gaunt, and in the course of the year he was called upon, and he consented, to undertake his defence in a highly questionable cause. Two knights had escaped from the Tower of London, in which they were imprisoned for refusing to deliver up a prisoner whose release the Duke demanded, and had taken refuge in the sanctuary at Westminster. Thither the Duke sent a band of armed men to recapture them, and in the fray which ensued one of the two was slain and the other taken prisoner. The Bishop of London thundered excommunications, and John, to elude the hostility of the Londoners, had to contrive that Parliament that autumn should meet at Gloucester. Here it was Wycliffe who supplied him with a set defence. In a state-paper which he afterwards incorporated in his book *On the Church,* he did not attempt to excuse the homicide, but he maintained strenuously the expediency of the violation of the sanctuary. He was so far in the right that the licence of asylum was open to frequent abuse; but the debatable antecedents of the case, apart from the violence with which it was attended made it difficult to defend on general grounds of principle.

Wycliffe as a Religious Reformer.

The same year, 1378, marks a crisis in Wycliffe's life. The Papacy had been restored to Rome in 1377, and now, on the death of Gregory XI., a double election took place. Urban VI. was chosen Pope on April 7th; but the French cardinals, desirous of being ruled by a Pontiff of their own race, with the further hope of returning to their beloved Avignon, declared the election void, and in September set up an antipope, Clement VII., who re-established the seat of his Papacy at Avignon. The Great Schism thus begun lasted for more than forty years, two lines of Popes reigning side by side in irreconcilable hostility. The allegiance of the various nations was divided, and while England adhered to the Roman Pope, France, except for a short interval, steadily acknowledged his rival at Avignon. The shock caused to the fidelity of Christendom acted with momentous force upon Wycliffe. Long critical of the immense range of the Pope's authority, he now came seriously to question its rightness altogether, and soon became its declared opponent. It is probable that he now set himself with all his might to the task of spreading his teaching broadcast among the English people. For this purpose he made use of two agencies, the plan and execution of which constitute his principal claim to honourable remembrance. He sent out a number of "simple priests," or "poor preachers," and he supplied them with an English Bible to direct their teaching. It is possible that the beginning of the work reaches back to an earlier time; but the Schism gives the date at which Wycliffe found it more than ever necessary to make his reforms widely popular. At the outset the poor preachers no more than the earliest Friars conflicted with the parish clergy: the object was to teach the simple truths of the Gospel to those who were strangers to them. And in this promoting of the English language Wycliffe but went in harmony with the general impulse of his day, in which he had support in the example of high dignitaries both in Church and State. But when the preachers passed from their plain expositions to criticism and denunciation of what they deemed to be evils in the existing system of the Church, jealousy and strife were inevitable.

Wycliffe's Bible.

The translation of the Bible made by Wycliffe and his disciples—the first complete version in English—gave their

efforts powerful assistance, as it became widely diffused and
read ; for texts were ready at hand, and were eagerly caught
up, which told in favour of simplicity and unworldliness, and

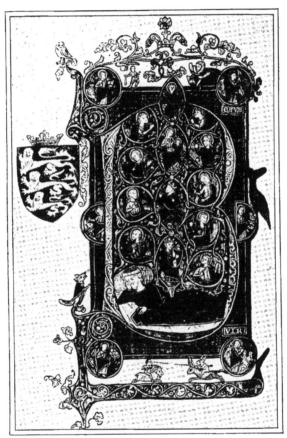

MINIATURE FROM A WYCLIFFE BIBLE (MS. Arundel 104).

rebuked the pomp and pride of endowments. In the meanwhile Wycliffe sent his message home by a multitude of short,
pithy tracts and sermons, in which he summed up the conclusions at which he had arrived in his ponderous and formal

Latin treatises.   His activity in the closing years of his life is almost incredible, since there is reason to believe that in seven or eight years, besides the translation of the Bible, he not only wrote nearly all his English works, but completed or revised a good half of his Latin writings, which may be estimated to fill at least thirty solid volumes of print.

Wycliffe Attacks Church Doctrine. Working thus upon the popular mind, and turning his attack now no longer against the endowed clergy and monks only, but also against his former allies the friars, he became by degrees persuaded that the root of the evils in the Church was to be found in the priestly power, and thus was led to assail the speaking symbol of that power contained in the doctrine of Transubstantiation.   It was the power, he felt, of "making the body of Christ" that declared most evidently the authority of the priest and contradicted most decisively that rule of equality among all Christian men, for which he found Scriptural evidence.   If he could once disprove the accredited position with regard to the Sacrament, the way was clear for the general reform of the Church system on the lines for which he earnestly strove; and thus in the summer of 1380 he ventured to make his public declaration that the elements in the sacrament of the altar suffered no *material* change by virtue of the words of consecration. He denied not the real presence of the body and blood of Christ, only the change of substance in the Host.   He promulgated the heresy in Oxford itself, and the Chancellor of the University, William Berton, lost no time in summoning a body of theologians and jurists to take action upon it. The doctrine was unhesitatingly condemned, but no better evidence could be desired of the high academic reputation which its author held, than the fact that in this decree his name was not mentioned.   Wycliffe at once appealed to the king, and John of Gaunt in hot haste sent a messenger to Oxford urging him to silence on the obnoxious subject.

In the following year, 1381, the rising of the peasants in the eastern parts of England might seem to point but too plainly to the unsettling influence of Wycliffe's teaching.   But such an inference is not sufficiently warranted by the facts.   There were reasons in the social condition of England to furnish an adequate account for the rebellion without the need of going further; and the circumstance that the insurgents vented their wrath especially against the Duke of Lancaster may be taken to offer a strong presumption that Wycliffe had no direct hand in inspiring the revolt. Still, his communistic views, however he might himself guard them with reservations, were only too well adapted to fan the flames of plunder when disseminated by less scrupulous disciples.

Archbishop Sudbury was one of the victims of the rising: his successor, Courtenay, a man of more resolute character, showed himself prompt in taking action against the doctrine which it was now impossible to let pass without a public challenge. He called a synod to inquire into the charges of false teaching at Oxford, which was held at the Blackfriars' convent in London—on the site of the present printing-office of the *Times* newspaper—on the 17th May, 1382. An earthquake, which troubled its first session and gave a name to the council, was joyfully interpreted by the Wycliffites as a manifest token of the Divine wrath. The heresy touching the sacrament was forthwith condemned, but here again no condemnation was uttered against Wycliffe himself; and we can only guess that now, as at Lambeth four years before, the influence of the Court was exerted to protect one who had proved so valuable a servant, or else that his personal ascendency at Oxford was too great for it to be prudent to attack him. In support of the former view we may note that, just before the sitting of the council, he had no fear of addressing a powerful memorial to Parliament in support of far-reaching reforms in the Church. Still, while he himself escaped, unnamed and unsentenced, rigorous measures were taken against his followers. We are told, indeed, that he was afterwards tried by a council held by Courtenay at Oxford, and that he abjured his doctrine; but this statement is accompanied by the professing text of his recantation, which is in fact a reassertion in English of the condemned doctrine: so that the story, which is otherwise unconfirmed, has in all probability arisen from a confused report of the Earthquake Council and the subsequent recantations of Wycliffe's disciples.

Nevertheless, his party at Oxford had received a heavy blow, from which it was some time in recovering; and it is likely that the leader, who was now rapidly aging, quitted the scene of his lifelong labours, and withdrew to the tranquillity of his Leicestershire rectory. Not his courage, but his physical strength was failing. Yet he continued restlessly engaged in writing. The crusade undertaken in 1383 by the Bishop of Norwich against the adherents of the antipope, Clement VII., in Flanders, roused anew all his old fire, and he poured forth tract after tract in English and Latin, not merely against the lavish misuse of money in that futile enterprise, but also in defence of all the reforms in doctrine and practice on which his heart was set. The disaster of the crusade told strongly in his favour, and Pope Urban deemed it necessary to summon him to appear at Rome. But Wycliffe was already

His Death. crippled by a paralytic stroke, and the journey, even had he been willing to take it, was impossible. He laboured on at Lutterworth until the 28th December 1384, when he was seized, while hearing mass, with a final stroke, and died two days later. He was buried in peace at Lutterworth. Nearly half a century later, in 1428, in execution of a decree of the Council of Constance passed in 1415, his remains were taken up and cast out. But his work was done; and if in England by that date his school had almost ceased to exist, he left behind him in Bohemia a tradition which, through the animating influence of Hus, penetrated a nation and stirred it to a heroic resistance to the forces of Catholic Christianity.

C. W. C.
OMAN.
The Art
of War.
THE hundred years of war which commence with the struggle of Edward III. and Philip of Valois, and end with the expulsion of Henry VI.'s troops from France in 1453, were the time of the military supremacy of the English archer. The use which Edward I. had made of archery had not been lost upon his grandson, and it was by the arrows of his yeomen more than by the spears of his knights that the third Edward won his successes. His Scottish victory of Halidon Hill was purely an archers' battle; the English horse were hardly engaged, and the bowmen alone riddled and turned to flight the great masses of Albany's pikemen.

In the number of mailed horse that she could put into the field, England could never have vied with France, now that France had become a large and united kingdom, instead of the small State with which Henry II. and Richard I. had contended. The French habitually took the field with four or five times as many cavalry as the English. On the other **Archery.** hand, the English archery were a force to which France had nothing to oppose. By the fourteenth century they had attained a fearful efficiency : both in length of range and in penetrating force the arrow had a power which it would be hard to credit, were it not for the universal testimony of the chroniclers as to its doings. The cloth-yard shaft had a range of quite three hundred yards, and at this distance could pierce everything that was not covered with good armour. At shorter range it could penetrate even plate-armour and the complicated coverings laid one over the other which formed the knightly panoply. We hear of breastplates pierced, of steel caps nailed to the owner's head, of leg and arm coverings easily shot through. It is true that his armour was still of much use to the knight: unless the shaft struck straight and fair it would probably glance off plate, though it would go through mail. But the one most certain way of disabling the horseman was to shoot at his horse, and this the archer soon learnt to do. The charger was either unprotected, or only partially covered on head and breast by iron plates ; he was a large mark, and an easy one. The killing and wounding of a proportion of its horses wrecked the charge of any body of knights. Those that fell broke the line, but far worse were those that had received a wound, who turned off, plunging to right and left "with the arrows jangling in them," carried their unwilling masters off the field, and checked or overthrew even those whose horses had been more fortunate. Froissart tells us how the front of a charging squadron often went down entire, man and horse, when it received the first flight of arrows at short range. The wounded were more numerous than the dead, and many were not even wounded, but the sudden check and confusion brought down the horses, and threw the unwieldy knights out of their saddles, so that the whole line became a confused heap of plunging and kicking horses and men, striving with more or less success to get to their feet again. After a few volleys and a few ineffectual attempts to close, the whole field in front of the line of archers was loaded with such a wreck of dead and wounded men and horses that succeeding squadrons could not get a fair ground to charge over.

It was the misfortune of France that the French infantry had never been noted for their skill in the use of missile weapons. The dismounted part of a French army were either the militia of the towns equipped with spear and mail-cap —as the English militia had been in the twelfth century—or the rude levies of the country-side armed with the miscellaneous weapons that had once been seen in the hands of the old English levy, or foreign mercenaries—Genoese crossbowmen, and Biscayan or Gascon javelin-men. But the French kings had never attached any importance to their foot-soldiery. As Froissart says, speaking of the days before Crécy, " they never used to count anything more than the number of *heaumes couronnés* " (crested helmets) of knightly horsemen that followed them.

A KNIGHT OF 1347.
(*Wimbish, Essex.*)

If Edward III. and the Black Prince had endeavoured to cope with their adversaries by leading charges of mailed horse against them, disaster only could have followed. The French were as gallant as and far more numerous than the English knighthood. It was the want of a sufficient force of cavalry that compelled them to give battle in a new style, acting on the defensive and making the infantry the more important element in the line of battle. The sole weak point of the archery was that, if unprotected on the wings, they might be taken at disadvantage and rolled up by cavalry assailing them from the flank. This was what had happened on the disastrous field of Bannockburn, where the archers, ill-placed,

and not aided by the cavalry, had been taken in flank
by Bruce's small body of horse and driven off the field.
The cavalry, unaided by bowmen, had been proved unable
to break the Scottish squares, and had finally grown demoralised and fled.

Edward III. never committed the fault of leaving his
archery unsupported, or of employing cavalry without first
preparing the way for them by the fire of his bowmen. His

Edward
III. as a
Tactician:
Crécy.

methods may be best illustrated by
his management of the battle of Crécy.
There the English line was composed
of two divisions, commanded respectively
by the Prince of Wales and the Earl
of Northampton.   In each about two
thousand archers and eight hundred
men-at-arms were placed.   The archers
were drawn up in wedge-shaped formation, "like a (triangular) harrow,"
as Froissart expresses it.   Between the
wedges and on the flanks of them
were the men-at-arms, a little drawn
back, *au fond de la bataille.*   The
king kept in second line a reserve
of two thousand archers and seven
hundred lances, while between the
two lines were scattered in small
bodies somewhat more than a thousand
Welsh and Cornish light infantry,
armed with javelins and long knives.
The position was on the slope of a
gentle hill crowned by a windmill, and
was covered at each end by two
villages with enclosures, which made
flank attacks difficult.

A KNIGHT OF 1365.
(*Cobham, Kent.*)

For the first time in English history, Edward made the majority of
his knights and men-at-arms dismount.   The sixteen
hundred horsemen in the front line all sent their horses
to the rear and acted in serried clumps as heavy infantry.
So the line was composed alternately of triangular bodies of

archery, and smaller squares of dismounted knights using the long lance. Only the seven hundred men-at-arms in the reserve remained on horseback.

Philip of Valois brought against the nine or ten thousand English an army at least five or six times as strong, and comprising as many mailed horsemen as Edward had troops of every sort. His front of battle, hastily and unevenly formed—for the fight was forced on against his wish by the ardour of the knights in his van division—was in four successive lines: first a vanguard of Genoese crossbowmen, then a line of squadrons

CROSSBOWMEN (MS. Roy. 16 G. vi.).

of mailed horsemen under the Counts of Flanders and Alençon. then in the third and fourth lines the rest of the horse and the unwieldy and ill-armed bodies of communal militia on foot.

The battle began with the rout of the Genoese, whose crossbows could make no impression whatever on the English line. The archers gave them back six arrows for every bolt, being able to let fly again and again while the Italians were winding up their clumsy weapons for a single shot. Moreover the arrow had a longer range than the cross-bow, and a not less penetrating power. Even had they not had the additional disadvantage of going into battle with their bowstrings relaxed by rain, the crossbowmen could not have held their ground for long. But the really instructive and epoch-making incident of Crécy came when the second "battle" of French knights pushed to the front, riding through or over the routed Genoese. It had not yet been guessed that a line of archers would be able to stop a cavalry charge well pushed home, but this was now seen to be the case. Horses and men went down in heaps, a barrier of dead and wounded built itself up before the English front, and it was only here and there that small bodies of men, or even individual knights, were able to thrust themselves through the quivering mass, and close with the English men-at-arms who stood in support of the archery. Those who got to handstrokes with the dismounted knights were soon disposed of, while the rest, unwilling to retire and unable to advance, surged for some hours along the English front, seeking in vain to close, and losing more and more heavily from

ANELACE.
(*Guildhall
Museum.*)

the archery as their masses grew more and more congested and helpless. Between the attacks the Welsh light in-fantry ran out from the intervals of the English line, and butchered the dismounted men strug-gling to gain their feet and get to the rear.

Without having moved a foot from their first position, the English slew off a quarter of the French host; and at last the whole mass turned bridle and rode off the hopeless field, to the great wrath of Philip of Valois, who still wished to continue the battle.

Crécy was an epoch-making field in the history

Photo: York & Son, Notting Hill, W.

SWORD AND SHIELD CARRIED BEFORE EDWARD III. AT CRÉCY.

(*Beside the Coronation Chair, Westminster Abbey.*)

of the art of war. It led to the discrediting of the use of cavalry charges all over Western Europe, much as the result of Sempach did in Central Europe. On the English side it inaugurated the regular use of the man-at-arms as a dismounted soldier to cover the archery from flank attacks. For the future the English knighthood habitually sent their horses to the rear and shared the fortunes of the yeomanry on foot. For a hundred years our armies always endeavoured to receive battle under the same conditions as at Crécy, in a good position with flanks covered by wood, marsh, or houses, and with an array composed of archery, interspersed with bodies of dismounted men-at-arms.

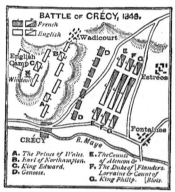

A. *The Prince of Wales.*
B. *Earl of Northampton.*
C. *King Edward.*
D. *Genoese.*
E. *The Counts of Alencon &*
F. *The Duke of Lorraine & Count of*
G. *King Philip.* [*Blois.*
[*Flanders.*

(From Oman's *" History of England"*: Edward Arnold.)

On the French side Crécy led to an even greater revolution in the art of war. . Finding that he could not close, because his horse would infallibly be killed if he tried to ride in, the French knight, like the English, resolved to try his fortune on foot. When next the nations met in pitched battle at Poitiers, in 1356 the French king bade all his knights, save a picked vanguard and two small wings, to dismount, send their horses to the rear, cut short their long lances to six feet only, and advance on foot.

The inspiration was not a happy one on the part of King John, for at Poitiers (or rather Maupertuis as we ought to call the field) the English were in position on a rough hill-side covered by vines and brushwood, and protected by lines of hedge. A dismounted knight was not suited for scrambling up a slope among tangled underwood. The vanguard of mounted men tried to get at the English through a gap in the hedge which covered their line, and were shot down by the archers who lined the front. The first line rolled slowly up-hill, and actually got to handstrokes with the English, but was beaten back. They fell back on the second line and threw it in disorder. Then the

Black Prince made his men-at-arms mount and ride down into the confused mass, while a detached body, who had circumvented a wood to the side, came down and charged the French in flank. The result was crushing : the main body of the French took to their heels, got back to their horses and fled. Only the king's division in the third line stayed to fight, and were riddled with archery, and then trampled down by a charge of horse.

The spirit of the French chivalry was so damped by the result of their second endeavour to cope with the English archery and dismounted men-at-arms, that for some years they never accepted another battle in the open field, but shut themselves up in towns and castles, and suffered their enemies to march through the length and breadth of the land without having to risk an engagement. They fell back, in fact, on the superiority of the defensive over the offensive in the art of fortification which had continued ever since the eleventh century. In 1373 the Earl of Lancaster was allowed to cross the whole of France, from Calais to Bordeaux, and to pass by the very gates of Paris without being assaulted. The policy of this abstinence on the part of the French was justified by the event—hunger, fatigue, and the cutting off of stragglers harmed Lancaster's army far more than a pitched battle would probably have done.

The only occasion on which the English got the opportunity of fighting an engagement on a large scale in these times was at the Spanish battle of Najera or Navarette. The usual results followed ; the Spaniards of Henry of Trastramara were

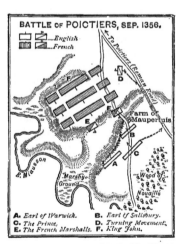

A. *Earl of Warwick.* B. *Earl of Salisbury.*
C. *The Prince,* D. *Turning Movement,*
E. *The French Marshalls.* F. *King John.*

(*From Oman's " History of England " : Edward Arnold.*)

still accustomed to fighting on horseback, and only a small part of the army, moved by the councils of the French auxiliaries who served in their ranks, dismounted and fought on foot. When the fighting began, the Spanish wings, where the horse were placed, were shot down by the hundred and soon left the field, while the only obstinate resistance was made by the phalanx of knights on foot in the centre, who took some hard strokes before they were surrounded and overborne.

The
English
Decline.
In the last years of Edward III., when the English cause fared so badly in France, the ill-success which followed the great

KNIGHTS AT POITIERS (MS. Sloane 2433).

victories of earlier years was not brought about by any marked decline of the efficiency of the English, but by the cautious defensive tactics of their adversaries, and the exhaustion in England, due to the long protraction of the war. The English ranks were more and more filled up with foreign auxiliaries, Flemings, Germans, Gascons, and the invincible archery made a small proportion in the host. But the reduction of the war to a series of long bickerings round fortresses was the thing that harassed the English most. The tactics of Bertrand de Guesclin, who was the soul of the French army, were to assault the small outlying garrisons on the frontier of Guienne. If left alone he took them, if a relieving army marched against him he made off, and laid siege to some distant stronghold where he was least expected. He fought by night surprises, ambuscades, escalades, and stratagems of all descriptions, but seldom or never in engagements in the open field. This system wore away the strength of the English, who were better suited for winning great battles than for carrying on long and harassing campaigns.

If the fourteenth century represents in the line of tactics in the open field the victory of the defensive over the offensive, of

ARMOUR ABOUT 1380 (MS. Add. 29,704).

the line of archers and dismounted men-at-arms over the **The Art of Attack.** charging squadron, it represents in the line of fortification the beginning of the opposite tendency—of the victory of the offensive over the defensive. Castle-building had arrived at its highest pitch of perfection in England about the time of Edward I., and magnificent works like Carnarvon and Caerphilly represent the triumph of the builder over the engineer's attack. But in the reign of his grandson England saw for the first time the employment of the new engine which was ultimately to reduce the embattled castle to impotence. It was in the second quarter of the century that gunpowder first began to be used in Europe; first in Italy, shortly afterwards in France, and then in

Cannon.

England. The first cannons—smaller firearms came in much later—were rude iron or brass engines, sometimes molten in a piece, but often made of bars welded together round a core, afterwards removed, and hooped about with rings to keep them together. They were small, slow in fire, and very liable to accidents. The cast guns often burst from a flaw in the metal; the hooped guns still more frequently flew to pieces and scattered destruction around. The English reader will remember a typical disaster of the kind in the explosion of the hooped gun which burst into its component parts and slew James II. of Scotland at the siege of Roxburgh. Another cause of the comparative feebleness of artillery in its first days was the badness of its powder; the right proportions for mixing the saltpetre, sulphur,

THE OLD ARTILLERY: A TRÉBUCHET. (MS. 264).
(Bodleian Library, Oxford.)

and charcoal had not yet been quite settled, and the impurity of the saltpetre which the chemists of the day produced was a perpetual hindrance.

Still, when once cannon had been introduced into warfare the offensive found itself in possession of a weapon which placed it on quite a new footing as regards the defensive, and as years went on the advantage grew more marked, for cannon and powder gradually improved. Slow as was their fire—three shots an hour was fair practice for a big bombard—and comparatively weak as was the impact of their stone balls, they were yet able to beat down a castle wall, if they could be brought near enough, and enabled to play long enough upon it. The mangonels and perrières and rams of a preceding age had never had any such decisive effect. When the attacking party nad once taken to employing guns against the besieged place, the defenders soon found that the counter-use of artillery was their best protection. Guns were, when practicable, mounted on the walls and directed on the artillery of the attack, so as to overpower its fire, beat down the mantlets and palisades erected to cover it, and disable its gunners. But two things hampered the defensive use of cannon: the old town and castle walls were not, as a rule, sufficiently broad and strong to provide a secure platform for artillery, and even if the guns could be hoisted up, the attack could always concentrate more fire on a given space than the defence. The narrowness of the old walls was, however, the chief hindrance; the recoil of the discharged gun tended to

THE OLD ARTILLERY: A SPRINGALD. (MS. 264).
(*Bodleian Library, Oxford.*)

throw it over; or if to avoid this the gun was fixed to its place, a few discharges began to loosen the stones of the wall and weakened the defence even more than the fire of the attack. In early days we hear of several occasions when the besieged had to slacken or cease their discharge of cannon because of the harm it was doing them.

The earliest record of the use of guns in the Hundred Years' War was on the French side; a fleet told off in 1348 to attack Southampton having been provided, as French archives show, with a *pot de fer*, and three pounds of powder (a not very magnificent provision!) for shooting iron bolts. Later in the same year a French Treasurer-for-War is found providing *poudres et canons* for the siege of the little English fort of Puy

Guilliem in Guienne. The English were not much later in applying the all-important invention. In 1344 Thomas de Roldeston appears in charge of "the king's engines," and is directed to make powder for them. Three years later the same Thomas was ordered "to buy at once all the saltpetre and sulphur he could find for sale," to make into powder. He could only get together 700 pounds of the former at eighteenpence the pound, and 310 pounds of the latter at eightpence.

The one chronicler—Villani—who states that the English brought a few cannons into the field at Crécy, "which threw little iron balls and frightened the horses," is probably wrong. No English source mentions them; their use was only just commencing for siege purposes in the armies of Edward III.; and their employment in the open field does not seem to have been contemplated. It is, on the other hand, quite probable that Froissart is correct when, in the next year, 1347, he states that King Edward placed some bombards in the fort which formed the central point of his lines of investment round Calais; cannon were used in position long before they became mobile and suited for the open field. But even in great fortresses guns were still very few; the Tower of London in 1360 mounted only four, all of brass; and ten years later Calais, now become

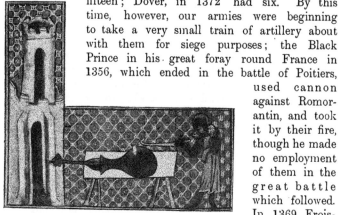

the chief of English strongholds, had but fifteen; Dover, in 1372 had six. By this time, however, our armies were beginning to take a very small train of artillery about with them for siege purposes; the Black Prince in his great foray round France in 1356, which ended in the battle of Poitiers, used cannon against Romorantin, and took it by their fire, though he made no employment of them in the great battle which followed. In 1369 Froissart tells us

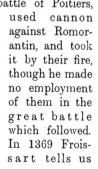

THE EARLIEST REPRESENTATION OF A CANNON.
(*By permission of the Dean and Governing Body, Christchurch, Oxford.*)

CAPTURE OF CALAIS. (*Lambeth Palace Library.*)

[*To face p. 246.*]

T

SPRINGALD.
(Bodleian Library, Oxford.)

EARLY CANNON AND SPRINGALD.
(Bodleian Library, Oxford)

that Sir John Chandos was *accustomed* to take about
"cannons and springalds" with his host, which implies that
the usage had come habitual.   But these were, as before,
for siege work; it is not till the fifteenth century that we
find them employed in the field; we believe that we are not
wrong in stating that Northampton was the first English battle
where they were so used by native generals, and Formigny the
first where they were used against us.   In all the chief fights
of that century—Agincourt, Verneuil, Cravant, Patay, St. Albans,
Towton, we find none.   At Châtillon and Formigny the French
used them to some effect; in the Wars of the Roses they were
brought into use at Northampton—where their discharge was
entirely frustrated by the rain—Barnet and Tewkesbury, but had
a decisive effect on none of these battles.   The only one among
those which we have cited where they really influenced the
event of the day was at Châtillon, where they were used
from a carefully entrenched position, and proved effective
in mowing down crowded charging columns who assaulted
their front.

But the day of field artillery had not yet arrived.   The
characteristics of the fifteenth century, as well as of the
fourteenth, were the predominance of the archer and the dismounted man-at-arms in the battlefield; the ever-increasing
efficiency of artillery was only felt in sieges.

W. LAIRD
CLOWES.
The
Navy.
EDWARD III. and his family brought the English Navy to a
pitch of glory such as it had never before attained.   The king
himself, the Black Prince, and the king's fourth son. John of
Gaunt, repeatedly fought at sea, and by their supervision, as
well as by their presence, benefited alike the general development and the spirit of the Service.   Not undeservedly was
Edward given by his subjects the title of "King of the Sea";
yet, owing to his Majesty's strange misapprehension of the real
power of his country, and to his conviction, especially in later
life, that the conquering mission of England had before it on
land an even finer field than it had upon the waves, Edward's
great naval victories produced no lasting direct results, and at
the close of his long reign, his fleet, neglected for the sake of
his army, had fallen into absolute decay.   For many years,

however, the reign was one of steady naval progress, and of magnificent maritime successes. The battles of Sluys (or the Swyn), when the French fleet was almost annihilated, and of "Les Espagnols sur Mer," when the Spaniards were crushingly defeated, were victories which in any age would have been remarkable, and which could not but exert immense influence upon the ambitions and future policy of the race that won them, and that then, for the first time, learnt to know its power.

In Edward's time the narrow seas were far better policed than in the days of any of his ancestors, and piracy in consequence decreased, but it did not altogether disappear, nor were the coasts completely protected against hostile raids. About the year 1338, persons who had goods and chattels near the sea were directed to remove them for safety a distance of four leagues inland. In 1339 a French squadron appeared at Southampton and summoned the town to surrender, but withdrew without effecting its purpose. Later in the same year a body of French pirates burnt some fishermen's huts at Hastings, and alarmed Dover and Folkestone, while another body entered the port of Plymouth and burnt some ships there. Reprisals were, however, promptly undertaken by the English, who entered the port of Boulogne, captured several vessels, hung up a dozen French captains, and burnt part of the town. Indeed, though the English coasts were harried much, the French coasts were probably the greater sufferers. The king more than once specifically reasserted the British claim to the dominion of the seas, and, it must be admitted, did more than any of his predecessors to substantiate it. So long as he persisted in this policy, trade flourished, but after 1360 the sea-borne commerce of the country greatly declined; and the English naval disasters of 1372 and 1375 placed it, for many years afterwards, in a most precarious position. But that these disasters occurred and went unavenged was the fault of the Government rather than of the maritime spirit of the people. In 1360, a most disgraceful order was promulgated and sent to all the ports directing that every vessel should be drawn up high on shore at a considerable distance from the water, so as to save her from the French, who were known to be in force at sea; yet, in that year, Nicholas of Lynn (or Lymne), a friar of Oxford and a good astronomer, is reported, in company with some other persons, to have made a voyage of discovery towards the North Pole (p. 483). He is said to have made his discoveries "by magic arts," for which we may, perhaps, read "exceptional skill in navigation." Whether the report of his having undertaken the expedition is deserving of credit cannot now be ascertained; but there is nothing antecedently improbable in it, and, if we accept it, we must place the name of Friar Nicholas at the head of the golden roll of Arctic explorers, the greatest of whom have been Nicholas's countrymen. Unfortunately, no account of the voyage remains.

Before the king left England, after the renewal of war with France in 1359, a measure which, at a later period of English history, had important developments, was adopted. In order to protect the national trade, the Council, with the consent of the native and foreign merchants who were summoned before it, but without the assent of Parliament, imposed a tax of sixpence in the pound on all merchandise imported or exported, so that a fleet might be maintained at sea. Another point of marine law that deserves notice is that from the records of certain proceedings of 1371 it appears that neutral ships carrying the property of the belligerent States of France and Spain were held liable to seizure, and that, in other words, free bottoms did not make free goods.

The Black Book of the Admiralty. From the reign of Edward III. dates that most valuable record of ancient naval manners and customs, the "Black Book of the Admiralty," the more important contents of which are here summarised.

An Admiral after receiving his commission, was immediately to appoint lieutenants, deputies, and other officers, who were to be well acquainted with the law and the ancient customs of the sea. He was then to ascertain from them the number and sizes of all the ships, barges, balingers, and other vessels in the ports, and the names of their owners. The deputies were also to discover by inquiry how many seamen available for defensive purposes were in the realm, so that the king might always know his force at sea. When a fleet was ordered to be equipped, the admiral, if a knight, was to be paid four shillings a day; if a baron, six shillings and eightpence; and if an earl, eight shillings and fourpence. For each knight in his retinue he was

A PAGE FROM THE "BLACK BOOK OF THE ADMIRALTY" (MS. Vesp. B. xxii.).

allowed two shillings; and for each esquire armed, one shilling; for thirty men-at-arms, £66 13s. 4d. a quarter; and for each archer sixpence a day. He was to take measures for the proper administration of justice in all cases brought before him, " according to the law and ancient custom of the sea "; for which purposes, and to assist him in the performance of his other duties, the king's letters were sent to mayors, sheriffs, and other officers, enjoining them to be obedient to him and his deputies.

As soon as a fleet was collected, the admiral was to choose the best ship for the king, or for the king's lieutenant, and this ship was called " the king's chamber." If the king himself were present, the next best ships were to be selected by the steward of the household—one for " the hall," in which presumably councils were held; one for " the wardrobe," or royal storeship; one for " the larder," and a fourth for " the kitchen "; and, if necessary, still other ships were to be taken by the steward. Should a son, a brother, or an uncle of the king be present, a good ship was to be provided for him. Before the admiral selected a ship for himself, he was to provide accommodation for the lords and captains about to be embarked, and for their stores. Every master and every constable of a ship was to be paid sixpence, and each mariner threepence-halfpenny a day, with an additional sixpence a week as a " reward "; and every " sea-boy " was to receive three-halfpence (some copies erroneously say twopence-halfpenny) a day; but for masters, constables, and boys, there was no fixed " reward."

Since the admiral was the commander of the sailors, and was bound to support them in all their laws and customs, to defend them, and, if needful, to sue for their wages, he was awarded fourpence out of every pound paid to them; for which fourpence he had, in return, to carry at his masthead at night while the fleet was at sea, two lanterns, in order that the masters might know what course he was steering. If the king were in the fleet, the admiral was to approach his ship every evening, and to take the royal commands as to the course to be steered during the ensuing twenty-four hours. If the king were not present, the same deference was to be paid to his lieutenant. The other ships were then to assemble round the admiral to learn the royal directions. At night the king's ship, or that of his lieutenant, was to be distinguished by three large lanterns arranged triangle-wise, but more lanterns might, if his Majesty pleased, be carried. A vice-admiral was to carry one lantern. The station of the Vice-Admiral of the West extended from the Thames to the south-west, and while upon it he might carry two lanterns, as might the Vice-Admiral of the North when to the northward and eastward of the Thames; but one of the vice-admirals, when on the station of the other, was to carry only one

WARSHIP LEAVING PORT (MS. Roy. 20 C. v.)

lantern. If the admiral desired to call together the captains and masters of the fleet in order to consult them, he was to hoist half-mast high " a banner of council," on seeing which they were to go on board in their boats.

All goods taken from the enemy by persons receiving the king's wages were to be divided into four parts, of which the king took one, and the owners of the ships another. The remaining moiety was to be thus divided: to the admiral, if present at the capture, two shares; if not present, one share; to others present, the rest, the share being, of course, proportionate to the numbers engaged. Of property taken by seamen not in the king's service, the king was to receive no part; but the admiral was to receive as before.

No man, when in an enemy's ship or country, was to touch the Holy Sacrament upon pain of being drawn and hanged, nor to commit sacrilege or rape upon pain of death. No master was to " cross his sail aloft," until the admiral had done so; but upon the admiral doing so, all vessels were to follow suit. Similarly no vessel was to anchor until the admiral had anchored; and when he had done so, all vessels were to anchor as close to him as they conveniently could. At sea, also, they were to keep as close to him as possible; and no ship was to enter or leave a port by day or by night without his permission. When a ship sighted an enemy at sea she was to hoist a banner. If any ship were permitted to leave the fleet and meet a strange vessel, she was to examine her cargo and papers; and, should it appear that the stranger was, or contained, property belonging to the enemy, she and her master were to be carried before the admiral, who was to release her if a friend, and to keep her if an enemy, " according to the custom of the sea." Should any vessel offer resistance, she was to be treated as an enemy, and carried to the admiral, but not to be pillaged nor needlessly damaged. In the event of any ship being captured, no one was to presume to take her out of the fleet without the admiral's consent, upon pain of paying double her value. The captors of an enemy's vessel were entitled to the goods and armour on the hatches and upper deck, except the tackle and other things belonging to the ship's equipment, and except also what was exempted by the ancient customs and usages of the sea. No seaman was to be beaten or ill-used, but offenders were to be brought by the captain or master before the admiral, to receive such punishment as the law of the sea provided.

In case of the separation of a fleet by stress of weather, the masters were to follow the admiral to the best of their ability, upon pain of being considered rebels. On arriving in an enemy's port the admiral was to appoint a sufficient force to protect people sent for fresh water and other necessaries. When a castle or city was to be attacked, no one was to make an assault without the admiral's orders. Troops landed on an enemy's territory for provisions were not to proceed until the harbingers (scouts) had first returned to them. No place was to be set on

fire without the admiral s orders. Soldiers and mariners were not
to be landed unless accompanied by responsible officers, lest they
might commit excesses. No boat, after the fleet had sailed, was
to be sent back to a port without the admiral's permission. No
ship, "from, pride, envy, or hatred," was to injure another.
Search was to be made in ports for such thieves as stole
anchors, ropes, boats, etc. He who was convicted by a jury of
twelve persons of having stolen an anchor or a boat to the value
of twenty-one pence, was to be hanged. Anyone stealing a buoy-
rope attached to an anchor was to be hanged, no matter how
small might be its value. For cutting a ship's cable, the
penalty, in case any loss of life resulted, was death. If there
were no loss of life, the offender was to make good the damage
and to pay a fine to the king. If he were unable to do so, and
if the owners prosecuted, he was to be hanged; but in this event
he was not to be condemned at the king's suit, and there was
not to be "an appeal of battle." The same penalties were prescribed for weighing an anchor without informing the master or
crew, in case death, or the loss of the ship, resulted. If a sailor
were condemned to death for stealing the goods of aliens, the
aliens, if not enemies, were to have the goods restored, provided
that they did not insist upon the felon's execution. If a foreign
ship were plundered and the crew ill-used at any port, the
warden and six or eight of the leading persons of the port were
to be arrested until the admiral had ascertained by whom the
felony had been committed. If there were many ships in the
port, the admiral was to take the masters and "bursers" and
four of the crew, and to cause the ships to be searched until he
found the criminals, or was informed by whom the robbery had
been effected. Stealing an oar, anchor, or other small thing was
punishable, upon conviction by a jury, with imprisonment for
forty days; a second offence, with imprisonment for half a year;
and a third, with hanging. No lieutenant of an admiral could,
without a special warrant, try matters involving life and death.
Divers minor offences, which are specified, were punishable with
fine or imprisonment, or with both. If a man injured another
in a quarrel and was the beginner of the fray, he was not only
to make the other amends, but to pay to the king a fine of five
pounds, or lose the hand with which he struck the blow, unless
he obtained pardon from the king or the high admiral.

Offenders were, pending communication with the admiral, to be imprisoned by the master of the ship. The master was to be assisted on such an occasion by the crew, and anyone refusing assistance was liable to the same punishment as the original offender. Process in the admiral's court against an absconded prisoner is described, and is said to have been settled in the time of Henry I.

If any ship that had been impressed for the king's service broke away, and if a jury were satisfied of the fact, the vessel was to be forfeited. A seaman refusing to serve at sea was punishable with imprisonment for one year for the first offence, and for two years for the second. Contracts between merchant and merchant beyond sea, or within flood mark, were to be proclaimed before the admiral; and hue-and-cry or bloodshed within his jurisdiction was punishable with two years' imprisonment and a fine. Merchants having sometimes gone on board vessels entering a port to purchase the whole cargo, and having then sold it at a higher price than the original owners would have demanded, it was ordered that such offenders should be liable to imprisonment for half a year, and to a fine equal to the value of the cargo so purchased. The same penalties were awarded to purchasers in gross of corn, fish, and other provisions within flood-mark. If a warden of a port, or a water-bailiff levied unlawful customs, he was to be imprisoned and fined the amount so levied. If anyone sued a merchant or mariner for a matter cognisable by marine law, he was, upon conviction, to be fined. Goods found at sea as flotsam, or at the bottom of the sea, were to be reported to the admiral on pain of fine and surrender of the value of the goods. All deodands,[1] as gold or valuables, found on a man killed or drowned at sea belonged to the admiral, who was to employ one-half for the soul of the deceased and one-half for the benefit of the deceased's family, if any. Carpenters of ships taking extravagant salaries to the prejudice of shipping were to be fined at the admiral's discretion. The exportation of corn without special licence, except to Bayonne, Bordeaux, Brest, and Calais, was punished with a fine equal to the value of the corn.

[1 Any inanimate object which accidentally caused, or was associated with, the death of a human being, was "given to God"—in practice, forfeited to the Crown or one of its officers for religious uses.]

Cases in the Admiralty Court were, it is clear, always tried by jury; and a very extraordinary penalty was prescribed for the juryman who "discovered the king's counsel and that of his companions in a jury." His throat was to be cut and his tongue drawn out of his throat, and cut from his head.

In Edward's day carpenters and pursers seem to have first attained to the dignity of naval officers. Large vessels carried two carpenters, and as a carpenter received sixpence a day he was evidently regarded as an important person on board. The clerk, or "burser," received similar pay, which put

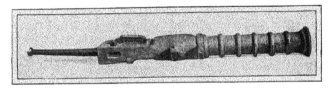

A PRIMITIVE BREECH-LOADING CANNON. (*Rotunda Museum, Woolwich.*)
(*By permission of the General Officer Commanding Woolwich District.*)

him on a level with the master and constable. All stores and provisions were placed under his charge; he sometimes provided them, and he also acted as ship's paymaster. A hint that, in certain circumstances, a kind of uniform was furnished is provided by a note in the wardrobe accounts, to the effect that the king gave the master, crew, and soldiers of his galley, the *Thomas*, a coat of ray-cloth, apiece.

The ships of the period are recorded to have been armed **Naval Armament.** with springalds, haubergeons, bacinets, bows, arrows, jacks, doublets, targets, pavises, lances, and "firing barrels." These last were, there is little doubt, guns of some kind; and the mention of them suggests a brief inquiry into the first adoption of cannon and gunpowder into the English Navy. "It is manifest," says Sir N. H. Nicolas, "that cannon made part of the armament of many ships as early as, and probably a few years before, 1338; that about 1372, guns and gunpowder were commonly used; that some guns were made of iron, some of brass, and others of copper; that there was a kind of hand-gun, as well as large cannon; and that gunpowder was formed of the same elements, and made nearly in the same manner, as at

61

present.   Among the stores of the hulk *Christopher of the Tower* in June, 1338, were three iron cannon with five chambers, a hand-gun, some article of iron (of which the name is obliterated in the Roll) for the cannon, and three old stone bags, no doubt bags to hold shot.   The barge called the *Mary of the Tower* had an iron cannon with two chambers, and another of brass with one chamber.   Two iron cannons 'without stuff' are mentioned; and in the king's private wardrobe were two great guns of copper.   Guns had, in some instances, handles; for among the king's expenses between 1372 and 1374, were payments for 'helvying.' or putting handles to, eight guns.   There are also numerous entries in the naval accounts for those years relating to gunpowder and shot for guns, of which the following are the most material :—A small barrel of gunpowder, a quarter full; one hundred and eighty-four pounds of powder for guns, made from one hundred and thirty-five pounds of saltpetre and forty-nine pounds of live sulphur; and also two hundred and forty-two pounds of pure live sulphur.   Payments occur to workmen for making powder and pellets of lead for guns at the Tower of London.   There were purchased coal and five hundred of 'talwode' for casting the lead and drying the powder; four trays of wood, and brazen pots and dishes for drying the powder over the fire and by the sun; also leather bags to hold the same powder; two brass mortars, three iron pestles, twelve iron spoons to make leaden bullets; ten moulds of 'laton' (a sort of brass) to make the same; one pair of scales to weigh the powder; thirty small barrels with hasps and staples to hold the bullets; thirty small hanging locks for the said barrels; two hundred and twenty pounds of saltpetre; two 'sarces' (sieves); eighteen bellows; earthen pots and pans to dry the powder by the fire and sun; and willows for making charcoal."

The chambers to cannon were movable breechpieces, which, being charged, were placed in the gun.   A gun with a chamber of this kind, but of the fifteenth century, was shown at the Royal Naval Exhibition of 1891.   It was formed of longitudinal bars of iron, hooped together with iron rings.   The guns which had handles were probably small ones, to be mounted on iron forks and used as swivels.   The guns were primed at the touchholes and discharged by means of fire-irons heated to redness.

Rates
of
Freight.

The expense of freightage was low in the fourteenth century. In 1370 the sum of £30 6s. was paid for a ship with a crew of thirty-eight men, carrying twenty soldiers and sixteen archers from Southampton to Normandy. In 1368 the transport from Dover to Calais, in thirty-nine ships and thirteen smaller vessels, of the Duke of Clarence, four hundred and fifty-seven men-at-arms, and one thousand two hundred and eighty horses, cost only £173 6s. 8d. But there had previously been a tendency on the part of the passenger-carriers to raise prices, for in 1330 it was enacted that, the keepers of the passage to France having increased their charges, no higher fare should in the future be exacted than the ancient rate of two shillings for every horse-man and sixpence for each foot-passenger. Long before 1330, it may be of interest to add, a company called "The Fare Ship Company," existed at Dover, its business being the management of trans-channel traffic. The vessels of this company sailed according to a pre-arranged roster, each ship apparently making three passages, and then not making any more until all the other ships had done likewise. The company was governed by four wardens, who were empowered to enforce their regulations by the infliction of fines upon members or shareholders who failed to comply with them. The fines went, however, not to the company, but to the king.

The relative commercial importance of the sea-ports of England during this period may probably be estimated with some degree of fairness from the number of ships supplied by the chief of them for the Calais expedition. According to the "Roll of Calais,"[1] the ports, with the ships furnished, ranked as follows:—Fowey, 47; Yarmouth, 43; Dartmouth, 31; Plymouth, 26; Shoreham, 26; London, 25; Bristol, 24; Sandwich, 22; Southampton, 21; Winchelsea, 21; Weymouth, 20; Looe, 20; Lynn, 19; Newcastle, 17; Boston, 17; Dover, 16; Hull, 16; Margate, 15; Harwich, 14; the Isle of Wight, 13; Ipswich, 12; Hook, 11; Grimsby, 11; and Exmouth, 10. The other ports furnished less than ten ships apiece, Portsmouth and Hartlepool sending only 5 each, Poole only 4, and Cardiff and the Mersey only 1 each. Ranked according to the number of mariners furnished, the order is Yarmouth, Fowey, Dartmouth, London, Bristol, Plymouth, Winchelsea, Southampton, Sandwich, etc.

[1] Printed in Nicolas' "History of the Royal Navy." App. vii., Vol. II.

The reign of Richard II. was, upon the whole, disastrous both for the royal and the commercial navy of the country. The royal navy was even more neglected than it had been in the last years of King Edward III.; and, although a naval victory was won off Cadsand in 1387, the country's normal condition during this unfortunate period was one of terror—often of abject terror—lest the French should invade and conquer it. The defective discipline of the fleet may be judged from the facts that in 1377, when the Earl of Buckingham and Lord FitzWalter

PORTION OF THE "ROLL OF CALAIS" (MS. Harl. 3918).

were supposed to be co-operating against the French at Brest, they were, in reality, fighting one against the other, and that, when the leaders did, in a half-hearted way, at length co-operate, the seamen mutinied. The ships seem to have been transformed, too, into floating dens of vice and barbarity; and a very lurid light is thrown upon the sea manners of those days by the record that when, in 1379, Sir John Arundel's squadron was overtaken by a storm, sixty women who were on board [1] were

[1] They had been inmates of a nunnery near Southampton that he had plundered before sailing—nuns, schoolgirls, and others. Some had gone voluntarily, others were taken by force. The story is told by Walsingham, i., pp. 420-424, Rolls Series.]

thrown into the waves to lighten the vessels. Almost every year the coasts were insulted by the French. In 1380, according to some historians, the Spaniards entered the Thames and burnt part of Gravesend; yet the English Government refused to be aroused from its lethargy, and the most brilliant naval actions of the time were the fruit of the patriotism and gallantry of private individuals. John Philpott, Mayor of London, fitted out at his own cost a squadron to oppose the combined French, Scottish, and Spanish pirates, who, in 1378, under John Mercer, ravaged the Yorkshire coast; and in 1385 the men of Portsmouth and Dartmouth, "hired," as Walsingham says, "by none, bought by none, but spurred on by their own valour and innate courage," put to shame the pusillanimity of the Administration by fitting out an expedition against the French at the mouth of the Seine. At the very moment when the kingdom was most in danger, the Government permitted the greater part of the fleet, as well as an immense army, to leave England in furtherance of the Duke of Lancaster's selfish pretensions to the crown of Castile; and the consequences were that trade was almost ruined, and that such ships as remained in England were, for the most part, laid up in harbours across the mouths of which chains were drawn. Nor did trade suffer only by the inability of the Government to protect it; for the king arrested, from time to time, all such merchant-vessels as would suit his immediate purpose, and seldom thought of making either compensation or restitution to their owners. Yet acts that were designed for the encouragement of the trade of the country were passed under Richard II. One measure, which was adopted in 1390, and which foreshadowed the Navigation Laws of a much later date, enacted that "all merchants of the realm of England shall freight in the said realm the ships of the said realm, and not foreign ships, so that the owners of the said ships may take reasonably for the freight of the same." This statute not being properly observed, the Commons in the following year petitioned the king that inasmuch as the navy of England was greatly weakened and impaired, no English merchant should be allowed to put goods or merchandise into a foreign vessel in any case where he could freight an English one, upon pain of forfeiting the goods shipped in a foreign bottom; and the king answered: "Let the statute thereupon made be kept and

observed "; though it does not appear that his Majesty's utterance led to the slightest improvement. That the merchants
were not always honest in their often expressed anxiety for the
welfare of the country may be inferred from Walsingham's
assertion that in 1383 a Genoese carack,[1] richly laden, was driven
into Sandwich by stress of weather, and that though her cargo
would have sufficed to supply the whole country with particular
commodities, the merchants of London induced her to proceed
to Flanders, lest the sale of the goods which they had on hand
might be prejudiced by the bringing into the market of goods
fresher and better.

REGINALD HUGHES. Architecture and Art.

BEFORE the mid-day splendours of Edward III.'s reign had
been lost in the gloom and confusion of its close, the decadence
of Gothic art had begun. But the processes of decay were
slow, and the change from the free grace of the earlier to the
stiff utilitarianism of the later style occupied forty years or
more. The period usually assigned to the transition from
Decorated to Perpendicular is from 1360 to 1399; but the
chronological line must not be too sharply drawn. Perhaps,
indeed, it would be safer to shift the first date a little further
back, for in Gloucester Cathedral we have typical mixed work
which is certainly not much later than 1350, and by the end of
the century the victory of Perpendicular forms was complete.

Transition to Perpendicular.

It is probable that the " plague of Froissart," that most potent
of all influences in the fourteenth century, had something to say
to the rise and progress of the new architecture. During the
winter of 1348–9 the pestilence had swept off the workmen like
flies, and the scarcity of labour was felt with prodigious severity
in every department of the national life. More than one
attempt was, as we have seen, made by Parliament to control
wages, not only those of the hedger and ditcher, but of the
skilled artisan, and in the twenty-fifth year of Edward III. the
amended Statute of Labourers actually fixed the wages of " a
master freemason " at fourpence per day. Such wages, no more
than the pay of a corporal of Welsh auxiliaries (who, besides,
had his dress, his long knife, and his rations for nothing), was
not likely to secure the highest artistic skill; and though the

---

[1] A carack was primarily a cargo-carrying vessel.

statute must, to some extent, have remained a dead letter, so far as it had any effect at all it operated to drive the artificer out of the country. It certainly is significant that Perpendicular forms, which, of all that are included under the name of Gothic,

EAST WINDOW, GLOUCESTER CATHEDRAL.

make the slightest demand on the invention, should have come into vogue at the very moment when the craftsmen of original talent (at no time a too numerous class) had almost disappeared.

During the quarter of a century which followed the pestilence new foundations were few, the work which was undertaken being generally in the nature rather of remodelling than of fresh construction.   Perhaps the earliest instance of this process of adapting the old work to the new fashion took place in the Abbey Church at Gloucester, an establishment which, in a time of almost universal depression, was specially fortunate in its finances.   The body of the murdered Edward II., removed thither from Berkeley Castle by Abbot Thokey, continued, through a great part of Edward III.'s reign, to bring in a vast revenue.   Hundreds and thousands of pilgrims came to worship at his tomb, and their offerings were spent, not on rebuilding the church, as the architects of previous ages would have done, but in recasing the surface, in forming new windows in the old walls, in inserting new glass, and generally, in clothing the twelfth-century body with a fourteenth-century dress.   For such purposes nothing could have been handier than the Perpendicular forms, and, in particular, the Perpendicular panel.   It does not, how-ever, appear that any new forms of moulding were adopted at Gloucester, the architects being satisfied to repeat those of the preceding style.   And we thus find the singular combination of mouldings that seem pure Decorated, and windows and walls that seem pure Perpendicular, while a pure Norman skeleton, though unseen, supports both.

The Perpendicular Style.   It is not difficult to summarise the more obvious charac-teristics of the style that was in act to supersede all the Decorated forms.   As its name implies, perpendicularity is its salient feature, and the chief instrument by which this effect is produced is the straight-sided panel.   It is not, indeed, that the Perpendicular architects, the remodellers and converters of so many old buildings, invented panelling—they merely raised it from obscurity and gave it predominance.   Instead of the panel being sparsely used to decorate comparatively small and narrow spaces, the whole surface inside and outside—wall and arch, screen, parapet, basement, and buttress—are now covered with it.   Even the windows, when, later on, the style gets thoroughly logical, become simply an arrangement of these panels pierced to let in the light.   But in the earliest time, no less than in the latest, the perpendicular lines are there.   As a rule, the partitions go straight up from sill to window-top.   They no longer bend and intersect above and cross each other in an ordered maze of springing curves.   Even when minor arches are introduced into the window, the straight, upright mullions are generally forced through them, regardless of every canon of good taste, or else the perpendicularity is more queerly emphasised, by perching small panel-shaped openings on the heads of the larger lights.   There is a certain consistency and strength of appearance in this upright stonework, and, as a vehicle for painted glass, these aggregates of panels — the only restriction on size being due to the fear of weakening the wall that supported the roof—were, no doubt, unrivalled.   But they form a poor substitute for the elegant grouped lancets of the Early English, or for the flowing tracery of the Decorated style.

DEVONSHIRE FOLIAGE, STOKE-IN-TEIGNHEAD CHURCH.

The doorways are of one set type—a depressed arch, the depression increasing **Doorways.** as the style advances, set in a square frame, and the whole enclosed in a label, outlining three sides of a rectangular oblong.   The sides usually carry shafts, the label-moulding and the spandrels being generally more or less ornamented with such things as shields, foliage, animals, or grotesques. The square frame and label are, indeed, characteristic features, and entirely supersede the earlier segmental-headed doorways, although window-heads of that form are common enough.   Stiffness and squareness extend their sway everywhere, ruling in things great and in things small, in things decorative and in things utilitarian.   Every sort of detail, as well as the employment and arrangement of detail, is thus affected, and the divorce from Nature in the representation of all natural objects is almost absolute.   An exception must be made, however, in regard to certain carvings in our western

Ornament. counties, which, though occurring in Perpendicular churches, and late in the style too, show an attempt to return to Nature. This work, which goes by the name of " Devonshire foliage," was no doubt a mere local development, probably due to the effort of some provincial artist to imitate in stone the wreaths of natural leaves and flowers, with which, on appropriate festivals, the church columns were decorated. With this exception the Perpendicular foliage is extraordinarily angular, not to say wooden. The crocket which we have noticed (Vol. I., p. 472) in the twelfth-century work of St. Hugh of Burgundy, lives on into late Perpendicular times, but it seems wholly to have forgotten the curled leaf from which it was derived. Yet, altered as it is, it looks almost an anachronism.

The Tudor Flower. More characteristic is the so-called " Tudor flower," an ornament, we should say, that was in use before any Tudor aspired

TWO EXAMPLES OF THE TUDOR FLOWER.

to an alliance with a Plantagenet or a Plantagenet's widow. It is founded on the *fleur de lis*, alternated with a trefoil or ball, but the principal flower is more like a heraldic lozenge than a lily. It is poor in invention, but not unfrequently has a rich effect, particularly in late examples, as, for instance, in Henry VII.'s chapel at Westminster, where the lily has an edging suggesting the fructification of the ceterach fern, and the small intermediate flower becomes an elaborate triple primrose. The battlement as an internal ornament for screens, rood-lofts, and the like, though by no means unknown to the Decorated artists, becomes quite fashionable now, and the date of such work can, in general, be fixed by the horizontal moulding which runs along the edge. This, in the Perpendicular period, is continuous, and carried not only along the top but down the sides, while the Decorated masons cut it off at each opening. The mouldings differ greatly from those of the preceding era, looking as if the workmen no longer cared to do their best, as was their wont in the early days. In dealing with the Decorated style we noticed that there was a great falling-off in the depth and fineness of the cutting, but that the deterioration of workmanship, as well as the shallower forms, was to some extent compensated for by increased sumptuousness of surface ornament. In the Perpendicular style the mouldings are flatter still, and the pateræ, grotesques, animals, foliag e, and the like, whichadorn the wide shallow cornices, are rarely rich in effect or spirited in execution.

EDINGTON CHURCH, WILTSHIRE.

There are not many entire buildings, or entire parts of buildings, in this mixed or Transitional style, though additions and alterations in it are plentiful. Among the earliest are the choir and transepts of Gloucester, the cloisters and porch of the Treasury (formerly the Garter Chapter House) at Windsor, and Abbot Litlington's work at Westminster. William of Edington's church in the parish of the same name, dedicated in 1361, is one of the rare edifices which seem to have been wholly constructed in the Transitional time. Here we find, in the west front, a great window, which is neither quite Decorated nor quite Perpendicular in feeling. The reticulations are numerous,

Early Perpendicular Work.

and the lower openings in the window-head, instead of being in the long panel shape, are so short as almost to form a hexagon. There are, indeed, no mullions carried right through from bottom to top, but from the tops of the lowest tiers of arches into which the window is divided, straight mullions start up, to affirm the Perpendicular principle. The small west windows of the side aisles are, indeed, hardly to be distinguished from work of the previous age, and their diamonded heads are a stiff example of a form of Decorated tracery, though one more common in lay buildings than in churches. But if the window-forms at Edington are neither frankly Decorative nor frankly Perpendicular, the doorway is frankly both ; nor could there be a more instructive example of the mixture of styles. The doors are not set in the square stone Perpendicular framework, but enclosed in the " segmental " headed Decorated arch. But the space between arch and door-head is filled with four typical Perpendicular panels, and the Decorated arch is itself enclosed in the square Perpendicular label.

The Work of William of Wykeham.   This William of Edington was a great builder, and later he began the modernisation of Winchester Cathedral. William of Edington developed, in fact, into William of Winchester, and the Transitional of the rector, doubtless, became the almost full-blown Perpendicular of the bishop. He died in 1366, but not before he had begun to clothe the Norman bones of Winchester with Perpendicular flesh, and his task was carried on without a break, and with greater energy, by his successor. It is to that successor, William of Wykeham, whom we may count the last of the great episcopal architects of the Middle Ages, that we owe the modernisation of three-fourths of the cathedral. But against a wrong which the antiquary finds hard to forgive, must be put, not only the imposing character of his work on the cathedral, but the construction of edifices like the chapels of Winchester and New College—really noble specimens of this ignoble style. Finest of all is the chapel at Oxford, which was begun in the first year of Richard II. and finished in the seventh year of the reign. As might be expected from its date, there is at least a hint of Transition in the building. The tall perpendicular mullions do not quite reach the window-tops unbroken, and the sub-arches spring from a central division as at Edington. A little later, this arrangement was abandoned, as in the choir of York Minster, which, though commenced as early as 1361, was not completed till 1408.

The nave and western transepts of Canterbury, begun about 1380, also belong to the period of Transitional and early Perpendicular, but the distinguishing marks of the Transition are not very observable there. Though much of

GATEHOUSE THORNTON ABBEY

the work was contemporary with that of Winchester, Canterbury is much more full-blown in style. In both a Norman nave has been replaced by a Perpendicular one, but at Winchester this was effected by clothing the old piers with new ashlaring, the old mouldings being altered to look like new; while in Lanfranc's nave, which was ruinous, they were pulled down and built anew from the foundation. Other well-known examples are the Chapter-house at Howden in Yorkshire, and the gatehouse at Thornton Abbey in Lincolnshire. The cloisters at Gloucester are generally spoken of as belonging to this period, though the windows are probably earlier. But the traceried cloister roof, the progenitor of the

Roofs.

later wonders in the royal chapels, may safely be ascribed to some early Perpendicular architect.

The redeeming features of the Perpendicular style are its towers and its elaborate stone vaulting, to which may be added its timbered roofs. Few of these last belong to the best and earliest period, but many are very fine, their late date not-withstanding. The roof of the palace at Eltham belongs to the reign of Henry IV. That of St. Stephen's, Norwich, one of the richest in all England, was built under Henry VIII., and a majority of the wooden roofs (which are oftenest found in the eastern counties) date from the beginning of the sixteenth century. But one noble example of the fourteenth century remains at Westminster—the roof that covers " the great Hall of Rufus," the scanty remnants of whose Norman work have been brought to light in recent years. The hall was practically rebuilt from its foundations in the last years of Richard, and retains to this day, both in the carving of the walls and the timbers of the roof, the form then given to

WESTMINSTER HALL.

FORTIFIED RECTORY, EMBLETON, NORTHUMBERLAND.

it. Such open timber roofs are incomparably more beautiful than any vaulted work of the same period, and show that, in the matter of carpentering at least, we are not wiser than our fathers were five centuries ago.

The lay architecture of the reign of Richard, and the last years of Edward III., is not very distinctive. The evolution of the country mansion from the castle went on, but it cannot be traced step by step with sufficient accuracy to admit of the story being told with anything like regular sequence. Taste and fancy played an increasing part, now that the uses of private war had finally ceased to be a dominating consideration. On the Scottish border alone was it necessary to live in a state of alarms. Elsewhere the determining factor was the personality of the proprietor. As a result, we have the noble hall at Penshurst, forming part of what was essentially a mansion-house in the reign of Edward III., built at the very beginning of the Perpendicular period, and contemporary with the very earliest work at Gloucester; while at Bodiam, which was not begun till the middle of the reign of Richard, we have a type, though a late one, of the impregnable feudal

Secular Archi-tecture.

castle. Subsequent alterations and additions, though they have left the hall at Penshurst[1] comparatively intact, make it hard to trace the outline of the old buildings, but it is clear that Sir John Devereux's manor-house could never have been capable of military defence. On the other hand, in Bodiam,[2] built by a veteran of the French wars, who had made a fortune by plunder, we have a stronghold that must have delighted the eye of a soldier and a free-lance. Massive walls with round towers at the angles and square towers in the centres at the sides look down on a moat of prodigious width and depth, filled to the brim with water. The great gateway is reached by a narrow causeway, and a long drawbridge defended by a barbican tower. The gate itself had three portcullises (one remains *in situ*), and the vaulted roof over the intervening spaces is pierced with meurtrières. Internally the arrangement is like a compressed Oxford college. On one side are the chapel, and beyond it probably the stables, and on the other side of a small court the living-rooms, the banquet-hall, the kitchens and ovens. Between, and alongside of, these two types, there were, unquestionably, all sorts of buildings erected at this time. Some like Bolton Castle, in the North Riding, were obviously not intended for military purposes, though retaining the military form. Others, like Dartington Hall, in Devon, were purely private houses with extensive farm-buildings attached. Dartington is also remarkable as showing the persistence of old forms, for the windows (which are of four lights) are built with shouldered arches, recalling the shouldered lintels of Carnarvon Castle, and carry us back to the beginning of the thirteenth century, and the vogue of the purest Early English. But such buildings as Bodiam reflect the arrogance, or at least the eccentricity, of the individual rather than the feeling of the times. That was in the direction of greater comfort, as is shown by the spacious double courts at Bolton and elsewhere; and this feeling grew with internal wealth and quiet, and was promoted by the increased intercourse with the higher civilisation of Italy and France.

[[1] Near Edenbridge, Kent. *See* the illustration, p. 167.   [2] Near Robertsbridge, Sussex; between Tunbridge Wells and Hastings.]

BODIAM CASTLE, NEAR ROBERTSBRIDGE, SUSSEX

IN continuation of the remarks in the last chapter, it will be convenient to say a few words upon the further development of dramatic literature down to 1500. A few mysteries, such as "The Burial and Resurrection of Christ," and the "Conversion of St. Paul," were produced in the North and Midlands during the fifteenth century. The latter, in seven-lined stanzas, is interesting because its subject is new, and because it is divided into sections which foreshadow the later division of plays into acts. Parallel with these in time and place (East Midlands) there grew up a new species of drama which was the outcome of the medieval love for allegory and the personification of abstract ideas. The Morality was the first step towards secular drama, and it was a false one. But this excursion into an artistic *cul-de-sac* at least taught the playwrights independence. The fight of the Seven Deadly Sins and the Seven Cardinal Virtues for the human soul, a life-long battle, is the theme of the earliest and best Moralities Humanity, his virtues and vices, are personified in the attempt to materialise what, after all, was only the general thought underlying the old collective Mysteries. This moralising tendency is even traceable in the *Expositor* of the Chester plays, and in the *Contemplacio, Veritas*, etc., of the Coventry "Salutation and Conception." The earliest extant [1] Morality (*temp.* Henry VI.) is the typical "Castell of Perseverance," the hero of which, *Humanum Genus*,[2] is beset from his birth till his final dissolution, by *Mundus, Belyal, Caro*,[3] and their henchmen. He is only saved at the last after an argumentative scene between Mercy and others, similar to one in the Coventry "Salutation." Other plays of the same type are "Mind, Will, and Understanding," "Mankind," "Mundus et Infans," and "Everyman." This last (*temp.* Edward IV.) was so popular that it was printed four times in the early sixteenth century. The Buddhist story of friendship tried, known to the West in the legend of Barlaam and Josaphat, forms the basis of the action, but the idea of suggesting the manner of a man's life by the light of his death-scene,

---

[1] *Cf.* Wycliffe, *De Officio Pastorali* (c. 1378), ch. **xv.**, p. 429, ed. Matthew; and Smith, *English Guilds*, p. 137 (first mention of a Morality).

[2] *I.e.* Mankind.]   [3] The World, the Devil, the Flesh.]

instead of presenting its whole course, marks a real advance **Lyric Verse.** in dramatic art.

To return to the fourteenth century, we find in lyric poetry, not only a constant increase in complexity of stanza, but a growing tendency to imitate the sensuous beauty of the French singers. This is quite as true of the religious as of the lay lyric. Excellent examples of this kind of writing, religious, erotic, and political, are to be found in a MS. collection[1] made in the fourteenth century. Among the best known political songs are those upon the evil times of Edward II.[2] and the famous songs of the north-countryman Laurence Minot. These last are ten in number, and celebrate the wars of Edward III. with burning patriotism and contemptuous hatred for the French, and still more for the Scottish. The verse he writes is of two kinds —a short-lined metre, sometimes tail-rime, sometimes short couplets; and the fluctuating Middle English Alexandrine, with strong cæsural pause connected by continued but not cross-rime into strophes, a typical measure for the wandering gleeman. In both forms he makes great use of alliteration, but naturally with more effect in the longer line.

The new national spirit found its expression, however, in **Ballads.** other than political song. The "good old times" of the twelfth century, when the Midlands were infested by outlaws, seemed to the men at the close of the next to be clothed with attractive, romantic colouring—a mantle cast over the reality by age. Round the stories of these men was gathered all the rough sense of justice, of revolt against oppression by the rich and the clergy, of sympathy with the struggling poor, which were a sign of the nation's new-springing life. Trappings of the court romances, incidents from the lives of historic and legendary heroes, were found useful in supplying details of colour and circumstance; while the very verse, the well-known ballad-metre, is but the worn-down derivative of the septenar so common in southern romances. And thus arose the Robin Hood ballads in the country around their beloved Sherwood. They became so popular that they were mentioned by Langland with blame[3] in 1377; and by Chaucer[4] as much appreciated of Pandarus in

---

[1] MS. Harl. No. 2253.
[2] "Political Songs," ed. T. Wright, Camden Soc., pp. 195 and 323.
[3] Piers Plowman, B., Passus V. 1. 402.   [4] "Troil. and Cres." v. 168.

1382—the first mention that we find of them in literature. In close relation to these, standing midway between the true romance,[1] to the form and verse of which it has much similarity, and the purely democratic Robin Hood cycle, with the spirit of which it is saturated, is the "Tale of Gamelyn," a story Chaucer probably intended to use as basis for his "Yeoman's Tale." After his death it was included in the "Canterbury Tales" as that of the "Cook," which the author had left with no more than its opening. The same story was long afterwards used by Thomas Lodge for his novel "Rosalind" (1590), in its turn the source of "As You Like It." "Gamelyn" is written in much the same dialect as that of Chaucer, but in the South-West Midlands a group of romances appeared about this time (the middle of the fourteenth century), which aimed at a large and popular audience by making use of the old alliterative, unrimed long line. The West had never come so completely under Norman and French influence as other parts of the country, and the old English measure had never completely died out. Both these facts, and the failure of the ordinary romance measures to reach any really artistic development in face of the linguistic disorder, rendered a revival likely; though phonetic changes in the language, the substitution of a logical for an artificial sentence-stress, and the change in many cases of word-accent, made, even here, an exact adherence to the old rule an impossibility. As it is, many Romance words are accentuated on the Germanic principle in these poems, though in ordinary usage this was not the case for more than a hundred years later; and naturally the total effect upon the ear is very different from the dignified roll of the older, slower line. The earliest and most important of these poems is "William of Palern," written by a poet named William, to the order of Sir Humphrey de Bowne (Bohun), Earl of Hereford (1355–61). Somewhat later, probably, is "The Chevelere Assigne," an English version of the Lohengrin saga, based on the French "Chevalier au signe." Fragments of a Graal romance called "Joseph of Arimathea," and of an Alexander-romance in this metre, have also survived. Remembering

---

[1] Contemporary examples are "Octavian" and "Sir Ferumbras," the latter being partly written in the same verse as "Gamelyn," *i.e.* Middle English Alexandrine, with the addition of middle rime.

this revival, it will only seem natural that William Langland, a man from the South-West Midlands, writing his popular allegory in the second half of the century, should use the same measure. But of this more presently.

Also in the West, but this time probably in Lancashire, was the home of the poet who did most towards the higher development of this form of romance, and more for the beautifying of Middle English poetry as a whole, than any writer before Chaucer. He was born about 1330. Like young Chaucer, the poet of the "Gawain" was dominated by courtly ideals; like him he had a love for Nature in all her moods, and clothed both with that beauty of language and melody of line, for which he, like his young London contemporary, had so fine a sense. But, unlike Chaucer, he was not one of the world's great poets, for he always had a clearly realised didactic aim in his work, and did not trust to the innate quality of his subject, and still less to the innate purity of his mind, as sufficient assurances of a right tendency. He was only saved from being a commonplace allegorist by his love of form, and a rich fancy that saw in every aspect of life and nature a symbol of the higher life. His chief, and only non-religious work, "Sire Gawain and the Grene Knight" (*c.* 1370), is the first of that school of romances of which "The Faery Queene" is the greatest example; in which the adventures of the heroes are all allegorical of the struggle of man against the world, the flesh, and the devil. "Sire Gawain" is one of Arthur's knights, and the story is of plighted word, of tried and victorious chastity; the whole adventure being due to the fairy Morgana, who intends it as a warning to Guinevere.[1] The verse is a skilful combination of the old alliterative line into strophes of unequal length, by means of a ballad-quatrain introduced by a line of one accent, rhyming with the second and fourth. Equally remarkable is his "Pearl," probably the earliest of his extant works, an elegy on the death of his two-year-old child. He sees her in his vision, the personification of all that is pure and innocent, on the far side of a clear stream, which prevents him from approaching her; and a conversation between them finally

"Sire Gawain."

"Pearl."

---

[1] Possibly the poet also had in mind the relations of Edward III. to the Countess of Salisbury, which led to the foundation of the Order of the Garter. —*Cf.* "Pearl," ed. I. Gollancz (David Nutt, 1891), p. xli. *seqq.*

leads him to resignation.   The form into which the poem is
cast is most complex, beautiful in itself, and most skilfully
carried out, but scarcely suited to the simple innocence of the child
who is his theme.   The strophes are of twelve lines, with four
accents, rhymed according to the scheme *abab abab bc bc;*
the last word of every stanza in each section of the poem being

SIRE GAWAIN AND THE GRENE KNIGHT (MS. Nero. A. x.).

repeated in the first line of the next stanza, and again as refrain.
The sections, of which there are twenty, each with five strophes
(the fifteenth has six), are also connected by the repetition of
the same or some allied word, while the last line of the poem
differs but slightly from the first.   The verse is certainly
Romance in origin, and, as Mr. Gollancz remarks, has much in
common with the sonnet; at the same time, there is little
doubt that the author learnt to know it from a rather older

contemporary poet on the Welsh border, whose work shows the same qualities and characteristics less highly developed.[1] The names of both poets arc unknown. Was the "philosophical Strode," to whom, with the "moral Gower," Chaucer dedicated his "Troilus and Cryseyde," the Gawain poet?[2] Mr. Gollancz

SCENE FROM "PEARL" (MS. Nero. A. x.).

thinks it possible. His "Cleanness" and "Patience" are didactic alliterative poems, written later, with vivid imaginative descriptions of the Flood and Jonah.

[1] *Cf.* "Early English Poems and Lives of Saints," by Furnivall, Phil. Soc. Trans., pp. 118, 124, 130, 133.

[2] The methods of the two poets were sufficiently in contrast, but Chaucer can scarcely have failed to appreciate his contemporary's mastery of technique; and, curiously enough, both "Gawain" and "Troilus" are romances in which

About the time that the elder poet was beginning to write, possibly in the house of some nobleman of Lancashire, the name of the young man, Geoffrey Chaucer, must often have been on people's lips at the court in London. He was one of the yeomen or servants of the King's chamber, and had won golden opinions for himself by his character and appearance. He was attractive in person, he was good-tempered, and had a dreamy expression of face which seemed to suggest the deep feelings of which he was capable. This quiet mien, however, did not prevent him from being an excellent companion, complaisant and modest, but withal lively, though sometimes given to silence. Now and again he would show a roguishness which took his companions by surprise, and gave promise, could they have appreciated it, of the great humorist to come later. He was known to be devoted to his books; indeed, he would often try to woo the god of sleep by reading in his Ovid or some other old manuscript; and his friends had read many a roundel and virelai that he himself had written in French, and even in English. But he was no mere bookworm, for before he was twenty-one he had already seen a good deal of the world. He was sprung from a citizen's family: his father John was a wine merchant in Thames Street, and Agnes, his mother, a niece of Hamo de Copton, a moneyer. From earliest childhood he must have heard stories of the court, and the great world that lay beyond London;[1] and, at the same time, have seen and heard much in his father's shop which recurred to him in after years, when he was painting the democratic life of the times in his Tales. The Chaucers seem to have settled in Ipswich before the grandfather Robert came to London, and they must have been of Norman extraction, as the name shows (Chaucier=stocking-weaver). The poet was born about 1340,[2] for in 1386 he de-

the plot turns on a mental conflict. In "Gawain" the hero is tried and is victorious in all essentials ; in "Troilus" the heroine is tried and fails. Of such a plot "Gawain" is almost the first, certainly the finest example in England before "Troilus and Cressida." What more natural than that Chaucer should have dedicated his first attempt at mental analysis to its author, though even then the sly smile was not absent ?—*Cf.* "Troilus and Cressida, v. 267.

[1] In 1338 his father had accompanied the King and Queen to Cologne and Antwerp.

[2] The date formerly given, 1328, was a mere guess ; *cf.* Professor Hales's life of the poet in the Dictionary of National Biography.]

scribed himself as forty years old and over, and as having borne arms for twenty-seven years. As a child he escaped the Black Death of 1348-49, though it must have left an impression on his memory. When sixteen, or thereabouts, he was made *squier* (page) to Elizabeth of Ulster, wife of Lionel, Duke of Clarence, daughter-in-law to the King, and thus came into direct contact with the court. About three years later he went with Edward's invading army to France (1359), and so learnt something of the most terrible side of life. This expedition was not exactly distinguished for its heroic deeds, nor for the success which it won. But still it was full enough of incident, which was new to Chaucer, and which certainly did not escape him in spite of the habit he had of walking with eyes cast on the ground. He took his part in those wearisome, useless marches and counter-marches through the north of France, and was present at the unsuccessful siege of Rheims, whilst the less busy hours not occupied in raids for booty and the like were enlivened by hawking and feudal sports; till at last he was taken prisoner on one of these minor expeditions, and ransomed by the King (March 1, 1360) for a smaller sum than he paid at the same time for a horse.[1] This was a rich experience for a youth of twenty. He then became a valet of the King's household, having under his care the royal bed and board, for which he was rewarded in 1367 with a pension of twenty marks (£140) a year. The tone of society, as he saw it at the court, cannot have been without effect upon one who was so completely the child of his time as Chaucer.

The brilliant trappings of chivalry already on the decline, **His** and therefore laying more stress on externals than the inner **Works.** chivalric ideal; the increase in luxury in every branch of life leading to an overloaded ornamentation in architecture, decoration, dress, and gardening alike; the anxiety to keep in check the unauthorised emotions and the consequent increase in seriousness and worldly wisdom; all this coincident with the old chivalric forms helped not only to mould the personal character of the poet, but offered him many interesting types of humanity, such as a time of transition alone can produce. The relations of the various grades of society to each other, and, above all, of men to women and of women to men, in

[1] The former sum was £16, the latter, £16 13s. 8d.

each of them, could not fail to be of deepest interest to his humorous observing spirit. As we should expect from what has been said, the first[1] extant work from his pen, "The Boke of the Duchesse" (1369), is wholly courtly in style, and serious and romantic in method of treatment. The poem is in form of a vision after the approved fashion of the "Roman de la Rose," and, as in "Pearl," the lost beloved is made once more to meet in a beautiful landscape the man she has left behind. Here, however, the lady is the Duchess Blanche, wife of Chaucer's patron, John of Gaunt, Duke of Lancaster; and the verse[2] is, with the exception of two short lyrical stanzas (ll. 475–86), in short rimed couplets. The poem has many of the faults of an early effort. Its many learned references, its long-spun allegories, its philosophical platitudes, all tend to destroy the effect aimed at. But a real power of character-isation, and the germs at least of the poet's later dramatic power, are evident. Though the speeches are too long and too full of digressions, the dialogue between the poet and the unknown knight is well conceived, but the retarded crisis intended to come as a surprise fails of its effect, because too long postponed. Among his early works may probably be included a roundel and a virelai,[3] both of which breathe the hopeless burning love expressed in the "Compleynte to Pite" (1370–72), the first poem in which Chaucer makes use of his famous seven-lined stanza, often called "rhyme royal," because it was subsequently used by James I. of Scotland. In this poem he tells how he intended to give "Pity" a petition against "Cruelty" for depriving him of his love, but found Pity dead, and Cruelty regnant. Eight years long, and more,[5] had Chaucer suffered from this hopeless passion. Brandl, on

---

[1] There is some divergence of opinion amongst authorities as to the chronology of Chaucer's works. Where this is so it shall be noted. Skeat, for instance, makes "Chaucer's A B C" the first work, and dates it 1366, fol-lowed by "The Compleynte to Pite" in 1367, whilst Brandl puts "The Com-pleynte" first, then the "A B C." "The Boke of the Duchesse" is thus third according to these two scholars. The order adopted in the text is that of Ten Brink.

[2] Borrowed like much of the matter from Machault's "Dit de la fon-taine amoureuse."

[3] A "virelai" is a lyric poem in short lines with only two rhymes: the first two lines recur in the course of the poem.   [4] vi. 304, 305.

[5] Cf. "Boke of the Duchesse l. 37 seqq.

OCCLEVE'S PORTRAIT OF CHAUCER (MS. Harl. 4866).

insufficient grounds, thinks the lady was the Duchess Blanche herself, and that Chaucer was asking for her generosity, not her love ; certain it is that she was of far higher rank than he, and that he never spoke happily of his own relations to women. Here, again, the "Roman de la Rose" is the source of the main ideas ; the verse, however, which consists of heroic lines of five accents, arranged thus, *ababbcc*, comes from Provence, though Chaucer has made it his own by the skill shown in its construction and the consistency with which he uses a new rhyme for the last couplet.[1]

Foreign Influences on Chaucer.
Already in 1370 he had been sent abroad on some important mission by the king, and in 1372-3 he was again despatched, this time to Italy, to conclude a commercial treaty with the Doge of Genoa. This journey marks an epoch in his literary development, the commencement of what is often called the "Period of Italian influence," whilst the previous one is spoken of as that of French influence. In the same way, the years from 1385 to his death in 1400 are called the "English Period," or that of "Ripeness." These terms are useful if it is remembered that the words "Italian" and "French" are not mutually exclusive, but imply that the literature of Italy exerted in the second portion of his life an influence side by side with that of France, and taught him truths that he was unable to learn from the latter. He possibly met Petrarch at Padua during this sojourn in Italy, and from him he obtained, either directly or through Boccaccio, the story of the patient Griseldis, which he afterwards translated literally from the Latin, and still later made use of as the "Clerke's Tale." Dante and Boccaccio he studied carefully, borrowing from the latter two complete epics and any number of minor suggestions, and learning from the former much about the technicalities of his art. Petrarch's art was too refined and sophisticated to make much appeal to the sturdy manliness of the English poet ; by Dante's greatness as a stylist he was deeply impressed, though scarcely capable of appreciating his genius to the full. Boccaccio, the least of the three as a poet, but greatest as a story-teller, was certainly the most sympathetic to him.

In 1374 Chaucer was made Comptroller of Customs in the

---

[1] *Cf.* Ten Brink, "Chaucer's Sprache," § 347.

port of London, a post which he filled unaided for ten years, **Chaucer in Middle** in addition to which he was several times abroad on various **Life.** errands, amongst others another journey to Italy in 1378. We know that in 1374 he was already married to a wife, Philippa, was settled in a house near Aldgate, and was rewarded by the Duke of Lancaster for the services of himself and his wife with a pension of £10 (£100 of our money). Whether the marriage was a recent one or no is uncertain. A Philippa Chaucer was one of the ladies of the Chamber to the Queen in 1366. Was Chaucer his wife's maiden name, and was she, perhaps, a descendant of the Richard Chaucer whom the poet's grandmother married as her third husband? or was the poet already married in 1366? Neither view is free from difficulties. On the whole, the former seems to agree better with the known facts.

Fortunately, the course of the poet's inner life is easier to **A New** trace. About the time of the first Italian journey he passed **Phase.** through a mental crisis which cast at first a serious and religious tone over his thoughts and tastes, leading in time to a higher, more independent view of life, which made possible at a later date, when his inborn *joie de vivre* returned, the humoristic and kindly ironical view of men and things, which are the distinctive marks of his genius. This crisis may have been the result of many concurrent causes. The great religious revival under Wycliffe, which was then at its height, cannot have been without its effect. The weariness of spirit, induced by his secret unanswered love and the hollowness of an intriguing court-life, doubtless helped. Not least was the influence of Dante, which is seen in the legend of St. Cecilia, translated into "rhyme royal" at this time from the "Legenda aurea" of Jacobus à Voragine, possibly with the help of a version contained in another cycle of saints' lives, and incorporated later in the "Canterbury Tales" as the story of the second nun (III. 29). About this time, too, must be placed his translation of Innocent's "De Contemptu Mundi," now lost, though fragments were doubtless made use of in later works, and that of Origen's "Homilia de Maria Magdalena." This work is mentioned in the prologue to the "Legend of Good Women," but is not extant. Ten Brink would place here his "A B C," a free translation of "Le Pélérinage de la Vie

Humaine," by Guillaume de Deguileville. The work is very uneven in quality, and has an artificiality about it which seriously detracts from its evidently earnest tone.

The purely religious phase was not likely to last long with a man of Chaucer's temperament, but his next work, a translation of Boccaccio's "Teseide" into "rhyme royal," made between 1374 and 1377, was completely in keeping with his serious tone of mind. Though only fragments of the original version of "Palamon and Arcite" remain embedded in later poems, such as "Anelida and the False Arcite" and "Troilus and Cressida,[1] yet they are sufficient to show that it was treated throughout in the serious romantic tone. Two noble kinsmen, Palamon and Arcite, love and fight for the person of one lady, Emelye. Arcite is thrown from his horse at the moment of victory, and the vanquished Palamon wins the prize, which his brother, with the fuller knowledge of the next world, sees to be worthless. In this spirit it was that Chaucer made about this time a prose translation of Boethius' "De Consolatione Philosophiae," a book which must have encouraged his natural tendency to intellectual scepticism, at the same time that it instilled him with neo-platonic ideas.

In this frame of mind the poet was found when John of Gaunt, his old patron, prompted him to produce his next two works. The first of these, "The Compleynt of Mars," an occasional piece, written in the spring of 1379, describes in skilful astrological allegory a recent court intrigue between John Holland (Mars) and Isabella of Castile (Venus), John of Gaunt's sister-in-law. Chaucer also began about this time his translation of the "Roman de la Rose," now lost. That the latter parts of this especially were not calculated to encourage the romantic spirit is certain.

Anyway, from this time, though he could be serious on occasion, and never lost his appreciation and honour for the "eternal womanly," yet he could never suffer the existence of anything bordering on sentimentality in his work, without placing in sharp contrast to it the other commonplace and material side of the question.[2] And so, when dissatisfied with

"Palamon and Arcite."

[1] *Cf.* Ten Brink, "Chaucer-Studien," p. 39 *ff.;* "Englische-Studien," II., 230.
[2] This has been well shown by Ten Brink ("Chaucer-Studien," p. 45).

PROLOGUE TO THE CANTERBURY TALES (MS. 686).
(Bodleian Library, Oxford.)

his " Palamon and Arcite," which certainly none but his most
intimate friends had seen, he reconstructed the whole tale in
manner suitable for the mouth of the knight, and introduced
many a humorous and ironical remark into the tragic love-
story, which was not only consistent with the experienced old
knight's character, but also with his own view of life. In 1377
Edward III. had died, and in January, 1382, the young King
Richard married the Princess Anne of Luxemburg, daughter
of the Emperor Charles V. Whilst the negotiations were still

"The Par-
lament of
Fowles."
proceeding Chaucer wrote his allegory, " The Parlament of
Fowles," in support of the king's suit. The princess is represented as a hen eagle wooed by three tiercel eagles, who have
come with the other birds under guidance of Nature to choose
their mates on St. Valentine's Day. The tiercelets represent
Richard II., a Bavarian prince, and a margrave of Meissen,[1]
with whom Anne had been betrothed at different times of
her childhood. In the poem, Nature, who shows much in
common with Boethius' Platonic conception of her, declares
the "formel egle " (*i.e.* the princess) old enough to make her
own choice, · and she accordingly decides to delay decision
for a year.

The poem shows Dante's influence again at work. The garden seen in the poet's dream is as beautiful, but not as carelessly
joyous, as the Garden of the Rose, for over the portal is an inscription of the same intent as the famous "per me si va nella
città dolente,"[2] and he enters not alone as of yore with careless
ease, but under guidance of the dead Scipio, as Dante had
entered the Inferno with Virgil. The fragment of Cicero's " De
Civitate " known in the Middle Ages as the "Somnium
Scipionis," had influenced Chaucer in this matter as it had
Dante before him. The poem, however, does not lack an
Aristophanic touch in the remarks passed by the other birds
upon the royal wooing.

"Troilus
and
Cryseyde."
In the same year as his " Parlament of Fowles" most
authorities agree in placing " Troilus and Cryseyde," the second
of the epics borrowed from Boccaccio. In the " Filostrato " the
Italian had enlarged an episode of the Troy saga into an important work. Chaucer, without altering the story in any

[1] Ten Brink, " Englische Studien," I., 288.

[2 "By me the·way lies ·to the city of sorrow."—" Inferno," III., 1.]

important particular, and without shifting the centre of interest in the tale, changed this epic into a poem, no less important and, if somewhat less harmonious, yet showing a far deeper knowledge of human nature. "Troilus" is the first analytical novel in the English language, and loses nothing by comparison with the work of Richardson and George Eliot, whilst it gains in its total effect when compared with Shakespeare's play. This advantage which it shows over the latter work, however, is due to the greater suitability of the story for narrative rather than dramatic form, not to the superior genius of the earlier poet. The story is one of the tragic fate awaiting a gentle, lovable character, for whom the influences of time and present impressions are too great to be resisted. Cressida's grief at leaving Troilus is described with ironical compassion, yet not without sorrow for the weakness of mankind; Troilus, the fervent Romeo-like lover, learns at last to laugh at the pettiness and worthlessness of the world; and in Pandarus the dramatic development of the story is centred, whilst the dash of naturalism is heightened in colour, but refined, with enormous gain in ironical humour, by making him an old man, instead of a young one as in Boccaccio. This was Chaucer's "litel tragedye," as he called it, praying God at the same time to grant him strength to write a " comedy," *i.e* a story with a happy ending.

The prayer was answered when he had written "The Hous of Fame," a vision-poem which shows the influence of Dante more strongly than ever. The poem was commenced December 10th, 1383, and is a playful, fantastic allegory, flowing over with good spirits, and yet showing beneath the surface an intensely personal, serious tone shadowing the unspoken dreams of the hard-worked poet. In many details of the poem we are reminded that Chaucer was thinking of the "Divine Comedy," and the "House of Fame" stands, as Ten Brink has finely remarked, in the same sort of relation to the former gigantic work of genius as the caprice of my lady Fame to the eternal justice of God. Chaucer fittingly returned to his old short-lined couplets for the last time in the fabric of this airy vision. In the next year the king allowed him to appoint a temporary deputy at the Customs-house, and three months later (February, 1385) this permission was made permanent. This

"The Hous of Fame."

63

date may be taken to mark Chaucer's entry upon his third and last period of literary activity, for the leisure which he had now gained led to the production of a number of important works—

The "Legende of Gode Women." two of them being series of stories enclosed within a common frame,[1] but neither of them ever finished. The "Legende of Gode Women," or "Seyntes Legende of Cupyde," as he himself calls it, commenced in 1385, stands at the entrance of this period, and stretches out a hand to both past and future. It reminds us of his early work because its spirit is the purely chivalric and romantic one which he had left behind in his youth, and for the last time he here makes use of the allegorical vision. It shows the influence of Italy, for it consists of a series of tales connected by a slight bond into one poem, and it anticipates the "Canterbury Tales" in this respect as well as in its use of the heroic couplet. The idea of writing a set of poems in praise of women who had been the martyrs of love was the queen's, for he sings her praises in the carefully executed prologue as the leader of "the ladies good ninetene," as he does in the person of Alcestis, and under the figure of the daisy. The translation of the "Roman de la Rose" and the "Troilus and Cryseyde" had not pleased her, and Chaucer may well have felt bound to make amends by writing this work in return for her advocacy in the matter of the deputy at the Customs-house. It is at any rate curious that only nine of the whole series planned are in existence, and that the queen survived just that number of years after the commencement of the poem. The general plan of the work is based upon Boccaccio's "De mulieribus claris,"[2] and to the same poet is due the general form of the "Canterbury Tales," on which Chaucer was at work, and to which he was giving his main thought and energy at this time.

The "Canterbury Tales." The "Decamerone" offered an example of a series of separate tales told by a company of men and women all come together with the same object; but here the likeness ceases. The object of the pilgrims was a worthy, not a selfish one, and the scene is ever shifting, not a quiet villa garden. The characters, too, are drawn from all sorts and conditions of

---

[1] Like the "Decameron" of Boccaccio.
[2] "Concerning Famous Women."

The Knight

The Miller.

The Reeve.

The Cook

The Man of Law.

The Wife of Bath.

THE CANTERBURY PILGRIMS.

(By permission of the Right Hon. the Earl of Ellesmere.)

men, except the very highest and the lowest, not all from the same rank of society as in Boccaccios book. The idea of representing the various grades of the commonwealth, and of making them undertake a pilgrimage, is without doubt due to Langland's "Piers Plowman" (p. 308), but in the method of adaptation the master's hand is again visible, for the goal of their journey is not an abstract Truth, but the ancient city and cathedral of Canterbury with all its ecclesiastical and historical memories; and the power of characterisation is far greater and more dramatic than that of the Malvern poet, though even Langland had gone much farther in this direction than the allegorical names of his personages imply. It is not impossible that Gower in a negative way had also helped to call this masterpiece into existence, for in 1383, or thereabouts, the "Confessio Amautis," Gower's great English work, had been commenced. This work came into direct competition with the "Legend of Good Women" in subject matter, and was far more ambitious in scheme and extent than anything Chaucer had yet produced. Did "that last infirmity of noble mind," or at least the desire not to be over-shot in his own particular province, act as a spur to the rather easy-going poet?

The Pilgrims. Chaucer's motley company start from the Tabard Inn in Southwark, under guidance of "mine host," a man who is genial enough, but quite capable of preserving the requisite degree of discipline. His following consists of the perfect gentle knight, just back from the wars which he has waged in all parts of the world, who has laid aside his armour but not his rust-stained jerkin to join this pilgrimage with his son, who is little more than a youth, is dressed in the latest court fashion, and is *au fait* in every point of chivalric etiquette. One servant only has this worthy knight, a sturdy yeoman-forester with arms well kept, well versed in woodcraft and the tales of Robin Hood. Another gentleman is the epicurean old franklin, well loved for his hospitality. The ecclesiastical profession is well represented. The prioress, "full simple and coy," is the most attractive of these. She is a very refined, amiable, and tender-hearted lady, who takes pains to be dignified, is very fond of her dogs, and is decidedly well favoured. With her was another nun, who acted as her

The Squire.

The Summoner.

The Clerk.

The Doctor.

The Pardoner.

The Merchant.

THE CANTERBURY PILGRIMS.

(By permission of the Right Hon. the Earl of Ellesmere.)

chaplain, and three priests.[1]   A monk there was who had but
one fault, forgetfulness of the rules of his order, and an inordinate love of hunting.   He was well mounted, well dressed,
and well fed.   Smooth-tongued Friar Hubert is no less im-
pressive a personage, and his acquaintances are drawn from
every class but the poor.   The appearance of the summoner
with his fire-red pimpled face, narrow eyes and loose morals,
is as little attractive as that of his friend the effeminate
pardoner, with his beardless chin, goggle eyes, dank yellow
hair, and squeaky nasal voice.   None the less, however, is
the latter a good man of business, with a wonderful power of
persuading people to buy his pardons.   This unedifying
group of clerics is contrasted with the unselfish, patient,
zealous country parson, who is learned but poor, and " Cristes
lore, and his apostles twelve,. He taught, and ferst he folwed
it himselve."   It is not without meaning that this man is made
brother to the ploughman whom Langland had taken as his
hero, and that the tales should close with his sermon upon
penitence as the " good way " for men to walk, on their
spiritual pilgrimage.   The canon and the canon's yeoman join
the cavalcade as they near Canterbury.

The other learned professions are represented by an Oxford
scholar, who cares more for books than aught else, and hence
grows not fat; a serjeant of the law. a clever, learned, and
experienced gentleman, who is of very different opinions with
regard to money from the scholar, and a doctor of physic,
equally fond of money, but a skilful practitioner, and a
moderate liver.   The manciple, who is quite as good a business
man, and the wife of Bath, the naïvely outspoken autobiographer,
much experienced in the holy estate of matrimony, belong to
no particular group.   Business and labour find their representatives in a merchant, a sailor, a cook, a weaver, a dyer, an
upholsterer, a haberdasher, a carpenter, a miller, a reeve, and the
ploughman already mentioned.   But these are little more than
sketches, and either did not attract the poet so much, or he

---

[1] This is inconsistent with the earlier statement (Prol., l. 24) that twenty-
nine pilgrims assembled at the Tabard, for three priests would bring the
number up to thirty-one. This is one of the evidences that the final revision
even of the Prologue was never made. For the nun-chaplaincy *cf.* Sussex
Archaeol. Soc , ix., p. 15 : "An Episcopal Injunction to the Prioress of Easeburn
in 1478," and Dugdale, Mon. III., p. 415, in a report on the Elstow nunnery.

The Friar.

The Sailor.

Chaucer.

The Franklin.

The Prioress.

The Monk.

THE CANTERBURY PILGRIMS.

(By permission of the Right Hon. the Earl of Ellesmere.)

intended to reserve their nearer characterisation for the prologues of their respective tales; an intention which, however, never found fulfilment, if it ever existed. Finally there is Chaucer himself, a figure of distinct value in the composition, both from a realistic point of view, and because the consciousness we have of the poet's presence all through lends extra point to the irony and pathos of the tales. Thus there are in all thirty-four characters.

Structure of the Poem. The greatest care is taken not only to bring the various tales into the most effective contrast by the order in which they are recounted, but also to put into the mouth of each speaker just such a tale as shall thoroughly suit, and thus help to illustrate his or her character. In this way Chaucer was enabled to make use of the long literary experience and of much of the actual production of his whole life. Nothing was thrown away. The various phases, fashions, and modes of thought and work through which he had passed, and which were his no longer, were thus no less useful than the work produced in the period of full ripeness. With an intense dramatic sense, unequalled until the end of the sixteenth century, he made the varied sympathies and tastes of his long artistic development expressive of the characters of his personages, and turned in this way even the faults and weaknesses of poems written in the past to account. Thus the hazy, romantic, completely mediæval tale of " Griseldis " is given to the Oxford scholar; the well-meaning sermon on " Repentance " is put into the worthy parson's mouth; and with excellent irony the interminably dull and moralising " Tale of Melibœus," the " *litel* thing in prose," is told by himself, after the company have rebelled against the satirical skit upon the tales of the ballad-mongers for its wearisomeness. Out of the frying-pan into the fire, it seems to us, and did no doubt to him, but to the average mind of Chaucer's day the " treatise " was acceptable enough.

The work reflects, not only society, but the literature of the time. Every type of mediæval writing is there—the chevalresque and the popular romance, sacred legend and epic saga, history and myth, fabliaux [1] and lais,[2] prosopopœia,[3] allegory and sermon.

[[1] Stories in verse.   [2] Short poems in eight-syllable verse, recounting some incident of legendary lore.   [3] Personification.]

The Nun's Priest.

The Second Nun.

The Monk's Dogs.

The Yeoman.

The Manciple.

The Parson.

THE CANTERBURY PILGRIMS.

(By permission of the Right Hon. the Earl of Ellesmere.)

The
Metre.

And the verse is varied, according to the subject-matter. The tragic stories, such as the " Monk's Tale," are written in an octave stanza of French origin, with rime order *ab ab bc bc.* The pathetic ones, such as the "Clerk's Tale," in the famous Chaucer stanza, or "rhyme royal," which is, without doubt, of Provençal origin (p. 282). In the "Rime of Sir Thopas" "rime couée" (tail rime) is adopted ; and lastly, in the Prologue, nearly all the interludes and the majority of the tales (in all the best ones) the heroic couplet is the measure. The line is of the same structure as that in the octave stanza and the "rime royale," and the idea of combining such lines into rimed couplets was probably suggested by the Southern cycle of legends of saints, which were in Middle English Alexandrines, rimed in couplets (*cf.* p. 123). It will be remembered that Chaucer first used this measure in his own legend-cycle the "Legende of Gode Women," the sub-title of which, the "Seyntes Legende o. Cupyde," showed that the poet had the sacred cycle in mind. Finally, two of the tales—that told by Chaucer himself and that of the parson—are in prose.

The comprehensive scheme of this great work was, however, never carried out. Death came to the cunning artist before the poem was half finished ; and though the arrangement of some of the tales in relation to the whole is clear enough, it will probably never be possible to assign to all their proper place. In some cases we may be sure that the poet himself had come to no definite conclusion. He seems originally to have intended that each pilgrim should tell four tales, two going and two on the return journey. Afterwards he determined to assign but half this number to each, but of this less ambitious plan not half was finished. This was the work on which Chaucer was almost wholly occupied from 1388 (the probable date of the Prologue) till his death in 1400—only twelve short years ! His wife had died in 1387, for soon after we find him mortgaging his pensions. Philippa Chaucer may have been an unsympathetic but careful housewife. A new royal pension of £20, granted in 1394 but paid irregularly, still left him in debt, and the post of Clerk of the King's Works, held from 1389-91, had but temporarily banished care. The respite had, however, been well used in producing the ironical "Wife of Bath" and "The Merchant's Tale."

In 1391 he wrote his "Treatise on the Astrolabe," a book *Chaucer's later Works.*
on astrology for his ten-year-old son Lewis. In the last ten
years of his life must also be placed his unfinished "Quene
Anelyda and False Arcyte," which contains fragments of the
original "Palamon and Arcite"; his "Complaynt of Mars and
Venus," translated from the French of Granson for the
Duchess Isabella of Lancaster: his "Praise of Women" and
the "Goodly Ballade of Chaucer," both addressed to the
queen, if, indeed, they are his work. Two ballads of warning
are addressed to Richard, whose unpopularity was rapidly
bringing his downfall, and the humorous "Compleynte to his
Purse" earned from the weak, good-natured king a letter of
protection against his creditors in 1398. When Henry IV.,
the son of Chaucer's old patron, John of Gaunt, seized the
throne next year, one of his first acts was to grant the poet
another pension of twenty marks. With new hope Chaucer
bought the lease of a house in the garden of St. Mary's
Chapel, Westminster, for fifty-three years. The sale was completed on Christmas Eve, 1399; on October 25th, 1400, the
poet was dead.

The works of which the names alone have survived are: *Lost Works.*
"The Book of the Lion," mentioned at the end of "The
Parson's Tale"; "Origenes upon the Mandeleyne," mentioned
in the "Prologue" to the "Legende of Good Women," l. 428;
a translation of Pope Innocent's "De Miseria Conditionis
Humanae," mentioned in the Cambridge MS. of the "Legende
of Good Women"; and a translation of the "Roman de la
Rose."[1]

The following works were at one time supposed to be
Chaucer's, and were consequently included in editions of his
works. They are now known not to be so. "The Complaint

[1] Lines 1-1705 of the Glasgow fragment are now accepted as genuine by
Kaluza ("Chaucer u. der Rosenroman, 1893") and Skeat ("Chaucer's Works,"
Vol I., 1894). Kaluza also accepts l. 5811—end. The matter is far from
settled. Lounsbury's defence of the whole ("Studies in Chaucer," II., l. 166)
is unreliable, and has been refuted by Kittredge ("Studies and Notes in Phil.
and Lit.," Boston, 1892). Ten Brink ("Chaucer-Studien," p. 14*ff.*, and "Gesch.
d. engl. Litt., 4") rejected the whole; so did Skeat formerly ("Essays on
Chaucer," Chaucer Society. No. 14, and Introduction to the "Prioress's Tale,"
Clarendon Press Series). Lindner ("Engl. Studien," x., 163) argues for a com-
posite authorship. Mr. A. W. Pollard, in his excellent little "Chaucer Primer."
summarises the arguments for and against fragment A.

of the Black Knight" is by John Lydgate; "The Cuckoo and the Nightingale" is similar to Chaucer in style, and takes its two opening lines from the "Knight's Tale"; "The Flower and Leaf" was written by a woman in the fifteenth century; Chaucer's "Dream" was first printed in 1598, and is certainly not his; "The Court of Love" was written about 1500; "The Testament of Love" and several short poems, included in the sixth volume of the Aldine "Chaucer," are likewise spurious.

A few words must be devoted to the language of Chaucer and of his time. In the second half of the fourteenth century the struggle for supremacy between the Anglo-Norman dialect and the native English had finally been decided in favour of the latter. Indeed, Anglo-Norman had given way even at the court to the more fashionable Central French, and hence Chaucer says of the prioress who had no relations with the court :—

> And Frensh she spak ful faire and fetisly,
> After the scole of Stratford atte Bowe,
> For Frensh of Paris was to hir unknowe.

At the same time the battle had left its marks on the victorious tongue in the loss of inflections, the addition of a large number of Romance words to the vocabulary, a general state of uncertainty as to the position of the stress in the borrowed words, and even, through analogy, in many native ones. This last phenomenon was greatly to the advantage of the poets of that time, who were thus enabled, without any offence to the ear, to make use of either accentuation. The example, however, led to evil results, for imitators of Chaucer, living in a later time, when the area of this fluctuation was far less wide in colloquial speech, extended the liberty, for which they found a limited authority in their master, to the violation of all music and rhythm in their verse. The secret of Chaucer's versification lay in the skill with which he was able to combine the spirits of two so utterly diverse metrical systems as the Germanic and Romance. And this secret could never be discovered by counting of syllables and neglect of the laws of stress; hence the monstrosities of Lydgate. But the service done by Chaucer for English literature was more than a metrical one. Him we have to remember and thank, not only as the "Father of English Poetry," but also as the "Father of Literary English." His works had more influence in directing the form of the written language than those of any other writer, Wycliffe not excepted. The dialect which he spoke was that of London, *i.e.* South-East Midland, and London was at that time the centre of the intellectual, commercial, and social life of England, even more than to-day, for then she had no rival Manchester, Liverpool, or Birmingham. It was from London and the royal court that the modern language of half the world sprang, not from the Universities, and not from the Church. And Chaucer was the directing and forming channel through which it was handed down to the use of future generations. An attempt has been made, but without success, to prove that the royal proclamations and other governmental documents were the chief agents in the production of a single literary language,[1] but though these, no doubt, were not without their effect, the main service must be ascribed to the poet. Wycliffe, doubtless, prepared the way for Chaucer by his polemical pamphlets, written in English, and the literary language once established was further defined by the printing-press of Caxton, another Londoner by residence though not by birth. (*Cf.* Chap. VIII.)

AMONG the men whom Chaucer must have met at John of Gaunt's Palace of the Savoy was undoubtedly John Wycliffe. This almost sternly practical man, by far the greatest thinker of his age, must have made an impression on the Court poet, were it only by his fearlessness in thought and deed, and by the idealism which raised his every act above the commonplace. Yet wanting as he was in the artistic sense, it is no wonder that he exerted less influence on the work of Chaucer than on that of Langland, who cared far less for the form than for the spirit. His attitude as a thinker and a religious reformer can only be understood in the light of previous events in the history of the Church, and this side of his activity is dealt with elsewhere. In ecclesiastical politics he was the follower of Bishop Grosseteste, who had already, in

Wycliffe and English Literature.

---

[1] *Cf.* Morsbach, "Ursprung der N.E. Schriftsprache" (Heilbronn, 1888).

the thirteenth century maintained the interests of the national Church in opposition to those of the Papacy. But Wycliffe, as a thinker, felt bound to find some philosophic basis for his action, and found it in an idealised form of the feudal theory of lordship based on reciprocity of service. This was his famous doctrine of Dominion: the development of a theory originated by Richard Fitzralph, Archbishop of Armagh (p. 222). His final theological position was equally conditioned by his metaphysical thought, for his denial of transubstantiation was based upon the theory that annihilation

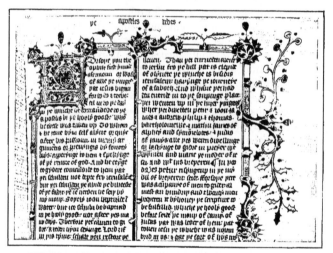

PORTION OF WYCLIFFE'S EARLIER ENGLISH BIBLE (MS. Egerton 617).

was a fiction, and that it was not in the power because not in the nature of God to annihilate anything. Indeed, all his works, even his sermons, show this love of theories and illustrations gathered from his philosophical and scientific studies, for he was scarcely less well read in science than in metaphysics. . This taste he owed to his early University training, possibly in some measure also to his Northern blood.

Wycliffe was a great and original thinker, a fierce opponent of superstition, and, in his later years, of the men-

dicant friars,[1] but he was no stylist; yet, though our literature
is not indebted to him for a single work of art, she owes to
him many new ideas. He had worked out a complete philosophical system in a series of treatises of metaphysical,

PORTRAIT OF WYCLIFFE.
(By permission of the Rt. Hon. the Earl of Denbigh.)

ethical, and political content, collected under the title "Summa

---

[1] He repeatedly brands them with the name of CAYM (Cain), taken from
the initials of their orders: Carmelites, Austins, Jacobins (or Dominicans),
Minorites (or Franciscans).

Theologia," and remarkable, not so much for the originality of their thought, as for the manner in which he deduces and finds philosophic bases for his ideas. His " Trialogus " (published 1383) treats, in four books written in dialogue, of God, the world, virtue, sin and redemption, the sacraments, the servants of the Church (especially the mendicant friars), and the last judgment. It gives, in strictly scientific form, the latest results of his researches made during the translation of the Bible. He was the first to uphold the absolute and sole authority of Scripture, and this, together with his translation, had much to do with the influence which the style and thought of that Book have exerted upon our best literature ever since. In this sense he was a true precursor of the Reformation, though he did not anticipate the Protestant doctrine of Justification by Faith alone. He was aided in the vast undertaking of giving the Bible for the first time complete in the vulgar tongue to the English people by Nicholas Hereford, an Oxford man, who was teaching at Queen's College, when, in 1382, he had to flee the country before the

Wycliffe's Bible. storm which was already breaking on the Lollards. The larger part of the Old Testament was translated under his direction,[1] and when he suddenly left England to appeal to the Pope in person against the sentence of excommunication passed on him, the translation had been completed to Baruch iii. 20. Wycliffe was responsible for the remainder of the Old Testament, and for the Gospels of St. Matthew and St. Mark. The rest of the New Testament was possibly by another hand, working under Wycliffe's direction.[2]

No sooner was the work completed (1383-4) than its many imperfections became evident. The laudable desire to be faithful in the rendering of each word had led the translators into grievous Latinisms which had their source in the Vulgate Version they were using.

Participial constructions and the use of the Latin perfect passive were common, especially in the work done under the direction of Hereford, who was far more painfully literal in his

---

[1] Much of it was the work of his own hand, but part was done by others. (Cf. Hermann Fischer : "Ueber die Sprache Wyclifs," Hallenser Diss., 1884.)

[2] Cf. Ernst Gasner : " Beiträge zum Entwickelungsgang der neuenglischen Schriftsprache," Inaugural Diss., Hanover, 1891.

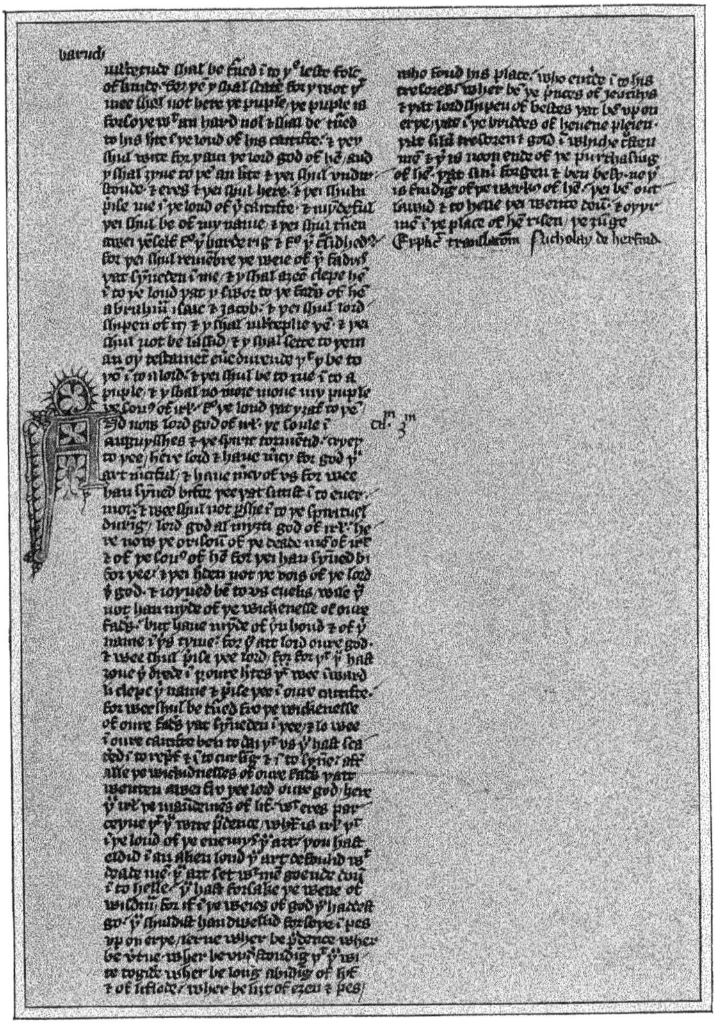

PAGE FROM NICHOLAS OF HEREFORD'S VERSION OF THE OLD TESTAMENT.

(MS. Douce 369: *Bodleian Library, Oxford.*)

rendering than his master ; so the work of revision began under Wycliffe's guidance. The task fell to John Purvey, but was not completed till 1388, four years after the master's death.

Wycliffe's Tracts. Wycliffe's English tracts and pamphlets stand in close relation to his translation of the Bible, for they constantly refer to the teaching found in that Book, and are written in the same strong and clear, if somewhat unformed, English. They are essentially moral, not theological, treatises, and deal with the same social and clerical abuses that had been matter for Walter Map's satire in the past, and were now the mark for Langland's irony. The most famous, because one of the most theological, called "The Wyket," speaks of the great temptation the faithful are under to leave the narrow path and the " strayte gate " which leads to "everlasting lyfe," and to wander into the " large and broad way" of belief in transubstantiation "that leadeth to dampnacion." The conception of human life as a pilgrimage, with Heaven our home, has always been popular, but was especially so in a time when the Renaissance had not yet taught men to see. the dignity and worth of the present life in the flesh.

Had the Government been willing to watch over and direct the impulses to thought and reform which had their source in Wycliffe, instead of crushing them, as they mercilessly did in the next century, England might well have seen a great advance made towards the establishment of a strong prose tradition some two centuries earlier than was actually the case. As it was, the fifteenth century had nothing to show but the beginnings of this in the sense of rhythm, and even occasional passion, with which Malory was inspired by his rambles through the mystic jungle of Arthurian romance. It was longer still before argumentative prose took form.

Langland. In Wycliffe's day reform was far more engrossing than form ; and artist though he was, this remark holds good for Wycliffe's great fellow-labourer, William Langland. Yet nothing could be more widely different than the temperaments, theories of life, and methods of work of these two men. Langland was every whit as much a man of ideals as Wycliffe, but his ideal polity is built up from the existing order of things by a reform of the individual. Both saw something rotten in the state of England ; but Wycliffe found it in the system, Langland in the men who worked it. Could men be made perfect, then law might be neglected; but he had no touch of the leveller, and could feel no sympathy with the catch-phrases of John Ball. He saw no reasons for altering the *rôles* allotted to the various figures in the feudal system of society; he wished to inspire each with the desire to play his part manfully. "Rightful reason should rule you all," is his answer to the query about the existence of gentlemen in the days "when Adam delved and Eve span"; and testing them by this touchstone, he does not spare his blame of begging

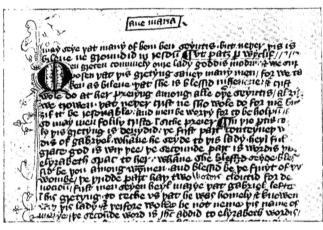

PART OF A TRACT BY WYCLIFFE (MS. Harl. 2385).

friars, lying pardoners, and such-like caterpillars of the commonwealth, or even of the king himself.

It is consistent with all this that the means he took of expressing his ideas was not a polemical pamphlet, but a dream allegory, in which this insistence on the importance of the individual, and his careful observation of men rather than Man, makes him a draughtsman of types of character, and a humorist rather than a logician. If as a reformer he is related to Wycliffe, he is quite as much the humorous dramatic poet whom Chaucer found suggestive. He came of a much humbler stock than either, and was probably in one of the lower orders of the priesthood. He had a wife and family, and does not seem to have had much personal intercourse with men outside his own home. He was probably born at Cleobury Mortimer, in Worcestershire (*c.* 1332), and was very likely attached as lector or exorcist to some chantry or mortuary chapel in London. This is about all we know of his life, yet there is no poet whose character is more clearly seen in his work.

" Piers Plowman. "The Vision of William concerning Piers the Plowman" is a religious allegory, which the poet was constantly revising and extending, probably up to the very last. The MSS. fall into three groups, of which the earliest (1362) is thirty years older than the latest (1393), by which time the poem had grown out of all compass, and had lost the little unity it originally possessed. The middle group of MSS. gives the poem as it was in 1377 : certainly the most interesting and most artistic stage of its development. "Piers Plowman" is divided into two main sections. The first, common to all three versions, is complete in itself, and, as literature, is the better. It tells in somewhat rambling fashion the pilgrimage of a company of men and women to the shrine of Truth, under the guidance of Piers the Plowman, who, as the poem proceeds, rises in the poet's conception from being only a representative English labourer to the type of Christ Himself. It is an allegory with a large number of digressions and discussions having small connection with the main action; but it is not mere abstract moralising allegory, like so much medieval art. The popular seven deadly sins are introduced, but the scene of their confession before Repentance is a piece of true comic drama, in which the characters are no personifications, but living English peasants and mechanics. These concrete figures are as different from the abstractions of "The Dance of the Seven Deadly Sins," or of "The Induction," or even the romantic procession in "The Faery Queene," as Volpone is from King Hart. It is not till we come to such plays as "The Roaring Girl," or such poems as "The Jolly Beggars," that a parallel to them can be found. Another notable feature of the first part in the version of 1377 is the introduction of the fable of belling the cat, which first appeared in literature in a Latin and French collection of fables in a Paris MS. of the year 1333.[1] The beast-fable was, however, no

---

[1] The Latin version is evidently the older. The fable later became very popular all over Europe. It is found in La Fontaine.

new idea in England, and it formed a part of the Pre-Norman tradition.which Langland represented. The cat typifies Edward III., the kitten Prince Richard, the " route of ratones . . . and smale mys myd hem," the Lords and Commons.[1]

The second section of the poem is that which varies most in the different versions. It is made up of three parts: the lives of Do-wel (*i.e.* do your duty on earth), Do-bet (*i.e.* translate the Bible and do deeds of charity), and Do-bèst (*i.e.* become a fisher of men). In the second and third versions

PRIDE.   A STERN FATHER.
(*MS. Douce* 104: *Bodleian Library, Oxford.*)

of the poem these parts are extended by a number of visions of theological and moralising import, such as that of Fortune, Nature, and Reason, that of Faith and Charity, and of the triumph of Piers, the whole concluding in deep depression and melancholy with the vision of Antichrist. Do-bet had closed triumphantly with the poet awakened by the clashing of the hopeful bells on Easter morning ; but in the conclusion, Conscience, who has fled for refuge to the church, hard set

---

[1] *Cf.* J. J. Jusserand, " Observations sur la Vision de Piers Plowman," *Revue Critique*, 1879, II. Semestre, and Skeat's small edition of Piers Plowman, 1888, in which he accepts Jusserand's conclusions.

by Sloth and Pride, starts out as a pilgrim through the wide world to seek Piers the Plowman, praying the while with tears for grace. That, after thirty years of labour and experience, was the utmost of the poet's hope. Thus the three greatest men of the time all thought of human life under the favourite figure of a pilgrimage, but Chaucer alone treated the conception in the modern spirit.

Structure of the Verse. It has already been pointed out that in form "Piers Plowman" belongs to that group of works produced in the West Midlands which revived in this century the Old English alliterative line, though in a freer form, which was largely the result of linguistic and accentual changes. At the same time, the tendency to introduce four instead of three alliterative syllables helped to hasten the conception of the old long line as two short ones: a conception which was destined to be confirmed when the ballad-singers added the ornament of end or even middle rime. Thus on the basis of such verse as Langland's there had grown up in the eastern counties, under French influence, the Middle English Alexandrine, as we find it in the Tale of Gamelyn, and from the use of middle rime a short-rimed couplet, of which the measure of "King Horn" is the typical example.

Langland and Richard II. In the third version of "Piers Plowman" Langland had spoken more plainly than ever of the ill-government of King Richard, but his next work was directed wholly as a warning to that unhappy palterer. "Richard the Redeless" was begun in August, 1399, when the king was captured, and closes with a welcome to Henry IV. The poem is from the third Passus, an allegorical beast-fable. It is in the same measure as his longer work, the central figure of which had become very popular, and had tempted other writers to imitation. Such a poem is the alliterative "Piers Plowman's Crede," written 1393–1400. By the same author is the "Complaint of the Plowman" (c 1400), a poem in an eight-lined cross-rime stanza of four-accent lines, which in the sixteenth century was included in editions of Chaucer as the "Plowman's Tale."

Gower. A very different person from any of the men we have been talking of was John Gower. Chaucer the artist, Wycliffe the reformer, and Langland the puritan, all in their way

were before their time. They all—even Chaucer—had the
medieval limitations, but in greater or less degree their faces
were set towards the dawn of modern life in the fifteenth
century. Gower was always looking back. He could not help
seeing that the times were out of joint; he could not help
acknowledging the advantages of the new methods in literature
used by Chaucer; but he only adopted the vulgar tongue
as his instrument under the stress of competition, and he saw

GOWER AS A SATIRIST (MS. Tib. A. iv.).

no hope for the land save in retraced footsteps. He was
wholly conservative, wholly medieval. He was a man of great
learning and with considerable sense of style, but he had no
instinct for variety. His English verse is fluent and harmonious, his language lucid, and even forcible at times, but
he has no touch of brilliancy, no play of fancy, still less any
imagination. He is earnest, sententious, and grave; he is never
profound. He can describe realistically the vices of which
the lover may be guilty, but he cannot delineate character.
He can tell a story with some sense of proportion, yet if his
original has failed to grip the dramatic kernel, Gower is

unable to make good the omission. Indeed, he often allows himself to boil down the most effective passages of his original into a dry summary of contents. His best and most poetical work is undoubtedly to be found in his " Cinquante Balades" and a few other French poems which have come down to us. His natural elegance and polish of manner find in these short poems a peculiarly fitting form.[1]   They are not long enough to make monotony of treatment possible, their complexity of form ensures sufficient variety of music, and their erotic theme keeps moralising at a convenient minimum.   The majority were probably written early in life, though some, such as the envoi of the " Cinquante Balades," addressed to Henry IV., and the thirty-fifth balade, which clearly refers to the " Parliament of Fowles," are evidently of much later date.

Gower s Life

John Gower, born in the second or third decade of the century, was most probably a member of the family of Sir Robert Gower, a large landowner in Suffolk and Kent, and was till the later years of his life closely connected with the southern county.   He writes of Wat Tyler's rebellion as an eye-witness. He married late in life, and died in 1408 as an old blind man in the priory of St. Mary Overies (now St. Saviour's), Southwark, of which foundation he was a great benefactor.   His first ambitious work was a long poem in French, now lost, on the

and Works.

virtues and vices, called " Speculum Meditantis."   This was possibly written before the death of Edward III.   Soon after Richard's accession he began (1381) another long moralising poem, which was not finished till near the end of the reign. This time writing in Latin elegiacs, with a tendency to punning and assonance, and no great regard to quantities, he described at length in the first book of the " Vox Clamantis " the peasants' revolt under Wat Tyler, making use of prosopopœia, as Langland had done in his fable of the rats and mice and his " Richard the Redeless."   In the six following books, which only make up three-fourths of the whole in length, he proceeds to preach the need for a purer faith, the sins of the clergy and lawyers, the dangers of Lollard doctrine, the sensuality of the serf, and the avarice of the merchant.   What with Chaucer

---

[1] Gower s "balades" are poems of three stanzas, each consisting of seven or eight lines, the last forming the refrain. followed by an envoi in four lines, thus *a b a b b c (b) C* thrice, followed by *b c b C* in the envoi.

gives rise to some humorous ironical trait in one of his characters serves Gower as material for sharp satirical invective. A
sort of sequel to this poem is the " Chronica Tripartita," which
gives in running Latin hexameters a hostile account of Richard's

GOWER'S TOMB, ST. SAVIOUR'S, SOUTHWARK.

conduct of affairs from 1386 till his death and the accession of
Henry IV. In two MSS.[1] ten short poems follow (most of them

---

[1] Those of All Souls' College, Oxford, No. xcviii., and the Cotton Collection
(Tib. A. iv.), British Museum.

Latin), which either inveigh against Richard or praise Henry of Bolingbroke.

The "Vox Clam-antis."   In the "Vox Clamantis," after describing the evil condition of his own day, the poet continued with a picture of the five ages of the world, based on the vision of Nebuchadnezzar, concluding with a description of the seven deadly sins. He adopted the same plan, though allotting different proportions to the various parts, in his best-known work, the "Confessio Amantis" (1393),[1] an English poem of about 30,000 lines, in the same metre as the "Boke of the Duchesse." He compressed the first two subjects into the prologue, the third he expanded into the framework of the actual poem. Taking from the "Roman de la Rose" the idea of the author as a lover, he makes Genius,[2] the priest of Venus, his confessor. The lovers' confessions make up the poem. Intermixed with much discourse on universal knowledge, philosophy, and morals, culled from the popular "Secreta Secretorum," Genius recounts a hundred and twelve stories, biblical, classical, and medieval, in illustration of the seven deadly and more numerous minor vices into which a lover may fall. No work shows so clearly as this the inconsistencies of Gower's character. The confessor is at one moment a true servant of the goddess, describing in sensuous detail the temptations of the lover, or in mystic subtleties the conventional code of love, as laid down in the "Roman de la Rose"; at the next he is the priestly exponent of science, religion, and morals. The poet and lover alternate constantly with the pedant and priest. The only really readable parts of the poem are the tales; their tone and substance, however, being sometimes curiously ill-fitted to point the good moral intended. With the tale of Dido in mind, as an illustration of carelessness, and remembering that all the poet's blame in "Canace" is for the father's rage, we shall not miss the full significance of the epithet Chaucer gave

---

[1] It is now certain that the first edition of the poem was finished in 1393 (not the second, as used to be thought), and that the second, in which the dedication to Richard is replaced by one to Henry IV., was not published until after Bolingbroke's accession. This makes Gower's transference of allegiance easier to understand, and more accordant with his conservative character. *Cf.* C. F. H. Meyer, "John Gower's Beziehungen zu Chaucer u. König Richard II." (Bonn, 1889).

[2] Genius, in the second part of the "Roman de la Rose," is father confessor to Dame Nature.

his friend. Whether the two poets were less friendly at the close of their lives, as has been said, is uncertain. Perhaps Chaucer's strictures upon "Tyro Appolloneus," and "such cursed stories," caused a coolness between them, but nothing can be argued from Gower's omission of the eulogy on his friend from the second edition of the "Confessio." for Chaucer was then dead, and it would have been meaningless to recommend him to cease writing on love. Equally inadequate is the suggestion that the plagiarism of either poet was the cause of the estrangement, if any, for where they told the same tale they evidently used a common source.[1] This is surely a case where "De mortuis nil nisi bonum" is consistent with a love of truth.

THE Black Death made special havoc among the clergy. It is expressly noticed in the statutes which the Countess of Clare gave to Clare Hall in 1359, shortly before her death; and a similar wish to replenish the supply of educated men no doubt stimulated the efforts of other benefactors of learning. Of these, by far the most brilliant and original was the great architect and politician, William of Wykeham, who became Bishop of Winchester in 1366, and Lord Chancellor in 1367. He was probably not at the University himself, but rose to eminence as a man of practical ability. He was the leader of the conservative Church party against the movement in theology and politics associated with the name of Wycliffe. But he was anxious to combat an intellectual movement by intellectual weapons only; and for this object he purposed to increase the production of capable men carefully trained at the centres of learning to support orthodoxy of every description. Walter of Merton and his imitators had devised means for the eleemosynary encouragement of promising students at the universities; and schools for the education in grammar of boys, too young to be matriculated with advantage, already existed in connection with the greater monasteries, such as Canterbury and York. But to Wykeham belongs the distinction of having combined and adjusted the requirements of elementary and higher studies by a scheme

H. E. D. BLAKISTON. The Universities.

The Work of William of Wykeham.

---

[1] They both tell the tales of Troilus and Cressida, Florent, Constance, Ceyx and Halcyone, whilst the stories of the "Legend of Good Women" all recur in the "Confessio Amantis."

which marks him out as the founder of the English public-school system, since his day the almost universal method of education for the upper classes. Subsequent endowed grammar schools, ·from Henry VI.'s Eton College downwards, merely imitate Wykeham's arrangements; and the influence of his Oxford statutes may be as plainly traced in those of later foundations up to the sixteenth century as the ground-plan of his buildings in colleges of a date even more recent.

Wykeham's school (St. Mary College of Winchester) was erected near his episcopal palace of Wolvesey. It was amply endowed for a warden, ten fellows, a headmaster, an usher, and seventy scholars, with chaplains and choristers. It was first started in 1373, but not finally installed in its spacious buildings till 1393. The Oxford College (St. Mary College of Winchester in Oxford) was for a warden and seventy poor scholars (to be rather older than the ordinary undergraduates), with ten chaplains and three other clerks and sixteen choristers for the chapel services. It commenced work about 1375, and took possession of New College in 1387. The founder continued to revise the statutes and safeguard the interests of his creations till his death in 1404, when he was buried in a splendid chantry in the nave of Winchester Cathedral, then lately rebuilt by him.

The scheme of Winchester and New Colleges shows that Wykeham intended them to be "not merely eleemosynary institutions, but great ecclesiastical corporations." The buildings show a grand adaptation of the common monastic plan to a different and more public use. At Oxford the lofty chapel and hall with gateway and muniment towers defended from the cold winds the large low quadrangle containing the sleeping-rooms and studies; the cloister on one side and the kitchen on the other are remote from interruptions. There was a large library, an audit-

WYKEHAM'S STAFF.
(By permission of the Warden of New College, Oxford.)

room; a brewhouse and a bakehouse outside the gate; everything, in fact, which could be needed for the various wants of the members. The warden's residence, allowances, privileges, and provision for hospitality, are on a level with

Photo : Gillman & Co., Oxford.

MERTON COLLEGE LIBRARY.

those of the abbot of a wealthy monastery. Every detail of the life of his scholars is minutely prescribed by Wykeham's statutes; in fact, perfection is the note of his whole design. The particular course of study to be followed within the college is marked out; and in this Wykeham, as " the first founder who contemplates any instruction being given to his scholars in college, is the founder of the Oxford tutorial system,' by which the teaching in the Faculty of Arts has been almost exclusively carried on. All recognised branches of learning were to be encouraged at New College; of the seventy scholars, ten were to study civil law, ten canon law, two might devote their time to medicine, and two to astronomy, while the rest were to pursue arts or theology. The text-books of the arts students were still those of the old routine of grammar and

QUADRANGLE, WINCHESTER COLLEGE.

logic, Donatus and the Latin Aristotle; of classical studies in the modern sense there was as yet no sign in England. A curious result of the strictness of Wykeham's rules survived till 1834, in the custom by which New College men could demand degrees without passing the ordinary examinations. This arose from the founder's prohibition to his students to sue for the " graces " or dispensations from the statutable conditions of residence, etc., which at last formed the only preliminaries to a degree. Wykeham provided that his Winchester scholars should have an exclusive right to places at Oxford; by this he secured a high standard of efficiency in the elements of learning.

But in the preferences which he left to his own kindred instead of his estates, he placed his colleges under an obligation which was fertile in litigation and inefficiency.

Wykeham's aim was in a great measure successful. New College produced no learned men at first, but several able ecclesiastics, among whom the statesman, Henry Chichele, Archbishop of Canterbury, and William Waynflete, Bishop of Winchester and Lord Chancellor, themselves founded colleges after Wykeham's design. At a later period the careful grounding given by the school began to tell, and the pioneer of the Oxford revival of learning, William Grocyn, was a Wykehamist.

BOTH sanitary and preventive, or quarantine, practices arose out of the experiences of the Black Death and of the outbursts of plague that followed it at short intervals. Scavenging of a kind there must have been long before; the force of public opinion, as expressed in the manorial and other courts, would have kept down nuisances offensive to the sight and smell. But the great difficulty, then as now, was the radical disposal of refuse. It was comparatively easy to deposit the clearings of scavengers in "laystalls," or rubbish-heaps, or to throw offensive matter into the town ditch, or into the river, or the nearest standing water. London in the fourteenth century saved appearance well enough; it was known to foreigners as the "White City," which one of our poets, an admirer of things archaic, took to mean "London small and white and clean." In a sanitary inquisition of the year 1343, it is worthy of note that the offensive latrines, dust-heaps, and the like, which were reported upon, were all, or nearly all, in the narrow lanes leading down to the Thames. The laystalls were outside the walls, or beyond the town ditch; in Henry V.'s time there was a common latrine on the Moor (the marsh, or fen, between Moorgate and Finsbury), which became so offensive that it was suspected of breeding sickness and was ordered to be removed. The shambles were inside the walls, not far from Newgate, and were a continual source of annoyance to the whole locality both from the blood flowing in the kennels and from the transit of offals through the streets and lanes to the jetty at Barnard's Castle, from which they were thrown into the Thames. The

CHARLES
CREIGHTON.
Public Health.

Sanitation.

first Sanitary Act ever made in England was passed by the
Parliament of Cambridge in 1388, and was chiefly directed
against the throwing of dung, garbage, and other corruptions,
etc., into ditches, rivers, and waters, whereby the air was rendered
greatly corrupt and infect, and many maladies were engendered.
But it should be remembered that, with all these sources of contamination, the town ditch of London contained " great store "
of excellent fish until the time of Henry VIII., that the Thames
ran clear and was frequented by salmon from the sea, and that
at so characteristic a medieval town as Chester, the Dee (which
encircled two-thirds of the city, and received the refuse) had
salmon fisheries of great value directly under the walls until
long after the medieval period. The real difficulties of sanitation
do not arise until population begins rapidly to exceed its old
limit, until suburbs begin to spring up in the old waste places
where laystalls were wont to be, and until the river and its
tributary streams can no longer absorb, so to speak, and oxidise
the refuse of the town. So far as domestic sanitation is concerned, its difficulties were naturally greatest in the houses without any ground attached to them situated in the poorer lanes
and alleys, which were usually close to the walls, either within
or without them. The houses of the richer citizens stood in
gardens; but it appears from a Paston letter (fifteenth century)
that the possession of a garden was no reason why there should
not be a " draught-chamber " within doors.

　　The scavengers, who were said in the time of Elizabeth to
be exercising their functions " as of old," corresponded more
to inspectors of nuisances than to the actual carriers of refuse.
Originally, the duty of removing refuse fell on the householder
himself; but by the year 1540 it appears from the burgh records
of Ipswich that men were appointed by the municipality
to remove the town refuse and deposit it at four stated places
without.

　　It is, of course, conceivable that our ancestors may have
been more tolerant than ourselves of gross offences to sight and
smell. But while that is doubtful, it is further clear that they
knew the same subtle or unperceived dangers of befouling the
air, the water, and the soil with putrefying matter, excremental
or other. The connection between infective or other diseases and
such befouling is the explicit motive of the Sanitary Ordinance

THE FIRST ENGLISH SANITARY ACT
(*Record Office.*)

of Edward III. in 1371, of the Sanitary Act of Richard II. in 1388, of the Sanitary Ordinance of Henry V. in 1415, and of the Act of Henry VII. against the shambles in 1488–89. These Sanitary Ordinances are so few and far between that it may appear as if the English people in early times had been indifferent as to sanitation; but it has been truly remarked by Hume that the frequency of a particular class of measures in the Statute Book goes to show, not so much that their object was attained in a high degree, having been a matter of special solicitude to rulers, but rather that negligence was so chronic and persistent as to demand incessant legislative checks.

The effects of the Black Death did not end with the thinning of the population and the rise of wages. The whole national life was demoralised. The surviving rich fell into unheard-of luxury, vulgar display, and avarice; the monks added whole manors to their estates, and rivalled the secular lords in their style of living; the parish clergy deserted their cures to live in London "in Lent and Yule," taking service as clerks of the Chancery and Exchequer. Many of the people lived out of wedlock, others made unhappy marriages; few children were born, and the rising generation was brought up in indulgence and ignorance. Meanwhile the king and his lords were engrossed with the wars in France. But the most disastrous consequence of the Black Death was that the seeds of bubo-plague remained in the country, to burst forth in widespread epidemics time after time. Langland, the realistic poet of the age, compares the prevalence of sickness to "the rain that raineth where we rest should." The second great epidemic, which fell most on the upper classes and the rising generation, was in 1361, the third in 1368–69, the fourth in 1375, the fifth in 1382, and the sixth in 1390–91. One or more of these may have been of some other type of disease than the plague, and there were certainly outbreaks of sickness during the same period (not counted among the six), which were due to scarcity or to spoiled grain and fruit. But, it is clear that plague of the same type as the Black Death—not so severe, doubtless, as in that primary visitation, but causing panic and mortality which called for the prayers of the Church and for plenary remission to the dying—formed part

The Recurrence of Plague.

of the epidemics which were numbered to the *quinta pestis* in
1382, or the *sexta* in 1390–91. The last-named was, indeed,
compared to the Black Death itself, and in the city of York
is said to have destroyed eleven thousand, an incredible
number, as it would have been three-fourths of the inhabitants.
Many of the towns were much decayed; probably none of
them, except London, York, Bristol, Coventry, and Plymouth,
regained the population they had in the first half of the fourteenth century until the Tudor period, and some of them, such
as Bodmin, Sarum, and Leicester, not until late in the reign
of Elizabeth. The old saying ran: "Lincoln was, London is
York shall be." The decline of Lincoln was certainly progressive, while that of Norwich, which came next to London
before the great malady, was relatively even more marked.
On the other hand, the county of Kent, which was the scene
of the Peasants' Revolt in 1381, came to the front in population, with its various ports, doubtless from its proximity to the
English possessions in France. The poll-tax of 1377 showed
a population of about two millions and a half in all England,
excluding Wales and the counties palatine of Chester and
Durham. That was a generation after the Great Plague; but
the numbers showed no recovery, for there is cause to think
that the population before the mortality had been some four
millions—a total which England did not reach again, or exceed,
until after the Reformation.

BEFORE proceeding to describe the final catastrophe of the
Peasants' Revolt, towards which England was now hurrying,
and the further impolitic steps on the part of the landowners
which brought them face to face with it, it will be pleasant
to turn for a moment to the doings of those agriculturists
who, even before this, had given up the struggle to keep down
wages, and being not too wedded to old fashions to accept
the inevitable, had already begun devoting their attention
to devising other and more original methods by which to
escape from the dilemma into which they had, by no fault
of theirs, drifted.

W. J. COR-
BETT.
The Agri-
cultural
Revolu-
tion.

So far as we have gone, we have found the demesnes of
the manors cultivated in one of two ways: either by the

Management of Land. customary and unpaid labour of villeins, who in return had holdings for nothing, or by the paid services of practically free labourers, who if they also had holdings, paid a fixed money rent for them to the lords, the rent in its origin representing a commutation of the older customary services. In either case it was the lord of the manor who found any capital that might be required, and who, either in person or through a bailiff, directed the various operations of agriculture : chief among which, however unsuitable to the land, was the growing of corn. It is obvious that these two ways of using the demesnes were not the only alternatives which were open to their owners if they wished to make a profit on them ; for they do not include either letting them on lease, which is nowadays the ordinary method, or using them as sheep farms, for which, in many instances, they were alone adapted. But neither of these ways had the sanction of custom ; indeed, both were directly in opposition to the old manorial traditions, and so as long as the older systems worked smoothly there was very little chance of either being introduced. As soon however, as the possibility of getting labourers to work on profitable terms vanished, and it became important to do with **Sheep Farming and Leases.** as few farm servants as possible, both these methods were seen to have attractions which outweighed the dominant aversion to trying novelties. For sheep farming almost dispensed with the necessity of having labourers, except in small numbers, while leasing transferred the burden of getting them from the shoulders of the landlord to those of his tenant. If, too, a demesne was not let in a block, but divided into a number of small holdings, even the tenants, who in this case would be small men, would, in all probability, be under no necessity of hiring labourers ; for in most cases they would find their own labour, aided by that of their wives and families, sufficient. In fact, by adopting this plan, many of the free labourers, tempted by the idea of becoming their own masters, could be induced to give a reasonable rent for being allowed to work a piece of land which, at the bidding of a master, they would not have worked except at unreasonable wages. All these considerations put together could not fail in the long run to have some effect on the more clear-sighted of the landowners, and it is not surprising to find that on the better-managed estates both sheep farming and the leasing of the demesnes came more and more into vogue at the very time when a great number of landlords seemed only bent on reactionary measures.

Of sheep farming not much need be said here, as it will be necessary to discuss it at much greater length when we come to the fifteenth century, at which date it assumed the position of a leading national industry. It may, however, be pointed out that its introduction just at this time was particularly encouraged by Edward III.'s commercial policy. For that monarch not only paid the greatest attention to regulating and developing the export trade in wool, which had always been carried on between England and Flanders, but also did all in his power to persuade Flemish weavers to come over and settle in this country, and so founded a home manufacture for draperies, which soon increased so greatly in volume that it easily used up all the fleeces that could be supplied

AULNAGER'S SEAL.
(*Ipswich Museum*)

by the English farmer. Its introduction, too, as long as the country was depopulated from the effects of the Black Death, was undoubtedly a good thing; for in this way much land could again be turned to good account which must else have remained waste from lack of persons to till it. In the end, however, as we shall see, it was fated to cause a great deal of social discontent. For to carry it out it was necessary for the lord to withdraw his share in the common fields from tillage, and lay it down in grass; while he further not infrequently was tempted to enclose the whole of the manor wastes without sufficiently compensating his tenants for the loss of their rights of pasture which consequently ensued; and both these measures, by interfering with their customary means of gaining a livelihood, tended to disorganise the peasants' agriculture, besides greatly restricting their chance of obtaining employment.

New Social Dangers.

Letting the demesne on lease, on the other hand, was not attended by any of these drawbacks, but rather by substantial advantages; for it was to the introduction of this method of cultivation that England, in a large measure, owed the rise of that class of sturdy yeomen farmers who, for about two centuries, formed the backbone of the country. The change thus brought about was by no means so revolutionary as that which accompanied the introduction of sheep farming, and, indeed, had little direct effect on the manorial system. Its indirect effects, however, as has been well said, were of the highest importance; for it helped to break down the personal dependence of the tenantry on their lords, on which feudalism was based, and set up a new middle class who had to trust to themselves, and who, in time, as they grew in wealth, gradually rose to a position not so very inferior to that of their former masters. It must not be supposed that this was accomplished all at once, or that the leaseholders on their first creation at once assumed the character and status of the later tenant-farmers. On the contrary, it took some time, and the earliest leases were not at all like those with which we are now familiar. For nowadays when a tenant takes a holding, he is usually expected to find the capital necessary to work it from his own resources, the landlord considering that he has done the whole of his part of the bargain when he has supplied the bare land and farm buildings. But the new tenant-farmers in the fourteenth century could not have done this, for none of them were wealthy men, and unless they had had the capital lent them in the form of the stock, both live and dead, which was already on the land and which the landlords no longer themselves required, they could not

Stock and Land Leases. have undertaken to farm their new holdings. The leases, therefore, which they took, were what have been termed "stock and land leases," in which both the land and everything required to begin cultivating it were let together, the tenant not only having to pay a yearly rent but being also bound on the expiration of his term to render up to his landlord the same amounts of seed-corn, live-stock, and implements as he originally received or else their estimated value in money. The leasing of cattle or sheep on these terms had become quite common even before the plague, five shillings a year being an ordinary rent for a cow; and there are early instances of the leasing of demesne land in the same way, but it only became a common practice in the latter half of the fourteenth century. And here, perhaps, we ought to note that leasing the demesne to a tenant, who did not thereby acquire his lord's manorial rights, is not at all the same thing as leasing the whole manor to a "firmarius" or farmer with all the seigniorial rights entire, a practice which had for long been a special feature of some estates. For we often find the manors belonging to the Chapter of St. Paul's farmed out singly to the various canons ; but this did not imply any abandonment of the system of cultivating under bailiffs. The stock and land lease proper, on the other hand, did, and when

THE TREASURY, MERTON COLLEGE, OXFORD.
(By permission of the Warden.)

once adopted seems to have lasted on most estates for about fifty years, after which it was in its turn abandoned and its place taken by the ordinary form of lease for a life or years. Thus the Merton College estates were nearly all let on these stock and land leases for short terms soon after the Black Death, but at the beginning of the fifteenth century they had all been changed for leases for long terms of the ordinary kind. From this it would appear that it took about fifty years from the introduction of leases in any manor for a fairly substantial kind of yeomen to grow up, and that it was only after a certain amount of tutelage that the class really became self-dependent. A single instance will be sufficient to show what kind of stock was supplied to the tenant with the land. In 1360 Merton College let its lands at Farley, in Surrey, and "the tenant took nine horses and a bull, valued at 10s. each; ten cows, valued at 11s. each; four oxen, each at 18s. 5d.; twenty-four quarters of wheat, at 6s. 8d. a quarter; six and a half of sprig, at 4s.; three quarters and a bushel of 'frumentum vescosum,' at 4s.; three quarters three and a half bushels of barley, at 4s. 8d.; two of pease, and two of vetches, at 3s. 4d.; and forty-nine and a half of oats, at 2s." [1] In all, that is to say the college supplied its tenant with capital to the amount of about £22, but this does not include either poultry or any agricultural implements, which in many cases were also supplied.

Efforts at Reaction. While some of the more versatile landowners were thus withdrawing from the direct cultivation of their estates, the more conservative and pugnacious were still engaged in their uphill struggle with the intractable labourer. Year by year, however, the chances of success became more remote, the population, if anything, declining, until at last the exasperated and baffled employers determined on the desperate expedient of reverting wholesale to the personal services of former times. Not only did further commutation cease to take place, but manumissions and exemptions, which for years had passed unchallenged, were set aside, and all the ingenuity and learning of the stewards of the various manors was invoked to hunt up informalities and omissions in the court rolls, which might serve as pretexts to the lords for reinforcing their antiquated rights. The law, it must be admitted, was apt to be on their side; for whereas the lords could usually produce some documentary evidence that the services had existed, there was very little to show how the labourers had escaped from performing them; and, even if there had been, the place where such disputes had to be tried was the manor court itself, in which the steward

---

Sprig was possibly a kind of barley, "frumentum vescosum" wheat and vetches sown together. *Cf.* Thorold Rogers, "Agriculture and Prices," I., p. 27.

presided, the king's courts always refusing to interfere in quarrels between the unfree and their lords. Parliament, too, as usual, could always be called in to assist the latter, and in the first year of Richard II.'s reign an act was passed annulling all claims to freedom based upon the evidence of Domesday. If such a venerable record was not respected, it is not likely that any others that the villeins could produce would be. Indeed, the statute seems devised to help the lords in any event, for it winds up by ordaining that they "shall have Letters Patent under the Great Seal, as many and such as they shall need, if they the same require." That they must have required them, and in great numbers, there can be no doubt, and very little either that, when they got them, they were of no avail. For the labourers had not stood out all these years to give in tamely in the end, and if . the lords had the Crown and Parliament to back them, their opponents by this time had found allies in the followers of Wycliffe, in the wandering friars, and

"WHEN ADAM DELVED AND EVE SPAN"
(MS. Roy. 1 E. iv.).

in John Ball, the mad priest of Kent The last-named boldly took up a socialistic position, saying that things never would go right in England so long as goods were not in common, and so long as there were villeins and gentlemen ; and the popularity of this view was shown by the rhyme which everywhere passed from mouth to mouth, beginning, " When Adam delved and Eve span, Who was then the gentleman ? " The bitterest feelings, in fact, soon became engendered among the peasantry, and a fierce spirit of resistance sprang. up, which led to the formation of what would now be called agricultural unions and other formidable combinations against their employers. As the statute already quoted says, they did "menace the Ministers of their Lords both of life and member and, which more is, did gather themselves together in great Routs and did agree by such Confederacy

that every one should aid other to resist their Lords with
strong Hand." When once things had got to such a pass,
very little more provocation was wanted to set the strong hand
actually in motion, and this little was quickly supplied by the
excessive taxation which had to be laid upon the country to
repair the growing disasters of the French War.

The
Peasant
Revolt. In 1377, just before Edward III. died, the financial position
of the kingdom had become so bad that a new expedient
had to be invented, and Parliament voted a poll-tax of a
groat, or four-pence, on all over the age of fourteen, both men
and women, excepting veritable beggars (p. 209). In 1379 this
imposition was repeated and made more productive by being
graduated from £6 13s. 4d. on wealthy nobles like the Duke
of Lancaster, down to a groat on the ordinary labourer.
Even so, "great grudging and many a bitter curse" followed
on the levying of the money; but the last straw which broke
down the patience of the peasantry altogether only came in
1380, when the graduation was abandoned and a new tax of
three groats laid on every person, of whatsoever state or condition he might be, who had passed the age of fifteen. In
money of the present day this would mean over fifteen shillings
a head, so it is not hard for us to realise what a burden the
tax must have formed on the slender resources of the medieval
cottar and farm labourer. Proportionately, too, it was on these
classes that it weighed heaviest, and many must have echoed
the complaint of the anonymous author of a political song who
wrote: "To seek silver to the king, I my seed sold: wherefore
my land lieth fallow and learneth to sleep. Since they fetched
my fair cattle in my fold: when I think of my old wealth, well
nigh I weep. Thus breedeth many beggars bold; and there
wakeneth in the world dismay and woe, for as good is death
anon as so for to toil." Anyhow, fresh rhymes at once spread
through the country summoning all to revolt and trample on
their oppressors. "John Ball," the doggerel ran, "greeteth you
all, and doth for to understand he hath rung your bell. Now
right and might, will and skill. God spede every dele. [1] The
die, in fact, was cast, and the end of the following spring saw
the whole of the peasantry of the home counties in insurrection, headed by their parish priests, and backed by the

[[1] *I.e.* every part of the movement.]

poorer inhabitants in the towns. The original outbreak began
in Kent with the murder of a tax-collector by one Walter the
Tyler, who afterwards marched to Canterbury to release John
Ball from prison, and then upon London at the head of a large

ANCIENT HOME OF THE CAVENDISH FAMILY, CAVENDISH, SUFFOLK.
(The murdered Chief Justice had purchased the Manor in 1359.)

rabble, computed at 100,000 men, slaying every lawyer and
burning all the manorial records he could find upon his way.
But this movement must have been preconcerted; for as Wat
Tyler, south of the Thames, was marching on Blackheath, north
of the river the Essex men were marching towards Mile End,

and the men of Hertfordshire towards Highbury. Riots, too, were going on all over the country—at St. Albans, at Bury St. Edmunds, at Winchester, Cambridge, and Norwich, at York, Beverley, and Scarborough, in Surrey and Sussex, and even as far west as Devonshire. Everywhere, too, the rioters seem to have been animated by the same ideas, and to have demanded emancipation from the power of the great landowners, or, as their petition expressed it, the abolition of villeinage as an institution, the reduction of rent to fourpence an acre, free access to all fairs and markets, and the establishment of a free peasant proprietary to be governed by the king directly.

When asked by their king at Mile End, "What will ye?" the Essex men shouted back, "We will that you free us for ever, us and our lands, and that we be never more named or held for serfs";

THE DAGGER THAT SLEW WAT TYLER.
(By permission of the Worshipful Company of Fishmongers.)

and it was in the same spirit that the villeins round St. Albans forced the abbot to give up the charters which proved them to be bondmen and broke in pieces the millstones which as bondmen they had been compelled to use. At first it seemed as if the movement would succeed (p. 210); but the peasants quickly alienated the sympathies of the townsfolk by their violence. In London they burnt the Temple and the palace of the Savoy, ransacked the Tower, and murdered the Archbishop of Canterbury, the Treasurer and the Chief Commissioner for the levy of the poll-tax. At Bury St. Edmunds they killed the prior and Chief Justice Cavendish, and all over the country they attacked the justices and the manorial officials. Many foreigners, too, lost their lives, while everywhere manor-houses and granges were pillaged and destroyed. When, therefore, their leader, Wat Tyler, was slain by the hand of the Lord Mayor of London, the crisis was over, and Richard II. found himself at the head of an army sufficient to stamp out the revolt in three weeks. . The

stubbornest resistance offered anywhere was in Essex, where
Richard was confronted with his own charters; but he now only
answered, " Villeins you were and villeins you are. In bondage
you shall abide, and that not your old bondage, but a worse."
And in this he was as good as his word. When Parliament met
in the autumn, the question of enfranchisement was, indeed,
submitted to it by the king and Council, but only to be summarily rejected. As the Commons pointed out, the charters of
enfranchisement granted by the king without their consent were
entirely illegal, and this consent they never had given and

TOMB OF ARCHBISHOP SUDBURY, CANTERBURY CATHEDRAL.

never would give, " were they all to die in one day." On the
contrary, they would do what in them lay still further to secure
the continuance of villeinage and increase the disabilities
of the bondmen. To this the king consented, and together
they passed statutes ordaining that all manumissions, releases,
and other bonds made during the late tumult should be void,
and that the Council should provide a sufficient remedy for all
who made complaints touching " charters, releases, obligations,
and other deeds and muniments, burnt, destroyed, or otherwise eloined" (made away with), on their furnishing sufficient

proof of the muniments so lost, and of the form and tenor of the same. Six years later they took further precautions against the supply of villeins diminishing by enacting that, if any person, boy or girl, should have served at husbandry at the plough and cart till the age of twelve, from thenceforth they should abide at the same labour, and that it should be illegal for them to be taught any other mystery or handicraft. Attempts were also made to prevent the children of the lower orders from being sent to school lest they should be advanced in the world by entering the Church.

The Measure of its Success. How far all these efforts to keep things stationary were really successful is not altogether clear. Some writers, indeed perhaps the majority, have assumed that they entirely failed, and that, though the revolt to all appearances was easily suppressed, the villeins really gained their ends. For in their eyes the very number of efforts at repression is evidence of their practical futility. The adoption of an argument of this kind, however, is hardly convincing, while actual manorial records can be found which testify to the continued exaction of services all through the fifteenth century and far into the sixteenth. At Wilburton, for instance, in the Isle of Ely, no change was effected until Tudor times, and we read of royal manors where Elizabeth found serfs to emancipate in 1574. In reply it is easy to characterise such instances as exceptional, but they certainly are in keeping with the lament of Fitzherbert, that when he wrote in 1523 the country was still disgraced by the retention of villeinage. On the whole, then, it seems more accurate to hold that no sweeping change followed the revolt, but that at the most it only accelerated changes already in progress, and assured for good and all their final triumph. The revolt, in fact, though it did not at once render serfdom a thing of merely antiquarian interest, must have more and more convinced the landowners that the game they were playing was not worth the candle. In increasing numbers they must have come to see that, though the labour services were of more value than the money payments for which they had been commuted, they would nevertheless be losers by their restoration ; for there were methods of using their land now within their reach which were more profitable than either of the older systems, and which, when adopted, would secure an income at the cost of far less trouble to themselves than could ever be hoped for if they continued to struggle on with unwilling agents in the old grooves. Such a view of the great revolt of course somewhat diminishes its importance, but only very slightly, and it must ever remain memorable as the first struggle on a large scale between capital and labour in England.

LONG before chapters on economic history found their way into text-books every schoolboy was familiar with some of the changes of the fourteenth century which have exercised a great and enduring influence on English social life. The Black Death and the uprising of the peasants have never been wholly neglected by English historians, while the encouragement which Edward III. gave to the woollen manufacture has been the first introduction of many to the story of the growth of English industry. The development of commerce during the latter half of the fourteenth century, and the elaborate system of organisation to which it gave rise, are not inferior in interest or importance to these more striking topics. For the commercial legislation of this period was not the work of men dominated by a set of economic principles which they believed could show them how to overcome all the difficulties in the way of progress· When we read the statutes or the Rolls of Parliament we are impressed with the absence of definiteness of aim or policy which characterises the legislation of this period. Principles of action which have now become axioms had to be found in the painful road of experience. In the fourteenth century subjects such as the incidence of taxation, the best method of organisation, movements of currency and the foreign exchanges, bristled with difficulties which could not be surmounted by the easy method of ignoring their existence. The commercial world was less homogeneous than it is now, the administration of justice less pure, commercial integrity less common. Legislation was of necessity largely empirical, and it is partly to this fact that we must attribute the frequent and almost · bewildering changes in the statutes. Acts of Parliament, again, were not so effectively administered as they are now; some were not enforced at all. Complete efficiency in the strict administration of a statute was not necessary to indicate its

W. A. S.
HEWINS
Industry
and
Commerce.

probable results. A brief trial of a measure might justify its repeal or more thorough legislation on the same lines, according as experience showed that it was likely to be mischievous or the reverse.

The Wool Trade.   Little experience was needed to show that friendly relations between Flanders and England were necessary to the prosperity of both countries. A dearth of English wool stopped the Flemish looms; when the markets of Flanders were closed to the staple product of England, English wool-growers were threatened with ruin. At the commencement of the period with which we have to deal, the woollen trade had been depressed for some years; from 1336 to 1363 the price of wool was only once, in 1343, above the average price of the fourteenth century; in 1349 it fell to 1s. the tod,[1] the lowest price touched during the century. The principal causes of the depression which we must briefly notice in order to understand subsequent legislation were four in number. The year 1328 was marked by a sudden reversal of the policy of the time. So far there had been a steady growth of the staple system. In that year, however, Edward decided to try an experiment in free trade, and all staples were abolished. Another statute to the same effect was passed in 1334. There can be no doubt that such an attempt was premature. In that age some regulation of commerce was necessary in the interests of the traders themselves. Confusion and uncertainty naturally followed, and in the absence of adequate means for their protection we may be sure that merchants would be unwilling to incur the risks of foreign trade. We may with confidence attribute part of the depression to this measure. In 1336 a still more serious blow was struck at the staple trade of the country by the prohibition of commerce between England and Flanders. From what has already been said about the importance of the Flemish market to English wool-producers, it is obvious that a prohibition must have been very injurious to both countries, and the measure of 1336 may be regarded as the second cause of the depression. Thanks to the good offices of James van Artavelde and Edward's need of Flemish aid in his war with France, friendly relations between England and Flanders were re-established, and in 1341 Bruges became the staple for English wool. For the next four

[¹ Usually the tod was 28 lb.]

years there was an improvement in trade, and the cities of
Flanders enjoyed great prosperity. The death of Artavelde
(July, 1345), and the troubles which followed, again caused some
falling off in the Flemish demand. Still there was no serious

Photo: Neurdein, Paris.

BELFRY AND CLOTH HALL, BRUGES.

interruption of friendly intercourse, and in 1347 the Flemings
resisted Count Louis' efforts to detach them from the English
alliance. But in 1348 it was found necessary to expostulate
with the cities of Bruges, Ghent, and Ypres, for trying to

66

prevent Lombard merchants from buying English wool, their object evidently being to keep down prices by securing a monopoly of the demand for themselves. The troubles in Flanders during the year, culminating in civil war, practically put a stop to industry, and made Bruges anything but a safe place for business transactions. The natural consequence was a fall in the demand for wool. The depression in trade, therefore, which began with the abandonment of an old policy, was probably accentuated by the prohibition of 1336, and the civil troubles in Flanders during the following years.

Effects of the Black Death. There was a fourth cause of great, though exaggerated, importance, viz. the Black Death. It would be easy to attribute to this visitation changes which were due to other influences. Had nothing of the kind occurred, there is no reason for supposing that subsequent commercial development would have been materially different. In his commercial policy Edward III. does not appear to have been influenced by the great calamity. The prices of the year 1349 show that it caused a restriction of the foreign demand for English goods and of the supply of foreign commodities. But so far as foreign commerce was concerned, the effect of the Black Death was immediate and temporary only. It had none of those far-reaching consequences in this sphere of economic activity which made it a turning point in agricultural history. The depression was, for the time, rendered more severe than it otherwise would have been. But it is noteworthy that the decline of trade was attributed not to its influence, but to the fact that the staple was out of the country.

The French War. The French war was not an unmixed evil so far as commerce was concerned. The wool subsidies, the purveyance of ships, the subordination of trade to the exigencies of foreign diplomacy, the insecurity of travelling, the ruin and havoc of France, the withdrawal of skilled artisans from the exercise of their trades at home, no doubt operated as a serious check on economic progress. But indirectly the country gained. The Flemings would, probably, not have so readily accepted Edward's invitation if their own country had not been involved in civil dissensions, and if England had not been relatively a place of security. It is possible that the same causes left the way more open for the development of the English cloth manufacture. By the capture

of Calais (August, 1347), followed by the defeat of the pirates
in the Channel, England secured commercial advantages which,
to some extent, outweighed the evils of the war. One of the
greatest difficulties in the way of foreign commerce was the
insecurity of the Channel owing to the ravages of pirates. It
was no slight gain to convert the home of some of the worst of
these robbers into a staple for English goods. The risks of
trading were diminished, and English merchants enjoyed by one
route comparatively secure ingress to Continental markets.
Edward's constant need of money for carrying on the war had
consequences of great importance in the economic sphere. It
impressed upon him, in regard to the collection of the customs,
the necessity of an effective organisation, the advantages of
which were great, although his exactions were a severe strain
upon the resources of the country. It made him more and
more dependent upon his people; and whether or not he cared
for the development of commerce, he was obliged to pay more
regard to the interests of the trading classes. On the whole,
therefore, it is probable that the French War hastened a
commercial development which, in the ordinary course of events,
would have been long delayed.

It is clear, then, that the time was ripe for new measures *Edward*
in commercial policy. Trade was depressed, but the country *III.'s*
had the means of starting on a career of great prosperity. The *Commer-*
experiment had been tried of doing without staples for English *cial*
goods altogether, and it had failed. Foreign staples had been *Policy.*
tried with unsatisfactory results. A dispute with the Hanse
merchants in 1350–51, in which not they, but the citizens of
Bruges, were to blame, did not diminish the friction with that
city. If a foreign staple were desirable, England had possession
of Calais; and it was now less necessary, in the interests of trade
or the French War, to cultivate friendly relations with Flanders.
Calais afforded easy access to France, and wool was so indispensable to the Flemish weavers that they would be obliged to
take it on whatever conditions England imposed. As long as
the staple was out of England it was impossible for the king's
officials to secure that ample flow of wealth into the English
exchequer which the French War rendered necessary. Hence
we have the great Ordinance of the Staple (1353).

The broad features of Edward's commercial policy are

strongly impressed upon this important measure; and although there were some modifications in subsequent years, they remained substantially the same for 200 years. On the occasion of the great wool grant (1338) special ports in England had been appointed for shipment of the wool, and a similar arrangement was made by the new ordinance. The following were the staple towns and the corresponding ports :—Newcastle-on-Tyne, York and Hull, Lincoln and Boston, Norwich and Yarmouth, Westminster and London, Canterbury and Sandwich, Winchester and Southampton, Carmarthen, Dublin, Waterford, Cork and Drogheda. The mayor and constables of the staple, who were to be elected annually by the native and foreign merchants of the place, were to exercise jurisdiction over all persons concerned in the business of the staples, and their proceedings in all matters of debt and contract were regulated by the Law Merchant, and not by the common law or the customs of the town. On taking office they swore that " well and faithfully they would serve the king in the office to which they were· chosen; that they would intreat the merchants of the same staple faithfully; and that they would do equal right unto all persons as well of this realm as unto strangers after the ordinances made by the king and his council and the Law Merchant." There was an important provision for the settlement of disputes. Two foreign merchants, one for the north, the other for the south of England, might be elected to sit with the mayor of the staple and watch the interests of alien traders. In trials, the jury was to consist of natives, if the parties to a dispute were natives; of foreigners, if foreigners; and if one was a native and the other a foreigner, the jury was to be composed equally of natives and foreigners. Alien merchants were treated very generously by this ordinance, but the policy with regard to them during the reign varied so frequently that we shall not further discuss its provisions. To give validity to contracts, the mayor of the staple was to attest them under the seal of his office, charging $\frac{1}{2}$d. for every contract under £100, and 1d. for more than that amount. All merchants had liberty to buy and sell goods in any part of the country provided they were taken to the staple, and special exemptions were granted to certificated carriers. Forestalling and regrating were prohibited; and, in the staple towns, special streets or warehouses were appointed; the rent of the latter was to be fixed by the mayor and constables with four of the principal inhabitants.   The customs duties were regulated and machinery provided for their collection, while the exportation of bullion was prohibited, except by merchant strangers, who might carry back the portion of their money which was not laid out in the purchase of English commodities.   Such was the staple organisation.   During the latter half of the fourteenth century the staple towns were frequently altered, and there were other changes in the ordinance from time to time.   But the general policy, except in the treat-

Lincoln.   Southampton.   Boston.
STAPLE SEALS IN THE FOURTEENTH CENTURY.

ment of foreign merchants, remained unchanged until the loss of Calais in 1558, which inflicted a death-blow on the staple system.   It should be noticed that at this time the merchants of the staple consisted of all those, trading in the specified commodities, who took the required oath of obedience to the king's officials.   They were less an exclusive trading company than an organ of administration.   In the bitter controversy about the trading companies at the end of the sixteenth and during the seventeenth centuries, many adherents of the old system looked back with regret to the comparative free trade of those days.

At this time the resort of foreigners to England was greater than that of Englishmen to foreign parts.   Chaucer's "Schipman"

"Knew well alle the havens, as thei were,
From Gothland to the Cape of Fynestere,
And every cryke in Bretayne and in Spayne."

**Foreign
Trade.**

So that he did not go very far from home. English merchants,
indeed, frequented the marts of Flanders, and were to be found
in the Mediterranean, but during the period under discussion,
the bulk of the foreign trade of the country was in the hands of
various bodies of foreign merchants. Of these the most important were the Hanse merchants, who had an extensive
provincial organisation in England. So powerful were they,
that in 1348 there was a complaint that one of their number
had bought up all the tin produced in Cornwall during that
year. The " Flanders galleys " already sailed from Venice and
periodically visited England, bringing the manufactures of
Venice and the produce of Persia and the Indies, and taking
back the staple commodities of the country. By these and
similar agencies all kinds of foreign commodities found their
way to the great English fairs, whence they were dispersed
through the country. Eastern produce, Italian silks and velvets,
glass, furs and amber from north-eastern Europe, the fine linen
and cloth of the Flemish cities, the wines of Gascony, Spain,
and Greece, millstones and candles from Paris, iron from
Norway and Spain, mercury from Spain and Transylvania, and
many other commodities too numerous to mention were bought
and sold in England.

**"Mercan-
tilism."**

With the reign of Richard II. signs are not wanting of the
approach of the "mercantile system," which dominated the
commercial world from the days of Elizabeth to the publication
of the "Wealth of Nations." We have already noticed the subordination of trade to foreign diplomacy. Under Richard II. we
meet with the first Navigation Acts, which were no doubt
rendered necessary by the injurious effect on the navy of
Edward's purveyance of ships. They were imitated a few years
later in Scotland; but they failed in their object, perhaps from
the want of adequate means of enforcing them, but more probably because the time was not ripe for such an experiment.
The Government could not call into existence a powerful mercantile marine by simply passing an Act of Parliament conferring a monopoly on English shippers to the exclusion of
foreigners. Foreign merchants continued to resort to England
and to carry away the staple commodities of the realm. But
the prevailing jealousy of foreign merchants found expression
in several Acts of Parliament; and, though the measures varied

considerably from time to time, there appears to have been a systematic attempt on the part of the merchant class to reverse the policy of Edward III., which had been, on the whole, favourable to foreigners. We can see the effect of this change more clearly in the fifteenth century.

Looking through the Statute-book, our first impression is that commerce, during the latter half of the fourteenth century, was so cramped by absurd regulations that progress was well-nigh impossible. But the measures of this period were the result of practical efforts to cope with difficulties, by men who were untrammelled by any theoretical system. Edward III. took counsel with his merchants in making provision for the regulation of trade. Many of the means adopted will not bear the test of criticism from the modern economic standpoint. But it must be remembered that the conditions of every economic problem have changed since that era. Practically it will be found that there was much more freedom than at first sight appears. In many cases the merchants obtained what was of greater importance than freedom in a wild lawless age, viz. security. If we subtract from the statutes of Edward III. all these regulations which were intended for the protection of property, for the repression of piracy and smuggling, for securing fair dealing between man and man, the regulations to which reasonable objection can be made become greatly reduced in number.

In the period which succeeded the Black Death little outward or visible change passed over English town life. It was already a settled thing that England was to be one kingdom in a sense in which no other country of Europe was at that time one. The danger that London would form an *imperium in imperio* such as Venice and Florence had formed within that geographical expression which men called Italy, the danger that the Cinque Ports would form a confederation as independent of the government at Westminster as the Hanseatic League was of the yoke of the Holy Roman Empire, was already past. Yet outwardly there was little difference to be recognised between the two kinds of municipalities. Almost all over Europe the municipal form was tolerably similar, while almost as wide powers and even wider immunities were accorded to a citizen of London than to a

C. R. L.
FLETCHER.
Town
Life.

citizen of Nuremberg. Would the titular head of the Germanic confederation, if he had ridden with his train of knights and followers into Lübeck or Augsburg, and sent his marshal, or the steward of his household, to choose lodgings for his suite in the houses of the citizens by the simple process of putting a chalk cross on the doors, have found those crosses rubbed out, and " the men and serjeants with horses and harness," belonging to the royal party, ejected by force because it was " contrary to the liberties of the city"? Scarcely; yet this is what had happened in London a few years before the Black Death; and the Sheriff of London being indicted for " the said contempt within the verge " (*i.e.* of the king's court) was triumphantly acquitted; and it was laid down that the mayor and citizens should in future " enjoy such liberty of livery of lodgings, within the city aforesaid, in such manner as their predecessors."

The power of regulating trades and crafts seems also to have been completely in the hands of the municipalities, and it was not until the sixteenth century that the experience of the craft-guilds was taken up and embodied in Parliamentary enactments binding on the whole kingdom. But the Customs, both export and import, and the control of the wool trade, had become matters of national concern; and one finds that towns constantly had to petition the king for leave to impose a new port-due or a new toll at their gates or bridges, and that they were not unfrequently refused. Above all, coinage was in England, as it never was on the Continent, entirely a national and nowhere a private concern. Professor E. A. Freeman struck the right note when he said: " The history of Exeter is a lesser one than that of Nuremberg only because the history of England is a greater one than that of Germany." So it was; and by the time that our period opens, miserably behind the German, Italian. and even Southern French cities as all English towns, except London, manifestly were, they were already fitting themselves to play their part actively in the harmony of English national life.[1]

---

[1] The genesis of the English town from one or more agrarian communities, and the rural character (Vol. I., pp 297. 520) which clings to it through the mediæval period, cannot be enlarged upon here. Nor can the curiously complicated rights of ownership in it, which raise problems still awaiting settlement. The student will find abundant illustration in F. W. Maitland's "Township and Borough," 1898.

The whole commercial and industrial activity of England **Seaports.** lay at present in the towns which dotted the eastern and southern coasts from the Wash to the Cornish headlands. Northward of this fringe, indeed, lay Hull, Newcastle, and the debateable town of Berwick-upon-Tweed, which was proud of possessing the longest bridge in England. This bridge, by the

ERPINGHAM GATE, NORWICH.

way, had to be frequently rebuilt, partly owing to the repeated inundations of the Tweed, partly owing to Border warfare ; and there were long periods during which it was suffered to lie in ruins, and " one half-quarter of pease " had to be allowed daily to " six cross-bowmen guarding the ferry of the Tweed " at Berwick. A toll of sixpence on each ship entering the harbour was granted in 1347 by the king towards the rebuilding of the bridge. To the west, too, lay the great port of Bristol and the somewhat less important Milford Haven both being utilised

chiefly as places of embarkation for Ireland, and, perhaps, already for pilgrimages to
St. James of Compostella. By a charter of
Edward III. (1373) Bristol was made into
a county, because the burgesses complained
that they were partly within the jurisdiction
of the sheriff of Gloucestershire, partly
within that of the sheriff of Somerset, and
consequently liable to attend county courts,
juries, assizes, and inquests at Gloucester and
Ilchester respectively, to their great detriment,
and petitioned " that Bristol be not burdened
to send more than two men to Parliament,"
as, perhaps, it had been asked to do as being
situate within two counties — a strange instance of the contempt of our ancestors for
the glorious privilege of heckling the King's
Government !

But it was from Lynn to Falmouth that
the real town life of fourteenth - century
England was concentrated. There stood the
Cinque Ports, now expanding into a considerable confederation of associated towns, still

BRISTOL STATE SWORD, surrounded with their ancient walls, still main-
1373.
(By permission of the Lord taining a rigorous and somewhat tyrannous
Mayor.) control over the lesser lights in their planetary
system, still jealously guarding their rights of fairs and markets;
above all, still remain-
ing the real nucleus
of the naval power of
England. And the
Thames, like a silver
wedge driven into
the heart of this strip
of coast, separated
the eastern associated
towns from the
Cinque Ports proper
and their western de-
pendencies. On the

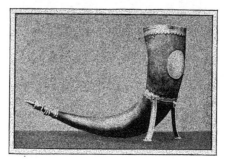

FOUNDER'S HORN, C. C. C., CAMBRIDGE.
(By permission of Messrs. Macmillan and Bowes Cambridge.)

THE LYNN CUP.

[To face p. 346.

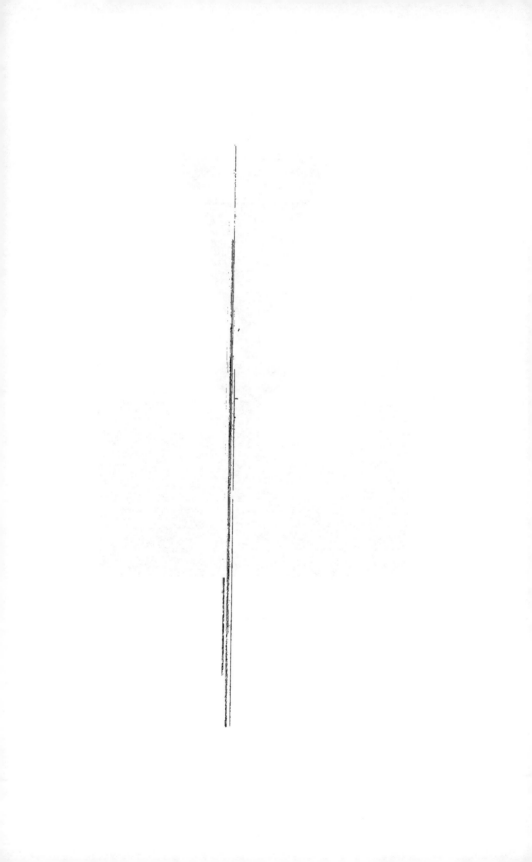

INGATHERING OF AN ORCHARD: BRASS OF ADAM DE WALSOKEN.

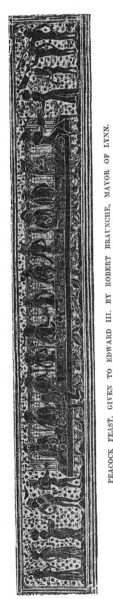

PEACOCK FEAST, GIVEN TO EDWARD III. BY ROBERT BRAUNCHE, MAYOR OF LYNN.

(From Memorial Brasses, St. Margaret's Church, Lynn.)

Thames, and within the jurisdiction of the lord mayor and aldermen of London, "from Staines to Yantlet Creek" (the first "conservators of the Thames"), the Yarmouth fishermen and the Sandwich sailors could meet in peace.

London Life.
Let us try for a moment to realise the life of fourteenth-century London. The houses of mud and timber were beginning to give way to stone and even brick—bounties were given to persons who built with these new materials. Upper chambers,

SHOP OF MEDIEVAL TYPE, ELMHAM, NORFOLK.

called "solars," were being added to the single-roomed houses of former days. These would be used for sleeping rooms, though we find no mention of "parlours," or talking rooms— *i.e.* rooms where a rich merchant would meet his customers and discuss business—before the fifteenth century. The "shop" would still frequently, though not invariably, be in a booth outside the door. The solar was approached by a wooden or stone staircase from the outside. Huge signs swung overhead, and were obliged to be at least nine feet above the level of the street, to allow of a man on horseback riding under them in compara-

DRINKING VESSELS. (*Guildhall Museum.*)
(*By permission of the Library Committee to the Corporation of the City of London.*)

tive safety. Even at that height it must have been an unpleasant task in a high wind. Footpaths there were none; but the road was raised by a slope from the middle downwards to the two "kennels" (canallos), into which the filth of the streets was supposed to run. A little before our period that useful animal the pig had served as scavenger; but it had recently been ordered that "no swine be found about the streets and lanes of the city and suburbs"; if they are found, anyone may kill them, but the owner has the right of pre-emption of the carcass at fourpence. "And he who shall wish to feed a pig must feed it at his own house" (*Liber Albus*, 235). The most minute regulation for prices, for apprentices, for trade of every kind, prevailed; and almost sovereign power over every department of life was in the hands of the lord mayor and aldermen. Every alderman was constantly obliged to go round testing measures and weights

DRINKING VESSELS, 14TH OR 15TH CENTURY.
(*Guildhall Museum.*)
(*By permission of the Library Committee to the Corporation of the City of London.*)

and wine cups; measuring the "ale stakes," *i.e.* long poles fixed over the doors of the innumerable taverns, to see that they did not exceed the regulation nine feet; examining the mesh of the fishing-nets to see that they were two inches in width at the least ("as appears after inspection of the memoranda in the chamber of the Guildhall, namely, the lesser Guildhall"), and that no "gorce, chotnet, chofnet, nor kidel" was used in fishing. Not unfre. quently he would be obliged to act as policeman, and to arrest "persons who should be so daring as to be found wandering by night about the streets of the city after curfew rung out at St. Martin's-le-Grand and St. Laurence, and at Berkyng-chirche [All Hallows, Barking], with sword or buckler, or with other arm for doing mischief"; to shut the taverns and ale-houses at the same time; to see that no suspicious persons were harboured therein. The mere testing of the bakers' materials, under the "assize of bread," must have been of itself a serious task to the city authorities. For instance, the "light bread which is called ' pouf' (puff?) ought to be of the same bolting (*i.e.* fineness) and weight as wastel bread"; "and as to demeisne bread (*i.e. panis dominicus*, the Lord's bread, from the image of Our Saviour stamped on it), it should weigh the same for a halfpenny loaf as a farthing loaf of wastel except nine pennyweights, which may be lost in baking." One does not quite understand why our ancestors, who drank such enormous quantities of beer, left the brewing business in London—and in all other towns apparently— so largely in the hands of alewives, who retailed their own brew on the spot. It was reckoned a low calling, and woe to the alewife who infringed the "assize of beer." After repeated fines she stood in the pillory at Westchepe, where the beer-drinking mob would probably not be very merciful to her. The windows of the houses seem pretty generally to have been made of glass by this time; Edward III. chartered the Guild of Glaziers, but chimneys were long a luxury of the rich.

The Topo-graphy of Old London.

Pauli[1] points out what a much greater effect the natural elevations of ground in old London had on the eye than at present, when we hardly realise that St. Paul's stands on a really considerable hill, and that Fleet Street once crossed a consider- able river, up which barges plied. Of the ground-plan of the present city it would still be possible for our ancestors to recog- nise Cheapside, Cornhill, Leadenhall Street, Thames Street, and perhaps Gracechurch Street. The mighty bridge of twenty arches that had been finished in the reign of King John, and which was spoken of as one of the wonders of the world, with

[1] "Bilder aus Alt-England," 1876, p. 372 *seq.*

its street or shops, its drawbridge in the middle, where the tolls
were levied on "foreign merchants" passing up to the little
wharf of Queenhythe, and over which frowned the Tower with
the grim remnants of mutilated traitors fixed on spikes, was the
scene in 1390 of a curious duel between Sir D. Lindsay, Earl of
Crawford, and Lord Welles, Ambassador at the Scottish Court.

The Scotsman, having been at the
expense and trouble of crossing the
kingdom under a safe-conduct from
Richard II., deserved to win, and did
win. But even London Bridge was in
constant need of repair, and direct
taxes, as well as charitable subscription,
had to be resorted to by more than
one of the Edwards to maintain it.
Naturally the tendency of the City to
extend westwards in the direction of
the great abbey, within whose precincts
the business of the law courts and of
Parliament was transacted, and south-
wards towards the Surrey hills (the
scarcely less important business of bear-
baiting, cock-fighting, and other less
reputable amusements, were chiefly
confined to Southwark; indeed, persons
of evil reputation were regularly hunted
out of the City, ferried across, and made
to pay the boatman for transporting
them), was continually showing itself,
though one finds constant complaint
of the almost impassable condition of
the road from Temple Bar to West-

ST. MICHAEL'S, CORNHILL,
BEFORE 1421.
(From an old Drawing.)

minster. In the reign of Edward III. a special tax on all goods
carried into the City, a sort of octroi in fact, was established for
the repair of the roadway. From London Bridge radiated the
great road to the west, and the high road to the Continent, along
which Chaucer's "Canterbury Pilgrims" had to pass from the
Tabard Inn at Southwark. The almost equally important
"pilgrims' way" to Walsingham, in Norfolk, started from the
eastern gate of the city; and as these two shrines had a

European reputation, it follows that these roads were not traversed by Englishmen alone; Jusserand quotes a decree of the Venetian senate authorising Lorenzo Contarini to visit from Sandwich the shrine of St. Thomas, while the Venetian galleys lay in that port; but he was to be sure to return to his ship the same day.

Other Towns. If other towns were far behind the London of the fourteenth century in splendour and extent of trade, we may be sure that they were tolerably accurate copies of its general principles of

ST. MARY'S HALL, COVENTRY.

life internal and external. The same minute provisions for over-seeing everyone from the cradle to the grave, the same publicity of life (the utter want of real privacy must have been the most serious discomfort of town-life in medieval times), the same outward conformity to the ordinances of the Church, the same secret growths of scepticism with regard to these ordinances, whether displayed in the good-humoured bourgeois banter of Chaucer, or the more serious attacks of the followers of Wycliffe, meet us everywhere. The great churches of Sandwich and Winchelsea, St. Nicholas at Yarmouth, and St. Nicholas at Newcastle, were in their glory in the fourteenth century; the high tide of the Decorated style of architecture had already been reached; but the spirit of unity and brotherhood, which had animated the original building of these monuments, was already passing away. The strife of the various religious orders—monks, friars black and white, parish priests, hermits, pardoners, and pilgrimage-mongers—was degrading the ideal unity, and rending the seamless garment. And in secular matters within the towns a somewhat similar spirit was displaying itself. The separate craft guilds were rising upon the ruins of the old Guilds Merchant, which had once embodied all the trading and industrial societies of each town. Although the municipal and parliamentary franchise still remained in the hands of all burgesses in nearly all cases, yet the time of the " charters of incorporation " was not far distant. When that time should come, the towns would be governed by a narrow oligarchy.

THE instinct which brought our forefathers from Central Asia to the shores of the Atlantic continued to exert an influence over the individual lives of their descendants long after the " Wandering of the Nations " had come to an end. The ecclesiastical system of Christendom with its outward unity,

D J. MEDLEY. *Wayfaring Life in the Midd.e Ages.*

ST. IVES BRIDGE, SHOWING THE CHAPEL AT ITS CENTRE.

its cosmopolitan priesthood, and its affiliated system of mon_asteries, gave occasion for much systematic and indiscrimin_ate travelling, while the stupendous mass of Crusaders of all ages and classes, witnesses to the eagerness with which the lay portion of the population welcomed an outlet for the exercise of the primitive instincts of their race.   In England and elsewhere piety and utility combined to preserve and improve the means of transit.   The danger which attended the traveller caused him to be placed alongside the sick, the prisoner, and the poor, as a special object for the prayers of the Church.   Hence ecclesiastical lands, freed from all other burdens, had from the first submitted to that "trinoda neces_sitas" or threefold obligation on all landowners, which comprised as one duty the maintenance of the bridges: while equally readily at a later age did they share with other lands the obligation of repairing the great highways.   As a matter of fact neither of these obligations was burdensome.   Pious motives often prompted the erection of a particular bridge, and not infrequently lands were left whose proceeds should be devoted to its maintenance.   Often, too, on the bridge or at one end of it, stood a chapel, where the passing traveller might rest his body and, if a pilgrim, refresh his soul. To the offerings of pilgrims at the chapels and the endow_ments of pious builders was sometimes added the grant to an individual of the right of taking toll from all passing over a certain bridge on condition that he kept it in repair.   And in cases where all these methods failed, the trinoda necessitas should have ensured the security of these important com_municating links.   But after the break up of the manorial

Aids to Travel.

A ROYAL TRAVELLING CARRIAGE

system and until the Tudor policy made the justice of peace the State's "man of all work," as he has been aptly described, local government was scandalously inefficient, and the great landowner, retaining the local influence without the responsibility, could laugh to scorn the demands of the neighbouring sheriff or justice for the performance of duties which from time immemorial had lain upon his lands. Consequently we find frequent notices of bridges which through sheer neglect had collapsed and were suffered to remain in ruin. Nor were the roads in much better plight. True, the method of travelling did not demand a carefully prepared surface. Everyone walked or rode on horseback; even the movable furniture and the personal luggage were carried mostly on horses and mules; while the springless carts used for agricultural purposes would not be much the worse for many joltings. But in the fourteenth century great ladies travelled occasionally in carriages gorgeously ornamented and resembling in size and structure a gipsy caravan, or were carried in horse-litters, borne on two long poles, slung on either side of two horses going tandem. No doubt when estates were much scattered, as they were in the centuries immediately following the Norman Conquest, and when the monastic orders were still active, it was to the interest of the chief landowners, both lay and ecclesiastical, to keep the highway in some kind of repair. But at the best of times such roads would have been little better than our country lanes, and a little neglect or intermittent repair reduced them to mere tracks which might be rendered impassable by a long continuance of bad weather. It was a

Modes of Travel.

AND ITS HORSES (*Luttrell Psalter*).

SADDLE HORSES (MS. 264: *Bodleian Library, Oxford*).

not unfounded grievance with Members of Parliament that
they might be subjected by the Crown to a heavy fine for a
late arrival at Westminster, which was due to the state
of the highroads which they had to traverse.

A collection of statistics has popularised the fact that in
the Middle Ages carriage of goods was cheap. But it has been
justly pointed out that this is not to be interpreted as evidence of the good quality of the roads so much as suggesting
the great quantity of the country carts which did the carriage.
These were the carts which the royal purveyors appropriated
without stint, ignoring the statutable claim of their poor owners
to compensation for the use. Even casual travellers were liable

**Royal
Progress.** to have their luggage turned out anywhere upon the road and
the cart which conveyed it impounded for the use of an
ubiquitous court. Indeed for sheer destructiveness, the royal
journeys resembled the flight of a swarm of locusts. The purveyors were without conscience, the king was without knowledge,
and nothing resulted from his attempts to meet the complaints of his people by statutes restraining the activity of his
caterers, even though they comprised a ridiculous attempt of
Edward III. to remove the stigma by altering the name of
the responsible official. The fault lay in the constant movement of the court. While the king journeyed it was not altogether the purveyors' fault if they could not get the peasants
to surrender their stock of hay and corn and their waggons
without some show of violence. The great men imitated
the king, and the retinue of a nobleman or a bishop in the
fifteenth century must have resembled the progress of an Anglo-

A HALT (MS. 264: *Bodleian Library, Oxford*).

Indian Lieutenant-Governor on a tour of inspection during the rainy season.

Even lesser folk, if they had anything to lose, preferred to move about in company. Yet merchants' caravans were not always free from attack. The "robber lords of the Rhine" have passed into a proverb; but even Englishmen of gentle blood were not always to be acquitted of the kind of evil reputation which we have learned to associate with the German knights. And if the nobles themselves were not often guilty, their retainers, sheltering themselves under the livery of some powerful lord, with impunity committed all kinds of outrages —robbery, arson, seduction, forcible detention. Furthermore, the free use of outlawry in the judicial procedure of the time filled the woods and waste places with bands of men, often of gentle blood, whose numbers made it inadvisable for their victims to protest. It is to ballads of the fourteenth century that we owe the idealisation of the career of Robin Hood. Not that those responsible for the law and order submitted to these things without some attempt at remedy. In the Statute of Winchester (1285), Edward I. among other things attempted to provide for the safety of the roads by directing all neighbouring landowners to demolish the brushwood in which robbers might lurk on either side of the highways to the breadth of two hundred feet. But the executive was weak, or rather its influence was intermittent; the patronage of some local magnate was easy to get, and, in the last resort, the privilege of sanctuary for the felon, which was insisted on by the Church, gave a protection which was freely used. And

Dangers of Travel.

TAKING SANCTUARY (MS. Roy. 10 E. iv.).

the sanctuary often extended for some distance round a specially favoured Church. Within this boundary felons and male-factors of every kind would assemble, forming a society among themselves, and safe from pursuit so long as they remained. Anyone who became tired of his confined life was at liberty to abjure the kingdom. The coroner exacted an oath from such an one that he would go straight to the nearest port and there avail himself of the first opportunity that offered of embarking for some foreign land. Armed with a little cross and clad in the scantiest of garb he could then leave the sheltering precincts without fear of molestation, though only too often the felon's original instincts proved too strong for the situation and he availed himself of his recovered freedom to return to his old bad ways.

Lodgings for Travellers. Before we place any more travellers upon the road it may be instructive to learn the kind and amount of accommoda-tion that they met with on their journeys. The king's court was billeted upon the inhabitants of any town through which he passed. The king himself would be received in the neigh-bouring monastery; so would any great lord who was travel-ling. The monastery might also be called upon to shelter their retainers. In this case accommodation would be found in the monastic guest-house, which was often built outside the walls of the actual monastery. The monastic guest-house would also be the night refuge of all poor travellers—wander-ing scholars, pilgrims, and such like. The merchants and all professional travellers would, as a rule, seek accommoda-tion in the inns. These seem to have been numerous if not very luxurious or even always very clean. In the earlier centuries they were often mere caravanserais where nothing except bare shelter was to be found; the traveller was forced to carry his own food. But in process of time the innkeeper on the main road became a substantial person. There was much going to and fro; a regular service of horses seems to have been established between important towns. The journey of the Warden of Merton College, in 1331, with two of the Fellows and four servants, to visit the northern estates of the College, has often been quoted. Beds for the whole party cost twopence a night. Food for the horses is one-third of the total cost; but inclusive of this the average expenditure of the whole party is half a crown a day, which even in terms of modern money would probably not be an extravagant amount. The travellers were, of course, going along a well-frequented track—the great northern road—and they seem to have found accommodation at regular intervals. It is to be noted that the English Boniface, like his Sicilian representative in comparatively recent times, did not go unsuspected of some kind of understanding with the bands of robbers whose existence often added to the dangers of the journey. When there were not inns the smallest village would certainly contain an ale-house where the casual traveller could slake his thirst. This was indicated by a pole or post

Inns.

COOKING OUTSIDE AN INN.
(MS. 264: *Bodleian Library, Oxford.*)

called an alestake, from the end of which hung a bunch or bush of ivy—the plant sacred to Bacchus. Hence the proverb that "Good wine needs no bush." Apparently these alehouses were kept ordinarily by women : in contemporary pictures it is invariably a woman who appears at the door, jug in hand : while the ale-wife was notorious for her dishonest dealings. They were for the most part places of bad repute, too often the scenes of the quarrels of drunken peasants and of the revels of all the disreputable characters, male and female, in the neighbourhood. The respectable traveller would quench his thirst and pass on.

Travellers Afoot. The travellers on foot would be far more numerous than those who journeyed either on horseback or in any kind of conveyance. They would fall roughly into the two classes of lay and religious wayfarers. The lay wanderers may be distinguished as those who supplied people's needs and those who administered to their pleasures. In the former category may be placed the pedlars who thronged the roads, and who, at a time when shops were scarce and buying and selling were limited to the weekly markets and periodical fairs, brought all kinds of wares, both necessary and superfluous, to the very doors of their customers. They supplied the wants, not as now, of a limited class—the farmer's wife in the country, the maidservant in the towns—but of all sections of society alike : they included in their stock substantial articles of clothing, no less than laces and trivial ornaments. Until the middle of the sixteenth century no legislation interfered with their coming and going. Alongside of the pedlars the opinion of the day would lead us to place the itinerant drug-sellers. They may still be found at fairs and in market-places, vending with loud voice and practised assurance their specific remedies for every human ill. Medieval legislation treated them captiously—at one time severely repressing their fraudulent traffic, at another time letting them loose without restraint upon their victims. But the accredited medical

A WAYFARER.
(Luttrell Psalter.)

science of the day was of so empirical a nature, that the encouragement or restraint of these charlatans by those in authority was not likely to have a sensible effect upon the general health of the inhabitants.

A PEDLAR.
(Luttrell Psalter.)

Equally numerous with the pedlars was the large class of strolling players comprehensively described as minstrels or jongleurs, and consisting of musicians, singers, jugglers, dancers, tumblers, and buffoons of all kinds. Before the invention of printing and the spread of literary pursuits long hours of idleness had to be filled somehow. Away from table there were games, both out of doors and in the house; while the company sat at table they were entertained with music and dramatic performances. The absence of sufficient copies, rather than the want of knowledge of how to read, was responsible for the universal presence of the minstrel. If stories could not be read they could be heard from the mouths of those who made it their business to compose them, or at least to recite them from memory. An early distinction seems to have been made between the "scop" (*i.e.* maker) —the bard proper — and the gleeman. The former was the Anglo-Saxon Homer chaunting the old national songs and legends to the accompaniment of his harp. The gleeman played various instruments, sang, danced, and did many feats of skill and strength; but the general tenor of the songs

A BIRDCAGE SELLER.
(MS. 264: *Bodleian Library, Oxford.*)

and the coarseness of the buffoonery caused him and his fellows to be reckoned among the disreputable class. On the other hand, both before and after the Norman Conquest, men of noble

birth did not disdain the accomplishment of minstrelsy, while
the trouvères or troubadours of the twelfth century, like the
Anglo-Saxon "scops," seem to have been genuine poets and
musicians.   Moreover, kings and great men had private
minstrels, among whom there might be individuals of
substance, if not of social position.   Even in Domesday a
jester of Edward the Confessor is noted as the holder of
three vills in Gloucestershire.   Again, at a later date, we find
the genuine minstrels forming themselves into gilds.   The
best known of these existed at Beverley, and although the
earliest extant copy of its regulations dates only from the reign

of Philip and Mary, yet we
know it to have been in
existence long before the time
of Henry VI., when its members gave a pillar to the new
church of St. Mary in their
native town.   There still survive regulations of similar
organisations at York, Canterbury, and perhaps Chester.
The formation of these gilds
only bears witness to the felt
need of distinguishing the
genuine   artists   from   the

KING AND JESTER (MS. Roy. 2 B. viii).

common crowd of entertainment providers.   In truth. by force
of his position the ordinary minstrel was professionally a
mere mountebank.   He finds his modern counterpart in the
troops of so-called "nigger" minstrels who frequent the
beach of seaside watering-places.

usical
struments.   The musical instruments of these performers changed in
the course of time.   The harp was succeeded by the vielle
played with a bow, and thus closely resembling the modern
violin.   It was susceptible of a good deal of skilful manipulation.   But the more common sort of minstrels took refuge
in the tambourine, which demanded little or no skill   Of
other medieval instruments the lavish illustration afforded
by the Minstrels' Gallery in Exeter Cathedral gains little
except confirmation from such sources as illustrated manuscripts and the capitals and bosses in churches and cathedrals.

Hurdy-Gurdy.
(*Luttrell Psalter.*)

Stilt Act (MS. Roy. 14 B. v.).

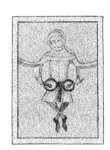

Cymbal Player.
(*Luttrell Psalter.*)

Bagpiper.
(*Luttrell Psalter.*)

A Troop of Jugglers (MS. Add. 24,686).

Regal-Player.
(*Luttrell Psalter.*)

Performing Monkey. (*Luttrell Psalter.*)

Performing Horse (MS. Bodl. 264).

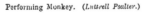

STROLLING PLAYERS OF THE MIDDLE AGES.

The most commonly used instruments seem to have been the bagpipe, the tabor, the double pipe, the horn or trumpet, and the shawm or psaltery. Many of these the real trouvère regarded as of an undignified character, for they were easy to learn, and capable of little development, and were used as the accompaniment of degrading performances. The vocal part of a musical entertainment took one of two complexions. The genuine bard or troubadour recited or, rather

Photo: N. M. Dodson, Bettws-y-Coed.
THE MINSTRELS' GALLERY, EXETER CATHEDRAL.

perhaps, chaunted versified romances embodying the exploits of the heroes of the race. These were often real epic poems of considerable merit. After the Norman Conquest they were naturally composed in French, the language of the court and the noble class; but as their audience became practically bilingual these romances of Norman origin were translated into English, or adapted for those who could not comfortably follow them in the original tongue. But in the course of time constant repetition made these old romances stale; new details were added, increasingly complicated adventures and ingenious escapes from impossible situations were invented. The old epics lost all poetry and all meaning.

Provided they were written in an easy metre at the necessary length, and filled with sufficiently impossible adventures, they satisfied the demand of their limited audience. Chaucer's "Rime of Sir Thopas" is so little of a caricature that it may be taken as sufficiently typical of the products of contemporary minstrels. And yet he represents his pilgrims, through the mouth of the host, as resenting his attempt to palm off such a tale upon them, and refusing to let him continue the jingling, meaningless stanzas. Chaucer's own works did something to supply the place of the moribund heroic romance with tales of ordinary life. The song of the ordinary minstrel was the popular or satirical ballad, sometimes commemorating the adventures of some local hero, often a mere fugitive satire on the political situation or social follies of the moment. For, the minstrel was a man of the people, living a free life himself, and in some sort privileged to utter thoughts which would be dangerous in the mouths of other men—he was, in fact, a licensed jester. Latin and English ballads form quite an important class of literature in the closing centuries of the Middle Ages, and the minstrels must share with the mendicant orders the responsibility of spreading the excitement which often ended in a popular rising. Nor did they hesitate to chaunt these revolutionary lays in the halls of the nobles, who, like the aristocratic class before and since, good naturedly tolerated in song, and even professed to approve the expression of, ideas which, if carried into action, would have undermined their whole social position. And as the minstrels were employed to spread political revolt, so they formed useful agents for the collection of private information. They entered every hall, they stopped at every inn, and even every tavern, they frequented every fair ; the presence of a band of minstrels was considered indispensable for every function, whether public or private. No question was asked of a wandering player, except what he could do to amuse the company. Hence the credibility of such stories as those of the visits of Alfred and Athelstan to the Danish camps in disguise, of which parallels are to be found in the French romances of the troubadours. Hence the part which the minstrel played as a go-between in intrigues of all kinds, and versatile as was his art, the rewards

which fell to him were by no means always the guerdon of
his performances.

Dancing.   For, singing and playing on instruments were merely
part of the jongleur's accomplishments. As the Anglo-Saxon
"scop" seems to have been absorbed in the more common
gleeman, so the troubadours became gradually indistinguishable
from the mountebanks of all kinds who ministered to the
multitude. To judge from extant illustrations, the Anglo-
Saxon gleeman danced as well as sang, and it did not need
the contact with the East, to which some authors have
attributed it, to introduce dancing women in the minstrel

DAUGHTER OF HERODIAS DANCING (MS. Roy. 2 B. vii.).

bands. Their dances were not the quiet domestic "carole"
in which those of gentle birth sometimes engaged. The
object of the professionals seems to have been rather to
excite mirth and, possibly, some admiration by the extravagance, if not the positive indecency, of their movements.
Closely allied to their dancing was the tumbling of these
mountebanks. The style of this may perhaps be judged from
a medieval illustration whose comparatively frequent reproduction in extant manuscripts may entitle us to regard it as
typical. The daughter of Herodias when dancing before
Herod appears in a long garment indeed, but with head
downwards, her feet poised in the air, and her hands resting
sometimes on the ground, sometimes on the points of two

Merelles.

Bowls.

Chess.

(MS. 264: *Bodleian Library, Oxford.*)

'LONG HOURS OF IDLENESS HAD TO BE FILLED SOMEHOW.'

swords stuck upright in the earth. With such performances were associated feats of juggling—the tossing and catching again of several knives or balls in quick succession, which is often depicted in early manuscripts. Along with such fry would go the keepers of performing bears and other captive animals, and lastly, the mere buffoon, who was appreciated in proportion to the coarse indecency and absence of all restraint in word or gesture.

This is not a pleasing picture of the things in which our forefathers took delight. But even exhibitions such as would not now be tolerated in public-houses or dancing saloons of the lowest type, may not have been altogether without a civilising influence. A violent and even sanguinary ending to a dinner-party was by no means unknown, and the soothing effects of music and song and the diverting games of tumblers and buffoons would help to keep the spectators from quarrelling over their cups. In its origin and development the song descriptive of heroic themes was intimately associated with the public feast of the chief, his friends, and retainers. The gradual displacement of the hall as the centre of social life, and the withdrawal of the lord and his friends into a separate room, did not abolish the need of the minstrel, but, by giving him a more select audience, it must have restrained his grossest performances. Meanwhile, the invention of printing and the spread of literary taste made the comfortable classes less dependent on constant amusement at the hands of others; while the rise of the modern English drama ministered to a passion that, apart from the efforts of the minstrels, had only found satisfaction in the intermittent performances of the miracle plays.

Friars, Pilgrims Palmers. Even more numerous than lay wayfarers were wandering ecclesiastics. The collapse of the Peasant Revolt of 1381 was followed by the enactment of severe measures against those classes who had used their professional mendicancy as a means of helping on the movement. On the one hand, these were the beggars and wandering labourers who were dealt with in the first Poor Law in English history: but alongside of them a series of statutes placed preachers wandering from place to place without any ecclesiastical licence, pilgrims who went unfurnished with the royal leave, and all hermits who could not produce letters testimonial from the Ordinary. All such were to be summarily imprisoned as vagabonds and preachers of sedition. But there were other classes of ecclesiastical wanderers every whit as mischievous as those mentioned in the Acts of Parliament, but protected against legislative interference by the supposed sacred character of their duties. Thus the friars might be touched by the Act against wandering preachers; but the use they made of their freedom from ecclesiastical restraint to undermine the family and parochial life of the country could not be dealt with by the legislature. Again, even those in authority in the Church grew ashamed of the pardoners, but the hostile resolutions of synods against their malpractices, and even the thunders of a Papal bull, could not outweigh the superstitious feelings of the age and the accepted ecclesiastical theories which gave rise to the calling of the pardoner. Each of these sections of vagrant ecclesiastics deserves separate treatment.

The hermits may be dismissed in a few words. They **Hermits.** were not wayfarers, but dwellers on the road. The inhabitant of the woods and solitary places was a being of a bygone age. Robert, or Richard Rolle of Hampole was an exception whose fame does not seem to have produced imitators. The cottages of hermits in the fourteenth century were to be found along the most frequented roads, and the inmates lived upon the alms of the passers-by. There was nothing religious about such mendicants except their garb. Langland pictures them as drunken, thievish rascals who had been turned from honest trades by the success of the lazy friars. Episcopal regulations seem to have been powerless to check their growth.

Langland's condemnation also descends upon the friars, **Friars.** who alone among the clergy retained some share of the popular good will. Chaucer is no less severe. The monks, of course, hated them, and monastic chroniclers are only more severe than Langland in attributing complicity in the Peasant Revolt to the friars. Wycliffe's poor preachers are generally regarded as the worst enemies of the friars, but the two bodies seem to have been equally energetic in the propagandist work which spread the news of the intended insurrection. The whole order of the friars is scarcely likely to have been so black as it was painted by its

68

numerous and virulent opponents; but there was a very substantial amount of truth underlying the satire of poets and story-tellers and the denunciations of such involuntary allies as Wycliffe and the monks.   The monstrous iniquities of the. friars, as of any other body of traditional sanctity, could always be explained on the principle of *corruptio optimi pessima.*   " However contemptible the man," says a recent writer, " one could never be certain that he had not the keys of heaven, and respect mingled with fear in the sentiment towards him." Not that the friars went personally unmolested.   In 1346 the Commons in Parliament demanded the expulsion of all alien friars, whose numbers alarmed them as a danger to the State.   In 1385 a royal proclamation was necessary to protect the preaching friars whose "proud behaviour" had brought on them persecution in London and elsewhere.   The friars were condemned officially by councils and synods, and unofficially by preachers and writers.   But they made themselves both felt and feared. Though everyone had a grievance against them, yet they were to be found everywhere.   Langland sketches them as the confessors of great men.   Chaucer's friar added the business of a pedlar to his ecclesiastical ministrations :—

> "His typet was ay farsud ful of knyfes
> And pynnes for to give faire wyfes." [1]

A caustic song of the end of the fourteenth century tells us in more detail that not only do

> "Thai dele with purses, pynnes, and knyves,
> With gyrdles. gloves for wenches and wives,"

but that their packs contain materials for dresses and robes of all kinds:

> "Some frers beren pelure (*a*) aboute,
> For grete ladys and wenches stoute.
>   *   *   *   *   *
> For some vaire (*a*). and some gryse (*b*),
> For some bugee (*b*), and for some byse (*c*).
> And also many a dyvers spyse
>   In bagges about thai bere." [2]
>   *a.* fur : *b*, cloth ; *c*, silk.

[1] Prologue to the "Canterbury Tales."
[2] T. Wright, "Political Songs and Poems" (Rolls Series), I., 264.5. The whole song is well worth reading, as a contemporary (unfavourable) opinion of the friars.

This and other songs of the fourteenth and fifteenth
centuries represent the friars as entering houses and cottages
at any hour, eating and drinking of the best, while, however
great might be his wish, the master of the house would not
dare to turn them out. But more important than pedlars
was the function which the friars performed as the news-
carriers of the day. Curiosity would often get the better even
of caution begotten of past experience, and to the inhabitants
of out of-the-way country districts the visit of a traveller
and a man of the world was an excitement for which they
would be willing to risk much peace of mind. Spiritually the

PRIEST, WITH PARDON.   BEGGAR.   PALMER.   HERMIT.
(MS. Douce 104: *Bodleian Library, Oxford.*)   (*Luttrell Psalter.*)

friars had an immense power at their disposal. Their irresponsibility to episcopal control enabled them to step in
between the parish priest and the individual members of his
flock in so important a means of influence as confession. Even
more potent was their device of "letters of fraternity." By these
they professed, in return for money, to pass on to credulous
and pious souls a share in the surplus merits laid up
through their prayers to the heavenly account of their Order.
"By such reasons," says Wycliffe scornfully, "think many
men that these letters may do good for to cover mustard
pots."[1] But this was a piece of pure rationalism which
would appeal only to a limited number even among the
educated. Nor, finally, was the political influence of the
friars to be despised. We have noticed the share attributed

[1] Select English Works, I., p. 381.

to them in the spread of the Peasant Revolt. It is equally significant to mark the trouble which they gave to Henry IV. for some time after his accession by their popularisation of the belief that Richard II. was still alive.

The friars took upon themselves to distribute the surplus merits of their Order. Their work in this respect was a small **Pardoners.** matter compared to that of the pardoners, whose entire business it was to dispense the surplus merits of the whole Church. The discipline of the early Church was carried out by the infliction of penances for spiritual offences. In course of time these penances, which often extended over long periods, came to be exchanged for a severe punishment of shorter duration. Such commutations were granted by way of indulgence. They were reduced to tariffs, of which one of the earliest and best known was the " Penitential" of our own Archbishop Theodore of Canterbury (690). Under this system a fast of so many years' duration could be commuted by a certain number of lashes, or the recitation of a fixed quantity of psalms. With laymen the commutation took the form of money, which was applied to such religious, or semi-religious, purposes as the building of churches or bridges. But this practice of commutation was gradually replaced by the theory of the " Treasury of merits." As the system became universal these indulgences could not be regarded as mere substitution of one kind of penance for another; they were a composition rather than a strict commutation. But the composition became so utterly disproportionate to the original offence that justice seemed to demand that the deficit should somehow be made up. This was supplied by the transference to the sinner of the surplus merits of Christ and the Saints. This super-abundance says a Papal bull of 1350, has been gathered into a treasury, the key of which has been entrusted to St. Peter and his successors. For the better distribution of the contents of this hoard officials were appointed, who were called some-times Quæstors, because they demanded worldly wealth in return for the gifts of which they disposed; sometimes Pardoners, because they were the agents of God's remission of sins. This traffic in the Church's power of absolution lent itself to enormous abuse; the country was flooded with ecclesiastics, whether secular priests or friars, tramping up and down without any licence, pretending to sell pardons, and exhibiting as their credentials all kinds of curious relics. Chaucer's description of a "gentil pardoner . . . . that streyt was comen from the court of Rome," and the Pardoner's own account of himself in the tale allotted to him, are amply borne out by notices which, whether official or merely satirical, are yet equally condemnatory. The gain of Chaucer's Pardoner was a hundred marks a year; this would have made the trade attractive, for the money would generally go into the pockets of the impostor himself. Sheer brazen-faced impudence carried him. along his successful career. Chaucer makes his Pardoner end a tale with a calm attempt to foist pardons and relics upon his fellow pilgrims. In order to further their traffic the licensed pardoners some-times formed associations, and employed inferior agents. If they were interfered with by an intrepid parish priest who demanded to see their licence, or refused to let them preach in his church, they would sue him before some distant ecclesiastical judge, and would make themselves far more troublesome to him than their original interference with him would have been. The relics which they exhibited were intended to impress simple people with an idea of their sanctity as pilgrims. Like the wandering friars, they were men of resourceful wit and ready anecdote, and displayed in the spiritual sphere all the qualities of the successful quack who dealt in charms and patent medicines.

Pedlars and minstrels, friars and pardoners were members   **Pilgrims.** of fairly definite classes of society. But anyone from the prince to the peasant might form one of the great company of pilgrims who unceasingly thronged the roads and even crossed the Channel. Pilgrimages—that is, journeys to places of reputed sanctity, in order to discharge a vow or to gain an answer to prayer—are among the manifestations common to all the great religions of the world. Christian pilgrimages began in visits to the scenes of Our Lord's earthly life. But the distance and the danger confined such journeys to the idle or the wealthy. Piety found some parallel in the tombs of distinguished martyrs and confessors. The chief of these was, of course, the tombs of SS. Peter and Paul at Rome, which proved a most powerful attraction to the great capital of Western Europe. No less attractive were the legendary shrines, the sites of some alleged vision, of the supernatural discovery of some hidden relic, or of the presence of a wonder-working image or picture. For English people the most important of such places were the shrine of St. James at Compostella in Spain, and, at home, those of St. Thomas Becket at Canterbury, and of Our Lady at Walsingham. These last were the English shrines which enjoyed something more than a local reputation. There were many others on this side of the Channel which were frequently visited—the shrine of St. Edward the Confessor, at Westminster; of St. Cuthbert, at Durham; of St. Alban; St. Edmund, at Bury; and St. David; while an attraction of a different kind was found in the holy thorn tree planted by Joseph of Arimathæa at Glastonbury (Vol. I., p. 115).

The pilgrimage to Canterbury has been immortalised by Chaucer. But scarcely less celebrated was that to the shrine of the Virgin at Walsingham. This was situated in a monastery of Augustinian Canons some twenty-seven miles distant from Norwich, and contained a miraculous statue of the Virgin, and a phial of her milk. The road to sites of pilgrimage was lined with chapels; the approach to Walsingham was known as the "Palmers' Way." The towns of pilgrimage were themselves a mass of inns and churches: many of them contained hostels for poor pilgrims, which were supported by local gilds. There was much encouragement to go on pilgrimage. Besides the benefits promised by the Church pilgrims were freed from toll, and their persons were inviolable, so that anyone injuring them was excommunicate. Moreover, they obtained shelter and sometimes food free of cost along the road, and those who were members of a gild were helped to a distant journey by the contributions of their fellow gildsmen. On arrival at their goal pilgrims put up at one of the numerous hostelries, or were taken in at some guest-house provided by charity; they visited the shrine, made their offerings and prayers, and, before departing, bought one of the little perforated pewter medals, which could be sewn on the hat or dress as a sign of the pilgrimage performed. For each shrine had its own peculiar form of token; from Canterbury the pilgrims would carry

away a bottle or bell with the image of St. Thomas
stamped upon it, while a shell was the mark of a visit to
Compostella. The professional pilgrim—the palmer—who
wandered from shrine to shrine, wore a peculiar garb and
hat, and carried a scrip for his food and a bottle. Moreover, the staff in his hand and the little medals which

CHAPEL AT HOUGHTON, NORFOLK, ON THE ROAD TO WALSINGHAM.
(From a photograph by the Rev. W. Martin.)

studded his clothes proclaimed his profession and marked
his assiduity.

But as pilgrimages became part of the penitential discipline of the Church they were undertaken by all kinds of
people, with all manner of ulterior motives. "Some," says
an author already quoted, "went like gypsies to a fair, to
gather money; some went for the pleasures of the journey
and the merriments of the road." This combination of
pleasure with business commended pilgrimages as forms of
penance to the amateur, and their continuance as an occupation was encouraged because, like friars and pardoners,
and, indeed, like all travellers living by their wits, pilgrims
were men of the world, news-bringers, and retailers of the

marvellous. But it was just this qualification that excited the wrath of reformers. Langland scornfully remarks that

> Pilgrims and palmers ply them together
> To seek Saint James and saints of Rome.
> Went forth in their way with many unwise tales.
> And have leave to lie all their lifetime.

Relics.   Among the most wonderful sights of which the pilgrims would have to tell would be the relics offered to their view at the various shrines. Nor would it be impossible for them to acquire relics of considerable interest, which to the devout would be irrefutable proofs of the sincerity, if not of the sanctity, of the pilgrims themselves. We need not go to contemporary satirists to appreciate the marvellous credulity of the Middle Ages. Certainly it is Boccaccio whose Frate Cipolla produces "one of the Angel Gabriel's feathers which remained in the Virgin Mary's chamber, whenas he came to announce to her in Nazareth." Similarly the pardoner in an old French farce offers to show "the comb of the cock that sung at Pilate's." But the relics known to history are quite as farcical. To Exeter Athelstan gave, among a large number of other treasures, such deeply interesting memorials as a piece of the candle which the angel of the Lord lit in the tomb of Christ, a portion of the burning bush whence God spoke to Moses, and one of the stones which slew St. Stephen. Medieval law punished with death thefts of even a trifling amount, but such was the inherent efficacy which was supposed to reside with genuine relics that their fraudulent removal, even by members of one religious house from those of another, was considered not only a condonable but almost a praiseworthy act. Even the losers dwelt not on the act of theft but on the danger which they suffered from the loss of a valuable fetish or talisman. Nor was it only satirists, whether rationalist poets or religious reformers, who scented mischief in indiscriminate pilgrimages. They were also at times a political danger. Thus, Edward II.'s cousin and rival, Earl Thomas of Lancaster, was considered a popular martyr, and after his execution in 1322 the pilgrimages to his tomb were intended as a political demonstration against the king. The crowds who shipped from English ports to visit Compostella might easily include spies from foreign courts. Hence the act of

PILGRIMS' SIGNS (*Guildhall Museum*).
(*By permission of the Library Committee to the Corporation of the City of London.*)

Richard II. which enforced the necessity of licences and passports for all would-be pilgrims.

The Social Value of Pilgrimage. Historically speaking, the indirect use of pilgrimages sur-
passes the various uses to which they were deliberately turned.
The coming and going of considerable crowds between different parts of the country and from one side of the Channel
to the other was a great instrument in the process of civilisation. It drew together different classes and so helped on the
growth of national sentiment. It broke down the provincial-
ism of speech and thought which comes of isolated life. It
spread the news: it gave a holiday and fresh air, and change
of life and scene. Finally, it introduced the pilgrim to foreign
lands and so helped on the growth of commerce. Neither
the frank cynicism of Chaucer's elaborate picture nor the
biting satire of the wailing Langland had the least effect in
checking the constant stream of pilgrims. Nor, a century
later, would the scathing sarcasms of Erasmus have borne
more abundant fruit, had not many other things already contributed to the disuse of the machinery of the medieval Church.

AUTHORITIES, 1348-1399.

(*a*) GENERAL HISTORY.

The contemporary authorities are the *St. Alban's Chronicle* (as in Chap. V.) and the
Evesham Chronicle; Knighton and Walsingham, both living under Richard II.; the
French *Cronique de la Traison et Mort de Richard Deux*, the *Chronicon* of Adam of
Usk, the *Annales Ricardi* and Capgrave's *Chronicle of England*, Gower's Poems, the
Political Songs (Wright's ed. and Rolls Series), the *Rolls of Parliament*. To the
modern authorities, as given at the end of Chap. V., may be added: Gairdner, *Houses
of Lancaster and York*; and for Wycliffe and the Lollards, the preface to *Fasciculi
Zizaniorum* (Rolls Series); G. M. Trevelyan, *England in the Age of Wycliffe* (1899),
and *The Peasant Rising and the Lollards*, and a good account of Richard II.'s reign
in Lingard, *History of England*.

(*b*) SPECIAL SUBJECTS.

Religion.—The standard life of Wycliffe is still that published at Leipzig by
Gotthard Lechler; but the English translation, which has appeared in three separate
issues, is neither complete nor altogether satisfactory, and in its last edition (1884)
has suffered a number of changes which remove it still further from the original.
Among English lives that by Mr. F. D. Matthew, prefixed to his edition of Wycliffe's
English Works hitherto unprinted (1880), deserves special mention; and the writer of
the section dealing with Wycliffe in the present chapter, while his statements and
opinions are based upon a study of Wycliffe's works and the records of contemporary witnesses, has made free use of his own sketch of *Wycliffe and Movements
for Reform* (1889). The student will be rewarded by much of interest on the subject
in W. W. Shirley's preface to the *Fasciculi Zizaniorum* (1859), though it requires
correction in the light of more recent investigation. For Wycliffe's connection with
politics no sounder guide exists than Stubbs, *Const. Hist.*, XVI. and XIX.

Law, Warfare, Naval Matters, Architecture, and Art.—As in Chap. V.

History of Universities and Schools.—The works referred to at the end of Chap. V., especially Maxwell-Lyte's *Oxford* and Clark and Willis's *Cambridge;* T. E. Kirby, *Winchester College;* Moberley, *William of Wykeham;* the (unedited) *Compotus Rolls of Durham College;* Macray, *Annals of the Bodleian Library;* volumes in the series of *College Histories* published by F. E. Robinson; articles in Dict. of Nat. Biography, especially on "Humphrey, Duke of Gloucester."

Medicine and Public Health.—Father Gasquet's *Great Pestilence* (1894) deals fully with the Black Death. Other authorities as for Chap. V. See also Jessopp, *The Black Death in East Anglia,* "Nineteenth Century," Vols. XVI., XVII.

Literature.—B. ten Brink, *Geschichte der Englischen Litteratur,* Bd. 1 and 2 (Berlin and Strassburg, 1877-93) ; Alois Brandl, *Gesch. d. mittelengl. Litteratur,* n Paul's *Grundriss,* II. 1 (Strassburg, 1889) ; *Altenglische Dichtungen des MS. Harl.* $22_{5}8$, ed. Böddeker (Berlin, 1878) ; Political Songs, ed. T. Wright (Rolls Series) ; *Political Songs of England from John to Edward II.*, ed. and trans. by T. Wright (Camden Soc., 1839) ; William of Shoreham's *Religious Poems,* ed. T. Wright (Percy Soc., Vol. xxviii.) ; *Pearl,* ed. and trans. I. Gollancz (D. Nutt, 1891) ; *Sir Gawayne and the Green Knight* (circ 1360), ed. R. Morris (Early Engl. Text Soc., 1864) ; Chaucer's *Poetical Works,* ed R. Morris (Aldine Poets, 1866) ; Chaucer, *Prologue, Knight's Tale,* and *Nun's Priest's Tale,* ed. Morris and Skeat ; Chaucer, *Man of Lawe's Tale, Prioresses' Tale, Minor Poems,* ed. Skeat (Clarendon Press) ; Kluge, *Gesch. d. Engl. Sprache,* in Paul's *Grundriss,* Bd. I., Lief. 5 (Strassburg, 1891) ; Ten Brink, *Chaucer; Studien zur Geschichte seiner Entwickelung,* etc. (Munster, 1870) ; Ten Brink, Chaucer's *Sprache und Verskunst* (Leipzig, 1884) ; Morsbach, *Ueber den Ursprung der N.-E. Schriftsprache* (Heilbronn, 1888) ; Dict. Nat. Biography, "Chaucer" (Prof. J. W. Hales). The critical edition of Chaucer's works, with Life, etc., by Prof. W. W. Skeat (6 vols., Clarendon Press) is now the standard edition of the poet. Wycliffe, *Works,* ed. by T. Arnold, 3 vols., Oxford, 1869-71 ; *English Works of Wiclif hitherto unprinted,* ed. F. D. Matthew (E.E.T.S., 1880) ; Wycliffe's *Latin Works,* ed. Buddensieg, Loserth, R. L. Poole, and others (Wyclif Soc., at present 17 vols , 1883-93) ; Morley's *English Writers,* Vols. IV.-VI. ; Buddensieg, *Johann Wiclif u. Seine Zeit* (Gotha, 1885) ; Lechler, *John Wickliffe and his English Precursors* (see above) ; E. Gasuer, *Beiträge zum Entwickelungsgang der neuenglischen Schriftsprache auf Grund der mittelenglischen Bibelversionen* (1891) ; Langland, *Works,* ed. Skeat (Clarendon Press) ; Jusserand, *Le Paysan Anglais au Moyen-Age et la Poème Mystique de Langland* (Paris, 1893) ; *Observations sur la Vision de Piers Plowman* (Paris, 1879) ; J. W. Hales, "Langland" (in Dict. of Nat. Biography) ; R. Kron, *William Langley's Buch von Peter dem Pflüger, Untersuchungen,* etc. (Göttingen, 1885) ; Rosenthal, *Langland's Metrik* (in "Anglia," I , 414) ; *Pierce the Ploughman's Crede and God Spede the Plough;* ed. Skeat (E.E.T.S., 1867). Gower, *Balades and other Poems,* Roxburgh Club, 1818 ; *Minnesang,* etc., ed. Stengel, *Ausgaben u. Abhandlungen . . . der Romanischen Philologie,* No. LXIV., 1882 ; *Vox Clamantis necnon Chronica Tripartita,* ed. Coxe, Roxburgh Club, 1850.; *Confessio Amantis;* ed. Pauli (3 vols. London, 1857) ; K. Meyer, *John Gower's Beziehungen zu Chaucer,* etc (Bonn, 1889) ; S. Lee, art. "Gower," in Dict. of Nat. Biography.

Agriculture.—Thorold Rogers, *History of Agriculture and Prices* and *Six Centuries of Work and Wages* ; Ashley, *Economic History* ; Nasse, *Zur Geschichte der Mittelalterliche Feld-Gemeinschaft in England* ; Vinogradoff, *Villainage in England* ; Maitland, *Select Pleas in Manorial Courts* (Selden Soc.) ; Seebohm, *English Village Community* ; Gomme, *Village Community.*

Industry and Commerce, 1349-1485.—For the commercial history in detail it is necessary to consult Rymer's *Foedera,* the Rolls of Parliament, and the Statutes of the Realm. Macpherson's *Annals of Commerce,* in addition to rather inaccurate abstracts of Rymer and other authorities, contains many useful details ; and Thorold Rogers's *Agriculture and Prices,* with its exhaustive records of the prices of English and foreign commodities, is indispensable. *Die Hanserecesse*, ed. by Koppman, is a mine of information on the commercial relations between England and the Hanse towns. Ochenkowski's *Englands Wirthschaftliche Entwickelung im Ausgange des Mittelalters* and Gross's *Gild Merchant* are the most useful works on the Staple ; and Cunningham's *Growth of Industry and Commerce* gives a good general view of English commerce in the fourteenth century. *See also* Ashley, *History of the Woollen Trade*, and, in general, Ashley's *Economic History*. Many of the *data* are only to be found in various county histories and local records.

Town Life.—Merewether and Stephens, *History of Municipal Corporations ; Liber Albus of London* (ed. Riley) ; Mrs. J. R. Green, *Town Life in the Fifteenth Century ;* Sharpe, *London and the Kingdom ;* Burrows, *Cinque Ports ;* Historic Towns Series ; Jusserand, *English Wayfaring Life in the Middle Ages ;* Pauli, *Bilder aus Alt-England ;* Loftie, *History of London. See also* Stubbs, *Constitutional History ;* Cunningham, *Growth of English Industry and Commerce ;* Rogers, *Six Centuries of Work and Wages ;* Maitland, *Township and Borough.*

Social Life.—Strutt, *Sports and Pastimes of the People of England* (revised by W. Hone, 1838) ; Jusserand, *Les Anglais au Moyen Age* and *English Wayfaring Life in the Middle Ages ;* Cutts, *Scenes and Characters of the Middle Ages ;* A. W. Ward, *History of English Dramatic Literature ;* Katharine L. Bates, *The English Religious Drama ;* A. W. Pollard, *The Miracle Plays.*

BOYS WHIPPING TOPS (MS. 264).

(*Bodleian Library, Oxford*).

CHAPTER VII.

THE CLOSE OF THE MIDDLE AGES. 1399-1485.

THE Henry IV. of Shakespeare sums up in his dying speech the whole course of a singularly eventful career when, in a famous scene, he cries out that God knew by what crooked ways he had won the crown: "I myself," he adds, "know well how troublesome it sat upon my head." It is the story of honour perverted by ambition, and avenged by disappointment and remorse. His Scottish and Welsh wars were marked by disaster. His old friends, his own kinsmen, proved traitors. The nation which had once loved him grew weary of his rule. His kingdom's great revenues, his own vast domains, melted away like fairy gold in his hands. His murdered rival seemed to live again in a mocking pretender, the false Richard. He slew his enemies only to find that men mourned their fate, and even canonised their memory. The crusading ideals of his youth were destined to be degraded into mere persecution; he was the first English sovereign who burned men in the name of religion. At first sight there is much that is inexplicable in the reign, much that is repulsive, much that seems weary and fruitless; little or nothing of the heroic, and no landmarks of progress.

Yet upon a closer view, features of interest and of promise reveal themselves. The medieval period is closing; its great ideas have faded. But a new era is dawning. The Church had already passed its climax of prosperity and independence; henceforth it prepares its own downfall by an even closer connection with the royal power. That royal power itself was beginning to show the influence of those theories and those events which were soon to cover all Europe with absolutist sovereignties. The new commercial classes, in whose support this absolutism was to find its practical basis, begin to manifest

[margin: A. L. SMITH. The Reign of Henry IV.]

[margin: Signs of a New Era.]

themselves; they even have their heroes, a Whittington, a Jack of Newbury.

Most rapid change of all, the feudal baronage had been, even in the preceding century, transforming itself into a more modern nobility, intriguing for places and pensions, instead of taking up arms for local independence.

Famil.
Feuds. Moreover, the reign of Henry IV. is a time of beginnings. That changeful drama, the political suicide of the baronage, which only closed with the extinction of Poles and Nevilles upon the Tudor scaffolds, had for its first scene the massacre at Cirencester. There the whole body of citizens, the women being specially conspicuous, rose in fury against those great lords, Montague, Holland, Lumley, whose selfish insurrection aimed at wrecking the reign of peace just inaugurated (February, 1400).

Those implacable family feuds, which not even the bloodshed of Towton Field, or Barnet, or Tewkesbury, could slake, had taken their rise in the personal jealousies which had gathered about the court of Richard II., but were fanned into flame in the court of his successor. The central issue of the Wars of the Roses was the claims of the Duke of York. These claims had been fostered by Humphrey of Gloucester as a means to excite popular prejudice against his rivals, Suffolk and the Beauforts. Traced to its root, this rivalry had its origin in the position of the Beauforts supporting the Prince of Wales in 1410 against the king, the Prince's next brother, and the greater nobles and churchmen.

Ideas of
Hereditary
Right. Again, the offence done in 1399 to contemporary belief in hereditary right was amply avenged in 1461. Bolingbroke set forth his claim as resting on God's grace, and on the fact "that the realm was in point to be undone for default of government"; but he went further, and challenged the Crown, as one descended by right line of blood from Henry III. This was probably not mainly intended to suggest the worthless gossip about Henry III.'s son, Edmund of Lancaster, Edmund "Crouchback," being rejected from his rightful place as heir to the throne, and the younger son, Edward, preferred in his stead. But the challenge did no doubt intend to discountenance the Mortimer claim, which rested on female succession as it came through Philippa, heiress of Lionel of Clarence, Edward III.'s

third son. The Lancastrian claim came through John of Gaunt, fourth son of Edward III., but was a claim through males. But Edward IV., who deposed Henry VI., was the great-grandson of that Roger Mortimer who had already been declared heir by Richard II., and whose little sons, aged eight and seven, now possessed a right, which a usurper less scrupulous than Bolingbroke would have found the means to remove by death. The same Yorkist. claim had to be recognised, much against his will, by the first Tudor sovereign; and his Queen, Elizabeth of York, was crowned by a right of her own which to most men was

SEAL OF HENRY IV.

probably better based than that of Henry her husband, heir as he was only to the weak Beaufort title.

Nor, obscure and gloomy as it is, does this reign lack episodes and subsidiary questions which invite inquiry. The obscurity is partly due to the surprising way in which the primary authorities for the period differ on decisive points. Even where all substantially agree, as in bearing out the traditions as to the wild escapades of Prince Henry's youthful years, their testimony is hard to reconcile with other evidence, such as the facts of his strenuous military career and his active leadership of the council. Nor, though we may discern some of the causes of the unusual success of the Welsh insurrection (p. 387) continued through the whole reign, is it easy to thread the intricate maze of contemporary Scottish history, or to trace the connection of Scottish affairs with the rebellion of the Percies. Very startling, again, are the reversals of policy, by which, in the wild duel of

Obscure
Episodes.

the two great parties in France, an English army is sent now to support the Burgundians (1411), and now in the Orleanist interest to attack the allies of Burgundy (1412).

The Rule of Parliament.

With so much in it that is futile and resultless, the reign of Henry IV. has yet bequeathed one result of inestimable value for English liberty. Parliamentary government came at this time to its maximum. True, it outran itself, and after thirty-eight years of precocious development, fell into anarchy, and gave place to the two centuries of Yorkist, Tudor, and Stuart absolutism; but when the Commons once more began, under Charles I., to assert their place in the constitution, it was to Lancastrian times that they looked back for their ancient rights, and to Lancastrian precedents that they had recourse for weapons in the struggle.

Henry IV. had come to the throne pledged to abandon the evil ways of Richard III. He would not govern by his " own voluntary purpose or singular opinion," but by common counsel and consent. He was " the new Judas Maccabæus." He was the first king anointed from the holy flask miraculously presented to St. Thomas, and revealed again to Duke Henry of Lancaster. He was the " boar of commerce " foretold by Merlin as destined to " recall the scattered flocks to their lost pastures." But above all he was the chosen man alike of clergy, barons, and nation. Yet for all that, it was not the weakness of his title that gave the Commons such a hold upon him from the

The King's Difficulties

first. It was the extraordinary difficulties of his position, and particularly the inexplicable financial difficulties, which beset him from the outset. Lord as he was of six earldoms, and of all the vast domains of the house of Lancaster, master of many confiscated estates, neither these nor the lands and revenues of the Crown sufficed to meet the expenses of garrisons and fleets, and of endless wars, and above all, the insatiable claims of those whose support he had to buy with promises beyond his means to fulfil. In his first year, the pensions already granted amounted to £24,000, a sum more than his whole royal and private revenues from land. Calais alone cost £30,000 a year; Ireland and Wales and the Marches at least as much again; the household about the same. On the other hand, even with all the subsidies and grants of increased customs, which the most moving statements of the royal needs won from

the reluctant Commons, his average annual revenue seems
to have reached little more than £100,000. The Chief
Justice's statement to Parliament in 1401 showed that at

TOMB OF HENRY IV., CANTERBURY CATHEDRAL.

least £150,000 was needed for the ordinary annual expenses
of the realm.

No wonder then that the Commons made bold so early as
1401 to claim that redress should precede Supply. This time

69

the king refused ; it was without precedent, he said ; but nevertheless the victory lay with the Commons; for henceforth they made it the rule to announce their money grant only on the last day of the session, when the answers to petitions had been declared. This gave the Commons control of the purse; and with that must go practical control of the whole government. Hence we find them insisting on their freedom of debate, forcing the king to accept advice on details of administration, complaining formally of the king's household, the royal pensioners, and the abuse of " livery." We find the old cry against "aliens" revived on occasion of Henry's marriage to Joan of Navarre, 1403 ; the household restricted to £12,000 a year ; and, above all, the names of those on the king's council submitted for the approval of Parliament. This last was the characteristic Lancastrian solution of that fundamental problem of politics, how to ensure harmony between the Legislature and Executive ; how to give to the legislative power ultimate control over the executive without unduly hampering the latter. It was a better plan than that devised by the Good Parliament in 1376, which was, occasionally, to "enforce" the council by adding ten or twelve lords whom the Commons could trust:

If redress before Supply was the first maxim of financial control, hardly second to it in importance was that of audit of accounts. In 1405, after declaring that kings do not render accounts, Henry had to yield and allow auditors to be appointed ; and from this date audit was never refused. The kindred practice of appropriating particular grants to particular purposes became more. and more an unbroken rule ; thus tunnage and poundage came to be appropriated for naval defence, the wool custom for maintenance of Calais and defence of the realm, and several sources of income were set apart for "the king's list" (the civil list, as it would be called now). Finally, the exclusive right of the Commons to originate all money grants was brought into notice through an accidental invasion of this right by the Lords in 1407.

This prudent submission to Parliamentary control brought its own reward. The Commons meddled with the king's most intimate affairs; they cut down his grants and pensions, they expelled his wife's attendants, they told him his household was a set of rascals, their Speaker bored him with allegorical homilies.

But amid universal treason and rebellion no shadow of treason was found in them. Over and over again they declared his title and confirmed his succession to his sons. The solid strength of this tie between the royal power and the gentry, yeomen, and burgesses of the nation is best proved by the strong position into which Henry V. at once stepped, and the unswerving and generous loyalty with which his people seconded his far-reaching designs. *Parliament Loyal.*

THE causes of the rebellion of Owen Glendower were partly political, partly social, and partly national. Owen was the hero of the student, of the labourer, and of the Welsh yeoman who had a grievance against sheriff or lord marcher. *O. M. EDWARDS. Owen Glendower's Rebellion.*

Between the death of Llewellyn in 1282 and the rise of Glendower in 1400 there had been three classes of rebellions in Wales. The first was the rebellion of the princes, who, in their jealousy of Llewellyn, had joined Edward I. The second, in 1294, was the widespread rebellion against taxes, when the king's collectors were hanged throughout the length and breadth of Wales. The third, in 1315 and 1322, was caused by the success of the Scots, and by the Bruces' attempt to build up a Celtic empire.

By 1400 there were new causes of discontent. The Justico and the lord marcher were more unpopular than ever, for the weakness of the Lancastrian central government enabled the lords to encroach on the territories of their Welsh neighbours, and to use the law for their own aggrandisement. "Bitter was the justice of the law; the injustice of the officers of the law was more bitter still." The great social upheaval which in England took the form of the Peasant Revolt had affected Wales also. Peasants flocked to the standard of Glendower after hanging their bailiffs, and Owen's bard sang the praises of the sons of labour and of the plough. The national spirit was rising still, in spite of Sir Edward Llwyd's failure to unite with the Bruces. Welsh students flocked home from Oxford to fight under Glendower's banner. *Welsh Discontent.*

Owen Glendower was a Welsh squire, whose property lay on the eastern and western slopes of the Berwyn. He had been a law student at Westminster, and was in the service of Henry of Lancaster before Henry ascended the English throne as

Henry IV. In Lord Grey of Ruthin he had a grasping and tyrannical neighbour, who was ever claiming some part of his mountain
patrimony. He had appealed to the king in vain for justice,
and he saw that Lord Grey was plotting his ruin by making him
appear a traitor to the king.

In 1400 Owen attacked Lord Grey, and found that the whole

BATTLE BETWEEN THE ARMIES OF RICHARD, EARL OF WARWICK, AND OWEN
GLENDOWER (MS. Jul. E. iv.).

The Early
Stages
of the
Revolt.

of the Welsh land subjected to English sheriff and lord marcher
alike was ready to rebel. Henry immediately recognised the
danger, and with the activity which characterised the early part
of his reign, he at once advanced into Wales. Owen retired into
the fastnesses of Snowdon before him, and Henry had to retire
without achieving anything beyond the destruction of Glendower's country, "the glen of the sacred waters," which had

been left undefended. The king offered pardon, and the country became quiet for a moment. But the danger continued, and there was rigorous legislation against the Welsh; no Welshman was to remain in office, the Welsh were to be forced to repair their rulers' castles, no meetings were to be held without the permission of the English officers, and the activity of the itinerant bards was to be mercilessly repressed.

The Justice of North Wales, and the custodian of the castles which guarded the north, from Chester to Carnarvon, was the headstrong and ambitious Henry Percy. In 1401 an attempt was made to break this line of castles by the capture of Conway, the key of mountainous Carnarvonshire. The castle was captured on Good Friday, when the garrison was in the town church, but violent Hotspur stormed it again. As long as Henry Percy held the castles, Owen's chief activity was further south, where the men of Cardigan and Carmarthen were ready to rise against the custodians of the castles which fringed their mountains. Percy's strength and almost empty exchequer were taxed to the full in the north, while Owen was vowing at Carmarthen that he would exterminate the English tongue. Before the end of the summer the king came to North Wales, then struck across Mid Wales to meet Glendower, sparing neither church nor child on his way, and stalling his horses near the high altar of Strata Florida Abbey, the resting-place of the kings of Wales. The land of the rebels was parcelled out among the loyal Welsh, and then, fearing winter, the king departed. Owen reappeared, as if by magic, and, in the depth of winter, made another determined attack upon the northern line of fortresses. He was, however, obliged to raise the siege of Carnarvon, and to retire with his white banner and golden dragon; and Harlech was relieved by an army which marched from Chester through deep snow.

Owen had revived the Bruces' dream of a Celtic empire. Before the end of 1401 he had begun to negotiate with Henry Percy, and his emissaries were on their way to the lords of Ireland and the King of Scotland. He aimed at uniting a number of powerful barons, dependent upon himself, against the King of England. The victory of the Fyrnwy, at the

Owen's English Allies.

beginning of 1402, gave him Lord Grey as an ally; the
great victory of Bryn Glas, in the summer of the same
year, won Sir Edmund Mortimer to his side.

STRATA FLORIDA ABBEY.

Owen had begun as the champion of the oppressed
labourer :

> "God and Mary ever shelter
> Every suffering son of toil."

But the widespread misery and injustice made his success
so rapid and great that he assumed the title of "our most

dread sovereign prince," and entered into an alliance with the discontented English nobles. In 1403 Henry was to be crushed by a great league. Glendower was to subdue the whole of Wales, and to march northwards to meet the Percies. Owen had not completed the reduction of Glamorgan, when the king marched rapidly and attacked the Percies before they could unite with the Welshmen, at Shrewsbury, in the summer of 1403. The defeat of the Percies foiled Glendower's first plan.

But he continued to work with unceasing vigour. During the autumn of 1403 all the castles along the South Wales coast, from Kidwelly to Chepstow, were in the utmost danger; and an alliance was formed in 1404 between Charles VI. of France and "Owen, by God's grace Prince of Wales, in the fourth year of our reign."

Owen, now Prince of Wales, aimed at dethroning Henry and placing the young Earl of March on the English throne. In this he was foiled by the capture of Lady Spencer. His good fortune, for the moment, seems to have left him. Raising peasant armies was as easy as ever, but in battle after battle, especially in the disastrous battles of Grosmont and Mynydd Pwll Melyn, they were routed by an English army soon to be commanded by the young prince Henry. It was believed for the moment that Owen was dead, in spite of his magic. He disappeared; his poet plaintively inquires about his habitation, and calls him home from all parts of the world to rule the Welsh as their prince. Tradition says that Owen went no further than a cave on the wild coast of Merioneth. *Owen, Prince of Wales.*

His Rout and Disappearance.

In 1406 Owen Glendower is Prince of Wales again, with views as statesmanlike and plans as great as ever. In a letter written to Charles VI. in this year, he defines his aims. They were chiefly three. The first was the independence of Wales, with Owen himself as its prince. The second was the ecclesiastical independence of Wales, with a Welsh archbishop at St. David's. The third was the revival of learning in Wales by the creation of two universities, one in South Wales and the other in North Wales. Owen's plans stand out in strange contrast to the narrow, selfish plans of that cruel, sensual, degenerate age. He himself stands head and shoulders above *His Return and Plans*

the warriors and statesmen of that iron time.   The truest
description of his character is well known, though he is
described as taking part in a scene which is not historical :—

> ' In faith, he is a worthy gentleman,
> Exceedingly well read, and profited
> In strange concealments, valiant as a lion,
> And wondrous affable, and as bountiful
> As mines of India."

The negotiations between the self-created Prince of Wales
and Peter de Luna, who got Charles VI. to support him as Pope
Benedict XIII., are not uninteresting, were it only on account
of the personality of the two men.   Peter de Luna was a man
of invincible courage, and Owen Glendower struggled against
unforeseen disasters and difficulties with as much success as
against the temptations of sudden gleams of good fortune.   And
his aims, after all, were not impossible.   Wales had been independent before, and a hundred years' subjection had not made
Welshmen forget the fact.   In his own country, and with a free
hand, Owen could remedy the condition of the labourer who was
his chief supporter, and who was now suffering from the tyranny
of his foreign master and from the agricultural depression at
the same time.   During his time of power, Wales was ecclesi-
astically independent.   Owen's bishops owed no allegiance to
Canterbury, and he fondly hoped to see a Welsh archbishopric
established by Papal authority.   The Pope was asked to establish two universities in Wales, in order, for one thing, to please
the students and bards who had done so much for Glendower.

**Owen
and
Welsh
Poetry.**
The character of Welsh literature had changed with the advent
of Glendower.   The love songs of Dafydd ab Gwilym, which
mark the golden age of Welsh poetry, give place to the martial
odes of Iolo Goch—a more masculine and more vigorous literature, but with the grace of the fashion of it perishing.   But
Glendower himself believed in education.   He knew that an
independent church must draw its priests from the colleges of
its own country, and his own love for reading made this student
of Dante aim at giving his people intellectual as well as political
freedom.

His plans were, for the moment, doomed to failure.   The
great French army which landed at Milford Haven to help him
could not invade England and put an end to the struggle ; it

KIDWELLY CASTLE.

Photo : Graphotone Co.

pierced as far as Worcester, and then the whole of England was
roused. So vast a garrison could not be maintained in Wales as
a purely defensive army, and it had to return. The weather
fought against Glendower as it had fought against Henry. The
condition of the labourer did not become immediately better.
In 1407 the winter was so hard that nearly all the little birds
died. Owen's magic, it was believed, could command storms,
but he could not make the sun to shine and the wheat to grow.
It became more and more difficult to find allies; the activity of
young Henry crushed one rebellion after the other. Owen's
Bishop of Bangor was taken with the Earl of Northumberland at
Bramham Moor in 1408, and a vigorous warfare was maintained
on the borders in 1409. From this time to Glendower's death
His Later Years. in 1415, the Welsh prince maintained his independence in the
old Wales of Llewellyn, though he was never allowed to remain
in perfect peace. Prince Henry often besieged one or other
of his castles, and placed his own men within the walls. "But
it availed nought, for Glendower came and put new men in the
castle."

The Absorption of Wales. After the death of Glendower, Wales takes a new attitude
towards England. Hitherto it had struggled for independence,
now it begins to unite with some English party. Its military
element, the wild element that had been used by Glendower in
his later days, was drafted off to the French wars, and the wild
Welsh fought for Henry at Agincourt as they had fought for
Glendower at Worcester. When the French wars were over, the
Welsh found employment in the Wars of the Roses, first taking
the Yorkist side, and then, under the guidance of Jasper of
Pembroke, supporting the Lancastrians in their darkest days,
and finally seating the Tudor on the English throne. It was
during the Tudor reigns that Wales was really subjected to
English law. Owen Glendower and Jasper of Pembroke had,
each in his day, ruled independently in Wales; and while no
strong hand was present, robber chieftains ruled over wide districts. The Tudor made Wales into an integral part of the
realm he governed.

But the ideals of Owen Glendower were not forgotten.
Tudor legislation Anglicised the landowner and the government official; the son of labour and the bard still dreamed
that, like Arthur, Owen Glendower slept until the day

came for the deliverance of his country. No one has taken such firm and lasting hold of the imagination of Wales.

WYCLIFFE'S power as a teacher rested upon his possession of two special gifts. In the first place, he was immensely thorough, and ready to take all possible pains before he satisfied himself of the correctness of his conclusions. He was not merely a profound theologian and philosopher, but his studies extended to almost every branch of learning which in his age formed part of the equipment of the trained schoolman. The classics were little cultivated in the fourteenth century, and Wycliffe's deficiencies in this department do not call for notice. But, on the other hand, he was skilled in the mathematical sciences, especially optics, and even in medicine. As a master of his craft he had probably but few equals. To this high degree of competence he added, in the second place, an absolute sincerity in his pursuit of truth, which carried his hearers with him. To estimate his method and style of reasoning by comparison with those of the great schoolmen of the century before him is to do him injustice; for he lived in a time when the scholastic method was fast losing its vitality and becoming confused in a restless striving after infinitesimal distinctions. It is no disparagement to Wycliffe to confess that his philosophy did not rise above his generation: he knew its wants, and gave them satisfaction; it was not in philosophy that he was destined to strike out a new line.

Nor, indeed, in the formal treatment of theology—except in his later teaching concerning the sacrament—does he sensibly depart from the method usual among his contemporaries. His novel views of what may be called theological politics—his doctrines of Lordship and of Evangelical Poverty—were not themselves original; and they were ingeniously superimposed upon, rather than assimilated with, the subject-matter of his theological exposition. Wycliffe acquired his ascendancy as a teacher not so much by what he innovated as by his complete mastery of the accredited system of divinity. Having won his position of authority, he was able to make use of it as a means for the propagation of the opinions he had formed in the course of his studies; and after 1380, even though his propositions touching the sacrament were officially condemned, the strength of his support at Oxford was such as to call for the most vigorous methods for its repression.

In May, 1382, as we have seen, the Council of Blackfriars condemned the heretical doctrine, and the Archbishop dispatched a Carmelite, Peter Stokes, to Oxford as his commissary, to put a stop to its dissemination. No mention was made of Wycliffe by name, but the intention of the mandate could not be mistaken. Besides, the university conceived itself affronted by the Archbishop's invasion of its privileges, and the old jealousy of Regulars and Seculars gave a turn in Wycliffe's favour. It was hardly an accident that the new chancellor, Robert Rygge, had just before nominated one of Wycliffe's loyalest followers, Nicolas Hereford, to preach before the university: he now appointed another staunch Wycliffite, Philip Repyngdon, for the same office. Stokes went about in fear of his life, and durst not publish the archbishop's mandate. When he attempted to defend his commission, he was terrified by the appearance of men with arms beneath their gowns. Not only the chancellor but both the proctors stood firmly against him. When, however, the Council summoned Rygge to London, his courage forsook him: he dissociated himself from any leaning towards the condemned doctrines, and was pardoned. He was supplied with a new mandate for the repression of Wycliffite teaching in his university, but at first protested that he dared not publish it. A royal order compelled him to do this; and so great a tumult arose in Oxford that Rygge went the length of suspending an orthodox disputant, and brought down upon himself a further peremptory mandate. Wycliffe's principal adherents were next suspended from their academical functions, and two of them, Hereford and Repyngdon, excommunicated. These implored in vain the protection of John of Gaunt, who would not be persuaded that the doctrine touching the Sacrament was anything but detestable. The duke's alliance with Wycliffe's party was now finally dissolved. The reformers lost heart, and before the year was out, with the exception of Hereford, who seems to have gone abroad, they all recanted their errors. The strength of their school at Oxford was broken for many years.

While, however, in his university Wycliffe's doctrines had

won the ears of the masters in most cases rather as theoretical and in the Country. positions which might be maintained with credit in argument, in the country at large it was their practical issues which attracted and held men's minds. Here they meant a resolute attack equally on the system of the Church and on its temporal endowments—not only a denial of certain dogmatic beliefs (in particular that of Transubstantiation), but also of the authority of the priest (especially the power of excommunication). Besides these negative propositions, Wycliffe's disciples dwelt with emphasis on the clergyman's duty of frequent preaching, and urged the reading of the Bible as an obligation alike on clergy and laity. These were some of the practical forms taken by the teaching which claimed to re-establish the law of the Gospel in place of the tradition and authority of the Church. All through Wycliffe's later years, assisted by the too manifest existence of evils in the English Church as it then was, and still more by the unsettling effects of the Papal schism, his followers increased and multiplied. They were commonly known as Lollards—a The Lollards. word of doubtful origin, which certainly in Wycliffe's lifetime was considered a term of reproach, but which is now sanctioned by usage as their distinctive name without any offensive connotation.

It is impossible to estimate their numerical strength. Knighton, a writer at the close of the century, says that every other man one met in the street was a Wycliffite: but he was a canon of St. Mary's, Leicester, and Leicestershire was the chief home of Lollardy. From Leicester the influence extended into Northamptonshire. There were Lollard settlements also on the borders of the counties of Gloucester and Worcester, and, at a later time, in Kent. Elsewhere, as in Herefordshire and Bristol, they seem to have been more scattered, but the prevalence of the opinions they maintained is abundantly attested by the steady support they received from the Knights of the Shires in Parliament. In 1382 a Statute was passed against heresy, but it was repealed at the petition of the Commons in the same year. The Lollards were reputed still to have friends at Court; and it is certain that a powerful party was at least willing to profit by the bias against clerical ascendancy which they set in motion. The measures taken against them were half-hearted, and an inquiry held by Archbishop Courtenay at Leicester in

1389 ended in the absolution of those who were charged with heresy. A remarkable evidence of their tenacity is found in the bill of twelve articles setting forth their conclusions in favour of reform both in organisation and doctrine, which was presented in the Parliament of 1395; some of the Lollards were compelled to abjure, and next year a council was held by the new archbishop, Arundel, which condemned their heretical opinions.

It may be conjectured that the reason for the unwillingness of the leading churchmen to proceed vigorously against the Lollards is to be found in the fact that the sincerity and honest hard work of the Poor Preachers in the country districts were held to outweigh the errors charged against them. It is certain that the tolerant spirit shown by the bishops called forth the bitter reproaches of contemporary chroniclers, who commend only Despenser of Norwich for the resolution with which he frightened the heretics in his diocese into obedience by a threat of the stake. The sentence of burning was, however, not explicitly authorised by law in the case of heresy (as distinguished from open apostasy) until the reaction in favour of a sterner churchmanship began with the revolution which placed Henry IV. on the throne. In 1401 Archbishop Arundel succeeded in passing the statute *de Haeretico* which provided **Burning of** machinery for dealing with heretics. So urgent seemed the **Heretics.** need for it that actually a few days before the statute became law a Lollard clergyman named Sawtre was executed by burning. The Act itself had but little operation: Badby, a tailor of Evesham, was burned in 1410, and Wyche, a clergyman, thirty years later. Sir John Oldcastle[1] and those who suffered with him in the reign of Henry V. (p. 401), though they were dealt with as ecclesiastical offenders, were so much mixed up with charges of treasonable

[1] It seems worth while to mention, as a curious fact in the history of English literature, that Sir John Oldcastle was undoubtedly the original of Shakespeare's Falstaff, and had been represented under his own name in more than one drama before Shakespeare's time, sometimes from a favourable and sometimes from a hostile standpoint. There is contemporary authority for stating that Shakespeare had intended to do likewise, but substituted the name of the builder of Caister Castle, in deference to the protest of Lord Cobham, Oldcastle's descendant *See* Gairdner and Spedding, "Studies in English History" (1881), and Mr. James Tait's article on Oldcastle in the "Dictionary of National Biography."

designs that they can hardly be classed without qualification among the victims of religious persecution. The same remark probably applies to the great majority of the twenty persons so executed in the half-century following. In truth, as time went on, the religious element in Lollardy became subordinate to the political or social. Under the House of Lancaster the Lollards were valued as the allies of the Opposition in Parliament. In 1410 the Knights of the Shire sent up a petition for the confisca-

GATEWAY OF COOLING CASTLE, NEAR ROCHESTER, KENT, SIR JOHN
OLDCASTLE'S RESIDENCE.

tion of the lands of the bishops and greater abbots; a proposal frequently repeated by the Lollards, notably in the rebellion of Jack Straw in 1431. When King Henry V. came to the throne, a more determined policy was adopted against the Lollards. The danger with which they menaced the State had been set out in an influentially supported petition in 1406: now, in 1414, an Act was passed which armed the secular officers of justice with new powers co-ordinate with those of the spiritual authorities, and strengthened the procedure under the Act of 1401. With this Statute legislation against the Lollards is completed. The sect soon lost still more its religious characteristics, and, except in the case of a few older men, its adherents became confounded in the common herd of rebels against social order. If any thread of tradition connects the Lollards with the reforming movement of the sixteenth century, it is one so attenuated as to claim the notice of the antiquary rather than the historian. When an English Bible was once more asked for, no one thought of revising and modernising the translation of Wycliffe; the work was put in hand entirely anew.

The Oxford Lollards.

It has been already noticed that the fortunes of the Lollards at Oxford were in some respects different from those in the rest of England. The cloud which fell upon them in 1382 obscured them for many years; yet vigilant supervision of the books read in the university was still necessary. After the accession of Henry IV., the Wycliffite school again grew strong. How far it was actuated by jealousy of Archbishop Arundel's strenuous exercise of his authority, how far by the more local, if more intellectual, instincts of an academic party, cannot be said with certainty. Still it is clear that the Wycliffites had recovered their position, and now formed an important element in the university. In 1407 the archbishop held a council at Oxford, when not merely were stringent orders issued against the reading of Wycliffe's works, but an attempt was also made to regulate the studies of the place. Two years later the convocation of the university was induced to appoint a committee to examine Wycliffe's writings; the committee sat long, and at last reported only by a majority in favour of the condemnation of an exhaustive list of 267 articles. Disturbances arose in the university, and party feeling ran high; in 1409 Arundel sent a mandate to the chancellor, bidding him denounce heavy penalties against the Wycliffites. The university sullenly carried out its instructions. The articles were ordered to be preserved in the public library; every graduate was to swear on admission to his degree that he would not maintain any of them, and every head of a college or hall that he would not admit into his society anyone suspected of heresy.

Their Decay.

The Oxford Lollards as a body had held their ground firmly, but after this they rapidly declined. Bishop Flemming, it is true, so late as 1427 founded a college with the object of encountering the heretical movement (p. 502), but it is likely that he thought of Oxford as he had known it twenty years before. A few expiring traces carry down the tradition even beyond the middle of the century; but as a vital force it was dead, and in its death the university decayed also the more quickly. For, whatever its theological aberrations, the school which Wycliffe founded embraced, on the whole, the more earnest and more sincere members of the university. The stimulus he gave to independent thought, even though it led to perilous issues, was better than the stupor of mechanical routine under which the university remained sunk for generations afterwards.

THE transformation of the wild Prince Hal of tradition into the austere, concentrated, and somewhat self-righteous King Henry V. has its counterpart in the change which came over the nation. Discontent, treason, and want of money are replaced by military enthusiasm and plentiful supplies. All was to be harmony; the body of Richard II. was moved to Westminster, and the heir of the Percies and the Earl of March and the Earl of Huntingdon were restored. Schism was to be put down, and the Lollards were struck at through Sir John Oldcastle, their head. Great captain as he was, and personal friend of the king, Oldcastle was arrested, tried, and condemned. The Lollards threatened that 100,000 men should meet in St. Giles's Fields in January, 1414; but the attempt was as great a failure as that of the Chartists in

HENRY V.
(National Portrait Gallery.)

A. L. SMITH.

The Reign of Henry V.

Sir John
Oldcastle's
Death.

1848. Oldcastle, who had escaped from the Tower, was declared an outlaw. In 1417 he was captured in Wales and hanged in St. Giles's Fields. He had become a great anxiety to Henry from his connection with the Scots, the Welsh rebels, the Mortimers, and the "mawmett" (puppet) still in Scotland—that is, the sham Richard. But with Oldcastle's stubborn defence and his death Lollardy had died out as a political and social force. Henceforth heretics were not to be left to the bishops in the first instance, but were to be proceeded against by justices of the peace.

The
Mortimer
Plot.

But a startling event in 1415 showed that in some other respects things were not so quiet as they looked on the surface. On the eve of the expedition to France, amid the forces mustered at Southampton and from among the king's kinsmen and confidants, there was disclosed a plot which was at once a revival of the old union of the Mortimers and Percies with the Scots and Welsh, and a presage of the union of the claims of Mortimer and of York to the throne. The chiefs of the plot were Richard of York, lately created Earl of Cambridge by Henry V.; Lord Scrope of Masham, the king's closest companion "at bed and at board, in council and in chase"; and Sir Thomas Grey, a North-country knight. Their plan was, as soon as the king had sailed, to carry off to Wales the young Edmund Mortimer, Earl of March. But the young earl rose superior to the casuistry of his confessors, and revealed the plot. The three chief culprits were executed.

France
Invaded.

With no greater force of regular troops than 2,000 men-at-arms and some 6,000 archers, Henry set forth on Sunday, 11th August, 1415, for the conquest of a realm many times greater and more populous than his own. This daring ambition was not the mere rejoinder to the Dauphin's mocking present of a case of tennis-balls; it had probably been in his mind from the first. To it we may attribute much of his policy of general conciliation, his resolute crushing of all elements of disorder at home, his favourable offers to the Scots. There are stories, too, of doubtful authenticity, but pointing the same way. Henry IV. was said to have recommended war as a mode of strengthening the dynasty. The clergy were said to have urged it as a mode of diverting a threatened attack on Church temporalities. Within three months from his accession Henry's envoys in France were claiming his rights. The demands he made seem outrageous. They comprised, besides 2,600,000 crowns in money, all the provinces granted at Bretigny, 1360; all provinces which an English king had ever held or claimed; and all this without prejudice to his general claim to the crown itself of France. It is probable that in asking so much Henry meant to throw on the French the responsibility for the war. But it is certain, at the same time, that the woeful state of France seemed to him a Divine call upon him to restore order by force. " Never was there greater sin than now is in France," he said to the Duke of Orleans; " no wonder God is wroth at it."

In this view he had negotiated simultaneously with each of the two parties now rending France asunder; he was ready to marry Catherine of France or Catherine of Burgundy. His invasion had almost a religious character; there were to be no outrages. It was noticed that the king was stern to repress the usual licence of a camp as to language and conduct. He was equally careful to appear as rightful lord of Normandy. When Harfleur, the key of Normandy, was taken, on 22nd September, 1415, after five weeks' siege, the inhabitants were well treated. The march to Calais, foolhardy as it may appear, had probably a definite object as a demonstration in the eyes of France. On the march a man was hanged who had stolen a pix[1] (this is the incident which Shakespeare utilises to make an appropriate close to Bardolph's career). The Battle of Agincourt **Agincourt.** itself (25th October) is easily explained by the incredible blunders of the French, and their blind contempt for their enemy, as well as by the deadliness of the English longbow and the excellent open formation of Henry's lines. But a battle in which some 3,000 archers and 1,000 men-at-arms defeated, with almost no loss, a fourfold number of all the chivalry of France, might well be claimed by the English invader as a judgment in his favour by the God of Battles. The effect of Agincourt was, in England, to revive the ancient war fever; in France, to produce an alliance with the Duke of Burgundy; in Europe, to bring Spain, Holland, and the Hanse League to Henry's side. In April, 1416, the Emperor Sigismund, as representative of the Council now sitting at Constance, came to Dover to bring about a peace between France and England. But when

[1 That is, the box containing the reserved Host.]

Alliance with the Emperor. he left England in August, the pressure of circumstances had made him exchange the ancient league of his family with France for a treaty, offensive and defensive, with Henry against France. The reunion of Christendom, the suppression of heresy, the reform of the Church, which were the objects of the Council, were objects as near to Henry's heart. Henry's influence in the Council, through his envoy, Robert Hallam, Bishop of Salisbury, and later through Bishop Beaufort, was now united with that of Sigismund; and this joint English-German action defeated the chance of a French Pope, and secured the election of Otto Colonna, Martin V., 11th November, 1417.

Conquest of Normandy. In 1417, with an army of some 10,000, Henry, beginning with Caen, reduced the chief towns in Normandy and Maine. Rouen, the second city of France, after a six months' siege, was taken January, 1419. The murder of the Duke of Burgundy by the Dauphin's men threw the new duke into Henry's arms. Paris itself, which was starving, welcomed him. In May, 1420, the great Peace of Troyes recognised Henry as present Regent and as heir of France, to the exclusion of the Dauphin; in June Henry married Catherine, daughter of Charles VI. In December the two kings and the Duke of Burgundy entered Paris in state.

Henry's Failure. Thus did Henry's great plan seem achieved. But in truth the hopeless part of his task had but just begun. The French already resented his curt and peremptory ways. "He made no answers but, 'It is impossible,' or 'It must be done,'" says the chronicler of St. Denys. In 1421 he was recalled from a month's stay in England by bad news. Clarence had been defeated and slain at Beaugé by Scots auxiliaries in the French service. The Duke of Brittany had joined the Dauphin. In vain did Henry endeavour to bring on a decisive engagement by pushing on to the Loire. Even reinforcements from England began to fail; "never was he in greater need," he told his people. The siege of Meaux cost him eight months; and the hand of death was already on him. He struggled hard to answer the Duke of Burgundy's call for help; but he had long suffered from ague, and now from dysentery, and he could not sit his horse. On August 31st he died at Vincennes.

His Death. Among his last words were a charge to his friends to prosecute the cause to the end; "the guilt of bloodshed was not his, he had been assured by holy men before ever he drew the sword." As the penitential psalms were being read, the chaplain came to the words " Build Thou the walls of Jeru-salem." The dying king was heard to say : " Good Lord, Thou knowest that my mind was to re-edify the walls of Jerusalem." He was, indeed, one of the last great medieval

MARRIAGE OF HENRY V. AND CATHERINE OF FRANCE (MS Roy. 20 E. vi.).

characters : medieval in his sincere fanatical religiousness, in his strict, somewhat narrow legality, in his concentrated, passionate, impossible aims. For many a generation his exploits and memory were an inspiration to Englishmen. But to his immediate suc-cessors he left the fatal legacy of a hopeless foreign policy, an exhausted kingdom, and a royal house divided against itself.

CHARLES LE BIEN-AIMÉ had died seven weeks after his great son-in-law. Thus, in November, 1422, the English at Paris proclaimed the young Henry VI. as King of France; the Dauphin a little earlier was proclaimed as Charles VII. The English held the most important part of France; by military and political position, by their allies and by their own generals, they seemed to have much the stronger position. Yet from this date the revival of a national spirit in France, and the consequent expulsion of the invaders, was only a question of time. For the first six years, indeed, the statesmanship, the tireless energy, and the high moral qualities of Bedford availed to suspend destiny. In 1423 he made the League of Amiens with the two Dukes of Burgundy and Brittany, himself marrying the Duke of Burgundy's sister, and sealing the alliance by the victory of Crevant, which repelled the French from Burgundian territory. In 1424 the politic release of James of Scotland from his eighteen years of English captivity was followed by his marriage with Joan Beaufort, whom he has celebrated in his poem as—

HENRY VI.
(National Portrait Gallery.)

A. L. SMITH.
The Reign of Henry VI.

The Struggle for France.

> "The fairest and the freshest younge flower
> That ever I saw methought before that hour."

The king now tried to recall his Scots subjects from service in France. Their impetuosity and uncontrollable detestation of the English had sometimes led to disaster. Thus the Earls

of Buchan and Douglas insisted on attacking the English at
Verneuil (1424), and both fell in this great battle, which demonstrated once more that the long-bow still counterbalanced
almost any inferiority in numbers. " At Agincourt were many
more princes and people; Crevant was a pretty affair; but

HENRY VI., AS A CHILD, PRESENTED TO THE VIRGIN (MS. Dom. A. xvii.).

Verneuil was the most terrible and the best fought of the
three." This is the judgment of Waurin, the Burgundian
chronicler, who was himself present on each field. In 1425
Maine and Champagne were subdued. In 1426 the invaders
were still advancing further south. In 1427, despite reverses,
they were still strong enough to undertake the great enterprise

of forcing the barrier of the Loire. Salisbury, who, in a letter to the Londoners, was able to enumerate thirty-eight places captured that year, in October began to invest Orleans. Despite Salisbury's death and the resistance of the garrison, the city began to feel want. Sir John Fastolf's skilful defence of a convoy and his decisive victory, the " Battle of the Herrings," over the large assailing force of French, was one more timely proof of the English superiority in the open field. Orleans seemed doomed. Normandy, Maine, Picardy, the Isle de France, Orléanais, and Champagne were in English hands; as, in the south, were large parts of Guienne and Gascony. Brittany on the west, Flanders and the Burgundian territories on the east, encircled France with English. Charles VII.'s council was torn by intrigues ; some even advised that the king should retire to Spain or to Scotland.

The English position, however, in spite of this appearance of strength, had already been undermined. For, even before the Treaty of Amiens, Humphrey, Duke of Gloucester, had married Jacqueline, heiress of Holland and Hainault, who had fled from her husband, John, Duke of Brabant. Such a marriage had been a part of Henry V.'s policy. But Philip of Burgundy was cousin both to John and to Jacqueline, and heir presumptive to the territories of both. These territories, moreover, were, in a geographical sense, of vital importance to Burgundy. Bedford therefore had, in 1424, to pacify him by grants of other territories. But Gloucester persisted in invading Hainault : he harried Brabant, gave the lie direct to the Duke of Burgundy, and accepted a challenge to a duel with him. Gloucester had ruined Bedford's policy and effected absolutely nothing for himself. He left Jacqueline in Hainault, discarding her for Eleanor Cobham, one of her own ladies. In two months Burgundy was master of all. Bedford succeeded in averting the duel ; but the mischief had been done. Jacqueline, moreover, had escaped to Holland, and was still keeping up her importunate claims.

In March, 1429, Joan of Arc, "the Maid of God," appeared at Chinon and convinced Charles of her Divine mission to relieve Orleans and take him to be crowned at Rheims. The former object she accomplished in ten days, the latter within three months. Bedford himself described her advent as a

great blow, and as having "withdrawn their courage in
marvellous wise"; such was their heathenish fear, he says, of
this " disciple and limb of the fiend, called the Pucelle, that
used false enchantments and sorcery." Probably her view
was right that a resolute attack on Paris would now have
struck a death-blow at the heart of the English power. But
Charles VII. was as incapable of courage as he was of gratitude;

STATUE OF JOAN OF ARC.
(*Musée Cluny, Paris.*)

in the first check he found an excuse for disbanding his
troops. Thus, in 1430, the English were able to commit
Paris to the regency of the Duke of Burgundy, and to bring
over Henry, who had lately been crowned King of England.
In May, the Maid, who had long felt her work was done,
had " wished the Lord would send her back to her father's
sheep," and had lately heard miraculous voices warning her
of the end, was taken captive near Compiègne. For just

**Her
Capture
and
Death.**

twelve months was she kept close prisoner, examined by officials of the Inquisition, threatened, insulted, entrapped, treated with inconceivable cruelty and treachery, driven to attempt her own life, and at another time to make a temporary recantation. At last, on May 30th, 1431, she was burned at the stake in Rouen market-place. The guilt must be shared between Burgundy, who allowed her to be sold to the English for 10,000 francs: Bedford and Warwick, who hated the creature who had foiled them ; Charles, who might easily have saved his chivalrous preserver: the University

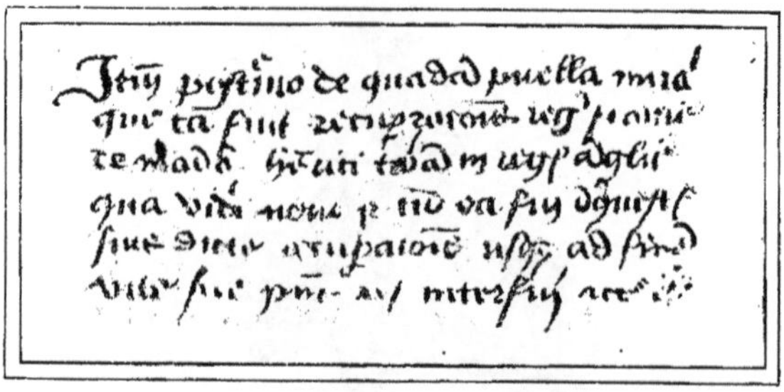

TESTIMONY AS TO JOAN OF ARC: BY AN EYE-WITNESS.
(*Book of Pluscarden: Bodleian Library, Oxford.*)

of Paris and the Norman clergy, whose actuating motives must have been the lowest time-serving or sacerdotal jealousy. The English could hardly be expected to rise above the prejudice to which even Shakespeare is not superior; but no words can be too severe to express the infamy of their accomplices.

**Henry
Crowned
Paris.**

The execution of Joan of Arc meant a temporary revival of English spirit. In December, 1431, Henry was crowned at Paris as King of France. But it was only temporary. Early in the year the three Estates of England had signified their desire for peace, and before the year closed Burgundy had made truce with France. In November, 1432, died Bedford's wife, Anne of Burgundy, "the fair and good lady, well beloved of the people of Paris." Bedford offended Burgundy by marrying, four months later, Jacquetta of Luxemburg, a Burgundian vassal. This practically ended the Burgundian alliance, the mainstay of Henry V.'s policy. In 1434 the refusal of quarter on both sides, and repeated risings of the peasantry in Normandy, showed the cause was lost. At the Congress of Arras, 1435, the French offers to cede Normandy were flatly refused. The English would not renounce

Photo: Neurdein, Paris.

PRISON OF JOAN OF ARC AT ROUEN.

the crown; such a renunciation would stamp their whole past dominion as a tyranny, and would preclude a future attempt to regain it. But this refusal warranted Burgundy in coming over definitely to the French side. And this proved the final blow to the stout heart of the Duke of Bedford. In September he died at Rouen; a good general and good ruler, a strong man sacrificed to a hopeless task.

"Noble he was by virtue as by descent; wise and liberal, both feared and loved," says the Norman Chronicle.   In 1436 the French recovered Paris; even Calais was besieged by the Flemings for a month.   Where Bedford had failed, other commanders were not likely to succeed.   One after another they resigned or died at their posts—the Duke of York, the old Earl of Warwick, the two Beauforts.   But gradually Cardinal Beaufort's peace policy began to prevail.   The Duke of Orleans was released in 1439, on a pledge that he would try to bring about a peace.   Still the war lingered on under the Duke of York from 1439 to 1445.   But in 1445 the Earl of Suffolk, a kinsman of the Beauforts, brought back Margaret of Anjou, a niece of Charles VII., to be the bride of Henry VI., but to be also the ruin of the Lancastrian dynasty. Fair as she was, high-spirited as her history shows her to have been,

SEAL OF HENRY VI. FOR FRENCH AFFAIRS.

she was daughter of the impecunious René, and came without a dower.   Men whispered that Suffolk had bought a queen not worth four marks at the price of a province; for he had been forced to purchase the truce and the marriage by the cession of Maine, as well as the surrender of claim to the French crown.   Henry was to be left in possession of Normandy and Guienne.   But aggressions by the unpaid and disorderly English garrisons gave the French king a fair excuse; the Norman fortresses fell rapidly, and the battle of Formigny, in 1450 (p. 450), broke the long tradition of English invincibility in the open field.   By August, 1450, the news ran in England that "now we have not a foot of land in Normandy."   The same fate rapidly overtook the ancient English holdings in Guienne.   These now consisted of the coast-lands from

Loss of Normandy and Guienne.

Bayonne to near Rochelle, with a wedge of territory reaching inland some eighty miles. But when the three great southern houses of Armagnac, Albret, and Foix "turned French," Bordeaux itself surrendered. At vespers, on June 23rd, 1451 the herald ascended a tower and formally cried aloud for "Succour from England." There was none to answer; a week later Dunois entered in triumph. Bayonne fell in August. Next year Talbot, Earl of Shrewsbury, the last of the fighting race of the Hundred Years' War, who had seen thirty-four campaigns, and who still lives in popular legends of the Garonne as Le Roi Talabot, was defeated and slain at Châtillon. Thus passed away the last remnant of the great inheritance with which Eleanor of Aquitaine had endowed the English Crown just 300 years before. It is easy to see the evil which the connection had caused; but it is easy, too, to overlook the effect it had had in raising England out of its narrow insularity and in converting to enterprises abroad those fighting energies which, for the next thirty years, are diverted into the channel of civil war. *France Finally Lost.*

In military history the Hundred Years' War decisively displaced cavalry by infantry, the feudal knight by the yeoman archer (pp. 235, 449); and it developed the application of artillery to siege purposes (p. 450). Before its close it was clear that the long-bow must soon yield to the musket, and that social order needed the support of standing armies. *Effects of the War.*

Its political effects had been to put together the splendid but hollow fabric of the Burgundian State, destined to endure a century, and to create for ever the intense patriotism of France—that patriotism which is a religion.

In English policy, neither under Edward III. nor under Henry V. had the war been mere military wantonness. The former had had a far-reaching though rather confused commercial aim underlying his attacks. The latter king had a very definite aim of reconstructing in Normandy another England, which would make him indeed "master of the narrow seas" and give him a decisive voice in European affairs. To this end many reforms were made, the gabelle and salt tax abolished, brigandage put down by patrols, English gentlemen were invited by offers of fiefs to settle in the country,

and an attempt was made to colonise the four great seaports
with English traders and artisans.   The native manufactures
were encouraged by bounties, and controlled by paternal regulations.   A system of three Estates was set up on the English
model, and to the Parliament thus constituted full powers
of taxation were committed.   The judicial system was re-
modelled on the English assizes and local courts.   Even a
militia was established.   Here, in fact, was a thorough and
honest attempt to apply the Lancastrian experiment to this
newer England—an attempt based, as in England itself, on
the gentry, the clergy, and the official classes, without whose
support, in fact, Normandy could not have been held so long.
All the defects, moreover, which ruined the Lancastrian scheme
of government at home were repeated here.   The political basis
was too narrow, the franchise too restricted, especially in the
towns.   The English settlers became French in one generation,
the Norman nobles proved irreconcilable, and the local spirit
was too strong to be mastered by an imported organisation.
It was a bold experiment doggedly carried out; but it was
tried too late.

Beaufort
and
Glou-
cester.

From 1422 to 1447 the internal history of England turns
upon the rivalry between Beaufort and Gloucester.   As
Gloucester ruined his brother's policy abroad, so with the same
arrogant self-seeking he ruined his family's chance of establishing their dynasty at home.   He began by claiming the
Regency in England; the lords would only allow him the title
of Protector.   He attacked every measure of his uncle, Henry
Beaufort, Bishop of Winchester, who was now Chancellor, and
raised the Londoners in arms against him.   In 1426 Bedford
had to return from France to mediate; and peace could only
be made by the bishop resigning the seals, and absenting
himself for two and a half years, on the ostensible plea of a
crusade against the Hussites in Bohemia.   Hard-pressed as
the treasury was for money, Gloucester succeeded in wringing
from it large sums as his salary, profitable wardships,[1] and loans
for his futile foreign schemes.   When Beaufort returned to
England in 1428, he had in the interval accepted a cardinal's

---

[1] [*I.e.* appointments of guardian and, as we should say, trustee for heirs
to large estates during their minority, a very lucrative incident of the
feudal system.]

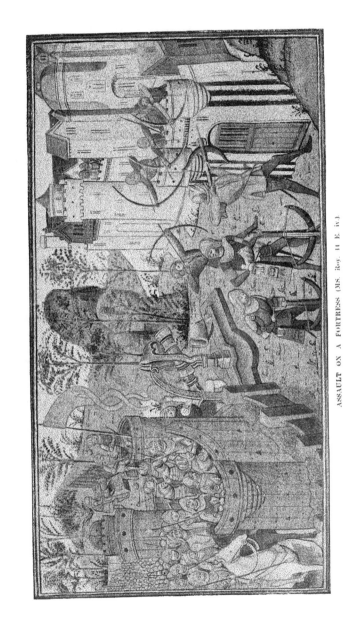

ASSAULT ON A FORTRESS (MS. Roy. 14 E. iv.).

hat. Gloucester took advantage of the old jealousy against
Papal legates in England, and of the recent irritation at the
Papal attempt to get the Statutes of Provisors repealed. Beaufort had to conciliate the national feeling by submission; but
by getting the king crowned next year, he forced his rival to
renounce his office of Protector. However, on the whole,
Gloucester still carried national feeling with him in his attacks
on Beaufort in 1431 and 1432, and was able to place partisans
of his own in the great offices of State, until his brother's return
to England ousted him from the chief place on the council,
and shamed him into a temporary sobriety and public spirit.
It was only temporary; for in April, 1434, he was criticising
his brother's conduct of the war; and Bedford sailed again
to France to spend the last year of his life on his hopeless
task. Bedford's death threw the Beauforts definitely on the
side of peace; and to this the king inclined more and more
Gloucester, therefore, as head of the war-party, and as patron
of the Duke of York, encouraged the people to clamour for
war while they refused to pay its cost, and to brand any attempts
at peace negotiations as " treason " and " corrupt dealing." But
his opponents were strong enough in the king's favour and
the lords' support to repel his virulent attack upon them in
1439. Next year they retaliated by convicting his duchess
of witchcraft, heresy, and treason; she had with magical arts
melted a waxen image before the fire that the king's life might
be wasted away; among her accomplices were a notorious witch,
and a clerk of Oxford, "most famous in the world for astronomy and necromancy." Barefoot and bareheaded she had
to do public penance for three days through London streets,
and was then imprisoned for life, her accomplices being
executed. Since 1435 her husband was presumptive heir to
the crown; but this incident seems to show his power was
waning. When he proposed that Henry should marry a
daughter of the Count of Armagnac, the Beauforts broke it
off; and they sent all the men and money the kingdom could
raise, not to succour York in Normandy, but to attempt a rival
enterprise in Guienne under the Duke of Somerset (John
Beaufort). When, however, the actual marriage took place
with Margaret of Anjou, Parliament and the nation, reflecting
Gloucester's attitude, were suspicious and mistrustful of the

Beauforts and Suffolk their representative. It is clear that in 1446, Suffolk, with the aid of the young queen, laid his plans for the duke's downfall. The Parliament of 1447 was called to meet at Bury St. Edmund's, for London was still under the spell of "the good Duke Humphrey's" popular policy and popular manners. On Gloucester's appearing he was arrested with his retinue. The shock, acting on a man of his temperament, and of a constitution long impaired by debauchery, brought on a paralytic stroke ; in five days he died. Dark rumours were current of his having been assassinated.

BEAUFORT'S TOWER, ST. CROSS, WINCHESTER.

But though there is a certain mystery about his and Suffolk's plots and counterplots at this time, there is little doubt his death was natural. Six weeks later his great rival the Cardinal followed him to the grave. Two days before his end he had a public funeral service performed over him, his will was read aloud, and he took solemn farewell of his household. Even in his last four years of retirement he had remained, as he had been throughout the forty-eight years of Lancastrian rule, the pillar of the State. His wisdom and devotion, his European influence, his immense treasures, had been given unsparingly in the public service. He was accused of personal and family ambition ; he held lucrative patents from the Crown, and was

Death of the Rivals: their Charac- ters.

71

"the greatest wool dealer in the realm"; he was ostentatious and imperious. In these respects he was no better than his time. Nevertheless he is not unworthy of his place in the list of great clerical statesmen of the Middle Ages, a list which begins with Dunstan and closes with Wolsey.

Very different must be the verdict on Humphrey, Duke of Gloucester, a notable instance of the worthlessness of contemporary fame. Headstrong, unprincipled, and greedy, a braggart and a debauchee, he earned a cheap reputation by a certain munificence, and a rather superficial patronage of literature and art. But his insane egotism ruined the war policy of his great brothers. He used his popularity to wreck all projects of peace. His intrigues reduced the administration to impotence and bankruptcy, and roused a blind irrational prejudice against Suffolk and the Queen. Above all, he pushed the Duke of York into the position of a rival to the reigning king, and so made the Wars of the Roses inevitable.

Fall of Suffolk. The fall of Suffolk was a sacrifice to Gloucester's memory. It was also the first step taken by the party soon to be identified with Richard of York. Suffolk, as now chief councillor of the king and the procurer of the French marriage, was made the popular scapegoat for the loss of Normandy as well as the cession of Maine and Anjou. An ominous sign was the murder of his coadjutor, Bishop Moleyns, at Portsmouth by the sailors. In the Parliament of January, 1450, Suffolk was impeached. In vain did he urge his services; that his father and four brothers had lost their lives in France, that he himself had spent seventeen years there under arms. The king had to abandon him; he was banished, but on his way to Calais was seized by ships of the royal navy, and after a form of trial his head was struck off on the gunwale of a boat. None who read his farewell letter to his young son will doubt that he died an innocent victim of popular prejudice and party rancour. Songs of the time still remain which show, in a horrible parody of the funeral service, the exultation with which the death of "the Fox" was received. Whether York's partisans were, as foreign opinion believed, the direct authors of this deed or not, at any rate it was followed by a strange event, which must be regarded as a direct challenge by the Yorkist party. On Trinity Sunday, 1450, a rising began in Kent under one

John Cade (p. 529), who called himself John Mortimer, cousin **Jack** of the Duke of York. Under this "Captain of Kent," "John **Cade's** Amend-all," the yeomen and gentry of Kent and Sussex rose **Rising.** in no tumultuous levy, but regularly arrayed under the constables of the hundreds. They formed a regular camp at Blackheath ; they drew up fifteen formal articles of grievance, and demanded that York .and his friends should take the places of the Suffolk party in the king's councils. Many in

TOMBS OF THE DE LA POLES, WINGFIELD CHURCH, SUFFOLK.

London, and eventually the king's own forces, were ready to fraternise with them. Cade was able to return to London, seize and behead Lord Say the Treasurer, and other unpopular officials. In Wiltshire about the same time, the Bishop of Salisbury, the king's confessor, was stoned to death by a mob. The Government had to make terms ; free pardons were issued to the rebels of Kent, Surrey, Sussex, Essex. They returned home. But Cade, remaining in arms, was slain by the sheriff of Kent a week later. In spite, however, of many executions, disaffection continued to show itself in these shires. And

Claims
of the
Duke of
York.

meanwhile the Duke of York threw up his duties in Ireland and came home to complain of mistrust, and to denounce the "lack of governance"; "he visaged so the matter that the king's household was right sore afraid." His position, in fact, was a very strong one. Not only was he heir presumptive, since Henry had no children, but, though his descent from Edward III. had to be traced through females, yet it was descent by an elder line than that of Lancaster; he had already in the eyes of men of that time a legal title to the crown superior to the king's, perhaps even an indefeasible title. Somerset could claim to be heir male of John of Gaunt, but only if the legitimation of the Beauforts by the canon law and by Parliament was to hold good against their deliberate exclusion from succession to the crown by Henry IV., and perhaps also by Richard II. At any rate, most men saw in York the true heir. For fifteen years also he had served in France and Ireland, with what, compared with the rest, seemed to stand forth as conspicuous success. His party was strong among the great nobles. He was brother-in-law to the four Nevilles, Lords Salisbury, Fauconberge, Latimer, Abergavenny, and to Humphrey Stafford, Duke of Buckingham, and Henry Percy, Earl of Northumberland; uncle to Mowbray, Duke of Norfolk, and Richard, Earl of Warwick. In his own person he represented the great house of Mortimer as well as the lineage of Lionel of Clarence and Edmund of York. Besides this, the Parliaments of 1450 and 1451 were strongly on his side. Thomas Young, member for Bristol, was sent to the Tower for petitioning that York might be declared heir. In 1452 York assembled an armed force to insist on the removal of Somerset as author of the loss of Normandy; but neither Kent nor London was ready to join him in arms, and he was forced to swear to use only legal means in future. Next year the final loss of Guienne, the king's going out of his mind, and the birth of a Prince of Wales, combined to stimulate York's action.

He is
made
Protector.

He was chosen Protector, and his rival was imprisoned. Salisbury was made Chancellor, and Thomas Bourchier, another kinsman of York's, Archbishop of Canterbury. The king's sudden recovery after eighteen months, and the restoration of Somerset, forced the Yorkists to arm in self-defence, and the first of the fourteen battles between the two Roses was fought at St. Albans, May 22nd, 1455. The number slain was "some six score" only; but Somerset was among them. York was victorious; his partisans were replaced in office; and the king again falling ill, the Protector resumed his authority, but only for three months, at which date the king recovered. Then followed three years of suspense; the Duke of York waiting on the queen and she on him, as the Paston Letters describe the situation. In March, 1456, a solemn "pacification" took place at St. Paul's, to which both parties marched in pairs, York hand in hand with the queen, and so on. This only meant a hollow truce, during which Warwick was gaining popularity as captain of Calais and warder of the seas. By September, 1459, the queen was ready; Salisbury was summoned to London; he mustered his Yorkshire tenants, sent for his son Warwick, repulsed a royalist force at Blackheath, and the two earls met York at Ludlow. But before the king's large army their scanty forces melted away; and they fled, Warwick and Salisbury to Calais, York to Ireland. Their return next June was a triumphal procession through Kent into London, followed by a decisive victory at Northampton, where many Lancastrian leaders fell, and the king was captured. In the subsequent Parliament York laid direct claim to the crown; but it is interesting to see that even then, though fourteen Lancastrian peers were dead or absent, the lords had the courage and common sense to resist, and to stand by their oaths to Henry. The result was a compromise: Henry to reign for life, York to be declared heir. But in a few weeks the Yorkists had been defeated at Wakefield; the leaders' heads were fixed on the walls of York by Margaret, the Protector's head decorated with a mock crown. The queen, however, once more ruined her own cause by the army of plunderers which she now gathered from the borders, and which did indeed win for her the second battle of St. Albans, but was so unruly that she dared not bring it into London. While the queen parleyed, Warwick and Edward, Earl of March pushed on from the west; and saved their cause by a few hours. For, "by counsel of the lords of the south," on 4th March, Edward IV. was proclaimed king. This was an immense stride taken by the doctrine of hereditary right; there was no recognition of the new king's title by Parliament till

The Wars of the Roses begin.

Wakefield.

Towton.

eight months later. In the interval was fought the skirmish at Ferrybridge, and the next two days the great battle of Towton (29th March). The disorganised Lancastrian host had retreated northwards, to gather fresh levies. But they were pursued by Warwick with his men of the Welsh borders and the men of Kent. Edward joined him at Leicester with fresh troops who had flocked in from the southern and home counties, eager for vengeance upon the wild northern folk " of strange speech, given to rapine and devouring of spoil." The fight of Palm Sunday, 1461, was the most stubborn of all in

Photo: G. W. Wilson & Co., Aberdeen.
BAMBOROUGH CASTLE.

these wars; it began at four in the morning, and was only decided in the afternoon by the arrival of the Mowbray retainers, who came up after long marches from Norfolk just in time to take the right wing and outflank the enemy on the east. It was fought in driving snow, and as the fugitives pressed across the flooded meadows, " that day the river slew its thousands." The chroniclers told that 48,000 men were ranged · on the Yorkist side, 60,000 on the Lancastrian; and that the heralds counted over 20,000 slain. These numbers can hardly be accepted. But it is certain that the Earls of Northumberland, Devonshire, and Wiltshire, and the Lords Clifford, Dacre, Neville, Wells, Manley, and many knights and squires fell on the field or were taken and executed. Henry

LUDLOW CASTLE.

Photo: Jones, Son & Iberzer, Ludlow.

and Margaret fled north, and finally into Scotland. Only a few fortresses still held out ; Alnwick, Bamborough, and Dunstanborough in the north ; Harlech in the west. The Nemesis of Henry IV.'s crooked ways, of Henry V.'s suicidal foreign wars, of Henry VI.'s favouritism and incompetency, had fallen upon the dynasty. England needed a strong ruler, and had found one in Edward IV.

Triumph of Edward IV.

A. L. SMITH. The Constitution under Lancastrian Rule.

THE Lancastrian reign, it has been truly said, saw the trial and failure of a great constitutional experiment. The most striking feature in this was the temporary harmony between the Council and the Parliament. From the accession of Henry IV. the Councillors were nominated in Parliament; their salaries, procedure, and rules fixed in Parliament. The result was a total cessation of the old hostility towards the Council. Its interference in justice, the relief it granted on petitions of all kinds, were no longer the subject of complaint as in the fourteenth century. The jealously guarded Statutes of the Staple and of Provisors were handed over to its discretion. The very power of taxation was entrusted to it, even to the details both of expenditure and of revenue. It became the regular practice for Parliament to grant a certain sum and leave the Council to raise it by loan on the security of the Customs. This practice even lasted to 1447, outliving by ten years the real harmony between the two bodies. For in the bankrupt state of the finances, a method that had at least been tolerably successful could not well be dropped, at any rate as long as Beaufort lived, with his willingness to lend of his great wealth, and his established fame as a financier.

Another feature in the constitutional experiment was the advance in the recognised position of Parliament itself. Freedom of speech was boldly claimed, and mercilessly exemplified by more than one long-winded speaker. In 1407 the Commons secured their exclusive right to initiate money grants. Their petitions were to be turned into statutes without alteration, and this led to the use of "bills"—that is, petitions drafted in statute form. By deferring their grants till the last day of Session, they ensured that redress should precede Supply. By ear-marking particular funds they ensured the exact appropriation of their grants. By their niggardliness in granting, they ensured that a full audit of past grants should be rendered to them.

More interesting still is the Lancastrian attempt to purify the representative system at its source. By many statutes from 1406 to 1445, the sheriffs' manipulation of elections was checked. The return was to be made under the seals of the electors. A false return was punished by a fine of £100. Residence was made a qualification for election. Orderliness was aimed at in the rules that no yeomen were eligible as knights, and that none under 40s. freehold should give votes.

Not without reason did Sir John Fortescue claim that the English realm in his day was a constitutional or limited monarchy. The sovereignty was "political" in that the king cannot legislate or tax without Parliament, or sit as judge in his own courts of law. But it was royal, too—a real monarchical rule in the large powers entrusted to the Crown, in its extra-legal powers in case of foreign invasions, in its prerogatives of pardon and of equity, and in its hereditary character.

The question is natural—Why was the attempt to make Parliament the direct instrument of government such a disastrous failure? The answer lies partly in the fact that the nation had not yet learnt the qualities needed for such a high stage of self-government, partly in the inherent defects of the representative system of the time. Why Parliamentary Government failed:

In the first place the representation was incomplete. The Commons represented an oligarchy of freeholders ruling over a vast unenfranchised body of villeins and artisans. The Commons themselves were a still more exclusive class of knights and burgesses, who tried to pass such tyrannical measures as that no one under the degree of freeholder should keep a dog, or that villeins should not put their sons to school. By the statute of 1430, this despotism of the freeholders was riveted on England for 402 years to come (p. 536). Incomplete Representation:

In the second place, the Commons were still the slaves of the blindest prejudices. To them, the ruffian Thomas of Lancaster was still a saint, and Humphrey of Gloucester a political martyr. When the local executive proved itself the victim of bullying nobles and truckling officials, they blamed the Crown and its ministers. When their own sumptuary laws and their laws against "regrators" proved futile, the only help they could see was a change of dynasty. When negotiations were made for peace they called it treachery— Popular Prejudice.

that peace which they had made inevitable by refusing to face the war bills.

Instability of the Administration. The third defect was the want of security for any permanence of the results of any one Parliament. A consciousness of this explains both their persistent tendency to see in some great noble a constitutional champion, and their eagerness for annual Parliaments and their long Sessions. It was a defect only to be remedied by Cabinet Government and an organised Civil Service.

Decay of the Shire System. Meantime, the basis and unit of the representative system, the old shire-moot, was itself falling into decay. The rise of the Justices of the Peace stripped it of much of its power. It fell once more into the hands of the sheriff, who returned his own candidates or nominees of some great lord. In the same way, the boroughs tried to shake off their Parliamentary duties and the accompanying burdens; their internal rule became narrow and oligarchical; their elections often fell into the hands of the Corporation, and their representatives at Westminster were timid and unpatriotic as well as reactionary.

The drastic discipline of Yorkist and Tudor absolutism, the awakening effect of the Reformation, and the educating influence of the struggle against Charles I. and Laud, against Cromwell's Major-Generals, and against James II.'s Declarations of Indulgence, were needed before the English people could take up once more the great task of Parliamentary self-government with some prospect of hard-won but assured success.

The Wars of the Roses. The Wars of the Roses have been described as a mere struggle of noble factions. As regards the actual fighting, from St. Albans to Tewkesbury, it is indeed characteristic that, as Comines noted, it was all done by the nobles and their retainers. But it would be a very superficial view which ignored the deep-seated causes leading up to so obstinate a struggle, or failed to discern the momentous results issuing from it. Without the deep popular discontent against the dynasty, the Yorkist party could have hardly formed itself. Popular discontent was the outcome of the long drain of the French wars, their demoralising influence, and the humiliation of their closing stages. It was also the outcome of a premature strain put upon Parliamentary institutions, overshadowed as these were by sinister influences; the nobles are "the weeds in the fair garden," which must be "mowed down full plain" to let "the pleasant sweet herbes appear." It was the outcome finally, of a long period of "lack of governance," shown

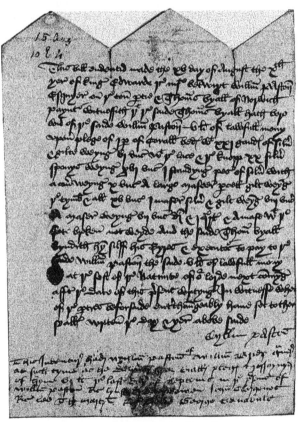

ONE OF THE PASTON PAPERS (MS. Add. 27,445).

most conspicuously in the bankruptcy of the central power and its failure to keep order at a distance. The revenue was, as to more than one-fourth, forestalled by "pensions to great lords and others." As early as 1433 there was a debt of nearly five times the revenue. New and "exquisite" means of taxation produced only mutterings of revolt. The judges themselves at one time had been unpaid for eleven years. The king had to live by purveyance[1]; and this was one more charge in the long account the nation meant to settle with Suffolk and Somerset. "Ye have made the king so poor that now he beggeth from door to door"; but they "swear by Him that harried hell" that there shall be a reckoning. Worse still was the local anarchy. Such private wars as that in the west between Lord Bonville and the Earl of Devon, and that between Percies and Nevilles in the north, were common occurrences. The Paston Letters show us the state of Norfolk and Suffolk; organised and open murders, gangs of ruffians holding the roads, a thousand men with guns assaulting and demolishing a manor-house, and the noble author of these proceedings acquitted because the sheriff has received orders by royal writ to empanel a favourable jury (such a writ, we learn incidentally, could be got for 6s. 8d. in London). The very scholars of Oxford and Cambridge "arrayed themselves in habiliments of war," and exercised a reign of terror and blackmail over the neighbouring counties. In fact, in the weakening of the central power a bastard feudalism had once more arisen in the great nobles. Their aim was not provincial independence, but personal aggrandisement and profit; and their instruments, the vast estates they held, the bands of men they "maintained" in their livery, and the Crown offices of which they acted as brokers. They kept almost royal state, each with his council, his writs, his assumption of the title of "Your Highness." We find the Duke of Norfolk appointing his men to be justices and sheriffs, empanelling his tenants on juries, exercising "notorious and horrible intimidation" over the courts of law, forcibly rescuing a murderer, buying up wrongful disseisins, besieging Caister Castle with 3,000 men on a private quarrel, sending "his menial servants" to Parliaments. No wonder that to Paston in Norfolk the secret of success in life seemed to lie in securing such a great lord's favour; "get you lordship, for thereon hangeth all the Law and the Prophets." When the Star Chamber made it its object " to

[1 Requisitioning goods and means of conveyance : *cf.* p. 201.]

bridle such stout noblemen," it came none too soon for the general welfare.

It was only natural that the geographical division of districts in the war should follow the lines of cleavage between the great houses. The Welsh marches went with the Yorkists as representing the Mortimer house. Norfolk and Suffolk were accounted for by the Mowbray influence. The great house of Neville carried Kent and Durham, Warwickshire and Wiltshire. That the great towns of the South, and the whole sea-coast, were Yorkist is explained by their looking to that party for stronger government and for better keeping of the seas, and by their hostility to the hierarchy regarded as largely identified with the reigning family. On the other side the Percies, Dacres, and Cliffords carried with them most of Yorkshire and Northumberland; the Earls of Westmoreland, too, though they were Nevilles, were of an elder line and were Lancastrian. The Tudors and Beauforts were strong in Wales. The chief lords in Bucks and Oxfordshire, in Stafford and Dorset, in Somerset and Devon, were Lancastrians. The old duchy of Lancaster had included the earldoms of Hereford, Derby, Leicester, Lincoln, Essex, and Northampton; and many retainers from these districts flocked to Queen Margaret's call. But a noble's estates rarely lay in a compact block, and there was much intermingling and confusion of parties. Thus in the North itself the Yorkists were strong about Raby and Middleham, Sendal and Wakefield; while the Yorkist Lord Lovel contested Oxfordshire with the Veres. On the whole it was a war of the more populous and more advanced South against the more baronial and wilder North. To some extent, too, it was a class division; townsmen and traders under a few great houses against the bulk of the nobles and gentry and the higher clergy. It may also be represented as a duel between hereditary right and Parliament; or between the ideals of absolutist and of limited monarchy; or between a new order and the old feudal and ecclesiastical system.

But the simplest and best clue is the personal relations of the small circle of nobles. This explains the insignificant numbers in the battles, the balanced state of parties and the suddenness of the revolutions of fortune, the personal hatreds and cold-blooded ferocity of the leaders, and, lastly, the curious way in which trade and business, and even judicial administration, went on in their normal course all the time.

"THE king should please the Commons in this cuntre; for they grudge and say how that the king resayvith sych of this cuntre as haff be his gret ennemyes and oppressors of the Commons; and such as haff assysted his Hynes, be not rewarded. And it is to be considered; or elles it will hurt; as me semeth, by reason." This significant threat from a Yorkist partisan explains why for ten years after the first Yorkist king's accession, the changeful scene of rebellions, battles, and revolutions still went on. Once on the throne, Edward IV. meant to be no mere king of a faction.· He would not, he said, show favour to one man more than to another; "not to one in England." But his old companions-in-arms had looked for a partisan triumph. To Warwick, the experienced soldier, sailor, statesman, diplomatist, Edward, a boy of nineteen, must have seemed an easy tool. As yet, indeed, the great earl and his house were indispensable. The unconquerable Margaret had landed in the North in 1462, and there was constant fighting around the northern castles till the last rally of the Lancastrians was crushed on the fields of Hedgely Moor and Hexham in April and May, 1464.

To complete the security of the new dynasty, it was necessary to cut off the Lancastrians from their foreign allies. Truces had already been made with Burgundy and with Scotland. Warwick now planned an alliance with France by a treaty to marry Edward to the sister of the French queen. When he was on the point of sailing to France to negotiate this, Edward coolly announced that he had already been five months married to Lady Elizabeth Grey. She was the widow of a Lancastrian knight, and daughter of the Lancastrian Lord Rivers, himself " a made lord who had won his fortune by his marriage." The blow to Yorkist feeling and Neville pride was immense. But worse was to come. By skilful marriages, six of the Woodville family were raised up to the high nobility. Two more such elevations followed in 1466. The power of the Nevilles was still immense; for John Lord

Montague, the second brother, had stepped into the confiscated estates of the Percies. But in the new group of the Woodvilles the king had raised a threatening counterpoise. Next he forbade the betrothal of his brother George of Clarence to Warwick's daughter Isabel. Finally, he sent Warwick on a fool's errand to conclude a peace with the king of France, while he was himself effecting a treaty of marriage and alliance with the Duke of Burgundy. All this had its natural result.

In April, 1469, Yorkshire rose under one Robin of Redesdale,

EDWARD IV., WITH HIS FAMILY AND COURTIERS.
(Lambeth Palace Library.)

and like Kent under John Cade, complained of the king's near kinsmen being kept away from his council. Lords Latimer and Fitzhugh of the Neville blood joined the revolt, Warwick joined them from Calais, where he had hastily concluded his daughter's marriage to Clarence. Defeated at Edgecott, Edward was Warwick's prisoner. With characteristic grace and dissimulation, the king conceded all demands, and declared his conquerors to be his best friends. But when next year a new rising took place in Lincolnshire, the king, after an easy victory over the rebels at Lose-coat Field, professed to have discovered proofs of

Popular Risings.

the complicity of Warwick and Clarence. Denounced as traitors, surprised by Edward's masterly promptitude they fled to France, there to make common cause with Queen Margaret, Warwick's ancient enemy, his father's murderess. In September, 1470, within eleven days of Warwick's landing at Dartmouth, he was master of the kingdom and Edward was flying to Flanders. King Henry, poor shadow of a king, was brought from the Tower and seated on the throne. But in March, 1471, by Burgundian aid, Edward was enabled to return, landing, as Henry IV. had landed, at Ravenspur, and declaring like him that he came only to claim his duchy. Men flocked to him, Clarence deserted to his side, and London opened its gates to the popular king. On Easter Day, at Barnet, the battle in the mist with its strange incidents, decided for ever, by the fall of the King-maker and his brother Montague, the long strife of the two Roses, and closed the stormy history of the medieval baronage in a typical confusion of bloodshed, treachery, and desperate courage. The

Barnet and Tewkesbury. defeat of Margaret's army at Tewkesbury, three weeks later, was a foregone conclusion. So, too, were the executions which were its consequence, and the fate of Henry VI.; one more murder, the secret of which has been well kept by the dungeons of the Tower.

Clarence. Edward's position was now secure. But he had still an enemy on whom to be avenged, his own brother, " perjured Clarence," who stood in the way of the ambitious hopes both of Richard, Duke of Gloucester, and of the queen's kindred, the Woodvilles. Left to himself, Edward would probably have almost forgotten, as he had professedly forgiven, Clarence's past sins against him. But Clarence himself kept the court in turmoil and the country in alarm with his quarrellings and recriminations. He disputed fiercely the Neville inheritance with his brother, who had married Warwick's other daughter, Anne. He took the law into his own hands against a woman whom he declared to have poisoned his duchess. He persisted in maintaining the innocence of two of his own servants executed for sorcery, and for " casting the king's nativity." He had even declared the king a bastard. At last Edward arrested him, and fearing his intrigues with Burgundy and Scotland, had him attainted and executed in 1478. The story that he was drowned in a butt of Malmsey rests on a general agreement of the chroniclers.

A contemporary French annalist declares that no king could long rule in England who did not embark on a foreign war. In 1475, Edward, with some 13,000 men, set out on the old adventure of an invasion of France. Bound as he was to this course by the terms of his alliance with Charles the Bold, Duke of Burgundy, Edward was, perhaps, also bidding for

EXECUTION OF THE DUKE OF SOMERSET AFTER TEWKESBURY.
(From a contemporary MS. in the Public Library, Ghent.)

popularity. But Charles was in no case to give him effective support. Louis XI. seized the right moment to offer terms. He bought off his foe cheaply enough; £15,000 down. and a pension of £10,000 a year for life. Within three months the best army that had yet left English shores was back at home, and bitter murmurs were heard against the corrupt councillors

72

on whom so shameful a failure was charged But the times
were growing such that men dared not murmur against the
king.   They submitted sullenly to the increasing severity of
the new rule. They would rather, they said, see the devil in
the Parliament-house than grant any more taxes; yet they had
to endure that the Crown should make each man contribute
"by way of benevolence what pleased him, or rather what dis-
pleased him."   They had to endure while "the rich were hanged
by the purse and the poor by the neck"; while the clergy were
treated "as if bound to grant any demand of the king": while
Parliament was reduced to a practical nullity: and while the
king ran unchecked that career of open profligacy and intemperance which brought him to a sudden death in his forty-first
year (1483). He had entered on public life with high promise;
a born general, a born popular ruler; sensual already and ruthless, no doubt, but capable of energetic action and of unbending
purpose; affable and courteous, interested in art and literature,
kindly to those around him, true to his ministers, gifted with
a singular talent for detail and for organisation, fully alive to
the new commercial spirit and its importance ; a man of great
gifts, mental and bodily. But the passions of that fierce time,
his own self-indulgence, the defection of Warwick and Clarence,
the promptings of evil favourites, ruined his character. He
died a worthless and worn-out debauchee.

A. L.
SMITH.
The
Reign of
Richard
III.
THE reign and character of Richard III. possess a singular
fascination. Brief as the reign is, it is crowded with dramatic
incidents and unsolved historical problems. It is marked also
by active and most significant legislation. The current view
of his character seems to ascribe to him such superhuman
villainy, that from Horace Walpole's "Historic Doubts" down
to the present days it has invited a series of attempts to re-
habilitate him.   But on the whole these must be regarded
as having failed. It is true, indeed, that More's account was
derived from Morton, a bitter enemy of Richard. It is possible
also that he was not the murderer of Clarence, and that his
story of Edward's betrothal to Lady Elizabeth Butler, which
would make Edward's issue illegitimate, is not a baseless
calumny. It is clear, too, that he showed generosity to the

widows of his victims ; that he had great ability, courage, energy, and foresight; that he had many of the qualities which might have made a great ruler. Moreover it must be remembered that he had been trained in a bitter school, and also that he found few or none whom he could trust. But when the utmost has been said for him, enough remains. The slaughter of Prince Edward at Tewkesbury, the murder of Henry VI. and of the two princes in the Tower, made Lancastrian and Yorkist alike abhor his memory. To the people at large, these murders, the executions of Hastings, Rivers, and Grey, the slanders cast upon his own mother, the cynical project of marrying his own niece in the face of all the bloodshed that lay between them, were crimes which proved too much even for that callous age.

RICHARD III.
(National Portrait Gallery.)

Upon Edward IV.'s death, Richard, by a skilful use of the general jealousy against the Woodvilles, secured the person of the young king and his brother, and in a council meeting suddenly arrested Hastings, who was summarily beheaded on a log of wood in the Tower yard. On June 25th, 1483, by the busy aid of the Duke of Buckingham, he procured an invitation to himself to take the crown, as "the undoubted son and heir of Richard, late Duke of York." But by September Buckingham was in revolt; Henry of Richmond was in Brittany preparing an invasion; and risings took place in the South, the Midlands, and the West. These were put down. The duke, whose army had been stopped by a great flood of the Severn, was taken and executed. The

Parliament convened in January, 1484, ratified the king's title, and granted him tunnage and poundage and the wool custom for life. The clergy also granted him a tenth, and recognised his "most noble and blessed disposition." His foreign policy, too, had a certain success. He made a truce with Scotland, and by another with the Duke of Brittany, he drove Richmond to take refuge in France. He conciliated the Papacy by a promise of the old "filial and catholic obedience" of England. The year was spent in untiring efforts to secure his position, by reorganisation of the navy, by progresses through the country, by lavish grants to greedy lords, to important cities as York and Hull, even to yeomen whose barns were burnt, or a clerk who had lost his place. In particular he aimed at popularity in Yorkshire and the North. Never did a man work harder to avert inevitable destiny. But his hope and pride, his son Edward, died suddenly, "so that his parents were almost insane with the sudden grief." By the queen's death some months later he lost the Neville connection, which was still a name to conjure with. Vere, Earl of Oxford, escaped from prison, and joined the exiles abroad. The king had to call out the arrays in every shire to meet the constant threats of invasion. In his extreme need he had even to over-ride his own recent statute against Benevolences. Perhaps the joy which he expressed when at last Henry of Richmond actually landed at Milford Haven on the 7th August, 1485, indicated a real sense of relief that the crisis had come. It was soon over. The treachery of Percy and the Stanleys left Richard with no ally but John Howard, the man whom he himself had made Duke of Norfolk. At Bosworth, on August 22nd, Richard fell, fighting desperately to the end. The long strife had come to an end. Richard had fallen, as Edward IV. nearly fell, before a coalition of Lancastrians and Yorkists. Henry, the descendant of John of Gaunt, the Beauforts, and the French Queen Catherine on one side, was to marry Elizabeth of York, the descendant of Lionel of Clarence and the Luxemburg Duchess Jacquetta.

Legisla-
tion.

Stormy and troubled as the reign had been, it yet found time for legislation remarkably expressive of the time, and significant of the changes about to come. To improve judicial procedures, the qualification for jurors was raised to 20s. a year of freehold land. The import was forbidden of all articles such as silks, bows, woollen cloths, that could be made in England; the only exception allowed was printed books. The decay of archery was checked by prohibiting other sports and the use of the cross-bow. A royal post service was established by relays of mounted messengers. Consuls were appointed to assist English traders abroad. One Act, which protected pur-chasers against "secret feoffments,"[1] anticipates the principle of the great Statute of Uses of 1536; another, which abolishes benevolences,[2] "which had ruined many men and left their children beggars," anticipated a con-stitutional result not finally secured till the Bill of Rights in 1689. The Act by which the first of the Tudors succeeded in putting down the abuse of "liveries"[3] had been already laid down by his predecessor. The Tudor severity against vagabondage was but a repetition of Richard's measures to clear the roads infested by discharged soldiers. But "not even the tyrant's virtues could avail." His statesman-ship was as ineffectual as his crimes.

"TRAYLEBASTON" (MS. Nero D. ii.).

The last of the great Plantagenet house, who summed up with its evils many of its good qualities, fitly closes that strange family story. The men of the twelfth century believed the line had sprung from an evil spirit in the guise of a beautiful lady. "From the devil we all came," said Richard I., "and to the devil we shall all go." And truly there was something almost demoniac in the brief and fiery career of Richard III., in his revolting unscrupulousness, in his fierce struggle against fate, and its sudden and furious ending. One after another the great kings of his race had wasted superhuman energies upon impossible tasks. Henry II. had vainly laboured to build up a Con-tinental empire, Edward I. to crush Scottish independence, Edward III. and Henry V. to make another England in

The End of the Plan-tagenets.

[1 Conveyances of "an estate in " landed property.]

[2 Forced loans : first levied under that name by Edward IV.]

[3 Maintenance of an armed retinue.]

Languedoc or Normandy, Richard III. to do violence to a nation's conscience. In their objects they had failed one after another, for all their force of will. But out of evil came good ; they had achieved other objects beyond their power to foresee ; the rise of English self-government, of Scottish nation-ality, of French patriotism ; and Richard III.'s failure meant the establishment of the undisputed title and the popular despotism of the Tudors.

C. W. C.
OMAN.
The Art
of War.

IT is surprising to note how little change had been made in the art of war, either by the English or the French, in the long in-terval between the two great acts of the drama of the Hundred Years' War. Agincourt found the enemies much in the same position with regard to each other as that at which Poitiers had left them. The fighting in which each had been engaged in the meantime had not been very instructive ; at Homildon the English had found their bowmen as effective as ever against the Scots, and had routed with ease a much superior force by the mere line of archery, the men-at-arms having hardly struck a blow. Shrewsbury fight had been the first pitched battle fought by Englishmen against each other since the bowmen had become the arbiter of battle. It had been very bloody and obstinate, and since the combatants fought with the same weapons and the same tactics, had been settled by mere force of numbers. The French, on the other hand, had nothing to learn from the feudal bicker-ings of Armagnac and Burgundian against each other—save, indeed, the lesson of the campaign of 1411, when a small body of English auxiliary troops lent by Henry IV. to the Burgundians, won the battle of St. Cloud, and turned the fate of a whole campaign. Two extensive military experiments made against foreign enemies—Roosebeque and Nicopolis—had also not much that was instructive for the French. At the former the dis-mounted knights of France and the pikemen of Ghent, both fighting in massive columns, had met on equal terms, and the more heavily armed column had ultimately trampled down and crushed the lighter. At Nicopolis the same tactics, tried against the light horse and disciplined infantry (Janissaries) of the Turks, had failed with fearful disaster the mass of armour-laden knights having been exhausted after their first successful charges,

SIEGE TRAIN, FIFTEENTH CENTURY. (MS. Roy. 14 E. iv.)

[To face p. 488.

and being unable to sustain a running fight with successive relays of foes who were individually their inferiors.

The only differences which may be noted between the character of the armies which fought at Agincourt and at Poitiers are comparatively slight. On both sides the men-at-arms were now more heavily armed than in the previous century. The

Armour and Weapons.

A HAND-TO-HAND FIGHT (MS. Harl. 4374).

last relics of the old mail armour had disappeared—the cammail [1] round the neck being superseded by solid steel gorgets,[2] and massive plate defences below the breastplate having been added to cover the thighs, in place of the mail skirt of the fourteenth century. The custom of fighting on foot had obliged the knight to drop his long lance and take to shorter and heavier weapons,

[1 Chain-mail protecting the neck and shoulders.]   [2 Throat-pieces.]

among which the mace, glaive,[1] axe, and halbert are prominent. Most of these weapons, and particularly the pole-axe, required two hands to wield them effectively, and so the shield had been almost discarded for actual use, and only survived for heraldic purposes. Beyond the change in armour there is only to be noted in the armies of Henry V. the fact that the proportion of archers to men-at-arms had increased : in the time of Edward III. it had sometimes been only two to one, seldom more than three or four to one ; but in the fifteenth century it had risen to six or seven, sometimes even to ten, bows to each spear. At Agincourt, however, the proportion was only five to one—an exceptionally low one for the time.

Henry V.'s campaign of 1415 in France gave at first little promise of leading to great things. The capture of the single town of Harfleur wasted many weeks, and cost the lives of a fifth of the army. The march through Northern France which followed looked like a mad adventure, so small were the king's forces and so many the troops arrayed against him. After wandering for some days among the marshes of the Somme, Henry appeared likely to be lost by the way, or surrounded and starved long before he could find his road to Calais. If subsequent campaigns had not proved him to be a capable general, we should feel inclined to call the whole scheme of the march the inspiration of a reckless knight-errant.

Agincourt.   The event of Agincourt, however, may be considered to justify Henry's rashness, though a capable man in command of the French army might certainly have crushed the English, even without committing himself to a pitched battle. Having got between the English and the only place where they could find safety and provision themselves, the Constable of France had the power of making Henry offer him battle, but need not have accepted it on any terms which gave the enemy an advantage. By only sitting still he could ruin the English as securely as by attacking. The fact was, however, that no ordinary feudal noble at the head of superior numbers dared to refuse a battle if it was offered him · his own army would have fought without his leave if he had denied it. Henry was no doubt aware of this when he drew out his little band and challenged the French to attack.

[1 A cutting weapon, composed of a short cutlass-like blade mounted on a stout staff.]

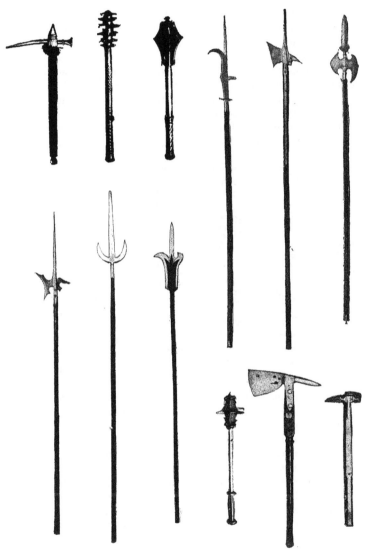

WEAPONS OF LATER MEDIEVAL TYPE.
(*Tower of London and Rotunda Museum, Woolwich.*)

The strength of the English position lay in the fact that it was well protected on both flanks by villages and woods, and was exactly wide enough to allow the army to develop its full front, and no wider. But another fact gave an additional advantage: for a mile in front the ground was slippery ploughed field, soaked with the inordinate rains that had fallen in the past week. Henry's line was composed on the old plan that had been seen at Crécy: right, centre, and left each consisted of a small body of men-at-arms, flanked by two bodies of archers, drawn up in the triangular harrow-shape, and protected by a line of stakes.

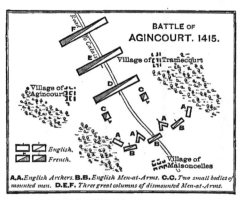

THE FIELD OF AGINCOURT.
(From Oman's " History of England " : Edward Arnold.)

The French repeated the mistakes of Poitiers. Once more they dismounted almost the whole of their men-at-arms, and formed them in three massive lines, one behind the other, on a front no broader than that of the English army. Only on the wings were small squadrons of mounted men under picked leaders, who were bidden to ride on ahead of the main body, and do their best to engage and clear away the archers, so that their comrades might advance unhampered. The fight commenced by the ineffective charge of these squadrons. Well-nigh every horse and most of the riders were shot down before they got near the stakes of the bowmen; hardly a man struggled in to perish fighting hand-to-hand. Then came the turn of the main body; with them the fact that really settled the day was the inordinate heaviness to which knightly armour had now attained. To walk a mile in full panoply of plate over sodden ploughed fields turned out to be an impossibility. For some time the first line lurched on, sinking to ankle, or even to knee, at

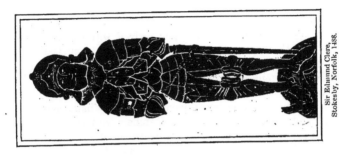

Sir John de Cressy,
Dodford, Northants, 1414.

BRASSES, SHOWING ARMOUR OF THE FIFTEENTH CENTURY.

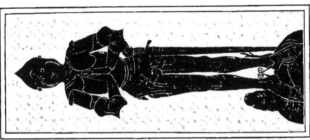

Sir W. Fitzwilliam,
Spotborough, Yorks., 1474.

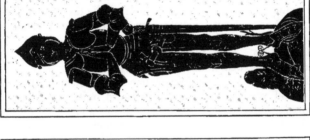

Sir Edmund Clere,
Stokesby, Norfolk, 1488.

Sir John Russell,
Strensham, Worc., 1405.

every step. But by the time they arrived within arrow-shot of the English they were utterly tired out, and stuck fast in the mud with the archery playing freely upon them. When the arrows gave out and the French had been well riddled, King Henry took the decisive step of bidding his whole army charge. His own men-at-arms must have been sorely hampered by the mud, and it was the onset of the archers with axe, mallet, and sword that settled the day. That unarmoured men should have prevailed over mailed men under the odds of six to one, and on plain open ground, is one of the marvels of history. But prevail they did; the chroniclers speak of the embogged knights as standing helplessly to be hewn down, while the archers " beat upon their armour with mallets as though they were hammering upon anvils," and rolled them one over the other till the dead lay three deep. Truly the knightly panoply was a deadly trap when once the wearer had grown fatigued.

The relics of the first French line were thrown back on to the second, which had now pushed forward, in its turn, on to the laboured ground through which their predecessors had struggled. The English followed hard on their heels, and a second slaughter was made, no less deadly than the first. The infantry and third line very wisely resolved not to meddle with the business, and left the field, save their leaders, the Counts of Merle and Dammartin, who refused to fly and went down to share the fate of their comrades in the second line.

So ended this astonishing battle, whose not least astonishing feature was that the whole English loss did not amount to a hundred men, though two great peers, York and Suffolk, were numbered among the dead: the former, who was a man of a stout habit of body, is said to have died not so much of his wounds as of fatigue and the weight of his armour. Meanwhile the French had lost ten thousand men, including well-nigh every commander of mark in the army, and those who had not fallen were nearly all prisoners. Agincourt had proved even more deadly than Poitiers, and for the reason that flight, comparatively easy in the lighter armour of the fourteenth century, was impossible in the weighty panoply of the fifteenth. If a man failed to struggle back and pick up his page and his horse at the rear of the battle, he was now doomed to death or capture.

Even Agincourt did not break the French of their in-

veterate belief in the power of the mailed knight, unaided by
other arms, to break the English line of archers and men-at-
arms mixed. The bloody fights at Cravant and Verneuil were
new variations on the same theme, coming to much the same
result, save in the mere detail of the exact amount of slaughter

SIEGE OF CALAIS (MS. Jul. E. iv.).

suffered by the beaten army. The "Day of the Herrings" was
a somewhat varied instance in the same line of fighting. A
very small English force (about one thousand archers, with one
thousand two hundred Parisian militia fighting on the English
side) was surprised in the open field while escorting a large

convoy of provisions to the siege of Orleans. Beset by five times their number of men-at-arms, they had just time enough to form a *lauger* of their waggons in a rough square. The archers got upon the carts, while the auxiliary French spear-men held the intervals between them. Against this extem-porised fortification the Dauphin's cavaliers dashed themselves, with the usual ineffective result, and withdrew when a large proportion had been shot down.

**Warfare,
1415-1471.**
From 1415 to 1471 England scarcely enjoyed a moment's peace, the Forty Years' War with France being almost imme-diately succeeded by the outbreak of the Wars of the Roses. From the point of view of military science the only discovery of first-rate importance in the whole period was the fact that after long years the French at last found out an effective way of dealing with the hitherto triumphant tactics of their opponents. Of first-rate generals very few were produced by either nation; the two English kings, Henry V. and Edward IV., are alone worthy of the highest commendation. Of capable hard-fighting officers who could conduct an army with discretion, but brought no new discoveries into the art of war, there were a considerable number on both sides—among Englishmen, Bedford, Salisbury, Talbot, and Warwick the King-maker might be mentioned—among the French the great condottiere-captains, Dunois, La Hire, Pothon de Xaintrailles, and the Constable of Richemont.

**The
French
War.**
The great French war from 1415 to 1453 might fairly be described as a war of sieges from first to last, though there were a considerable number of battles to diversify the long story. Stated in the simplest form, the problem set before the English was to find out whether, with very small armies and with a rather meagre supply of money, they could persevere long enough to capture, one by one, the thousand strongholds of a land which bristled with castles and fortified towns. The problem would have been a hopeless one from the first but for two facts: a considerable proportion of the French nation—the "Burgundian" party—throughout the North of France lent a more or less active aid to the invader, and the resources and taxes of the conquered districts of the country helped to maintain the English army. Henry V. and Bedford, like Napoleon, "made war maintain war." There are figures which show that King Henry only relied on England for about a

quarter of his military expenses; the unfortunate districts of
Northern France were made to pay and feed well-nigh the
whole of his army. It is only thus that we can understand
how the war was kept up so long;
without their Burgundian auxiliaries, and without the taxes of
Paris, Normandy, and Champagne,
the English would have been
wholly unable to maintain themselves in their conquests. When
the Duke of Burgundy made his
peace with the French king, and
when the exhausted region of North
France at last began to stir in
revolt, the English attempt to hold
down the country collapsed. That
the war lingered so long after the
treaty of Arras had drawn the
Burgundians from the English side,
can only be attributed to two
causes — the exhaustion of the
French, and the vast number of
fortresses in Normandy, Maine, and
Guienne which were still in English
hands. If Henry V. and Bedford
had taken laborious years to win
these fortresses, it was now to take
no less a time for Charles VII. to
win them back. But after 1438
all the gains were on one side, and
the English were—like the losing
player at chess—merely persisting
in playing out to the end a game
that could only end in defeat
however long it might be pro-
tracted. A mistaken sense of

FRENCH ARMOUR ABOUT 1460.
(*Musée de l'Artillerie, Paris.*)

national pride made them persevere, and caused them to visit
with wrath any statesman who, like the unfortunate Suffolk,
tried to put an end to the war and retain some small remnant of
territory instead of striving to win back the unattainable whole.

The depressing time from 1438 to 1453 when England was striving to maintain the French war from her own resources, trying to accomplish the impossible, yet mourning at every tax that became necessary, and grudging every man that was sent across the Channel, is one of the most dreary periods of our history.   How inadequate were the efforts made may be judged from the fact that the same nation which sent 3,000 or 4,000 men into the field to defend its last possessions in France at Formigny or Châtillon, put 60,000 men in line a few years later at Towton in a deplorable civil war.

How Troops were Raised.

The armies of Henry V. and those which, after his death, followed Bedford or Talbot were, so far as English troops were concerned, raised by the principle of contract.   The peers or knights who purposed to go to France undertook to find so many hundred spears or bows while the Government took them into its pay.   The leaders were recompensed by the grant of great lands and titles in France, while the archer and man-at-arms received high pay and had the chance of much plundering.   Thrifty men like Sir John Fastolf made large fortunes out of the war, even when half their outstanding claims against the Crown had never been paid.   As the years rolled by without a peace, there grew up a whole army of veteran mercenaries who had spent the best part of their lives in France.   The return to England, when Normandy and Guienne were finally lost, of dozens of castellans who had lost their castles, and thousands of archers who had lost their pay and plunder, was not the least of the many causes which made the outbreak of the Wars of the Roses possible.   For the noble verging toward rebellion, what temptation could be greater than the presence, at his elbow, of hundreds of trained soldiers out of employment ?   Every man of resources could, without trouble, procure for himself as many of the " waged men " or " household men " of whom we hear in the Civil War as he could afford to keep up.

The English Failure in France.

But before proceeding to speak of the Wars of the Roses a few words are needed to explain on the purely military side the loss of the last English possessions in France.   The English force, small at the best, was cut up into so many garrisons—from the need of occupying every fortified place that was taken—that only 3,000 or 4,000 men were, as a rule, to be found in the field.

[1485]

Even a great undertaking like the siege of Orleans only brought together 7,000 or 8,000. The native bowmen were largely mixed with foreign mercenaries, but there were still enough of them to form the line which had hitherto been unbreakable. But the French had at last forsworn the habit of letting the English get into array, and then attacking them in great masses.

KEEP OF ST. SAUVEUR-LE-VICOMTE, NORMANDY.

Beaugé, the first isolated French success, was won by pouncing on the men-at-arms when they were separated from the archers by a river, and were not expecting an engagement. Patay, the fight which broke up the English host that had beleaguered Orleans, had a similar character. The retreating army of Talbot was retiring on a position where its commander intended to receive battle, when the mounted men of the French

73

vanguard charged in upon them " before the archers had time to fix their stakes." The unformed array was broken up, the whole battle lapsed into confused hand-to-hand fighting, and numbers carried the day.   At Formigny, the engagement in 1450 which lost us Normandy, the little English army had time to form its line, in the old traditional style, with archers and lances supporting each other.   But the French very wisely refused to charge it, and brought forward some cannon with which they commenced to play upon the English from a distance out of bowshot.   This, after a while, provoked the harassed English to leave their position and rush on the cannon which galled them.   The fighting then became confused and the lines were intermingled, but the day might yet have been saved when a new French force appeared on the field and fell upon the unprotected flank and rear of the English, who were now outside their position and engaged in the open.   The arrival of this fresh corps settled the day, and the whole English army was cut to pieces ; not five hundred men escaped out of four thousand.   Châtillon, the last battle of the great French war, was similar to Formigny, in that the English attacked, instead of waiting in position in the old style.   The veteran Talbot, hoping to catch the French unprepared, essayed the desperate task of storming an entrenched camp, lavishly garnished with artillery, by the rush of a phalanx in which men-at-arms and archers were combined.   The attempt was hopeless ; the column of attack was blown to pieces, and though a few men got within the palisades the result of the battle was never for a moment doubtful.   Such was the end of the English attempt to hold France.   A form of tactics which required the defensive to be assumed, lost its efficacy when the enemy refused to attack.   When once the French learnt to stand back and force their adversaries to take the offensive, the methods of Edward III. and Henry V. began to prove comparatively ineffective.

Artillery.   It should be mentioned that siege artillery was regularly used throughout the French war, and proved far more effective than in the fifteenth century.   Where a relieving army did not drive off the besiegers, the siege train did its work as a rule with success.   The campaigns of 1451 and 1452, which expelled the English from Normandy and Guienne respectively,

SIEGE OPERATIONS, SHOWING CANNON (MS. Harl. 1319).

were both notable for the large amount of siege artillery used and the rapidity with which Jean Bureau, the great master gunner of Charles VII., battered the English out of stronghold after stronghold.

The Wars of the Roses.

Nothing, as we have already observed, is more extraordinary than the way in which England, which had found the greatest difficulty in providing armies of 3,000 or 4,000 men for the French war, was able to put really important forces into the field in the fratricidal Wars of the Roses. But the explanation of the phenomenon is not very hard : the national Government, in raising men for the struggle over-sea, took them into its pay for long periods, and had to maintain them far from home. The armies of the Civil War were "tumultuary," hurriedly raised, and soon disbanded, and were mustered and kept together by the personal efforts of the lords and knights who had taken sides and knew that their estates and their heads depended on their being able to put as many men in line as possible. A typical army during this time consisted of three elements. First, came the "household men" of each lord, the professional fighting men whom he always kept about his person, largely veterans of the French war; second were the armed men whom both sides raised by the system of "commissions of array"; these levies ultimately represented the old national militia, but it was difficult to get together the shire force when two commis- sioners, each bearing mandates in the king's name, were engaged in enlisting men for different camps. The wise gave heed to neither summons, and waited for the event of battle to decide which king they should acknowledge. In especial the towns preserved a most Gallio-like attitude, and permitted the rivals to tear each other to their hearts' content before giving their judgment as to who was their rightful lord. But the third and most important element in the armies of the day were the men gathered together under the system which was known as "livery and maintenance." This arrangement recalled the characteristics of pre-Conquest feudalism; it consisted in the knights and squires of each district binding themselves by written agreement to serve the great lord of their neighbourhood, to espouse his quarrels in every place, from the law-court to the battle-field, in return for the promise of his protection and assistance in any troubles of their own. The great lord gave his adherents his "livery"; that is, he allowed them to wear his badge—the Bear and Ragged Staff, the Stafford Knot, the White Swan, or whatever it might be—and engaged to "maintain"

ASSAULT ON A CASTLE, EARLY FIFTEENTH CENTURY (MS. Sloane 2433).

them; that is, to protect them and champion their cause. They, on the other hand, contracted to take the field under his banner with all the tenants and retainers that they could raise. An example will suffice to show the character of these bonds: in 1449 Walter Strickland, a Westmorland squire of considerable local importance, contracts with Richard Neville, Earl of Salisbury, to follow him to the field with all his tenants, "bowmen horsed and harnessed 69, billmen horsed and harnessed 74, bowmen without horses 71, billmen without horses 76," in all a compact body of 290 men. The bond has a saving clause that the call to arms is not to infringe Strickland's loyalty to his sovereign lord the king: but this was a mere formality. In the early part of the war the Yorkists always pleaded that they were the king's best friends, and wished to deliver him from evil counsellors; in the second part of the war they had made a king of their own. When we see that a single squire could covenant to put nearly 300 men into the field, we can understand that a peer who had gained many such adherents and "given his livery" far and wide could bring several thousand men to the host. Every powerful personage in England practised the custom: the most extraordinary instance was perhaps when in 1459 Queen Margaret of Anjou went into Cheshire with the Prince of Wales and enlisted the whole of the gentry of the county, giving them all the badge of the White Swan. The army which fought at Blore Heath seems to have been composed almost entirely of these adherents in the queen's livery. It is obvious that when the system of livery and maintenance had once spread abroad, the power to raise the national forces by commissions of array became comparatively unimportant to the combatant parties. The great lords had the fighting strength of the counties already in their hands by this method, and a commission of array to put their followers under arms only legalised an already existing fact. Yet it was usual for the sake of legality to issue such a document, though Northumberland followed a Percy, or Warwickshire a Neville, not because he held the parchment, but because the local squirearchy were already bound to him, either as being his vassals or as wearing his livery.

Tactics in the Wars of the Roses. The battles of the Wars of the Roses for the most part followed the type of which Shrewsbury fight had hitherto been the only example. Each side fought in the old orthodox English fashion, with a line composed of bowmen and men-at-arms intermixed, arranged in three great "battles." All the fighting was on foot, though in the last years of the French war the English might have learnt something from their opponents as to the advantage of keeping part of their men-at-arms mounted. The good and abundant supply of archery on both sides made the fighting bloody, but as the bowmen neutralised each other it was not they who won the field. Both sides found the arrows too hard to bear, and closed as soon as they could. The only battle settled by archery was Edgecott, where the Yorkists, being mainly Welsh, had few bowmen among them, and were beaten off the field by the overpowering shower of shafts from the northern rebels. At Towton the Yorkists had the best in the preliminary interchange of missiles, but as the armies soon closed and got to hand-to-hand fighting, it was not the bow which won the day, but the bill and sword.

Artillery was largely used by both sides. At Northampton **Artillery.** the Lancastrian entrenched camp was lined with guns, but small use was made of them, for a fierce storm on the battle morning flooded the entrenchments and damped the powder, so that few shots or none were fired. At Barnet both Edward IV. and Warwick were well provided with guns; a desultory cannonade was kept up during the night that preceded the battle, but in the mist of the next morning neither general found his artillery of any use. At Tewkesbury Edward IV. is said to have employed cannon to harass the strongly posted Lancastrian left wing, in order to induce it to leave its position and charge. But the skirmish near Stamford, called "Lose-Coat Field," is the engagement where the guns seem to have been most effective. There the Lincolnshire rebels, who had attempted to surprise King Edward's camp, were scattered to the winds by the fire of massed artillery, and fled home without making any attempt to rally (1470). In the few sieges of the war the power of gunpowder asserted itself with unmistakable efficiency: the best known instance of its use was the occasion when Warwick battered to pieces the Norman walls of Bamborough, "so that great cantles flew into the sea," and then stormed the breaches which had been made by the new train of cannon that the king had cast in London during the preceding winter (1465).

It is noteworthy that the first use of the smaller firearms

Musketry. in England is to be found in the Wars of the Roses.   In 1461 Warwick brought to the second battle of St. Albans a body of Burgundian arquebusmen, whom he had hired in Flanders: they did little service, and the chroniclers remark that the

WARWICK THE KING-MAKER.
(From the Rous Roll, by permission of the Chapter, Heralds' College.)

heavy squalls of wind which raged on that February day sufficed to blow out their matches and spoil their shooting.   The second use of the arquebus was in 1471, when Edward IV. raised, also in Flanders, some hand-gun men to accompany him in the daring attempt to reconquer his kingdom which he was

about to make. They landed with him at Ravenspur, but we
have no particular mention of their doings at Barnet. In fact
the efficiency of the long-bow was still so great when compared

BATTLE OF TEWKESBURY.
(From a MS. in the University Library, Ghent.)

with that of the arquebus, that it was not likely that the latter
should gain any footing in England. Down to the middle of
the sixteenth century the archer held his own against the
arquebusier ; on the few occasions when they met he had
decidedly the advantage. In Elizabeth's reign, when firearms

were already long. established in use all over the Continent,
archers were still found in the army which followed Leicester
to Flanders, and in the fleet which scattered the Armada. It
was not till the seventeenth century that the long-bow finally
disappeared; even as late as 1642 there was a proposal to arm
some of the London militia with the old national weapon !

We have already mentioned that the Wars of the Roses

EARLY FIREARMS (MS. Burney 169).

only brought to the front one general of the first class,
Edward IV. Warwick the King-maker, the most prominent
fighting-man of the period, was only a capable leader after
the manner of many of the English commanders in the Hundred
Years' War. He introduced no new ideas into the military
art: nor could he boast, like Edward, that he had never lost
any battle in which he had engaged. If he failed by ill-luck

at Barnet, it was rather by mistaken generalship that he lost the second fight of St. Albans.

The Yorkist king, on the other hand, never failed in any task that he undertook, from Northampton to Tewkesbury. Nor is the reason far to seek: he was not only a hard fighter,

ATTACK ON LONDON BY THE "BASTARD OF FAUCONBERGE." ·
(*From a MS. in the University Library, Ghent.*)

and a genial leader of men, but he was one of the first commanders who learnt the value of time in war. Edward's marches were as noteworthy as his battles; his seizure of London by a forced march in the face of the Lancastrian army the week after St. Albans, the rapid descent which dispersed the Lincolnshire rebels in 1470, the long and toilsome chase after Queen Margaret, which culminated in his thirty-two-mile march on the eve of Tewkesbury, were all great feats of war. The armies of Edward's enemies seem always to have been commanded by a council of war rather than a single chief, and, wanting the impulse communicated by a single brain, they were never able to parry his rapid blows by corresponding alertness. Even the veteran soldier Warwick was in the campaign of Barnet completely outmatched and outwitted by his old pupil.

The Wars of the Roses did not on the whole bring about any great change in the art of war in England. The lesson was not a military but a political one, and it was a lesson which was not soon forgotten. The nation learnt that anything was better than a war of disputed succession, and gladly recognised anyone as king who could give it "strong governance," even if his title to the throne was so imperfect as that of Henry Tudor. And it was not less clearly seen that the crying evil of "livery and maintenance" must be made to cease out of the land. The first and last efforts of Henry VII. were devoted to crushing this abuse (p. 662), and by the end of his reign there was no great baron left who could trouble England either by hordes of swashbuckling household retainers, or by confederacies of unruly squires and knights contracted to him by treaty, and wearing his badge on their sleeves.

Never again were armies raised like those of the Wars of the Roses to be seen in England. The next age saw as great a change in the composition of the English national forces as it did in their tactics and equipment. The Middle Ages ended at Bosworth Field.

W. LAIRD CLOWES. The Navy. VERY many technical terms which are used in the royal and mercantile navies of to-day were used in those of the beginning of the fifteenth century. We read in the various expense accounts of "shrouds," "stays," "backstays," "hawsers," "seizings," "tow-ropes," "bowsprits," "yards," "forecastles," "sheeves," "swivels," "slings," "davits," "leads," "sounding-lines," "buoys," "buoy-ropes," "head-ropes," "deadman's eyes" (deadeyes), "cabins," "breaming," "blocks," "tacks," "capstan spokes" (capstan bars), "hatches," "pumps," "poops," etc., all used apparently in the modern senses of the words.[1] Vessels were measured by "ton-tights," or tons of burden, and seem occasionally to have been of three or four hundred tons, old measurement. The decorations were sometimes gaudy, if not tasteful, in the extreme. In 1400 one of the king's barges and her mast were painted red, and the vessel was adorned with collars and garters of gold, each collar encircling a fleur-de-lys and each garter a leopard; together with gold "lyames," or leashes, having within each of them a white greyhound and a gold collar. Another ship, called the *Good Pace of the Tower*, was also painted red, but her bulwarks, cabin, and stern were of other colours, and a large gold eagle, with a crown in its mouth, was placed on the bowsprit. The *Trinity of the Tower* was likewise red. Figures of St. George, St. Anthony, St. Catherine, and St. Margaret stood in the stern, together with four shields of the king's arms within a collar of gold, and two shields with the arms of St. George within the Garter. Two large eagles on a diapered ground were painted in the cabin. The *Nicholas of the Tower* was painted black and "powdered" with white ostrich feathers, the "stems" and scroll-work being of gold. In one part of the cabin were large escutcheons of the king's arms and of the arms of St. George, and in another part was an image of St. Christopher. Many ships had their sails painted or worked with arms or badges; and when not embroidered or painted they were often parti-coloured. Vessels were also decked with numerous flags, banners, and pennants; so that a large fleet at sea upon a fine day must have been a magnificent sight.

[1 The "stays" are ropes carried to the stem from the upper part of a mast to prevent its being sprung by the pitching of the ship; the "backstays" are similar ropes carried to the ship's sides; "seizings" are small ropes used to lash the ends of larger ropes together; "sheeves," the wheel on which the rope works in a block; a "head-rope" is the upper bolt-rope (*i.e.* the rope which is sewn round the sail) of a square or oblong sail (the term is also used of the small ropes used to hoist flags); "tacks" are the ropes employed to haul out the studding sails ("stunsels"); "deadeyes," the flat, oblong pieces of wood, pierced with holes, and attached respectively to each of the shrouds and the ship's hull by the chainplates; small ropes or lanyards connect each pair of deadeyes, passing through the holes, so that by tightening them the shrouds can be tightened; "breaming" is burning off seaweed, etc., from the vessel's bottom when she is laid high and dry for the purpose. The other terms are too familiar to require explanation.]

Anglo-
French
Sea-fights.
Sir Harris Nicolas remarks as extraordinary that although, in the reign of Henry IV., England was never actually at war with France, the two countries were for several years in constant hostility one with the other. There was no regular peace, but there was a truce, which, though it was almost daily expected to end or be ended, was never formally broken. Yet the reign was full of sea-fights, coast-raids, piracy, and reprisals ; and there could scarcely have been more bloodshed or less security had the nominal truce been non-existent. The English were generally to blame. With them the truce had been unpopular, because war had, on the whole, been rather profitable. They let slip, therefore, no opportunity for plundering the French ships and ravaging the French coasts. They even collected large fleets for these purposes; and many considerable actions were fought, in some, at least, of which the ships destroyed were to be numbered by tens and the men by thousands. The situation was complicated by the fact that the French were, in a more or less unofficial way, assisting the Welsh and the Scots in their struggle with England ; so that, though there was truce between the monarchs, there was the utmost hatred between the peoples. The ambition of every Englishman, and of many an Englishwoman, was to fight a Frenchman. When, in 1404, the French appeared off the Isle of Wight, the inhabitants invited them to land and promised them six hours for rest and refreshment, if then they would vouchsafe the delights of a pitched battle; and when, in the same year, the French landed at Dartmouth, the women of the town fought bravely and assisted in their rout. Peace was not for kings and governments to arrange, save on paper. The English people made war as of yore, the very existence of a Frenchman within their reach providing a more than sufficient inducement.

In the early part of his reign, being fearful of a regular war with France, and being in actual presence of one with Scotland, Henry IV., to avoid rendering himself unpopular by the imposition of a tax for naval purposes, prevailed upon the spiritual lords to give him a tenth of their property, and upon some of the temporal lords to bear voluntarily some of the charges for the maintenance of a fleet at sea. These arrangements proving insufficient, Henry, in 1401, caused instructions to be sent to the sea-ports, and to many other cities and towns, for the building in each of a vessel for the defence of the sea; but the Commons promptly protested against the issue of such orders without their consent, and frightened the king into cancelling his instructions. No adequate Royal Navy being consequently maintained, Henry, a year or two later, endeavoured to compromise matters by making contracts with the merchants and shipowners for the defence of the sea; but this experiment proved unsatisfactory, and at the end of 1406 the king made up his mind to depend

TRANSPORTS (MS. Harl. 1319).

no more upon the merchants, but to create for himself such fleet as he could, with the co-operation of the Commons. The failure of the attempt to do with merchant vessels what ought to have been done with warships is interesting, because similar attempts have often been made in England, and will no doubt be often made again. In the fourteenth century a merchant ship could be transformed—so far, at all events, as outward appearances were concerned—into a passable warship by the placing in her, at the cost of a few pounds, of fore-, after-, and top-castles—structures which, indeed, at that period formed no part of the permanent fabric, even of war-ships, but were removable at will, being only raised upon stanchions above the deck. Merchant ships had not, however, the structural strength of vessels built expressly for war; nor had merchant sailors the discipline, trustworthiness in action, and knowledge of arms that were to be gained by service under the king's officers in king's ships.

Terrors of the Sea. A characteristic story illustrative of the ignorance of sea affairs that prevailed amongst landsmen, and of the superstitions of the time, is related by Walsingham. About the Feast of St. Martin (1406), he says, when the English ships were going to Bordeaux, they entered a sea which had not been frequented by the sailors of this country, and four vessels belonging to Lynn were suddenly engulfed by a whirlpool, which existed somewhere in the Spanish Sea, and which, thrice every day, swallowed up the flood and vomited it forth again. As preservatives against such awful dangers, silver images of saints seem to have been very generally carried in ships; and as votive offerings after preservation from disaster, small silver ships were commonly vowed and given to noted shrines.

"Admiral of England." Henry IV. is the first who appointed to the office of "Admiral of England." Officers had previously been commissioned as "Admiral of the Southern, Northern, and Western Fleets," or of some of them; but in 1405 Thomas of Lancaster, afterwards Duke of Clarence, was made Admiral of England.

Piracy. The prevalence of piracy in the English Seas has more than once been spoken of (p. 249: I., pp. 444, 588). Henry V., a chivalrous sovereign and an upright man, who took warm interest in all that appertained to navigation and commerce, did not wholly repress it, but, greatly to his honour, he did his best to do so. Impressed, in the year of his accession, with the importance of the subject, and anxious to put down piracy in England, irrespective of whether or not other Powers chose to concern themselves in the reform, he instructed the Chancellor at the opening of Parliament to call attention to the frequent infraction of truces upon the high seas, in the ports, and on the coasts of the realm, whereby many persons who were protected by undertakings, or who possessed safe-conducts, had been killed, or robbed and pillaged to the great dishonour and scandal of the king and against his dignity; and to the fact that the offenders 'had been encouraged and supported by the people in many counties. It was in consequence enacted that such proceedings should be considered high treason; that a conservator of the truce should be appointed in each port to inquire into such offences, and to punish the parties; and that two lawyers should be joined in all commissions issued to that officer. Masters of ships, barges, and other vessels were to swear before the conservator, previous to sailing, that they would observe the truces; and that, if they captured anything, they would bring it into their port, and make a full report to him before the goods were sold. This measure was not inoperative; for, in 1415, two barges of Newcastle, that had been fitted out against the Scots, captured two Flemish ships laden, as was alleged, with goods of the enemy, and carried them into Shields, whence they appear to have been seized by the conservator and taken up to Newcastle pending inquiry. This officer, though complained of by the captors, did his duty nobly, and, after ascertaining the facts, delivered up the prizes and everything on board of them to their Flemish owners. We do not, however, learn that the captors were otherwise punished. Piracy was further discouraged by an order of 1413 that no merchant vessels should proceed to sea singly; and by an arrangement of 1414 between England and Spain that for a year no armed ship belonging to either nation should leave port without first having given security not to molest the subjects or property of the other State.

Henry let slip no opportunity for increasing and improving his navy. He arrested, or impressed, ships and men; he built ships, and he purchased ships abroad. A very fine ship of his own, the *Holy Ghost*, was built in 1414 at Southampton, at a cost of £496. She was adorned with images of the supporters of the royal arms, a swan and antelope, and she is probably the vessel which is described as having borne Henry's motto, "Une sanz pluis." Another king's ship, the cog *John*, bore a crown and sceptre, and the royal crest, the lion of England crowned, as a truck, or vane, to the mast. Her capstan was decorated with three fleurs-de-lys, and she carried five smaller lanterns and one great one. By 1417 the

Henry V. and the Navy.

74

country had a royal, as distinct from a hired, war navy of twenty-seven vessels, of which three, the *Jesu*, the *Trinity Royal*, and the *Holy Ghost*, were of the first class, eight were caracks, or large ships, six were nefs, or ships, and the rest were barges, or balingers. For these Henry seems to have permanently retained officers, for he granted annuities to the masters of each of them, paying £6 13s. 4d. a year to the masters of the great ships and caracks; £5 to those of the nefs: and £3 6s. 8d. to those of the balingers. At about the same period the private owners who provided vessels for temporary service were encouraged by the issue of an order for the punctual payment of the "ton-tight" allowances—allowances at the rate of 3s. 4d. per ton per quarter on account of the wear-and-tear of hired craft. The Commons' petition which secured this order is remarkable as containing the expression "because the Navy is the great support of the wealth, profit, and prosperity of the realm." These words may well be accepted as the origin of those in the preamble to the modern Acts of Parliament for the maintenance of naval discipline. There the expression is that it is on the Navy that, "under the good providence of God, the wealth, safety, and strength of the Kingdom chiefly depend."

Another Commons' petition, noticed by Nicolas, throws light upon the manners and customs of the merchant seamen of the first quarter of the fifteenth century. A ship called the *Christopher*, of Hull, laden with 240 tuns of wine, while lying at Bordeaux and about to return home, was, " by election of all the merchants, masters, and mariners of England there, chosen to be one of the admirals of all the fleet of England on the voyage to England for the security and protection of the whole fleet "; or, as we should now say, her captain was elected commodore of the homeward-bound flotilla. At this election all the merchants, masters, and mariners swore before the Constable of Bordeaux, according to the ancient custom at all times used, to remain by their "admiral" until they arrived in England. But the *Christopher*, being attacked on the passage, was basely deserted by her friends, and fell into the hands of Genoese pirates. The *Christopher's* owners represented that the capture of their ship was ruinous to them and disgraceful to the whole marine of England, and prayed that the owners of the other ships might be made responsible to them for her value. The king commanded that all who had been present in that fleet should be summoned before the Chancellor, who was, with the advice of three or four of the judges, to take such measures as he might deem fit: and power was given, not only to compel the cowardly merchants and masters to make good the loss, but also to punish them by imprisonment.

In 1416, as in later days, there were fishery disputes, the Fisheries. fishing industry of the country being already very extensive. It appears that for some time previous to that year the fish had deserted certain parts of the English coasts, and that the fishermen had, in consequence, gone to the coasts of Iceland, Norway, and other lands. They must have fished in what are now called territorial waters, for the Norwegians and Swedes protested, and requested Henry to forbid his subjects from thus trespassing. The fishermen represented that, if the foreign requests were granted, great injury would result to the realm; and they begged Henry to ordain that fishermen might go where they would to fish and might fish as they pleased; but the king, being an enlightened sovereign and having no desire to attempt any infringement of the reasonable rights of other sovereigns, replied, " Le Roy s'avisera "; and so the matter dropped. Henry never, however, abandoned in the smallest degree the old pretensions of the English sovereigns to be monarchs of the waters nearer home; and, as the author of "The Libel of English Policie" (about 1430) explains, the reason of Henry V.'s great care for his Navy

". . . . was not ellis but that he cast to bee
Lorde round about environ of the See."

In this reign Portsmouth was fortified. In March, 1418, Portsmouth Fortified. money was paid for building a tower there for the protection of the king's ships and the defence of the town and neighbourhood; and in 1421 further money had to be found for " building the new tower at Portsmouth," and for providing for the office of clerk of the king's ships. The port had been blockaded by the French in 1416. Hence arose, no doubt, the wise decision to strengthen it as a naval arsenal.

Henry VI. neglected his Navy and his seamen, and disgusted Henry VI. the merchants by his lawless treatment of them. On one occasion he mortgaged the Customs of London and Southampton to the Cardinal of Winchester, and engaged by indenture to do his best to turn the trade to those ports to the detriment of others. On another, he seized all the tin at Southampton and sold it for his own profit. He also, in contravention of the statutes, granted to foreign merchants licences to transport wool, and favoured the Hanse Towns and the Italians to the prejudice of his own subjects. The king's naval and commercial policy led to tumults in the great commercial and shipping centres, and was the chief cause of his downfall, inasmuch as it alienated the fleet, and rendered it an easy matter for Warwick, in the interests of the Yorkists, to corrupt part of the Navy, and, without very serious opposition, to vanquish the rest. The Yorkists, on their part, followed exactly the opposite plan. They showed distrust of strangers, and they cherished English seamen.

His Ships. In 1843, Mr. C. D. Archibald discovered, embedded in the sands and shingle of the coast of the Isle of Walney at the mouth of Morecambe Bay, a number of very interesting naval relics, which, there is very little doubt, date from the reign of Henry VI. It is to be assumed that an armed ship had been wrecked upon this spot. Some of the relics deserve description. One was a gun about ten feet long. It was made of hammered iron, and was constructed upon the principle of the oldest guns of which we have any account. The tube or inner lining consisted of three plates of iron, each of one-third of an inch thick, disposed in cylindrical form and arranged longitudinally side by side, like the staves of a cask, but apparently not forged nor welded together. These were strengthened or held in position by means of bands or hoops which had been driven on one after another, and then overbound at their points of junction with strong iron rings. But the extraordinary feature of this gun lay in the fact that it had two muzzles and two touch-holes; the breech being midway between the two ends, and the piece being capable of being fired in two opposite directions simultaneously Near each muzzle was a ring for the purpose of suspending the weapon. A second gun was two feet long and of two-inch calibre, formed, as in the other case, of longitudinal bars; these, however, were welded together as well as hooped. It had no trunnions or cascable, but, by means of staples, two large rings were attached to it, one on each side near the middle of its length.

A cast-iron spherical ball suited to its calibre was found. Two other guns, of cast iron, were very short and heavy, and were conjectured to be " chambers," or movable breech-pieces. They were lined with iron tubes, and each contained a charge of powder. Yet another " chamber " had a wad of oakum over the powder. At the same place were found two iron tubes, 15 and 18 inches long respectively, which may have been the barrels of hand-cannon. Of shot there were discovered many specimens, including six of granite, varying from 3½ to 6 inches in diameter;

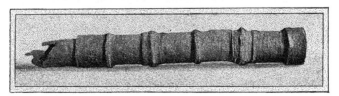

NAVAL GUNS FOUND AT WALNEY ISLE. (*Rotunda Museum, Woolwich.*)
(*By permission of the General Officer commanding Woolwich District.*)

one of grey sandstone, 6 inches in diameter; one of clay iron-stone of the same size; one hammered-iron ball of 5 inches in diameter, weighing 18 pounds; a cast-iron 2-inch ball; a cast-iron 1-inch ball enveloped in lead; and two leaden balls apparently cast upon kernels. In one case the kernel was a flint pebble; in the other, a square piece of hammered iron. It is curious that in the present day some of the tribesmen on the northern frontier of India cast bullets in this way. Colonel Durand, during the Hunza-Nagar Expedition of 1891, was wounded with a ball the centre of which was a garnet. A large gun, described as a wrought-iron serpent gun of the period of

Henry VI., was shown by the British Government at the Royal Naval Exhibition of 1891. It had two rings attached, and was 8 feet 6 inches long. The calibre was 4¼ inches, and the weight 8 cwt. 70 lb. The appropriate iron spherical ball would have weighed between 10 and 11 lb.

At Walney, from the same mass of wreckage, there was recovered a pair of compasses of a pattern so ingenious that it was at once adopted by one of the best nautical-instrument makers of fifty years ago, and is now as common as it doubtless was in the fifteenth century. The legs cross, and are so made that external pressure near the upper part will open them, while if it be applied below the crossing of the legs it will close them.

Naval Arma-ment.

The adoption of guns on shipboard did not, for many generations, have the effect of doing away with bows and cross-bows. In a MS. written by one John Rous, a chantry priest of Guy's Cliff, who illustrated the life of his contemporary the Earl of Warwick, there is a picture of archers firing over cannon, which last are placed *en barbette*, so as to look over the bulwarks of the ship in which they are carried. Another picture in the MS. shows a ship which is identified as one that was fitted with streamers, etc., for Warwick, by William Seburg, painter, and John Ray, tailor, of London. The ship is clincher-built,[1] with a rudder and roofed stern-cabin or round-house. In the bulwarks of the waist are apertures (not port-holes) through which cannon are pointed. The mainmast has shrouds, a top and one large square sail. The mizen is much smaller, and has one sail, which is reefed. The top is ornamented with the earl's device—a ragged staff. From above it floats what, in the bill (still preserved) of Seburg and Ray, is described as "a grete Stremour of forty yardes lenght, and seven yardes in brede, with a grete Bear and Gryfon holding a ragged staff, poudrid full of ragged staves, and a grete crosse of St. George." The St. George's cross was next the staff, and the other ornaments were in the fly. The "lymming and portraying" of these decorations cost £1 6s. 8d. Rous died in 1491. It is therefore clear that openings for guns in the bulwarks of ships were invented in England some years before the time at which they are commonly supposed to have been first devised by the French.

[1 *I.e.* the ribs are slight, and the planks overlap one another—a method of construction common in small rowing boats to-day.]

The Union Jack.

It is just possible that the germ of the present Union Jack may be found in a flag which appears to have been occasionally used during the minority of Henry VI. It seems that at that period, or before, a favourite French ensign was a blue flag

ARCHERS FIRING OVER CANNON (MS. Jul. E. iv.).

bearing a white, upright cross, and that John, Duke of Bedford, took this flag, and, surcharging the white cross with the red cross of St. George, adopted it, if not as an English banner, at least as his own. In the modern union, the white edging or

fimbriation of the St. George's cross is wider than that of the
Irish saltire. The reason of this is not certainly known; but it
may well be that the edging of the St. George's cross is not a
fimbriation at all, but a survival of the white French cross, and
so of our old claim to the sovereignty of France.

Edward IV. so much improved his fleet and so completely

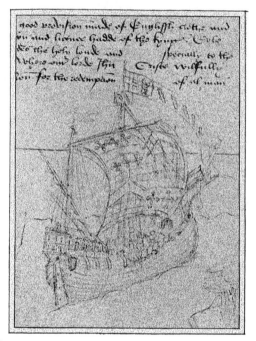

SHIP FLYING THE FLAG OF THE EARL OF WARWICK (MS. Jul. E. iv.).

re-established the naval power of his country, that in 1475, in
spite of the disorders and decadence of the previous reign, he
was able to collect for his expedition to France no fewer than five
hundred vessels. Fully appreciating the value of an extension
of commerce, he spared no pains to encourage the numerous
English merchants who had settled in the Low Countries; and
made enlightened treaties with Denmark, Castile, Burgundy, and

the Hanse Towns (p. 744). Richard III. also paid attention both to the royal and to the commercial Navy of England, and took every care to promote trade and to preserve the dominion of the sea. In all probability, as Campbell suggests, these measures were primarily intended to strengthen the position of himself and his family; yet the people did not the less benefit. It is strange that, at the critical moment of his reign, he committed exactly the mistake which had been committed by Harold four centuries earlier. When invasion was pending he suffered his fleet to be laid up, because either he imagined that the danger had ceased to be pressing, or he experienced difficulty in maintaining the force at sea; and thus, although he possessed the necessary ships and men, and probably the devotion of the Navy, he was unable to oppose Henry where opposition would have been most likely to be successful.

THE share of England in that expansion of Europe and Christendom which went on slowly but steadily throughout the Middle Ages is indeed a contrast with its share in the great development of the sixteenth century. The Catholic missionaries and the Italian cities, the Spanish Crusaders and the Norse pirates, were all alike far more active than the English before the age of Elizabeth. The seafaring merchants or adventurers of the Mediterranean and the Baltic easily outstripped the people of the British Isles as pioneers of that Western Society whose capital was Rome. None of the great medieval explorers were Englishmen; none of the great medieval discoveries can be laid to our credit. It was the Wickings of Norway (I., p. 209) who found the way to Greenland and America in the tenth and eleventh centuries, who rounded the North Cape of Europe in the ninth; it was the Italian land-travellers and sea-captains of the thirteenth and fourteenth who made known the overland routes to India and to China, and who began the ocean voyages towards the west and south at the very same time that Marco Polo had reached Cathay; it was the Portuguese in the fifteenth century who brought these slow and painful efforts of the earlier time to a brilliant issue. Up to the age of the Cabots our own discoveries in the Unknown were mainly accidental, and some of the most

CHARLES RAYMOND BEAZLEY. English Travel and Exploration, 650-1485.

successful explorers of the medieval time who served the English
Crown were foreigners, like the Northmen Ohthere and Wulfstan
in King Alfred's day. But such as it is, the early story of our
national exploration, though it has long been forgotten in the
result—in the history of our colonies—may be worth remembering, by itself. For, all this time, the English as a maritime
people were slowly but surely forcing themselves into the front
rank of Christian nations. And if, between the seventh century
and the fifteenth, we did not do much for the theory and
practice of European discovery, for the conquest of the world
by Christian civilisation, yet the little we did achieve was at
least something. Our share in that work can be fairly set
against the share of France, of the Hanse Towns on the North
German coast, of medieval Spain, or Hungary, or Russia. As
in other Christian States, so in England, pilgrims, traders,
and travellers succeed one another as leaders of Western exploration, before the age of the colonists brings us to the political
expansion of Europe. A religious movement is followed by a
mercantile, and that again by one of adventure, in which the
passion of wild freedom goes along with something of the
patient wish to know.

**Pilgrim-
age.**
The beginnings of English exploration take us back to the
first age of English Christianity, to the start of Anglo-Saxon
civilisation in the seventh century (I., p. 230). The time of the
Irish missions, of Theodore of Tarsus and of Bede, is also the
time of the first English record of travel. And though this is
merely a piece of information for pilgrims, it is our first book-
evidence of English interest in the great world beyond these
islands. Arculf and Willibald, the two chief western travellers of
the two hundred years between the rise of Islam and the death
of Charlemagne, are both connected with England, and both
are known to us through the Christian movement of our own
conversion and of our attempts to hand on that Christianity
to our brothers in the old homeland of heathen Germany.

**The
Impulse
from
Ireland.**
But the impulse of travel to the holy places of the Continent
and of Syria had sprung from the still earlier devotion to the
holy places of Ireland. The greater part of England was converted by the Irish missions between 633 and 664, and by the
middle of the century a fashion of Irish pilgrimage had already
set in among Bede's countrymen in Northumbria, among the

Southern English, and even among the Franks of Gaul.[1] Bishop
Agilberct of Dorchester spent a long time in Ireland "for the
sake of reading the Scriptures"; others, like Chad of Lichfield,
went to the holy island to "lead the monastic life while still
young, for the sake of the eternal kingdom."   Iona, the most
famous of Irish monasteries, the home of Columba and of Aidan,
was the spiritual capital of the Northumbrian empire, till in 664,
at the Synod of Whitby, King Oswy gave up the Irish obedience
for the Roman (I., p. 231).   And, as the Church of Patrick had

Photo: McIsaac & Riddle, Oban.

IONA CATHEDRAL.

planted colonies as far as North Italy, the Juras, and the Lake
of Constance, as at a later time (795) it sent its monks across
the ocean to Iceland, and set up a claim in St. Brendan to the
finding of a western continent, so the wider interest and outlook
which it gave to English converts may be fairly reckoned as
of some account in our preparation for the discovery of the
outer world.

   With Arculf's pilgrimage we get our first English manual of
travel.   More than this, we have in it the first guide-book of the
Middle Ages proper, of the dark time that followed Mahomet,
when Christian civilisation came most nearly to an end.   Arculf

[1] Bede, III., 7; IV., 3, 4; V., 9, 10.

was a Frank or Gallican bishop who had been to the Holy Land about 690, and on his return was driven by storms to Iona, where he found a home in the half-English, half-Irish monastery of Columba, then governed by Abbot Adamnan. He told his story ; it was written down by the abbot and presented to the last of the great Northumbrian kings, Aldfrith the Wise, in his court at York. Of this account two summaries, one longer, one shorter, were made by Bede of Jarrow, the great scholar of the time, to help Englishmen on the road to the holy places. The main interest of the time in these descriptions was purely devotional, but the secondary purpose of wider knowledge, though it were only for the sake of pilgrimage, was also realised. The connection of Northern England with the wider field of Irish proselytism, and of Southern England with Continental Christendom, were alike illustrated in the accident of Arculf and his journey becoming known to Europe through his stay at an Irish house of religion, through the reports of its abbot and through the summaries of that report made by the first English historian.

The great world became known both to Franks and Saxons through pilgrimage, first to the nearer, then to the farther and holier, of the holy places. The Englishmen who crossed and re-crossed the Irish Channel for piety or learning, and who were roused to unusual interest by the visit of a pilgrim from Jerusalem, made their way to Rome, Constantinople, Egypt, and Palestine in the course of the first hundred years after conversion (655–750 c.).

As early as 721, while Bede was still collecting all the knowledge of his time for the use of English religion, there started for Palestine an Englishman named Willibald, nephew of Boniface of Crediton, the Apostle of Germany, who, in later days, took up his uncle's work, and became the leader of those English missions in Central Europe which decided the fortunes of the Roman Church in the immediate future. As the earliest of English-born travellers, and the source of one of the most interesting medieval records of travel in Palestine, he deserves a special notice. His road seems to have been along one of the main routes of pilgrims and traders—by Southampton and Rouen, and over the Alps to Naples and Catania, " where is Mount Etna, and when this volcano casts itself out, they take

St. Agatha's veil and hold it towards the fire, which ceases at once." Thence by Samos and Cyprus Willibald reached North Syria and arrived at Emessa, " in the region of the Saracens," where the whole party, who had escaped the Moslem brigands of Southern Gaul, were thrown into prison as spies. They were released at the intercession of a Spaniard, but Willibald went up to Damascus in person and relieved himself of all suspicion before the caliph : " We have come from the West, where the sun has his setting, and we know of no land beyond—nothing but water." This was surely too far for spies to come from, he pleaded, and the caliph agreed and gave him a pass for all the sites of Palestine, with which he traversed the length and breadth of the Holy Land four times during the next five years, finding the same trouble in leaving as he had found in entering, for the age of persecution was beginning for the subject Christians of the East, and Willibald carried his life in his hand.

Like Arculf, he saw all the wonders of Syria—real and legendary—the fountains of Jor and Dan, " which are collected in the river Jordan," the top of Mount Tabor, " where our Lord was transfigured "; the " spot where Paul was converted," the Sea of Galilee, " where Christ walked with dry feet, and Peter tried, but sank "; the mountain of the Temptation; the " dry land once covered by the water where our Lord was baptised "; the " glorious church " of St. Helena at Bethlehem, and all the marvels of Jerusalem. Especially was he moved at the sight of the two columns, " against the north wall and the south wall," in the Church of the Ascension on Mount Olivet; for " that man who can creep between the columns and the wall will be free from all his sins." He saw the tombs of the patriarchs and their wives at Hebron; the great convent of Mar Saba near the Dead Sea, in the Kedron gorge; and, as he returned from Judæa to the Bay of Acre, " through the furthest borders of Samaria," he met a " lion, who threatened us with fearful roaring." Coming at last to the " head of Mount Lebanon, where it runs out into the sea, at the Tower of Libanus," Willibald and his friends were sent under escort to Tyre, " *six*[1] miles from Sidon," where he took ship for Constantinople. " But before this the citizens examined us to

[1] The distance is really more than fifteen.

see if we had anything concealed, and if so, they would have
put us to death.   Now, Willibald, when at Jerusalem, had
bought some balsam and filled a gourd with it, pouring in
rock-oil at the top; and at Tyre, when they opened the gourd,
they smelt the oil, and did not suspect the balsam that was
within. So they let us go."

They were at sea all the winter in their voyage through
the Levant and Ægæan, and, once safe in New Rome, stayed
there two years in full communion and friendship with the
Greeks, under the Iconoclast Emperors of that time. Willibald was lodged in the church "where was the body of John
Chrysostom, that he might behold daily where the saints
reposed."

At last he sailed with the "envoys of the Pope and the
emperor" to Sicily, "and thence to Vulcano, where is Theodoric's Hell.[1] And they went on shore to see what sort of
a hell it was, and Willibald wished to go to the top of the
mountain where the opening was, but he was driven back by
the cinders that were thrown up in heaps round the brim,
as snow settles on the ground.   But he saw "how the
column of flame and smoke rushed up from the pit with a
noise like thunder, and how the pumice stone, that writers
use, was thrown up with the flame from the hell and fell into
the sea, and so was cast on the shore, where men gathered it."

Willibald's account was read before Pope Gregory III., and
was published, as far as the age could publish anything, with
the imprimatur of the Church. To us it is of special value
as the record of the first and typical English pilgrimage, as
our earliest native Itinerary, preserving to us the actions and
thoughts of a great Christian leader at the time of the lowest
ebb of Christian civilisation, when the newly converted
northern nations were but just beginning to redress the
balance against Moslem advance, when Roman Empire and
Catholic Church were as yet united, and when the Byzantines
had just begun to recover from the conquests of Islam in the

---

[1] A hermit of Lipari told a friend of Pope Gregory I. ("the Great") that
he had seen the soul of King Theodoric, who ruled in Italy 493-526, thrown
into the crater of Vulcano for his Arianism and for his murders of the
senators Boëthius and Symmachus. This story was published to the world in
Pope Gregory's *Dialogues.*

seventh century. Willibald, a "Latin" and an Englishman, has perfect freedom of intercourse with the Greeks of Constantinople; compared to most Westerns, his outlook is wide indeed. A Spaniard helps him in Emessa and Damascus, the Isaurian emperors befriend him, the Pope endorses his book. His voyage was the practical discovery of the Bible-world for Englishmen, as his life in Germany, like the lives of Willibrord and Boniface, helped to spread a practical knowledge of Central Europe among us. Again, this "Hodœporicon" or Guide-Book of Willibald's was the outcome of the great social and religious movement that followed the conversion, and as that movement died away, English exploration died with it; for discovery is but a natural activity of any vigorous society, and is in proportion to the healthy and, as it were, over-flowing life of the State as a whole.

The next revival came with the revived national life of Alfred's reign. The great West Saxon king describes how the Norse captains, Ohthere and Wulfstan, had explored the north and north-east coasts of Europe, in voyages that were truly of discovery, where the object was to know more of the world for the sake of the new knowledge itself. This was not all. He himself sent yearly embassies to Rome in the last period of his life, and in 813 despatched Sighelm and Ethelstan with presents to India, " to St. Thomas and St. Bartholomew," by way of Jerusalem. He created a fleet and revived trade and learning among his people with the same unconquerable energy with which he tried to find what the world was like beyond his coasts. It is only of the first-named of these expeditions that we know anything more than the bare fact; but the reports of Ohthere and Wulfstan were written down by the king and copied into his Description of Europe—our first scientific geography — by which Alfred tried to make the outline of Paulus Orosius something of a really "Universal History." After a wonderfully clear and good account of the "borders of Germany," the courses of Rhine and Danube, the divisions of the great German tribes, and of the nations to east and south-east, "from the land of the Carinthians south to the Alps, and east to the Bulgarians and the Greeks," the king comes to the Danes and the ocean that divides Britain from them. Then he talks of the sea to the north of the Danes, and the coasts of Old

Voyages of Ohthere and Wulfstan.

Saxony, the mouth of the Elbe, and the course of the strait that runs between Swedes and Danes, and stops with the mention of Finns and Northmen, to north and west of the Swedes, for the story of Ohthere's voyage.

The First Arctic Explorer. "Ohthere told his lord King Alfred that he lived to the north of all the Northmen, on the mainland by the West Sea, with only the waste land to north of him, save for the Finn hunters and fishers. He wished to find how far this land went, and whether any lived north of the waste. So he sailed three days north, as far as the whale-hunters ever go, and then three days more, till the land turned eastward [round the North Cape]. Then he sailed four days east till the land began to run southward [into the White or "inland" Sea], and he followed the coast five days more, to a river mouth, which he entered, where the land was all peopled" [round the Archangel of our own day]. Then after talking about the habits of these "Biarmians," or Russians of Perm, Ohthere goes back to speak of his own land, "very long and narrow," with a little strip of fruitful land between the wild inland moors and the coast—a strip that was never more than sixty miles across, and at the narrowest only three miles, with Sweden and Lapland on the other side of the moors, where there were "great meres of fresh water."

Another voyage of Ohthere's was to a port one month's journey south of his home, "sailing along the coast, with Ireland (*sic*) on his right, and then the islands that are between Ireland (*sic*) and England, while all the way to the left is Norway. To the south a great sea runs up a vast way into the land, so wide that none can see across it," dividing Norway from Jutland. "In five days more" Ohthere sailed to the "lands where the English had once lived," on the German mainland, with Denmark on his left, and on his right the wide sea and the islands subject to Denmark.

Exploration in the Baltic. From the same point, the old English homeland, Wulfstan, another Norse captain in Alfred's service, sailed up the Baltic coasts, first by Gothland and the land of the Swedes, then by the Gulf of Riga, to the opening of the Gulf of Bothnia, about which he says nothing to decide the vexed question whether it flowed into the Arctic Sea, as the Greek geographers mostly thought, making of Scandinavia one vast island.

But we must come back to Alfred's Description. After reciting these three voyages, the king then turns to describe the coasts and rivers of Greece, Bulgaria, Macedonia, Thrace, Dalmatia, and Istria, south of which last is "that part of the Mediterranean called the Adriatic," while "west are the Alps, and north is that desert between Carinthians and Bulgarians." Italy, " of great length," is "surrounded by the sea on every side but the north-west, where are the Alps, that begin in the land of Narbonne, and end in Dalmatia." So far it is all very clear. The geography of Gaul is more curious: of its three provinces, Belgium or the " Belgic Gaul " has the ocean on the west, *south,*

THE FRANKS CASKET.
(*British Museum.*)

and north ; and Aquitaine, "*west* of the Loire, has the ocean to the *south,*" with the Narbonnese. Spain, "which is a triangle," has Aquitaine on the north-*west*, one angle over against Cadiz island, one against the Narbonnese, one against "Braganza of Gallicia." Opposite to Ireland, across the sea, Spain lies in a straight line with the mouth of the Shannon. Britain is of great length to the north-east, four times as long as it is broad : west of it is Ireland, to the north the Orkneys. Ireland or " Scotland " is "surrounded on every side by the ocean: so, because the rays of the setting sun strike on it with less inter- ruption than on other countries, the weather is milder." North- west of Ireland is " that utmost land called Thule, known to so few, from its great distance."

75

In spite of its errors in detail, it would not be easy, in the whole range of the earlier Middle Ages, to find a better and juster account of the lie of European countries than is here given by the West-Saxon king, or a clearer evidence of that expansion of Christian knowledge and enterprise which was so steadily, though slowly, recovering from the barbarising attacks of foreign enemies. But there are not many men like Alfred of Wessex, and till the age of Elizabeth we do not find, even in the first days of crusading energy, the same union of thought and action in English discovery. The king was fortunate in being able to use the Wickings' new knowledge of the Northern Ocean, but all the work actually done by him and for him was not the result of lucky accident, but of heroic perseverance. He, if any man ever did, truly rose above his people and his age; it was not an easy thing to make an enterprising and seafaring nation out of a dispirited, beaten, and brutalised race of landsmen, who had long forgotten that they had ever been ocean-rovers.

Between the death of Alfred and the time of the Crusades England is not to the fore in exploration. Her people are little inclined to struggle with the men of Amalfi and the other commercial republics of Italy for the great trade routes of the south; in the north, the discoveries of the Wickings, from Labrador to Novgorod, are nearly all exclusively their own. The only traces of English interest beyond England between 900 and 1100 are first the maps of the tenth and eleventh centuries, of which two remain to us from the Anglo-Saxon period, which, with all their shortcomings, stand to the thirteenth-century Hereford Map much as fact stands to fiction, and secondly the records of a few formal pilgrimages, such as those of Andrew Whiteman, in 1020; of Sweyn Godwinson, in 1052; of Bishop Eldred of Worcester, in 1056. We may pass over the doubtful travels of the Welsh monk, Teilo, and of John Scotus Erigena in Alfred's day, and the flight of so many Englishmen, like the sons of Edmund Ironside, to Hungary and to Constantinople, where some of them found a place in the Varangian Guard of the Eastern Emperors. All this was only partial evidence of that reopening of the great European land route to the south-east which followed the conversion of Hungary, under King Stephen, and prepared

Geography in England, 901-1200.

the way for the Crusades; it did not represent anything very new or important in exploration. Every stage of this route was well known by the time of the Norman Conquest, and in the strictest sense there is no discovery of the unknown world which can be set down to the credit of Englishmen between the time of Alfred and Macham's discovery of Madeira about 1360. But the travels of Saewulf in 1102 and of Adelard in 1114, with the exploits of the English Crusaders, in 1147 and 1190, on the coasts of Spain and Syria, give us too good a view of English enterprise in the twelfth century to be quite passed over, although they add nothing to our knowledge and stop well within the limits of both southern and Scandinavian exploration. For it is in this time that

CONSTANTINOPLE.
(*Luttrell Psalter.*)

we have the beginnings of the permanent English navy and merchant fleet, the opening of our really important trade with Continental countries; it is now that we see the foundation laid for our steady progress towards the achievements and discoveries of the sixteenth and seventeenth centuries. To come to the later Middle Ages. In the thirteenth century we **1200-1485.** have the geographical theories of Roger Bacon and the Hereford Map. In the fourteenth there is published the famous English collection of popular medieval tales of foreign lands, under the name of Sir John Maundeville. Before the end of the fifteenth we hear something of the fish trade of the eastern ports with Iceland, of the mysterious voyage of Nicholas de Lymne (p. 250), to all the countries "situate under the North Pole," of the intercourse of English seamen

with the Hanse towns, with the Baltic, that "Mare Clausum"
of the north, with the Teutonic Knights of Prussia, and with
Portugal.

But before the age of the Cabots there is no continuous
exploration; the position of Catholic England, except for intervals of foreign conquest, is purely insular throughout most
of the thirteenth, fourteenth, and fifteenth centuries, and we
must be content with instancing two or three of the more
interesting points of English enterprise and geographical know-

INHABITANTS OF THE FAR EAST (MS. Roy. 15 E. vi.).

ledge in this central period of the Middle Ages, not because
they are of any general importance, like the adventures of
Elizabethan explorers, but as showing that national energy
was not always at so low an ebb as to be bounded by the
four seas of Britain.

Saewulf and Adelard.   1. Saewulf of Worcester and Adelard of Bath were two
Englishmen who made their way to Syria in the early years
of the twelfth century.   Of Adelard's account, which professed to give news of Arabia, Egypt, and Bagdad, nothing
remains; we only know of his journey through the allusions
of chroniclers, but Saewulf has left us the fullest guide-book
of any early English pilgrim—fuller than others, because

A THIRTEENTH-CENTURY MAP OF THE WORLD (MS. Add. 28,681).

written with the eye of the merchant and the traveller, as well as of the devotee.

Starting, perhaps, as the story goes, at the instance of his confessor, Bishop Wulfstan of Worcester, some three years after the first Latin capture of Jerusalem in 1099, Saewulf describes six different routes from Italy to Syria, thus giving us fair evidence of the vast commercial development of Southern Europe since Willibald wrote. His own route, by Corfu, Corinth, and Athens, took him to Rhodes, "which once had the idol called Colossus, one of the Seven Wonders of the World, but destroyed by the Persians, with nearly all the land of Rome, on their way to Spain. These are the Colossians to whom St. Paul wrote." Then by the port of "Myra in Lycia, the harbour of the Adriatic" (for so Saewulf terms the Levant) "as Constantinople is of the Ægæan," to Jaffa, after a sail of thirteen weeks. The wonders of Jerusalem, like those of the other holy sites, had not grown less since the eighth century. In the Church of the Holy Sepulchre Saewulf saw the "Navel of the Earth, which Christ measured with His own hands, working salvation in the midst, as say the Psalms, 'For God is my King of old, working salvation in the midst of the earth'"; across the Jordan he looked into Arabia, "hateful to all who worship God, but having the mount whence Elias was carried into heaven in a chariot of fire"; at Hebron he found the "Holm-oak of Abraham" still standing, where, as the pilgrims said, the patriarch once "sat and ate with God"; in Cana of Galilee he noted the "house of Saint *Architriclin*"—Saint-Ruler-of-the-Feast. After traversing the Holy Land, he was content to go no farther, and returned by sea as he had come, escaping the Saracen cruisers and weathering the storms that wrecked in the roads of Jaffa, before his eyes, some twenty of the pilgrim and merchant fleet then lying at anchor.

Saewulf is the first traveller who followed in the wake of the Crusaders and has left us his note-book. That note-book is valuable evidence of the great inward revival in medieval Christendom of which the Crusades were outward and visible signs; but it is not in any sense a record of new ground explored, the religious interest is credulous, beyond the earlier standards, almost beyond belief, and we may well regret, by the side of this, that Adelard's more scientific treatise of his "search for the causes of things and the mysteries of Nature," throughout the nearer East, has not come down to us.

2. The English share in the Spanish crusade against the Western Moslems comes out chiefly in the second and third Crusades. In 1147 a fleet of one hundred and sixty vessels, largely English, sailed from Dartmouth for Syria, and on their way decided the siege of Lisbon, and won it finally for Christendom. In 1189–90 the main fleet of Richard I. helped, in the same way, to win and hold Sylves, near Cape St. Vincent. In both these enterprises there was more of exploration than at first appears; Southern Spain had been alien ground to Christians for four hundred years, and its recovery was a real extension of the horizon of knowledge. *English Sailors Rescue Spain.*

3. In connection with Edward III.'s sea-fights in the Channel we have a muster-roll of English shipping (p. 259) which is hardly in any sense a part of the chronicle of English discovery, but suggests, on the one hand, a recollection of the older prominence of such forts as Dartmouth in the fleets of the twelfth century, still in great part maintained in the fourteenth, and, on the other hand, prepares us for the voyage of Macham as something more than an accidental piece of good luck to a nation of mere landsmen. Somewhere about the year 1360 Robert Macham escaped from Bristol with Anne d'Arfet, and was driven by storms off the French coast to the island of Madeira, where both the lovers died of exhaustion and despair. This is the whole story of the one original discovery of any Englishman in that great age when the Middle Ages were passing into Modern Europe, when Italians and Portuguese and Spaniards were pressing on to the finding of a new heaven and a new earth. It is our one achievement in the course of that long preparation of the fourteenth and fifteenth centuries for Columbus and Da Gama and Magellan. *Discovery of Madeira.*

4. Lastly, the Hereford Map of 1275–1300 is a great picture, as it were, of vulgar English ideas of the world in the later Middle Ages. Our maps of earlier times, with few exceptions, are mere sketches; this thirteenth-century "Mappa Mundi" is at least an attempt to represent the whole world, with the main features, the people and the products of each country, on a great scale. *The Hereford Mappa Mundi.*

But its faults are like an ocean in which its few merits are soon lost. Unless we possessed some evidence, in Arabic drawings, that a worse parody of geography were possible, it would be hard for a modern to believe that anything wilder than the Hereford Map had ever been tried in plan or chart. In this short space it is only possible to say that almost everything is

THE "MAPPA MUNDI."
(*Hereford Cathedral.*)

either legendary or grotesquely misapplied. The true shape of the Mediterranean and of the Northern seas, of each one of the European countries, disappears as much as that of Asia or Africa. And the farther we get from England, the larger grow the legendary figures, the Minotaurs and Gog-magogs of Tartary, the horse-footed, dog-faced, flap-eared monsters of the far East,

SECTION FROM A FACSIMILE OF THE HEREFORD "MAPPA MUNDI."

the one-legged, four-eyed, headless, and hermaphrodite tribes who fringe the torrid zone.

We may read with it as our commentary the strange passages in which Roger Bacon wastes his time and genius in explaining the Arabic *mélange* of geographical fact and fancy, the theory of a centre of the world, from which equal lines can be drawn to any point on its circumference. We may get what further light we can from the travels of Sir John Maundeville,

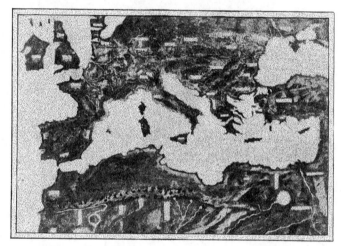

SECTION FROM THE LAURENTIAN MAP.
(British Museum.)

that wonderful collection of fashionable travellers' tales which so long imposed upon men as a real if fanciful record of a real journey. We may also, if we like, contrast these absurdities with the wonderful accuracy and finish of the Italian coasting charts, or Portolani, of the same period. And all these together will perhaps leave us with a true, if a rather humiliating, confession of prolonged national short-coming in what became the special pride of Englishmen. For until the national awakening in the age of Henry VIII. and Elizabeth we were not a great discovering, or even a great commercial, nation. At the most, we satisfied an average standard.

REGINALD
HUGHES.
Architecture
and Art:
The Decay
of Gothic.

THE high-water mark of the style which we call Perpendicular was reached before the end of the reign of Richard II. A little more than a century and a half brings us to the accession of Elizabeth, when the end had come. The history of this period is the history of the decadence of what was itself the decadent style of Gothic. Little by little all that the early Gothic builders prized disappeared. The manner has ceased to be regarded— the utilitarian result is everything. Thus the windows become mere contrivances for the admission of light and the exhibition of glass. The mullion becomes a mere beading, and the window itself a frame of many transparent panels. The knot of the difficulty of making beautiful curves in stone work is got rid of by the simple method of making them straight, till at length under the Tudors we have window-heads consisting of two straight lines inclined at an obtuse angle, or only slightly rounded. The style has, in fact, ceased to be a pointed style at all. The downward movement was, however, exceedingly slow, and the old tradition exercised its restraining influence on masons and workmen.

Towers of
the later
Perpendicular
Period.

The architects of the reigns of the Lancastrian and Yorkist Plantagenets deserve, however, to be remembered for the towers which they built. The great central tower of Canterbury, "the Bell-Harry Tower," is unquestionably their *chef-d'œuvre*. It is the first object that catches the eye of the modern pilgrim, and forms a superb centre to the group formed by the subsidiary roofs and towers. It is of no great height—235 feet, which, by comparison with Continental standards, is very low. Neither is it remarkable for elaboration of ornament, the shallow Perpendicular work producing a soft rather than a rich effect. But in matter of proportion it is faultless. Chaucer and his fellows, however, never looked on it, for it dates from the last decade of the fifteenth century. Moreover, the tower at Canterbury is not a solitary success, nor were these successes of the Perpendicular style confined to one period. Almost as imposing is the central tower of York, though that is nearly a century earlier. The central towers of Gloucester and of Bristol are also to be put to the credit of the later Perpendicular architects, the latter being of the same date as the Bell-Harry Tower at Canterbury. The smaller church towers which form the chief architectural glory of Somersetshire belong to the same time. Many of these—at Wrington, Brislington, and Taunton, for example—are elaborately ornamented, having several storeys with large canopied windows, double buttresses at the angles, and frequently the small hanging pinnacles, which last are distinctive. The separate campanile, so usual in Italy, is almost confined to this epoch. They are a not uncommon addition to parish churches, though occurring in only one cathedral, that of Chichester, where the detached campanile is in this style. Occasionally, too, one is seen which exhibits something of the chasteness and, if one may use the word, the Attic simplicity of the pure Early English. Such an example is the tower of Magdalen College at Oxford, which, as originally built, stood alone as a belfry, though the effect has now been marred by later additions, huddled against two sides of its base. The lower storeys are here quite plain, the ornament, in which great moderation is displayed, being reserved for the belfry windows, the parapet, and the pinnacles. By this arrangement an effect of solemnity and repose is obtained which is lacking in more decorative examples.

Fan Tracery.

The famous ornamental vaulting known as fan tracery must also be given to the Perpendicular architects, and, indeed constitutes the veritable swan-song of Gothic architecture. In the earlier examples, such as the cloisters at Gloucester Cathedral, these great fans with their wide, stretching circular outline, spring apparently from a narrow piershaft on each side, and meet in the centre. If rather heavy, they are extremely beautiful, and the irregular space left between them, being covered with most elaborate tracery, sufficiently satisfies the eye. In the retro-choir at Peterborough the size of the fans is increased so as to include two bays of the side aisles in one of the centre, but this expedient was not generally followed ; and at King's College Chapel at Cambridge, and the later St George's at Windsor, there was a return to the arrangement at Gloucester, although the shape of the fans was altered. In the former case, a great rib was carried to the centre, without being broken, and in the latter a broad flat band was introduced, the idea (though it may be a false idea) of structural stability being thus finely suggested. Nothing, however, seems to have been farther from the mind of the architect of Henry VII.'s chapel than any such suggestion of constructive strength. Not only is

Bell Harry Tower.

Magdalen College, Oxford.

Brislington Church.

Chichester Cathedral.

TOWERS OF THE FIFTEENTH CENTURY.

the need of introducing any explanation of the means of support, for the benefit of the puzzled worshipper, not admitted, but his bewilderment seems to have been studiously aimed at by the architect. Enormous pendants hang from the roof, looking as if they needed to be supported by pillars from the floor. As a matter of fact, they are supported by brackets from the wall and internal flying buttresses ; but the effect on the eye is such as to suggest the miraculous. A late example of this sort of roof is that erected by Cardinal Wolsey, in the sixteenth century, over the choir of Oxford Cathedral, which is extremely elegant, though hardly, perhaps, justifying the praise given it by an eminent architect, as one of the most remarkable ever executed. The ornamental details of these chapel roofs are, it must be confessed, somewhat monotonous, but their grand dimensions (King's College is 78 feet in height), the prodigality of enrichment on every square foot of the interior, and the amazing ingenuity of their construction, justify the saying that, under the Tudors, "the style went out in a blaze of glory." But the glory was confined to the interiors of the churches, to the stone vaults and screens and rood-lofts, to the wooden canopies and stalls and bench ends. Externally they are apt at this late period to be very commonplace, and, in the Tudor period, even the richest decoration, such as that on the outside of the chapel at Westminster, has a distinctly paltry effect. Many, perhaps most, of **Market Crosses.** the conduits and market crosses which still adorn England belong to the Perpendicular period ; but these may be thought to belong to the province of the lay architect.

Domestic Architecture. During the reigns of the houses of Lancaster and York castle-building gradually fell into entire disuse. The number of licences to build them, which had declined from one hundred and eighty-one in the reign of Edward III., to sixty in the reign of his son, fell suddenly to eight in the reign of Henry IV. ; the succeeding reigns showing one granted by Henry V., five by Henry VI., and three by Edward IV. The name of castle was still retained, and occasionally much of the form, but there was no longer any pretence of building a genuine fortress. Still, although their military value was small, these pseudo-fortresses have a most imposing appearance. Internally, they present the ordinary type of a grandee's country house—a series of open courts with rooms built round them, and a large hall on one

Lady Chapel, Peterborough Cathedral.

The Cloisters, Gloucester Cathedral.

Photo: E. Clennett, Cambridge.

The Chapel, King's College, Cambridge.

TRACERIED ROOFS OF THE FIFTEENTH CENTURY.

side of the principal court.   There is no better type of the manor-house castle than Hurstmonceux in Sussex, which retains its outer walls, although, by the vandalism of a proprietor in the last century, the interior has been swept away.   It was built under Henry VI., in the first half of the fifteenth century—in the middle, therefore, of the Perpendicular period.   It is a nearly square building, more than 200 feet along each side.   The

Photo : R. Wilkinson & Co., Trowbridge.

THE MARKET CROSS, MALMESBURY.

walls were flanked with turrets over 80 feet high.   A moat surrounded it, and the entrance was by a strong gateway and drawbridge.   It enclosed one large and two small courts, a large and lofty hall and kitchen, a bakehouse, a lock-up or dungeon, and numerous suites of apartments and domestic offices, a stable, and a chapel.   There were two storeys, at least in parts, connected with galleries to which access was obtained by winding staircases.   But though the convenience of the place is unmis-

Photo: Graphotone Co., Enfield.

HURSTMONCEUX CASTLE.

takable, its martial appearance is not less marked. Probably this was the fashion ot the time, and no doubt the builder, John de Fienes, who had fought at Agincourt, preferred to be housed in a dwelling of military aspect. Hurstmonceux is essentially a manor house enclosed by castle walls and a castle moat, and forms the connecting link between the castle and the stately Tudor pleasaunces, from which the castle attributes were altogether omitted. That form was the one adopted by great benefactors like William of Wykeham and William of Waynflete in the colleges they founded at this time, and may be seen in the quadrangle and chapel of All Souls', and the cloistered court at Magdalen with the founders' lodgings, the chapel, and the hall. The greater part of Penshurst, Chalfield, and Thornbury, and numberless other famous seats, also belong to this period, and on them was founded a tradition which persisted to a much later date. Wolsey's work at Hampton Court and at Christchurch shows the style of lay architecture in its most grandiose mood; and in these examples the idea of a sumptuous palace has altogether replaced that of the strong place of arms.

Painting and Sculpture.   Architecture, even in its decline, remained the one art in which Englishmen exhibited anything like genius. Painting remained a foreign art almost down to a period within the memory of the grandfathers of people still living. English sculpture—which in the thirteenth century was full of promise, and was, as far as sepulchral sculpture is concerned, still advancing at the beginning of the fourteenth century—stood still for a century. Some Perpendicular tombs are, no doubt, imposing structures, but their merit is mainly architectural, and most of them are, more or less, imitations, or variants, of such earlier masterpieces as the tomb of Edward II. But the makers of such monuments as that of Lady Arundel at Chichester, and of William of Wykeham, in the great cathedral which he restored out of all knowledge, certainly deserve to be remembered. It is, moreover, curious to see how thoroughly the artist of William's monument anticipates the realism of our best or only modern sculptors—not a vein or wrinkle overlooked on the folded hands. Nevertheless, down to the middle of the fifteenth century, we are unable to identify any English artist, either sculptor or painter, worthy of the name of artist; for the

earlier artists, the Master Walters and Master Williams, who, in
Henry III.'s reign, painted pictures at Windsor and Westminster,
the Odos and Edwards who carved "trees of Jesse" and the
like for the king's and queen's chamber, were, probably, scarcely
more artists in our modern sense than the sheriffs of Wiltshire

TOMB OF EARL RICHARD BEAUCHAMP, ST. MARY'S, WARWICK.

and Southampton who received the king's command to have
such works executed.

It is not till we come to the reign of Henry VI.—the very William
middle, that is, of the Perpendicular period—that we meet Austin.
with an Englishman who has left his name to a sterling work
of art. This man is William Austin, the author of and con-
tractor for the noble tomb of Earl Richard Beauchamp, at
St. Mary's Church, Warwick. It is a brass casting of "the
image of a man, armed" with sword and dagger, a helm and
crest under his head, and "at his feet a bear musled," and

rests on a tomb " with fourteen images embossed, and eighteen less images of angels." The whole expense of the tomb and the chapel in which it was placed is worked out at £2,458 4s. 7d., an enormous sum for the time, A.D. 1442–1465. It is curious as showing that England could produce a metal casting at this date not far inferior to the similar and almost contemporaneous work of Ghiberti.[1]

Decorative Painting. In a former chapter, in dealing with the reign of Henry III., attention was called to the introduction of fresco work (chiefly in oil) as an advance on the earlier (and also later) practice of merely colouring or gilding carved stone or woodwork. The same decorative-practice sort of art continued throughout the Decorated, and was largely followed in the early Perpendicular times. Most of the paintings in the Chapter-house at Westminster belong to the latter period, though it is not improbable that some of them, at least, were restorations of earlier designs. Probably this is true of the paintings on an octangular pillar of Faversham Church, where the costumes clearly suggest an Early English origin. Similar works exist at Arundel and elsewhere, though at Arundel the date is approximately fixed by the date of the church, which was rebuilt in 1380. These mural paintings are more plentiful in some counties than in others; but there is no reason to suppose that the art ever attained great excellence, or that the work of the later half of the fourteenth century was materially better than that of the earlier half, or that that, in its turn, showed any marked advance. That it rapidly deteriorated in the fifteenth century may be taken for granted; for, almost without exception, the best of these frescoes are generally the earliest. For instance, the larger and older figures at Westminster are unquestionably superior to the details of later date. There is, of course, great difficulty in fixing the precise date of these scraps of painting: one of the few about which there is absolute certainty is the canopy of the tomb of Anne, Richard's queen, erected shortly after her death, and the date is valuable because a trustworthy archæologist, who had seen the now destroyed frescoes in St. Stephen's Chapel, declared that these were by the same hand. The receipt for £20 to Master Peter Sacrist for painting this canopy, dated 19 Richard II. (1396), is extant, but its terms

[1 The designer of the famous gates at Florence.]

suggest that it was a payment for work generally, and that he was the middleman, in the transaction, so that, although the date is fixed, we have no clue either to the name, the nationality, or the position of the artist.

The use of raised surfaces, the insertion of imitation jewels, and actual gilding or silvering in various metals, were certainly

FRESCOES AT CHALGROVE CHURCH, OXON.

practised in England, and a certain kind of work, though An English probably it belonged rather to the embroiderer's than the Art. painter's art, was at that date essentially national. This was the manufacture of transparent paintings on cloth for church banners and similar purposes. It was a water-colour process, and we have conclusive evidence that it was employed on a scale sufficient to attract the attention of foreign students. An

Italian artist working in Bologna, in 1410, mentions copies, made by his order, of recipes lent to him by a resident of Pavia, one Theodoric of Flanders, "who had obtained them in London from the artists who worked in them there." Special mention is made in this curious passage of historical figures and other subjects; but as to their artistic qualities the MS. is silent. How far there was anything like a school of English art, in the time which corresponds with the Transitional and early Perpendicular architecture, has never been worked out; but probably we may safely accept the late Sir Charles Eastlake's verdict, which was, that, as far as the mere materials and technical processes are concerned, the practice of the English painters closely resembled that of the followers of Giotto. Unfortunately England had no Giotto.

H. E. D. BLAK-ISTON. The Universities.

Lincoln and All Souls' Colleges.

WYKEHAM'S magnificence probably combined with other causes to daunt for a time intending patrons of learning, and it was not till nearly half a century later that Bishop Flemming of Lincoln, a Wycliffite turned ultra-orthodox, commenced the "College of the Blessed Virgin Mary and All Saints of Lincoln in Oxford" (Lincoln College), and this was quite immature till its refoundation in 1479 by his successor, a Cambridge man, Thomas Rotheram, Lord Chancellor 1474, and subsequently Archbishop of York. His idea was unique: he contemplated a collegiate church of theologians who were to strengthen the resistance of the University to heresies, presumably Wycliffism in particular. In 1437, Chichele built St. Bernard's College on the site now occupied by St. John's College, Oxford, as a small house for Cistercian student monks, and in 1438 a "College of the Souls of All Faithful Departed at Oxford" (All Souls) for a warden and forty fellows or scholars studying arts and philosophy or theology (twenty-four), and law canon or civil (sixteen). The statutes follow those of Wykeham, though Chichele's special purpose of providing for the destitution of the clergy, and the peace of the souls of those slain in the French wars (which he had encouraged), renders the scope of his foundation more limited. At Cambridge a London parson, William Bingham, founded God's House (now merged in Christ's College), a very small institution for grammar students; while a few years later Henry VI. rivalled Wykeham by his two equally magnificent colleges of Eton and St. Nicholas (King's), though at first he had thought only of a school at Eton with a small house at Cambridge. The statutes, dated 1443, show that the young king intentionally established his school and college upon the ideal of the great bishop; and eminent as Eton has been since, it must be acknowledged that it was not in any way an original conception. Queen's College was founded soon afterwards under the patronage first of Margaret of Anjou, and then of Elizabeth Wydeville, but it was a very small affair; St. Catherine's Hall (1475), even smaller, was the last foundation at Cambridge before the series of transformations which occurred in the Reformation period. At Oxford, Bishop Waynflete, some time headmaster successively of Winchester and Eton, founded St. Mary Magdalen College out of an old almshouse, the Hospital of St. John Baptist, on the same lines as New College, but with more

King's College, Cambridge.

Queen's College, Oxford.

Magdalen College, Oxford.

ARCHBISHOP CHICHELE.
(From a portrait in glass at Lambeth Palace Library.)

stress laid on the study of theology, and with the first clearly defined division into senior and junior[1] members of the foundation, with different studies and privileges.

When Wykeham procured estates for his colleges by purchase on easy terms from monastic bodies, it was the first symptom of a growing discontent with the monastic system which found definite expression when another Bishop of

[1 The latter called demies (pron. dĕmȳs: from Latin *dimidium*, half), as being only entitled to half the Fellows' allowances.]

Winchester, Richard Fox, was persuaded by Bishop Oldham, of Exeter, to found Corpus Christi College, Oxford, rather than "provide livelihoods for a companie of bussing monks." Accordingly the ample revenues of All Souls', Magdalen, and King's Colleges were provided by the suppression of Alien Priories—that is, cells established as dependencies of the great French monasteries at a time when the kings of England were also dukes of Normandy. During the long wars with France, it was out of the question that English rents should be sent abroad; they were sequestrated under Edward III., and the total confiscation of 122 such cells, enacted in 1402, was completed in 1414. Chichele bought various lands from the Crown at a reduced price, and Henry VI. lavished on his noble foundations, though not the entire revenues which it is said his father had designed for one large college at Oxford, yet many broad acres wrested from the abbeys of Bec and Caen, from St. Peter de Conches and St. Nicholas d'Angers.

Decline of the Universities. In spite, however, of all these splendid endowments for arts, theology, and law, the decay of the Universities and of learning generally in England proceeded rapidly from the date of the Black Death till the introduction of classical studies under the early Tudors. This retrogression may be traced to various causes. In the first place the value of the older endowments had greatly decreased with the drop in the profits of agriculture. Durham College, for instance, provided with ample funds in 1389, was in great straits fifty years later. This deficiency was only partly made up by the new foundations. Secondly, the scholastic philosophy and theology had worn itself out, and there was as yet nothing to take its place. In consequence, the absorbing attention which was paid to the professional and lucrative studies of the civil and canon law was unchecked; and though Holcot and De Bury might speak scathingly of the civilians as Hagars, or enemies of God, there was no competing with a pursuit which not only gratified minds trained in scholastic subtleties, but also provided a royal road to the highest posts in administration or diplomacy. Thirdly, the various Statutes of Provisors, especially that of 1390, which were directed against the encroachments of the Popes on the rights of the holders of Church patronage, were found to discourage the pursuit of theological learning, at least in the

Universities.　No doubt the appointment of mere foreigners to
the more valuable benefices was a serious wrong to Church and
State ; but it was felt to be quite as serious an evil when the
claims of real students, which had been recognised by the
Popes, were postponed to those of the uneducated relations of
the patrons.　In 1417 and 1438 Convocation tried to make a
degree a necessary qualification for a large proportion of livings,
and exemptions from the penalties of Præmunire were obtained
by the Universities from time to time.　This agitation is
perhaps the only attempt ever made in England to secure that
the "open career" provided to any poor but able youth should
be made of value by the requirement for certain public posts of
the certificate of the University education, to acquire which the
gains of an ordinary profession have to be abandoned.

The Universities naturally became deeply involved in the The Uni-
two most difficult controversies of the time, and this also pro-　versities
and the
duced listlessness in matters more purely intellectual.　The Papacy.
first of these disputes was about the Papal Schism, which also
seriously damaged the cause of order generally.　Paris, which
was then regaining its activity, took the lead in the negotiations
for restoring the unity of the Latin Church.　Oxford was soon
pledged to the Italian against the French claimant; but her
main contention was a consistent demand for a General Council
to end the scandal.　At Pisa an Oxonian graduate, a friar from
Crete, was made Pope as Alexander V., while at the Council of
Constance, a former chancellor of Oxford, Bishop Halam of
Salisbury, was one of the most active prelates present.　Both
Oxford and Cambridge displayed decidedly ultramontane tendencies during this period.　Oxford resisted the visitation of
Archbishop Arundel in 1411 to the verge of a serious conflict
with the Crown, only arrested by the mediation of Prince Hal.
In 1430 Arundel's attempt to visit Cambridge ended in the
"Barnwell Process," after which the rights of the University
were asserted by Martin V.　The chief advocate of this ultra-
montanism was the eccentric Bishop of Chichester, Reginald
Pecock, formerly a Fellow of Oriel College, whose objection to
authority in intellectual matters eventually led him into the
heresies which brought about his downfall and the repression of
his doctrines.

Still more distracting was the ferment produced by the

DUKE HUMPHREY.
(Oriel College, Oxford.)

teaching of Wycliffe, which was a sort of medieval "Oxford movement." It is sufficient here to point out with regard to Lollardism that at Oxford the disputes and councils it involved would have wrecked studies more secure than those of the later Schoolmen. Wycliffe's itinerant preachers were mainly Oxford masters of the less learned class, though his opinions were kept out of the Oxford schools, and the efforts of his supporters, Dr. Nicholas Hereford and Dr. Philip Repyngdon (afterwards Bishop of Lincoln, a Cardinal, and a persecutor), were so popular at Oxford that they were only silenced by the most high-handed measures of Archbishop Courtenay. The University was long embittered against the monks and friars, especially the Carmelites, to whose officiousness it ascribed the interference with its privileges; and Oxford continued to be the headquarters of the reforming movement till after the provincial council held there by Archbishop Arundel in 1407 (p. 400).

The final stroke was put to the old learning by the Wars of the Roses. Discipline was relaxed, the higher degrees were hardly ever taken, and the University of Oxford showed its weakness by the way in which it trimmed between Lancaster and York, with a Nevill and a Wydeville succeeding one another as chancellors. English learning suffered much from its isolation from the Continent, though Poggio Bracciolini and some few eminent scholars came over early in the fifteenth century.

It must not, however, be overlooked that during this period the Universities were accumulating, not only endowments destined to increase in the remote future, with beautiful

PAGE FROM MS. PRESENTED BY BISHOP GREY.
(*Balliol College, Oxford.*)

buildings, but also the tools by which the new learning might
in time be operative in English education.   Many distinguished
Englishmen visited Italy, and heard of the new lights there.
They collected books, and in many cases disposed of their
collections nobly and wisely.   Duke Humphrey of Gloucester,
at the suggestion probably of his physician, Gilbert Kymer, a
chancellor of Oxford, presented to the old University library
from 1439 to 1443 so great a number of valuable MSS., that
at last, with the help of Thomas Kemp, Bishop of London, a
new library was erected over the superb Divinity School.
Though the books were carried off at the Reformation, this
part of the Bodleian still retains the name of Duke Humphrey.
He was not only the patron of Occleve, Capgrave, Lydgate,
and all that was in the least valuable in the English literature
of the day, but also a man who saw that the classics were
coming to the front.   The great scholar Lionardo Aretino was
among his friends ; and the books which he gave to Oxford
include beside philosophy, medicine, astronomy, and history
(there is very little theology), specimens of pure literature
such as the works of Ovid, Cicero, Seneca, Quintilian, and even
Dante, Petrarch, and Boccaccio.

The learned and butcherly[1] John Tiptoft, Earl of Worcester,
gave a valuable collection of MSS. ; and another patron of
learning, like Tiptoft a pupil of Guarino at Ferrara, was
William Grey, Chancellor of Oxford 1440–42, and Bishop of
Ely 1454.   In his prolonged studies, under the Humanists in
Italy, he had acquired 200 MSS., which he left to his old
college, Balliol, where 152 of them are still preserved.   The
Cambridge University Library seems to have taken form about
the same date, and Archbishop Rotheram was a liberal benefactor about 1475 ; but at Cambridge there are hardly any traces
of classical literature.   Such literature was to be found in
England ; for the monks of Durham in 1416 had copies of
various works of Virgil, Ovid, Terence, Claudian, Juvenal, Lucan,
and Horace, as well as the more ornate and popular Statius ;
but it was some time before the diffusion of taste, together with
the re-introduction of Greek, produced the English Renaissance,
the interest of which centres mainly in Oxford.

[1] Like an Italian of the Renaissance : cf. W. Hunt's life of him in the
Dictionary of National Biography.]

UNTIL the middle of the nineteenth century, the most learned W. S. ROCKSTRO. Music in Medieval England. and painstaking art-historians in Europe were entirely mistaken in their chronological theories concerning the famous Schools of regular musical composition, founded in England and on the Continent during the Middle Ages. They were unanimous in the belief that the so-called *First Flemish School*, which flourished so brilliantly under the leadership of Gulielmus Dufay in the latter half of the fifteenth century, was the earliest that had ever existed. We know now that this theory was as false as it was baseless. The researches of Mr. William Chappell, supplemented by those of Mons. de Coussemaker, conclusively proved that two distinct and highly developed Schools of Composition existed in England a hundred and fifty years, at least, before the art was systematically taught by Gulielmus Dufay in the Low Countries.

The *First English School*—really the earliest[1] of which any "Sumer is icumen in." trace has ever been discovered—was founded in the third decade of the thirteenth century by John of Fornsete, a monk attached to the famous monastery at Reading, in Berkshire. Its records have been transmitted to us in a volume written by the founder himself, in the year 1226, and now preserved, under the name of the Reading MS., in the British Museum. This priceless codex contains, among other treasures, the earliest secular composition in parts which has hitherto been discovered—a Canon, or Round, for six voices, now known as the Reading Rota; as melodious as an Italian *Fa la* of the best period, and, considering the date at which it was written, wonderfully free from contrapuntal defects. The poem to which the music is adapted is a " Song of Spring," written in a northern dialect, and graphically describing the sights and sounds of a bright May morning, with its fragrant blossoms, its pastoral beauties, and its rich chorus of the voices of Nature, dominated throughout by the song of the cuckoo. And so genial is the treatment of the subject that the Rota, though composed so long ago, can still be sung with effect, and listened to with pleasure.

In addition to this most interesting relic, the volume contains

[1 Since this was written attention has been called to the existence of an English song written, with the music, in a Latin Psalter of about 1200, in the Bodleian library (MS. 14755 in Madan's Catalogue).]

four Latin Motets, for three or four voices, also in John of Fornsete's handwriting, together with some quaint poetry and other literary fragments which throw much valuable light upon its chronology.

An Early English Hymn. Another volume, written a few years later, though certainly not later than the middle of the thirteenth century, and unquestionably belonging to the same early School, contains three more Motets of similar character, and a beautiful English Hymn—*Quen of euene, for* y^e *blisse* (Queen of Heaven, for the bliss). This volume, which is also preserved in the British Museum, and which, in another work,[1] the present writer designated as the *Chaucer MS.*—in allusion to a copy it contains of the *Angelus ad Virginem* mentioned in the Miller's Tale—furnishes, in conjunction with the still more valuable Reading MS., the only record believed to be now in existence of the First English School. But the information conveyed through the medium of these few short and beautifully written pages is priceless.

John of Dunstable. The *Second English School* was founded during the second decade of the fifteenth century by John of Dunstable; the date of whose birth is uncertain, though he is known to have been buried in the old Church of St. Stephen, Walbrook, in 1453. Until within the last few years two unimportant fragments only of his compositions were known to be in existence; but some important works have lately been discovered in the Vatican Library, and in a very valuable MS. volume formerly known as the *Piacenza Codex*, but now the property of the Liceo Filarmonico, at Bologna. The patient researches of Mr. William Barclay Squire have lately brought to light a still larger collection preserved in the library at Modena.

The Cambridge Roll. In addition to these interesting compositions, written in a very advanced style for the period, the library of Trinity College, Cambridge, possesses a MS., now known as the *Cambridge Roll*, which may fairly be considered as the most valuable record of the Second English School hitherto discovered.[2] This contains twelve Carols and an interesting MS. National

---

[1] Rockstro, "General History of Music."

[2] A complete edition, edited by J. A. Fuller Maitland and W. S. Rockstro, is published, entitled "English Carols of the Fifteenth Century."

A SONG OF SPRING, BY JOHN OF FORNSETE (MS. HARL. 978).

Song, inscribed on a roll of parchment seven inches wide and six feet seven inches long, on one side of which the music is written in triangular black notes on a stave of five red lines, while the other side is occupied by an ecclesiastical treatise unconnected with the subject. The Carols are written in English poetry, accompanied, in most cases, with a Latin refrain. The National Song is a poem celebrating the Battle of Agincourt, fought in 1415, and is entitled *Our Kyng went forth to Normundy*, each verse being preceded by the refrain—

Deo gracias anglia
Redde pro victoria.

The actual authorship of these compositions is unknown, but their style so nearly resembles that of John of Dunstable himself, that it is by no means improbable that we are indebted to him for the entire series.

The First Doctors of Music. Of the *Third English School* no certain record remains, its archives having, in all probability, been destroyed during the ravages which accompanied the Wars of the Roses. All that we know of it is that its founders, John Hamboys, Thomas Saintwix, and Henry Habengton, were the first composers who took academical degrees in music.

The *Fourth English School* was founded by Robert Fayrfax, Mus. Doc., who took his degree in 1511, and has left numerous works, most of which are preserved in the *Fayrfax MS.* at the music school in Oxford, together with compositions by Syr John Phelyppes, William of Newark, and other masters of the same period.

ROBERT STEELE. Magic and Alchemy. DURING the fourteenth century, cases of sorcery came to the front in sufficient numbers to prove popular belief in it, but not to show an exaggerated dread. Chroniclers still speak of demoniacal agreements, with, perhaps, a note of incredulity, and Chaucer tells us with a smile that the fairies that used to haunt each grove are gone—banished, no doubt, by the good friars who wander over the land. The cases of sorcery we meet with are dealt with by the archdeacon, or by the King's Court; thus, a man found with a book of magic and a dead man's head in his wallet was released for lack of evidence, though the book and head were burnt. In the fifteenth century

THE SONG OF AGINCOURT.
(*Trinity College, Cambridge.*)

77

the crime of sorcery became important in its political bearings—
the ease with which the charge could be made, the little
evidence necessary to support it, and the difficulty of proving
a negative, made it a convenient engine for hampering or
removing an opponent. Consulting a diviner as to the king's
death came perilously near compassing and devising it, and
the ancient connection between witch and poisoner (the same
word is used for both in the classical languages) was neither
forgotten nor non-existent. The diviner who uttered the
prophecy could find the means for its fulfilment. The change
of popular feeling towards the crime, the growth of fear and
horror, is shown by the Lollard tracts, the Bishops' Visitation
inquiries, the Sorbonne Articles of 1398, and such documents
as the Commission to the Bishop of Lincoln in 1406.

Sorcery in
Politics.

It was probably on some charge of consulting a diviner
that Joan, the Queen Dowager, was imprisoned in 1419; but
the case which first struck men's minds was that which led
to the murder of James I. of Scotland (1437) by Walter, Earl of
Athole, who had been told by his magician that his destiny
was to wear a crown. The unfortunate issue of this prophecy
only increased public alarm when, as Henry VI. was approaching
manhood, it was told that the wife of the Protector, Eleanor
Cobham, Duchess of Gloucester, had been consulting the fiend
as to the life of the king and her own destiny, and had roasted
a wax image of Henry slowly before a fire to waste away
his frame with that of his likeness. A witch, Margaret
Jourdain (who had been brought ten years previously before
the Council, but had then escaped for want of evidence), from
whom she had obtained the charms by which she captivated
the debauchee Protector, had furnished her with the king's
image, and had introduced a certain Master Roger, a magician,
to her. Roger had obtained the services of Southwell, a canon
of St. Stephen's, Westminster, to bless his preparations for
raising the fiend, and, through his servants Gloucester's enemies
obtained their information. Stow tells us of the public ex-
posure of Roger Bolinbroke in his curious garments, sword
and sceptre in hand, standing beside his painted chair, with
copper figures at each corner. The result is well known;
Gloucester fell, his duchess did public penance, the magician
was executed, and the witch burned as a heretic. Another

execution for sorcery—discreditable alike to the English, the French Clergy, and the University of Paris—was the burning of the Maid of Orleans, whose sorcery chiefly consisted in wearing a branch of " mandragoras " and in believing in a " fairy " well.

A more purely political case was the charge against the Duchess of Bedford, investigated at her own request in 1470.

CONSULTING A WITCH (MS. Roy. 17 F. ii.).

One Thomas Wake, a squire, produced a leaden image of a man-at-arms, broken in the middle, and bound together with wire, which had been left at a country parsonage by a troop of soldiers, and said that by this the Duchess had charmed the king to wed her daughter Elizabeth Woodville. The council cleared her of the charge; but it was revived in 1483, and formed one of the grounds for deposing Edward V. Another case, happening in 1477, shows the way in which a charge of witchcraft was utilised by the great. A certain Thomas Burdet, son of Henry VI.'s Grand Butler of Normandy, was annoyed that, in one of his progresses, Edward IV. had shot a favourite deer, and, it is said, wished that the head, horns and all, were in the man who had killed it. For this he was brought to trial, condemned for poisoning, sorcery and enchantment, and executed at Tyburn.

Conjura-tion.

It is interesting to notice that neither Stow nor Shakespeare mentions the wax image of Henry VI. ; probably both believed it too serious a matter to speak of, much as elementary chemical manuals do not describe the manufacture of explosive compounds. Some curious processes for making these images remain. In a treatise under the name of Artephius, a process is described where a hollow cross is made for the reception of a spirit, and under it an image corresponding to the object required, *e.g.* a chair, if pre-eminence is sought. The reason for the cross is that, since the shape of the spirit is unknown, a cross possessing length and breadth is a most suitable and universal substitute for the proper form. We can form a picture of the conjurations of such a "clerk" as Master Roger. His stock-in-trade consisted of a book of magic, pentacles[1] on cover, each opening containing on the left an image of a spirit in its accustomed form, on the right the magical characters representing it, the invocation by which it must be called, the place, time, and incense to use. This book is consecrated by being buried with fitting ceremonies three days, at a spot where three roads meet. Some days before the incantation the seer prepares himself for the ceremony by hearing mass, his instruments being, if possible, laid on the altar ; a

RAISING A GHOST (MS. Harl. 1766).

[1 A mathematical figure used in incantations ; apparently a five-pointed star.]

suitable spot is chosen, and at the planetary hour the ceremony begins. Clothed in priestly garments, his companions dressed in white linen and chanting litanies and gospels, a circle is traced, the divine names are inscribed in it, and those of the angels of the day who guard and assist in the ceremony. Pentacles are traced round the circle, and the characters of the evil spirits to be summoned, then the circle, the fire, and the incense are blessed in order, and the angels of the four winds and the seven planets

A MAGICIAN IN HIS CIRCLE (MS. Tib. A. vii.).

are invoked, while all the while the assistants keep up their chant. Then the magician stands up and summons the spirit he requires, and all the air round the circle swarms with frightful visions, but not yet does the spirit appear. He calls stronger and louder, and, showing the pentacle, orders it to appear. At last it comes under its own form, answers the questions, and obeys the orders. The magician bids it depart in peace, the incense is extinguished, and, re-forming the procession, the company retire, chanting a litany as they go. Opinions differed as to the spiritual status of the seer and his companions: most theologians held that they entered into an implied contract with the Fiend, the popular view more than suspected the·existence of a direct one, while the magician represented himself as taking the advantage of his knowledge of certain powers which the Church possessed but did not use, running very definite risks if he was unskilful or negligent. Legally, it appears that the crime of sorcery was punishable at common law if injury was caused in any way; or, if the case was brought before the ecclesiastical courts, the sorcerer was burnt by virtue of a writ " de hæretico comburendo." Probably, the majority of the burnings for heresy from 1440 onward were for witchcraft.

Alchemy.   A MS. list of alchemists gives the names of a score of English writers on the subject during the fourteenth century and towards the close of it much attention was paid to the science. Gower and Chaucer picture for us the theory and practice of alchemy respectively; indeed, it was probably owing to Gower's influence that Chaucer was led to engage in the study. The current theory still was that metallic substances consist of a mercury or fusible principle, and a' sulphur or hardening one, and as these were pure or otherwise, so the qualities of the metal varied. Accordingly, alchemists sought a drug to purge metals of their impurities, and make them perfect. Gower tells us of three stones of this nature—one which acts on the body, a second on the senses and intellect, and a third on minerals, driving out the rust, the odour, and the hardness. Chaucer gives us the alchemist at work, with a minute accuracy of detail which shows his personal interest in the result, and with only the portions of theory which would be caught up by the practical man. He shows us the charlatan cheating his victim by sleight of hand or false bottoms to his crucible, and the genuine worker, using actual mercury and sulphur, with many substances, mineral, animal, or vegetable ; every now and then losing their material by an explosion of their tightly sealed vessels, or by their borax and lime forming a flux and dissolving their earthen crucible. But charlatan or worker alike brought ruin to all who believed them, and we may fairly trace the Statute of 1403, forbidding the multiplication of gold and silver, to the Canon's Yeoman's Tale, and the state of things therein described.

Two generations passed, and no more was heard of alchemy till Duke Humphrey found his finances exhausted, and set the alchemists to work again. The works of Lully were translated from Provençal into Latin in 1443, and many persons sought the king's leave to engage in the study, some of the licences being of exceptional interest. Soon the royal exchequer became

Alchemy and Finance.

ALCHEMISTS AT WORK (MS. Add. 10,302).

low, and as alchemists were not wanting to point out "useful methods by which coin of gold and silver may be multiplied in our Kingdom of England," Henry VI. issued, in 1456–7, three Commissions to examine and report on the schemes submitted to them. The second thus describes the Elixir: "By it all infirmities may be cured, human life prolonged to its utmost limit, and mankind preserved in health and strength of body and mind, clearness, and vigour; all wounds are healed by it without difficulty, and it is the best and surest remedy against poisons; with it, too, many other benefits to us and the community of our realm may be wrought, such as the transmutation of metals into actual gold and the purest silver." The effect of these commissions seems to have been to lessen Henry's hopes from alchemy, and the pursuit gradually dropped on the accession of Edward IV. (perhaps from the dearth of great patrons), though licences continue to be granted up to 1477.

The Dangers of the Alchemists.   We get much information as to the popular alchemy from some little-known poems of the time. Ripley (who, tradition asserts, sent gold to Rhodes to fight the Turks), in his "Compound of Alchemy" (1471), dedicated to Edward IV.. gives an account of the fraternity of London Alchemists. They harboured, it seems, in Westminster (the Archdeacon being easily satisfied there), and came to London to seek their dupes, who followed them up and down, hoping by their means to come to great riches. The goldsmiths and merchants who have lent them money would, however, be glad to get back even a part of it ; so they are arrested and led off to Newgate or Ludgate, where they are questioned. Their ready excuses win on the merchants, and they are released and depart to Westminster.

> "And when they there sit at the wine,
>   'These monks (say they) have many a pound.'
> 'Would God (saith one) that some were mine,
>   Heigho, care away, let the cup go round.'
> 'Drink on (saith another), the means are found:
>   I am a Master of that Art,
>   I warrant us we shall have part.'"

And Ripley ironically advises the abbot to cherish men who will soon restore the poverty of St. Benedict.

Thomas Norton (1477) tells us how all classes, even weavers and tinkers, had joined in the search for riches, and the land was brought to poverty. In one chapter he tells of the dangers of an alchemist, and illustrates them from the life of a contemporary, Thomas Dalton, a monk of Gloucester, formerly clerk to Sir John Delvis, whose son was at the court of Edward. On Delvis' information, the king sent for Dalton by Thomas Herbert, who arrested him, and, after some rough handling, brought him to court. Here Dalton admitted having made gold for Delvis, but refused to attempt it again, saying that he had destroyed all his material, and Edward dismissed him with a small gratuity. On his way from court, however, Herbert seized on the unlucky alchemist, and endeavoured by promises and threats to make him engage in the work, imprisoning him for three years in Gloucester Castle, and even bringing him out for execution; threats and promises alike in vain. But Norton believed in the art, and laments how this violence had lost great ease to the country:

> " To have ceased taxes and tallages of this loude;
> Whereby much love and grace would have be,
> Between knighthood, priesthood, and commonalty."

Probably the only practical result of the study of alchemy in this period is seen in the great number of distilled waters, essences, spirits, etc., the preparation of which was the work of the ladies of Tudor days. Most of them were known centuries before, but were popularised by this wide extension of alchemy. An example of this occurs later, when it is thought a legitimate excuse if an alchemist, who may be a small yeoman, to hide his real object, tells his still-maker that he is about to make an eye-water for his father.

THE supremacy of Chaucer is in nothing more clearly seen than in the fact that for more than a century after his death he was the sole source of inspiration for the poets. In Scotland this was not inconsistent with a measure of originality; in England it was. A time of religious persecution and foreign war, followed by internecine feud, is not favourable to the continuation of such an open-minded, sympathetic, and humorous conception of life as that seen in the "Canterbury Tales." It was Chaucer the student of the "Roman de la Rose," not Chaucer the poet of his fellow-men, nor even Chaucer the student of Italian literature, after whom the younger versifiers stumbled.

H. FRANK HEATH. Literature.

Of these, Thomas Occleve (b. 1369, d. *c.* 1450) stood near to Chaucer personally, and his verse recalls more often than any other his master's lighter manner. His character and

Occleve.

life remind one of Robert Greene. He had the same love of pleasure, the same weakness of purpose, the same fatal ease of expression, the same high ideal of womanhood. All that we know of his life is to be found in his " Male Regle,"[1] his "Complaint," and his "Dialog" with the old beggar in the prologue to his " Governail of Princes" (1411 or 1412), his longest and most ambitious work. Written with the aim of winning the patronage of the young Prince Henry, this " Mirror

OCCLEVE AND HIS ROYAL PATRON (MS. Roy. 17 D. vi.).

for Princes" was chiefly based on Ægidius Colonna's " De Regimine Principum," composed for Philip the Fair. The various aspects of a prince's duty, with illustrative examples from the Bible, classics, Church fathers, and English history, are dealt with in " rhyme royal," a measure ill-suited for such a theme. In the prologue occurs the touching passage in which, addressing Chaucer as " maistere deere and fadir reuerent," Occleve laments that his "deth hath harme irreparable unto us doon," adding, with only too much truth :

[1 So called as containing the account of his ill-regulated life.]

"She mighte hau taryed her rengeance a while
Til that some man had egal to the be.
Nay lat be that! sche knew wel that this yle
May never man forth brynge lyk to the."

Occleve also told with success two stories from the "Gesta Romanorum," the "Tale of Jerislaus' Wife," and the "Tale of Jonathas," both in Chaucer stanza. His many balades are neither lyrical in tone nor correct in form. His best work is undoubtedly to be found in those passages where his reverence for women is heightened and refined by the religious emotion. Consequently, his finest poem is the "Modir of God," which, on the authority of an Edinburgh MS., was long thought to be Chaucer's. The close of the "Letter to Cupid" in the same metre (rhyme royal) is dominated by the same spirit. Had Occleve only possessed more sense of proportion, been content to restrain the expression of his remorse, and been gifted with a finer instinct in the choice of his measures, much of his work would rank higher than it does.

John Lydgate (*c.* 1372—*c.* 1451) was a man of greater **Lydgate.** robustness and with more real insight and a greater sense of humour than Occleve. He had in him the making of a really effective fabliau writer—*e.g.* "The Chorle and the Bird"—and light satirist, but he was a monk of Bury—a profession ill-consistent with the themes most sympathetic to him—and he had an overpowering admiration for Chaucer, which was his ruin as a poet. The first half of his life was spent in the attempt to bring his rule of conduct and that of the monastery into some accord. This was no easy matter, for his youth, as his "Testament" shows, was as wild as Occleve's. None the less, he was a most voluminous writer, producing narrative, devotional, hagiological, philosophic, and scientific poems, besides many occasional pieces. He was already past middle life when he began his first important poem. The "Troy Book" (1420), a rendering of Guido delle Colonne's "Historia Trojana," was begun (1412) at Prince Henry's request, and was intended to serve as a completion of the partial view taken in "Troilus and Cryseyde," to supply the pre-Britannic history of our race, omitted by Layamon and his predecessors. The poem is in 30,000 lines of heroic couplets, which run more smoothly than much of his later work. In Lydgate's youth Chaucer had consented to "amende and correcte the wrong

traces" of his " rude penne,"[1] the loss of which help he laments in
the "History of Troy," confessing that he follows "the sentence":—

> " And trouthe of metre I set also a-syde,
> For of that art I had as tho no guyde,
> Me to reduce when I went a-wronge,
> I toke noue hede nouther of shorte nor longe,
> But to the trouthe, and lefte curyosyte
> Both of makynge and of metre be." [2]

Lydgate's Verses.   One soon discovers that he had no appreciation of the strict
limits Chaucer had set himself in grafting the Romance prin-

THE PILGRIM TESTED : FROM A POEM BY LYDGATE (MS. Tib. A. vii.).

ciples of metre upon the native strongly rhythmical stock.
Lydgate allowed himself the same freedom in the position of the
verse-accent which he found in the work of Machault and Granson : a freedom that Chaucer's interest doubtless held in check in
his first attempts ; and he made no effort to vary the position of
the cæsura, which with him always follows the second foot. The
explanation of much that is rough in his verse is due rather to
an ignorant imitation of Romance principles than to a lack of
ear. His most important work, " The Story of Thebes (*c.* 1422),
suggested by the " Knight's Tale," and designed to form one of

[1] "Life of Our Lady," fol. E₇, *b.*
[2] "History of Troy," Pynson, 1513, fol. E₅, *b.*

the " Canterbury " series, was in the same heroic couplet, whilst
his most popular but dullest poem, the " Falls of Princes,"
written for Humphrey, Duke of Gloucèster, between 1430 and
1438, is a rendering in " rhyme royal " of a French translation of
Boccaccio's " De Casibus Virorum Illustrium." The theme was
sympathetic to a people which saw three of their kings within a
century come to a tragic end. The source of inspiration was
again Chaucer (" The Monke's Tale "), and the subject did not
lose its popularity till the issue of the last edition of the " Mirror

LYDGATE (MS. Harl. 1766).

for Magistrates," in 1620. Lydgate also wrote the " Complaint
of the Black Knight," and in his younger days (*c.* 1403) the
" Temple of Glas," an allegorical poem, formerly attributed to
Hawes. In his later calmer years he versified to order the lives
of SS. Alban, Edmund, and Margaret. There was nothing that
came amiss to his easy, somewhat slipshod muse. To modern
taste, Lydgate's occasional pieces on social subjects, such as his
" Satirical Description of his Lady " or his " Ballade on the
Extravagant Head-dresses of the Day," will always prove most
attractive, and cause regret that he wasted his energies on any-

thing more ambitious.[1] When, in the next century, one comes
to the endless and moralising allegory of the "Pastime of
Pleasure" (c. 1506) shambling along on the utterly weak-kneed
line of Hawes, one feels that the revolt of Wyatt and Surrey
came none too soon.

Prose:
Pecock. A few words must suffice for the prose of this period. In
Reginald Pecock's "Repressour of overmuch Blaming the
Clergy" (written 1449), we have an acute and ingenious
attack on the Lollard position, written in the pedantic style
of a purist who rejected, as Ascham did in the next century,
the riches of the Romance vocabulary which Chaucer and
Wycliffe had placed at his disposal. The only master, because
Malory. the first artist of prose, was Sir Thomas Malory, whose version
of a number of French Arthurian romances, called the "Morte
d'Arthur," was finished in 1469-70. His style was peculiarly
his own. It has been well said that Malory's work marks a
similar stage in the development of English prose to that
of Chaucer in English verse. Both had personally to beat
into form, or at least to temper and give polish to, the instrument of their thought; and this preliminary service should
never be forgotten in our estimate of them. Such writers as
Malory and Herodotus, says Prof. Paton Ker, "though they
have preserved many of the beauties of the uncritical childhood of literature, . . . are both of them sophisticated; it
is their craft or their good genius that makes one overlook
the critical and testing processes, the conscious rhetoric,
without which they could not have written as they did."[2]

Fortescue. Another writer, one who used prose as a means of argument
rather than with the love of the artist, was Sir John Fortescue
(1394—c. 1476), whose best known work, "The Governance of
England" (written after 1471), reproduces in brief the arguments of his Latin "De Laudibus Legum Angliæ" as introduction
to a study of the causes underlying the evils then affecting the
State. He sees the chief cause in the poverty of the Crown:
an ill Henry VII. later took care to remove. Fortescue's style

---

[1] A full bibliography of Lydgate's works (he wrote in all over 130,000
lines) will be found in Mr. Sidney Lee's excellent article on Lydgate in the
Dictionary of National Biography. "London Lickpenny," in its present form
at any rate, is not his.

[2] Introduction to Craik's "English Prose Selections." Vol. I., 1893.

is clear and sometimes rhetorical, though his thoughts are not always systematically arranged.

At the close of the century, on the border-line between **Caxton.** medieval and modern times, himself an active worker in the spread of knowledge, stands William Caxton, printer, translator, and editor. His most important work, the foundation of the first English press, will be dealt with in the next chapter, but his services as translator and editor, and in making certain the final triumph of the London dialect as Chaucer had shaped it, are no less real, though perhaps less evident. He saw clearly how "before that (Chaucer) by his labour embellished, ornated, and made fair our English, in this realm was had rude speech and incongruous, as yet appeareth by old books"; and he determined to issue no book from his press unless in the dialect of the capital. Thus, he would not print Trevisa's west-country translation of Higden's "Polychronicon" until he had revised it in accordance with his determination. He himself rendered "Le Recueil des Histoires de Troye" and "The Game and Play of Chess," by the Dominican, Jacobus de Cassolls, and nineteen other works, into a free and clear idiomatic English. Yet he was no slavish adherent to the English of Chaucer. His object was, as he said himself,[1] to adopt the average dialect of the educated Londoner in his own day, and we therefore find the Kentish peculiarities of the great poet absent from Caxton's work, and the presence of a larger number of Northern forms.[2] He dealt with the problem he had set himself in a moderate but progressive spirit, and his work is, therefore, next to that of Chaucer, of the highest importance in the history of standard literary English, whilst the aid of the printing-press gave assurance of permanent results for his labour.

WITH the suppression of the Peasants' Revolt and the passing of **W. J.** the Acts of 1389 for ensuring an undiminished supply of villeins, **CORBETT.** we take leave of one of the most abnormal epochs in the history **Rural** of English agriculture, and once more find ourselves in the midst **England.** of a prolonged period of slow evolution, during which there is

[1] In the Prologue to his "Eneydos."
[2] *E.g.*, the third pers. sing. Pres. Ind. in *s*. *Cf.* also *infra*, p. 732.

little that is either exciting or extraordinary to relate. Over the life of the country districts there once more settles down a calm dulness, which for more than a century is unbroken by any epoch-making events, all the changes that can be observed being of the gradual silent kind which only become recognisable when they are completed, and which to contemporaries are almost imperceptible. So rare, in fact, are the notices of agriculture in the chronicles and records of the time, that even to-day, after much research has been expended in collecting them, there are still several schools of interpretation, and historians still hold the most contradictory opinions even as to the general character of the period. On the one hand we are invited to believe that

Character of the Period. the fifteenth century and the first quarter of the sixteenth form the "golden age of the English labourer,"[1] and that "no European community has ever enjoyed such rough plenty as did the English yeoman during these years"[2]; while, on the other hand, there are writers who regard the same period as one of unmitigated disaster, and who confidently assure us that there were few years at this time "unmarked by famine and pestilence."[3] Others, again, though they admit that a good deal of distress and discontent existed at the end of the period, still claim the earlier years as prosperous, and think that of all epochs "the first half of the fifteenth century most nearly realised the peasant's dream of Arcadia."[4] And, lastly, yet a fourth school[5] has arisen, who hold that arable farming almost continuously decayed, but that a growth in the clothing trade and the consequent introduction into rural districts of domestic manufactures, more or less counterbalanced the loss so suffered.

So great a variety of opinions reveals how little is really known, and warns us to show caution in adopting or rejecting any one of them. Nevertheless, there need be little hesitation in regarding both of the more extreme views as exaggerations. For had the lot of the labourer been even moderately prosperous throughout all districts down to Henry VIII.'s reign, it is impossible to suppose that it could suddenly have become

---

[1] Rogers, "Six Centuries of Work and Wages," p. 326.

[2] Hyndman, "Basis of Socialism," c. I.

[3] Denton, "England in the Fifteenth Century," p. 213.

[4] Prothero, "Pioneers and Progress of English Farming," p. 14.

[5] Cunningham, "Growth of Industry and Commerce," I. 393.

so bad as to lead Sir Thomas More, in the sixteenth century, to declare that the state and condition of labouring beasts were much better. On the other hand, had the whole period been one of famines and pestilences, it is hard to see why the same results did not follow as in the fourteenth century, and why the country was not distracted with agitations and revolts. True, the great civil war between the partisans of the White and Red Roses occupied a great many of these years, but the authorities generally agree in seeing in this only a faction fight of the nobles, and in asserting that the bulk of the nation took neither interest nor part in it (p. 426).

Even when Cade rebelled, in 1450, social grievances do not seem to have been the cause (p. 419), and the complaint of the commons of Kent, which was laid before the royal council, contains only political demands, except in so far as it reiterates well-worn denunciations against the Statute of Labourers. Sir John Fortescue, too, writing just about the same time, and wishing to account for the apparent inferiority of the Frenchmen, says of the Englishmen, " the people be wealthy and have all things necessary to their sustenance "; a remark hardly more in keeping with famines than is that of Polydore Vergil with pestilences, when he tells us that " in England disease reigns seldom, and there is less

RUDE COMFORT
(MS. Harl. 2332).

use of physic than in other countries." The critically inclined say that this only shows the fearful state of other countries, but that is really begging the question.

And now let us turn for a moment to the evidence on **Evidence.** which the advocates of either of these extreme views rely. Those who hold that the peasantry were exceedingly prosperous seem to base their views entirely on records of prices that have come down to us. The most praiseworthy energy has been displayed in collecting these, so that historians have now at command a perfect mine of valuable facts. Regarded as evidence of the state of given districts at particular times these are incontrovertible, but it is hard to draw conclusive inferences from them for general purposes. For clearly it is often necessary to eke out the information applying to one period by adding facts from another and then striking an average, a process which often produces very different results according as the limit of time is slightly varied. A good deal, too, has to be assumed in applying the figures. For instance, it has been computed [1] that at the beginning of the fifteenth century an ordinary farm hand with his wife and child earned about £3 15s., while his living only cost about £3 5s. This clearly leaves a fair margin between receipts and expenses, and so it is quoted to show the prosperity of labour generally. The calculation, however, not only omits the case of the labourer with several children, but assumes that work was to be got for 300 days a year, wages then being about threepence a day. This sounds reasonable, but there seems to be no proof of it. On the contrary there are some indications that, even if the labourer was constantly employed, he only earned wages for about five days a week, or two hundred and sixty days a year. For in 1403, under Henry IV., an Act was passed ordaining that no labourer should be retained to work by the week, and that " labourers should not take any hire for the holy days, nor for the evens of feasts, when they did no labour but till the hour of noon, but only for the half day "; that is, the labourer was only to get half a day's wages on Saturdays and saints' days, and on the vigils of saints' days, and these together must have averaged nearly one day a week. As compared with the supposed £3 15s., the wages for two hundred and sixty days would only amount to £3 1s. 8d., or less than the supposed amount of expenditure, which shows that the whole calculation is somewhat arbitrary. The case, too, which we have been considering is that of the labourer constantly employed, but it cannot be doubted that this was rather the exception than the rule, and that in the fifteenth century as at present many men often found themselves out of work, and had the greatest trouble to scrape together a living. Altogether it seems unlikely that as a class the labourers were very much better off than they had been, and certainly the fifteenth century saw no improvement in the direction of shortening the hours of labour. What they were can be seen from an Act passed in 1495, and at no time can they

[1] Gibbins' " Industrial History of England," p. 79.

well have been longer. From the middle of March to the
middle of September work was to go on from 5 a.m. till between
7 and 8 p.m., with half an hour for breakfast, and an hour and a
half for dinner and for the midday sleep. In winter work was
to be during daylight. These legal ordinances were not perhaps

A CALENDAR FOR NOVEMBER (MS. Harl. 2332).

always kept, but they at least show the standard at which
employers aimed.

The evidence, again, by which it is sought to show that
England during all these years was a prey to famine and
pestilence would seem to be equally insufficient, being chiefly
drawn from the records of the towns. Thus it is pointed out

Health in the Country.

that in 1406 the plague was so bad in London that Henry IV.
preferred not to pass through the streets; that in 1483 the
London chronicler was almost in despair over its ravages; that
in 1449 Parliament had to be removed hastily from Westminster
to Winchester for fear of the infection; that in 1476 Hull lost
more than fifteen hundred of its inhabitants, and of the rest so
many fled that the town became desolate; that in 1477 an
"incredible number" of persons died at Norwich, and, finally,
that in London alone, the sweating sickness caused the death of
thirty thousand people on the occasion of its first outbreak.
All these notices of pestilence, however, even supposing there is
no exaggeration in them, are somewhat beside the point if the
object is to show that disease was extraordinarily rife all over
the country; for there is not a word in them about the rural
districts, nor does there seem to be any evidence for supposing
that these were suffering from any unusual amount of mortality.
Occasionally, indeed, the London chronicler talks vaguely of a
great pestilence throughout all England, but in all probability he
only means in all the towns, just as Sir John Paston did when
he assured a correspondent that in 1471 it was the "most
universal death" that ever he knew in all England, for he
hastens to add, "I cannot hear of any borough town in England
that is free from the sickness" (p. 570). Unless, too, there is some
definite evidence that the peasantry were particularly affected,
it is useless to bring forward "the undrained, neglected soil, the
shallow stagnant waters which lay upon the surface of the
ground, the narrow, unhealthy homes, the insufficient food,
and the abundance of stale fish which was eaten,"[1] as pre-
disposing the agricultural population to disease; for all these
conditions existed just as much in the thirteenth century, when
it is admitted that the people were prosperous, as in the
fifteenth. All the descriptions, in fact, given of the fifteenth
century, both by those who believe it to have been a time of
wretchedness and by those who think that it was a golden age,
would seem to be too highly coloured, while without a doubt
they are far too sweeping. For just as in other centuries
there have been endless varieties of fortune, so in the fifteenth
one class may have been going up while another was going
down. · Even members of the same class need not in every

[1] Denton, *op. cit.*, p. 103.

locality have fared alike, and it is quite likely that at the very moment when one great section of the daily labourers and small holders of villein allotments was developing into prosperous tenant farmers, another was rapidly sinking, until at last there grew up that great mass of pauperism which so burdened the country in Tudor times.

The term "golden age," too, provokes yet another objection, for it challenges comparison with all succeeding ages, and implies that even at the present day the labourer is no better off than in the fifteenth century—indeed, is not so well off. This, however, can hardly be, when we take into consideration some of the facts of modern life. For instance, the alarms of war are now absolutely unknown; even riots are unlikely; pestilences are very rare, and famine inconceivable; work, on the whole, is more regular, and the hours of labour are much shortened. Add to this, too, the fact that, though the cost of living has increased tenfold, the rate of wages has at least risen in proportion, and in most localities is now far higher. The goods, too, that a labourer can buy with his wages are probably of better quality nowadays, and certainly far more varied in character. In two points only has the average labourer lost. Besides being landless, he has now no common rights either of wood or pasture with which to supplement his income; and there is a greater gap than in the fifteenth century between himself and most of his employers as regards the amount of material comfort each can respectively command. Neither of these points, however, is of much importance when compared with the substantial improvements that have undoubtedly taken place, and neither would even now be considered a grievance had not an improved education been at work upon the rustic, dispelling his time-honoured ideas as to knowing his place, and opening his eyes as to the possibility of bettering his lot.

The Gain and Loss of the Modern Labourer.

It is to be hoped that enough has now been said to discredit the idea that the state of England at this time can be summed up in any one formula, or that any true picture of the nation can be drawn that will do equally for all classes, and for both the beginning and the end of the period. On the contrary, in dealing with the agricultural classes the evidence to hand is found to be so scanty and contradictory that it is almost

Obscurity of the Problem.

impossible to form an opinion, and the only thing to do seems to be to put as much of it before the reader as possible, and leave him to form his own conclusions if he feels inclined. To begin with, therefore, we will mention some of the facts which seem to prove, though indirectly, that a certain amount of prosperity must have marked most years of the century, even though the lower classes may not always have enjoyed an enviable existence.

One of the most striking of these, and one that any one can still test for himself, is to be found in the activity in building that still went on. For all over the country there

Photo: Spanton, Bury St. Edmunds.
LONG MELFORD CHURCH, SUFFOLK.

are still parish churches to be seen which were built at this time, some of them, as those at Lavenham and Long Melford, in Suffolk, among the finest in the kingdom, while there are a still greater number that were enlarged and added to in the late but more decorative Perpendicular style: all of which shows that there were both wealth to spare and an increasing population.

**The Use
of Bricks.** A fact of a similar kind and telling in the same direction is to be found in the general revival of the use of bricks, the art of making them having been practised only in very rare instances[1] since the departure of the Romans. This revival occurred about

[[1] *See* a paper in *Archæologia Cantiana*, Vol. IX.

[485]

1400, the bricks in the first instance being most probably imported from North Germany by sea for use in the eastern counties. Thus in 1406 we find them being used in Essex, in 1438 at Cambridge, and in 1442 at London. In this last year they

BRICKWORK AT CAISTER CASTLE, NORFOLK.

also began to be manufactured, as we hear of a " breke kylne " being made in April of that 'year to supply bricks for the building of the boys' chambers at Eton, and of 66,000 bricks being ordered to be made there. In fact, between 1442 and 1451 Henry VI. seems to have used up about 2,469,100 bricks about his new foundation; and in 1475 the "Brekmakerrys," who are said to have been London men, had to look about for a new brickfield. Not many relics of this outburst of brick building now remain, but it is natural to connect with it the great improvement in domestic architecture which also took place, and which led to the erection of the first country houses that at all deserve the name, and to the first intro- duction of chimneys into farm-houses. For now a comparatively cheap yet durable material was everywhere to hand, and it was no longer necessary to go to the great expense of getting stone from the distant quarries of Yorkshire or Normandy. Manor houses consequently increased in size, two or three rooms being added to the hall and grange, and sometimes even a second storey. A single bedroom, however, was usually thought sufficient, and not much was done in the way of ceiling or wainscoting; while houses that contained even four beds for the accommodation of their inmates were thought to be very extravagantly furnished. Of the more movable articles of household furniture there were still next to none, and what little there was chiefly appertained to the kitchen. For though men have always appreciated feasting and were now beginning to appreciate good houses, they had still no idea of comfort, and, if any internal magnificence was indulged in, it was in the form of glittering rows of plate and pewter.

Forty Shilling Free- holders.

The constitutional history, also, of this period may be used to show that on the whole the country people were improving. In 1406 the electoral franchise for the counties was declared to reside in all the suitors at the county court; but in 1430 this was repealed (p. 425), and the vote limited to those who had freeholds worth forty shillings yearly above all charges (or about twenty pounds of our present money), the reason being that with the growth of leases there had sprung up a rapidly increasing class of fairly well-to-do people, who, though " of no value " in the eyes of the House that passed the repealing statute, nevertheless "pretended, every one of them, to have a voice equivalent with the more worthy knights and esquires," and threatened in no long space of time to take all power over the elections out of the hands of the " gentlemen born." Facts like these speak with no uncertain sound, but should any clearer evidence be wanted it is to be found in the Statutes of Apparel of 1463 and 1482, which are directed against the farmer and the labourer clothing themselves excessively, and in the successive editions of the Statute of Labourers, in which the rate of wages to be allowed is constantly enhanced. The Act of 1482, it is true, somewhat illogically complains that because of the "non due observance" of former sumptuary laws "the realm had fallen into great misery and poverty, and was like to fall into more greater"; but if this were true, it is not very likely that, in 1495, the Commons would have sanctioned the following statutory wages: for a bailiff 26s. 8d. instead of 24s. 4d.; for a common servant in husbandry whose food was found, 16s. 8d., and 4s. for clothes, instead of 15s. and 3s. 4d.; for other workmen without food, 5d. and 6d. a day in winter and summer respectively, where before they had received 4d. and 5d.

All through the century, too, the Statute Book is encumbered with Acts against the giving of liveries (p. 452) or the maintenance of large troops of retainers. This was forbidden as a political danger, but incidentally it testifies to the luxury and ostentation of the great nobles of the time, and to the wealth which enabled them to gratify their desires. Six hundred liveried servants, for instance, followed the great Earl of Warwick to Parliament, while no fewer than two hundred and ninety formed, in 1449, the retinue of a much less important personage, one Walter Strykeland, deputy-steward of Kendal in Westmoreland. These men, too, were not merely tenants as in former times, but for the most part hired servants, who had to be fed, clothed, armed, and lodged, and who, in many cases, took even wages in addition. The prosperity of the gentlemen who could long maintain such state cannot well be called in question, and cannot have materially deteriorated from that enjoyed in the fourteenth century by the same class, as typified in the person of the Sir John Arundell mentioned in an earlier section of this book (p. 260), who, in 1380, was drowned off the coast of Brittany, and lost "not only his life but all his apparel to his body" to the amount of "two and fifty suits of cloth of gold." The wealth lavished in this way, whether by nobleman, gentleman, or esquire, must nearly in every case, be it remembered, have been derived from the profits of successful agriculture. For the only trade

Livery and Maintenance.

that the landowners of this period could engage in without loss of dignity was the export of agricultural produce, and not very many of them even did this, but lived entirely off their rentals.   The famous Sir John Fastolf (the builder of Caister Castle) and Lord Cromwell, two of the richest men of the fifteenth century, may have added to their great fortunes by war and by shipping barley and malt to the Continent (the estate of the latter after his decease was valued at £66,334), but in most cases the gentleman's farm was his fortune, and there could have been no magnificence without a prosperous tenantry.

Landlord and Tenant.   People who take a gloomy view may prefer to hold that the landowners were enabled to gratify their passion for display, not because their tenants were prosperous but because their rents were excessive.   It would seem, however, that in reality this was rarely the case, and that in the fifteenth century rents were exceedingly low and landlords very lenient.   This may be seen not only from the study of the terms of actual leases that have been preserved, but from the way in which the men of the next century, when the practice of rack-renting un- doubtedly did become usual, lament the olden state of things. Antecedently, too, this is the more likely, for it is obvious from what has already been said of the introduction of stock and land leases, that at their origin it must have been hard for the landlords to find any suitable tenants, that nevertheless there was a constantly increasing number who wished to let, and that consequently they could never impose any onerous terms.   If we want to confirm this reasoning, we have only to turn to the leases granted by some Oxford colleges, and we shall find that, not only was the tenant provided with stock, but that it was also the rule for the landlords to pay for all repairs and for losses of the stock if they occurred through no fault of the tenant and were of a sufficiently serious character to embarrass him materially.   For example, in 1430, New College gave up farming its manor of Alton Barnes, in Wiltshire, on its own account, and let it to a tenant on the stock and land lease principle.   The amount of arable land let is said to have been 108 acres, and this was furnished with stock valued at £74 7s. 3d.   The term taken by the tenant was a short one, but there is evidence that the system in its main out-

lines remained in force for upwards of a century, the lease
being renewed usually to the same tenant every five or ten
years ; for in 1530 the stock is still entered as unrepaid.
During all this time the rent only varied from £14, at the
outset, to £14 10s. in 1484, and £15 10s. with a quarter of
oats in 1530; in other words, if we consider the arable alone,
from 2s. 5d. an acre to a little under 3s. This, however, must
be rather an over-estimate ; for, as in this case the tenant
took the whole demesne, he must also have got the wastes and,
apparently, some of the manorial rights. Further, it was
stipulated that the college should pay for all repairs and for

REAPING (MS. Canon. Liturg. 99).
(*Bodleian Library, Oxford.*)

all losses from murrain if they exceeded ten per cent. Thus,
in 1484, the rent-collector paid the farmer £1 12s. 2d. for
repairs, and charged it to the college. Similarly as to stock,
in 1447, the college pays on twenty-two wethers, that had
died in the previous year, twenty-four ewes and seventeen
hoggs ; in 1448 on ninety-two wethers, fourteen ewes and ten
hoggs ; and, in 1452, on fifteen wethers, twenty-five ewes and
six hoggs. The risks undertaken by the college were, in fact,
by no means slight, and in the long run must have greatly
reduced the burden of the rent upon the tenant, even supposing that it had always been paid. This, however, was by
no means always the case, for we find from the accounts that
the rent collector was almost constantly in arrear.

Alton Barnes has been given as a good typical case, but in the matter of arrears it is, if anything, hardly up to the average, and so for exact figures let us go to the accounts for Takeley, in Essex, another of the estates belonging to New College. Here, according to the account for the year 1475, the total receipts of the college, including both the old commutation fees and the rents of three separate demesne farms, ought to have amounted to £65 12s. 6d. annually. The rent collector, however, cannot often have collected this amount, for in 1474 he was already £220 in arrear, and by 1475 this had increased to over £240. No little portion, in fact, of the estimated rental consisted of irrecoverable claims and hopelessly bad debts; one of the arrears that kept mounting up being a rent that had not been paid for ninety-five years, while another had been due for twenty-two. The misfortunes of the tenants may, of course, account for these being still owing, but if so, it is not likely that they would still have been reckoned in the rolls as debts; for our records contain many instances of remission of rents when there was any real call for it. Facts of this sort show how long-suffering many of the landlords were, and recall the testimony of a writer of a much later date who, in talking of the monasteries and commending them as landowners, says: "They never revenged themselves of any injury, but were content to forgive it freely; they never raised any rents nor took any fines of their tenants. Yea, happy was that person who was tenant to an abbey, for it was a rare thing to hear of any tenant that was removed by taking of his farm over his head, nor was he not afraid of any re-entry for non-payment of rent if necessity drove him there-to." When this was written, in the reign of Edward VI., such landlords had become extinct, but in the fifteenth century it was still the great monastic houses that set the examples to which the rest of the farming community usually conformed.

The Yeoman Class.　　As practical illustrations of how the yeoman might thrive under this treatment, two stories may be given, one from the beginning and the other from the end of the century. The first is to be found among the Paston papers, and sets forth the rise of that noble family from one Clement, a good plain husbandman, who in the days of Richard II. rode his horse bare-backed to the mill, and drove his own cart to market, " as a good

husband ought to do." Whether he was actually a villein or a
small freeholder is not related, but anyhow he held bond-land
of the manor of Gimmingham, a parish lying on the coast of
Norfolk, between Paston, whence the family took their name,
and Cromer, and is said to have married a bond-woman, the
sister of a serf in the neighbouring township of Somerton, who
had become a pardoner and attorney. Being a thrifty man, as
years went on he gradually increased his holdings until he had
in Paston about six score acres, whereon he kept a plough at all
times in the year, and sometimes two, and a little water-mill;
but "no manor had he there nor in none other place." By the
time that a son, William, had been born to him and had grown
to be a boy, he had thriven sufficiently to be able to set him to
school and give him a good education. All his life the father
kept to his farm, but the son did so well that he was sent to
the Bar, though Clement Paston had to borrow money to provide for him. And there, we are told, William begat much
good, becoming a right cunning man at the law and steward
to the Bishop of Norwich. His reputation, indeed, soon rose so
high that in 1421 his father had the pleasure of seeing him
become a serjeant, and in 1429 a justice of the Common Pleas,
a wealthy man, in fact, and esquire, who could marry into a
gentleman's family, and who purchased not only much land in
Paston, but the manors of Oxnead and Gresham, together with
a seigniory at Bacton and a free warren and market at Cromer.
In later times the family residence at Oxnead became a famous
house, and its masters the Earls of Yarmouth. The second story
is the well-known one of Hugh Latimer's father, the Leicestershire farmer, whom the Bishop thus described in a sermon to
Edward VI.: "My father was a yeoman, and had no lands of
his own; only he had a farm of three or four pounds by the
year at the uttermost, and hereupon he tilled so much as kept
half a dozen men. He had walk for a hundred sheep, and my
mother milked thirty kine. He was able, and did find, the
king a harness with himself and his horse. He kept me to
school and my sisters he married with five pounds apiece. He
kept hospitality for his poor neighbours, and some alms he gave
to the poor; and all this he did of the same farm." The entire
credibility of the first of these stories ought not perhaps to be
assumed, for it is related by an enemy of the Pastons; but

none the less each in its own way shows that the view current at the time of a small farmer's prospects was no gloomy one, and warrants us in believing that to many of them the expression "Merry England" must have been no unmeaning formula. It must be noted, however, that already, at the date the bishop preached, all this was altered, for he adds: "He that hath the same farm now payeth sixteen pounds by the year or more, and is not able to do anything for his prince, for himself, nor for his children, or give a cup of drink to the poor"—a startling contrast, which may serve to remind us that as yet only the brighter features have been inserted in our picture, and that the shadows still remain to be presented. To a certain extent these darken the whole of the fifteenth century, but, as the chief causes of complaint only became very prominent in the early years of the Tudor period, it will be more convenient to defer treating them till then.

W. A. S. HEWINS. Industry and Commerce.

GREGORY KING estimated the "artisans and handicrafts" and their families, at the end of the seventeenth century, at 240,000, and the "labouring people and outservants,' at 1,275,000, out of a total population of 5,500,520. The latter class included all wage-earners, but not cottagers. Writing forty years later than King, Defoe states that "those who make the goods they sell, though they do keep shops to sell them, are called handicrafts; such as smiths, shoemakers, founders, joiners, carpenters, carvers, turners, and the like; others who only make, or cause to be made, goods for other people to sell, are called manufacturers and artists." Below these in the social scale were the "workmen, labourers, and servants," corresponding to the second class in the quotation from Gregory King. "By labour," says Defoe, "I mean the poor manualist, whom we properly call the labouring man, who works for himself indeed in one respect, but sometimes serves and works for wages as a servant or workman." King made his investigations, and Defoe wrote his description, at a time when the changes which were only just beginning in the fifteenth century were very widely extended. They cannot, therefore, be an entirely trustworthy basis for an estimate of the number of the industrial classes at the earlier period. But the extension of the domestic system, and the growth of manufactures and commerce during the sixteenth and seventeenth centuries, did not so completely alter the relative numbers of the various classes that King's estimate cannot furnish a rough means of giving some definiteness to the conditions which prevailed in the fifteenth century. Making allowance for the probable alterations, the industrial popula-

tion may be estimated at from 500,000 to 600,000 out of a total of about 2,500,000 persons. The following account of the state of England from 1399 to 1486 applies to these people, but not to the wealthier classes, nor to the paupers and vagrants, of whom there were probably not less than 40,000, and the condition of those engaged exclusively in agriculture will only be touched upon incidentally.

CARPENTER'S TOOLS.
(MS. Nero D. vii.)

The great collections of Thorold Rogers are the best foundation to build upon for any period between the thirteenth and the eighteenth century. The inferences he drew from the record of prices which he made with such extraordinary thoroughness were not always correct. But the facts themselves are a trustworthy record of actual transactions, and anyone willing to take the trouble may test the accuracy of his conclusions, and reconstruct from his materials a picture of past times. Thorold Rogers's information was derived from such a variety of sources, and the entries are so numerous, that no future investigations are likely to involve any very important alterations in the averages for the period under consideration. It may be pointed out, however, that the overwhelming preponderance of information derived from districts south of a line drawn from the Severn to the Wash should make one hesitate before accepting the average for the northern counties.

The average rate of wages of skilled artisans or craftsmen from 1401 to 1485 was, if we may take the carpenter as typical of the whole class, about 5¾d. a day. During that period they effected a rise from 4¾d. to 6d. a day, or, in modern numbers, from 28s. 6d. to 36s. a week. These particulars, however,

Numbers of the Industrial Population.

The work of Thorold Rogers.

Wages.

convey only a vague impression of the actual condition of the workers. Fortunately the record of prices is so complete that there is no difficulty in estimating the purchasing power of wages for every year. There are obvious objections to the adoption of the standard of comfort of any modern class of artisans in investigating the condition of the working classes in the fifteenth century. Household economy and the lives and habits of the people have changed so greatly since the intro-duction of machinery, that it would be unsafe to use a working-class budget of the present time. The basis of our calculations will be formed by the standard of comfort of the class of small manufacturers of South Staffordshire before their industries were revolutionised by the introduction of machinery. These men had their labourers and apprentices, but their social status was little, if at all, higher than that of ordinary artisans. They lived plentifully, but they had none of the luxuries which changes in the conditions of supply have converted into necessaries, and their habits of life had not substantially altered for many years. Another difficult question to decide before a clear idea of the state of the industrial classes in the fifteenth century can be obtained, is the amount of employment a skilled artisan might reasonably expect in the course of the year. The Act of 1403, referred to on a previous page (p. 530), may not indeed have been universally observed, and Thorold Rogers gives numerous instances of continuous employment for more than three hundred days in the year. To be on the safe side, however, we will assume that, taking one year with another, the artisan was employed on an average for only 260 days.

If then we estimate the amount of food, clothes, and other commodities which a craftsman, his wife, and four children would require during the year, with a fixed allowance for other expenses, it is found that the mean proportion of this standard which the average craftsman could purchase was, from 1401 to 1442, from 132 to 136 per cent., or from 32 to 36 per cent. more than he required; and from 1443 to 1485, from 149 to 153 per cent., or from 49 to 53 per cent. more than he required. To put the same statement into another form, skilled artisans could, from 1401 to 1485, live comfortably, and save on an average 30s. or 40s. a year. But there were sharp contrasts between one year and another, and a thriftless

The marginal notes:
The Standard of Comfort.

Skilled Crafts-men.

person might easily be involved in great difficulties in bad times. In this estimate the addition to the resources of the family which the small holding might afford is entirely neglected, as also are the possible earnings of other members of the family besides the father. At this period the furniture of the wealthiest merchants was "poor and mean," and an artisan could probably have furnished his house comfortably, in accordance with the ideas of the time, for £3 or £4.

Inferior artisans and most of the agricultural labourers *Lower* were paid at a rate between 30 and 40 per cent. lower than *Grades.*

BUILDERS AT WORK (MS. Harl. 2278).

that of the skilled craftsman, but there was a slightly greater proportional increase in their wages during the period. It is clear that they could not have lived so well as the better class of workman, nor had they the same opportunities of saving. Their employment was less regular, and they must have felt the pinch of dear years more acutely. But the standard of comfort here supposed in the case of skilled workmen might be considerably depressed, and there would still be more than enough for comfortable subsistence. It is plain from the numerous entries in Thorold Rogers's tables of the allowance for food to labourers when they were boarded, that this class lived well, and that a decided improvement in their condition took place during the fifteenth

79

and the early part of the sixteenth century. A thrifty labourer might have saved, and so have raised himself and his children in the social scale, without deprivation of the comforts or the necessaries of life usual at the time. On the whole, therefore, the industrial classes were amply provided with the means of subsistence, and their standard of comfort was rising. They lived in houses, better indeed than the single rooms and hovels in our large cities, which many English workmen inhabit, for they could at least escape into the fresh air; but not so comfortable as an ordinary artisan's dwelling in Yorkshire or Lancashire. They suffered from the constant recurrence of the plague (p. 570), which baffled the medical skill of the time. The perils of infant life and the perils of disease were infinitely greater than they are now. Only the hardy could survive, and the average duration of life was less than it .is at the present time. But these hardships were not the result of economic causes, and their diminution or removal in modern times must not be credited to the competitive system, but to improvements in sanitation and progress in medical and surgical science. By dwelling exclusively on such drawbacks, to the neglect of the plain record of wages and prices, it is possible to paint the fifteenth century in very dark colours. There were probably more paupers in proportion to the population, but there was certainly less poverty; and if we try the fifteenth century by the best criterion, namely, the capability of improvement, and the degree of hopefulness of the industrial population, it will compare very favourably with any other period in English history.

Policy of the Crafts.   It remains to trace the influence of the rising standard of comfort, and the increasing accumulations of capital on the industrial system, on legislation, and on the growth of manufactures. The crafts, naturally, insisted more generally on apprenticeship for a definite term, usually seven years, and imposed higher fees and other restrictions as their members became more wealthy (p. 560). In this policy they were aided by statutes, instinct with the same spirit of monopoly and protection. A similar policy has been at all times adopted by organised trades and professions, as a defence against the competition of workers accustomed to a lower standard of comfort than their own; nor can a generation which views with approval the efforts in this direction of lawyers, doctors, dentists, teachers, and artisans, reasonably find fault with the

A GREAT BUILDING SCHEME (MS. Add. 18,850).

craftsmen of the fifteenth century. It is doubtful whether any real hardship was inflicted on inferior classes of workers; the increase in their wages has already been pointed out, and

the outcome of the policy in England was the growth of a
numerous body of manufacturers, who were wealthy enough
to pass successfully the ordeal of the sixteenth century, yet
poor enough to keep in touch with their workpeople, and
whose productions gradually forced their way into the markets
of Europe. An Act of 1410 imposed a property qualification
for apprenticeship to certain trades of 20s. per annum in
land or rent. The London citizens complained in 1429 that
they were "grievously vexed and inquieted" by this Act, for
it was the custom of London that anyone, not of villein
estate and condition, but of free estate and condition, might
put himself, his son or daughter, apprentice to any freeman
of the city, and that any freeman might take such apprentice. An Act was therefore passed, giving legislative sanction
to the custom, and excepting London from the operation of
Henry IV.'s statute. But the complaint of the London citizens was not due to sympathy with the agricultural labourers,
whose prospects of rising in the world would be likely to
be curtailed by a property qualification of the kind imposed.

**Journey-
men's
Societies.**
The supposed oppression of journeymen by the masters is
said to have brought into existence associations of the former
for the protection of their interests. But when all the evidence relating to these so-called journeymen's associations is
strained to the utmost, it does not show that they were of
any importance in the industrial system of the fifteenth
century. It is doubtful whether they were of any economic
significance, and they certainly have nothing in common with
the true journeymen's association, which does not appear in
England until the eighteenth century. There is no evidence
of the systematic oppression of journeymen by the masters
in the fifteenth century. Occasional disputes between master
and man on quite trivial subjects cannot be regarded as
evidence of a social revolution. The masters were the last
people in the world against whom the journeymen of the
fifteenth century would have combined. If the Statutes of
Labourers had been enforced, the endeavour to keep up the
rate of wages might have brought such combinations into
existence. An Act of 1425, indeed, states that "by the yearly
congregations and confederacies made by the masons in their
general chapiters and assemblies, the good course and effect

of the Statutes of Labourers be openly violated and broken, in subversion of the law, and to the great damage of all the commons," and "at the special request of the commons" all persons taking part in such assemblies were to be adjudged felons, and to be punished by imprisonment.

The Statutes of Labourers (p. 195) were several times re- Regulation of
Wages. enacted and extended under the Lancastrian sovereigns. Their general tenor was very similar to the great statute of apprenticeship passed in the reign of Elizabeth, which, indeed, codified the thirty-four Acts of the same kind which were unrepealed in 1563. It is a mistake to suppose that Elizabeth's Act first authorised justices of the peace to fix the rate of wages. Extensive powers were granted to them in the fifteenth century for the regulation of wages. The law which relates to work on holy days and the eves of feasts has already been mentioned, and the clause in the Act of Henry IV., imposing a property qualification for apprenticeship. The certificate of property was to be produced before a justice of the peace. Fresh powers were given to the justices in 1415, and two years later penalties for excessive wages were imposed on the taker only. But in 1424 the justices were empowered to proceed against masters as well for giving wages in excess of the ordinance. It is evident from the language of the statutes themselves that they were rarely enforced, a conclusion fully borne out by the record of the wages actually paid. But some labourers appear to have felt the hardship of attempts to force down their wages by government authority. The case of the masons has already been mentioned. In 1415 the Act states that "servants and labourers flee from county to county, because the ordinances and statutes for them are not executed in every shire."

The rise in the standard of comfort and the growth of The
Woollen
Trade. capital during the period led to a great development of the woollen manufacture. That there was a considerable demand in the home markets is evident from the many varieties of cloth mentioned amongst the purchases of individuals and corporations in Thorold Rogers's great work. English cloth had been exported as early as 1265, and the foreign demand must have been by this time very considerable. Capital flowed into the trade, and the clothier, the middleman of

the woollen manufacture, rose to importance in the industrial system. With the greater division of labour, the industry afforded opportunities of employment to carders, spinners, winders, and other labourers, both men and women, formerly unknown; and rapidly extended in the rural districts. Thus arose what is known as the domestic system, a system which no doubt had its advantages, but which was destined in the long run to introduce many evils, and to retard the progress of the working classes. For industries organised on this plan lend themselves easily to practices collectively known as sweating at the present time. Weak and isolated, the labourers combine with difficulty for the protection of their interests. They are completely in the power of the middleman, and their employment, dependent to a large extent on the will or caprice of a single individual, or a small group of individuals, in their district, is insecure and irregular. As early as the reign of Edward IV. it was found necessary to pass an Act to check the truck system. The Act provides that "whereas before this ' time, in the occupations of cloth-making, the labourers thereof have been driven to take a great part of their wages in pins, girdles, and other unprofitable wares, under such price [as stretcheth not to the extent of their wages], and also have delivered to them wools to be wrought by [very] excessive weight [whereby both men and women have been discouraged]. . . . Therefore, . . . every man and woman, being clothmakers, . . . shall pay to carders and spinsters, etc., current coin, and give due weight of wools." The statute book at this period is full of Acts regulating the woollen manufacture, too numerous to give in detail, but showing the variety and importance of the industry.

Although the subsidiary branches of the woollen manufacture were perhaps generally combined with some agricultural occupation, it is clear that a class of labourers was appearing who depended entirely on the wages of industry for their subsistence. An Act of 1448-9 mentions "men, weavers, fullers, and dyers, and women [websters], carders and spinners," who "do know none other occupations," and "of very necessity" are "constrained for their living to do the same occupations." The earliest accounts we have of the wages of women workers under the domestic system show that they were very poorly paid. The greater diversity, also, of the conditions in which the manufacture was carried on, the fact that many of the workers were drawn from the poorest class in the community, who had never been under the discipline of the guild system and the absence or ill-success of the means to keep up a

BRASS OF A WOOL MERCHANT AND HIS WIFE.
(Northleach, Gloucestershire.)

high standard of workmanship, gave rise to abuses which were kept in check in the better organised trades of the country. There is, in fact, reason to believe that the period of transition from the old system to the new was marked by evils analogous to those which attended the greater changes of the eighteenth century, although some of the causes, such as the excessive dearness of provisions, the heavy taxation for the French war, and a bad poor law, which made the latter so disastrous to large bodies of workers, were absent in the fifteenth century. The vacillation of the Government, exhibited in the frequent changes of the law, shows how difficult it was found to regulate the rapidly extending manufacture.

EARLY IRONWORK.
(*Lewes Museum.*)

It was not only in the woollen industry, however, that great progress took place during the fifteenth century. The catalogue of trades in the statutes of Richard III. and Edward IV. for the protection of native industries against foreign competition, shows that

Protection. there was a growing demand for other commodities. In addition to textile fabrics, iron and hardware goods, harness and saddlery, and many other home products are mentioned. The cry for protection probably did not arise before English manufacturers had discovered that they could compete with foreigners in more than the merely local markets they had hitherto supplied. In the same way the growth of a separate and distinct class of tradesmen and shopkeepers led to restrictions on the retail business of foreign merchants, a course which was keenly resented by the Hanse merchants as a violation of their privileges.

The Merchant Adventurers. Amongst other signs of the growth of capital and industry in the fifteenth century, the rise of the Merchant Adventurers is one of the most important. An offshoot of the Mercers' Company of London, they obtained their first charter as an organised association in 1407, and grew rapidly in influence and wealth. The appearance of a body of English merchants engaged exclusively in the exportation of woollen cloth shows how greatly the foreign demand for English cloth must have extended since the reign of Edward III. For three hundred years the new company was destined to play an important part in the commercial history of England. It became the type of several other companies in the sixteenth and the seventeenth centuries, and was associated throughout its history with the growth of the mercantile system. Their trade was carried on chiefly with the Netherlands, where they had their mart, first at Bruges and afterwards at Antwerp. Even during the period here described there are not wanting signs of those quarrels and dissensions with foreign merchants and the Staplers which grew to such a pitch in the sixteenth century. But the history of these controversies must be deferred to a subsequent chapter.

English foreign trade was still mainly in the hands of the **Foreign** merchants of the Staple, and various bodies of foreign merchants **Trade.** —such as the Hanse merchants, the merchants of Venice, whose fleet, known as "the Flanders galleys," periodically visited Southampton and other ports, and the merchants of Florence. Many Acts of Parliament were passed during this period regulating the Staple trade of the country. The merchants of

Genoa, Venice, Catalonia, Aragon, etc., and the merchants of Berwick are generally exempted from the operation of these Acts, which confined the Staple trade to Calais. After the sketch of the general outline of the Staple organisation which has been given in a former chapter (p. 340), it is unnecessary to describe in detail the various modifications of this period; the system of regulation remained substantially unchanged. It should be pointed out, however, that the Staple

ARMOURERS AT WORK (MS. Roy. 20 G. v.).

Acts appear to have been very successfully evaded by merchants who found their restrictions too irksome. In the absence of an adequate system of supervision, a country like England, which abounds in creeks and quiet havens, affords great facilities for an illicit trade. Penalties for evading the statutes of the Staple were imposed in 1430, and another Act of the same year complains that "divers foreign mariners of Flanders, Holland, etc., in divers ports and creeks of the realm smuggle Staple commodities." Another Act withdrew all the licences to export Staple commodities, elsewhere than to Calais, from the merchants of Newcastle and Berwick. In 1432 it was enacted that the value of staple merchandises exported elsewhere than to Calais should be forfeited, except wools exported by special licence. It was also made felony to ship such commodities in creeks, etc.; but this statute was evaded. It was, however, re-enacted and amended in 1435 and 1439. An Act of 1448-9 complains of the decrease of Customs at Calais and the decay of the Staple from various causes. The merchants of the Staple were to enjoy all their former privileges, and elaborate regulations of the trade were imposed. Such were some of the attempts to maintain a system of control over the foreign trade of the country which was fast becoming unsuitable for the times. The fact is, there was a growing divergence of interest between the associations of foreign merchants, the staplers, who were a mixed body of foreigners and Englishmen, the native merchants, anxious to create a national trade, in the hands of Englishmen, and the growing class of outsiders who found it more profitable to engage in illicit commerce than to trade in accordance with the accepted principles of the time. The disputes with the Hanse merchants illustrate the disintegration of the old system. Their constant complaints of the seizure of their ships and goods, of the violation of their privileges, and of the serious delays and loss thus occasioned, show how jealously they were regarded. Englishmen, on the other hand, brought counter-charges of "colouring," of unfair trading, of evasions of statutes, etc.—charges which eventually (in the reign of Edward VI.) caused the withdrawal of their privileges and the victory of the merchant adventurers.

Regulation of Trade. The difficulty of regulating commerce in accordance with the old system was felt not only in the relations between one body of merchants and another. The Statutes of Employment and those regulating the importation and exportation of bullion were constantly being amended.　In 1401 gold and silver found in course of exportation were to be forfeited, except reasonable expenses, and merchant strangers were compelled to employ one-half the bullion they brought with them in the purchase of English commodities.　Gold and silver money of Scotland or Flanders was to be "voided" out of the realm and its

A FLEMISH LOOM (MS. Roy. 17 E. iv.).

importation was forbidden.　Two years later, to remedy a scarcity of halfpence and farthings of silver, it was provided that one-third of the silver bullion imported should be coined to meet the deficiency, and goldsmiths were forbidden to melt such halfpence and farthings.　Another Act of the same year provided that the money received by merchant strangers or denizens for goods imported should be laid out in English commodities.　This statute was confirmed in 1404, and customers were directed to take surety of foreign merchants to observe the law.　Aliens were to sell their merchandise within a quarter of the year, but this clause was repealed in 1405, because it was "found hurtful and prejudicial as well for the king and his realm as for the said merchants, aliens, and strangers." Aliens were not to sell merchandise to each other, and posts were assigned to them. Other Acts on the same lines, more or less stringent, were passed under Henry V. and Henry VI. An Act of 1410 states that "certain merchants, aliens, in London and other towns, have taken and hold great houses, and sometimes bring in the year 1,000 or 2,000 cloths of fine white, dye it themselves, make garments and pack the same in their houses, and in the parks pack fine wool, gold and silver in barrels, and bring the same out of ·the realm without paying subsidy or custom." It is not surprising that such practices, all of which were contrary to the law of the land, aroused great hostility against foreign merchants.

Treaties of Commerce. One of the most usual methods employed during this period for securing markets for English goods was the negotiation of commercial treaties. Few years passed without some international agreement affecting English trade in a greater or less degree; and they show how widely extended English commerce was becoming. The most important treaties are those dealing with the trade between England and Flanders. That of 1467, one of the long series leading up to the Magnus Intercursus (1496; pp. 613, 626, 745), is a good example of the arrangements made at this time for regulating the most important branch of English commerce. The subjects of both countries, whether dealers in wool, hides, or provisions or other articles, were to have free access by land or water, with liberty to buy and sell all kinds of merchandise, except warlike stores, on paying the duties, established when commerce had free course between the two countries. Each prince, in case of scarcity, might prohibit the exportation of provisions. The fishermen on both sides might freely fish in any part of the sea, without needing formal licences or safe-conducts, and, if driven by necessity into any port on the opposite coast, they should be kindly treated, provided they paid the customary dues, committed no fraud, and did no damage. Then followed several clauses relating to neutral vessels, and the prevention of piracy —the merchant's principal danger in the fifteenth century. There were other treaties during this period—with France, Castile, Portugal, Prussia, Denmark (p. 668), and the Mediterranean

cities. The contracting parties did not, it is to be feared,
strictly observe the conditions they imposed upon themselves,

A GLASS FACTORY (MS. Add. 24,180).
(Probably after Flemish originals.)

though they were drawn up with great elaborateness of detail.
The Duke of Burgundy prohibited the sale of English goods in

Flanders, in spite of a direct obligation to permit freedom of trade. Foreign ships and goods were seized by English seamen contrary to treaties granting them immunity, and foreigners retaliated. The merchants of Venice complained that they durst not avail themselves of the permission to resort to England, unless they had a special safe-conduct as well. The existence of a commercial treaty, therefore, was no guarantee that merchants would be allowed to pursue their calling unmolested. Notwithstanding this drawback, however, there can be no doubt that trading connections increased in number, and that greater uniformity and equality of commercial privileges was the outcome of the numerous commercial treaties between the countries of Europe. By these means, also, much was accomplished in building up the fabric of international law, and in promoting the extension of trade and commerce by peaceful negotiations.

It would be wrong to infer from the prevalence of piracy at this period (p. 249) that commerce must have declined. On the contrary, it was probably the increase of commerce, unaccompanied by the growth of adequate means for its defence, which made the pirate's calling so profitable. Nor was the evil confined to the professional pirate class, if we may use the expression. Even recognised associations of merchants frequently indulged in practices which can only be characterised as piracy. Commerce, in fact, was deeply imbued with the spirit of lawlessness, and in these circumstances it is probable that the depredations of pirates did not excite the same alarm nor discourage trade in the same degree as would be the case in more law-abiding times. In the fifteenth century the profession of Christianity and extreme respectability were not incompatible with a life of violence and outrage, and it is to be feared that in some cases the Governments, which should have repressed pirates by the severest measures, encouraged their depredations. Certainly they have never enjoyed such immunity from the strong arm of the law as in the fifteenth century (pp. 464, 465). Outrage and robbery went on unchecked along the coasts and in the track of merchant vessels. No trader was safe even in the rivers and ports of his own country. The pirates burnt and sacked towns as important as Sandwich and Southampton; they carried off not only the goods they could lay their hands on, but men and women, and even children, whom they held to ransom. Unable to look to the Government for protection of life and property while they were engaged in trade, the merchants were thrown upon their own resources to provide security. The best method of grappling with the pirates, and that which was most frequently adopted, was for merchant vessels to sail together in such numbers that they could repel attack; and these voluntary efforts were sometimes aided by the Government. In 1406 Henry IV. granted the merchants 3s. on every cask of wine imported, and certain payments on staple exports for purposes of defence. Two admirals were appointed, one for the north and the other for the south, with full jurisdiction in maritime affairs and power to organise naval forces. But this scheme was unsuccessful. A similar expedient was tried in 1453, but abandoned two years afterwards. The only satisfactory remedy would have been a strong navy, but the conditions necessary for this had not yet been realised. The country could not have supported the charge of maintaining a strong naval force; and although Henry V. devoted much attention to ship-building, and built at Southampton three famous ships—the *Trinity*, the *Grace de Dieu*, and the *Holy Ghost*—and Edward IV. revived for three years the navigation policy of Richard II., the development of English shipping was left to individual efforts. That merchants were beginning to realise the importance of the subject, and were becoming wealthy enough to build vessels of a considerable size, is evident from the operations of John Taverner, of Kingston-upon-Hull, and the famous William Cannynge, of Bristol, the latter of whom is said to have possessed 2,470 tons of shipping and some vessels of 900 tons burthen.

The commercial ideas of this period are very well illustrated in the "Libelle of Englyshe Polycye," a political poem written about the end of the year 1436. The author appears to have been well informed, and gives many interesting particulars of the commerce of the period. Throughout the poem we are reminded of the arguments which had so much weight with the writers of the sixteenth and seventeenth centuries. The author complains that English merchants exported their commodities in foreign bottoms, to the discouragement of native shipping, and that foreign merchants had more privileges in England

Commercial Policy.

than English merchants in foreign parts. He condemns the importation of luxuries in terms which would have pleased a writer of the mercantilist school. His arguments relative to Ireland and Wales remind us of the language of the age which saw the deliberate subordination of the interests of colonies and dependencies to those of the mother country. The sentiments, and in part the language, of the author of the "Libelle" are reproduced in a poem of a somewhat later date on the commercial policy of England.[1]

THE GUILDHALL, NORWICH.

R. L.
ETCHER.
wn Life.

If we are to take a last glimpse at the life of the English towns before the Middle Ages close, we shall find little real difference between the fourteenth and fifteenth centuries. The disintegrating tendencies, which broke up their internal economy into a lot of separate trades and crafts, were still at work, and had resulted in the almost complete triumph of the craft guilds. The new "charters of incorporation," which began to be given to the towns from the reign of Henry VI., confined the franchise, both parliamentary and municipal, almost wholly to the freemen of the guilds, and the guilds were every day narrowing themselves. Instead of being societies for the maintenance of small capital and labour in the same hands, and for securing an equal remuneration to all labourers engaged in the craft, they were tending to become associations for the investment of capital. Where this was the case, the journeyman would already be sinking in the social scale, and would gradually lose his chance of rising to be a master.

[1] "Political Poems" (ed. Wright), Rolls Series.

Though competition had not yet supplanted custom as the mainspring of trade, its germ was already there, and the mercantile ideas sometimes attributed to Edward IV. probably helped to foster it.

If the early part of the fourteenth century was the golden age of the Cinque Ports, the early part of the fifteenth was the golden age of the towns of Norfolk. Before the close of the reign of Richard II. the French navy had amply avenged on Winchelsea and Rye, on Hastings and Portsmouth, and even on places as far distant as Dartmouth and Yarmouth, the crushing defeats of Sluys and of " Les Espagnols sur mer." Matters did not improve under the Lancastrian kings. No complaint is more frequent in Parliament than the neglect " to keep the sea," *i.e.* the narrow seas between Dover and Calais, and the whole of the English Channel. Piracy abounded, and town after town woke up to find itself in ashes. Not but that there were occasional fits of energy displayed: Henry V. had been, when Prince

Decay of the Cinque Ports.

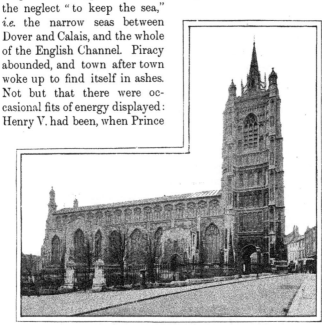

ST. PETER MANCROFT, NORWICH.

of Wales, Lord Warden of the Cinque Ports; and Henry Pay, of Faversham, had won some useful victories over French and

80

Spaniards in the preceding reign. It was from Southampton, long the principal post for the Venetian galleys, that Henry V. sailed, with the most considerable fleet medieval England ever saw, to the barren conquest of Northern France; but the reign of Henry VI. is more conspicuous for the burnings repeatedly inflicted on English coast-towns by French squadrons or privateers than for any active measures of retaliation. Hence the Cinque Ports appear as enthusiastically Yorkist as early as. 1450, if indeed Jack Cade's insurrection can be considered a Yorkist movement. But even the Earl of Warwick, who was already taking the lead in English naval affairs, was unable to protect Sandwich from being fearfully plundered by the French in 1457.

Norfolk.

There can be no doubt, however, that if any portion of England was prosperous in the fifteenth century, it was the county of Norfolk. Though Norwich does not invariably appear on the assessment rolls as the second city of the kingdom, being more than once surpassed by Bristol and once by York, it is oftener in the position of "proximus sed longo intervallo" to London than any other place. And Thorold Rogers has well pointed out that the assessment of the *county* of Norfolk, *i.e.* the county including the greatest number of small clothing towns, was greater than that of any other county (London being excluded from the rating of Middlesex). The great Norfolk churches belong largely to the fifteenth century. Little places like Aylsham and North Walsham were famous each for its own special kind of woollen manufacture. Little old-world havens, more stranded now if possible than the smaller Cinque Ports themselves like Lynn (before modern improvements) and Wells, towards which sluggish tidal channels now crawl and wind—nay, ridiculous villages like Cley and Blakeney, in comparison with which nineteenth-century Winchelsea is a roaring mart—counted their tonnage by the thousand and their vessels by the score. There is an old tradition that the merchants of the Hanseatic League once traded with Cley in such numbers that a special portion of the churchyard was reserved for them to be buried in; and it is certain that the Cley men had a complaint to make to the king along with the men of York, London, Colchester, Yarmouth, Norwich, Lynn,

Cley Church.

Photo: Poulton.
St. Margaret's, Lynn.

Worstead Church.

Photo: Chester Vaughan, Acton. W.
St. Nicholas', Lynn

CHURCHES OF NORFOLK, FIFTEENTH CENTURY.

etc., against the merchant-pirates of Wismar and Rostock, who had robbed their ships on the high seas. Lynn was important enough to have an establishment of its own at that great outport of the Hansa, Bergen, in Norway. All visitors to North Norfolk are familiar with the splendid church of Worstead, which may be seen from the Great Eastern Railway between Norwich and Cromer; but perhaps not everyone realises that the humble domestic thread of which our stockings are knitted was named after the place.

The Woollen Industry.

But it would be as great a mistake to imagine that the woollen industry was confined to Norfolk as to imagine that it dated only from the fifteenth century. It must always be remembered that medieval statistics are the most fluctuating and untrustworthy things in the world. Temporary causes, such as fire, Frenchmen, famine, and pestilence, constantly caused towns to lose their position for a few years—perhaps never to recover it. There was a regular practice of allowing £6,000 for "decayed towns and districts" out of the £38,000 to which the tax called a tenth and fifteenth amounted; and over and over again we are surprised to find even such towns as Yarmouth, Lincoln, and Cambridge claiming their share of this exemption. Yarmouth possibly fell somewhat rapidly from the contemporary decay of its former rivals and later allies—the Cinque Ports. Indeed, Lynn certainly appears as the more important Norfolk port throughout the fifteenth century, so that, on the whole, it is extremely hard to get an accurate idea as to the prosperity, or the reverse, of the period. Perhaps we should not be far wrong if we put it somewhat in this shape: (1) The woollen manufactures were extending. We may cite two pieces of direct evidence for this: first, the great falling-off in the produce of the export custom on wool, which shows itself almost parallel with the increase of pasture-land and the decrease of tillage; and, secondly, the repeated efforts of the Government, to which the statutes bear witness, to keep the children of agricultural labourers to the profession of their fathers, while their tendency, which such statutes vainly endeavoured to check, was to go off into the towns and seek employment in the new industries. Rogers has no doubt that the depopulation of the country districts in favour of the towns had been going on ever since, if not before, the peasant revolt of 1381 (indeed, it must be remembered that one of the principal ways in which a villein could become a freeman was the residence for a year and a day in a privileged town); and he quotes an instance of a "plea of villeinage" being set up against a free burgess of Gravesend by Sir Simon Burley, as one of the causes which immediately hurried on that rising.

But (2) this very influx of labourers into the towns— Class Dis-men who would at first be glad to take any service and tinctions. at any rate—would naturally deepen the cleavage of classes, which was already beginning within the town. We find,

CLEY TO-DAY.

therefore, alongside of much wealth and richness of living among the great merchants, of whom we shall soon be able to speak as capitalists, much misery and poverty among the journeyman class; probably, indeed, even more than in the previous century, in proportion as the monasteries and other similar institutions wore themselves out, and ceased to fulfil their charitable as well as their religious duties; and as the craft guilds more and more lost their original character of friendly societies. And (3) there seems little reason to doubt that the wool trade, though still largely localised in East Anglia, was spreading itself also over a considerable portion of the country in driblets. The population of

England in the early years of the fifteenth, as in the early years of the sixteenth century, has been guessed at about two and a half millions; and it has also been guessed that the proportion of urban to rural in this estimate is only as one to twelve. But while such various figures as 40,000 are assigned by one writer and 130,000 by another as the total for the metropolis, it would not be wise to build too much upon these calculations.

A Forgotten Mart. Yet the more one rummages into medieval documents, the more does one come across evidences of trade or municipal life unsuspected before. Who would suspect that the grey old Somersetshire village—it is hardly more—called Ilchester, the "camp on the Ivel," or Yeovil river, which has probably had an almost unbroken municipal life from Roman times, was in the fourteenth and fifteenth centuries regarded as of almost equal importance with Bristol? It stands on the old Roman road, called the Fossway, about half-way between Bath and Exeter. Like London, it had its "Chepe," or market street. It possessed five churches, two great crosses, a nunnery, a leper hospital outside the walls, a Dominican friary, whose buildings originally within them soon extended without also, and a famous almshouse, founded by one Robert Veel as late as 1426. Veel's endowment of the hospital was so large and increased so rapidly that it practically amounted to an endowment of the corporation of the town.[1] Under these circumstances, seemingly, the bequest was not long in bearing natural fruits of a premium on idleness. The aldermen of Ilchester no doubt grew fat, and the incentive to industry being taken away, the town appears never to have shared in the woollen trade, which in the sixteenth century began to fix itself in many of the towns of eastern Somerset. Its decay was rapid, and in 1540 Leland found only one church which was not in ruins. Ilchester, however, depended for its importance not so much upon any special branch of trade as upon being a sort of provincial capital, and the centre of a great district. But such towns as Kendal in the north, Salisbury and Winchester in the south, Colchester in the east, were renowned for special woollen manufactures before the accession of Henry VII. The fact that Coventry had long been important as the centre of the dyeing industry probably points to other

[1 Hayman, in the *Antiquary*, Sept., 1883.]

localities for cloth manufacture in the Midlands; and the statutes of Edward IV. teem with allusions to various and distinct employments, such as those of carders, spinners, weavers, fullers and shearmen. Division of labour, which was to be characteristic of the new age of competition, may be reckoned therefore to have already begun.

It would be a mistake to attempt to give any account of town life in the fifteenth century without alluding to the great frequency of pestilence and local famines, which seem to have recurred intermittently ever since the Black Death. In 1400 we hear of the importation of corn—probably in Hanseatic vessels—from the shores of the Baltic (*cf.* Vol. I., p. 679). The conditions of life in a crowded English town at the present day are, though doubtless less "beautiful," probably healthier, owing to improved drainage, than in rural districts. The reverse was certainly the case in the Middle Ages. Each of the leading Oxford colleges possessed a pest-house at some convenient distance from the city, to which the Fellows migrated when the "sickness" was hot under the shadow of St. Mary's spire. In 1406 the plague was so violent in London that Henry IV. preferred to run the risk of being captured by pirates in the Thames on his way from Kent to Essex rather than take the natural route over London Bridge. After six fierce attacks within twenty-eight years, four months of plague in 1477 swept off three times the number of people who had perished in the civil wars during the previous fifteen years.[1] Six years before that, Sir John Paston writes: "I fear that there is great death in Norwich and in the other towns in Norfolk, for I assure you it is the most universal death that ever I wist in England." In 1485 we first hear of the "sweating sickness" (p. 753), which was to be the typical epidemic of the succeeding seventy years.

The Recurrence of Plague.

Yet it cannot be denied that luxury was on the increase so far as outward show was concerned. The account of the splendid entertainment offered to Edward IV. by William Cannynge, merchant of Bristol, in 1461, in his magnificent home with its tiled floors, rich stained-glass windows and sumptuous hangings; the beautiful timbered houses which still overhang the old streets of Tewkesbury, in one of which Prince Edward

[1] Denton, "England in the Fifteenth Century," pp. 89, 103, 104.

[1399

of Lancaster is said to have been stabbed in 1471, after the battle; above all, the splendid buildings in the collegiate foundations of our two universities which owe their origin to Chicheley and Waynflete and the sainted Henry of Windsor,

Photo: R. Wilkinson & Co., Trowbridge.

TIMBERED HOUSE AT TEWKESBURY.

all point to an age which, in the upper ranks at least, was beginning to understand comfort. Yet, as Mr. Cunningham points out, Cannynge's guests probably slept very many in a bed, and his tables were probably mere tressels such as we should be ashamed to put up for a school treat, while other furniture there would be little or none.

As the most widely divergent views have been taken of the social state of England in the fifteenth century, so have the conceptions been variously coloured regarding the public health in that period. Of one thing we may be sure—there was no longer leprosy in the country. In the reign of Henry VI. new charters were made for two of the most distinctive of the old leper-hospitals, those of Durham and Lincoln. The new charter of the former makes provisions

CHARLES
CREIGH-
TON.
Public
Health.

for two lepers (where there had once been sixty), "if they can be found in these parts"; and that of the latter, while assigning the hospital to other uses, provides for the contingency of leprous applicants, adding the pious wish that it might never arise. The disappearance of leprosy

[1485]

from England in the fifteenth century may be taken as Leprosy Disap-
pears. absolute; and there could be no better index of the fact that the weight of misery, such as it had ever been in the Middle Ages, was already lifted. The period was for England one of peaceful development, notwithstanding the Wars of the Roses. It was the great time of the thrifty yeoman and his stalwart sons, of the decent burgher and his industrious apprentices, of fine churches in town and country—the time when Chief Justice Fortescue contrasted the commons of England with the commons of France to the infinite advantage of the former: " They eat plentifully of all kinds of flesh and fish. They wear fine woollen cloth in all their apparel; they have abundance of bed-coverings in their houses, and of all other woollen stuff; they have a great store of all hustlements[1] and implements of household; they are plentifully furnished with all instruments of husbandry, and all other things that are requisite to the accomplishment of a quiet and wealthy life according to their estates and degrees." And Philip de Comines, towards the end of the century, confirmed the happy contrast of the English commons with those of France, from the side of his native French experience, specially remarking that the civil wars were not of a kind to touch the domestic peace and prosperity of the nation. It happens that the records for the fifteenth century are few, so that one is apt to project into it the better-known history from the times of Edward III. and Richard II. preceding it, or from the time of Henry VIII. following it. The latter part of the fourteenth century was certainly an unhappy period in the history of England; the first Tudor reigns were, for the common people, not less distressful, although in another way. In the earlier period Wycliffe has a significant remark, that the friars came no longer to poor men's houses, " for the stink and other filth "; which may mean, either that the friars were become more fastidious, as indeed they were. or that the dwellings of the poor were more sluttish than they had been before the great mortality came to shake the foundations of society and to demoralise the nation in all its ranks. For the first Tudor reigns we have evidence of the country swarming with poor people evicted from their old manorial holdings, of crowded

[1 Utensils: akin to the modern French *outil*.]

gaols, and gaol-fever, and of the sudden establishment of pauperism on the great scale as a permanent British institution. But there is no warrant to carry the earlier state of things forwards into the fifteenth century, nor to carry the later state of things backwards into it. Fifteenth-century England had recovered from calamities on the one side, and had not yet plunged into those on the other. Even of famines, which were at the mercy of the skies, it had only one of greater magnitude than a local scarcity, the great famine of 1438, which was still more acutely felt in Scotland and in France, and was the climax of two or more bad seasons.

Plague.

Although the fifteenth century is undistinguished in the annals as a time of famines or of a poor level of general well-being, yet it had its own share of plague. But it should be remembered that plague in England was a direct inheritance from the foreign invasion of the Black Death, having reappeared four, or perhaps five, times in the fourteenth century in general outbursts over the country, although far less disastrous than their great original. These general outbursts of sickness (for the most part the plague) continued into the fifteenth century; one of them fell sometime between 1405 and 1407, and is said by the St. Albans annalist to have left desolate many humble homes which had been gladdened by a numerous progeny; another attended and followed the great famine of 1438, and was most felt in the year 1439, being called "the pestilence," and said more commonly than usual to be universal throughout the realm. (In Scotland the first effects of famine are known to have been dysentery in 1438, which was followed by proper plague, or "the Pestilence sans Mercy," in the end of the year.) Then, in 1464–65, we hear again of universal sickness and of many thousands dying, as the Croyland Chronicle says, "like sheep slaughtered." A few years afterwards, in the autumn of 1471, Sir John Paston writes from near Winchester: "I cannot hear by pilgrims that pass the country, nor none other man that rideth or goeth any country, that any borough town in England is free from that sickness," which we know from other sources to have been the true plague. The special mention of the borough towns is important; for from that time onwards plague was almost restricted to the towns, and to a few of these in one and the same season; the succession of general epidemics, which were counted to the "fifth" or "sixth," in the fourteenth century, and might have been continued to "ninth" or "tenth" in the century following, comes to an end probably with the epidemic of 1464. The Black Death had as if spent itself, so far as concerned the country at large; and, although the same type of sickness occurred in villages and country-houses to the very end of the plague, in 1666, yet, for the last two hundred

CHAPEL OF ST. MARY'S HOSPITAL, GREAT ILFORD, ESSEX.
(*By permission of the Archdeacon of Essex*)

years of its stay in England, it was distinctively a disease of the summer and autumn in the poorer quarters of the towns. Of these London always took the lead: even from the scanty records of the fifteenth century, the existence of plague in the capital to a more or less dangerous extent can be traced in most years. Among the larger provincial towns, Norwich, Exeter, York, Newcastle, and Hull, are known to have had severe visitations, the last especially having been reduced to absolute desolation by three outbreaks between 1472 and 1478. But the fullest record of fifteenth-century plague comes from Oxford. Anthony Wood counted in the various college registers

no fewer than thirty pests, great or small, which had so interrupted the studies of the place, and had so encouraged idleness
and "several sorts of vice," that it was consulted of great
personages whether the university seat should not be removed
elsewhere, many colleges and halls having ceased to be, while
the best were slenderly tenanted, and whole quarters of the
town decayed.

The Wars of the Roses and Public Health.   The wars of York and Lancaster, says De Comines, did not
touch the lives and homes of the common people, but were
restricted in their effects to the nobles and their retainers. But
some of the battles were bloody, there was much military stir,
and doubtless plague was helped thereby, as it most certainly
was by the grim struggle between Parliament and the king two
centuries afterwards. By all accounts, the most severe plague-
period of the fifteenth century was between 1464 and 1479; the
autumn of 1471, when Sir John Paston heard of plague in
the towns from every passing pilgrim or packman, was the year
of Barnet and Tewkesbury. We may believe Chief Justice
Fortescue and Philip de Comines when they contrast the happy
lot of the English common people with those of France; but, inasmuch as war, with the occupation of towns and the slaughter
of men and horses, gave new vitality to the lurking seeds of
plague, the people suffered indirectly from the strifes of their
rulers. The peculiar effects of plague upon the population, and
upon the average of well-being, which were doubtless felt as
much in the fifteenth century as in later times, will be considered under the reign of Henry VIII.

D. J. MEDLEY. Costume in Later Medieval England.   THE history of change of fashions in civil dress is very
largely the history of human folly and caprice. From time
to time a developing commerce introduces new materials—the
fur of strange animals, silk, linen, and even wool of finer kinds,
and the character of these gradually works a change in the
shape of necessary garments. But often investigation will prove
that the apparent introduction of a new garment is little more
than a change of name in one with which we have been long
familiar. For our means of knowledge in such matters are
so slight that conjecture must needs play an important part.
In the first place, we depend on illuminated illustrations of

romances, chronicles, and even missals—the work, for the most part, of monks or skilled craftsmen who did not habitually live in the world which they essayed to portray. Rich colouring and artistic beauty would be more important than truth of representation. The most magnificent or picturesque or curious or extravagant costume would be likely to be chosen. The same may be said of the parallel means of information afforded us by the far scantier source of monumental effigies. Neither heir nor artist would choose that we should associate the deceased with the costume that he wore every day. The armour of the knight, the robe of his lady, would be typical of the position which they occupied in contemporary society. A second source of our information is the casual descriptions of romancers and chroniclers, written for literary effect and with a view to the development of a character or a story, and whose value is often seriously discounted by the confused use of names for the garments which they are endeavouring to denote. The most detailed information about costumes in all ages comes from the social satirists of the period. It is the source on which historians are most tempted to draw, and yet it is just the source which should be used with the greatest caution. Exaggeration is of the essence of their work, and the indignation of a Juvenal or the desire to provoke a laugh invests their pens with an irresponsibility of description that should put us on our guard against their accuracy and good faith.

On the other hand we have a scanty but absolutely trust-worthy means of knowledge of contemporary costumes in the inventories of personal effects made for various purposes. Naturally these only relate to kings and individuals of wealth and position, and cannot form the basis of too wide a gener-alisation. It is also necessary to remember that medieval society was far more dominated with the idea of caste than the society with which we are familiar, and that this caste, whether social or merely official, was outwardly marked by a difference of costumes. The rich bourgeoise might attempt to emulate the dress of the lady of noble birth, but the two did not move in the same social sphere. In the country the knight and his dame need have no fear that his steward or any of his tenants had so far forgot what was due to

Trust-worthy Evidence.

their respective positions in the social scale as to seek to imitate his lord. In modern England the clergy alone never lay aside the mark of their profession. It is true the satirists of the fourteenth century accuse the clergy of bedizening their clerical garments with so much finery that they lost all professional distinction and became assimilated to the costume of the laity. But the clerical garb was not the only distinctive dress. In England, no less than in France, it was their official costume which gained for lawyers, when they had

REGAL COSTUME (MS. Add. 32,097).

ceased to be clergy, the descriptive title of "gentlemen of the long robe." Thus, with the qualifications already mentioned, for our purposes we may make shift to use the illuminations of manuscripts, the effigies on tombstones, the chance descriptions of romancers, and the savage detail of satirists. One does not always confirm the other; indeed, sometimes they flatly contradict each other. But the information will be sufficient. We are not engaged in compiling a dressmakers' book of fashions. We are investigating a curious and by no means uninstructive side of human history, which has its own witness to bear to the display and development of national no less than individual character.

The Upper Classes. But a history of costume must needs be chiefly a history of changes in the shape of outward garments. Thus the classes whose dress remains almost stationary from generation to generation do not occupy a large portion of our attention. It is with the well-to-do, those of noble birth and of high position, those who formed the "society" of the time in the technical sense, that we must chiefly concern ourselves. The comparison of the costumes of various classes is little more than antiquarianism. The object before us is the manifestation of a certain phase of the human mind. Now, before we examine in detail the various garments in which gentlemen and ladies of the fourteenth and fifteenth centuries clad their persons, one or two general remarks fall to be made. Notwithstanding the comparative scantiness of the information on which we can draw, a period of two centuries is sufficiently long for us to be able to trace in it the alternation of simplicity and extravagance which is more or less characteristic of costume in all ages of civilised society. Thus the reign of Edward I. was a time of serious work. The king set a good example in simplicity of costume, and although the satirists must have something to talk about, there is no such complaint of extravagance and foppery as the sober Matthew Paris indited in the preceding reign. But with the reign of Edward II. serious objects for a time were gone ; for some generations politics became a mere selfish scramble for power; every side of life was infected; the nobles and gentry became more selfish and irresponsible, the clergy more careless of their duties, the bourgeois more exclusive, the commons more discontented. The French wars only postponed the inevitable result of callousness in the governing classes. As a matter of fact the foreign fashions which the warriors introduced only helped to emphasise the luxury of the noble classes. This reached its height, as we should expect, in the disgraceful days of Richard II. Nor was this useless luxury confined to those in high position. " The commons," says an anonymous writer whose work has been assigned to this reign, " were besotted in excess of apparel, some in wide surcoats reaching to their loins, some in a garment reaching to their heels, close before and strutting out at the sides, so that at the back they make men seem like women, and this they called by a ridiculous name, *gowne.* Their hoods," he continues, " are little, tied under the chin, and buttoned like the women's, but set with gold, silver, or precious stones. Their liripipes or tippets pass round the neck, and, hanging down before, reach to the heel, all jagged. They have another weed of silk which they call a paltock. Their hose are of two colours, or pied with more, which they tie to their paltocks with white latchets called perlots, without any breeches (*i.e.* drawers) ; their girdles are of gold and silver, and some of them worth twenty marks. Their shoes and pattens are snouted and picked more than a finger long, crooking upwards, which they call crackowes,

Dress under the Edwards.

Growth of Extravagance: Richard II.'s Reign.

Dives (MS. Arundel 83).

Pauper (MS. Arundel 83).

Wayfarers in the Fourteenth Century (MS. Roy. 2 B. vii.).

Mistress and Maid.
(*Luttrell Psalter.*)

A Domestic Pet.
(*Luttrell Psalter.*)

Lady and Squire
(*Luttrell Psalter.*)

COSTUME IN THE FOURTEENTH CENTURY.

resembling the devil's claws, and fastened to the knees with chains of gold and silver." This detailed description of the spread of extravagance in apparel to all classes is confirmed by the remark of the contemporary chronicler, Harding, that

> Yemen and groomes in cloth of silk arrayed,
> Satin and damask in doublettes and in gownes,
> In cloth of greene and scarlet for unpayd [*i.e.* unpaid for].

Chaucer's Parson, whom we shall have occasion to quote more

DAGGING (MS. Harl. 1319).

than once, has much caustic censure to bestow on the extravagant fashions of his day. And it was an extravagance of all kinds. Not only were materials more costly than necessary, but in shape and size the long gowns or robes worn by men and women alike were so long that they trailed in the mud and had to be carried over the arm, or, rushing into the other extreme, men wore their tunics so short as, in the eyes of moralists, to expose the person indecently. Nor did this extravagance easily subside. One comprehensive attempt was made in the reign of Edward III. to regulate the expenditure of the various classes upon their dress. In the Acts of the Parliament of 1363 a number of provisions (caps. 8–14) define the apparel of themselves

Sumptuary Legislation.

81

their wives, and families in the cases of ploughmen, yeomen, handicraftsmen, merchants, clerks of various kinds, esquires, and knights owning land of the annual value of four hundred marks. These Acts remained upon the Statute Book until they were superseded by a new Act of Henry VIII. But, despite the penalties attached, they remained for all practical purposes a dead letter. The fashions of Henry IV.'s

Its
Futility.

DRESS AT THE COURT OF RICHARD II. (MS. Roy. 20 B. vi.).

reign were more fanciful if not more extravagant than those of the preceding period. The toes of the shoes could not well get longer, but the head-dresses of the ladies became continually higher. The sleeves were longer, wider, fuller, and their edges "dagged" or cut into extravagantly fanciful shapes. But every other method of fantastic ornamentation sinks into insignificance before the use of posies or mottoes as a means of embroidery. Chaucer tells us of a lady who had the words "bien et loyaultment" embroidered on the borders and facings of her dress, and Holinshed, writing in the reign of Elizabeth, but doubtless copying some contemporary authority, says that when the Prince of Wales, afterwards Henry V., went to make peace with his

HEADDRESSES IN THE FIFTEENTH CENTURY. (*MS. Reg. 15 E. v.*)

(*To face p. 578*)

father, he was dressed "in a gowne of blewe satin, full of small eylet holes, at every hole the needle hanging by a silken thread by which it was worked." But any English example pales before the account of the houppelande of Charles Duke of Orleans, on the sleeves of which were worked in pearls and gold the

BEDROOM, WITH LADIES, UNDER HENRY VI. (MS. Harl. 2278).

words and music of a song, the lines of the music represented in gold thread and the notes formed each of four pearls. In the reign of Henry V. there are some indications of a slight attempt to return to simplicity. The toes of the shoes for a while lose their long pikes; the women's head-dresses are less fanciful, if equally extravagant. But these are mere momentary aberrations from the normal line of development. The gallants of the following reign reproduce in an emphasised and exaggerated form all the eccentricities of former generations. The long toes to the shoes become longer than ever; the tippets or liripipes

Dress under Henry V. and Henry VI.

hanging from the hoods sweep the very ground as their wearers move along; the sleeves are more monstrous in size, or the sleeveless armholes are so wide that the garment thus per- forated scarcely hangs together. Hitherto the chief means of ornamentation had lain in the dagging or cutting into jagged patterns of the edges of the sleeves and the borders of the long robes. This had been carried as far as seemed practicable or possible. It was now transferred from the borders to the body of the garment, and results in the "slashing" or slitting which, first heard of in the reign of Edward IV., becomes the most conspicuous method of ornamentation in the dresses of the sixteenth century. It was first applied to the elbows with the object of allowing the shirt beneath to appear; it was gradually extended to every part of the dress which was in the least degree susceptible of such treatment. An additional advantage was that, unlike the outside dagging whose effect depended on the length of the garment to which it was applied, the slashing was equally effective in the shorter dresses which came into vogue in the sixteenth century. Its supposed origin is sufficiently curious. It is said that after the defeat of Charles the Bold of Burgundy at Grandson in 1476 the magnificent garments and stuffs found among the plunder were cut up by the Swiss soldiery and fantastically sewn upon their clothes. The effect of a variety of colours thus obtained was afterwards systematically reproduced by the makers of garments in all the countries of Western Europe. Nor was this the only instance of the influence of foreign fashions. Indeed, a great deal of the caprice which is so conspicuous in the rapid changes of fashion in costume during these two centuries is due to the successive waves of foreign influence which swept up against the shores of English social life. The indecently short tunics of which moralists complain in the reign of Edward III. are said to have been an importation from Spain, and set the fashion in France and Italy no less than in England. The extravagances of the court of Richard II. were due to German influences coming through his Bohemian Queen. Gower in "Confessio Amantis" alludes to the new guise of Beme (that is, Bohemia). To the same influence, perhaps, is especially due the introduction of the piked shoes stretching to monstrous length which went by the name of "crackowes." Poland, after whose chief city they

Under Edward IV.

Foreign Influences.

were called, had been incorporated by Anne's grandfather with his kingdom of Bohemia. Again, from Italy is supposed to have come the fantastic embroidery of mottoes and similar devices; while, finally, the constant influence of France, or of more distant countries through France, is to be found in the names of the most familiar garments. *Gown* may be Anglo-Saxon, or even British, but *robe* is undoubtedly French; *hanseline*

DETAILS OF COSTUME, LATE FIFTEENTH CENTURY. (MS. Roy. 18 D. ii.)

comes from Germany, and *paltock* perhaps through the Spanish; but of the French origin of cote-hardie and court-pie no less than of the more familiar surcoat and doublet, there can be no reasonable doubt. Many of these, of course, came into use at a time when French was the language of the court and the nobler classes, but they continued long after this had ceased to be the case. Our enumeration of the caprices of fashion during the period under review is by no means finished; but it will be enough to note, in the first place, that the high head-dresses became distinctly higher until they culminated in the well-known steeple or horn-shaped adornment of the reign of Henry V.—monstrous in itself, but a simplification of preceding shapes—and then suddenly all such disappear in the closing years of Edward IV., and are replaced by a low, flat covering of the nature of a cap. Again, whereas **Dress under Henry VII.** in the reign of Henry VI. dresses were worn high in the neck by both sexes, under Henry VII. the neck was left very bare, and, as a slight protection, the hair was allowed to grow longer on both sides of the head. Finally the piked shoes disappeared

MEN'S DRESS, LATE FIFTEENTH CENTURY.
(*Tapestry in St. Mary's Hall, Coventry.*)

in the reign of Edward IV., and as a compensation the toes were so expanded that their breadth became limited by law. So far we have been at pains merely to trace the extravagance and caprice of the fashions of costumes in general and to account for them, as far as it is possible to account for anything which is only limited by the unfathomed limits of human folly, on the ground of successive waves of foreign influence. Hitherto, perhaps, the antiquarian interest has been too studiously avoided. A closer study of the principal parts of the costume will be useful, if for no other reason, in enabling us to date monuments, illuminations, and all other pictorial representations of the men and women of past ages.

Little, if any, of the modern Englishman's costume is studied with a view to artistic effect. The man of taste and position Details of Costume. to-day is contented to know that his clothes fit him more accurately and are of a better quality of cloth than those of his poorer neighbour. The duty of looking graceful and of dressing beautifully he leaves to his wife and daughters. Not so the medieval gallant. Men as well as women were at pains to adorn their bodies with splendour, if not with such taste as we can admire. No article of modern male attire is so hideous as the recognised head-dress—the top hat or the " billy- Men's Head-gear. cock " of social life. They are certainly not artistic, they are

WOMEN'S DRESS, LATE FIFTEENTH CENTURY.
(*Tapestry in St. Mary's Hall, Coventry.*)

not even comfortable. But the male of the fourteenth and fifteenth centuries sought at first comfort and convenience, and then, as fashions grew more extravagant, he aimed at what we may presume that he considered magnificence if not beauty. Not infrequently men and women of all classes in the Middle Ages wore no headgear at all, or were contented with a simple fillet or ribbon to keep back the hair off the forehead, or with a chaplet of real or artificial flowers whose sole object was adornment. Caps and hats, however, were worn from the earliest times of which we have record in this island. The Norman " fusion," as a writer calls it, introduced the hood as a species of covering common to both sexes alike, while mere convenience soon gave vogue to the ugly coif which resembled a nightcap

tied under the chin. Caps were of various shapes and materials
and colours ; hats were sometimes worn over the hood, and were
made of felt and of the skins of various animals. Chaucer's

THE CHAPERON OR HOOD (MS. Add. 10,204).

Merchant wears " on his head a Flaundrish bever hat." Women,
too, wore hats. The Wife of Bath has one " as broad as is a
buckler or a targe." The gallants of the fourteenth century wore
high felt hats rounded on the crown, the brims turned up either
in front only or all round, often cut or jagged into fancy shapes
and of a different colour from the hat itself. In front one immensely tall feather was stuck into an ornamental pipe or
socket, in which it was fastened by some band or jewelled
ornament.

But the commonest head-dress was the chaperon or hood,
which has been described as " a sort of pointed bag with an
oval opening for the face ; the point, sometimes of great length,
hanging down behind or twisted round the head, or, if short,
sticking up or dangling, according to circumstances." These
pointed ends were the tippets or liripipes already mentioned.
So worn, the epithet " smug," applied by another writer to the
close fit of the hood, appears not undeserved. But at the end of
the fourteenth century some more fanciful covering for the head
appears to have been aimed at. The cloth was cut and twisted
until it was piled upon the top of the head something in
the shape of a turban, while, for the sake of ornament, the part
of the hood which had hitherto covered the shoulders was
turned over the crown of the head and was cut into fanlike and
other imaginary shapes. The hood, in fact, disappeared, but the
tippet or liripipe was represented by a long band or streamer

depending from one side of the turban. This was often dagged into various shapes, and was worn so long that convenience caused it to be wound round 'the neck or tucked into the girdle of the wearer. The hood and the hat had now changed places. Formerly the hat, when carried at all, would be slung behind, and the head ordinarily covered by the hood; but in the fifteenth century a hat or cap was usually worn, and the hood, or what now represented it, was slung by the tippet over the shoulder to be assumed at pleasure or necessity. Towards the end of the century these elaborate turbans pass away; the caps lie flatter on the head, and the gallants wear them with broad brims and a profusion of enormous feathers. These were the " Milan bonnets," whence we are told the word " milliner " was imported into the English language to denote the maker of ladies' caps and bonnets.

Meanwhile the women's head-dress had undergone even swifter transformation. In the thirteenth century the hair was first confined in a caul or net, and over it would be worn a wimple of silk or linen which would be secured on the forehead by a simple fillet. But this was too plain for a generation whose resources were enlarging, and early in the fourteenth century developments begin. We will not embroil ourselves in the

(margin: Women's Head-gear.)

HEADGEAR UNDER HENRY VI. (MS. Harl. 2278).

acute controversy over the earliest appearance of the celebrated horned head-dresses already mentioned. To judge from extant illustrations the wimple or gorget or coif (the exact difference is too slight for any need of distinction) was raised off the head by all manner of fantastical devices. The earliest of these in use were protuberances from the side of the head which are quite adequately described by a contemporary satire as "bosses," or even, to use the disputed word, as horns. These protuberances were raised gradually higher from both sides of the head, and were so bent over and shaped as to form what came to be known as the heart-shaped or reticulated head-dress. Finally, the depression which made the heart was itself raised until the two side horns twisted up perpendicularly on either side of the head or amalgamated into one on the top, and there was obtained the "steeple" shape, which modern tourists may still see on the heads of the women of the Pays de Caux in Normandy. But it was ugly and cumbersome, and after a short vogue during the reigns of Henry VI. and Edward IV. it gave way to flatter coverings. These were chiefly small round caps with lappets called clogs or clocks on either side, or that near return to the hood, the diamond-shaped head-dress so familiar on monuments and in pictures of the early sixteenth century.

Body Garments: the Cote.

The chief difficulty in describing the body garments lies in the confusing multiplicity of names used at various times to denote what must have been similar, if not identical, articles of apparel. Among men the place of the classical tunic or tight fitting under-garment was taken in the fourteenth century by the *cote*, and among women ultimately by the gown. The Anglo-Saxon name *kirtle* was unknown to the Normans, but was revived in the course of the century and is frequently used by Chaucer. But all over Europe the common name for this garment was *cote-hardie*. It was worn by both sexes and buttoned all down the front. The male cote just covered the hips and round it was buckled the military belt; in the case of ladies it varied in length, sometimes even reaching to the ground, but in all cases fitting closely to the shape of the body. It was this close fit combined, in the case of the men, with the scanty length, which provoked the rage of the satirists. Nor was this the only cause of offence. The Crusades had introduced heraldry, and families were distinguished by colours as well as by crests, arms and mottoes. What more natural than an attempt to distinguish in the garb of daily life the family, by birth or dependence, of the wearer? Hence came the parti-

Lady de Creke,
Westley Waterless, Cambs., 1326.

Ismayne de Wynston,
Necton, Norfolk, 1372.

Eleanor Corp,
Stoke Fleming, Devon, 1391.

Philippa Byschoppeston,
Broughton, Oxon., 1414.

Lady Walsche,
Wanlip, Leicestersh., 1393.

Margery Argentine,
Elstow, Beds., 1427.

BRASSES ILLUSTRATING WOMEN'S DRESS, FOURTEENTH AND FIFTEENTH CENTURIES.

coloured dresses which distinguished in the two colours of the two sides of the cote, or of the sleeves, or of the hose, first the lords and then their followers. Chaucer's Parson combines these two faults in one condemnation and speaks of "the horrible disordinate scantiness of clothing as be these cut slops or hanselines (varieties of the cote), that through their shortness and the wrapping of their hose—which are deported of two colours, white and red, white and blue, white and black, or black and red—make the wearer seem as though the fire of S. Antony (*i.e.* erysipelas) or some other mischance had cankered and consumed one-half their bodies."

Contemporary representations of rustic labourers without their tunics exhibit them as bare from the waist upwards. And the earlier illustrations give us no reason to suppose that the wealthier classes were more elaborately clad. From other sources, however, we learn that beneath the cote was commonly worn a shirt. By Chaucer's day this was becoming a means of ornamental dress. His Parson indignantly asks, "Where then the gay robes, the soft sheets, the smal (*i.e.* thin or delicately fine) shirts?" The similar garment worn by the other sex was known as a smock. Even of the carpenter's wife Chaucer tells us

> White was her smock, embrouded all before,
> And eke behind on her colore about,
> Of cole-black sylke within and eke without.

Its
Varieties.

For the garment which we have hitherto distinguished as the cote, a number of alternative names are found. These may denote some slight variety of form or merely a difference of origin. Thus the *paltock*, of which we know little for certain beyond its name, is probably of Spanish origin. Of a few others something more certain can be said. The "jack" was, at least in England, a military garment, a loose coat or tunic of the gambeson kind, made of "jacked" leather, and often stitched and quilted. The *jacket*, a garment of civil life, was a little jack, a short body garment. In the middle of the fourteenth century Froissart speaks of "une simple cotte ou jaquette," which his translator, Lord Berners, renders by "a syngle (*i.e.* unlined) jacket." Again, "Hans" was the German equivalent for Jack. Hence the *hanseline* already mentioned would be the little jack or the jacket. In the same connection may be mentioned the later

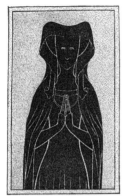

Annabella, wife of Sir Thos. Straunge,
Warkworth, Northants, 1430.

Unknown Lady,
Minehead, 1440.

Lady Clavell,
Swanwick, Dorset, 1490.

Wife of John Gouge,
Chipping Norton, 1440.

Isabella Cheyne,
Blickling, Norfolk, 1485.

Wife of Edmund Clere,
Stokesby, Norfolk, 1488.

BRASSES ILLUSTRATING WOMEN'S DRESS, FIFTEENTH CENTURY.

ferkin which seems to have denoted the same garment when used for military purposes, or as worn by the handicraftsman or the rustic. Finally, in a passage already quoted, with hanselines Chaucer's Parson classes *slops*. The name is one of the most bewildering in the whole nomenclature of clothes, and was apparently applied in turn to almost every kind of garment. Herein, perhaps not unreasonably, has been found the meaning of the term slop-shop, as applied to the dealer in all sorts of clothes.

The adaptation of garments of military origin to civil use seems also to explain the origin of the *doublet*, which in the middle of the fifteenth century superseded the cote-hardie and all its equivalents. For it was merely a form of the military gambeson, the stuffed and quilted body garment worn under the hauberk. Like its military prototype, the doublet at first bore no sleeves. These were afterwards added, and it became a universal garment of male attire, constantly changing its form until it passed into the modern waistcoat.

The "Petti-coat.'

In the "Boke of Curtasye" the chamberlain is told to get ready for his lord "a clene shirt and breeches, a *pettycote*, a doublette, a long cote, a stomacher." In the "Boke of Kervynge" the squire is directed by his instructor to "warme your soverayne his petticote, his doublett and his stomacher." At the close of the fifteenth century, therefore, a petticoat was an article of male attire; in fact, as the name implies, it was a little coat worn under the long coat or gown. Henry V. had a petite cote of red damask, unlined and with open sleeves. while in the inventory of Sir John Fastolfe's wardrobe (1459) there is mention both of a "pette" cote of linen cloth stuffed with flokys and of a "petticote of linen cloth without sleeves." The garment was evidently worn between the shirt and the

Stom-acher.

cote-hardie or doublet. These directions mention a *stomacher*. This also appeared at the end of the fifteenth century and was at first worn equally by both sexes under the doublet or bodice which was laced across it. It was often made of rich materials and adorned with jewels. It may or may not have been identical with the "placard" of Tudor times.

Surcoat.

So far we have attired our gallant in shirt, petticoat, and cote or doublet. Above these would come the *surcoat*, which represented the supertunic, cyclas or bliaus of the thirteenth century. It denoted especially a military garment worn over the hauberk to protect it from the weather, or the garment which women wore over their close-fitting cote. It also denoted generally the outer garment worn by men of gentle blood when in civil dress. It was of every shape and size, sometimes with sleeves, sometimes without. In its most extravagant and least artistic form it resembled a lady's waterproof without the cape. But the surcoat ordinarily gave way to the *gown*. Strutt Gown. believes that the name " was first applied to the supertunic of some of the religious orders. . . it was afterwards given

A GENTLEMAN AT HIS TOILET, FOURTEENTH CENTURY (MS. Roy. 2 B. vii.).

to the upper vestment of the burghers and magistrates of corporate towns and cities, and at last became a common appellation for a garment substituted in the place of the supertunic." We have seen that an anonymous author, writing at the end of the fourteenth century regards it as a " ridiculous name." These gowns were of infinite variety. In the inventories and wardrobe accounts of the next century mention is found of " long gowns, short gowns, half gowns, straight gowns, and loose gowns; others, again, denominated from the purpose for which they were used, as riding gowns, night gowns and tenice gowns; or named from the fashion or the country the fashion was borrowed from, as cassock gowns, Turkey gowns and Spanish gowns. They were also lined or single—that is, without lining—as the weather required; they had sometimes hoods, sometimes standing capes and square capes, and sometimes high collars; they were made also with sleeves and without sleeves, and the sleeves were sometimes wide and loose, sometimes straight and sometimes open." These gowns were frequently so magnificent as to invite the rage of the satirist, and so long that they had to be carried over the arm. Chaucer's Parson complains of the "costly furring of the gowns and the superfluity in the length of them, trailing in the dung and in the mire, on horseback and eke on foot, as well of man as of woman." Except for old men and men of official rank the gown went out of fashion as a garment of male attire in the middle of the sixteenth century. Meanwhile, women's gowns had gone through several phases. Under Richard III. and Henry IV. they were worn high in the neck and with a tight-fitting collar like those of the male sex. Under the last two Lancastrian monarchs the collars were turned over, and a short waist was the prevailing fashion. Then the waist was lengthened and the front of the gown was opened down to it, so as to display the gorget round the neck and the stomacher beneath it. But these changes did not affect the extravagant length of the gown whether in front or in the train itself. So long as it continued to be worn, the gown was the only visible garment which escaped the slashing and puffing which were all-prevalent in the dress of the sixteenth century.

Sleeves.   The sleeve is so conspicuous a feature of medieval dress that it calls for separate treatment. "Many sleeves," says Mr. Planché, "in the Middle Ages did not form a portion of the dress, but were separate articles themselves, and worn with this or that garment according to the fancy of the owners." It may be remembered that the middle Norman period was an era of luxury and extravagance. One outward manifestation of the latter was the monstrous length to which the dresses were extended, which necessitated their being tied in knots to avoid the trailing in the dust. But, perhaps, as an author has observed, on the principle "reculer pour mieux sauter," the sleeves of thirteenth century garments were moderate in dimensions, those of the undertunic fitting fairly closely and reaching to the wrist, while those of the supertunic were loose

and wide, and halted at the elbow.   But a song from the time
of Edward II. tells us that

Because Pride hath *sleeves*, the land is without *alms*.

Apart from the testimony to fourteenth century wit—" a pun

LADIES' CLOAKS, EARLY FIFTEENTH CENTURY (MS. Roy. 2 A. xviii.).

sufficiently bad to make the fortune of a modern burlesque "---
this seems to suggest the recrudescence of extravagance in
this particular portion of contemporary dress.   Certainly the
cote-hardie had short sleeves from which hung " streamers," that

82

is, long strips of some material, generally white, but sometimes of costly stuff, the edges of which were dagged and cut into fanciful shapes. The long gowns which became prevalent at the close of the fourteenth century gave far more scope for the development of this particular extravagance. All classes and both sexes wore the sleeves of their outer garments enormously long and wide. The satirist had a peculiarly favourable field. Says Occleve :

> But this methinketh an abusion,
>   To see one walk in a robe of scarlet,
>   Twelve yards wide, with pendant sleeves down
>   On the ground, and the furrier therein set
>   Amounting unto twenty pounds or bet (*i.e.* better):
>
> . . . .
>
>   Now have these lords little need of besoms
>   To sweep away the filth out of the street,
>   Since side sleeves of penniless grooms
>   Will up it lick, be it dry or wet.

The shapes of these long sleeves were innumerable. An anonymous monk of Evesham, who wrote a life of Richard II., speaks of gowns with deep, wide sleeves " called pokys, shaped like a bagpipe, which were rightly termed devil's receptacles because they were so convenient for concealing stolen goods." Illustrations from the reigns of Henry IV. and his son give examples of long pointed sleeves like those of a University Bachelor's gown. The inconvenience charged against such appendages when worn by servants who dipped them into the dishes as they served at table, is sufficiently obvious. But we have to wait for the reign of Henry VI. before we find pictorially represented the less trailing, though too capacious, bagpipe sleeve of our author. The dagging or escalloping of the edges of the sleeves was perhaps more fanciful than that applied to any part of the costume. It was probably because all classes had taken to this rude method of ornamentation that at the end of the fifteenth century the gallants evolved the slashing or slitting which was only a transference of the same principle to the body of the garment itself. The law was not altogether silent on these eccentricities. The better sense of the community speaking through an Act of Parliament in 1403 forbade any man below a certain rank to wear any kind of large, hanging sleeves. Again, when to the slashing was added the puffing, first at the shoulders and then in almost any part of the costume, an Act of 1464 endeavoured to check the growing fashion by enacting that "No yeoman or any other person under the degree of yeoman shall wear, in the apparel for his body, any bolsters nor stuffing of wool, cotton, or caddis in his pourpoint or doublet, but a lining only according to the same."

Over all these articles of attire would be thrown, in cold or Cloaks. inclement weather, a garment called from very early days a

SLASHED AND PUFFED SLEEVES, UNDER HENRY VI. (MS. Harl. 2278).

mantle or *cloak*, and sometimes capa, balandrana or supertotus. It was originally worn with a hood attached, but gradually this came to be restricted to the religious orders. For cold weather this "overall" was lined partially or entirely with fur of various and varying kinds: the summer cloak was of lighter material. Both the stuff of which the cloak was made and the lining were adapted to the means and social position of the wearer. The garment was at first fastened with a fibula or brooch; latterly it was for the most part laced across. It was some times short, but most often reached some length; it was worn both with and without loose sleeves and a cape. Perhaps, as Strutt urges, the short mantle became a cloak. At any rate we are told that "in 1372 they first began to wanton it in a new curtall weed which they called a cloak, and in Latin "armilausa," as only covering the shoulders." Mr. Planché, however, holds that from this date "mantle" became an official term, and the ordinary outer wrap was known simply as a "cloak." The question may, without any material loss of knowledge, be safely left to the antiquarian, and in the same careful, if contentious, guardianship we may repose any discussion as to the exact shade of difference denoted by numerous other words such as pyke, pilche, and pelisse, which suggest a covering of a similar kind.

Breeches and Hose. We have seen that the "Boke of Curtasye" mentions *breeches* as part of the ordinary dress. These were the modern "drawers" extending from the waist and covering the knees. Below them the legs would be clothed in what the Anglo-Saxons called *hose*, the Normans chausses. In the fourteenth century the Anglo-Saxon name was revived. Whether in all cases they were drawn over the breeches or were not infrequently worn in place of them does not appear. But they seem to have reached in one piece from the sole of the foot right up to the cote or doublet on which they were fastened by latchets or points. When Falstaff is recounting his valorous engagement with the men in buckram, he exclaims, "Their points (*i.e.* the points of their swords) being broken—" when he is interrupted by the ribald Poins, who interpreting the word "points" as the latchets just mentioned, aptly remarks, "Down fell their hose." Like the cotes and other garments the hose were parti-coloured and were hence included in the castigation of the satirist. They do not escape the minute analysis of fashionable follies put in the mouth of Chaucer's Parson. This and similar criticisms may have produced an effect at last. At any rate, whatever the reason, after the middle of the fifteenth century these parti-coloured hose were worn only by attendants until their complete disappearance a century later. The hose of the fourteenth century were usually made of cloth, but the wealthier classes sometimes wore velvet, while the poor were contented with a wrapping of blanket. At the beginning of the sixteenth century the tops of the hose began to be padded and puffed, and finally there came a distinction between the upper stocks which we know as breeches or trunk hose, and the nether stocks or stockings. The term thus lost its original meaning, and its use was confined to denote the outer covering for the thighs.

Shoes and boots of various kinds (p. 580) complete the attire. **Shoes.** We have already seen something of the extravagant fashions in this part of the dress. A satirist already quoted tells us that the long "crackowes" of the reign of Richard II. were fastened to the knees of the wearers by chains of precious metals. This is borne out by no extant illustration. On the other hand Chaucer, in his description of the dress of the priest Absolon, says he had "Paule's windowes carven on his shoes." In contemporary illustrations the shoes of the "people" are always painted black, but the fanciful geometrical patterns represented on the shoes of the wealthier classes enable us to understand the poet's allusion.

LEATHERN SHOE OF MEDIEVAL TYPE.
(British Museum.)

AUTHORITIES. 1399–1485.

General History ; Contemporary.—Walsingham (to 1422), Rolls Series; Otterbourne (to 1419), Hearne's ed.; *Eulogium*, and Henry IV.'s letters, both in Rolls Series; *Gesta Henrici V.*, Eng. Hist. Soc.: lives of Henry V. in Rolls Series, and by "Titus Livius" (ed. Hearne) ; Gregory's *Chronicle*, Camden Society, to 1467 ; volumes in the Rolls Series on the Wars in France ; the St. Albans *Chronicle* (1421–1461), and the Chronicles of John Hardyng, Fabyan, the *Recueil des Croniques* of the Burgundian Waurin, and Monstrelet's great work ; and the works of Chastellain, Jean le Febvre, Olivier de la Marche, and Commines for the Wars in France ; chronicles relating to Joan of Arc, collected by M. Valet de Viriville ; the *Croyland Chronicle*, printed in Fulton's collection, for Henry VI.'s reign: William of Worcester's *Annals* and John Blakman's book (both edited by Hearne); volumes in the Camden Society's series (including *Camden Miscellany*, Vol. I.) dealing with the reigns of Edward IV. and Richard III. ; the letters of Bishop Bekynton, Bishop Pecock's *Repressor*, the Correspondence of Henry VI. (all in Rolls Series) ; the letters of Margaret of Anjou, and the Plumpton Correspondence (Camden Society) ; Ellis, *Original Letters ;* Fortescue, *Governance of England ;* and especially the Paston Letters: Chronicle of London, edited by Sir Harris Nicolas; Sir T. More, *Life of Richard III.* (ed. Lumby). The Political Songs, Parliament Rolls, Foedera, Privy Council Records, as before. Hall's work, written under the Tudors, has some of the value of a contemporary account.

Modern Works.—The best account, both narrative and critical, covering the whole period, is that contained in Stubbs's *Constitutional History*, Vol. III. ; to which Ramsay's *Lancaster and York* adds many useful details. Much valuable critical work is to be found in the prefaces to the various works (named above) of the Rolls, Camden, and other series. Gairdner's *Lancaster and York* gives a discriminating summary. The social and literary side of the period is treated in Green's *Short History of the English People*. On special periods, Wylie's *History of Henry IV.*, Kingsford's *Henry V.*, Oman's *Warwick the Kingmaker*, and Gairdner's *Richard III·*

Welsh History.—The *Chronicles* of Capgrave and Adam of Usk, Ellis's *Original Letters*, the Poems of Iolo Goch; Bradley, *Owen Glendower* ("Heroes of the Nations"); Edwards, *Wales* ("Story of the Nations"); Rhŷs and Jones, *The Welsh People.*

Religion.—Besides the books previously mentioned on Wycliffe, reference may be made to Foxe's *Acts and Monuments*, Maxwell-Lyte, *History of University of Oxford*, Antony à Wood, *History and Antiquities of the University of Oxford*, and Stubbs's *Constitutional History of England.* Latin Authorities.— *Chronicon Angliæ* 1328-1388 (ed. Maunde Thompson), Adam of Usk's *Chronicle* (ed. Maunde Thompson); Knyghton, *de Eventibus Anglicis* (Rolls Series); Malverne and other continuations *of Higden's Polychronicon;* Wilkins, *Concilia Magnæ Britannicæ;* Loserth, *The Trial of Richard Wyche* (*Eng. Hist. Rev.*, V., 531–544); Loserth, *Mitth. d. Inst. für Oesterr. Gesch-forsch.*, XII., 254–269; R. L. Poole, in *Eng. Hist. Rev*, VII., 306-311.

Warfare and *Naval History.*—As in Chap. V.

Discovery and Exploration.—Hakluyt, *Voyages;* Pilgrim-memoirs in the publications of the Société de l'Orient Latin, Série Géographique, and D'Avezac's *Recueil de l'Histoire de la Géographie;* Bede's *Historia Ecclesiastica;* King Alfred's *Orosius;* old maps (*see* text); Sir John Maundeville's *Travels*, ed. Warner, Roxburghe Soc., and *see Edin. Rev.*, 1889; Galvano's *Discoveries of the World* (for the story about Macham); Roger Bacon on the centre of the world, in the *Opus Majus.*

Art.—As in Chap. V., with the addition of Lübke, *History of Sculpture.*

Music.—There are general histories of music by Dr. Burney (4 vols., 1776-1789), Sir John Hawkins (5 vols., 1776), Dr. Busby (2 vols., 1819), and W. S. Rockstro (London, 1886). *See also* C. E. H. Coussemaker, *Histoire de l'Harmonie du Moyen Age* (Paris, 1832); A. W. Ambros, *Geschichte der Musik* (4 vols., 1868), and various articles in Grove's *Dictionary of Music* and the *Encyclopædia Britannica.* But the most valuable information is usually derived originally from stray passages in works not wholly devoted to the history of music.

Magic and Sorcery.—The introduction to T. Wright's *Proceedings Against Dame Alice Kyteler* contains many official documents referring to sorcery in England. The works of Delrio and Cornelius Agrippa give full information as to rites and beliefs. *See also* works cited for Chap. V.

Literature.—Occleve, *De Regimine Principum*, Roxburghe Club, 1840; *Minor Poems*, ed. Furnivall (E.E.T.S., Extra Series, LXI., 1892); Lydgate, *The Temple of Glas*, ed. Schick (*ibid.*, LX.); *Guy of Warwick*, ed. Zupitza (*ibid.*, XXV.); *Select Minor Poems*, ed. Halliwell (Percy Soc., 1842); Sidney Lee, art. "Lydgate," in Dict. Nat. Biography (contains bibliography of early editions); Pecock, *The Repressor*, ed. Babington, 1858; *Treatise Proving Scripture to be the Rule of Faith*, ed. Wharton, 1688; Malory, *La Morte d'Arthur*, ed. H. O. Sommer, with essay on Malory's prose by A. Lang (London, 1889-91); Fortescue, *Works*, ed. Lord Claremont, 1869; *De Laudibus Legum Angliae*, with trans. by F. Gregor, Cincinnati, 1874; *The Governance of England*, etc., ed. C. Plummer; Blades, *Life of Caxton* (the standard authority); H. Roemstedt, *Die Englische Schriftsprache bei Caxton*, Göttingen, 1891; T. Schipper, *Englische Metrik.* For Gower, *see* ed. by Macaulay. *See also* Dict. of National Biography, arts. "Gower," "Lydgate," "Malory," and "Caxton," by Sidney Lee, and "Fortescue," by G. P. Macdonell.

Agriculture, 1389-1509.—Denton, *England in the Fifteenth Century;* Rogers, *Six Centuries of Work and Wages*, and *History of Agriculture and Prices;* Cunningham, *Growth of English Industry and Commerce;* Fortescue, *De Landibus Legum Angliæ;* Fitzherbert, *Surveyinge.*

Industry and Commerce.—As in Chap. VI.; and the *Cely Papers* (Camden Society).

Town Life (besides the works mentioned in Chap. VI.).— *Privy Council Records;* Denton, *England in the Fifteenth Century; Paston Letters,* ed. Gairdner; Toulmin Smith, *History of Guilds;* Historic Towns Series; Mrs. Green, *Town Life in the Fifteenth Century;* Miss Dormer Harris, *Coventry* (Social England Series); Miss M. Bateson, *History of Leicester; Cely Letters* (Camden Society); Dowell's *History of Taxes and Taxation;* Leland's *Itinerary;* Gregory's *Chronicle;* The *Antiquary* magazine, *passim.*

Public Health.—As in Chaps. V. and VI.

Costume.—J. R. Planché, *Cyclopædia of Costume;* Fairholt, *Costume in England,* revised by Dillon, 1885 (Bohn's Series); Strutt, *Dress and Habits of the People of England;* Shaw, *Dresses and Decorations in the Middle Ages;* G. Hill, *History of English Dress from the Anglo-Saxon Period,* is of use rather for post-medieval times. The illustrations in Fairholt's and Strutt's works are drawn in part from French sources, and histories of costume must generally be used subject to the limitations stated in the text. For brasses, Boutell, *Monumental Brasses of England.* Those given in the text are taken from the superb Addington collection of rubbings in the British Museum (MS. Add. 32,490) in forty-four volumes, classed according to the period and station of the persons commemorated.

LADIES IN MOURNING, TEMP. HENRY VII. (MS. Roy. 18 D. ii.).

CHAPTER VIII.

THE BEGINNINGS OF MODERN ENGLAND. 1485–1509.

A. L.
SMITH.
The
Rule of
Henry VII.

IN his life of Henry VII., Bacon joins him with Louis XI. and Ferdinand of Aragon. " They may be esteemed the three magi of kings of those ages." Each of the three was a great founder. Louis XI. "took the crown of France out of wardship"; that is, brought the royal power to maturity. With Ferdinand and his high-souled wife, Isabella, began the hundred years' domination of Spain over Europe, alike in war, in diplomacy, and in government. But Henry Tudor not only founded a strong dynasty, and set the key-note of a decided and successful policy ; he was also the originator of that peculiar Tudor character, the union of immovable resoluteness with the highest degree of tact, by which these rulers accomplished so much.

To high natural gifts, fortune in his case added that training in the uses of adversity which monarchs rarely get. Left with a widowed mother, himself a prisoner at eleven years old, an exile at fifteen with his proscribed uncle, his life aimed at by Richard III., and exposed to the intrigues of the petty court of Brittany, it was not till he was twenty-eight that his chance came. Once it had come, however, he made full use of it. The hunted fugitive, the questionable adventurer of 1485, died in 1509 with the highest reputation in Europe for wisdom and wealth. In the taste of the time, Bernard André compares his labours to those of Hercules. Edward IV. and Richard III. answered to the Nemean lion and the Erymanthian boar ; the factions of the Roses to the Hydra, and John de la Pole to the Arcadian stag. Margaret of Burgundy corresponds to the Amazons ; the Scots king to the Cretan bull, and Martin Swart, by some violence of metaphor, to the horses of Diomedes. His Stymphalian birds are lawless subjects : his three-headed Geryon the power of Burgundy under Maximilian, Philip, and Margaret ; his

Cacus hiding in a cave, is Perkin Warbeck in Ireland ; and the Hesperides' apples, the golden fleurs-de-lis of France.

. He was truly, as Bacon says, ever in strife, but ever coming out victorious. His history is apt to be overshadowed by the tremendous issues of the next four reigns. It has even been called dull. On the contrary, it forms a varied and dramatic story. Its chief defect is the extraordinary lack of actual con-

HENRY VII. (MS. Roy. 18 C. xviii.).

temporary evidence. The Parliamentary records are bald and brief; the State papers, so full under Henry VIII., are as yet meagre. The only historians of the time are two foreigners; and of these, Polydore Vergil did not actually write till somewhat later. André has the empty copiousness of a panegyrist. Thus on several grounds, the history of the reign tends to resolve itself into a biography. At the same time, it is peculiarly exposed to the modern fault of reading history backwards. The danger is of antedating effects. To the men then living, no sharp line indicated a new era. They were slow to realise even that the Wars of the Roses were over. We are apt, on the other hand, in viewing the period, to read into it too much of the **A Time of Begin-nings,** future. The truest way to regard it is as a period of transition. It is marked by new ideas and new influences; but they are only as yet in germ. The printing-press is at work; but its first result is destructive, almost paralysing to literature. America is found, both South and North, but the effect on English industry and commerce is hardly marked till Elizabeth's reign. The "new learning" had made its way to Oxford with Colet and Erasmus; but no breath of hostility can yet be detected against Church dogmas. Morton and Warham both attempted a reform of the monasteries; but the movement was ineffectual till revived by Wolsey. The earlier dealings with Brittany, the later with Castile, suggest to us that the era of diplomacy was coming in; but it was to be long before the balance of power would be adopted as a clear principle; long even before Popes and legates would be replaced by conferences and diplomatists. So, too, with the relations of classes: the nobles were cowed and discredited, but there is little change in their ranks; not till after fifty years of popular despotism does the new nobility of Russells, Cavendishes, Parrs, Dudleys, Pagets, Seymours, begin to arise on the spoils of the Church. From this transitional character of the times there arise some strange contrasts. The first free trade treaty is almost side by side with a law wholly **and of Contrasts.** prohibiting "usury"; a crusade and a search for the North-west Passage jostle against each other. The Yorkist claims of in-defeasible right do not cease to be formidable till 1505; yet in 1495 the Statute of Treasons seems a precocious expression of seventeenth-century theories of popular sovereignty. The medi-eval is constantly confronted with the modern. The king's own **The King.** character seems to reflect now the one, now the other aspect. His favour to churchmen and his religious foundations, a certain reserve and aloofness in his bearing, a habit of suspicion, a just but great self-confidence; even his appearance, "reverend and like a churchman," all these remind us of medieval rulers. Then, again, he was a man of business, like Henry II.; he loved able men and used them well, as Edward I. did; he was as fair-spoken as Edward III.; his chapel at Westminster, "one of the stateliest and daintiest monuments in Europe," is typically

HENRY VII.'S CHAPEL, WESTMINSTER ABBEY.

medieval. But his aversion to war, his punishing by fines rather than by bloodshed, his system of espionage, his sense of the importance of finance, his liberal expenditure on objects that made a good show, the concentration of the whole State in his hands, are characteristics of a Frederick the Great or a Czar Peter. So, too, are his skilful and intricate diplomacy, his care for social legislation, his "paring of the privilege of clergy." There was about him a certain breadth and tolerance which was far from insular; and was, no doubt, partly learnt in the life of an exile and a refugee. There are some anecdotes which seem to show that he was not so immovable and uncongenial a man as is often supposed. At any rate he was a just and able sovereign, and in many ways a great one. His life and household were pure and frugal; he worked hard, and that for his country's good; he found England torn by factions, he left her peaceful, united, orderly; he found her isolated, he gave her a weighty voice in the councils of Europe.

The Opening of the Reign.

The crown which Richard had worn at Bosworth, Henry boldly set upon his own head before leaving the field of battle, 22nd August, 1485. This was not to claim the realm by conquest, so much as to manifest the verdict of the God of Battles given in his favour. Doubtful as his title may seem to modern eyes, there was no one else left to represent the Lancastrian line, and his engagement to marry Elizabeth, the eldest daughter of Edward IV., guaranteed him the support of the Yorkists. He took, however, the precaution of at once securing in the Tower the person of Edward, Earl of Warwick, son of Clarence; and on his triumphal entry into London he publicly renewed his engagement to Elizabeth. He felt strong enough to celebrate his coronation on October 30th, and left it to Parliament, which met a week later, to ratify accomplished facts by their declaration "that the inheritance of the Crown should rest, remain, and abide" in him, and his heirs. Soon after he procured a papal bull sanctioning this declaration. And as in January, 1486, he had united by marriage the two lines of Lancaster and York, his title, resting now on five foundations, seemed beyond cavil. But it was to prove far otherwise. At Easter came the rising of the Yorkist lords, Lovel and Stafford. It proved, indeed, abortive; Lovel fled abroad, and the Stafford brothers were taken. But the event was ominous. The long struggle of the two factions had left implacable hatreds. Yorkist feeling was a fire that smouldered beneath its ashes. It was fanned into flame by the king's refusal to have Elizabeth formally crowned as queen, by his keeping the Earl of Warwick a close prisoner in the Tower, and by rumours that Richard, Duke of York the younger of the two princes supposed to have been murdered by King Richard, was alive and would appear to rally the old friends of his house. The Yorkist party had always been strong in Ireland. When, therefore, a youth presented himself at Dublin, early in 1487, as Edward Plantagenet escaped from the Tower, he was eagerly accepted and crowned in the cathedral as " Edward the Sixth." His real name was Lambert Simnel, a baker's son of Oxford. He *Lambert Simnel.* had been trained for his part by a clever and unscrupulous priest, and probably encouraged by the queen dowager, a vain and intriguing woman, resentful of the slight done to her daughter the queen. Henry's measures were characteristic of his usual policy in dealing with such emergencies. He called his council, and had the queen dowager banished to a nunnery. He had the real Edward Plantagenet paraded through the streets of London. He offered pardon to all rebels who should come in by a certain day. The rebels meantime had won the adhesion of John de la Pole, Earl of Lincoln, brother-in-law to Edward IV., and of Margaret, Duchess Dowager of Burgundy, and eldest sister of Edward IV. This lady, wealthy and vindictive, "having the spirit of a man and malice of a woman," provided 2,000 mercenaries under Martin Swart. The Earl of Lincoln had in the last reign been declared heir to the crown. Both were ready to use this occasion as a stepping-stone, whereby a Yorkist might once more reach the throne. But when Lincoln and Lovel brought their forces from Ireland, they *The last* found Yorkshire and the North would not rise for a cause *of the* supported by Irish and German troops. At the battle of *Yorkists.* Stoke, Lincoln fell; Lord Lovel escaped only to perish in a secret chamber of his own house at Minster Lovel. Simnel was taken, and, in contemptuous pardon, made a varlet in the king's kitchen. But the rising had taught Henry a lesson; and in November, 1487, he allowed the coronation of his Queen Elizabeth. It had also distracted his attention somewhat from the attack which Charles VIII. of France was making upon the Duchy of Brittany, hitherto a practically independent territory, and an old ally of England. This attack, however, gave him an opportunity to call a Parliament, and to take advantage of their jealousy of France to grant him two "fifteenths." Edward Woodville was also allowed to take over English volunteers to the Bretons' aid. The total defeat of the Bretons at St. Aubin in 1488, and

the death of the Duke of Brittany, whose daughter and heiress, Anne, was already betrothed to Maximilian, made relations with France still more critical. Small bodies of English troops were thrown into Brittany and into Flanders. The French king was forced to make peace with the young duchess, restore her towns, and allow her marriage by proxy to Maximilian, December,

SEAL OF HENRY VII. FOR FRENCH AFFAIRS.

1489. The Parliament of this year had granted a large subsidy for the wars. But the attempt to levy it had provoked a dangerous rising in Yorkshire. It seemed that popular hatred of new modes of taxation would give new opportunities for Yorkist intrigue. And this perhaps explains why Henry, though leagued with Maximilian and with Ferdinand to defend Brittany, yet, in 1491, allowed it to be overrun by the French, and the young duchess, despite her proxy-marriage to Maximilian, forced or persuaded into actually marrying Charles VIII. This meant the final consolidation of the French realm. It shut one of the English "doors into France." It made possible the French invasion of Italy in 1494, an event which is generally reckoned as the beginning of distinctively modern history.

The marriage was a triumph for France, and an apparent humiliation for England. But there went with it the solid gain of a lasting peace; for the Treaty of Etaples, November, 1492, and its renewals kept off war between England and France till 1512. For himself, Henry secured a great sum, over £100,000, from France. And when we regard the fact that the expedition accomplished nothing else beyond besieging Boulogne for some twenty days, we may well suspect now, as did his disgusted soldiery at the time, that the king scrupled not "to plume his nobility and people to feather himself." His subjects, indeed, now found a point before unexpected in the king's original declaration that "the war once begun, it should pay itself"

But the truth is that his throne was not yet stable enough for the risks of a foreign war. In 1492, Perkin Warbeck appeared in Cork. The Irish were eager to thrust upon him the character of a Yorkist prince, whether Warwick, or a bastard son of Richard III., or Richard, the younger of the princes in the Tower. He settled on the last, and was in this character received, first in France, and then by Margaret of Burgundy. She acknowledged him as her nephew, helped to perfect him in his part, and kept him at her Court two and a half years. Henry appealed in vain to the rulers of Flanders to dismiss "the garçon." Then he retaliated by breaking up the commercial intercourse between England and the Flemings. But the French party in Flanders continued to support the pretender. Maximilian also aided him, from an idea that a new English king might be willing to take the field against France. It is not to be supposed that these princes and the Yorkist exiles themselves believed in Perkin's claims. But they saw in him a convenient instrument. He was to be pushed forward as a pawn in the game of Yorkist intrigue, and to be replaced when he had served their turn. But meantime, Henry, "working by countermine," had by his spies learned who were supporting the plot from England. He seized the leaders, and beheaded the chief of them as traitors, including Sir William Stanley, his own chamberlain and relative, the man to whose action at Bosworth he owed his life and his throne. This prompt severity embarrassed, if it could

Perkin Warbeck.

not wholly frustrate, the plot. Not till 1494 was Perkin able to offer a descent on English coasts. Beaten off by the country people at Deal, and repulsed at Waterford, he took refuge in Scotland. James IV. received him cordially, married him to his kinswoman, Katherine Gordon, and took him on a raid into England, 1496. But James, too, soon tired of the futile enterprise. In 1497 Warbeck returned to Ireland. From Ireland he sailed to try his fortune once more on English ground, and landing in Cornwall, was joined by some of the disaffected Cornishmen. But the lords and gentry armed against him; he was repulsed from Exeter, and fled to sanctuary at Beaulieu. His life was spared, but he was paraded through London, and then put in the Tower. In 1499, after attempting to escape, he was executed, and the Earl of Warwick, too—his fellow-prisoner. Henry was, no doubt, determined to this act of policy rather than justice by the appearance of another impostor impersonating the imprisoned earl. It is clear, too, that Ferdinand of Aragon was anxious before allowing his daughter to marry Prince Arthur that there should be "not a doubtful drop of royal blood" left in the kingdom to endanger the succession.

Relations with Scotland and Spain. During the seven years' episode of Perkin Warbeck, Henry had been exposed to constant hostility from Scotland. James III., who felt and acted up to his Lancastrian relationship, fell in battle with rebel subjects in 1488. James IV. revived the old Scottish connection with France; and not till 1498 was a marriage between him and the king's eldest daughter, Margaret, agreed upon. It had been proposed long ago in 1491, but

¶ Innocenti⁹ et Alexand pontifices predicti ad perpetuā ꝑ fuꝛ turam rei memoriā ad omnes diſcoꝛdias q̄ olim inter domos Lanꝯ caſtrie et Eboꝛaceñ vigueraũt tollendas atꝗꝫ in ꝑpetuo abolendas motu ꝑpꝛio et de certa ſciẽtia ꝉ nõ ad inſtantia alicuius inter alia in iſta bulla contẽtis pnunciauerũt ius ſucceſſionis Regni Anglie ad ſereniſſimā dñm henricū .vij. Anglie regem ſuoſꝗꝫ heredes inꝯ dubitanter et de iure pertinere.

¶ Jtem predicti pontifices monent precipiũt et requirũt motu ſcꝯ entia et auctoritate p̄dictis omnes Anglicos ꝉ alios ſubditos prefati henrici Anglie regis cuiuſcũꝗꝫ ſtatus ſeu ꝯditionis exiſtant ne ipſi aut aliquis eoꝛ tumultus occaſione iuris ſuccedendi vel quouis queꝯ

PAPAL PROCLAMATION

at last was effected in 1502. There had been two centuries of warfare between the two countries. The Tudor marriage inaugurated a period which, despite Flodden and Solway Moss and Pinkie, was, on the whole, a time of peace; and peace made possible the union of the two under Stuart kings. This result was won by the skill of Ayala, the Spanish envoy to England; for Spain saw that England must feel secure before she could join "the Holy League," to protect Italy and the Pope from French aggression. The Spanish alliance constituted the most fixed point of Henry's foreign relations. With Ferdinand of Aragon, the type of a successful ruler to Macchiavelli and Guicciardini, Henry Tudor "had ever a consent even in nature and custom." Their circumstances and their interests, as well as their characters, were alike. When Prince Arthur was a year old the marriage to Catherine of Aragon was mooted. Friendship between England and Spain was in accordance with the old traditions of both countries, and was almost indispensable to Ferdinand and Isabella, who were at this time engaged in the last stages of their struggle with the Moors of Granada; and who saw themselves threatened both by the French occupation of Roussillon and Cerdagne, and by the French designs against the Aragonese house at Naples. It seemed also natural that Maximilian, King of the Romans should be included in the treaty. Between him and France there were manifold causes for war—in Flanders and Burgundy, in Switzerland and Italy, besides the affair of Brittany. But before a final treaty could be ratified, there was much diplomatic fencing. "Maximilian the Moneyless" was the most changeful

Foreign Alliances.

ſtio coloꝛe auͭ quanqͭq; alía canſa ín eodem Regno per ſe vel alíͭ mouere ſeu mouerí facíáͭ auͭ pauenͭ ſub excoͭícatíonís eͭ maíoꝛís anathematís pena ipſo facto íncurríſſe aquo quídē excoͭícatíonís eͭ anathemaͭ; vínculo ab alío q̄ ſede aplíca p̄fata nequeanͭ abſoluͭ tíonís benefíciū obtínere vͭ latíus ſupꝛa contínetur.

¶ Item pꝛoprío motu ſcíentía ⁊ auctorítate p̄dictís phíbenͭ quoſcūq; tam príncípes exteros q̄ díctí regní Jncolas p̄ſtantes opem ⁊ ſuccurſū eídem ſereníſſíno ꝥenríco regí eíuſq; deſcendētíbꝫ ꝛtra eoꝛ rebelles auͭ alíq̄ ꝛtra p̄míſſa quouís pacto molíētes auctorítate aplíca bene dícūͭ íllís eͭ quos ſíc facíendo ín tam íuſta cauſa deceder̄ ꝛtíngerͭ vlenaríā oĩm ſuoꝛ pccōꝛ indulgentíā eͭ remíſſíonē elargíunͭ.

RECOGNISING HENRY VII. AS KING.

of the three; Ferdinand the most unscrupulous; Henry perhaps the greatest gainer in the long run. In July, 1496, he joined the Holy League. This was a sign that he had made his terms and secured his price; the abandonment of Perkin, the restoration of trade with Flanders, the initiation of a treaty with Scotland, and the resumption of the marriage project for Prince Arthur. Nor did the sudden death of Charles VIII. of France and the accession of Louis XII., and the consequent break up of the League, annul these solid results. In November, 1501, the marriage of Arthur and Catherine was celebrated at St. Paul's. Six months later the young prince died. But it had probably never been more than a marriage in form : Arthur was only in his sixteenth year; and his brother Henry was by papal dispensation betrothed to the young princess, though not actually married to her till after his accession, 1509.

In his later years Henry VII. had some idea, as the State papers show, of taking advantage of Ferdinand's weak hold of Castile, after Isabella's death. With this idea he made a close treaty with Ferdinand's son-in-law the Archduke Philip, who was driven by a storm into an English harbour in 1506 ; he proposed a marriage between himself and Philip's sister, Margaret; he even offered to marry Joanna, Ferdinand's daughter. She was known to be insane; but the marriage would have given Henry the Regency of Castile. Finally, he effected a marriage by proxy between the Princess Mary, a girl of twelve, and Philip's son, Charles of Castile, a boy of eight. Ferdinand, we know, was seriously alarmed by these designs. They were, perhaps, only intended to produce this result. But they exhibit the diplomacy of the period in its most repulsive light; and Henry himself shows at his worst in the marriage projects he formed after the death of Elizabeth of York in 1503. His minute inquiries as to the person of the young widow, the Queen of Naples, belong to an age not very delicate in such matters. But his proposal to marry his own son's widow would be revolting in any age; and is hardly made pleasanter by the probability that it was chiefly intended to serve as a diplomatic move to avoid a restitution of the dower paid with her. There is something, too, which can only be justified by the tyrant's plea of necessity, in Henry's dealing with the De la Pole family, the last scions of the White Rose. In

1506 he had made it a point with Philip, his guest and prisoner, that Edmund de la Pole, Earl of Suffolk, should be surrendered on a promise that the fugitive's life should be spared. But it was reported that the king left to his son instructions like those of David to Solomon; and certainly Henry VIII., soon after his accession, executed the earl without further trial. Not till the very end of the reign of the first Tudor king would foreign Powers believe in the stability of the new throne. But there is ample evidence that, long before that, they had recognised in Henry a sovereign of first-rate diplomatic importance. " He is admirably well informed," writes an Italian envoy; " he receives special information of every event ; the merchants never cease giving him advices." Not only his detachment from English prejudices, and his unsleeping vigilance and industry, but the concentration of European politics around the Court of France, contributed to give this position to the English king. His almost unbroken successes deeply impressed a generation who worshipped fortune. He himself boasted that his alliances, with Scotland on one side, Burgundy and Castile on the other, had built a wall of brass about England.

It is clear, too, that his throne, so insecure in the first **Heavy Taxation** twelve years of his reign, was firm enough at its close. As early as 1495 his consciousness of strength was shown in the Act which legalised obedience to a *de facto* sovereign. It appears also in the greater unscrupulousness in amassing treasure which was the mark of Empson's and Dudley's tenure of office. Archbishop Morton's had probably been a restraining and constitutional influence while he lived; certainly after his death there is only one Parliament called in the nine years. Yet Morton himself was popularly credited with the invention of a dilemma—" Morton's fork "—to use upon reluctant contributers to the benevolence : the thrifty could pay out of their savings, the prodigal proved by their manner of life that they could pay. But after 1499, these two " horse-leeches " kept in prison men committed for trial till they paid heavy fines ; imprisoned men without verdict of a jury ; exacted the uttermost farthing of feudal dues ; " ruffled with jurors " to extort the verdicts desired; and " raked over " all old penal laws to exact the penalties. No doubt hoarding became a mere passion with Henry. But he had begun this policy, by which he left in his coffers at his death nearly two million pounds, on a sound principle. He saw that finance was the rock on which his Lancastrian predecessors had split; he felt that the ordinary revenue of the Crown must be independent of Parliamentary parsimony. In nothing was he more unflinching than in the levying of taxes. The new tax, the

TOMB OF CARDINAL MORTON, CANTERBURY CATHEDRAL.

subsidy, had caused a serious rising in the North in 1489; in 1495 Cornwall rose against it, and the rebels occupied Blackheath and threatened London, and could only be dislodged by a regular battle. Besides the large war-grants made by each of his seven Parliaments, he ventured on the great benevolence of 1492, and in 1495 had an Act passed which gave it legislative sanction. In 1504 he got the Parliament's sanction to the feudal aid for his eldest son and daughter. Measures that had shaken the position of former kings seemed only to strengthen that of the Tudor. Even Ireland, the standing failure of English sovereigns, was handled by him not wholly without success. The House of York had a deep hold over the settlers in Ireland, partly from memory of Richard of York and from his territorial influence, but mainly, no doubt, from the Irish instinct of opposition to the Government. They joined eagerly in setting up Lambert Simnel in 1486, though not even Irishmen could seriously believe in the impersonation. They submitted nominally to the new dynasty in 1488, but the Earl of Kildare, head of the Geraldines, who had been chief promoter of the rebellion, had to be left in the office of Lord-Deputy. Moreover, Warbeck found his first and his last adherents in Ireland. But if we look closely at the facts, we find that the disaffection in Ireland had on each occasion less life and body in it. And even when complaints against Kildare grew so loud that he was removed in 1492, he boldly faced his enemies at Westminster, and claimed to have none other for counsel on his side than the king himself. At last, when his foe, the Bishop of Meath, said, "You see, all Ireland cannot rule him"; "Then he" (said the king) "must rule all Ireland." But meantime Sir Edward Poynings had done two years' good work in the country (1494–96), especially in the famous Poynings' Act, which subordinated the Irish Legislature to the English. He also did much to establish royal authority in the English Pale; the assertion of it beyond the four counties (Dublin, Meath, Kildare, Louth) was left to Kildare, who was deputy from 1496 to 1513. Thus, even in Ireland, the close of Henry's reign offered at least the appearance of peace and order, though underneath the surface, what with the struggles between Fitzgeralds and Butlers, between the English Pale and the "Wild Irish," and between the various Irish chieftains and tribes, the usual policy was being adopted of "letting Ireland stew in its own juice."

One of the most important events of the reign was the Intercursus Magnus (pp. 556, 626), the great treaty with Flanders which followed on the two years' suspension of commercial intercourse (149–496). The suspension was bitterly felt in both

[margin: Ireland.]

[margin: Treaty with Flanders]

countries: as Bacon puts it quaintly, " Being a king that loved
wealth and treasure, he could not endure to have trade sick, or
any obstruction in the *vena porta* which dispersed the blood."
The treaty, therefore, was received with processions and feastings,
both at Antwerp and in ·London. It made traffic between the
two countries absolutely free in all commodities; each was to
aid the other against piracy, and each to open its law courts to
merchants of the others. Its result, however, was to transfer to

A FLEMISH TOWN (MS. Aug. A. v.).

England the cloth manufacture of Flanders, a transference completed by Alva's sack of Antwerp in 1585.

The New World. In one matter, Henry VII. let slip a great opportunity. In
1487, Columbus, despairing of Portugal, sent his brother
Bartholomew to the English Court to get his great project taken
up. Bartholomew was captured by pirates; and before he could
win the ear of Henry VII., Christopher discovered the West
Indies. It is curious to speculate on what might have been, had
the New World fallen to England and not to Spain. It was not
the fault of Bristol merchants that this did not happen. In
1480 they sent out two ships to find " the Isle of Brazil," and
in 1497 John Cabot, acting for them, perhaps discovered

1509|

Labrador (p. 674.) Henry now took it up; but Spanish jealousy was aroused, and Cabot was tempted away till 1517. With Spain claiming the West, and Portugal all the East, English enterprise was forced into searching for a North-West Passage.

THE New Monarchy is the term applied by Mr. Green to the period when England was governed by kings who were practically absolute. It was, in a word, the outcome of the executive weakness of the Lancastrians, it was "the source of the violent collision under the Stuarts of Crown and Parliament, of the executive and the representative or legislative sides of one constitution." During this period the position of Crown, Parliament, and Church is altered. A new era in foreign policy sets in, a great expansion of commerce takes place. The period sees a remarkable outburst of life and freedom in enterprise, art, literature, and religion, and later in politics.

ARTHUR HASSALL.
The New Monarchy

The New Monarchy dates from the accession of Edward IV., and was firmly established by Henry VII. Its advent not only marks the beginning of a new period, and with it a new development of kingship, which alone was able to cope with the turbulence of a widespread revolution in all departments of thought and life, but also involves the triumph of the new executive over the old legislative powers.

The relations between Crown and Parliament, between the executive and the legislative, may be based on three grounds. The legislative may be subservient to the Crown, and absolute monarchy is the result; or the executive may be controlled by the legislative, as in the case where constitutional government flourishes; or the two powers may be equal and independent to a great extent, as they are in the United States. The period of the New Monarchy saw the legislative completely subservient to the executive. During the fourteenth century, in spite of the growth of constitutional life, no fixed limit had been set to the definite growth of royal assumption. "For every assertion of national rights," says Bishop Stubbs, writing of the fourteenth century, " there is a counter-assertion of royal autocracy. Royalty becomes in theory more absolute, as in practice it is limited more and more by the national will." But though the strenuous assertion of divine right and the claim to indefeasible monarchical privileges by Richard II. were checked by the revolution of 1399, followed by the development under the Lancastrians of a kind of medieval constitutionalism, the check to this assertion of a factitious theory of absolutism turned out to be only temporary.

Parliamentary Supremacy,

After Richard's deposition, for the first time in English history the Legislature got the upper hand, and during the minority of Henry VI. the Council, itself subordinate to Parliament, carried on the administration. But the Council found itself unequal to the work of government, and its incapacity to preserve order, together with the weakness and misgovernment of Henry VI., necessitated the adoption of what has been called a new theory of English kingship, though on closer examination it will be seen to be in many particulars similar to that which Richard II. had in vain attempted to assert. A variety of circumstances now combined to give it weight and popularity.

and the Reaction.

The violence of the times brought home to men the monarchy as the ultimate protection and support of the weaker classes. The view that in the permanent sovereign power lay the source of all the rights of the upper classes, and that the king was the living embodiment of that sovereign power, found popular expression and ready acceptance. When once the Commons fully realised that the Lords had retired from their position as leaders of the people, and had plunged the country into an internecine war for their own factious purposes, they rallied round the Crown, and while becoming its greatest support, saw in it their protection. Parliament thus recognised willingly the necessity of a strong monarchy, and did all in its power to secure a vigorous succession. In the constitution of Parliament, therefore, at the close of the Middle Ages, " there is," as Hallam says, " nothing of a republican aspect. Everything appears to grow out of the monarchy, and redound to the honour and advantage of the king. The voice of the petitioners is, even when the Lower House is in its most defiant humour, always respectful ; the prerogative of the Crown is always acknowledged in broad and pompous expressions."

The Elements of Royal Power.

In legal theory the king was the ultimate and sole landowner, and the succession to the throne was treated by the jurists like succession to real property according to primogeniture. The idea of legitimacy, the indefeasible right of the lawful heir, had made great progress during the fourteenth and fifteenth centuries. Henry IV., Edward IV., Richard III., and Henry VII. all claimed the throne by inheritance amongst other pretexts, and the existence of such claims " testifies to the growing belief in a doctrine which was one day to become a part of the creed of loyalty." Regarded as the source of all private rights in the soil, standing since Edward I.'s time on the foundation of heredita- bility—no interregnum being legally recognised in the succession to the throne—the Crown was in a very strong position. The king held in his hands all the executive power which "is the source and basis of the royal prerogative." He had the right of appointing to offices of State, and the tenure of such offices was determined by him. He was the fountain of justice, the supreme guardian of the peace, the sovran arbiter in ecclesiastical and commercial matters. Political government was centred in the king, aided by Courts of Justice and his councillors. In practice, too, the king at times exercised legislative power, though it was understood that he did not repeal what the Three Estates had resolved upon; he was not obliged to summon Parliament, and his right of legislating by ordinance was rarely questioned. In theory, then, the king could do everything; but in practice he found it very difficult to carry on the work of government without the counsel and consent of the Estates.[1]

Such is the summary of the actual position of the king at the end of the Middle Ages. Richard II. had lost his life in mis- taking "the theory for the truth of fact." The Tudor monarchs found that the nation believed firmly in the theory and were not at all unwilling to hold to the fact. It was only when the Stuarts attempted to continue and develop a theory which had lost all reality, that the nation rose and discarded absolutism for ever.   *Uses of Abso- lutism.*

During the period of the Tudor Dictatorship, however, the nation would look only at the better side of the theory of royalty. A strong king was required, and while the clergy insisted on obedience as a religious duty, the lawyers supported it by the system of allegiance, fealty, homage, and the law of treason These obligations had, under weak kings, proved insufficient to maintain order, but aided by the political suicide of the baronage and strengthened by the support of the clergy and

[1] In England it can be proved that the king never had the legislative power alone.

commons, the Tudor dynasty, in preserving the peace of the country and enforcing the obedience of its subjects, found a ready acquiescence in the religious and legal sanctions with which the theory of kingship had been fenced in.

Political Development.

It has, indeed, been asserted that, from a constitutional point of view, the whole period from 1460 to 1640 is a blank, and that the Great Rebellion "took up the thread of the political development just where it had been snapped by the Wars of the Roses." But this statement is manifestly inaccurate. The changes at first effected by the New Monarchy amounted, indeed, almost to a revolution, and for some sixty years the parliamentary constitution was practically suspended; yet with the fall of Wolsey the political development of the country went on apace, and the advance made was, though slow, thorough and continuous.

The government of the House of York was a despotism, but, unlike the Tudor rule, it was not generally popular. During the reign of Edward IV. the executive freed itself from the trammels imposed on it, partly under the three former Edwards, but mainly under the house of Lancaster. The Crown had not possessed such power since Edward I., and thus the great constitutional struggle between the executive and legislative was stopped for the time by the predominance of the executive. Edward IV., it is true, paved the way for the Tudors, but he anticipated the methods rather than the spirit of their rule. Under him discontent was kept down simply by a reign of terror. He had slight power of foresight, his personal rule was almost as disorderly as the weak government of Henry VI., and his system was continued under his successor.

"Though never before and never again for more than two hundred years were the commons so strong as they were under Henry IV.," many of the rights claimed had been claimed prematurely. The victory of 1399 had been premature, hard facts had proved that the nation was not in reality ready for the parliamentary self-government offered it by the Lancastrians, and Parliament was decidedly not fit to become the direct instrument of rule. The monarchy of the Tudors was not in any formal sense a break in the continuity of English constitutional life, the Tudor princes were popular, and the absence of a standing army proves that even Henry VIII. could rely on the support of all classes. To secure a respite from the troubles of an age of dynastic and social revolution, men were prepared to recognise that a dictatorial and paramount authority, generally known as the king's absolute power, was involved of necessity in the very conception of kingship.

The strength, then, of the Crown at the close of the Middle Ages " lay in the permanence of the idea of royalty, the wealth of the king, the legal definitions and theory of the supreme power." Till the fall of the Lancastrians it might seem that in proportion as royalty became more absolute in theory, in practice it was limited more and more by the national will. But when the nation as a whole was interested in supporting the pretensions of the Crown, it became easy for the kings to exaggerate the royal attributes, and to extend the region of undefined prerogative. Henry VII. took advantage of the absence of competitors, and the desire for a safe succession, to obtain from a submissive Parliament statutory prerogatives ; he wielded with success the indefinite judicial and executive powers of the Crown, strengthened and organised the main instrument of his authority, the Royal Council, raised loans without consent of Parliament, and increased the representation. But the people were willing to be so governed, and Parliament was complaisant. For the sake of order and peace, the country was ready to forego some measure of constitutional liberty.

THE New Monarchy was based on the new forces of a new age—on commerce, which replaced feudalism, and on individualism, which replaced the old ecclesiastical system. With the accession of Henry VII. changes in the balance between Church and State, and between the Crown and the Estates, were begun, which were consummated under Henry VIII. Between the Norman Conquest and the Battle of Bosworth the centre of gravity in the great ship of the State had varied. From 1066 to Magna Charta, the Crown, clergy, and commons had united against the feudal instincts of the baronage ; from Magna Charta to the revolution of 1399, the barons, commons, and to a certain extent the clergy, had banded together against the aggressive policy of the Crown. From the deposition of Richard II. to the accession of Henry VII., the royal house, baronage, and commons were a prey to internal division. After

ARTHUR HASSALL. The Balance of Classes.

the Lancastrian and Yorkist reigns the clergy, which alone of the three estates did not suffer during the Wars of the Roses, appeared to be united and fairly strong. From their ranks were still chosen ministers of State; they had a secure majority in the House of Lords; they possessed great wealth. But though the Church retained so much power, it had lost its hold on the people. Its influence, which in the eleventh, twelfth, and thirteenth centuries had so successfully been used in the struggle for liberty, was now undermined from a variety of causes. The Lollard movement, the Renaissance, the growing secularity of Churchmen, the alliance with, or dependence on, a foreign authority—each contributed something to the unpopularity with which, during the fifteenth and earlier portion of the sixteenth centuries, the clergy were regarded. Threatened with spoliation, and no longer able to look for support to the already weakened and humiliated baronage with whom they had latterly identified themselves, the clergy now sank into complete dependence on the king, became a bulwark of the Crown, and endeavoured in this manner to save themselves from their impending fate.

Till the Wars of the Roses the noble class had paramount influence in the country. "Taken in the aggregate the landed possessions of the baronage were more than a counterpoise to the whole influence of the Crown and the other two estates of the realm." The clergy could not withstand them, and though the commons had taken up an important constitutional position in Henry IV.'s reign, it is quite evident that in reality they depended on the great lords, and that the advance made during the Lancastrian period was premature. The nobles and the clergy then were the governing classes, and the rest of the nation acquiesced in the predominance of their influence. The commons most distinctly had not learnt to act independently of the great lords when the Wars of the Roses came upon them. During the Wars of the Roses the nobles had. as is often said, committed political suicide. "Attenuated in power and prestige rather than in numbers," the House of Lords lay at the mercy of a strong ruler. The battles of Barnet and Tewkesbury in 1471 had destroyed the temporary union of the Lancastrian and Yorkist factions against Edward IV., and the fate of the medieval baronage as a political force was sealed.

The triumph of the nobles at Bosworth was but momentary. Readjustment by Henry VII. united both the Lancastrian and Yorkist parties, and then proceeded to restore the national balance.

The weakness of the Crown had been due to merely transient causes, and a strong sovereign with a well-defined policy could, with the support of a united people, re-arrange the political factors in the State so as to allow room for a more healthy development in the future. And this was the policy pursued by Henry VII.

The balance of forces was on his accession thrown out of gear by the absence of all political energy in the baronial estate. The commons, deprived of their natural leaders, the barons, in whom they had now lost all confidence, and neither able nor willing to withstand a powerful king, ceased to take an interest in politics, left the nobles, the wealthy merchants, and the rich landowners at the king's mercy, threw themselves into commercial

TUDOR ROSES (MS. Roy. 18 C. xviii.).

or literary pursuits, and began that accumulation of wealth which enabled them to withstand Charles I. in the Civil War. The higher clergy, unpopular with the nation, and dependent on the Crown, acted in complete harmony with the wishes of the king, and offered no resistance to the concentration of all the powers of the State in the hands of Henry himself.

Henry VII. was thus enabled to crush the old baronage, to begin tentatively the construction of a new nobility, and to aid in the growth, if not in the creation, of the middle classes. In his severity towards the nobles and rich landowners the nation fully acquiesced. Order was the one great need of the time, and in return for order men were prepared to stand by while the king pursued his policy for guarding the popular interests, levelling class privilege and depressing the baronage. Since the days of Edward III. the sovereign power had been weak, and consequently all authority had been weak. The constitutional experiment of the Lancastrians had failed, England had lost her foreign possessions and had suffered a diminution of her trade. The country itself, too, was a prey to disorder, which culminated in the Wars of the Roses. As far, however, as the trading classes were concerned, the Wars of the Roses were but the expression of a determination on the part of the nation to get rid of an incompetent ruler. For the only hope of order lay in the accession of a strong line of kings. Men had, in a word, to choose between anarchy and despotism. The revival of ancient learning, the outburst of commercial enterprise, the weariness of political strife, the selfishness of the nobles, the unpopularity of the clergy—all these circumstances reconciled the nation to the dictatorship of the Tudors. As long as he did not ask for money, the king could do as he liked. He might exact supplies from rich individuals provided that he did not interfere with the middle classes.

Henry VII. then, having no strong baronage to thwart him, and supported by his Parliaments and by the nation, still further depressed the old nobility. This was done mainly by the expansion of the treason laws, by heavy fines for all sorts of offences, and generally by means of the Royal Council. In 1487 the Act which founded the Court of Star Chamber was passed, and henceforward maintenance was put down, the misconduct of sheriffs was severely punished, and riots and unlawful assemblies were suppressed. Henry VII. definitely aimed at levelling class privileges. Some of the old nobles held office under him, but they were reduced to the same level as the rest of the new officials who aided the king to carry on the government. The power of the medieval nobility passed away, and gradually the old race of nobles, with slight exceptions, disappeared. Only a few like the Duke of Norfolk remained to connect the era of the Plantagenets with that of the Tudors. "The civil wars turned up a new soil to the surface," and the construction of a new nobility out of the ruins of the old was at least begun by

Henry VII., and definitely continued by Henry VIII. and Elizabeth.

At the end, then, of the fifteenth century, and at the beginning of the sixteenth, this process of filling the ranks of the nobility with new men was begun. The class which came forward to fill the gap caused by wars, confiscations

The New Nobility.

TOMB OF LORD DAUBENY, WESTMINSTER ABBEY.

and attainders, was what might be termed the upper rural class, a class which had been formed by the fusion of the knights of the shire with the non-noble free landowner, who had after Edward I.'s reign tended to separate from the class of barons. This new class had in the fifteenth century devoted itself to agriculture and to the selling of wool and the produce of its herds. It was mainly from this class that Henry VIII. chose his new peers. The new peerage was thus distinctly based upon wealth, it was ignorant of the traditions of the earlier nobility, it was at first absolutely dependent on the monarch to whom it owed its position, and to whom it

looked for future favours. Though the baronage of the latter
Middle Ages were ambitious, selfish, "with little conscience
and less sympathy," they always possessed a more ennobling
sense of their responsibilities than did their successors, the
new nobility of the Tudors.   The policy of the medieval
baron was insular, but "he was a wonderful impersonation
of strength and versatility."   The mercenary characteristics of
the new nobles were indeed at first as repulsive as were the
relentlessness and anarchical habits of the old race of barons.
The real meaning, however, of the change was that the feudal
lord was turned into the country gentleman.

Henry VII. himself only created five new peerages during
his reign—the earldom of Bath, the Irish earldom of Ormond,
and those of Daubeny, Cheney, and Burgh.   It is true that
we find that only twenty-nine lords were summoned to Parliament in 1485, but the smallness of the numbers was due
to accidental causes, to the suspension of some peerages, to
the fact that others were represented by minors, and to the
unexplained absence of others such as Lords Ogle, Dacre, and
Scrope.   As the reign proceeded, the suspended peerages were
revived, and the Howards and Ferrers returned to favour,
and in spite of a certain number of attainders, the later
Parliaments of Henry VII. contain a lay peerage of forty
members—which is the average number for the century.
Thus, though we can see a tendency in all Henry's policy
to raise and employ new men, though we can point to the
class out of which future creations would be made, it is an
exaggeration to say that Henry VII. did more than indicate
the policy which was followed by his successors.

Rise of the Commons.   In the sixteenth century the Commons for the first time
assumed that leading position in Parliament which they have
since retained.   "By bestowing representations on the towns
and counties of Wales, Calais, and Chester, Henry VIII. added
in 1543 thirty-two members, knights and burgesses to the old
number"; and in 1549 we find the first instance of a peer's
son seeking election in the House of Commons.   Moreover, in
the sixteenth century the altered position of the county and
borough members to each other is another significant proof
of the growing importance and cohesion of the middle class.
In the fifteenth century, though the borough members were

regar..:d as authorities in matters of finance, they had little voice in matters of State. The knights of the shire had always taken a decisive lead in the Lower House. With the sixteenth century a change came about. The citizens dis-

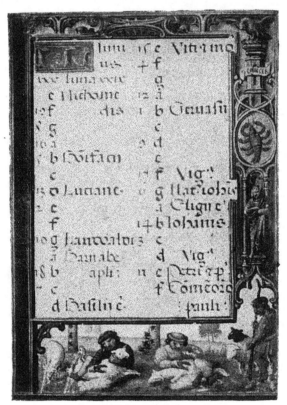

FLANDERS: SHEEP SHEARING (MS. Add. 24,098).

cussed political matters on an equality with the knights of the shire, and in the Parliament of 1529 the leading member of the Commons, Thomas Cromwell, sat for Taunton.

The prominent place taken by the borough members in the reigns of Henry VIII. and Elizabeth was in some measure

Social
Policy. due to the enlightened policy of the first Tudor sovereign. Henry VII. was as anxious for the prosperity of the new

commercial class as he was for the extermination of the old nobility. It was the definite aim of the Tudors to pose as social reformers. Their whole policy is marked by a systematic care for trade, and

FLANDERS: SUMMER.

for the middle and lower orders. They took up questions bearing upon wages, and upon the relations between labour and capital. They evinced an interest in agriculture and sheep-farming, they were equally careful for the advancement of education. During the fifteenth century a merchant class was steadily rising. It was this class which was especially interested in the establishment of a strong government capable of keeping order in the country. It had been encouraged by Edward IV. and Richard III., both of whom had made commercial alliances abroad and had fostered and protected trade by numerous statutes. Henry VII. did all he could to advance this middle class. He encouraged manufactures and

FLANDERS: SHEEP AND SHEPHERDS.

commerce, he furthered the interests of English shipping by requiring that "wines and woads of Gascony and Languedoc should be imported in English bottoms," he endeavoured by means which would not be approved by political economists of our day to prevent the importation of useless luxuries such as ribbons, to regulate the prices of different kinds of wool, and to prevent the exportation of gold. By his encouragement Sebastian Cabot sailed from Bristol (p. 674), by his diplomacy the Intercursus Magnus (pp. 556, 613, 745) was concluded in 1496—an epoch in the history of English trading relations with Flanders—and later, in 1506, another treaty

for regulating commercial intercourse between England and
Flanders was arranged, which was so greatly to the interest
of the former country that it was called in the Netherlands
the *Malus Intercursus.* Henry VII.'s policy, continued by
Henry VIII. and Elizabeth, transformed England from a poor
and thinly populated country into a rich and populous one.
The Tudor period saw the creation of a disciplined middle
class, and with it the introduction of a new political force
into the country. The mercantile influence tended undoubtedly
to widen the national mind, it had a beneficial effect on foreign
policy, it aided in the development of political economy. But

FLANDERS: CARRYING HAY.

at the same time the
trading spirit was as
inclined to engross
power and exclude
competition as any
class had done in pre-
vious times. England
required and secured
in the reign of
Henry VII. "constitutional and governmental consistency."
The balance of forces in the State was changed. The strength,
weight, and influence of royalty were increased by the temporary loss of prestige and political status by the nobles, by
the subservience of the clergy, and by the acquiescence of the
Commons.

Many circumstances, in addition to the prostration of all
classes before the royal power, contributed to place the Crown
in Henry VII.'s reign in an unusually strong position. In the
union of the
houses of York
and Lancaster
there was a
union of es-
tates. The
lands of con-
fiscated nobles
fell to the
Crown, and even when attainted lands were restored, the king
managed to keep a portion. All the rebellions of the reign added

*Strength
of the
Crown.*

FLANDERS: A WINTER SCENE.

largely to these acquisitions, and it has been said that " treason was more profitable to Henry VII. than any other branch of his revenue." He was always careful in money matters, and by the use of the system of loans and benevolences, and by the feudal exactions in connection with which Empson and Dudley achieved so unenviable a notoriety, he so increased his revenue as to do without Parliaments in the latter portion of his reign. His miserly habits and his expedition to France also contributed to this result. " His wars," says Bacon, " were always to him as a mine of treasure ", and again, " They slack not to say that the king plumed his nobility and people to feather himself." The power and supremacy of the Crown were by these means placed on a footing they had never been placed on before.

Henry VII.'s reign thus saw a great change in the balance of the constitution effected. The Crown was in reality absolute, and though the Tudors had no standing army and no organised police system, they established their power with little difficulty. Had it not been for the extravagance of Henry VIII. and the troubles of the Reformation, their absolutism might have become permanent, and the balance of the constitution fundamentally disarranged.

W. H. HUTTON. The Church under Henry VII.

THE history of religion in England during the reign of Henry VII. centres round one man, who may be taken as the representative in many ways of the Church of his age. John Morton, cardinal and chancellor, Bishop of Ely and Primate of All England—who planned the Union of the Roses, who brought about Buckingham's revolt, who was the right hand of the wise King Henry—seems at first sight to belong rather to the State than to the Church. The mixture of functions led indeed, as a great historian has noted, to occasional awkwardness and inconsistency, as when the chancellor-archbishop allowed his judgment on a fraudulent executor to be modified by the reflection that he would be " *damné in hell* " (*sic*).[1] But Morton discharged his ecclesiastical obligations with as much regularity and vigour . as his administrative and legal duties, and he was a man keenly interested in all the movements of a complicated and stirring period.   He was

[1] Stubbs, "Lectures on Medieval and Modern History," p. 317.

alive to the social changes of the time, and was eager to promote the material prosperity of the classes that were suffering by the agricultural revolution. He repaired at his own cost the palaces of his different sees, carried out many works at Oxford (including a share in that matchless monument of Perpendicular architecture, the Divinity School), cut the great drain from Peterborough to Wisbech still known as Morton's Leam, built the tower of Wisbech Church, and rebuilt Rochester Bridge. It was he, we cannot doubt, who supplied to Sir Thomas More the information on which is based the one standard English record of the reign of Richard III. Of his great household, his wide interests, his kindly manners, we may well conjecture that we have a close reproduction in the introduction to the *Utopia*. The whole scene rises before us: the talk before the big fire, the eager listeners to the tale of adventure, the sycophants ready to catch up their patron's words, the calm, wise tolerance of the cardinal himself. The chief social evils of the new era come into debate, and the great churchman touches on them as befits one "in his speech fine, eloquent and pithy, gentle in communication, yet earnest and sage." From him it may well be that More learnt first to see with sympathetic eyes the sorrows of the people, and to speak what was in his mind so boldly and clearly. He belongs half to the past, half to the future: in him the interests of the Middle Ages and those of the Tudor times, if not of modern life, seem to find a connecting link.

And, first, we may illustrate from his career the way in which ecclesiastical patronage was used by the kings of the fifteenth century. Sir John Fortescue,[1] in his scheme for the reconstruction of the Royal Council, notes that "it shall not be necessary that the twelve spiritual men of this council have so great wages as the twelve temporal men"; and the reason of this is clear from the appointments of the time. Gascoigne, reformer as much as satirist, says: "Churches and bishoprics are now the maintenance and reward of kings' servants and of worldly lords." The Popes winked at the abuse, so long as the Church paid their toll. The services which Henry VII. rewarded in Morton were certainly political, but his richest rewards were drawn by the king's hand from the Church. The great bishops of the age

[1] Plummer's ed., p. 146.

Ecclesiastics as State Officials. were either servants of the Crown or scions of the great noble families. Thomas Bourchier was made archbishop " because of the great blood he was of " ; the richest preferments in the land belonged to George Neville, the King-maker's brother. Good men, it may be, were often appointed, but the system was a corrupt one, and contained the seeds of its own decay. Such a method of appointment did not tend to make the holders of great offices active, though it might secure that they were men of toleration, of hospitality, of dignified splendour. Thus it is not surprising that in the reign of Henry VII. " there is little or no religious persecution, little or no literary or ecclesiastical activity."[1] It was, for the higher clergy at least, a comfortable age, and the tradition of ease spread to the monasteries themselves.

Decay of the Monasteries. On many of the great religious houses their obligations sat lightly. The abbots were sprung from noble families, and they lived as country gentlemen affecting the state of their social equals, kindly landlords, and showing a somewhat antiquated beneficence to the poor. For at their best the monastic houses stood forth in opposition—short-sighted and hopeless, indeed, but unselfish—to the competitive tendencies of the age. On their lands the old agricultural system lingered long after the lay land-owners had betaken themselves to pasture-farming and driven forth their villeins and labourers to seek work in the towns, or to be hanged for sturdy beggars on the highway. The monastic estates were still managed on the old system of bailiff-farming, and tillage was kept up upon them long after it had become economically unprofitable. The rustic population, when able-bodied, found employment at their hands; and when old and past work, were supported by their alms. Such a condition of affairs was obviously only a transition : monasteries which were to be a refuge for the needy cadets of great houses could not long continue to carry on unprofitable husbandry, or to be the sole support of the indigent. Throughout the reign of Henry VII. bankruptcy was approaching with rapid strides. The great houses still held their heads proudly aloft, but lesser ones were beginning to be closed from lack of object and lack of means. In 1494, by bull of Alexander VI.,[2] the houses of Mottisfont and

Stubbs, " Lectures." p. 369.
Gasquet, " English Monasteries," p. 62.

Suffield were suppressed: in the one case there were but three canons remaining, in the second only two monks under the prior, while the buildings were in ruins. And the earlier colleges at Oxford and Cambridge were founded and endowed by the dissolution of religious houses which had fallen into decay. The precedent was ominous.

But the condition of the monasteries was not only financially unsound; it seems, in some cases at least, to have been morally corrupt. Here it is necessary to sweep away the interested exaggerations of the greedy and prejudiced men who were responsible for the suppression of thirty years later. But that the condition of monasticism was not satisfactory is clear enough from the measures which were taken by Morton, with the sanction and authority of the Popes.

In 1489, on the request of the king and archbishop, Innocent VIII. granted to the latter authority to visit the religious houses in his province, to treat with all ecclesiastical censure, and, where necessary, to call in the secular arm.[1] The necessity of such visitation is shown by the statement that in divers monasteries some were leading a life dissolute and lascivious " to the ruin of their souls, the offence of the Divine Majesty, the shame of religion, and the hurt and scandal of many." The most flagrant instance was that of the great abbey of St. Albans. For this we have Morton's own letter to the abbot, which unfolds a terrible record of profligacy.[2] Not only did the monks resort to the company of depraved women, but one such woman was placed high in authority at a cell under their governance; and the priories of Pray and Sapwell were become nests of corruption. " Virtue is neglected, and religion is abased." Morton did not rest till he was armed with all powers, civil as well as ecclesiastical, to correct and amend. Parliament[3] gave him large authority to imprison for incontinency and other offences; and the Statute of Præmunire was disregarded in the tacit assent given to the Pope's bull for the legatine visitation. Morton visited the dioceses of Salisbury, Rochester. and Worcester twice, and once the dioceses of Winchester, Exeter, Bath and Wells, Lichfield and Coventry, and Lincoln. We have, happily, full records of local visitations at the collegiate church of Southwell and in

Visitations of the Monasteries.

---

[1] Wilkins, "Concilia," iii., 630–32. [2] *Ibid.*, pp. 632–4.
[3] Statutes at Large, ii., 65.

the diocese of Norwich as well as the acts of the Ripon Chapter. At Southwell—a secular college—the archbishop does not appear to have visited, but triennial inquiries were conducted by the chapter into the conduct of the inferior ministers.[1] In the records offences great and small are mingled without distinction —brawling, Sabbath-breaking, spitting during service, refusing to sing *pryksonge* (*i.e.* harmony), and frequenting taverns, are common ; adultery stands side by side with sleeping in church. There is great laxity in performance of the offices, and Thomas Cartwright has a singular way in singing, and gives not ear in his singing to the music of the others. The diocese of Norwich —a wider field—contained some worse scandals; but the accounts, on the whole, do not show much that is seriously wrong. We have record[2] of episcopal visitation of forty-four houses during the reign, the visitation taking place, somewhat irregularly, every six years. East Anglia was rich and prosperous, and there is little sign of a falling off in the numbers of those who adopted the religious life; but even in these shires there are reports of the financial distress from which monasteries elsewhere were suffering. The visitation of Bishop Goldwell, in 1492, illustrates this in the case of the Abbey of Wymondham. Under the abbacy of John Kyrteling, who had been abbot for more than twenty years, everything had gone wrong. The discipline was bad, the buildings were out of repair. There were no accounts of revenue or expenditure. The abbot was made to retire, and a further inquiry was ordered. In 1514 Bishop Richard Nicke had to take sterner measures, for the monastery was utterly corrupt and decayed. Licence of all kinds flourished, drunkenness and revellings, mad brawlings, and complete disregard of the rule prevailed. The prior was dismissed; but we have no report of any measures of reform. The priory at Norwich has no better record. In 1492 the monastic rule was found to be greatly relaxed, though no grievous scandals were observed. The gates were often not closed at night, frivolous laymen joined the monks at their repasts; there was talk of embezzlement, and, at any rate, there was far too much gossip and chatter, even in church. Women were not excluded from the house, and the servants of the monastery had their families living within the precincts. In

[1] Southwell Visitation (Camden Society, 1890).
[2] Norwich Visitation (Camden Society, 1888).

1514 the condition of affairs was much worse. The prior, it was said, had furtively abstracted the common seal, and used it to seal a presentation, doubtless to his own profit. Suspicious women were about, and there was dancing in the great hall by

WALSINGHAM ABBEY TO-DAY.
(*From a photograph by the Rev. W. Martin, M.A.*)

night. Sheep fed within the cloister, the brethren were neglected, there was no schoolmaster, and the number of monks had fallen short by ten. It appears that something was done to improve matters, for at the next visitation the complaints are either too wild to be credible, or are concerned with the sad folly of the juniors, who played cards and backgammon, and the gross vanity of the precentor, who would wear red dancing-shoes and a riding-coat. Lesser houses show lesser blots. St. Benet's at Hulme, and the great priory of Walsingham, brought into European note by the visit of Erasmus in 1511, the houses of Augustinian canons, and the many nunneries scattered over East Anglia, all were visited. Either there is some scandal, particularly if the house, like Walsingham, be rich, or there is decay and debt. But in the great majority of cases the cloistered life of this time seems to have been tranquil and uninteresting; and the religious, it they did little good, did no harm. They were either rich men furnished with ability, living peaceably in their habitations, or poor men praying for their neighbours, on whose alms they eked out a scanty subsistence. The great tide of time seemed, in this reign, at least, to pass them by. They did not go out into the world, and the world came not to them. Those who had land were good landlords but bad farmers (p. 737). Their religious duties were mostly performed, but with no great spirit. There was no stir of any sort in their humdrum life.

The Parish Clergy.

All this was not, however, suffered by all without a struggle. The monasteries sometimes sent up an able and aspiring abbot to high office in the Church; and the parish clergy, if we may believe Dean Colet in his sermons, and Erasmus in his Colloquies, were thirsting for preferment.

"How much greediness and appetite of honour and dignity," says the former, "is nowadays in men of the Church. How run they—yea, almost out of breath—from one benefice to another, from the less to the more, from the lower to the higher. Who seeth not this? who, seeing, sorroweth not? . . . . For what other thing seek we nowadays in the Church than fat benefices and high promotions? Yea, and in the same promotions, of what other thing do we pass upon than of our tithes and rents? That we care not how chargeful, how great benefices we take, so that they be of great value."[1]

And that the race was not always unsuccessful there are many instances to prove. Perhaps the most striking, as has been shown was the case of Colet's own predecessor in the deanery of St. Paul's. Dr. Robert Sherbourne held prebendaries in St. Paul's from 1489 to 1496; was Master of St. Cross Hospital, Master of the Hospital of Holy Trinity, near Kingsthorpe, 1492: Arch-

[1] "Convocation" Sermon, in Lupton, "Life of Colet," p. 121.

deacon of Bucks, 1495 ; Archdeacon of Taunton and Prebendary
of Wells, 1496 ; Archdeacon of Hants, Dean of St. Paul's, 1499 ;
Rector of Alresford, Hants, 1501 ; Bishop of St. David's, 1504 ;
and Bishop of Chichester, 1508. Such a man as this easily
distanced the parish clergy in the race. But his list of preferments looks poor beside that of Morton.

We turn from the monks and the parish clergy to the chantry
priests. Of these there were very large numbers : by far the
greater part of the English clergy had no cure of souls and no
parochial duties, but merely said mass for the souls of the
departed in chantry and other chapels. It was, doubtless, from
these men that the greatest discredit came upon the Church :
they dwelt often in private families, in a mean position, and
sank to the level of those with whom they lived.

The Chantry Priests.

The friars, too, had fallen from their first estate. It is impossible to resist the testimony which shows that by the end of
the fifteenth century, as a class, they had sunk low indeed.
They had suffered from their popularity : the offscouring of men
had rushed into their ranks, to enjoy their exemptions and live
more securely on alms than they could without the mendicant
habit. "At eating and drinking,' says the innkeeper in Erasmus,
"you are more than men, but you have neither hands nor feet
to work" ; yet in the same colloquy he bears witness to the
simplicity and religion of the lives of many Franciscans. The
best men among them aimed and rose high ; but the old vows of
poverty had often lost their meaning and served only to shelter
a multitude of sturdy and not too religious beggars. The worst
were utterly ignorant, the best were the leaders, the pioneers, of
that intellectual movement which was to change the face of
England. If Chaucer and many a later satirist mock alike at
monk and friar, if the leader of the New Learning in England,
Sir Thomas More, suffered from the assaults of the illiterate
religious, it was to the Charterhouse that he went when he
needed the deepest counsel and when he took the step which
turned him from a recluse into a man of affairs.

The Friars.

In spite of satire, well or ill deserved, there can be no doubt
that, during the reign of Henry VII., the clergy as a whole
were popular and the Church outwardly strong. The clerical
body was a caste with its own feelings and interests, but it was
the very reverse of an exclusive caste. It had its ties with

Signs of Vigour.

St. Mary Redcliffe, Bristol.

Photo: London & Coventry Photo. Co.

St. Michael's, Coventry.

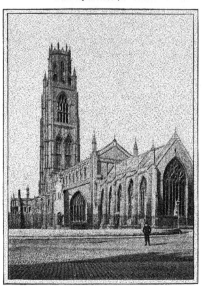

St. Botolph's, Boston.

St. John's, Cirencester.

GREAT TOWN CHURCHES OF THE FIFTEENTH CENTURY.

every family in the land. Where it was corrupt, the laity were too much interested in the corruption to endeavour to reform it. And the interest of the people in the system of the Church was more worthily attested than by the eagerness with which laymen sought ordination for their sons. It was the age of great churches—churches not of the diocese, but of the parish. The vast size, the splendid workmanship, show the popular feeling. St.

Michael at Coventry, St. Mary Redcliffe, Holy Trinity at Hull, the churches of Newark and Boston, and many a country village church, were clearly built for the people and by the people. It was an age of church restoration as well as church building. The in-junctions at episcopal visitations often enjoin work of this kind, and among the entries on the Lancaster roll are many grants of material for repair of sacred fabrics. If the finest work is that done in the universities in the beginnings of the new intellectual revival, the country is not far

CHURCH OF ST. PROBUS AND ST. GRACE.
(Near Grampound, Cornwall.)

behind. With the beautiful tower of Magdalen College at Oxford, the work of Wolsey's bursarship, we may compare alike for grace and massive grandeur so distant and unnoticed a monument of the finest architecture of the age as the tower, like its Oxford rival in many noticeable ways, of the parish church of St. Probus and St. Grace in Cornwall. And this zeal in church-building was no local fancy. As in Cornwall and Lincolnshire, so in Norfolk and the Midlands—the great church at Cirencester, for example—we find the same richness and profusion of work. And it is significant of the popularity of the Church in her material aspect that church-building in

MONASTIC PLATE: GOLD INCENSE BOAT.
(By permission of Messrs. Macmillan and Bowes, Cambridge.)

the towns stands side by side with municipal building and municipal growth. Most of the civic buildings of importance that we have are akin in date and workmanship to the great Per-

Church and People.

pendicular churches which are so plentiful. The mass of the people were loyal churchmen: yet there were stirrings, observed by the keen eye of foreign visitors, of new beliefs in things sacred. "There are many," says the "Italian Relation of England,"[1] "who have various opinions concerning religion"; but the general aspect of the people, as the same acute observer saw it, was distinctly religious. "They all attend mass every day, and say many paternosters in public (the women carrying long rosaries in their hands, and any who can read taking the office of our Lady with them, and with some companion reciting it in the church verse by verse, in a low voice, after the manner of the religious); they always

MONASTIC PLATE: CENSER.
(By permission of Messrs. Macmillan and Bowes, Cambridge.)

hear mass on Sunday in their parish church, and give liberal

[1] Camden Society, p. 23.

alms, because they may not offer less than a piece of money whereof fourteen are equal to a gold ducat; nor do they omit any form incumbent upon good Christians." From such a people, as might be expected, the offerings were large, and in spite of the poverty of many of the monastic houses, the appearance of the churches was one of great opulence. "Above all," says the authority already quoted,[1] "the riches of the people are displayed in the church treasures; for there is not a parish church in the kingdom so mean as not to possess crucifixes, candlesticks, censers, paten, and chalice of silver, nor is there a convent of mendicant friars so poor as not to have all these same articles in silver, besides many other ornaments in the same

DEDICATION OF A CHURCH.
(MS. Roy. 2 B. xiii.)

metal, worthy of a cathedral church. You may well imagine what the decoration of those rich Benedictine, Carthusian, and Cistercian monasteries must be, which are indeed more like baronial than religious houses, as you may have seen at the shrine of St. Thomas of Canterbury."

The offices of the Church, at the end of the fifteenth century, were distinctly popular. Even the choir services, those to which the monastic clergy were bound by their rule, and the secular canons by the custom of their churches, were well attended. The Norwich visitations, it is true, contain complaints of their neglect; but the neglect is only in the case of individuals, or of peculiarly lax houses, and is always severely reprehended. A canon of Hereford, writing some eighty years later of facts within his own memory, gives what may be taken as a fairly accurate picture of still earlier custom. At midnight, the whole of the cathedral clergy rose for matins, and the services were

[1] *Ibid.*, p. 29.

practically continuous from five in the morning till at length it rang to evensong.

"And every Sabbath and festival day St.

NUNS IN CHOIR (MS. Dom. A. xvii.).

Thomas's bell should ring to procession, and the dean would send his somner to warn the mayor for the procession. And then, upon the somner's warning, the mayor would send the sergeants to the parish churches to command all the freemen to attend on the mayor to the procession or lecture. For want of a sermon, there would be a lecture in the chapter-house every Sabbath and holy day, notwithstanding they were at high mass in the choir. And then by the mayor and commons it was agreed at a general law-day that if the mayor did not come to processions and sermons, he should pay 12d. for every default, and every alderman 8d., and every man of the elections 4d., and every freeman or gild merchant 4d., if it were known they were absent, and within hearing of the said bell, and did not come, which ordinance was and is recorded in the custom-book of the city. So zealous," admits the stout reformer, "and diligent were the temporality then in observing those dregs of the clergy"; and he adds, somewhat sadly, "then such heavy burdens were but light." [1]

The preaching of sermons here mentioned was not so common as in later days. Gascoigne says that the bishops sent out virtually no one to preach, and the reluctance of the bishops to give the preacher's licence is evidence of the ignorance of the clergy at large. But the mass was both a popular service and one which, though in an unknown tongue, must have been almost universally "understanded of the people"; and they were taught, not merely by significant ritual, but by constant issues of a popular work called the "Lay-folks' Mass Book," [2] which

[1] Quoted in Gasquet, "Edward VI. and the Book of Common Prayer," p. 11.
[2] Edited by Canon Simmons for the Early English Text Society.

was at once an explanation and a devotional commentary on the great service of praise and thanksgiving. The "Primer,"[1] too, in its different forms, was a book both of public and private devotion, and was in the hands of all well-to-do families. Printing had begun to aid in the dissemination of Church teaching: such a book as Pynson's issue of the Sequences (1497) shows the steps made in the popularising of religion.

Still, the part taken by the people in the Church service at this time was, on the whole, rather passive than active. Activity, on the other hand, was shown to a very considerable extent in the pilgrimages which were so popular. Interrupted and eventually diverted from their course by the Mohammedan conquest of the Holy Land, pilgrimages, as a custom, had grown

Pilgrimage.

MONKS IN CHOIR (MS. Dom. A. xvii.).

rather than diminished by time. Many journeyed far afield, and came back strengthened by the change; many were con-

---

[1] A book containing—partly in English and partly in Latin, or sometimes wholly in English—the "Hours of Our Lady," Evensong and Compline, the Seven Penitential Psalms, the fifteen Psalms on the Seven Deadly Sins, the Litany, the Placebo and Dirge, the Psalms of Commendation, *Pater Noster*, *Ave Maria*, the Creed, the Ten Commandments, the Seven Deadly Sins. [Perry, "Student's History of the Church of England," I., 513.]

tented with their own land and the water of St. Thomas at
Canterbury. Amid so many pilgrims, not all were religious; and
the picture of their journeyings is written for all time in the
Canterbury Tales. The wife of Bath, it will be remembered,

> Thries hadde sche ben at Jerusalem;
> Sche hadde passed many a straunge streem;
> At Rome sche hadde ben and at Bologne,
> At Galice, at Seynt James, and at Cologne;

PILGRIMS LEAVING CANTERBURY (MS. Roy. 18 D. ii.).

and it is recorded that in one year of Henry VI., 2,433 English
pilgrims went to Compostella.

At the close of the Middle Ages pilgrimages had not greatly
changed their character since Chaucer's day. We have vivid
pictures in Erasmus's account of his visits to Walsingham and
Canterbury. The shrine of St. Thomas was the most gor-
geons, as it was the most popular, in England. Erasmus, who
saw everything with the keenest eyes, yet not without an

PILGRIMS PAYING TOLL ON LANDING AT JOPPA (MS. Add. 24,189).

antiquarian and a devotional reverence for the past, thus describes what he saw:—

> "Iron screens prevent ingress, but allow a view of the space between the extreme end of the church and the place which they called the choir. Thither you ascend by many steps, under which a vault opens entry to the north side. There is shown a wooden altar, dedicated to the Blessed Virgin, but mean and not remarkable for anything save as a monument of antiquity, putting to shame the extravagance of these times. Here the saint is said to have made his last farewell to the Virgin when his death was at hand. On the altar is the point of the sword by which the head of the most excellent prelate was cleft. . . . Descending to the crypt, which has its own mystagogues, we were shown the perforated skull of the martyr." "Did you see the bones?" asks the inquirer. "That is not allowed. But a wooden shrine covers the golden shrine, and when that is drawn up with ropes, it lays bare inestimable treasures. The meanest part was gold, every part glistened, shone, and sparkled with rare and very large jewels, some of them exceeding the size of a goose's egg The prior, with a rod pointed out each jewel, telling its name in French, and the name of the donor, for the chief of them kings had sent as off rings."

Church and State.   In all the material furniture of the churches, the reign of Henry VII. marked the climax of richness. Pilgrimages spread the knowledge of the treasures, which the cupidity of the next generation was to seize or to destroy.

Amid these signs of material prosperity, the Church was becoming more and more Erastian year by year. Her riches were due to popular favour mixed with a good deal of corrupt interest. Her position, supported by ecclesiastics who were at the same time the king's ministers, depended more and more upon the Crown. The Church courts, indeed, retained their powers and multiplied their activities. Secular prohibitions, even the writ "Circumspecte agatis" of Edward I. (p. 26), had done little to check their encroachments. There was a large area of temporal jurisdiction upon which the ecclesiastical tribunals had made incursions, and much of what had been debatable land in the earlier conflicts of jurisdictions had now passed into the power of the Church. Chiefly, all testamentary and matrimonial suits were in the hands of ecclesiastical lawyers. Benefit of clergy was but slightly restricted, and a vast number of persons, clerical only in name, could claim its privilege; but it is clear, on the other hand, that the Church by no means always interfered on behalf of a clergyman brought up before the civil courts, and many a convicted clerk suffered the same punishment from the same court as if he were a layman.

The Church's position thus, though uneasy, was still one of magnificence and power. Reforms were needed, and were being, perhaps too slowly, taken in hand. The characteristic of the age—a richness of life, absorbing and secular, had thrown its glamour over the religious bodies, and infected the priestly ideal. For the moment the Church appeared at the crest of the wave, and the Italian observer could say with conviction, thinking, no doubt, of the great churchman who stood at the king's right hand: "The clergy are they who have supreme sway over the country, both in peace and war."[1]

THE desire for continuous legislation is modern. We have come to think that, year by year, Parliament must meet and pour out statutes; that every statesman must have in his mind some programme of new laws; that if his programme once become exhausted he would cease to be a statesman. It was otherwise in the Middle Ages. As a matter of fact a Parliament might always find that some new statute was necessary. The need for legislation, however, was occasioned (so men thought) not by any fated progress of the human race, but by the perversity of mankind. Ideally there exists a perfect body of law, immutable, eternal, the work of God, not of man. Just a few more improvements in our legal procedure will have made it for ever harmonious with this ideal; and, indeed, if men would but obey the law of the land as it stands, there would be little for a legislator to do.

During the fourteenth century a good deal is written upon the statute roll, and a good deal can still be said in very few words. "Also it is agreed that a Parliament shall be holden once a year or more often if need be." This is a characteristic specimen of the brief sentences in which great principles are formulated and which by their ambiguity will provide the lawyers and politicians of later ages with plenty of matter for debate. Many of these short clauses are directed against what are regarded as abuses, as evasions of the law, and the king's officers are looked upon as the principal offenders. They must

F. W.
MAITLAND.
English Law,
1307-1600.

Legislation
in the
Fourteenth
Century.

---

[1] "Italian Relation," *ut sup.* p. 34.

be repeated with but little variation from time to time, for it is difficult to bind the king by law. Happily the kings were needy; in return for "supply" they sold the words on the statute roll, and those words, of some importance when first conceded, became of far greater importance in after times. When we read them nowadays they turn our thoughts to James and Charles, rather than to Edward and Richard. The New Monarchy was not new. This, from its own point of view, was its great misfortune. It had inherited ancient parchment rolls which had uncomfortable words upon them.

Its Scope.   But Parliament by its statutes was beginning to interfere with many affairs, small as well as great. Indeed, what we may consider small affairs seem to have troubled and interested it more even than those large constitutional questions which it was always hoping to settle but never settling. If we see a long statute, one guarded with careful provisos, one that tells us of debate and compromise, this will probably be a statute which deals with one particular trade; for instance, a statute concerning the sale of herring at Yarmouth fair. The thorniest of themes for discussion is the treatment of foreign merchants. Naturally enough our lords, knights, and burgesses cannot easily agree about it. One opinion prevails in the seaports, another in the upland towns, and the tortuous course of legislation, swaying now towards Free Trade and now towards Protection, is the resultant of many forces. The "omnicompetence," as Bentham called it, of statute law was recognised by all, the impotence of statute law was seen by none. It can determine the rate of wages, the price of goods, the value of money; it can decide that no man shall dress himself above his station.

On the other hand, the great outlines of criminal law and private law seem to have been regarded as fixed for all time. In the twentieth century students of law will still for practical purposes be compelled to know a good deal about some of the statutes of Edward I. They will seldom have occasion to know anything of any laws that were enacted during the fourteenth or the first three-quarters of the fifteenth century. Parliament seems to have abandoned the idea of controlling the development of the common law. Occasionally and spasmodically it would interfere, devise some new remedy, fill a gap in the register of writs, or circumvent the circumventors of a statute.

But in general it left the ordinary law of the land to the judges and the lawyers. In its eyes the common law was complete, or very nearly complete.

And then as we read the statute-roll of the fifteenth century we seem for a while to be watching the decline and fall of a mighty institution. Parliament seems to have nothing better to do than to regulate the manufacture of cloth. Now and then it strives to cope with the growing evils of the time, the

THE GAME OF KAYLES (MS. Roy. 2 B. vii.).

renascent feudalism, the private wars of great and small; but without looking outside our roll we can see that these efforts are half-hearted and ineffectual. We are expected to show a profound interest in "the making of worsteds," while we gather from a few casual hints that the Wars of the Roses are flagrant. If for a moment the Parliament of Edward IV. can raise its soul above defective barrels of fish and fraudulent gutter tiles, this will be in order to prohibit "cloish, kayles, half-bowl, hand-in-hand and hand-out, quekeboard,"[1] and such other games as interfere with the practice of archery.

In the end it was better that Parliament should for a while register the acts of a despot than that it should sink into the contempt that seemed to be prepared for it. The part which

[1 "Kayles" is a variety of ninepins; "cloish" (*Fr. cloche*) seems to have been a game in which a ball was driven through a hoop surmounted with a bell—a sort of rudimentary croquet; "half-bowl" and "hand-in-hand and hand-out" were ball games of some sort; "quekeboard" seems beyond identification—unless it is shovel-board.]

the assembled Estates of the Realm have to play in the great acts of Henry VIII. may in truth be a subservient and ignoble part; but the acts are great and they are all done "by the authority of Parliament." By the authority of Parliament the Bishop of Rome could be deprived of all jurisdiction, the monasteries could be dissolved, the king could be made (so far as the law of God would permit) supreme head of the English Church, the succession to the Crown could be settled first in this way, then in that, the force of statute might be given to the king's proclamations. There was nothing that could not be done by the authority of Parliament. And apart from the constitutional and ecclesiastical changes which everyone has heard about, very many things of importance were done by statute. We owe to Henry VIII.—much rather to him than to his Parliament—not a few innovations in the law of property and the law of crime, and the Parliaments of Elizabeth performed some considerable legal exploits. The statutes of the Tudor period are lengthy documents. In many a grandiose preamble we seem to hear the voice of Henry himself; but their length is not solely due to the pomp of imperial phrases. They condescend to details; they teem with exceptions and saving clauses. One cannot establish a new ecclesiastical polity by half-a-dozen lines. We see that the judges are by this time expected to attend very closely to the words that Parliament utters, to weigh and obey every letter of the written law.

Statute and Common Law.

Just now and then in the last of the Middle Ages and thence onwards into the eighteenth century, we hear the judges claiming some vague right of disregarding statutes which are directly at variance with the common law, or the law of God, or the royal prerogative. Had much come of this claim, our constitution must have taken a very different shape from that which we see at the present day. Little came of it. In the troublous days of Richard II. a chief justice got himself hanged as a traitor for advising the king that a statute curtailing the royal power was void. For the rest, the theory is but a speculative dogma. We can (its upholders seem to say) conceive that a statute might be so irrational, so wicked, that we would not enforce it; but, as a matter of fact, we have never known such a statute made. From the Norman Conquest onwards.

SERJEANTS AT LAW. (*Long Melford Church, Suffolk.*)

England seems marked out as the country in which men, so soon as they begin to philosophise, will endeavour to prove that all law is the command of a "sovereign one," or a "sovereign many." They may be somewhat shocked when in the seventeenth century Hobbes states this theory in trenchant terms and combines it with many unpopular doctrines. But the way for Hobbes had been prepared of old. In the days of Edward I. the text-writer whom we call Britton had put the common law into the king's mouth: all legal rules might be stated as royal commands.

Still, even in the age of the Tudors, only a small part of the law was in the statute-book. Detached pieces of superstructure were there; for the foundation men had to look elsewhere. After the brilliant thirteenth century a long, dull period had set in. The custody of the common law was now committed to a small group of judges and lawyers. They knew their own business very thoroughly, and they knew nothing else. Law was now divorced from literature; no one attempted to write a book about it. The decisions of the courts at Westminster were diligently reported and diligently studied, but no one

CHIEF JUSTICE CAVENDISH.
(By permission of the Rev. Sir W. Hyde Parker, Bart.)

thought of comparing English law with anything else. Roman law was by this time an unintelligible, outlandish thing, perhaps a good enough law for half-starved Frenchmen. Legal education was no longer academic—the universities had

The Legal Profession. nothing to do with it, they could only make canonists and civilians—it was scholastic. By stages that are exceedingly obscure, the inns of court and inns of chancery were growing. They were associations of lawyers which had about them a good deal of the club, something of the college, something of the trade-union. They acquired the "inns" or "hospices" — that is, the town houses — which had belonged to great noblemen: for example, the Earl of Lincoln's inn. The house and church of the Knights of the Temple came to their hands. The smaller societies, "inns of chancery," became dependent on the larger societies, "inns of court." The sergeants and apprentices who composed them enjoyed

AT THE JUDGMENT SEAT.
(*Wynkyn de Worde, "Dives and Pauper."*)

The Inns of Court. an exclusive right of pleading in court; some things might be done by an apprentice or barrister, others required a serjeant; in the Court of Common Pleas only a serjeant could be heard. It would take time to investigate the origin of that power of granting degrees which these societies wielded. To all seeming the historian must regard it as emanating from the king, though in this case, as in many other cases, the control of a royal prerogative slowly passed out of the king's hand. But here our point must be, that the inns developed a laborious system of legal education. Many years a student had to spend in hearing and giving lectures and in pleading fictitious causes before he could be admitted to practice.

It is no wonder that under the fostering care of these

societies English jurisprudence became an occult science and its professors " the most unlearned kind of most learned men." They were rigorous logicians, afraid of no conclusion that was implicit in their premises. The sky might fall, the Wars of the Roses might rage, but they would pursue the even course of their argumentation. They were not altogether unmindful of the social changes that were going on around them. In the fifteenth century there were great judges who performed what may seem to us some daring feats in the accommodation of old law to new times. Out of unpromising elements they developed a comprehensive law of contract; they loosened the bonds of those family settlements by which land had been tied up; they converted the precarious villein tenure of the Middle Ages into the secure copy-hold tenure of modern times. But all this had to be done evasively and by means of circumventive fictions. Novel principles could not be admitted until they were disguised in some antique garb.

A new and a more literary period seems to be beginning in the latter half of the fifteenth century, when Sir John Fortescue, the Lancastrian Chief Justice, writing for the world at large, contrasts the constitutional kingship of England with the absolute monarchy of France, and Sir Thomas Littleton, a Justice in the Court of Common Pleas, writing for students

TOMB OF SIR JOHN FORTESCUE.
(*Ebrington Church.*)

of English law, publishes his lucid and classical book on the tenure of land. But the hopes of a renascence are hardly fulfilled. In the sixteenth century many famous lawyers

added to their fame by publishing reports of decided cases and
by making "abridgments" of the old reports, and a few little
treatises were compiled; but in general the lawyer seems to think
that he has done all for jurisprudence that can be done when he
has collected his materials under a number of rubrics alpha-
betically arranged.   The alphabet is the one clue to the maze.
Even in the days of Elizabeth and James I. Sir Edward Coke,
the incarnate common law, shovels out his enormous learning
in vast disorderly heaps.   Carlyle's felicity has for ever stamped
upon Coke the adjective "tough"—"tough old Coke upon
Littleton, one of the toughest men ever made."   We may well
transfer the word from the man to the law that was personified
in him.   The English common law was tough, one of the
toughest things ever made.   And well for England was it in
the days of Tudors and Stuarts that this was so.   A simpler,
a more rational, a more elegant system would have been an
apt instrument of despotic rule.   At times the judges were
subservient. enough : the King could dismiss them from their
offices at a moment's notice ; but the clumsy, cumbrous system,
though it might bend, would never break.   It was ever awk-
wardly rebounding and confounding the statecraft which had
tried to control it.   The strongest King, the ablest Minister,
the rudest Lord-Protector could make little of this "ungodly
jumble."

**Growth
of the
Judicial
System.**
    To this we must add that professional jealousies had been
aroused by the evolution of new courts, which did not proceed
according to the course of the common law.   Once more we
must carry our thoughts back to the days of Edward I.   The
three courts—King's Bench, Common Bench, and Exchequer—
had been established.   There were two groups of "Justices,"
and one group of "Barons" engaged in administering the law.
But behind these courts there was a tribunal of a less deter-
minate nature.   Looking at it in the last years of the thirteenth
century we may doubt as to what it is going to be.   Will it
be a house of magnates, an assembly of the Lords Spiritual
and Temporal, or will it be a council composed of the King's
Ministers and judges and those others whom he pleases for
one reason or another to call to the council board ?   As a
matter of fact, in Edward I.'s day, this highest tribunal seems
to be. rather the council than the assembly of prelates and

King's Bench.

Exchequer.

Chancery.

COURTS OF JUSTICE, LATE FIFTEENTH CENTURY.

(Inner Temple Library. By permission of the Masters of the Bench).

barons. This council is a large body; it comprises the great officers of state—Chancellor, Treasurer, and so forth; it comprises the judges of the three courts; it comprises also the Masters or chief clerks of the Chancery, whom we may liken to the "permanent under-secretaries" of our own time; it comprises also those prelates and barons whom the King thinks fit to have about him. But the definition of this body seems somewhat vague. The sessions or "parliaments" in which it does justice often coincide in time with those assemblies of the Estates of the Realm by which, in later days, the term "parliaments" is specifically appropriated, and at any moment it may take the form of a meeting to which not only the ordinary councillors, but all the prelates and barons, have been summoned. In the light which later days throw back upon the thirteenth century we seem to see in the justiciary "parliaments" of Edward I. two principles, one of which we may call aristocratic, while the other is official; and we think that, sooner or later, there must be a conflict between them —that one must grow at the expense of the other. And then again we cannot see very plainly how the power of this tribunal will be defined, for it is doing work of a miscellaneous kind. Not only is it a court of last resort in which the errors of all lower courts can be corrected, but as a court of first instance it can entertain whatever causes, civil or criminal, the king may evoke before it. Then lastly, acting in a manner which to us seems half judicial and half administrative, it hears the numerous petitions of those who will urge any claim against the king, or complain of any wrong which cannot be redressed in the formal course of ordinary justice.

In the course of the fourteenth century some of these questions were settled. It became clear that the Lords' House of Parliament, the assembly of prelates and barons, was to be the tribunal which could correct the mistakes in law committed by the lower courts. The right of a peer of the realm to be tried for capital crimes by a court composed of his peers was established. Precedents were set for those processes which we know as impeachments, in which the House of Lords hears accusations brought by the House of Commons. In all these matters, therefore, a tribunal technically styled "the King in Parliament," but which was in reality the House of Lords,

appeared as the highest tribunal of the realm.   But, beside
it, we see another tribunal with indefinitely wide claims to
jurisdiction—we see " the King in Council."   And the two are
not so distinct as an historian, for his own sake and his
readers', might wish them to be.   On the one hand, those of
the King's Council who are not peers of the realm, in particular

THE COURT OF COMMON PLEAS *(Inner Temple Library)*.
(By permission of the Masters of the Bench.)

the judges and the Masters of the Chancery, are summoned
to the Lords' House of Parliament, and only by slow degrees
is it made plain to them that, when they are in that House,
they are mere " assistants " of the peers, and are only to speak
when they are spoken to.   On the other hand, there is a widespread, if not very practical, belief that all the peers are by
rights the king's councillors, and that any one of them may
sit at the council board if he pleases.   Questions enough are
left open for subsequent centuries.

Its Work
and Use.
Meanwhile the Council, its actual constitution varying much
from reign to reign, does a great deal of justice, for the more
part criminal justice, and this it does in a summary, administrative way. Plainly there is great need for such justice, for
though the representative commoners and the lawyers dislike
it, they always stop short of demanding its utter abolition.
The commoners protest against this or that abuse. Sometimes
they seem to be upon the point of denouncing the whole
institution as illegal; but then there comes some rebellion or
some scandalous acquittal of a notorious criminal by bribed or
partial jurors, which convinces them that, after all, there is a
place for a masterful court which does not stand upon ceremony, which can strike rapidly and have no need to strike
twice. They cannot be brought to admit openly that one
main cause of the evils that they deplore is the capricious
clumsiness of that trial by jury which has already become
the theme of many a national boast. They will not legislate
about the matter, rather they will look the other way while
the Council is punishing rich and powerful offenders, against
whom no verdict could have been obtained. A hard line is
drawn between the felonies, for which death is the punishment, and the minor offences. No one is to suffer loss of life
or limb unless twelve of his neighbours have sworn to his
guilt after a solemn trial; but the Council must be suffered
to deal out fines and imprisonments against rioters, conspir-
ators, bribers, perjured jurors; otherwise there will be anarchy.

Its Pro-
cedure
The Council evolves a procedure for such cases, or rather
it uses the procedure of the canon law. It sends for the
accused; it compels him to answer upon oath written inter-
rogatories. Affidavits, as we should call them, are sworn upon
both sides. With written depositions before them, the Lords
of the Council, without any jury, acquit or convict. The
extraction of confessions by torture is no unheard-of thing.

and
Iniquities.
It was in a room known as the Star Chamber that the
Council sat when there was justice to be done, and there, as
"the Court of Star Chamber," it earned its infamy. That
infamy it fairly earned under the first two Stuart kings, and
no one will dispute that the Long Parliament did well in
abolishing it. It had become a political court and a cruel
court, a court in which divines sought to impose their dogmas

and their ritual upon a recalcitrant nation by heavy sentences; in which a king, endeavouring to rule without a Parliament, tried to give the force of statutes to his proclamations, to exact compulsory loans, to gather taxes that the Commons had denied him; a whipping, nose-slitting, ear-cropping court; a court with a grim, unseemly humour of its own, which would condemn to an exclusive diet of pork the miserable Puritan who took too seriously the Mosaic prohibition of swine's flesh. And then, happily, there were doubts about its legality. The theory got about that it derived all its lawful powers from a statute passed in 1487, at the beginning of Henry VII.'s reign, while manifestly it was exceeding those powers in all directions. We cannot now accept that theory, unless we are prepared to say that for a century and a half all the great judges, including Coke himself, had taken an active part in what they knew to be the unlawful doings of the Council—the two Chief Justices had habitually sat in the Star Chamber. Still we may be glad that this theory was accepted. The court was abolished in the name of the common law.

It had not added much to our national jurisprudence. It had held itself aloof from jurisprudence; it had been a law unto itself, with hands free to invent new remedies for every new disease of the body politic. It had little regard for precedents, and, therefore, men were not at pains to collect its decisions. It had, however, a settled course of procedure which, in its last days, was described by William Hudson in a very readable book. Its procedure, the main feature of which was the examination of the accused, perished with it. After the Civil War and the Restoration no attempt was made to revive it, but that it had been doing useful things then became evident. The old criminal law had been exceedingly defective, especially in relation to those offences which did not attain the rank of felonies. The King's Bench had, for the future, to do what the Star Chamber had done, but to do it in a more regular fashion, and not without the interposition of a jury.

Far other were the fortunes of the Star Chamber's twin sister, the Court of Chancery. Twin sisters they were; indeed, in the fourteenth century it is hard to tell one from the other, and even in the Stuart time we sometimes find the Star Chamber doing

The Court of Chancery.

things which we should have expected to be done by the
Chancery. But, to go back to the fourteenth century, the
Chancellor was the king's first minister, the head of the one
great secretarial department that there was, the President of the
Council, and the most learned member of the Council. Usually
he was a bishop ; often he had earned his see by diligent labours
as a clerk in the Chancery. It was natural that the Lords of the
Council should put off upon him, or that he should take to himself, a great deal of the judicial work that in one way or another
the Council had to do.   Criminal cases might come before the
whole body, or some committee of it.   Throughout the Middle
Ages criminal cases were treated as simple affairs ; for example,
justices of the peace who were not trained lawyers could be
trusted to do a great deal of penal justice, and inflict the punishment of death.   But cases involving civil rights, involving the
complex land law, might come before the Council. Generally,
in such cases, there was some violence or some fraud to be complained of, some violence or fraud for which, so the complainant
alleged, he could get no redress elsewhere.   Such cases came
specially under the eye of the Chancellor. He was a learned man
with learned subordinates, the Masters of the Chancery. Very
gradually it became the practice for complainants who were
seeking the reparation of wrongs rather than the punishment of
offences, to address their petitions, not to the King and Council,
but to the Chancellor.   Slowly men began to think of the
Chancellor, or the Chancery of which he was president, as having
a jurisdiction distinct from, though it might overlap, that of
the Council.

Its Sphere.   What was to be the sphere of this jurisdiction ?   For a long
time this question remained doubtful.   The wrongs of which men
usually complained to the Chancellor were wrongs well enough
known to the common law—deeds of violence, assaults, land-
grabbing, and so forth.   As an excuse for going to him, they
urged that they were poor while their adversaries were mighty,
too mighty for the common law, with its long delays and its pur-
chasable juries.   Odd though this may seem to us, that court
which was to become a byword for costly delay started business
as an expeditious and a poor man's court.   It met with much
opposition : the House of Commons did not like it, and the
common lawyers did not like it ; but still there was a certain

half-heartedness in the opposition.   No one was prepared to say
that there was no place for such a tribunal ; no one was prepared
to define by legislation what its place should be.

From the field of the common law the Chancellor was slowly
compelled to retreat.   It could not be suffered that, merely
because there was helplessness on the one side and corruptive
wealth on the other, he should be suffered to deal with cases
which belonged to the old courts.   It seems possible that this
nascent civil jurisdiction of the Chancellor would have come to
naught but for a curious episode in the history of our land law.
In the second half of the fourteenth century many causes were
conspiring to induce the landholders of England to convey their
lands to friends, who, while becoming the legal owners of those
lands, would, nevertheless, be bound by an honourable understanding as to the uses to which their ownership should be put.
There were feudal burdens that could thus be evaded, ancient
restrictions which could thus be loosened.   The Chancellor began
to hold himself out as willing to enforce these honourable under-
standings, these " uses, trusts or confidences " as they were called,
to send to prison the trustee who would not keep faith.   It is an
exceedingly curious episode.   The whole nation seems to enter
into one large conspiracy to evade its own laws, to evade laws
which it has not the courage to reform.   The Chancellor, the
judges, and the Parliament seem all to be in the conspiracy.
And yet there is really no conspiracy : men are but living from
hand to mouth, arguing from one case to the next case, and they
do not see what is going to happen.   Too late the king, the one
person who had steadily been losing by the process, saw what
had happened.   Henry VIII. put into the mouth of a reluctant
Parliament a statute which did its best—a clumsy best it was—
to undo the work.   But past history was too strong even for that
high and mighty prince.   The statute was a miserable failure.
A little trickery with words would circumvent it.   The Chancellor, with the active connivance of the judges, was enabled to
do what he had been doing in the past, to enforce the obligations
known as trusts.   This elaborate story we can only mention by
the way ; the main thing that we have to notice is that, long
before the Tudor days—indeed, before the fourteenth century
was out—the Chancellor had acquired for himself a province of
jurisdiction which was, in the opinion of all men, including the

common lawyers, legitimately his own. From time to time he would extend its boundaries, and from time to time there would be a brisk quarrel between the Chancery and the law courts over the annexation of some field fertile of fees. In particular, when the Chancellor forbade a man to sue in a court of law, or to take advantage of a judgment that he had obtained in a court of law, the judges resented this, and a bitter dispute about this matter between Coke and Ellesmere gave King James I. a wished-for opportunity of posing as the supreme lord of all the justice that was done in his name and awarding a decisive victory to his Chancellor. But such disputes were rare. The Chancellors had found useful work to do, and they had been suffered to do it without much opposition. In the name of equity and good conscience they had, as it were, been adding an appendix to the common law. Every jot and tittle of the law was to be fulfilled, and yet, when a man had done this, more might be required of him in the name of equity and good conscience.

Equity.   Where were the rules of equity and good conscience to be found? Some have supposed that the clerical Chancellors of the last Middle Ages found them in the Roman or the Canon Law, and certain it is that they borrowed the main principles of their procedure from the canonists. Indeed, until some reforms that are still very recent, the procedure of the Court of Chancery was the procedure of an Ecclesiastical Court. In flagrant contrast to the common law, it forced the defendant to answer on oath the charges that were brought against him; it made no use of the jury; the evidence consisted of written affidavits. On the other hand, it is by no means certain that more than this was borrowed. So far as we can now see, the Chancellors seem to get most of their dominant ideas from the common law. They imitate the common law whenever they can, and depart from it reluctantly at the call of natural justice and common honesty. Common honesty requires that a man shall observe the trust that has been committed to him. If the common law will not enforce this obligation it is failing to do its duty. The Chancellor intervenes, but in enforcing trusts he seizes hold of and adopts every analogy that the common law presents. For a long time English equity seems to live from hand to mouth. Sufficient for the day are the cases in that day's cause-list. Even in the seventeenth century men said that the real measure of equity was the length of the Chancellor's foot. Under the Tudors the volume of litigation that flowed into the Chancery was already enormous; the Chancellor was often sadly in arrear of his work, and yet very rarely were his decisions reported, though the decisions of the judges had been reported ever since the days of Edward I. This shows us that he did not conceive himself to be straitly bound by precedents: he could still listen to the voice of conscience. The rapid increase in the number of causes that he had to decide began to make his conscience a technical conscience. More and more of his time was spent upon the judgment-seat. Slowly he ceased to be, save in ceremonial rank, the king's first minister. Wolsey was the last Chancellor who ruled England. Secretaries of State were now intervening between the king and his Great Seal. Its holder was destined to become year by year more of a judge, less of a statesman. Still we must look forward to the Restoration for the age in which the rules of equity begin to take a very definite shape, comparable in rigour to the rules of the common law.

Somehow or another, England, after a fashion all her own, had stumbled into a scheme for the reconciliation of permanence with progress. The old medieval criminal law could be preserved because a Court of Star Chamber would supply its deficiencies; the old private law could be preserved because the Court of Chancery was composing an appendix to it; trial by jury could be preserved, developed, transfigured because other modes of trial were limiting it to an appropriate sphere. And so our old law maintained its continuity. As we have said above, it passed scathless through the critical sixteenth century, and was ready to stand up against tyranny in the seventeenth. The Star Chamber and the Chancery were dangerous to our political liberties. Bacon could tell King James that the Chancery was the court of his absolute power. But if we look abroad we shall find good reason for thinking that but for these institutions our old-fashioned national law, unable out of its own resources to meet the requirements of a new age, would have utterly broken down, and the "ungodly jumble" would have made way for Roman jurisprudence and for despotism. Were we to say that that equity saved the common law, and that the Court of Star Chamber saved the constitution, even in this paradox there would be some truth.

ARTHUR
HASSALL.
The Trans-
formation of
the Army.
DURING the reign of Henry VII. the peculiar characteristics of the English army of the fourteenth and fifteenth centuries were passing away. A general change and transformation of the forms of the art of war was in progress. But this change was a gradual one, and was not very noticeable during the reign of the first Tudor king, whose policy was pacific, and tended to keep the English soldiers at home. Henry VII. was more occupied with the suppression of the customs of livery and maintenance than with schemes of foreign aggression.

On his accession the whole military organisation was out of gear. The period of disorder known as the Wars of the Roses had had disastrous effects on the existing military system. Great difficulty had been experienced in raising troops before the Battle of Bosworth, and complaints of the decay of knighthood and the degeneracy of the English as soldiers were frequent. We have seen that during the incessant warfare of 1455 to 1485 the old national militia had been almost entirely replaced by the bands of "household men" and the liveried dependents of the great peers. These dangerous bands had to be swept away before the old military system, with modifications necessitated by the change in the character of the nobility and by the introduction of gunpowder, could be restored and placed on a satisfactory footing.

Concentration under the Crown. To adapt the existing arrangements for purposes of defensive and foreign warfare, to destroy the influence of the great lords, to place the whole military system in the hands of trustworthy men, whom he could direct and on whom he could rely, was the definite policy of Henry VII. Though the great European monarchies were establishing permanent military forces, England had no standing army. The nearest approach to such an institution was to be found in the Yeomen of the Guard and the Gentlemen-at-Arms, formed by Henry VII. England, however, was not without military resources, adequate for defensive purposes, and not wholly insufficient for occasional intervention on the Continent.

We have seen that in the fourteenth and the early part of the fifteenth centuries (p. 55) all men from sixteen to sixty were liable to be called out for the protection of the country against invasion, and even expected "to be well and defensibly arrayed," and to be so arrayed as to be ready upon a day's warning to resist the king's enemies and rebels, and to defend

SOLDIERS AND CIVILIANS (MS. Roy. 18 D. ii.).

the realm. Commissions of array had long been the recognised constitutional means of collecting forces for the protection of the realm. The law as settled in 1402 was that "except in case of invasion none shall be constrained to go out of their own counties," and as wars with Wales and Scotland were always, and rightly, regarded in the light of invasions, the militia of the counties were liable for such service. The Welsh and Scottish wars of Henry IV., and the Scottish war

of Edward IV. and Richard III., were carried on by troops
levied by Privy Seal letters, issued by the king and paid for
by the districts which supplied them.   Only the battles of the
Civil War had been fought out by the liveried retainers of the
baronage.   Henry VII. utilised the existing system and found
it sufficient for his purpose.   The attempted rising (p. 605) in
Yorkshire, instigated by Lord Lovel and the Staffords, old
followers of Richard III., collapsed at the appearance of a
strong muster of nobles, gentry, and yeomen; and as soon
as Lambert Simnel's rebellion assumed dangerous proportions,
Henry sent most of the southern nobility to their own districts
to muster men.   The desperate courage of Simnel's host was
as unsuccessful at Stoke against these hastily summoned levies
as was that of the Scots some years later at Flodden.   For
foreign war, troops were raised by voluntary enlistments under
Henry VII. just as they had been under Edward III. or
Henry V. (pp. 55, 448).   The enlistments were generally made
through the medium of some nobleman or gentleman who bound
himself by indenture to serve the king " for a fixed sum, and
with a fixed force for fixed wages."

Troops
Raised by
Contract.
When the system of livery was abolished, the necessity for
private defence removed, and the power of the great barons
destroyed, Henry VII. took in hand and continued the system of
contracting with county magnates for troops for foreign service.
For example, we find him in 1492 contracting with different
lords and gentlemen in order to make his army as effective as
possible, while in this same year he, in like manner, contracted
with the Earl of Kent to provide " vj. men of arms, his owne
person comprised in the same, every one of them having with
him his custrell[1] and his page; with sixteen demi-lances,[2] sixteen archers on horsbak, and sixty archers on fote, of good
and hable persons for the ware, horsed, armed, garnished, and
arrayed, sufficiently in all peces, and in everything as after
the custome of ware ought to appertayne."   This indenture is
exactly similar · to the business-like agreements by which
Henry V. had raised his troops eighty years before.   To pay
for the maintenance of an army raised for the defence of
Brittany in 1490, and for the expedition to France in 1492,

[1 Servants; so called because armed with daggers (Lat. *cultellus*).]
[2 Light horse, armed with a short, light spear.]

Henry VII. secured grants of money from his Parliaments. The people were heavily taxed for what was really not a war, and the unquiet spirits at home did not appreciate the fact that peace had been gained without a battle.

The contracts made always expired at the end of the wars, and the armies were disbanded. The rehabilitation of cavalry

A SCENE IN CAMP (MS. Roy. 18 D. ii.).

had not yet begun in England, though on the Continent the horseman was again in favour. But in Henry's time the knights and squires still descended from their horses to fight on foot, as their fathers had done at Towton and Tewkesbury. We therefore find that although light horse were used for raiding and for scouting, yet during the early Tudor period the common infantry formed the real fighting strength of the army, and were commanded by officers who had no personal connection with the men. Owing to the absence of a commissariat, to the inefficiency of the officers, and to the disorganisation of forces, " unaccustomed to discipline, unused to command, and brought at haphazard from the plough," the performances of the Tudor army abroad did not as a rule redound to the credit of the Government.

ARMOUR OF A KNIGHT UNDER HENRY VII.

(*Rotunda M^{u}'seum ; by permission of the General Officer commanding Woolwich District.*)

The invention of gunpowder brought about many important changes in the history of warfare in the sixteenth century. We have seen how Edward IV. had scattered the Lincolnshire rebels by the fire of his cannon at Lose-Coat Field. Not less effective was the fire of Henry VII.'s artillery at Blackheath, when the Cornishmen fled in dismay from the volleys which ploughed clear lines through their serried masses. It is hardly possible to exaggerate the advantage which the king had over rebels of all sorts through possessing the only parks of artillery within the four seas. But though the adoption of gunpowder thus gradually revolutionised warfare, and though artillery was used throughout the Wars of the Roses, the longbow retained its superiority. In the small engagements with the French which gave the only opportunity for the trial of weapons in the time of Henry VII., the archer still showed himself as effective as at Crécy or Agincourt. When Lord Morley defeated the French at Dixmuide and stormed their camp, all the credit is given to the bowmen. At Flodden the Lowland pikemen were shot down by the English archers, and in Edward VI.'s reign Ket's followers defeated a corps of German hackbut men with their archery fire.[1]

Henry VII.'s policy, then, in things military, was to destroy utterly the custom of livery and maintenance which had superimposed itself upon the old national system, and to render the county levies free from all baronial influence and loyal to himself. Livery and maintenance were ever the signs of faction and oppression, and for their suppression the Court of Star Chamber was set up. To secure the services of soldiers during the period for which they had contracted to fight, an Act was passed in the seventh year of Henry's reign inflicting penalties for desertion, and in Edward VI.'s reign another Act was passed "Touching the free service of captains and soldiers," which was somewhat of a Mutiny Act. Thus Henry VII. inaugurated a policy which was continued by all the Tudors. His aim was to provide a national and trustworthy force. In order to effect his purpose he revived the militia system, and compelled counties to supply a certain number of men according to their means. No better illustration of the

practical wisdom of the Tudors, in developing the county and parochial institutions, can be afforded than by observing the way in which they supported and extended the militia system. As long as a policy of peace was definitely pursued, the militia arrangements were probably adequate. But as soon as a nation engages in war, a standing army is a better and more economical instrument. "Armies raised by hasty levies from a rural population

"THE BROCAS HEAUME."

(Rotunda Museum; by permission of the General Officer commanding Woolwich District.)

are among the costliest, as they are the worst, of all political expedients." Industry is disturbed, the labourer acquires dis-

---

[1 The longbow, indeed, as will be shown in the next volume, was not displaced till the end of the sixteenth century.]

organised habits, and after the war the country is full of disbanded soldiers. Such was the condition of England at the time of the Wars of the Roses; such was its condition, to a modified extent, after Henry VIII.'s first experiences of Continental warfare. From such a state of things the wise policy of Henry VII. preserved England during his reign.

WARSHIPS ENTERING A RIVER (MS. Aug. A. vi.).

W. LAIRD CLOWES.
The Navy under Henry VII.

THE sovereignty of the Narrow Seas was worthily maintained by England under Henry VII., a monarch who not only understood that the only way to ensure peace is to be prepared for war, but also comprehended the principles, and realised the importance, of commerce. In 1487 the Archbishop of Canterbury, who was also Lord Chancellor, opened Parliament with a speech in which he conveyed to the Estates of the Realm the king's views on these subjects; and during the session that followed, much attention was devoted to them. In 1490 a very advantageous treaty was concluded with Denmark (P. 745) which secured to the merchants, and particularly to those of Bristol, the trade which they had long enjoyed with

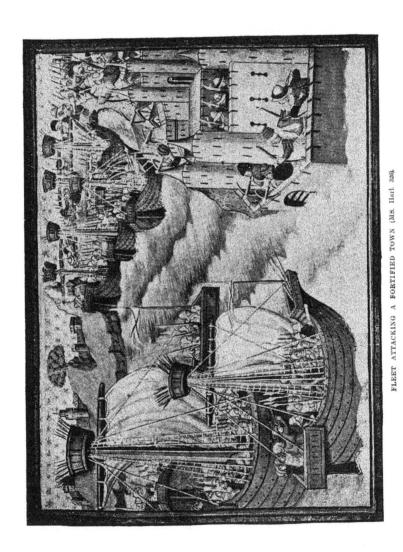

FLEET ATTACKING A FORTIFIED TOWN (MS. Harl. 326).

Iceland, but which, since the Civil Wars, had suffered some disturbance.

By the stipulations in this compact it was agreed that the English were to furnish the Icelanders with all kinds of provision, with coarse cloth, and with other commodities, without hindrance on the part of Denmark. This was an exclusive privilege, and was, no doubt, well worth obtaining.

DRAWING OF THE *HARRY GRACE à DIEU.*

(*In the Pepysian Library, Magdalene College, Cambridge. Reproduced from "Archæologia,"
Vol. VI.*)

In 1506 an almost equally advantageous treaty was concluded with Castile.

The
"Henri
Grace à
Dieu."

It seems to have been the practice all through the fifteenth century, as a ship became useless, to pass on her name to a new vessel built to replace her. It was also the practice to reserve certain names for vessels of the largest kind. One of the names so reserved was *Grace à Dieu.* When Henry VII. determined to replace a *Grace à Dieu* that had been left him by his predecessors, he decided that the new craft should be larger and more splendid than anything then belonging to his Navy; and, when he had at length completed her, he called her, in his own honour, the *Henri Grace à Dieu.*

She is said to have cost £14,000, and she appears to have had four pole-masts, each with two circular tops, a bowsprit, three square sails on each mast, a built-up poop and fore-castle, and two complete and two partial tiers of guns mounted in ports. There is some reason for believing that a drawing of the *Harry Grace à Dieu*, in the Pepysian Library at Cambridge, is intended to represent this vessel and not the next

Photo : W. H. Rau, Philadelphia.

SHIPS OF COLUMBUS, AS REPRODUCED FOR HIS QUINGENTENARY.

Henri Grace à Dieu, which was built by Henry VIII. What her guns were can only be conjectured; but some grounds appear for supposing that on her lower-deck she carried sixteen 24- or 32-prs.; on her main-deck, eighteen 12-prs.; and on her upper-deck, poop, and forecastle about thirty-six 5-prs. and 2-prs.; or seventy guns in all. It must, however, be admitted that little is known about her. It is very likely that, re-named the *Regent*, she was the ship which was lost in the engagement with the French on August 10th, 1512. If so, she was of 1,000 tons burthen, and carried a complement of 700 officers and men. James says that she was built in 1488, but so much that is contradictory has been written

concerning her, that almost all that can be said with certainty
is that Henry VII.'s *Henri Grace à Dieu* was a bigger vessel
than had ever before been built in England, and that, by the
beginning of the next reign, she had either disappeared or
received a new name.

**The Dis-
covery of
North
America.**
Henry's known zeal for the Navy, and his recognised
commercial and general ability, induced Christopher Columbus,
who had met with but a cool reception at the Court of Spain,
to turn, in 1485, to England, whither he despatched his brother
Bartholomew, within a few months after Henry's accession.
Bartholomew was unfortunate.   On his way to England he
was taken by pirates and made by them to labour as a slave,
and when he escaped and reached London, he was first so ill
and then so poor as to be unable to press his brother's designs
upon the king until 1488.   In the interval he supported
himself by making charts and globes, and, on being at length
introduced to Henry, he presented his Majesty with a map
of the world.   The king listened to Columbus's plans, and
readily promised to assist in carrying them out; but delays
supervened, and ere Bartholomew was in a position to carry
a definite commission to his brother Christopher, the latter
had not only obtained the co-operation of Spain, but had
actually accomplished his first voyage and made his great discovery.   The news of this naturally created great stir in all
the seaports of Europe, and induced John Cabot, or Caboto,
a naturalised Venetian, who had long been settled at
Bristol and who was already favourably known to Henry, to
make application to the king for encouragement to attempt
further discoveries to the westward, and especially to look for
a north-west passage to India.   According to some, Cabot had
already made a voyage to the north-west, and had sighted
Labrador in 1494.   The story of his two ascertained voyages
is told in detail in the succeeding pages.   In both these
voyages he made observations of the variation of the
compass, a phenomenon which had been already noticed by
Columbus.

In 1502 Henry granted further letters patent for maritime
discovery under English colours to Hugh Ellyot and Thomas
Ashurst, merchants of Bristol, and to John Gonzales and
Francis Fernandez, natives of Portugal.

THE great age of English discovery, it is often said, begins CHARLES RAYMOND BEAZLEY. with the Cabots, John and Sebastian, Italians and Venetians, who took the lead in the exploration of the North American The Cabots. continent. As in other countries, so in England, Italians were the first pilots and shipmasters of exploring voyagers.

RIB OF A WHALE FROM NEWFOUNDLAND.
(*St. Mary Redcliffe Church, Bristol.*)

but English exploration was slower in its growth than Spanish or Portuguese. The enterprise of 1497 was a generation too soon for national feeling, and is chiefly to be noted as an evidence, not so much of Northern and English as of Southern and Italian daring and seamanship. It belongs more to the world of Columbus, Da Gama, and Henry of Portugal, than to that of Henry VII. The native English movement rather starts with Chancellor and Willoughby and the seamen of Edward VI.

But the achievement of the Cabots, as being performed in

87

the service of the English Crown, became one of our national glories (P. 615). It is the one successful venture of seamen from our ports into the unknown world throughout that fifteenth century which witnessed the steady advance of the Portuguese round the African continent to India, the further opening of the new land routes to the Far East, the discovery of the Western continent by Columbus.[1]

First Voyage. On the 5th of March, 1495, a patent was granted to John Cabot and his three sons, Sebastian[2] and two others, for the discovery and conquest of unknown lands: in the spring of 1497 (May) these Venetians sailed from Bristol with two vessels, the *Matthew* and another, and on June 24th, after a straight course west of nearly two months, they sighted land. Their "Prima Vista," as Hakluyt calls it, was probably not Cape Breton Island, as stated in Sebastian's planisphere of 1544, but eight or ten degrees farther north, on the coast of Labrador,[3] which was then ranged by the discoverers, probably as far as Cape Chudley.

"On the 24th of June, 1497," says Hakluyt's Testimony, "John and Sebastian Cabot discovered that land which no man had before attempted." On landing, they found barbarous islanders dressed in skins. Three of these they brought home, and presented to Henry VII.

"When the news came of Columbus' finding of the passage by the West to the East," says Sebastian in his own account, ". . . I sailed N.-W., not thinking to find any land but Cathay [China], and thence to turn towards India." On failing to hit the passage "as the land ran even North and East," he turned down towards the tropics and ran along the coast to Florida. Then, as provisions began to fail, he turned back to England.

---

[1] This being at first mistaken for Eastern Asia, the real importance of the achievement lay not in its discovery as a new world, which was only realised later, but in its supposed proof of the possibility of sailing round the globe. *Cf.* Hakluyt's original, "The Voyage of Sebastian Cabot to the N.-E. part of America for the discovery of a N.-W. passage, as far as 58 degrees of latitude, and thence back again along the coast to Florida, in 1497. Confirmed by six testimonies."

[2] The Letters Patent authorised the Cabots—"John, Lewis, Sebastian, and Sancius, to sail to all places, lands, and seas, of the East, West, and North." First, they were to discover; second, to annex, any new-found heathen lands.

[3] *Cf.* Harrisse, "Discovery of North America," pp. 6–9, 36–37, which greatly discounts Sebastian's version, as that of a braggart or a charlatan.

In another account, it was only a mutiny of the shipmasters and mariners that prevented his making his way straight to Cathay; for, " on the 11th of June, still finding the open sea without impediment, he thought verily to have passed on" to Asia. He had sailed so near the Pole that he met "monstrous great lumps of ice swimming in the sea, and continual daylight," while to his own seeming he had got so·far west that, as he said afterwards, "Then I had Cuba on my left."

The whole of this famous voyage was made, it would seem, between the beginning of May and the end of July, when the discoverers were back in English waters with their reports of a new-found world in the Northern Ocean, which offered the attractions of mines of copper, and barbarous islanders. Whether this was an outlying part of Cathay or a great unknown land between Asia and Europe, could not yet be proved. In any case, though little was done by Englishmen for many years to follow up this Prima Vista, the Cabots had sailed in the service of the Crown, and Henry VII. had to give them a dole. It was not quite the sort of thing to draw seamen from the ports of Spain and Italy. In the Privy Purse expenses, under date of the 10th of August, 1497, there is the entry : " To him· that found the New Isle, £10 " (equal to about £100 now).

The discoverers gained their patent for a second venture on February 3rd, 1498. By this deed, " John Kabotto " is allowed to take six ships in any haven of the realm up to 200 tons burden " to convey and lead to the land and isles of late found by the said John, in our name and by our commandment "—and between May and July of this year (1498) the next voyage seems to have been made[1] with the most doubtful results.

Second and Third Voyages.

The second voyage of 1498 is followed by a disputed third in 1499, of which we have an entry that it was to the "Gulf of Mexico"; shortly after this is to be placed the death of John Cabot, and Sebastian disappears from sight till the year 1512. But in 1501, 1502, 1504, and afterwards, English ships went the Newfoundland voyage, chiefly for fishery.

---

[1] Possibly guided by Portuguese and Italian information. From the D'Este map, it seems clear that the Portuguese knew the outline of the North American coasts from Florida to Cape Cod in 1502. The landfall on this occasion was probably S. of that on the former voyage; and the exploration is said to have included the whole E. coast of the·present United States as far as Florida. (Harrisse, *op. cit.*, p. 34.)

REGINALD
HUGHES.
Architecture
and Art.

WE have seen how, in the matter of architecture, each new style arose and reached a comparative degree of perfection, not only during the lifetime of its predecessor, but while the predecessor

WINDOW IN FAIRFORD CHURCH, GLOUCESTERSHIRE.

was in the plenitude of its power. The same holds true of the work of the painter on glass. There is rarely any apparent difference between the texture or colour of the latter part of the Early English glass and the early part of the Decorated glass, or between the later Decorated and the earliest Perpendicular. The magnificent depth of colour of the earliest times of glass

Painted Glass.

[1509]

mosaic did not last long, and, indeed, in point of colour, the falling-off was tolerably continuous throughout the whole of the Decorated and Perpendicular periods. Nor was there, so far as we can judge, much original talent then, or at any time, displayed in England in this department. The borders are, as a rule, either copies of architectural details, or borrowings from French work. The stipple method of shading, which, no doubt, immensely increased the power of the glass painter, may be considered the great achievement of the Perpendicular period. Still, its results in England, at least, were unfortunate. For while it never at any time produced work of really fine pictorial character (such as the sixteenth-century glass of Montmorency), its influence was ruinous to the more decorative effect. At any rate, the desire to show off the minuter delicacies of their work led the glass artists to introduce large masses of white glass, and to eschew the deep and gem-like tints of their forefathers. This is equally true of Perpendicular picture-windows and of Perpendicular pattern-windows; and the tendency may be traced without breakdown, to the corruption of everything connected with Gothic under the influence of the classical Renaissance. The completest specimen of Perpendicular glass decorations in the kingdom is in Fairford Church in Gloucestershire. It dates from the first year of the sixteenth century, and shows, if we can be sure that it is English work, that in matter of drawing, and in harmonious though not rich colour, England was not far behind France at this time. It is only right, however, to say that the nationality of this glass is impugned by a tradition that the church was built by John Tame, in 1493, for the reception of the glass which he had just captured piratically. On the other hand, the Prince of Wales's Feathers appear in one of the lights; so we may feel sure that one window, at any rate, was of home manufacture. *The Fairford Windows.*

The enfeeblement and exhaustion which followed the Wars of the Roses seem to have extinguished the flickering light of English sculpture, and the superiority of the foreign painters and sculptors justified the fatal practice of their introduction. The statues and apostles in Henry VII.'s chapel, some fonts, chiefly in East Country churches, the reliefs at Tewkesbury, and a few monuments, like those of Cardinal *Sculpture under Henry VII.*

Beaufort at Winchester and Giles Lord Daubeney at Westminster, make up most of the best of our indigenous sculpture down to the end of the reign of the first Tudor sovereign. It is to the Italian Torrigiano that we owe the tomb of Henry VII. and his queen at Westminster, with its noble figures dignified

TOMB OF HENRY VII., WESTMINSTER ABBEY.

in character and naturalistic in treatment; but this, of course, brings us to the reign of the second Tudor sovereign.   The contract between the executors of Henry VII. and the Florentine artist still exists. The work was to cost £1,500, and was finished in 1518. The king, in his will, gave minute directions for the monument, and justified the saying that the only expense which Henry VII. ever willingly faced was that which was to be incurred after his death. The black marble tomb has a finely carved frieze, adorned with medallions in copper gilt, and, at each end, the royal arms supported by brass cherubs. It is a fine work of purely Italian character.

For a century, or thereabouts, after the death of Richard, Painting. the history of pictorial art in England is a blank. The marriage of Henry V. and Katharine after Agincourt produced nothing but a long and exhausting war. Nor was the connection between the courts of King Edward IV. and Duke Charles of Burgundy productive of more important results, although the one great northern school of painting was included in the dominions of the Duke. It is, no doubt, probable that Flemish pictures, as well as Flemish horses and French wines, found their way across the seas, but there is no evidence that the Englishmen of that day cared for anything of the kind. The art of the painter, in the highest sense of the word, was unknown in England until the sixteenth century, and then it came in one of its humblest manifestations in what we may call superficial, as distinguished from characteristic, portraiture. In Italy the dramatic presentation of human life had been achieved with brilliant success two hundred years before; but England could only show a manuscript here and there which did not exhibit the general indifference. Even the best illuminations, such as the Bedford Missal, belonging to Englishmen, were executed abroad. Portraits, or things called portraits, were no doubt painted in the fifteenth and even the fourteenth centuries. Here and there we come across a king who ordered the portraits of his ancestors, or a bishop who placed the portraits of all his predecessors on the walls of a chapel or chantry. A few rude panels, mostly copies, apparently made in the reign of the first Tudor, preserve the likenesses, or what were supposed to be the likenesses, of the earlier Plantagenets. In this way we see, or fancy we see, what manner of men were Edward IV. and Richard III., and Jane Shore —the picture of that unhappy woman possessing more than common interest, as answering, though not fully, to the description of the portrait seen and minutely described by

Sir Thomas More. Henry VII. deserves credit at least for this—that he was the first English sovereign since Henry III. who cared in the slightest degree for art. The long wars with France had left neither princes nor people time to cultivate anything but arms, and during the Wars of the Roses the one art really studied was that of cutting throats The reign of Edward IV. provided the first breathing-term,

FRIAR JOHN SIFERWAS PRESENTING HIS BOOK TO LORD
LOVELL (MS. Harl. 7026).

and after the union of the two rival houses by the marriage of Henry Tudor and the White Rose of York, a new and more promising era began.

Henry seems to have extended something like a welcome to the foreign artist. and has the credit of having invited

PAGE FROM THE "BEDFORD MISSAL" (MS. Add. 18,850).

Mabuse and his School.

Jan Gossaert to our shores. He came from Maubeuge, in Hainault, and is better known by the local sobriquet of Mabuse. The actual date of his birth, as well as the date, and indeed the fact, of his arrival in England, is indefinite, but early in the sixteenth century he was probably here. He is familiar to Englishmen by one of his noblest works, "The Offering of the Magi," at Castle Howard, which, however, was not painted for an English patron, but for the Abbot of Grammont. He had studied in Italy, and acquired fame in the Low Countries, if he quitted them for England, and the immediate cause of his doing so is uncertain. It is not, however, improbable that, having got into some scrape (the Cinque-cento painters were a wild crew), he determined to try the Court of one who was accounted the richest prince in Europe. He is said to have painted portraits of the king's children—Prince Arthur, Prince Henry, and Princess Margaret—and such a picture by a Flemish hand, though hardly that of Mabuse, exists. Grave doubt has, however, been thrown on the identity of the persons represented. It is by no means impossible that the picture was painted in England, though the better opinion is that it represents the three children of Christian II. of Denmark. At the same time, the fact that the group was several times repeated—there are no less than four replicas in England—certainly favours the view that it was supposed to represent the English royal family. It is probable that Mabuse, or a skilful countryman of his, established some kind of Flemish atelier in London, whence works, the nationality of which cannot well be disputed, were disseminated throughout England. There are several other pictures of this period which have been long attributed to Mabuse, such as the Adam and Eve, and the Virgin and Child, with St. Michael and St. Andrew, at Hampton Court. But however few the works by his hand may be, the number painted by Flemings, or the pupils of Flemings, or which belong to his Flemish school, is considerable. More than one portrait of "the Lady Margaret" Beaufort, the mother of Henry VII., remains, preserved by the piety of the colleges at Cambridge, of which she was a benefactress. And though many of them are copies, ordered by the filial piety of those who enjoyed her bounty, there must clearly have been at least one original of considerable character. The famous "Marriage of Henry VII. with Elizabeth of York," formerly the property of Horace Walpole, probably came from the studio the existence of which we have inferred. The famous virtuoso's description of this picture hits off the qualities of a most important work, and probably the most ambitious production of the first school of art which was planted in England :—

ANGELET OF EDWARD IV.

"It represents the inside of a church—an imaginary one—not at all resembling the abbey where those princes were married. The perspective and the landscape of the country on each side are good. On one hand, in the foreground, stand the King and Bishop of Imola, who pronounced the nuptial benediction. His Majesty is a trist, lean, ungracious figure, with a downcast look, very expressive of his mean temper and of the little satisfaction he had in the match. Opposite to the bishop is the queen, a buxom, well-looking damsel, with golden hair. By her is a figure, above all proportion with the rest, unless intended, as I imagine, for an emblematic personage, and designed from its lofty stature to give an idea of something above human. It is an elderly man, dressed like a monk except that his habit is green, his feet are bare, and a spear is in his hand. As the

ANGEL OF EDWARD IV.

frock of no religious Order ever was green, this cannot be meant for a friar. Probably it is St. Thomas, represented, as in the martyrologies, with the instrument of his death. The queen might have some devotion to that peculiar saint, or might be born or married on his festival. Be that as it may, the picture, though in a hard manner, has its merit, independent of the curiosity."

Coins.   From the reign of Edward III. to that of Henry VII., the
art of the medallist in England made no progress. The
noble, half-noble, and quarter-noble in gold; the groat, half-
groat, penny, half-penny in silver, continued to be coined
during the intervening reigns, but were nothing but more

SOVEREIGNS OF HENRY VII.

or less successful copies of the second and later coinage of
Edward. Henry IV., in the thirteenth year of his reign,
reduced the weight of the groat and of its subdivisions, and
in this step was followed by his son and grandson. But all
the while money grew steadily searcer and led to the introduction, not only of the Scottish silver, which was of inferior
quality, but of various foreign pieces, including a large coinage
made in Venice specially for the English market. Numerous

proclamations forbidding the use of these foreign coins, and an equal number of petitions for a further issue of small English coins, sufficiently attest both the scarcity and the illicit efforts to mitigate it. Under Henry VI. two new gold coins appeared—the angel and the angelet, so named from the figure of St. Michael trampling on the dragon, borne on the obverse—and under his successor a variation was made in the noble by adding a full-blown rose on the side of Edward's ship.

The reign of Henry VII. marks the beginning of our modern coinage. In the fifth year of that king the sovereign appeared (p. 751). It was double the weight of the royal or noble; but that coin, as well as the angel and angelet, continued in use. The design of the sovereign was new, the king appearing in his royal robes, crowned, seated on an open throne, with a background of fleur-de-lis diaper. There is also another type extant, in which the throne is surmounted by a canopy, but in both the double rose of Lancaster and York appears on the reverse. Like our own coin, the Tudor sovereign was of the value of twenty shillings, and in this reign, for the first time, an actual shilling in silver makes its appearance (p. 751). There were also many changes in the dies. The arched crown, after an absence of many centuries, re-appears; at first, upon a head of the conventional angelic type, which had done duty for all the Plantagenets, from Henry of Winchester downwards. But in the nineteenth year of Henry VII., if not earlier, there is an issue of coins, with a profile of the king, wearing his crown. Probably these were the best specimens of metallic portraiture which had been coined in this country since the time of Constantine, and in truth from this time the cabinet of the English numismatist assumes the character of a national portrait gallery.

The First Sovereigns.

AMID the richness of interest which marked the life of England at the end of the fifteenth century, the intellectual aspect must not be forgotten. The Universities were passing through a period of change, reflecting in their own way, then as ever, the fashions of the nation at large. In Cambridge, colleges were founded—Jesus, in 1497, famous for its

W. H. HUTTON. The Universities.

beautiful gardens, on the site of a Benedictine nunnery, and Christ's, in 1506, endowed by the devout and learned mother of the king, Margaret, Countess of Richmond. Each of these new colleges was to train a prominent reformer: Cranmer studied at Jesus and Latimer at Christ's. The glorious chapel of the royal foundation of King's College received also some addition at the hands of Henry VII. But at Cambridge the intellectual movement of the time

MARGARET, COUNTESS OF RICHMOND.
(National Portrait Gallery.)

became prominent rather under Henry VIII.; it had its beginnings at Oxford while the first Tudor still sat on the throne.

Probably at no time in the history of the University were there gathered within its walls men more eminent as scholars or more famous in the national annals. The founders of the Royal Society, or the leaders of the Tractarian movement, do not cover so wide a field as the men in whose hands the English Renaissance began to shape itself. Not long before,

1509]

it had been recorded that at least five Oxford students were pupils of the elder Guarino, at Ferrara. Now the "barbarians beyond the Alps" were beginning to teach and

GATEWAY OF JESUS COLLEGE, CAMBRIDGE.

to study for themselves. Within the reign of Henry VII. an Italian traveller might have met at the same time in Oxford William Grocyn, Thomas Linacre, Thomas More, John Colet, Thomas Wolsey, Cornelio Vitelli, and Desiderius

Erasmus.   On Christmas Day, 1488, three Italian scholars dined with the President of Magdalen; and it appears that a few years later Cornelio Vitelli was lecturing in the schools.

Greek taught at Oxford.   But to William Grocyn belongs the honour of first teaching Greek at Oxford.   He had travelled in Italy in 1488, and had studied under Chalcondylas and Politian.   He had been a fellow of New College, and was now living in Exeter College.   Thomas Linacre, who had been a fellow of All Souls', had also breathed the delicate atmosphere of the Florentine Academy.   He was More's special instructor. and from him, too, Erasmus first learnt Greek.   More was a typical student of the English Renaissance, and both his studies and their earliest fruits belong to the reign of Henry VII.   He was entered, in 1492, at Canterbury College, one of the foundations which afterwards made way for Christ Church, and he seems to have occupied a room also at St. Mary Hall.   There he remained for two years.   The old learning still held the field in England, and there was no such support for the humanists as was afforded in Italy by the circles of distinguished patrons, but the attempt to transplant Italian culture was being made with energy and success.   English scholars translated Greek into Latin, wrote Latin letters and poems with a new freedom and courage, and began to lecture on the literatures of Greece and Rome.   The reconstruction of the great world of the past was being undertaken in Oxford as seriously as at Florence.   Boys like More were sent by wise fathers, like the old Justice Sir John, away from the "distractions of public affairs" [1] to profit by the quietude of an academic training.   Already at work in the world, professed ecclesiastics and parish priests gave up active life to enter on the new course of study for which the relics of Scholasticism had given but slight training.   John Colet was already twenty-six, and a Master of Arts, when his eager pursuit of Greek brought him into relations with the young student of fourteen, with whom he formed a lasting friendship.   In 1493, not satisfied with all that Grocyn and Linacre could teach, he went to learn in France and Italy.   In 1496 he was back again, and lecturing on St. Paul's Epistles with all the eagerness and devotion of a disciple and a discoverer.

[1] Cresacre More, "Life of More," p. 9.

It is characteristic of the English scholars and of those Colet, More, Wolsey whom they gathered round them that their classical knowledge was used for religion rather than secular learning. The Bible and Dionysius the Areopagite, the Creation, Sacrifice, the Origins of Things—subjects wide enough, but within a range where clerks and ecclesiastics should be at home— these were the topics on which Colet dwelt. When Erasmus first came to Oxford, in 1498, men pressed him to lecture on Isaiah or the Pentateuch. When More first lectured it was on Augustine's "City of God." How far the great statesman of the next reign mingled in these spiritual matters we have no means of judging, but it is impossible that he was uninfluenced by the movement around him. Thomas Wolsey was even younger as a scholar than Thomas More. He was made bachelor at fifteen, and fitly dubbed the "boy bachelor." In 1497 he was a fellow of Magdalen. He became, for a while, Master of the College School, and, in 1499 and 1500, he was Senior Bursar of the College. It is most likely that More first met him in Oxford, and that their close relations as statesmen in later years, of which the State papers of Henry VII.'s reign give so full a record, began when they were scholars of the New Learning. But Wolsey was from the first given to practical affairs, while More was but gradually weaned from the contemplative life. Wolsey may have looked in upon the friends as they talked of ancient letters, but we cannot think of him as one of the small circle among whom Erasmus moved. "When I listen to Colet, my friend, I seem to hear Plato himself. Who wonders not at Grocyn's wide knowledge? Whose judgment could be more piercing, deep, and clear than Linacre's? And when did Nature form a character gentler, more loving, or more happy than that of Thomas More?" So wrote the Dutch scholar to his foreign friends. A very happy party of scholars, indeed, but not a training ground, Wolsey may have thought, for the stern world outside. So, at least, thought Sir John More, Justice of the King's Bench. He had kept his son very strictly at the university, "suffering him scarcely to have so much money in his own custody as would pay for the mending of his apparel," and demanding a strict account of his expenses. The treat-

88

ment had answered, for the young man had been "curbed
from all vice, and withdrawn from many idle expenses,
either of game or keeping naughty companions, so that he
knew neither play nor other riot." But while it had made
him a sober scholar, it had not made him a sound lawyer.
The medieval universities of the North were, as a rule,
unfavourable to the study of Jurisprudence and of Medicine.
At Oxford a degree in Law could not be obtained without
seven years' study after the completion of the Arts' course,
and this might well seem a waste of time to the practical
judge. More, then, was withdrawn from Oxford, and set to
study, in 1496, at Lincoln's Inn. By the beginning of the
sixteenth century the students who had met in Oxford
were near each other in London—Grocyn, as Rector of St.
Lawrence, Jewry, and More lecturing in his church, Linacre
and a new friend, Lilly, also a scholar from Italy, and at
St. Paul's, early in 1505, the new Dean, John Colet. Wolsey
had left Oxford in 1500 With the withdrawal of these
great names Oxford underwent a period of quiescence. Warham was elected Chancellor, in 1506, and Richard Fox, as
Bishop of Winchester, had already begun to visit the colleges with which he was connected. He gave Balliol its new
statutes, in 1507, treating it entirely as a home for poor
scholars. He was preparing to found a new college, which
should preserve his name. Under Henry VIII., a king who
was himself a scholar, the university was to begin a new era.

**H. FRANK
HEATH.
Early
Scottish
Literature,
1350-1600.**
THE kingdom of Scotland took its name and dynasty from a
race which in early time had emigrated from Ireland ; but
these people formed little more than a fourth of the whole
population of the land. Besides these, there were the Picts
in the north-west, the Anglians in the south-east, and the
remains of the old British kingdom of Strathclyde in the south-
west. Until the war of national independence broke out with
the English, after the death of Alexander III. (1286) had
left the succession to the Scottish throne doubtful, no political
solidarity had been possible. The sense of political unity grew
up under the fear of foreign domination. It was still longer
before this sense became sufficiently self-conscious to find its

expression in literature. Until the middle of the fourteenth century the Scots dialect was nothing more than a part of the Northern English manner of speech, and there was no literature with independent or national characteristics.

The earliest work that has come down to us which can lay claim to the name of Scottish was produced in the second half of the fourteenth century, and it was clearly the offspring of that school of poets in North-west England, of whom the author of "Gawain" was the chief. As a consequence, the author of the "Grete Geste of Arthur," and other works has been claimed both as an Englishman and as a Scot. Huchown (a variant of Hugon, or Hugh) of the Awle Ryale (*de aula regia*), as Wyntown calls him in his "Originale Cronykil of Scotland," written at the opening of the fifteenth century, is a person of whom we know nothing beyond his authorship of several poems ; unless, in leed, we are justified in identifying him with a certain Sir Hugh of Eglintoun, whose castle and lands lay in Ayrshire, and who had married a sister of Robert II., the founder of the Stuart dynasty. Sir Hugh's life must have fallen in the second and third quarters of the fourteenth century ; and his connection with the royal house might justify the phrase "of the Awle Ryale." Andrew of Wyntown speaks of Huchown as author of the "Grete Geste of Arthur and the Awntyre of Gawaine," which, though the names of two distinct works, are both most probably incorporated in an alliterative romance, "Morte Arthur," at one time ascribed to the Gawain poet.[1] Wyntown's account of the contents of the "geste" agrees in most points , though not in all, with the matter of the "Morte Arthur" as it has come down to us ; and there are similarities in style and diction which make some connection between the two works clear. That is all one can be sure of. It is probable, however, that Huchown's "geste hystoriale" (as Wyntown sometimes calls it) was amplified early in the fifteenth century by some Northern poet, who added a detailed account of Arthur's death and burial, and combined with it an altogether disproportionate episode, the poem called "the Awntyre of Gawaine." This theory would at least account for the double title given by Wyntown, which Trautmann believes to stand for a single work, and for the

The Differentiation from English: Huchown.

---

[1] *Cf.* Trautmann, "Anglia," I., pp 109–149.

discrepancy as well as the agreement between the contents of the "Morte Arthur" and the abstract given by the Scottish chronicler.

The "Pystyll of Swete Swsane," also referred to by Wyntown, is most probably to be identified with a poem of that name existing in three MSS., and printed by Laing in 1822. The poem is written in a strophe combining rime and alliteration, the "major" being of long lines, the "minor" of short ones with alternate rime. A similar form is found in a Lancashire poem, the "Anturs of Arthur at the Tarnewathelan," and (omitting the rime in the major part, which is, moreover, of varying length) in "Sire Gawain and the Grene Knight" (p. 277). Huchown, like all the poets of the North-West School, has a keen appreciation for the beauties of Nature and for the brilliant chivalric life which was passing away. His was not so emotional nor so delicately organised a nature as that of the poet of "Pearl," but he understood how to present his story vividly, and he had, as Wyntown has remarked, a sense of style as well as a love of the truthfulness, which, as he believed, characterised his authorities. But he was, nevertheless, not destined to have much influence on the growth of a national literature in Scotland. He was one of that group of poets who expressed most clearly the survival of the old Germanic and purely English tradition south of the Border. Just because this tradition was essentially English, the newer forms of literature which had grown up in the east of England under French influence became the models of the truly national poets. For with France Scotland was always in sympathy.

Barbour.   The first of these poets was John Barbour (1320 ?–1395), a man whose way of thought and choice of theme are unmistakably Scottish. If as little were known about the man as is known about Huchown, there yet could be no shadow of doubt as to which side of the Border owned his work. He was of lower birth than his fellow poet, and rose to be Archdeacon of Aberdeen. We know that he visited Oxford twice, France once; was several times auditor of exchequer, received two life pensions, probably for his literary work, and that he mortified the smaller of them in favour of the cathedral of Aberdeen fifteen years before his death, on condition that a mass for the souls of himself and his parents were said in perpetuity on the anniversary of his death. He himself records that he wrote the poem of the "Brus" [Bruce]—his most important work—in 1735. In the short and pithy rimed couplets of "King Horn"—lines which had grown weightier and more pointed, if less musical, by the disappearance of weak inflections—Barbour told the life and adventures of the saviour of his country.

In doing this he produced a work unique of its kind, equally history, epic, and romance. The same note which is heard so clearly in Dunbar, Douglas, and in the work of all Scottish poets down to Burns, the praise of "freedom," is sounded for the first time by Barbour, though, as is natural, Barbour lays stress upon "freedom" as the result of the national virtue of independence, whilst with the eighteenth-century poet it is the individual man who is thought of. None the less, it is impossible to miss the relationship between

> "A king can mak a belted knight
> A marquis, duke and a' that;
> But an honest man's aboon his might—
> Guid faith be maunna fa' that!"

and such lines as these—

> "A! fredome is a noble thing!
> Fredome mays man to haiff liking;
> Fredome all solace to man giffis:
> He levys at es that frely leyvs!"
>
> *Brus, I.* 225 *ff.*

Barbour deals skilfully with the material at his command, both written evidence and direct personal information, though a large legendary element is undoubtedly present. After a short introduction, he brings us quickly to the event which he looks upon as the dramatic cause of Robert the Bruce's many trials, the murder of the traitor John Comyn. The Nemesis of his sin has to be lived down, but once expiated, his progress is a constant one from victory to victory, the story of which is told with great consistency and healthy sentiment, and motived in a way which would have been impossible for a man with less insight into political problems than Barbour. He is far inferior in humour to his great successor Dunbar, but he is far less coarse.

The Brus was finished in 1378. Wyntown tells us that

he also wrote a poem on the genealogy of the Stuarts, now lost, in which he is said to have traced the descent of Robert II. from "Dardane Lord de Frygya." A Troy-romance, which has perished, with the exception of two passages of 596 and 3,118 lines, belonging to its opening and its close respectively, is ascribed to a poet named Barbour by two rubrics in a MS.[1] of Lydgate's "Troy Book," which contains the first of the two fragments and the opening half of the second.[2] These fragments, though

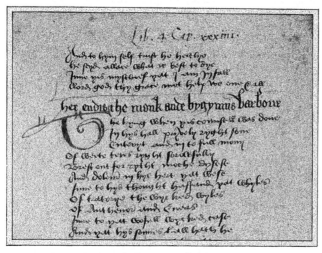

RUBRIC INSCRIBING A POEM TO BARBOUR.
(University Library, Cambridge.)

they show some command of form, do not compare favourably with Lydgate's poem on the same subject, which, like the Scot's, is a translation of Guido delle Colonne. They are in the same dialect as the "Brus," but there is considerable difference of phraseology, and the rimes point to a date later than that of the Archdeacon of Aberdeen. The large collection of Scottish lives of the saints attributed to Barbour by Horstmann is very inferior to the "Brus" as literature, and is certainly not from his pen.

[1] Camb. Univ. MS., kk. 5. 30.
[2] The whole of the longer fragment is in MS. Douce 148 (Bodleian).

Upon the death of Barbour in 1395, there comes a pause Ballad
Literature. of something like a quarter of a century in the formal literature of Scotland. During this period the ballad literature was growing, and the minstrels just south of the border produced ballads like that on " The Battle of Otterburn " (fought August 19th, 1388, between the Scots under Douglas and the English under the two sons of the Duke of Northumberland), which was later re-cast as " The Hunting of the Cheviot"; and such nondescript work as the pseudo-prophetic "Thomas of Erceldoune," which dealt with the Scottish wars down to 1399. Similar work must have been produced north of the Tweed, for Barbour quotes the opening lines of a ballad upon the death of Alexander III., the first two stanzas of which are given by Wyntown in his "Cronykil."[1]

There is considerable doubt about the right ascription of Thomas the
Rhymer. any particular work to Thomas of Erceldoune, or Thomas the Rhymer as he is often called; but it is quite clear that he himself is a historical personage, and that he held a large place in the popular imagination as a prophet and a poet. It is known from two thirteenth-century charters[2] that a Thomas of Erceldoune (or Earlstown) lived in the South of Scotland during the close of that century, and died shortly before 1294. The poem with which his name is most closely connected is the romance of "Sir Tristrem," a work standing midway between the metrical romance and the ballad, which in its present form seems to belong to the first quarter of the fourteenth century. Early French romances on the same subject allude to one " Thomas " as authority for their facts, and Gottfried von Strasburg refers to " Thomas von Britanje." This, and the reputation of the Scottish prophet, may well account for the belief Robert Mannynge of Brunne seems to have had some thirty-six years after his death, that "Sir Tristrem" was by Thomas of Erceldoune. The opening lines of the poem itself point rather against his authorship than otherwise, for they mention him by name, but in the third person. The author, whoever he may have been, took more

---

[1] *Cf.* "Brus," I., 37 *seq.*, with " Cronykil," VII. 3610 *seq.*

[2] *Cf.* "Liber de Melros," Bannatyne Club, I. 298, and a deed (date 1294) in the chartulary of the Trinity House of Soltra, now in the Advocates' Library, Edinburgh.

interest in venery than in the passionate tragedy of the love-potion. He makes no attempt to supply the gaps in his French original, and seems chiefly concerned to heighten the effect of his tale by condensation and omissions, which result in a frequent sacrifice of lucidity. The stanza in which the poem is written consists of four Alexandrines, divided into double that number of short lines by middle and end rime, connected by a bob-line[1] of one accent with a fifth Alexandrine line which is similarly divided.

The Poet-King. The next Scottish poet was a king—one of the poets who gave their allegiance to Chaucer, and one of the best of them. But James I. (1394–1437) was not only a good poet, he was one of the most accomplished statesmen of his time, and he made a brave, though unsuccessful attempt to introduce an orderly and strong government in the place of the faction and misrule which had characterised the regency of Albany, and had grown beyond endurance under the weak hand of his son Murdoch. The English Government, at war with France, had welcomed the hopes of peace and alliance with Scotland which young James's love for the Lady Joan Beaufort held out, and through Bedford's influence the marriage had been celebrated, and the young king, who had lived in captivity for eighteen years, had been sent back to Scotland with his bride in 1424. His brief but brilliant reign, and his tragic death at Perth at the hands of Sir James Graham and his Highland savages, need no emphasis. The devotion of Catherine Douglas was only surpassed by that of the queen herself, who received two wounds in her effort to save the man who, as a lover had prophetically sung of her, that

> " Thus this floure · . . . . . .
> So hertly has unto my help attendit
> That from the deth hir man sche has defendit."

The "Kingis Quair." The "Kingis Quair" ("King's book"), written in the first half of 1423, tells how the poet had first seen the Lady Joan, daughter of the Earl of Somerset and niece to Henry IV., from

---

[1] The stanza therefore looks like one of eleven lines with this rime-order: ababababcbc, the ninth being the bob-line. The same form occurs in the last three strophes of Laurence Minot's song on the siege of Tournay. A similar form, due to the division of septenars by middle-rime. is seen in Dunbar's "Ballat of Our Lady" (*cf.* p. 710).

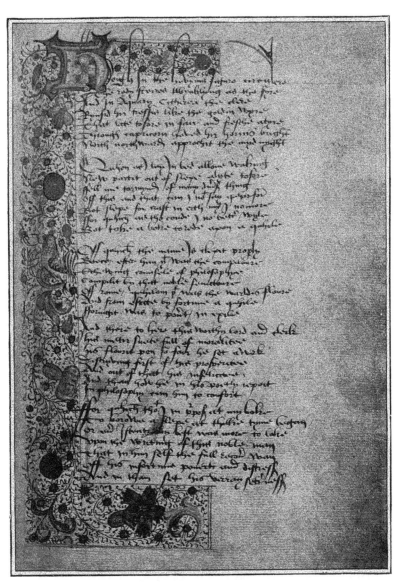

PAGE FROM THE "KINGIS QUAIR" (MS. Arch. Seld. B. 24).
(*Bodleian Library, Oxford*).

his dungeon window, as Arcite had seen Emilye walking in the garden beneath, and, like Arcite, had loved the lady who seemed to him to possess "Beautee eneuch to mak a world to dote." The poem is in Chaucer stanza, and affords clearest evidence of a very careful study of the English poet's work. There are constant reminiscences of passages and scenes not only from the "Knight's Tale," but from the "Parlement of Fowles," the "House of Fame," and "Troilus and Cryseyde." The allegorical form into which the facts of his experience are cast, and the frequent reminders one gets that the author is a pupil, not a master, would be apt to prove wearisome were it not for his evident sincerity—his highest quality, and a certain grace of manner which is his own. James is quite without Chaucer's ironical humour, and has little of his power of characterisation. On the other hand, he is more introspective. He takes six stanzas to describe the Lady Joan's appearance, and does it in pretty and fanciful phrase, but leaves no definite picture in the mind. It is the king—the "verray parfit gentil knight," with his high chivalric ideals, who, to judge from his poem, "nevere . . . no vileinye ne sayde In al his lyf," not his lady-love, that we learn to know; the poem is lyrical not dramatic. The dialect of the poem is artificial, the language of a Northerner trying, like the author of "Lancelot of the Laik," to write Chaucerian English, and the verse is smooth and musical, in marked contrast to that of Lydgate, though James undoubtedly allowed . himself licences which are not found in Chaucer.[1] Other poems have been assigned to him, amongst them "Christis (Christ's) Kirk on the Green," which is probably by James V. There seems little doubt that a balade ("rhyme royal") called "Good Counsel," and evidently inspired by Chaucer's "Fle fro the prees" (*i.e.* the crowd), is rightly ascribed to James I.

---

[1] *E.g.* he rimes together two lines ending with the same word and the same meaning more than once, and does not distinguish between rimes in *y* and *ye*, but this is Northern. After making all allowances for confusion on the poet's part concerning Chaucer's use of final *e*, and for its .probable omission in many cases by the copyist of the MS., there still remain several lines where James evidently allowed the pause to supply the place of an unaccented syllable, or where uncertain accent (*schwebende Betonung*) extends beyond the second foot. Anakrusis is omitted more frequently than in Chaucer's heroic line.

Andrew of Wyntown, born about the middle of the fourteenth century, though he wrote in verse, was no poet, but
rather the first Scot to write the history of his land in the
vulgar tongue. John of Fordoun, a contemporary of Barbour,
the author of the first five books of the "Scotichronicon," and
Walter Bower, Abbot of Inchcolm, who had written the conclusion from the death of David I. in 1153, in another eleven
books, had anticipated Wyntown as historians, but their appeal

Andrew of
Wyntown.

THE PRIORY OF ST. SERF, LOCH LEVEN.

was only to those who could read Latin. The same remark
applies to Fordoun's "Gesta Annalia," added as supplement to
his Chronicle, which gave a record of events from the time of
Stephen down to the year 1385. But Wyntown's book was
meant to be and was a popular handbook, and, therefore, was
written in Scottish, and, above all, in verse of the popular
four-accent romance measure adopted by Barbour. Andrew of
Wyntown became in time (1395) Prior of St. Serf's, a foundation
within the jurisdiction of the powerful priory of St. Andrews.
He began to write his "Orygynale Cronykil of Scotland" at
the request of his friend, Sir John of the Wemyss; he finished
it between the death of the Duke of Albany in 1420, and
James I.'s return to Scotland in 1424, and he probably did not

live long after this happy event. The "Orygynale Cronykil" is divided into nine books in honour of the nine orders of angels, and it is called "Orygynale" because the history in it is traced from the beginning of things. Adam and Eve were not "original" enough for this teleological historian, so after a prologue and summary of contents one reads—

> "Off Angellis now sall ye heir
> In this followand next Cheptere."

Thus even the headings of the chapters are decked out with the attractive tinkle of a rime. By the time one has reached the close of the ninth book events have advanced to the death of Robert III. in 1406.

Robert Henryson.   Robert Henryson or Henderson (*c.* 1430–*c.* 1506) was, after James, the next Scottish poet of note. He, like the king, was a Chaucerian, and he had a distinct knack of writing in his master's pathetic and romantic vein with not more exaggeration of these qualities perhaps than is the natural fate of imitators. But Henryson was more than a Chaucerian, for he was the first writer of pastoral poetry in these islands. It is no small praise to his "Robene and Makyne" to say that it anticipates "Duncan Gray"—which tells the same tale with the *rôles* of the lovers reversed—by something like four centuries and a half. Not that no pastoral poems of this description were written between the two referred to—not that Henryson's poem can compare with Burns's for either melody or dramatic condensation—but there is a freedom and originality of handling in both poems, at the same time that the pastoral spirit is maintained, which justifies one in saying that with Henryson, as with Burns, the pastoral lyric was an independent and indigenous growth, rather than the often sickly and always artificial importation which obtained south of the Tweed. Scottish pastoral is more expressive of a real social condition than anything since Theocritus, and though, of course, it is far rougher and less graceful, it is less sophisticated. The English pastoral of the eighteenth century was both artificial and sickly; that of the sixteenth cannot escape the former charge in spite of the exquisite melodies of some numbers in the "Shepherd's Calendar." "Robene and Makyne" is neither the one nor the other; "Duncan Grey" needs no apology nor justification. But

Henryson's chief and probably one of his latest works is his pathetic sequel to " Troilus and Cryseyde," which, until Urry's edition of Chaucer in 1721, was included among the English poet's works. As Chaucer conceived the tale, it was a " tragedye," and no other end was possible for Troilus than to meet his death on the battle-field by the hand of Achilles. The Scottish poet, however, continues the tale where Chaucer left off, and punishes Cressida suitably for her perfidy. She is deserted by Diomed, and when she reviles Cupid for this she is attacked by leprosy as a punishment. The meeting between this woeful wreck of beauty and Troilus as he returns victorious from

THE SWALLOW PREACHING (MS. Harl. 3865).

the field of battle is one of the most pathetic passages in all literature. He throws her a purse and gay jewels, seeming to find amidst the horror of her disfigurement a recollection of his love; while she, hearing from those who surround her the author of the boon, dies in the passion of remorse, bequeathing to him the " rubie red" which he had sent her as " drowrie." With the exception of the seven stanzas of her "Complaint," which are in a nine-lined strophe with rime-order *aabaabbab*,[1] the "Testament of Cresseid" is written in the Troilus stanza.

[1] This is the same stanza as that used for the "Complaint of Anelida" in Chaucer's "Compleynt of feire Anelida and fals Arcite."

Henryson used the same measure in his other long work the "Tale of Orpheus," the chief interest of which lies in the evidence it offers of the poet's knowledge of the scholastic learning of his time, and the special interest he took in music, which was one of the sciences of the Quadrivium. Th school-master of Dunfermline—for there is reason to think he was appointed to the Grammar School there—made good use in this way of his learning, and transformed the old fairy tale of Orpheus and Eurydice, as it was conceived of by the older Scottish poet of the romance of "Sir Orpheo," into a work which, if it does nothing else, gives a proof of the culture which was growing up in Scotland as the result of James I.'s short reign.   Another work of this poet was a series of thirteen "Fables of Æsop" in "rime-royal," probably written between 1470 and 1480.   Their style is light and the power of dialogue considerable, but they are too long; and yet the "Taill of the Uplandis Mous and the Burges Mous" is really excellently told, is much the brightest of the series, and will bear comparison with Wyatt's version of the story without any diminution of the impression it makes.   Finally, mention must be made of his reflective poems, such as "The Abbey Walk"—teaching the duty of submission, the quaint "metaphysical conceit of the "Garmond of Gude Ladeis," and his satirical "Reasoning betwixt Aige and Yowth."   The first of these is in an eight-lined stanza of octosyllabics with cross-rime, and the refrain, "Obey and thank thy God of all"; whilst the quatrains of the "Garmond" show no less than the "Robene and Makyne" his mastery of cadence and pause.   Closely allied to the tone of these is his allegorical ballad of the "Bludy Serk."   This is one of the oldest examples of ballad poetry extant, and it is significant for the literary history of the ballad in Great Britain that it should so early have taken this distinctly moralising form.   The love for pointing a moral has been fatal to the development of this kind of literature on both sides of the Tweed.   Be this as it may, Henryson must be remembered as the introducer of pastoral and as the first pure lyrist in Scottish literature.   It is only because he wrote so comparatively little that was wholly original that he cannot be ranked along with Dunbar; though even when he imitated others he always added something of his own.

With Dunbar (*c.* 1460–*c.* 1517),[1] the greatest of Scottish poets
before Burns, we reach the close of the Middle Ages; and
though scarcely to be described as a Humanist himself, yet
he lived in a time when the humanities were beginning to
gain ground   William Dunbar was the poet, as James IV.
was the king, of that short bright day which shone on Scotland
before the cataclysm which overwhelmed the land after Flodden
Field.   There is something pathetic, if not tragic, in the happy
ring of the rimes which were sung by this poet-friend of James,
the melancholy and romantic king-errant who threw away his
life and men at Flodden.   With all the limitations of his genius,
Dunbar was yet a pioneer who might have done much for
the future of Scottish poetry had not ruin, disorder, and fanatic
protest against the corruptions of the Church cast a cloud
upon the people's capacity for joy which was not easily to be
dispelled.   Dunbar was no poet of the stronger passions, the
writer of no epic or drama, but he records for us a variety of
quieter, pleasanter moods.   His poems deal chiefly with the
vanities of life, but this was largely a natural reaction against
the threadbare themes of the older serious poets; it was reaction
in a direction different from that of Wyatt and Surrey in
England, but this was because the poet's genius was not
philosophic and melancholy, but humorous and satiric.   Dunbar
has more in common with the Chaucer who met the pilgrims
at the Tabard Inn than all the other Chaucerians put together.
They only knew the Chaucer who mooned in the " Garden of
the Rose"; he gave a new interest to literature by calling
attention in occasional epicurean verse to the passing moods
of the poet's own life, which was also the life of his readers.
In "How Dunbar was desyred to be ane freir" he gives the
record of his early vagabond years in the dress of St. Francis.
In his "Old Gray Horse" he playfully tells, in form of fable,
his quest after the benefice that did not come; at another time
he gives the dull fit that stops his riming—but that does not
prevent there being a rime ("Of his Headache") to tell about
it.   Sometimes the low sad note of such an exquisite little

---

[1] Dunbar may have died any time between 1513, the year of Flodden, and
1530, when Lyndsay, in his "Papyngo," praises him as a poet of the past, and
speaks of Douglas (d. 1522) as the greatest of the poets who had recently
died: so Dunbar's death would fall about 1517, or, at least, before 1522.

poem as " What is this life but a straight way to death " makes itself heard through his laughter—through even the boisterous humour which produced " The Dance of the Seven Deadly Sins " (probably 1507), perhaps as a picture of an actual revel held on Shrove Tuesday at the gay court of the doomed king. The grotesque figures of the cardinal vices and their followings are rapidly sketched in their dance before " Mahoun " with an almost bitter humour, which culminates in the satire of the last stanza reserved for the Highlanders, who, it is suggested, are far worse than all the Deadly Sins together.   The quick movement of the tail-rime (I., p. 637) in the twelve-lined stanzas heightens the dramatic effect of the whole description.

And yet Dunbar did not altogether desert the older allegorical forms in spite of his numberless occasional pieces of the kind suggested.   " The Thrissil and the Rois " (" The Thistle and the Rose ") and the "Goldyn Targe " are both artificial poems of the same order, and every whit as well executed as the " Kingis Quair "; indeed, the former reminds one especially of James's poem and of the " Parlement of Fowles."   It is probable that Dunbar, who had graduated at St. Andrews and had entered the priesthood after a short and unpleasant experience of the Franciscan habit, was sent in 1501 with the ambassadors to the court of Henry VII. to negotiate the marriage of the Scottish king with the Princess Margaret Tudor.   This visit may have inspired his poem " In Honour of the Cite of London "; and the handsome gifts given by the king to " the rhymer of Scotland " may well have been rewards for this and other poems[1] when the poet next visited London on the occasion of the actual betrothal.   In January, 1502, the twelve-year-old princess was betrothed to James IV. by proxy, and on May 9th, 1503, Dunbar had finished his poem in honour of the match (*cf.* last line of the " Thrissil and the Rois "). He also wrote to welcome her arrival the short ballad " Now fayre, fayrest off every fayre,"

---

[1] *Cf.* Privy Purse Accounts of Henry VII.   Two sums of £6 13s. 4d. were paid to " the rhymer of Scotland " on December 31st, 1501, and January 7th, 1502.   The MS. Chronicle (Vit. A. XVI., fol. 200, Cotton Collection) in which the poem on London occurs, relates that it was made at a dinner given by 'the mair" to the Scottish ambassadors by " ane of the said Scottis givying attendance upon a Bishop ambassador."

which was set to music, still in existence.[1] He soon became a privileged favourite of the queen, and probably accompanied her when she visited the North of Scotland in 1511, for "The Queen's Progress at Aberdeen" is evidently the result of personal observation. His intimacy with her is shown by some playful lyrics on her wardrobe-keeper Doig, and by his "Dance in the Quenis Chalmer" (chamber), the description of an uncouth dance he arranged for her amusement. But the ecclesiastical promotion for which he did not cease to hope was withheld, though we know of a pension of £10 granted in 1500, which had subsequently been increased to £20, and then to £80, "during life or until promoted to a benefice of the value of £40 or more yearly." With this and various occasional gifts he had to rest content, though the queen pleaded for him, and he expressed the wish that the king were "John Thomsonnis Man."[2] James would not easily give up so bright an ornament to his court.

"The Thrissil and the Rois" is an heraldic and symbolic allegory which sings the praises of the young couple under the figure of the national flowers. Interweaving with this praise a description of the royal arms of Scotland, the poet symbolises the king by the lion, and makes Dame Nature— who, after the manner of the "Parlement of Fowles," has summoned all the birds and beasts to choose their leaders— commend to him the exercise of "justice with mercy and conscience," with the warning to "lat no small beist suffir skaith na skornis[3] Of greit beistis that bene of moir piscence."[4] But though one naturally thinks of the similarities with Chaucer and James I.—for the poem is essentially a Chaucerian one and is written in the Chaucer stanza—yet there are important characteristics which give it a strongly personal tone. Dunbar's genius was nothing if not lyrical, and this has saved him from the danger of wearying us which beset the "Kingis Quair." James's praise of his lady is more than seven times the length of Dunbar's praise of his king's marriage, and the latter's greater sense of proportion in the handling of a fashionable but dangerous form marks his strong poetic sense. It is a pity that the same praise cannot be given to his diction. This

---

[1] Royal MSS. 58, Append. fol. 15 v. and 16 r.   [2] The husband of a masterful wife.   [3] Harm or scorn.   [4] Power (puissance).

is certainly something new in Scottish literature, and is undoubted proof of the nation's growing culture, and of the increasing influence of French art and politics, but the "aureate" style which Dunbar was the first to introduce, and which Gawin Douglas readily adopted and exaggerated, was a form of "conceit" similar to the Petrarchan affectations of the sonneteers and the Guevaran extravagances of the Euphuists, laughed at later by Sir Philip Sidney. The old forms of expression were, no doubt, growing effete. Dunbar must have felt, as Wyatt and Surrey did, that some new method of expression was needed, and he sought a solution of the problem in an extension of the vocabulary by musical epithets of foreign origin and a freshening of the poetic style by ingenious comparisons. But neither of these devices is a substitute for the poetic imagination. Dunbar maintains a more even level than Chaucer ; he keeps his allegory well in hand, he is skilful in the choice of words, but he is far less imaginative, far less suggestive.

"The Golden Targe." Unfortunately, "The Golden Targe," Dunbar's other courtly poem, is even more "aureate" in diction and style. Though the basis of the allegory is much slighter and in less close touch with concrete reality—for it tells of the powerlessness of Reason before Love when aided by Beauty and the loved one's presence —yet the description of the conflict between "Resoun with the Scheld of Gold so schene" (*i.e.* bright) and the forces of Venus is drawn out to considerably greater length than the poem of the "awfull Thrissil" and the "fresche Rois." It is, indeed, consistent with the increased use of conceits, such as the "cristall teris" of "Aurora" for the dew, and "the purpur hevyn our-scailit in silver sloppis," that a more complicated stanza form should have been selected—the nine-line stanza of "Anelida's Complaint" (p. 710, note), used only two years previously by Douglas in his "Palice of Honour"; but the subject-matter is too slight for the heavy embroidered finery in which it is decked.

Dunbar's Verse The verse in both poems is musical, but it differs in several important respects from the Chaucerian technique. Dunbar makes as little approach as King James and less than Henryson to Chaucer's skilful use of *enjambement*[1] for lending variety

[1 The sense runs on to the next stanza without a clear break.]

to the rhythm of his line; on the other hand, he employs the "epic" cæsura more frequently than the English poet. His study of the unrimed alliterative metre makes itself felt in the use of alliteration in almost every line; a point which also differentiates his work from that of the earlier Chaucerians.

Ryght as the stern of day begouth to schyne
Quhen gone to bed war vesper and lucyne.
J raise and by a rolere did me rest
Up sprang the goldyn candill matutyne
With clere depurit bemes cristallyne
Glading the mery foulis in thair nest
Or phebus was in purpur cape reuest
Up raise the lark the hevyns menstrale fyne
Jn may/in till a moroW myrthfullest

Full angellike thir birdis sang thair houris
Within thair courtyns grene in to thair bouris,
Apparalit quhite and rede Wyth blomes suete
An amalit was the felde Wyth all colouris
The perly droppis schake in silvir schouris,
Quhill all in balme did branch and leuis flete
To part fra phebus did aurora grete
Hir cristall teris J saW hyng on the flouris
Quhilk he for luke all orank vp Wyth his hete

For mirth of may Wyth skippis and Wyth happis,
The birdis sang vpon the tender croppis
With curiouse note as venus chapell clerkis
The rosis yong neW spreding of thair knoppis
War poWdit bryp Wyth hevinly beriall droppis
Throu bemes rede birnyng as ruby sperkis,
The skyes rang for schoutyng of the larkis
The purpur hevyn our scailit in silvir sloppis
Ourgilt the treis branchis lefs barkis

Doun throu the ryce a ryuir ran Wyth stremys
So lustily agayn thai lybrand lemys
That all the lake as lamp did leme of liche

PAGE FROM "THE GOLDEN TARGE."
(*The Advocates' Library, Edinburgh.*)

Both the Eastern and Western traditions are represented in Dunbar's work, and this helps to give it a truly national character.

The unrimed alliterative measure was selected by him for his "Tua Mariit Wemen and the Wedo" (widow)—a bitterly satirical narrative poem, very different in tone from those just discussed. *His Satire.*

It is full of dramatic characterisation and drastic humour. The opinions of the three ladies upon the obligations of marriage remind one of the Wife of Bath's Prologue, and were certainly inspired by it; but there is all the difference in the world between salt satire and cynicism expressed in language of extreme licence from the mouths of young and beautiful women, and the irony, combined with *bonhomie*, which is felt through and beneath the profligate boasting of the Wife of Bath. It is not sufficient explanation of this difference to remark that the society of James IV.'s court was very corrupt. The difference of tone is due to the poets, not to their material. If any excuse be sought it is to be found in the fact that the poem is an early work. It is worth notice that the rhythm of the verse is very different from that of Langland and the Gawain poet. The further loss of final inflections, the increasing number of Romance words, and a consequent further misunderstanding of the principles which underlie the Old English alliterative line, have reduced the music very much to that of the "Tumbling verse" with anapæstic lilt described by James I. of England in his "Reulis and Cautelis (rules and cautions) of Scottis Poesie."[1] Dunbar also adopts a device apparently borrowed from Huchown, and seen in the "Morte Arthur," that of accumulative alliteration, *i.e.* the carrying of the same alliterative letter through several lines. The short rimed poem on "The Twa Cummeris" (Gossips) has been often compared with the "Tua Mariit Wemen and the Wedo," but its coarseness is not licentious, and it is far more like Skelton's "Tunnyng of Eleanor Rumming" in tone. One is reminded again of Chaucer's skill as a teller of *fabliaux* in the "Freiris of Berwik," a satirical poem in rimed couplets, about the authorship of which, however, there is some doubt.

lytings."   Closely related to his satires are his lampoons. His vituperative "Flyting of Dunbar and Kennedy" (a contemporary poet) reminds one of Skelton's similar abuse of Garnesche, of the French "jeux partis,"[1] and the Provençal "sirventois."[2] But such "Flytings," or poetic tournaments of wit and raillery, are found in Gaelic and in the Scandinavian "Loki Sennar," or "Flyting" of Loki with the gods of Asgard, and further

[[1] Poetic dialogues (under strict rules as to form) in which alternatives are proposed and defended by the interlocutors.   [2] Satirical poems]

parallels might be cited in the poetical duels of Callimachus, Ovid, Poggio with Philelfo, and Luigi Pulci with Matteo Franco. A similar "Flyting" is the subject of Dunbar's "Tournament against the Telyouris and Sowtaris" (Tailors and Shoemakers), a poem which seems, somewhat naturally, to have offended these handicrafts, and to have called forth an " Amendis " (apology), which made them still more ridiculous. So this abuse-flinging became fashionable, and was practised with zest by Lindsay, James V., and other later poets, until the fashion died out

Thou devillis member thou curfit homycide
Thou tigir tene fulfild of birnyng fyre
Thou fchryne fecrete of ftynkand voke & pride
Thou cocatras that with the ficht of thy ire
Affrayit has full mony a gudely fyre
That effward in warld had newir plefance
Grete god J pray to tak on the vengeance
Jn maidynhede fen was oure firft remede
And fra the hevyn oure haly fader fent
The fecund perfone his fone in a god hede
To tak mã kynde apon the maidyn gent
Clene of hir corfe / and clenar of entent
That bure the barne quhilk couit vs fra care
Scho being virgyn clenar than fcho was are
Grete was the luft / that thou had for to fang
The frute vetit throu thy falfe counfailing
Thou gert mankynde confent to do that wrang
Declyne his god / and brek his hye bidding
As haly write beris futhfaft witneffing
That for thou fro the foy of paradife
And thyne of fpring was banyft for thy vice
Explicit.

PASSAGE FROM ' THE FLYTING OF DUNBAR AND KENNEDY."
(The Advocates' Library, Edinburgh.)

with Byron's ridicule of the Lake poets. The only one of Dunbar's satirical poems which still calls for mention is his humorous account of the attempt made by John Damian, the French "leich," to fly from the top of Stirling Castle to Calais. In the "Ballad of the Fenyeit Freir of Tungland," the poet has pilloried this charlatan with the happiest ridicule, had left his reputation as innocent of honour as the friar was of his borrowed plumes after the visitation of the birds. The measure is the tail-rime (*rime couée*) natural to the ballad.

At the close of his life in the dark days which fell upon him after Flodden, the gay poet grew more serious and lost his buoyant spirit. Already in his "Lament for the Makaris" (poets) (1508), the sight of his fellows falling around him, and his own sickness, forced upon him the transitory nature of things and the moral—

> "Seu for the deid remeid is non,
> Best is that we for dede dispone,
> Eftir our deid that lif may we."

But he could not feel that the joyous view of life had been a false one. In a pensive but characteristic poem, with the refrain "For to be blyth me-think it best," he thus apologises for his natural temperament:—

> "Had I for warldis unkyndness
> In hairt tane ony haviness,
> Or fro my plesans bene opprest,
> I had bene deid langsyne, dowtless:
> · For to be blyth me-think it best."

The transition from the moral to the religious key was a natural one, and this is marked by his "Merle and the Nychtingall," which in the manner of the earlier southern "Owl and the Nightingale," sings the contest between the earthly and the heavenly love. To the same class belong the hymns for Christmas Day, Ash Wednesday, and Lent. The, "Ballat of Our Lady" is noticeable for its complex stanza, which consists of twelve lines rimed alternately, the ninth "Ave Maria gratia plena," forming a refrain. Dunbar was a lyric poet of many moods. That he was also a successful satirist of the lighter humorous sort need not surprise us, if we remember that Catullus among the Romans, Sordello among the Provençal poets, and Burns in modern times, were at one moment lyrists and at the next writers of personal or Archilochian satire. But to say this is to imply what is equally true, that Dunbar had neither the calm deliberation of the epic poet—though he undoubtedly had the gift of telling a story—nor the directness and objectivity which are necessary to the systematic draughtsman of human nature.

Among the poets mentioned in Dunbar's "Lament" is "Blin Harye," or Henry the Minstrel (*c.* 1450–92), who was one of the poets at the court of James IV., and the author of a long romance in rimed heroic couplets on "Schir William Wallace" (written before 1488, the date of the unique MS.), that, next to the "Brus," which suggested its inception, was the most popular poem of the day. Blind Harry says, at the close of the poem, that he based it on a Latin History by Wallace's chaplain "Blair," no longer extant; but it doubtless owes quite as much to national ballads dealing with episodes in the hero's life. This, and the fact that the period dealt with is more remote than that of the "Brus," accounts for its many historical inaccuracies. The early life of the hero is crowded with deeds of daring otherwise unknown, and Wallace is made to defeat Edward at a battle of Biggar previous to that of Stirling, though it is known that the English king was not in Scotland at the time.

"Blind Harry."

Dunbar's younger contemporary, Gawin Douglas (*c.* 1474-1522), was the third son of Archibald Douglas, Earl of Angus, who was surnamed "Bell-the-Cat" for his bold demeanour amongst the nobles who were conspiring against Cochrane and Rogers, the hated favourites of James III. His nephew, the young Earl, married after Flodden, the Queen Margaret, who was even then only twenty-three; so, though like Dunbar he was a priest,[1] his life was much mixed up with the feuds and strife which make up the larger part of Scottish history from Flodden till the accession of James VI. Douglas, like Dunbar, was a Chaucerian, and like him, was yet original and a true poet. But he was less interesting. His most important works, "King Hart," and his translation of the "Aeneid," fall outside the scope of this volume, but his first and longest poem, "The Palice of Honour," was finished in 1501. It was written at a time of life when he was beginning to feel its seriousness and the need for earnest effort on the part of himself and his countrymen. So he shows in a conventional allegorical form, which reminds one much of the "Parlement of Fowles," the inconstancy and uncertainty of earthly renown—the need and worth of honour, which is the reward of virtue and steadfastness. Considerable skill is shown in the grouping and introduction of the countless allegorical

Gawin Douglas.

---

[1] He was afterwards (January, 1515) made Bishop of Dunkeld, but could not enter on the see, owing to the opposition of the Earl of Athol and the Duke of Albany (who imprisoned him), till eighteen months later.

figures, and his extensive learning is visible at every turn. The poem is full of reminiscences of classical history, mythology, and poetry. And yet the note of originality is not lacking. At the opening, for instance, though the traditional dream introduces the story, the scene is not the usual May morning, but a wilderness of despair, where all the incidents and surrounding accidents of the scene help to heighten the effect. The appreciation of the colder, bleaker aspects of Nature is characteristic of the Scottish poets in general (*cf.* Dunbar's "Meditatioun in Winter"), and particularly of Douglas. But perhaps the chief interest of the "Palice of Honour" lies in the fact that it was probably the cause of Dunbar turning his attention to allegorical poetry, for both "The Thrissil and the Rois" and "The Goldyn Targe" were written after Douglas's poem. It is, at any rate, a curious coincidence that Dunbar should have chosen for. his second and more elaborate poem the same metre as that used by Douglas in what must rank as the earliest Scottish romance with a purely allegorical theme.

E. G. DUFF. The Early History of Printing. DURING the thirteenth and fourteenth centuries printing of a certain kind had been practised in Europe, but it was only in the fifteenth that the printing of books was reached. The first attempts were single-sheet prints, images of saints, or playing-cards; but at a later date certain consecutive. series of prints in book form were attempted, which are now known as block-books. The whole of the page, text as well as illustration, was cut on wood by the wood-engraver. These books contained generally religious histories, the most popular and best known being the "Biblia Pauperum." Each page contains pictures of well-known Bible incidents, with a few words of letterpress. Other books of the same kind were the "Speculum Humanæ Salvationis," the "Cantica Canticorum," and the "Ars Moriendi." The real invention of printing, however, was the invention of movable types, capable of being used again and again in different combinations; and for centuries there has been endless argument and strife upon the question of which city has the honour of being the birthplace of printing. Modern research has done much to narrow the question, and the two rival parties are now those who favour the claim of

PAGE FROM THE "BIBLIA PAUPERUM"

John Gutenberg and the city of Mentz or Mayence on the one hand, or Lawrence Coster and Haarlem on the other.   While the claims of Mentz are in a measure supported by direct evidence, the evidence in favour of Haarlem is entirely circumstantial, and in some cases imaginary, though upheld with no less vigour.

Guten-berg and Mentz.   The earliest information we have about Gutenberg is derived from the record of a lawsuit tried at Strassburg in 1439.   We learn from it that he was there employed in experimenting on printing.   In 1455 we learn more about him as a printer from the record of another lawsuit, brought, like the first, to recover money which had been lent to him.   By 1468 we may presume he was dead, for his stock of printing materials was handed over to his chief creditor.   The real interest, however, belongs to the books

COLOURED CAPITAL FROM PSALTER OF 1457.

rather than the printer, and we find that the earliest specimen of printing known to exist is "The Indulgence of Nicholas V.," issued to obtain assistance against the Turks.   The earliest editions have the printed date, 1454, and the earliest date filled in upon any of these in manuscript is November 15.   We may, therefore, consider November 15, 1454, as the earliest date connected with printing. From this time onwards the art was practised in Germany without a break, and the first efforts were almost the finest.   The "Maza-rine Bible" of 1455–6, the Psalters of 1457 and 1459, with their wonderful coloured capitals, rival, if they do not surpass, any later productions.   From Mentz the art spread before 1460 to Bamberg, where Pfister printed popular books in the vernacular, and to Strassburg where Mentelin printed Bibles and theological books.   The capture and sacking of Mentz in 1462 by Adolf von Nassau, is supposed to have scattered the printers of that town, and not long after that date we find Ulric Zel printing at Cologne. A large number of printers seem to have worked there, among them Arnold ther Hoernen, who introduced title-pages and the practice of numbering the leaves.   Henry Keffer, who had been a workman of Gutenberg's, introduced printing into Nuremberg

in or about 1470. In this town Anthony Koburger, one of the best known of the early printers, worked as many as twenty-four presses, sending his books over all the country. Basle, Augsburg, Spires, follow rapidly, and within the next few years hardly any important town in Germany was without at least one printer.

Coster's Claims. Turning to the claims of Coster at Haarlem, what do we find? In the first place, there is no evidence that any printer called Lawrence Coster ever existed; even his name was never heard of till more than a hundred years after his supposed invention took place. While the invention of Gutenberg at Mentz was continually being spoken of, no dissentient voice was raised till 1499, when in a not altogether accurate account of the invention of printing, given in the "Cologne Chronicle," it is stated that the first prefiguration of the art came from Holland, and that copies, of the "Donatus" printed there suggested the invention to Gutenberg. The first date in any book printed in the Low Countries is 1473, and in that year the art was introduced into two places—Utrecht and Alost. There are, however, a very large number of small pamphlets, editions for the most part of such school-books as the "Donatus" or the "Doctrinale of Alexander Gallus," a few of which must, and many of which may, have been printed before 1473. Believers in the Haarlem invention date all such fragments before 1473, and take them back thirty or even forty years earlier. It is, however, not reasonable to suppose that a press would have existed for so long in a country without giving birth to others, and would print only school-books and a few unimportant tracts, while so many important books were waiting to be printed. Until the claims of Haarlem have some reasonable basis of fact, its partisans cannot hope for any intelligent support. In 1473 also printing was introduced into Utrecht and Alost, and, once it had gained a footing, soon spread to all the larger towns—a strong argument against the existence of a solitary press in the Netherlands for the previous thirty years.

Early Italian Printing. Printing was brought to Italy in 1465 by two Germans, Sweynheym and Pannartz, who settled first at the monastery of Subiaco, near Rome, where they printed a few books, moving on in 1467 to Rome itself, where they set to work in the house of the brothers De Maximis. In this city the number of printers rapidly increased, as, indeed, it did throughout Italy, for within five years of the introduction of printing at Subiaco, more than twenty towns in the North of Italy were supplied with presses. The most important of these places was Venice, where the art was introduced by John of Spires in 1469, and where it prospered so greatly that by the year 1500 over two hundred printers were printing or had printed there. Foligno, Milan, Bologna, Florence, in turn received the art, and increased the reputation of Italian printing. If we study the productions of the Italian press

En hic ille eſt de illis maxime:qui irridere:atq; obiurgare
me ſolitus eſt:quod me non tecum(præſertim cum abs te
honorificentiſſime iuitaret)coiungeretē. ἀλλἐμόν ὁντο
Τεθυμόνἐνι ςήθεσἰΝ ἐπειθεν audiebā eni ꝑceres clamitātis.
Sed tamē idem me cōſolatur etiam hominē peruſtum :
& inanem : gloria uolunt incendere atq; ita loquuntur.

A SPECIMEN OF EARLY VENETIAN PRINTING.
Horatio Brown, "Venetian Printing Press"; J. C. Nimmo.)

the immense influence of the Renaissance can be clearly traced. While the Germans were turning out volume after volume of theology in their Gothic type, the Italian printers issued all the more important classics, in a graceful Roman letter, itself an outcome of the revived interest in classical studies. Greek literature was first to be found only in Latin translations, but in 1488 the magnificent first edition of Homer appeared, and the reputation of Italy for classical books was carried far into the sixteenth century by Aldus Manutius and his successors.

Although we have documentary evidence that some kind **Early** of printing was being used at Avignon so far back as 1444, **French Printing.** no product has come down to our times, nor can it be definitely settled that the printing spoken of was what we understand by the word. The first printing press in France, putting the Avignon story on one side, was naturally started at Paris, the centre of learning and culture, and the seat of one of the most renowned universities of Europe. Through the exertions of Heynlyn and Fichet, doctors of high position in the university, three printers—Crantz, Gering, and Friburger —were induced to settle in the precincts of the Sorbonne, and there in 1470 they issued their first book, "The Letters of Gasparinus Barzizius." In the first two years they printed about thirty books, strongly representative of the classical tastes of their patrons. Towards the end of 1472 they removed to the Rue St. Jacques, where some other rival printers were already settled. From this time onwards printers at Paris increased rapidly in numbers, and it became as important a printing centre as Venice or Basle. In 1473 Guillaume le Roy introduced printing into Lyons, and the art soon spread to other towns. French printers soon found that it was to their advantage to print books for the English market, especially books of an ornamental character, such as books of hours and missals, which the resources of the English press were not adequate to produce. These books were sent over with stationers to the fairs in the English towns, where they met with a ready sale. They even printed books in English, such as grammars and festials (exhortations appropriate to Church festivals), and this competition must have seriously affected home production.

In Spain printing was first practised about 1474, in which year it was introduced into Valentia, though no dated book is known earlier than 1475. In this latter year it is said to have been introduced into Saragossa, and shortly afterwards to Barcelona and Seville.

The first English printer, William Caxton, was born about 1442 in the Weald of Kent (p. 731). His parents gave him a good education, but we know nothing of his personal history until we find him bound as an apprentice to Robert Large, a mercer, in 1438. This Robert Large was an important and influential merchant, who in 1430 was Sheriff, and in 1439–40 Lord Mayor of London. He died April 24, 1441. At the time of his death he had eight apprentices, of whom Caxton was the youngest, and to him was left a legacy of twenty marks. The death of his master did not release Caxton from his indentures, and he must either have been supported by the executors or bound to a new master. What happened we do not know, but

English Printing: Caxton.

we learn from the prologue to " The Recuyell [Collection] of the Histories of Troye," in which he says that he had then, in 1471, been abroad thirty years, that he must have left England and gone to the Low Countries about 1441, very shortly after his master's death.

He settled in Bruges, then one of the most important of foreign mercantile towns, where his affairs seem to have prospered, and where he rapidly rose in estimation and position, for we find that by 1463-65 he was governor of the " English nation residing abroad," or merchant adventurers. With the exception of a few short journeys to England and elsewhere, Caxton seems to have carried on his business till about 1470, when he entered the service of the Duchess of Burgundy. The consequent increase of leisure which this appointment afforded him was spent in literary pursuits, in learning foreign languages, and in translating books into English. In 1477, however, a great change occurred in Caxton's position. The reverses sustained by the Duke of Burgundy at Morat, in his battle with the Swiss, and his death at the battle of Nanci, caused Caxton's mistress to be no longer the ruling power at the court of Bruges, and she retired into comparative privacy. Caxton's services would now no longer be required, and he determined to return to England. His career as a merchant was finished ; his career as a printer about to begin.

In 1471 Caxton had gone on a journey to Cologne, and while living there had finished the translation of " Le Recueil des Histoires de Troyes." The art of printing had been practised at Cologne for some years previously, and at the time of Caxton's visit several printers were at work there. From one of these he, no doubt, learnt the practical details, and, perhaps, assisted in the printing of some books in order to gain experience. Wynkyn de Worde, Caxton's assistant and successor, tells us that Caxton printed a Latin edition of " Bartholomeus de Proprietatibus Rerum " at Cologne. We know a Latin edition, printed at Cologne, about 1471, and Caxton very probably assisted in producing it.

On his return to Bruges he entered into partnership with Colard Mansion, who had been an illuminator and calligrapher, but who gave up such work to become a printer about 1474-5. These two together printed three books : " The Recuyell of the

Histories of Troye" (the first book printed in the English language), "The Game and Playe of the Chess," and "Les Quatre Derrennieres Choses."

In 1477 Caxton returned to England and settled in a house which his advertisement shows to have been in the Almonry, within the precincts of Westminster Abbey, where alms were distributed to the poor, and where Margaret, Countess of Richmond (p. 686), built almshouses. Here in November, 1477, with type brought from Bruges, Caxton issued the first edition of the "Dictes or Sayengis of the Philosophers," the first book printed in England. It was translated from the

CAXTON'S ADVERTISEMENT.
(Bodleian Library, Oxford.)

French by Earl Rivers, and "overseen" by Caxton, and a chapter was added "touching wymmen." His next book was the Ordinale Sarum, and though its existence is only known from fragments, there are still preserved two copies of his advertisement of it.[1]

[1 The last line signifies "Please let this notice remain up." "Commemorations" are services in honour of (1) the Virgin, (2) the patron saint of the church. (3) some local saint, which at this time were commonly held twice or thrice weekly according as the church was or was not dedicated to the Virgin. If any of them clashed with the celebration of a saint's day, there were rules for their postponement, called "the pye," "the number and hardness" of which is specially reprobated in the Preface to the English Prayer Book. *See* Mr. E. W. B. Nicholson's Introduction to his reproduction of Caxton's Advertisement, from which this explanation is condensed.

Robert Copeland, an apprentice of **Wynkyn de Worde's**, speaks of Caxton as "beginning with small stories and pamphlets and so to other," and the small books thus alluded to are no doubt the series of writings of Lydgate, such as "The Temple of Glas," "The Horse, the Sheep, and the Goose," and "The Churl and Bird," each of which contains but a few pages, and which must all have been printed soon after Caxton's settlement at Westminster. The most important of the early books is the first edition of Chaucer's "Canterbury Tales," a folio of more than 700 pages. The productiveness of Caxton's press at its commencement is most surprising, for in the first three years he had printed more than thirty books. Of these, certainly many were small, but, on the other hand, we have "The Canterbury Tales" (748 pages), "The History of Jason" (300 pages), Chaucer's "Boethius" (188 pages), "The Rhetorica Nova of Laurentius de Saona" (248 pages), "The Cordyal" (156 pages), the second edition of "The Dictes or Sayengis of the Philosophers" (152 pages), and "The Chronicles of England" (364 pages). Caxton was not only the printer, but corrector as well, and in some cases even editor, so that his diligence was remarkable.

In 1480 another printing press was started in London by John Lettou, and his books possessed several technical improvements which were wanting in Caxton's. The result of the rivalry or competition between the two presses is at once apparent, for Caxton immediately copied all the improvements. At the beginning of the year Caxton had printed an Indulgence of John Kendale, appealing for help against the Turks at the siege of Rhodes, in his large ragged type. Another edition issued promptly from the rival press, printed in a small neat letter very much better suited for such work. Caxton in self-defence had a fount of small type cut, and used it in the same year for another edition of the Indulgence. **Lettou's Press.**

So, also imitating Lettou, Caxton began to use signatures in his books, and to space out the lines on a page to an even length. It was about this time that he began to illustrate some of his books with coarse woodcuts, the first work so illustrated being "The Mirrour of the World," published in 1481, which contains a few cuts of men engaged in teaching and practising scientific pursuits, and also a number of **Caxton's Improvements.**

90

diagrams. The execution of these cuts is so bad as to make them appear the work of a beginner, and it is probable that

"THE CROW WHICH WAS ATHIRST."
(*Caxton,* "*Æsop's Fables.*")

there was so little demand for the art at this time in England that Caxton was unable to obtain the assistance of any skilled wood-engraver. In the next six years Caxton printed about thirty-five books, many being of great interest. Amongst them are " Reynard the Fox," " The Polycronicon," Lydgate's " Pilgrimage of the Soul" and " Life of Our Lady," " The Festial," Gower's " Confessio Amantis," " Æsop's Fables," " The Golden Legend," " The Morte d'Arthur," " The Life of Charles the Great," and " The History of Paris and Vienne." In addition to these **we** have second editions of " The Chronicles of England," " The Game of Chesse," and " The Canterbury Tales." Several of these books are illustrated. " Æsop's Fables " has a cut to almost every fable, and " The Golden Legend " is equally lavishly adorned, though the same cut often does duty **for** various saints. In 1487 Caxton seems to have been anxious to produce a missal of Sarum use, but not having suitable type he commissioned a Paris printer, George Maynyal, to print it for him. In this book Caxton's device first appears. It consists of the initials of his name divided by his mark,

THE COCK AND THE JEWEL.
(*Caxton,* "*Æsop's Fables.*")

and it was used for the future in almost all his publications, printed at first on the front page, but afterwards in the more usual position at the end. From 1487 till his death in 1491 he printed some thirty books, among which are "The Four Sons of Aymon," "Blanchardyn and Eglantyne," "The Doctrinal of Sapience," "Eneydos," and many religious books. Caxton died about the end of the year 1491, and was buried in the churchyard of St. Margaret's, Westminster. He is known to have left a will, as there is a record in the parish accounts of St. Margaret's of fifteen copies of "The Golden Legend" bequeathed to the church by William Caxton. Unfortunately, this will has never been found, though it may very probably be amongst the large number of un-examined documents be-

KING LOG AND KING STORK.
(*Caxton*, "*Æsop's Fables.*")

longing to Westminster Abbey. From it we should have been able to gather more of the personal history of the printer than can be found in the introductory portions of his books. Many of the details of his life as a printer are known to us from this source, and exhibit his extraordinary industry. Besides print-ing at least a hundred works, he translated no less than twenty-four, many of these being the largest of his publica-tions; and the "Vitæ

KING AND PHILOSOPHER PLAYING CHESS.
(*Caxton*, "*Game and Play of the Chesse.*")

Patrum," the last of these works, was finished by him on the day of his death.

For the next two years the business was more or less at a

standstill, and we find foreign printers producing books for the English market, almost all being reprints of Caxton's books. Wynkyn de Worde, a native of Lorraine and an apprentice of Caxton's, succeeded him in business at the printing office at Westminster. In the first two years after his master's death he produced only four books, but in 1493 we find him becoming more active. In the next year his name first appears in a book, and he uses as his device either the old mark which belonged to Caxton or else a smaller one of similar design. The activity of the apprentice was as great as his master's, for by the end of the year 1500 he had printed nearly a hundred books, many of these were reprints of Caxton's books, such as "The Golden Legend," the "Morte d'Arthur," "The Canterbury Tales," and others. Such books as he printed on his own initiative were, as a rule, small, and many are exceptionally curious. He also obtained assistance from abroad in printing service books, and it was probably through his means that Julian Notary, with two assistants, came to print in London about 1496. De Worde continued to live at Westminster till the end of the fifteenth century, removing in 1501 to a house in Fleet Street, with the sign of the Sun, where he stayed till his death in 1534. He was the most important and the most prolific of all the early English printers, for during his life he must have printed over five hundred different books.

The year after Caxton began printing at Westminster a press was started at Oxford. From the date of the first book having been misprinted 1468 in place of 1478, many writers have attempted to claim for Oxford and an imaginary printer Corsellis the honour of having produced the first book in England. The press was in existence from 1478 to 1486, a period of nine years, and the printers, Theodoric Rood of Cologne, and Thomas Hunte, an Englishman, produced some fifteen different books, for the most part of a learned character. Amongst these was an edition of "Cicero pro Milone," the first classic printed in England, "The Letters of Phalaris," and the first edition of "Lyndewode." The last book they printed was a "Liber Festivalis," the only book from this press in English, and the only one with woodcuts.

At St. Albans, a schoolmaster whose name is unknown began to print about 1480. His types bear great resemblance to

Caxton's, and for a short time he was in possession of a fount **The** Latin and for the most part theological, but the two last were **St. Alban** which had belonged to Caxton. His first six books were all in **Press.** Latin and for the most part theological, but the two last were in English and of a popular character. The first was "The Chronicles of England," an edition founded on Caxton's, the

"FISHING WITH AN ANGLE."
(*From Wynkyn de Worde's edition of the " Boke of St. Albans."*)

second the well-known "Boke of St. Albans." It contains treatises of Hunting, Hawking, and Coat-armour or Heraldry, and is full of the most curious information. Many cuts are given of the coat-of-arms, and most of them are printed in colours, the first attempt at such printing in England. A later edition of the same book was issued by Wynkyn de Worde in 1496, with a chapter added on Fishing with an Angle. The St. Albans press, like that at Oxford, ceased in 1486, and was not revived till about 1535, when a few more books were issued.

In 1480, under the patronage of William Wilcock, a London merchant, a foreign printer named John Letton settled, as we have seen, in London. That he was a practised printer is clear from the workmanship of his early books, but he seems to have met with little encouragement, for in 1480–1482 he had printed only two. About this time he was joined in business by William de Machlinia, and together they printed five law books. About 1484–85 Lettou disappears, and Machlinia continued to print alone, the workmanship of his books very much deteriorating. Nearly all his productions, however, are small, with the exception of "The Chronicles of England," and some law books. Among the others are one or two of interest, such as "The Revelation of St. Nicholas to a Monk of Evesham," "The Speculum Christiani," which contains some curious specimens of verse, and a treatise on the Pestilence, of which three editions were issued. One of these has a title-page, the first used in an English book. Machlinia lived first at Flete-bridge, but moved at a later date to Holborn. He disappears about 1490, and his materials passed into the hands of Richard Pynson, a Norman. The first dated book with Pynson's name appeared in 1493, but he must have begun printing before that time. He is generally considered to have been an apprentice of Caxton, and in one passage speaks of Caxton as his master, but it is more probable that he learnt to print in Rouen. He lived first outside Temple Bar, but moved a little later into Fleet Street, where he lived until his death in 1528. He printed far fewer books than his contemporary, Wynkyn de Worde, but his editions were more scholarly, and he was the first to introduce Roman type into England. Between the time of Caxton's first beginning to print and the end of the fifteenth century, a period of thirty-four years, nearly four hundred books issued from the English press.

A DULL and pedantic but conscientious critic writing in the year 1589, gives the following advice to the poets of his day: "Our maker, therfore, at these dayes shall not follow *Piers plowman*, nor *Gower*, nor *Lydgate*, nor yet *Chaucer*, for their language is now out of vse with us: neither shall he take the terms of Northern-men, such as they use in dayly talke, whether they be noble men or gentlemen, or of their best clarkes, all is a matter: nor in effect any speach vsed beyond the riuer of Trent, though no man can deny but that theirs is the purer English Saxon at this day, yet it is not so courtly nor so currant as our Southerne English is, no more is the far Westerne man's speach: ye shall, therefore, take the vsuall speach of the Court, and that of London, and the shires lying about London, within lx. myles, and not much aboue." He then goes on to acknowledge that the gentlemen and educated people in other counties generally speak, and especially write, "as good Southerne as we of Middlesex and Surrey do." The reason for that, however, he finds in the influence of English dictionaries and of literature.

From these lines the following important conclusions can be drawn: (1) That in the last quarter of the sixteenth century there was already a common literary language for English; (2) That this language was partly, at least, the common *spoken* language of the educated throughout the country; (3) That it was the native dialect of an area of country extending about sixty miles round London as its centre. It remains for us to show how this state of things came about. We have seen that up to the time of the Norman Conquest the West Saxon dialect of Old English had, since the days of Alfred, been gradually winning for itself the position of a common literary language. The defeat at Senlac, and its consequences, reduced the mother-tongue to fight for mere existence, and the centrifugal forces always present in language made themselves felt directly the unifying influence of an English court and an English clergy was withdrawn.

The fight, therefore, between French and English for supremacy was accompanied, as we have seen, by the splitting-up of the latter into almost as many different dialects as there are counties, in the kingdom. During the twelfth, thirteenth, and the first half of the fourteenth centuries, no common language for literature could possibly arise. English had to make good her right to existence as against both Norman and Central French in turn before this was anyway to begin. John Trevisa, of Cornwall, a Southerner and a contemporary of Chaucer, says, in his translation of Higden's "Polychronicon": "All the language

<hr/>

[1] George Puttenham. "The Arte of English Poesie," 1589. Prof. Arber's "English Reprints," 1869, p. 157.

of the Northumbrians . . . is so sharp, slitting, grating, and unshapen, that we Southern men can with difficulty under-stand that language." "Therefore it is that the Mercians, that are men of Middle England, being as it were partners of both extremes, understand the side languages Northern and Southern better than North and South understand each other." It is evident from this that there was a demand for some common tongue, and that from the nature of the case, the dialect most likely to supply the want was the Midland.

Its Nu-cleus the London Dialect.   Towards the end of the fourteenth century the necessary conditions were present, and just as the dialect of the Isle de France was the source of modern French, and that of Castile the source of standard Spanish, so London, the centre of political, commercial, and intellectual life in England, became the home of the standard English which was to be. Not that the dialect of London had always been Midland. On the contrary, it was originally distinctly Southern and Saxon in character, as the oldest London document, the famous Proclamation of Henry III. (1258; I., p. 403), makes certain.[1] There is evidence in this document of Midland influence, especially in the frequent use of the Present Indic. plural-ending in -*en ;* but both the Midland contamination and the predominating Southern character are the natural consequences of London's geographical position. Even so late as the middle of the fourteenth century, the London dialect, though by this time distinctly Midland, shows a larger proportion of Southern characteristics than the language of the Parliamentary and State documents. This can be proved by a comparison of these documents with such an example of the London records as "A Petition from the folk of Mercerye," of the year 1386 printed, in the Rolls of Parliament.[2] The work of Chaucer shows both some Midland and some Southern, especially Kentish, elements not found in the London dialect of his day This is accounted for partly by the fact that his family was of East-Midland origin, coming from Ipswich, and partly by the fact that he was a great reader and a man of very wide culture, conservative in tendency, and far from the radical innovator he has often been thought to be. His not infrequent

---

[1] *Cf.* Dr. L. Morsbach, "Ursprung der N.E. Schriftsprache," pp. 161, 2.

[2] Vol. III., p. 225, *f.* Reprinted from the MS., by Morsbach (*op. cit.,* Appendix I.).

use of Kentish forms, such as *fulfelle* for *fulfille* and *hed* for *hid*, has been shown to be due to his probable continued residence at Greenwich after 1385, and to his other connections with the county.[1]

It is not difficult to see now how it was that the dialect of London changed in character from Southern and Saxon to Midland and Anglian. London was the meeting-place for all sorts and conditions of men, the centre of English commerce, the seat of government and of the court. Midland was the only dialect in England fairly well understood by all. Inhabitants

The East Midland Dialect.

JOHN TREVISA'S ACCOUNT OF ENGLISH DIALECTS.

(*From Caxton's edition of his translation of Higden.*)

or London, if only from purely commercial considerations, were bound to give up in the main their Southern peculiarities of speech, and geographical position naturally led to the adoption of the East in preference to the West Midland. In the Parliamentary and other State documents the most serviceable form of speech would naturally have preference; and as the Midland and Northern portions of the kingdom were far greater in extent than the Southern, it is only natural that a smaller Southern and larger Northern element should be present than in the dialect of the Londoner, which

[1] *Cf.* Skeat, "On Chaucer's use of the Kentish Dialect," Phil. Soc. Trans., 1894.

was conditioned by geographical position in a way that of the Government was not.[1]

There now remain two questions to be considered. How did this East Midland dialect become the language of literature? And how did this literary language become the usual speech of all educated people, as we have seen it was on the way to becoming in Puttenham's time? To deal with them in order:—attempts have been made to show, on the one hand, that London was not the home of standard English, but rather the Rutland neighbourhood.[2] On the other hand, Morsbach has tried to prove that modern literary English is the direct descendant of the English used by London citizens of the second half of the fourteenth century, as seen in the documents of the time. He does not deny that Wycliffe and Chaucer had some influence, but it was no essential one. The

The Influence of Literature: Chaucer

truth seems to lie between these two extremes. Morsbach has completely failed to show how the dialect of the London merchants could ever become the language of literature without the authoritative stamp of some great literary genius, such as Chaucer, more especially as all the literature produced for a hundred years after his death was the work of a school of poets who were his slavish imitators. Chaucer was a Londoner, but he was also a member of the court, and his dialect, therefore, though essentially that of London, was more catholic, and incorporated elements both Midland and Southern not found in the speech of the average Londoner. Had there been no Chaucer there would have been no " Chaucer School," very possibly no English work from the pen of Gower; and though these are but fancies, it does not seem unlikely that Langland would, in that case, have been the father both of modern standard English and of English poetry. The tradition in both language and literature would then

---

[1] A typical example of each of the chief M.E. dialects in the fourteenth century may be useful: Northern—(*a*) East, the York Plays; (*b*) West, "Sire Gawain and the Grene Knight"; Midland—(*a*) East, Chaucer; (*b*) West, the Chester Plays, Langland; South—"Bevis of Hamtoune"; Kent—"Ayenbite of Inwit."

[2] *Cf.* Freeman, "Norman Conquest," v. 541, *ff.* Kington-Oliphant in his "Old and Middle English," p. 449, says, "Our classic speech did not arise in London or Oxford"; though, in his later work, "The New English," 1886, he has considerably modified this crude statement—*c*. especially Vol. I., Chap. II.

have been a West, instead of an East Midland,[1] and if we remember the strong influence which the West Midland tradition exerted on Spenser as it was. this will not seem a far-fetched hypothesis. The West was the home of conservatism—-the home of archaic forms, of the alliterative revival. Chaucer represented the East Midland tradition. The East Midlands came most under Danish and most under Norman-French influence, and this is seen in both language and literature. In this sense, the earlier East Midland writers, and among them Robert Manning of Brunne, may be considered as the forerunners of Chaucer in the M.E. period. Robert was doubtless one of the most important links in the chain immediately preceding Chaucer, but he cannot be called the "patriarch"[2] of modern literary English with any more justice than Wycliffe, or the authors of "Havelok" and "King Horn," or the poets of the "Cædmon School." This title can only be given, if given at all, to him who being at once a citizen of the capital, a courtier, and a genius, produced works which were widely popular, and as widely read; and which being written, to all intents and purposes, in the same dialect as that of his fellow-citizens, a dialect which national experience had shown to be more widely useful than any other, gave at once the best possible guarantee of universal acceptance and the stamp of a literary language to what before had only been a spreading form of speech. ' Wycliffe," to quote the words of the greatest authority on this subject, "prepared the great mass of the people for the reception of a common literary language; but Chaucer is the originator of the literary movement to which the development of this language during the following centuries is due."[3] It would be almost as hard to prove that Luther was not needed in the production of modern German as that Chaucer was so for the development of modern English. ·The influence of his art and of his language can be traced in poetry through the whole fifteenth and a large part of the sixteenth century,

Robert Manning of Brunne.

---

[1] It is to be remembered that the differences between East and West Midland are not nearly so great as between Southern and Midland.

[2] Freeman, and Kington-Oliphant following in his wake. see in Robert Manning the father of standard English.

[3] B. ten Brink, "Chaucers Sprache und Verskunst," 1884. p. 4. .

Caxton. and the language, though not so much the style, of prose, as seen in Caxton, owes its origin to him. Caxton did much to make the future of the new literary language certain; firstly, by always making use of it in his translations,[1] and, secondly, by the fixity and wide circulation ensured for it by his printing-press. He had, however, many difficulties to contend with, Some people, he tells us in the prologue to his translation of the Æneid, complained because he used "ouer-curyous termes, whiche coud not be understande of comyn peple, and desired me to use olde and homely terms [*i.e.* dialectal forms] in my translacyons." Others, and especially the scholars, "desired me to wryte the moste curyous termes that I coude fynde." "But," he concludes, "in my Judgemente, the comyn termes that be dayli used ben lyghter to understonde than the olde and auncyent Englysshe." And it is quite evident that he means by this the dialect of London, for, in another part of the same prologue, he remarks "that comyn Englysshe that is spoken in one shyre varyeth from another,"; and goes on to tell a story of a good wife of Kent who could not understand some travellers when they asked for "eggs," for she only knew the pure English word "eyren." Caxton, then, by using the London dialect and putting it into print, fixed it as the language of literature for the future; but he could never have done this had not Chaucer originated the movement in the previous century. Not only are the phonetic forms and vocabulary of standard English to be traced back to that time, but, so far as investigation has yet gone, it is clear that the syntax of modern standard English had its birth in the same century. There is no form of speech used at the present day which cannot be traced either in germ, or already fully developed, in the fourteenth century. It is noticeable, moreover, that the English language at that time came enormously under the influence of French syntax, and adopted French forms of speech, not only in cases where the native idiom was inadequate, but even where the Old English idiom was ready to hand. So far did this go that no less than three-fourths of the Old French idioms are to be found

---

[1] In printing Trevisa's translation of Higden's "Polychronicon" in 1482, he altered the South-Western dialect to that of London throughout, as already noted, p. 380.

reproduced in fourteenth-century English. As the East Midland writers were precisely those which came most strongly under the influence of French in other ways, such as vocabulary, literary forms, etc., the comparatively new study of historical syntax only offers another correlative proof of the truth of the main position.[1]

The part of this subject about which least is known is the course of development after Caxton's time, and the exact way in which the literary language became the spoken tongue of the

DIFFERENCE OF ENGLISH DIALECTS, AS NOTED BY CAXTON.

educated classes throughout the country. So far as the first of these points goes, the difficulty is enormously increased by the fact that although in the sixteenth and seventeenth centuries very widespread and important changes took place in our pronunciation, there was no corresponding break with the old orthography similar to that which took place in German, and which serves to mark the commencement of a literary language for that tongue. Our orthography, in the main. is the same to-day as it was in the Middle Ages, but our pronunciation is very

The Written and the Spoken Tongue.

[1] *Cf.* for proofs and an elaboration of these remarks. Chap. IV., in Kluge's "Geschichte der Engl. Sprache" (Paul, Grundriss der germ. Philologie, I.).

different.[1]   The changes which were made in the sixteenth
century in orthography only tended to confuse matters further.
Most people tried to write phonetically, but some followed the
English system and others the French, whilst the scholars spelt
many Romance words in accordance with their Latin etymolo-
gies, forgetting that they had come to us through French, had
thus become altered in pronunciation, and therefore in spelling.
This accounts for the presence of the Latin *d*, and *l*, in such·
Romance words as " adventure " and " assault." The second of
the two points mentioned above is also far from clear.   It must
be remembered that at the end of the sixteenth century there
was only a partial coincidence of the spoken and written language
amongst educated people, as we see from Puttenham's statement;
and that even in the present day the spoken language of educated
people is, in most cases, only an approximation to standard
English. Doubtless the popularisation of literature, and especially
the Authorised Version of the Bible, have been the chief factors
in its spread.

"Scots."   Finally, it must be remembered that the Northern dialect, as
spoken in the Lowlands of Scotland, possessed, in the fourteenth
and fifteenth centuries, a literature of its own, and gave promise
of becoming a separate standard language for the North. At
the commencement of the sixteenth century it began to be called
" Scotis," or " Scots," instead of " Inglis." as hitherto.   But even
Gawin Douglas, though he spoke of his tongue as " langage of
Scottis natioun," came so markedly under Chaucer's influence
that his dialect was no pure Northern one, and by the end of the
sixteenth century the life of the Northern dialect as a literary
medium was at an end. The chief cause for this was the absence
of an authorised Scots translation of the Bible. In 1542 the
New Testament, " in Inglis wulgare toung," was given to the
people, and the English Bible was printed in Scotland in 1576-9.
Even Knox's translation of the Psalms was much oftener printed
in English than in Scots, and the many books which he wrote in
the latter dialect show frequent evidence of English influence.
Thus, at the beginning of the seventeenth century, the whole

---

[1] Chas. Buttler, in his " English Grammar," 1633, p. 3, says : "We have in
our language many syllables which, having gotten a nue pronunciation, doo
yet retain their old ortographie, so that their letters do not now rightly
express the sound."

domain of English literature had been conquered by the London dialect.

IN giving an outline of the Lancastrian and Yorkist period, we only just alluded to the darker features which can be traced in the agricultural history, and which, though trifling at first, gradually kept increasing in intensity as the fifteenth century advanced. These now must claim our attention.

W. J.
CORBETT.
The Agri-
cultural
Revolution:
The Cessation
of Progress.

The first of them that may be mentioned is the absolutely stationary character of the farming of the period. During the whole of the years between the revolt of the peasants under Wat Tyler and their revolt in 1549 under Ket, hardly a single improvement was introduced. The uses of clover, turnips, and artificial grasses still remained unknown; ploughing continued to be little more than a scratching of the surface; draining and manuring were neglected, and even marling went somewhat out of fashion. For draught purposes horses were still hardly ever used, oxen being preferred because they cost less to keep in winter, wanted no shoes, and when dead were man's meat, whereas horses were carrion. And yet the common pastures were in many places so bare and unsheltered and the grass was so poor that we are assured it was almost impossible to keep working oxen in condition upon them. As to gardening and the cultivation of " such herbes, fruites and roots as grow yearlie out of the ground of seed," which had been very plentiful in the land in the days of the Edwards, we are told that "in process of time they grew also to be neglected, so that from Henry IV. till the latter end of Henry VII. and beginning of Henry VIII. there was little or no use of them in England; but they remained either unknown or supposed as food more meet for hogs or savage beasts to feed upon than mankind." The general interest, in fact, in estate management which had led under the Plantagenets to the production of such manuals as " Le Dite de Husbondrie" had entirely died out, and in the fifteenth century no writer arose who even attempted to improve on Walter of Henley's treatise. On the contrary, this was left with the field entirely to itself as the one and only guide for farmers, and it was not till 1523, when a new book of husbandry was published by Fitzherbert, probably a Justice of the Common Pleas, that people for the first time began to realise that the suggestions of

the thirteenth-century author were becoming a little antiquated.
The first fruits of this feeling are to be seen in the introduction
of hops into the south-eastern counties, the legend being that

' Turkies, hoppes, reformation and beer
Came into England all in one year.''

But hop-growing even long after the Reformation must still
have been in its infancy and very little practised, as it is not
mentioned by Fitzherbert, and the first treatise on it by Reginald
Scot was not written till 1574. The same view must also be
taken of the chief scheme for improvement advocated by Fitzherbert himself, though none of his contemporaries seem to have
disputed its advantages. This is to be found in his "Book of
Surveying," in the last chapter of which he recommends the
adoption of enclosing on a large scale, meaning thereby that the
system of having only open or " champaign " villages with their
unenclosed common fields and wastes should be abolished, and
that instead the land should be cut up into a number of "several
closes"—that is to say, into the endless small fields, each surrounded by its separate hedge, with which to-day we are so well
acquainted. To do this, of course, meant to put an end once
and for all to the old communal tillage, and to the scattering of
holdings into a number of acre and half-acre strips, dispersed up
and down over the arable. It would also require the suppression of the common right of pasture, enjoyed equally by all on
land from which the crops had been removed. When once,
however, this had been effected and the land equitably redis-
tributed, every one would be the gainer, so that townships that
had formerly been worth twenty marks yearly would instead be
worth twenty pounds. For under the new system every one
would have a compact holding to do what he liked with, free
from the interference of his neighbours, while the husbandman's
returns might naturally be expected to be larger, both the stock
and the crops being better protected. Even to mere labourers
who held no land the change would be no loss, for though there
might be less employment for herdsmen, there would be more
for hedgers and ditchers. After enclosing, too, a better proportion might be effected between the areas devoted to corn-growing
and pasturage respectively, the latter having hitherto been decidedly deficient, for with better harvests a smaller area of arable

Enclosures.

would suffice. All these arguments and others were urged by
Fitzherbert, but they can have done very little towards over-
coming the conservatism of his readers, except, perhaps, in
Essex and Suffolk. For outside these counties we know that
England remained almost totally unenclosed until well into the
eighteenth century.

The causes of this absolute standstill are somewhat mysterious, **Causes of Stagnation.**
and may be sought for in several directions with equal proba-
bility; in the extension of leases, for example, and the consequent withdrawal and absenteeism of the landlords from their

THE LABOURER.
(Caxton, " Game and Playe of the Chess.")

estates; in the general turmoil of the civil wars, which
undermined all steady effort; in the growth of commerce and
its absorption of all the enterprise in the country. All these, no
doubt, had something to do with it, but we have yet to mention
what was in all likelihood the most effective cause of all; one,
too, that was at work all through the fifteenth century, and
forms one of the darkest features of the period. This was the **Decline of**
unmarked, but nevertheless uninterrupted and unmistakable, **the Monas-**
decay that was gradually stealing over all the monastic houses, **teries.**
both great and small alike (p. 630). In earlier centuries these
had always taken the lead in farming, and if improvements
were introduced it was sure to be the monks that were the
pioneers. But now they had in one way or another nearly all
become impoverished, and though, as we have seen, they were

91

still lenient landlords, they were no longer energetic ones. The first symptom of their withdrawal from the agricultural leadership is to be seen in their reluctance to adopt the system of leasing, many of them not trying it till late in the fifteenth century, and even then continuing to manage their home farms. by bailiffs. Fortunately in this matter the want of their good example was not very much felt, but it soon made itself so in other things. Thus the old monks had always been excellent. men of business, and had firmly enforced all their manorial rights however trivial; but now the manorial courts began to get out of order. Records were badly kept; stewards and bailiffs abused their powers; and had it not been that the court. rolls formed the title-deeds of the copyholders, and that there was still money to be made from fees, the ancient jurisdiction would have run some danger of falling altogether into disuse. Similarly as to the internal communications of the country—in the old days the monks had been the great road-builders and repairers, but now both roads and bridges went to decay, and no one could be found with sufficient public spirit to prevent it.

The Effect on the Poor. How useful the monasteries had been, and what an important. factor they were, are, however, perhaps best seen from the effect their decline had upon the poorer classes. For from their first. foundation they had been the great dispensers of charity, and so, as they sank into poverty, or began wasting their means in luxury, there ceased to be any one to whom either the impotent. or the indigent could turn for aid. To the great body of the labouring class, whose wages, as we have seen, were kept down as low as possible by statute (p. 195), this was a very serious matter, for now if they were thrown out of work their customary resource failed them, and they had neither savings of their own nor any public system of relief to fall back upon. Absolute destitution consequently largely increased, and the country tended to become full of beggars, while, to make matters worse, there was at this very time a change passing over agriculture which tended constantly to throw more and more people out of employment.

Sheep Farming. The change referred to, though we have delayed speaking of it till last of all, is really one of the most important features of the period. It consisted in a continuous extension of sheep-farming at the expense of tillage. In a former chapter we.

have noticed the beginnings of this movement (p. 324), and connected it with the scarcity and expensiveness of labour after the Black Death, one of the chief advantages of sheep-farming being that it dispenses with the necessity of employing many farm servants. In the fourteenth century, however, it never assumed any very large proportions, and it was not till the fifteenth that its growth began to excite any very active opposition. In the language of the time, the change we are discussing is described as "enclosing"; but this is somewhat misleading, for there is nothing in common between it and what Fitzherbert recommended under that name. A few fences indeed might be run up, but the chief part of the process consisted in laying down as much land as possible in permanent pasture, and using it solely as a sheep-run. If there were any houses, they were either allowed to decay or taken down as encumbrances as soon as ever their inhabitants could be induced to quit.

A WOOL-MERCHANT.
(Chipping Norton, Oxon.)

To begin with, of course, the landowner might only enclose as much of the waste as he was entitled to do under the Statute of Merton, and then no destruction of buildings or eviction of tenants followed; but when once he had found out the advantage, it was not often that he would be content to stop at this point. The demesne share in the common fields usually followed the waste, the farm labourers were for the most part dismissed, and the manorial buildings dismantled. At Chesterton, for instance, near Cambridge, enclosing had reached this point in 1414, much to the damage of the tenants, who complained that "there was gret waste in the manor of Housing, that is to say, of Halles and Chambers, and of other houses of office, and none housinge left stondinge thereon but if it were a shepcote, or a berne, or a swynsty, and a few houses byside to putte in bestes." In acting thus, however much it might impoverish the labourers, who were thrown out of work, or the village artisans who no longer had the farm buildings to keep in repair, the lords were well within their rights. Many, however, did not stop here, but unscrupulously drove their tenants completely off the wastes, either by force or by buying out their rights, and then it could only be a matter of time before they also deserted their holdings, arable land without pasture being in the long run of very little use. In all cases, too, where the tenants had only been small cottagers, supplementing a too scanty income by working for wages, the same result must have been achieved even without the landlord adopting any unwarrantable measures. In this way manor after manor became depopulated, or, if the tenants held out, so hopelessly pauperised that it was no wonder that they sometimes broke out into riots, and assembled in warlike array for the purpose of beating down the enclosures. Quite early in the fifteenth century we hear of disturbances of this sort, and by 1436 corn growing had so decreased that politicians became

Attempts to check Agricultural Decay. alarmed for the food supply and passed an Act to keep up the price of corn and so encourage tillage. In 1463 this was supplemented by an Act against the importation of foreign corn unless the price was over 6s. 8d. Efforts of this sort, however, do not seem to have been of much avail, and all through the reigns of Edward IV. and Henry VII. enclosing went rapidly on. At Stretton Baskerville, for instance, in Warwickshire, we read that Thomas Twyford began the depopulation thereof in 1489, decaying four messuages and three cottages whereunto 160 acres of arable belonged. He then sold it to Henry Smith, who following that example five years later, enclosed 640 acres of land more, whereby twelve messuages and cottages fell to ruin, and eighty persons these inhabiting, employed in tillage, were constrained to depart and live miserably. In similar tones the Statute-book for 1489 tells us that the Isle of Wight " is lately become decayed of people, by reason of many towns and villages having been beaten down, and is desolate and not inhabited, but occupied with beasts and cattle." Throughout England, too, we are assured that " idleness daily doth increase; for where in some towns 200 persons were occupied and lived of their lawful labour, now there are occupied only two or three herdsmen." Starkey, the royal chaplain in the next reign, only puts this more epigrammatically when he says, " Where hath been many

houses and churches to the honour of God, now you shall find
nothing but shepcotes and stables to the ruin of men, and that
not in one place or two, but generally throughout this realm."
Finally, if any further evidence is wanted to show that great
hardships were being entailed upon the peasantry, there are
the indignant words of Sir Thomas More, in which he bids us
sympathise with " the husbandmen thrust out of their own, or
else by covin and fraud or by violent oppression put beside it,
or by wrongs and injuries so wearied that they sell all," and goes
on to denounce " the noblemen and gentlemen, yea, and certain
abbots that lease no ground for tillage ; that enclose all into
pasture, and throw down houses ; that pluck down towns and
leave nothing standing, but only the church, to be made a sheep
house."

WE have seen (p. 533) that the fifteenth century was by no
means the " golden age for labour " that some writers have
depicted. Nevertheless, it seems probable that the masses of
the English people were better supplied with the bare neces-
sarles of life in the reign of Henry VII. than in any other reign
before that of Victoria.   Under Henry VII. an artisan could
generally earn between two and three shillings a week, without
working more than eight hours a day,[1] while the prices of
necessaries were on an average about one-twelfth of what they
are at present.   Good meat could be obtained at a farthing
a pound, beer cost a halfpenny per gallon.   House rent and
fuel were, in most places, more than proportionally cheap.   On
the other hand, wheaten bread, and many commodities which
the poor now consume in large quantities, were not pro-
curable by the corresponding classes in the fifteenth century;
and many of their conditions of life were more unhealthy,
dangerous, and disagreeable than those now endured by any but
the very poorest.   There was much violence and oppression,
little opportunity for travel, little education, no newspapers.
Pestilence and epidemics were frequent.   Thus, in the very year

J. E. SYMES. Industry and Commerce.

The Standard of Comfort.

---

[1] This is said to have been the ordinary length of a day's work in the
middle of the fifteenth century.   But an Act of the eleventh year of
Henry VII. lays down as a maximum twelve hours between March and
September, and from daybreak to nightfall during the rest of the year. This
is, no doubt, only given as a maximum, but it is difficult to believe that an
eight-hour day was the rule when this Act was passed.

of Henry VII.'s accession (1485) the terrible "sweating sickness" made its first appearance in England (p. 753). It spread over the country and raged for two months, killing most of those whom it attacked. Then it passed away; but it returned at intervals. The doctors could neither account for its arrival nor discover any effective way of treating it.

Policy of Henry VII. The gradual abolition of serfdom, and the ending of the Wars of the Roses had diminished some of the evils from which the poor suffered; and the able rule of Henry VII. established an unusual amount of security and order. His wise policy of peace and economy husbanded the national resources; and, though his government was grasping, and in some ways oppressive, his exactions scarcely affected the mass of the people. In fact, Henry VII. distinctly favoured the industrial classes. He saw that their prosperity might bring money into his treasury, and that their growing influence would help to balance the power of the turbulent nobles, whose ancestors had involved the country in so many civil brawls and shaken the power of so many kings.

AN OPPORTUNITY FOR TRAVEL.
(MS. Harl. 1892.)

England was still mainly agricultural. The chief industry **Growth of Manu-factures.** was still the producing of wool and other raw material which foreigners worked up (p. 336). But we had already begun to manufacture our own cloth. As early as 1331, Edward III. had invited Flemish weavers, fullers, and dyers to settle in England. These had taught their trades to Englishmen; and by the accession of Henry VII. our artisans were able not merely to supply much of the home demand, but also to sell their goods to foreigners. The agricultural changes under which much arable land had been turned into pasture diminished the demand for agricultural work, and many of the displaced labourers flocked into the towns and gradually found employment in manufacture. So that cloth now began to rank with wool, hides, lead, and tin among the chief exports from England.

The export trade was chiefly in the hands of foreigners. Nevertheless the English Merchants of the Staple (chartered in 1313) had long been considerable exporters of raw material. In the reign of Henry VII. there was a great further development of the English carrying-trade. The Merchant Adventurers

The Export Trade.

"FLEMINGS' HOUSES" AT KERSEY, SUFFOLK.

(p. 552) got a charter in 1505, and we have evidence that by 1497 they monopolised much of the important trade with Flanders. A petition of that year asserts that English merchants were finding their way to Spain, Venice, Holland, and in fact to most of the chief ports on the coasts of the Atlantic, the Mediterranean, the English Channel, and even the Baltic. Nevertheless our foreign trade was still chiefly in the hands of Italians, Flemings, and, above all, of the merchants of the famous Hanse League (pp. 342, 554). This German association had made an arrangement with Edward IV. (in 1474) under which Englishmen were to be allowed to trade freely with the Baltic ports.   In return for this and for other concessions, the Hanse merchants received various payments and privileges, and their position in England was even more advantageous than it had previously been.   Their colony, which was situated in the part of London where Cannon Street Terminus now stands, became a great centre of prosperous trade, and excited much jealousy among their English rivals.   It was not finally abolished till 1597.

The New World.   Among the ultimate effects of the discovery of America (p. 674) we may specially notice the advantages which it gave to

ROOD SCREEN AT KERSEY CHURCH, SUFFOLK.

the more westerly nations of Europe.   Hitherto the countries round the Mediterranean had been the best placed for purposes of commerce.   Some of them had naturally become the richest and most prosperous of the European nations.   But now Spain, Portugal, France, Holland, and England advanced rapidly to the front; and a glance at the map of Europe will show that these were just the countries best situated for communication with America.   England was the last to profit by this new advantage.   But in the long run she outstripped all her competitors, and even before the death of Henry VII. there were many signs that she was entering on a period of nautical activity.

The growing commerce of our country, and the interest taken in it by the king, is indicated by the provisions of the various commercial treaties made in this reign. Among these we may notice the treaty with Denmark (1490), with Florence (1490), and with Flanders (1496). All these were for the encouragement of free trading between the contracting nations. As a specimen of these treaties, we may take the so-called Intercursus Magnus of 1496, of which some mention has been

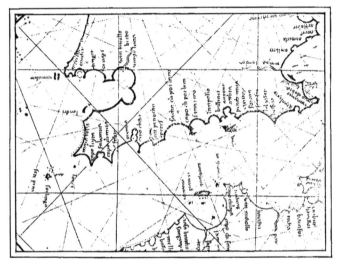

A VENETIAN CHART OF THE ENGLISH CHANNEL, 1489 (MS. Egerton 73)

made already. It guaranteed freedom of trade between England, Ireland, and Calais on the one hand, and Brabant, Flanders, Hainault, Holland, and Mechlin on the other. Merchants from each party might own houses in the dominions of the other. Custom-house officers were to be careful and considerate in dealing with imported merchandise; neither nation must allow pirates or privateers within its harbours, and merchants must deposit double the value of their ships and cargoes as a security that their sailors shall not be guilty of piracy. The trade in foreign bullion was to be free.

Another side of Henry's commercial policy may be illus-

**Naviga-
tion Laws.** trated by the fact that the trade between England and the South of France was limited by law to goods carried in English ships and manned by English sailors. Bacon shrewdly describes this as " bowing the ancient policy " of England " from consideration of *plenty* to consideration of *power*." He points out that " almost all the ancient statutes " had encouraged foreigners " to bring in all sorts of commodities, having for end cheapness," but that Henry VIII. was willing to sacrifice cheapness of goods for the sake of encouraging the merchant navy. In the long run this " protective " policy not only strengthened, but also enriched our country, England could scarcely have attained to her maritime pre-eminence without those Navigation Laws, of which Henry's were the first.

**The Mer-
cantile
Theory.** It was natural, however, that much of Henry's commercial legislation should be based on erroneous principles. The Chancellor, Cardinal Morton, called on Parliament to set the people " on work in arts and handicrafts " in order "that the realm may subsist more of itself," so that " *the draining out of our treasure* for foreign manufactures" might be stopped. This feeling, that the national wealth depended on the amount of gold and silver that could be brought into the country, continued to be for more than three centuries the basis of much of our commercial legislation. It still survives in the widely spread idea that what brings money into a country is the thing to be desired. But in modern Protectionist doctrines this idea holds a subordinate place. Their more common defence at present is that Government may profitably interfere for the protection of British industries. Of this, too, there are

**Protec-
tion.** signs in Henry's legislation. Thus an Act of one of his Parliaments (19 Henry VII., c. 21) prohibits the importation of "any manner of silk wrought by itself, or with any other stuff . . . in ribbons, laces, girdles, corses, cauls, corses of tissues or points"; but " all other manner of silks " may be freely imported. The object of the Act was, of course, to exclude those kinds of silk that were being manufactured at home.

The *internal trade* of England was still very largely carried on in the fifteenth century by means of Fairs, which were held annually at many centres, and often lasted several days

[509]

(I., p. 524). The Stourbridge Fair, near Cambridge, lasted a month
every year. Buyers and sellers flocked to it, not only from all parts
of England, but from many distant lands. In its stalls and booths
were sold Italian silks and velvets, French and Spanish wines,
fine linen from Flanders, as well as Derbyshire lead and Cornish
tin. Thither sheep and cattle were driven from all the counties
round, and Hanse merchants brought timber, iron, copper, grain,

A SEA-PORT, FIFTEENTH CENTURY (MS. Egerton 1065).

and many other commodities from ports on the Baltic and the
German Ocean. Among buyers, too, many strange nations were
represented. Some bought for consumption, others for exportation, while many were chiefly attracted by the fun of the fair.
Similar gatherings, on a smaller scale, were held in most parts of
England. In days when the population was small and scattered
there were, naturally, few shops, and these were seldom well
stocked. The modern organisation for distributing goods had

not grown up. The distinction of merchants, manufacturers, shopmen, and artisans only existed in germ; and the fairs provided the chief opportunities for all but the simplest commercial transactions.

Manu-facture. Manufactures, however, were beginning to grow in importance, and were already widely spread. "There was probably hardly a home without a spinning-wheel, hardly a manor without half-a-dozen hand-looms"; but in most parts of England the artisans were also agriculturists (p. 550). The same might indeed be said of almost all classes of the community, from the king to the monk and the poor student. In some places, however, and especially in Norfolk, large sections of the population depended for their livelihood chiefly upon manufacturing industries (p. 562). In others mining was pursued with great energy. Derbyshire lead found its way to many parts of the Continent. The tin mines of Cornwall retained much of their ancient fame. But little coal or iron was as yet produced.

The Dis-tribution of Wealth. The assessment of 1503 throws much interesting light on the distribution of wealth and industry among the towns and counties of England. London was, of course, far the richest of the towns. Bristol had once more reached the second place. This was, no doubt, owing to the growth of trade with the South of Europe; for the discovery of America cannot as yet have produced a very considerable increase in the population and wealth of Bristol. The same cause, no doubt, explains why Gloucester now stood as high as fifth among the English towns. Of the counties, Oxford came next to Middlesex, probably on account of its rich pasture lands. Norfolk took the third place. Its pre-eminence in manufactures and its extensive trade with Flanders failed to outweigh the pastures of Oxford. Cumberland, Northumberland, and Lancashire were the very poorest counties in England; and the West Riding was not much richer.

In manufactures, the chief change which the fifteenth century introduced was the growth of the class of capitalist artisans. At the beginning of the century, labourers were simply hired to work on materials owned by landlords, monasteries, etc. But by the time of Henry VII. we find that the artisans frequently provided their own materials. The class of manufacturing employers did not yet exist. There were, of course, no large factories. But the workman was now often his own employer, and he often sold the products of his labour to **Guilds.** the consumer or customer without the intervention of any middleman. But the price at which he sold it was generally fixed by his guild, or by custom, if not by law. The medieval organisation of labour has been described previously (pp. 155, 560). But we may here repeat that almost every industry had its guild, which laid down the rules under which alone it might be pursued, at least in the towns. These rules were chiefly directed to benefiting those in the guild, and preventing what was considered unfair competition between them. Sometimes they existed by royal authority, sometimes by that of the

municipalities. They often had a practical, and not unfrequently a legal, monopoly of the trade in their district, and they seem to have done something to keep up the standard of work and of character among their members.

No one was admitted to, or allowed to remain in, any trade, unless the guild authorities were satisfied both as to his moral character and his

THE MERCHANT.
(*Caxton, " Game and Playe of the Chess."*)

efficiency as a workman, and this efficiency had to be proved **Appren-** during an apprenticeship which generally, in England, lasted **ticeship.** for seven years. The admission of an apprentice was a solemn ceremony, by which he became a member of the family of his employer or master, who was expected not only to instruct him in his trade, but also to exercise supervision over his moral conduct. At the expiration of his apprenticeship he might become a full " citizen " by paying the accustomed fees, and going through the established forms. No member of a guild might possess tools which were not testified to be of good quality. Stringent regulations had to be observed as to the methods of working and the quality of materials. No one might begin his work before sunrise, or continue it after curfew;

and it was also forbidden to work on Church festivals, or after noon on the eve of a double feast. There were restrictions as to the number of apprentices any member might have, and regulations as to prices. Any member impoverished by misfortune had a claim to relief. Members might not go to law with one another till they had submitted their dispute to the arbitration of the guild wardens. Religion played a prominent part in guild life. Each guild had its patron saint, and often its chaplain, one of whose chief duties was to say mass for the souls of dead members. The extent to which the guilds regulated their trades led sometimes to serious evils. Henry VII. tried to check these by an Act of 1503, which prevented these guilds from making any new laws or ordinances concerning the prices of wares and other things for their singular profit, until first examined and approved of by the Lord Chancellor, Lord Treasurer, or king's justices. We shall see that this policy was carried further in the following reign. But meantime the growth of foreign trade struck a severe blow at the whole guild organisation. With every extension of markets, and every step in the direction of division of labour, it became increasingly difficult to regulate wages and prices by any force except that of competition, and the great intellectual revival that we know as the Renaissance tended to make men break through the bonds of custom, and the traditional ways of doing business.

Shifting of Industrial Centres. From quite early in the sixteenth century we get many complaints of the decay of towns; and this was probably partly due to the spread of the woollen and linen manufactures into rural districts in order to avoid the restrictions of the guilds. From various Acts of Parliament between 1515 and 1545 we gather that a very large proportion of English towns were in this decaying condition. On the other hand we may notice that the rise of the capitalist artisan, referred to above, seems to indicate a considerable accumulation of wealth in the hands of the labouring class.

"Usury." But though capital was growing, there was as yet little borrowing or investing for commercial or manufacturing purposes. All lending at interest was regarded as usurious and wrong (p. 159). The Chancellor Morton urged Parliament to repress it on the express ground that it was a " barren " employment of money, diverting wealth from its natural use in trading. In other words, he took for granted that lending must be unproductive. Accordingly an Act was passed in the third year of Henry VII., making all lending at interest criminal. The usurious bargain was to be null and void. The lender was to be heavily fined, and further punished, for his soul's good, under the ecclesiastical laws. Morton's language, and that of this Act, make it clear that the modern practice of lending at interest for business purposes was practically unknown. The usury aimed at was the lending at interest to spendthrifts or unfortunates. The building up of industries by means of credit, which transfers

SHILLING OF HENRY VII.

the use of capital to the hands that can use it most efficiently, was as yet scarcely thought of.

Henry's care for trade extended to the currency. Unlike **Currency.** many of his predecessors and successors, he never debased the coinage. He was greedy and covetous, but he was too shrewd to suppose he could permanently enrich himself by tampering with the amount or standard of the metal. He introduced, however, some important changes. Thus, he was the first to coin shillings and sovereigns. The word *shillings* had hitherto frequently been used in accounts, but the first actual shillings were coined in 1504 (p. 685). They were called *large groats*, and afterwards *testors*, from the king's head (teste) on one face of them. The gold sovereigns were at first called *double rose nobles*. In the next reign a perplexing variety both of gold and silver coins were issued, partly, it is to be feared, with the direct object of deceiving the public.

Signs of a New Era.   Externally and politically Henry VII.'s reign was a period of tranquillity. But in the social history of our country it was a period of general unsettling of old ways and habits of living, working, and thinking. Men's minds were awakening after the long sleep of the Middle Ages; and the new intellectual move-ment revolutionised industry as well as all the other departments of the national life. First came the great revival of study, especially of the study of Greek (p. 688). In Italy this move-ment began about the time of our Wars of the Roses, and several Englishmen, including Grocyn and Colet, journeyed to Italy for the express purpose of learning Greek, and then returned to teach it to their fellow-countrymen. Oxford became the great centre of this revival. There Grocyn began to lecture on Greek in the year 1490, and soon the University was split into two parties—the "Greeks," who threw themselves into the new movement, and the "Trojans," as the more conservative and reactionary section was called. The former party included all the more active and intelligent students, and soon Cambridge was similarly awakened from sloth, and the old learning passed into contempt. It was only indirectly that this movement affected industry. But it was inevitable that the new intellec-tual activity should make itself felt in business; that men should refuse to be bound by customs handed down from an ignorant past; and should try new processes in manufacture, agriculture, and commerce. The invention of printing must have had a similar tendency, and this too began to influence England in the reign of Henry VII. It was eight years before the beginning of this reign that Caxton brought his printing press to our country (p. 720). But the early presses were so clumsy and inefficient that the number of books produced by them was at first small. Nevertheless, by the year 1500 nearly 400 books had been issued (p. 726). Copies of them were circulated in all parts of the country, and a fresh stimulus to thought and originality was thus given. When we add to this the nautical discoveries already referred to, and those that now followed in quick succession, revealing new worlds, opening up new routes for trade, and stirring men's imaginations with the stories brought home by travellers, we can better understand that our country was entering on a new and revolutionary era—the age of the Reformation and of Shakespeare. And it was inevitable that the new spirit and temper which we call the Renaissance should make itself felt in the national industries. The struggle to grow rich became more intense. Men would not submit to the old restrictions, or be content with traditional ways of doing business. Custom was more and more displaced by competition, with consequences that will be traced in future chapters.

For the present it must suffice to say that the changes were by no means unmixedly good. In fact, they at first probably brought in their train more misery than happiness. Custom is a great protection of the poor. Changes in industrial processes alter the demand for labour, and make many kinds of skill almost useless to those who possess them. The eighty years that followed the death of Henry VII. enormously increased the wealth of England, and introduced many luxuries unknown or almost unknown to the earlier generations. But the *distribution* of wealth became far more unequal. The problem of pauperism acquired a quite new significance, and the question what to do with the unemployed became almost insoluble.

HENRY TUDOR had occupied the royal palace in the Tower of London only three weeks when a strange and fatal malady began, on September 19, 1485, to prevail among the citizens. It became well known during the two generations following as the English sweat; but in the autumn of 1485 it was a new disease, which the most experienced physician had never seen before nor the most learned ever read of. Only the numerous empirics in London, who "wrote and put letters upon gates, and church doors, and upon poles," pretended that it was known to them of old, and that they held the secret of its cure. It took men and women suddenly everywhere—when they were abroad in the streets, or conversing with their neighbours; an aguish shake warned them to hasten to bed; the chill was followed at once by great redness and turgescence of the skin, an intense feeling of heat and pricking which made clothing intolerable, and an agonising thirst which led the sufferers to drink immoderately, to their undoing. In a short time they were running with sweat at every pore, a sweat that drenched their linen and bed-clothes over and over again, differing from the sweat of rheumatic fever in being steady and as if in-

CHARLES CREIGHTON. Public Health: The Sweating Sickness.

92

exhaustible, but resembling the latter in having a peculiar but far more striking odour. By the twelfth or fourteenth hour from the first sudden warning, the patient was either out of danger or sunk in fatal collapse; in the latter event his limbs were cold, his features pinched and blue, the stony coldness creeping nearer and nearer to the heart, just as Shakespeare has described with the most perfect medical correctness for Falstaff in the play. It was mostly men of Sir John's habits and position that were seized, men who lived well, such as the portly alderman, the easy citizen, the swashbuckler, the courtier, the priest, with a small proportion of women, but with hardly any of the poorest class, who were the usual victims of the old plague. The Lord Mayor died, and his successor, who was immediately chosen, died three days after him; four more of the aldermen died. In a few weeks the epidemic was over in London, and the coronation of Henry VII. was celebrated by a great procession from the Tower and a feast in Westminster Hall on October 30, as if nothing unusual had happened.

Meanwhile the same disease had been spreading all over England; it is heard of in Croyland Abbey, where the abbot died after an illness of eighteen hours on October 14. It is mentioned in a Bristol diary, and as prevailing among the Oxford students for a month or six weeks. If there had been parish registers at that time, we should doubtless have found its traces in a rapid succession of burials for a week or two in many small towns and country villages, as we find during the last sweat of 1551, in parish registers of Devonshire, Leicestershire, Yorkshire, and Lancashire. A physician of the time says that fifteen thousand died of the sweat in 1485; but the number is ten times too large for London, and he had no means of knowing how many died all over England.

Its Source.   By one of those popular verdicts, which are often a true intuition or a divination of the truth, the outbreak of the sweat in England was laid to the account of Henry Tudor's expedition, which landed from Rouen at Milford Haven on August 6. The chronicle of Croyland goes so far, indeed, as to make Lord Stanley excuse the absence of himself and his troops from Bosworth Field on the ground that he was suffering from the sweat; but the reason is clearly an afterthought, and perhaps a jest, for, although Stanley refused to marshal his men

THE TOWER OF LONDON ABOUT 1480 (MS. Roy. 16 F. ii.).

under the banner of Richard III., and held aloof at the beginning of the fray, he came up in time for the victory, and with
his own hands placed Richard's crown on Henry's head. The
outbreak in London on September 19 is clearly stated by a
physician who saw it to have been the first signal of the disease
in England; another chronicler says September 21 in London;
still others place the death of mayors and aldermen early in
October, "then being the sweat of new begun"; and it is
certain that the abbot of Croyland did not die of the sweat until
October 14, although Croyland was only some twenty miles
from the spot in Leicestershire, where the annalist of the abbey
vaguely speaks of the disease as prevalent six or seven weeks
before. The beginning of it was almost certainly in London
three or four weeks after Henry Tudor's triumphal entry; it
befell suddenly in a crowded and redolent city, a city filled with
the soldiers from Bosworth (Welshmen and Frenchmen), attendants upon the Court, and place seekers of every kind and degree.
If the disease had been plague, one could have understood the
sudden outburst; for one of the greatest London plagues, that
of 1603, broke out amidst the bustle attending the accession of
James I. and the new dynasty; while the next great London
plague happened during the months immediately following the
accession of Charles I. But this disease was an absolute novelty
to England, to all Europe, to the whole globe; and it was not a
disease of the crowded tenements of the poorer classes. Henry
VII.'s French mercenaries, who numbered some two thousand or
more, and were doubtless all in London at the time, are not
above suspicion of having brought the new disease in. But they
had been in England since August 6, the hardships of their
voyage were past, they had fought and won, they were resting
on their laurels, and there is nothing to show that they suffered
from the sweat at any time from first to last, neither they nor
any of their countrymen in any of the five great epidemics down
to that of 1551. At the same time they were just the men to
have bred a pestilence, as troops have sometimes done even when
they did not suffer from it. There is an instance in English
history during the Civil War, in 1644, when a severe epidemic,
called in the parish register "the sweating sickness," broke out
at Tiverton, after it had been occupied for a fortnight by the
army of the Lord General Essex. The character of the French

mercenaries is described in the speech put into the mouth of Richard III. on the morning of Bosworth Field—" vagabonds, rascals, and runaways, base lackey peasants, rags of France, famished beggars weary of their lives, whom our fathers have in their own land beaten, bobb'd, and thump'd," as Shakespeare amplifies and varies the language of Hall's Chronicle. Let us imagine two thousand or more of them enjoying the pleasures of London for a season, quartered on its citizens, carousing in its taverns, swaggering in its narrow streets and lanes. London had never been occupied by such foreigners since the Conquest. And the most significant fact of all is that more than two

hundred years after-wards, when the English sweat had been long forgotten, a disease very like it, called by the name of sweat, and differing only in being a less swift and less deadly infection, began to be noticed year after year, as if native to the soil, here and there in the towns or villages of that very region of France — the lower basin of the Seine—in

THE APOTHECARY.
(Caxton, " Game and Playe of the Chess.")

which Henry Tudor had enlisted his army of free lances in the summer of 1485.

The first sweat, of 1485, came and went in a few weeks of autumn, like an influenza—the disease being no more seen until twenty-three years later, in 1508. In that year it broke out in July—the household of the Lord Treasurer being among its first victims—caused much mortality and panic in the king's households in and near London, as well as *per omnia loca*, according to the poet-laureate of the time, cut off several of the Court, called for public prayers at St. Paul's and kept Henry VII. moving in strict isolation from one hunting-lodge to another, just as the next sweats, of 1517 and 1528. permitted no abiding-place to Henry VIII. so long

Its Return in 1508.

as they lasted.   There is nothing to explain this second epidemic, except that an unusually mild winter, a dry spring, and a very warm May had been followed by rains in June. Like the first sweat, that of 1508 had spread over England; it is known to have caused ninety-one deaths (only three of them women) at Chester in three days, and it was probably the "sore pestilence" of that year which caused the Oxford students to disperse.

The two epidemics of the sweat in the reign of Henry VII. would both together, and all over England, have caused hardly more mortality (although the mortality was of greater personages) than one great epidemic of plague in London, in 1499–1500.   It is vaguely estimated to have destroyed twenty thousand of the citizens ; but if it had destroyed only half of that number, it would have taken the usual toll of a London plague of the first degree—namely, one-fifth or one-sixth of the inhabitants, and these chiefly the poorer classes, who could not seek safety in flight from the plague-laden air of the towns in the summer heat.   That was not the only out- break of the old plague in Henry VII.'s reign.   It is heard of also in 1487, and again in 1504, when it drove the richer classes away from the city.

It is clear, also, that the infection was not confined to London; it was at Oxford and Exeter in 1503, and it was still recent enough at Gravesend in October, 1501, to prevent the young Princess Catherine of Aragon from landing there, so that she had to sleep on board the royal barge after "her great and long pain and travail upon the sea."

Sanitation.   Two sanitary measures mark the reign of Henry VII.: one an ordinance against the nuisance of the shambles in London and other walled towns, "and in the toune of Cambridge" (which was not walled); and the other a deter- mined attempt to put down the stews   The latter, in London, some eighteen houses on the Bankside across the water above London Bridge, each with a distinctive sign, such as the Cross Keys or the Cardinal's Hat, painted on its river front, were shut up in 1506 (they had been shut up once before in the reign of Henry V., and were closed once more at the instance of Latimer, in 1546).   Some regulation had, indeed, been introduced a few years before 1506, not in London only, but also in such provincial towns as Bristol and Gloucester, the latter of which, at a date between 1500 and 1504, was "too abomynable spokyn of in alle England and Walys," by reason of "the vicyous lyvyng of dyvers personez, as well of spyrytuell as temperall," with the exceeding number of immoral and disorderly women dwelling in every ward of the said town, and more especially by reason of "the abomynable levyng of prestez and other relygious within the same toune," who were too often found walking by night suspiciously or "onlawefully demeanyng" with the ill-reputed persons aforesaid. The Gloucester measures in restraint of these practices (long before the Reformation, be it observed) were avowedly modelled upon those already in force in the worshipful city of London and in the town of Bristol.

HITHERTO our acquaintance with the social life of medieval times has been confined to a study of the material conditions of existence. But these are of permanent value only in so far as they enable us to understand the thoughts and feelings and ideas which underlay the particular form of outward expression at any given period. Before, then, we drop our acquaintance with the men and women of medieval England it is important that we should dig a little below the surface of their lives. It is interesting to know something of the kind of houses in which they lived, of their churches and their furniture, of the food they ate, and the clothes they wore. But, behind these temporary manifestations lies unchangeable human nature with its hopes and fears, its passions, and its capacities This is the truly fruitful study; for it is by this and this alone that we can gauge our real progress in all that makes for that complex phenomenon which we call civilisation. There is no reason to despise the study of changing fashions. More perhaps than is commonly allowed, more certainly than often appears at first sight, are they the index of the thoughts within. The substitution of carpets for rushes and of forks for fingers may not mark any serious diminution in brutal crime, but it does denote a search after a refinement of outer life which must needs set its mark on the mode of expressing the ideas, if not on the texture of the ideas themselves. A thoughtful writer[1] reminds us that

Mrs. Bernard Bosanquet, "The Standard of Life," p. 17.

" there is nothing essentially progressive in comfort," and she adds that " if it has been attained before wider interests have been aroused, it may prove to be a more insuperable barrier to progress than poverty itself." It is to the condition of these " wider interests " during the closing centuries of the Middle Ages that we must for a short while turn our attention.

Size of the Communities. It is necessary to notice at the outset the absence from medieval surroundings of much that is of the very essence of modern life. In the first place, there were not ten communities throughout the length and breadth of England which were larger than a small country town of the present day. London, of course, led the way with a population of 40,000, Bristol may have had 12,000, Norwich a rather smaller number; but neither York, Coventry, Lincoln, Lynn, Gloucester, nor Salisbury (to mention the most prominent) could boast of more than 10,000 inhabitants. Thus, with the possible exception of London, so far as their occupations and manner of life were concerned, the dwellers in any medieval city or country town differed in degree rather than in kind from the population of the neighbouring villages. There would be rather more buying and selling in a market town than elsewhere ; but there, no less than in the adjacent hamlets, the main interest of the inhabitants would be in agriculture. In the undeveloped condition of foreign trade the home harvest was a question of the utmost importance. The constantly recurring famines show the absolute self-dependence of the medieval population for the primary necessaries of life. But an agricultural population spends the greater part of its life in the open air, and the general prevalence of agricultural pursuits accounts, even more than the absence of foreign trade, for the slow advance in the material comforts of existence. Among such absent comforts **Life in Public.** nothing strikes us so much as the absence of privacy. Work, family life, religious observances were all carried on in company with the whole household or villages. Under these circumstances character conforms to a prevailing type, individuality is suppressed for all except the strongest characters. Again, in an agricultural society social ranks are far more clearly and sharply divided than when commercial wealth is setting a new standard of income and expenditure. Under such conditions familiarity between classes is far easier than in modern life. Chaucer's Knight can chaff with the other pilgrims and interfere to compose their quarrels because his position is assured and he has no fear lest his dignity should be compromised.

Now, the combination of clear social distinctions with the utmost publicity in daily life resulted in the prevalence of ceremony. Nearly every function in life was reduced to rules of the minutest kind, which often lost their basis in reason and became mere arbitrary dicta, accepted on authority and maintained for their own sake. Hence the numerous treatises, noticed in a previous section (p. 177), which contained minute directions on behaviour for every class and under every condition. Medi- **Ceremony.**

ORGAN.
(*Luttrell Psalter.*)

eval writers certainly held that " conduct " (in the sense of outward behaviour) " is three-fourths of life." They even sought for it a supernatural sanction. One rhyming teacher tells us that

" Clerkis that the vii artes canne
Seyn that curtesy from hevyn come;
When Gabryelle our lady grette,
And Elizabeth with Mary mette."

Another writer impresses on parents the duty of teaching children " in learning and good manners, for it is a nye servyce to God, it getteth favour in the syghte of men, it multiplyeth goods, and increaseth thy good name, it promoteth to prayer by which

God's grace is obtayned, if thus they bee brought up in vertue, good manners and godly learning." But, in comparison with modern ideas, book learning formed a small part of education. It is true that, even outside the clerkly ranks, reading and writing were not uncommon accomplishments, and perhaps even books in manuscript were more attainable than we usually imagine. Large numbers of copyists were at work in every monastery and nunnery throughout the land. Moreover, for those intending to be clerks, there were the monastic and cathedral schools whence boys proceeded to the Universities. For townsfolk there were, even before the middle of the fifteenth century, some score of free and endowed Grammar Schools. But the members of the knightly class chiefly obtained their education in the families of friends of their own rank. Here they would learn from the priest enough Latin to follow the services of the Church. For the rest, the chief part of their training would consist of accomplishments; and the aim of the good squire would be to know how to serve his lord in the bedroom and the hall, and how to make his society acceptable to the ladies. Thus the ceremonial side of life was esteemed above every other. This did not prevent the outbreak of violence any more than the social ostracism of anyone who is drunk at table prevents all men of good position from ever imbibing more than they ought. But the minuteness of the ceremony and the importance attached to it for its own sake must have been a real check on the instincts of the "natural" man. The idylls of ignorant authors in the last century invested the life of savage men with a glamour which a more travelled age has ruthlessly dispelled. We now know that, instead of being the freest of human beings, as Rousseau imagined, primitive man is the most fettered, for he is in bondage to an immemorial custom, generally of the most minute and meaningless kind. But this bondage marks a stage in the history of civilisation. Some nations have been caught in the net of custom and have ceased to struggle. But to the progressive nations of the world there has come a time when, by one means or another, they have shaken themselves loose. Some by degrees have substituted new customs for old, others have suddenly at one blow stripped themselves of a garment which threatened to act like a Nessus-shirt upon their vital activities. The history of France since the Revolution shows how much the framework of a nation's life is due to a very gradual growth, and that, for such an historical setting, it is difficult to find an efficient substitute. Modern minds are apt to be impatient at the machinery of life: ends rather than means are kept before our eyes. It is worth remembering that the forging of custom, the reduction to routine, in fact machinery, forms the first step in the eradication of the purely selfish impulses of the animal part in man. The strength of those impulses accounts for the tightness of the bonds which were gradually formed for the purpose of holding them in check.

Undoubtedly the most important civilising agency in medieval times was the Christian Church. It took in hand the ordering of man's life from the cradle to the grave; it sought to teach him what he should think and to guide him in what he should do. Its splendid attempt to associate belief and practice deserved a better fate than it obtained. So long as the Christian Church was a sect in the Roman Empire, clergy and laity were mutually dependent. But when it became the accepted religion of the State and the Emperor used its organisation as one of the most effective means of police at his disposal, the clergy had less inducement to remain in close connection with the laity. Backed by the authority of the State they became dictators rather than guides. Indeed, the wholesale baptism of heathen tribes at the bidding of their chief, who had been led to substitute the Christian God for the deities and fetishes of his race, gave the missionary a position of material advantage which substantially affected his whole subsequent teaching. On the one side, forgetting, like many of his modern representatives, that the Church had gradually grown into the formulated system of belief of which he was himself possessed, he sought to impose it in all its details of doctrine and ritual upon his recent converts. It is a great and important question how far abstruse doctrinal points can be, or indeed need be, made plain to simple worshippers. At any rate, to an ignorant and superstitious people such an attempt is impossible by words alone. The Church resorted to concrete representations, and endeavoured not only to drive home the Bible story and the legends of the saints, but even to interpret the doctrines of the Trinity and of the Eucharist by means of material symbols. On the other side,

The Church and the World.

Christianity endeavoured, as far as possible, to accept and to consecrate already existing customs and institutions. Thus Pope Gregory, in answer to St. Augustine's queries, tells him to convert the pagan temples into Churches by sprinkling them with holy water, in order that the new converts might continue to worship in the usual places. Under such circumstances it need not perhaps astonish us that Raedwald of East Anglia, after his conversion, set up side by side in his temple one altar to the Christian God and another on which he might continue to offer sacrifice to demons. Again, the early Church found existing in the Roman Empire a highly localised system of religion. For the old heathen deities of

RESCUE BY THE VIRGIN OF A MONK FROM DROWNING (MS. Roy. 10 E. iv.).

grove and stream it substituted the Christian saints. But it is not altogether strange if in the midst of ignorant people the saints assumed a position not far removed from that hitherto occupied by the local gods.

The Sacraments.

But the attempt to spiritualise every action of the daily life reached its most characteristic form in the sacraments of the Church. Every important act of the individual became a sacrament. Birth into the material world was paralleled by the baptism which admitted into the Church; on the civil ordinance of marriage was superimposed the blessing of the Church which transformed it into a sacrament; to the dying, the sacrament of extreme unction formed the symbol of their passage from the ranks of the Church militant to those of the Church triumphant. The sacraments, however, were only a supreme attempt to represent spiritual acts and relations in a material form. The Church acted on the belief that symbolic acts performed with frequency and regularity would ultimately Religious Material-ism. induce faith in the doctrines which they symbolised. But among a people hide-bound by superstitions the insistence on the material side made what was intended to be a spiritual symbol into a mere fetish or magical formula endowed with a

THE DEVOUT THIEF AND HIS REWARD.
(From a Fresco in the Lady Chapel, Winchester Cathedral.)

mystical power which acted quite independently of the moral or spiritual condition of those who made use of it. Now, as all religious ordinances are symbolical of spiritual relations, this feeling of their supernatural effect extended to every department of religious life. Penance was a fetish which cancelled the original sinful act; relics were fetishes which wrought wonders and conferred benefits often irrespective of the will or intention of the person on whom they were wrought. On the translation of the relics of St. Martin of Tours in 887, two impotent beggars who lived comfortably on the profits of their infirmities determined to quit the district of Tours before the procession carrying the relics arrived, for fear lest they should be involuntarily healed. Their fears were well grounded; the relics reached the soil of Touraine before they quitted it, and they found themselves healed and their occupation gone. Nor did the power of the saints cease with their relics. Their devotees might always expect serviceable aid in moments of distress. A fresco in the Lady Chapel of Winchester Cathedral preserves the legend of a notorious thief who had always been careful to do reverence to the altar of the Virgin. He was caught and hanged; but on the third day he was found still alive, for the Virgin had upheld the feet of her very mechanical worshipper, and had prevented the rope from strangling him. Apparently the merit obtained from the veneration of a worshipper was transmissible. At any rate a lady whose veneration for St. Thomas of Canterbury caused her to be constantly ejaculating, "St. Thomas, have pity on us," taught it to her pet bird. The bird was carried off by a falcon. But on its uttering the words, the grip of the falcon relaxed, and the bird escaped unhurt to its mistress.

The Host as a Touchstone.

The greatest fetish of all was the sacrament of the Eucharist, and stories of its use as a test of innocence or guilt are painfully abundant. St. Paul's warning to the Corinthians that " he that eateth and drinketh unworthily eateth and drinketh damnation to himself," was accepted literally. A story of the fourteenth century tells us of a priest, an habitual drunkard and evil liver, who, when warned of the danger which he incurred by his daily celebration of the Mass and partaking of the consecrated elements, owned that he never consecrated the host, but that he carried about with him a small round piece of wood of the size of a wafer, which he pretended to be the body of the Lord. This employment of the greatest of the sacraments as a talisman or form of ordeal did not pass without occasional protest from scandalised and enlightened Churchmen; but the use to which Pope Gregory VII. put it in the closing scene of his triumph over the Emperor Henry IV.

gave an authority to the popular view of its efficacy which would override any number of verbal protests. After Gregory had accepted Henry's humiliation at Canossa, he celebrated Mass, and having consecrated the elements, he turned to the Emperor and, referring to the charges of simony and worse acts laid against the Pope by the Imperial party, declared his desire of making an appeal of his innocence to God. "Here," he concluded, "is the Lord's body; may this either clear me from all suspicion if I am innocent, or, if guilty, may God strike me with sudden death." The Emperor refused the papal challenge that he should submit to a similar test the charges made by the princes of Germany against him. Another class of stories illustrating the talismanic power of the consecrated elements shocks our gravity rather than our reason or our sense of reverence. Nothing less than a triumphant vindication of the power of the Church could result from the fortunate thought of the priest who, when the flames failed to consume a heretic, brought a consecrated host which at once successfully dissolved the spell. And we may well doubt whether the force of superstition could further go than in the story of the consecrated wafer which a woman put into her beehive in order to stop an epidemic among her bees. Whether it had the desired effect, we are not told; but the reverent insects built round it in wax a complete miniature chapel, including even an altar, on which they placed the sacred talisman.

To a great extent this materialisation of Christian ordinances was due to an attempt to meet and vanquish by a mightier magic the superstitions of races emerging from barbarism. In no race, probably has the supernatural occupied a larger part of their customs and beliefs than in the Teutonic race. The Church took over and consecrated as much of these customs as could in any way be harmonised with its own practices; the rest were condemned as magic, as an invocation of the powers of darkness. Not that the Church did not believe in the existence of such powers. Belief in the personality of the devil is amply warranted by Scripture. What is not warranted by either the Old or the New Testament is the medieval conception of the devil ruling over a kingdom of darkness in rivalry with God. This seems to have been an importation from the Jewish writers of the Captivity, whose contact with Persia inoculated them with

Dualism.

a belief in a dualistic system of creation. Here Ormuzd, the good
spirit, and Ahriman, the evil spirit, both self-existent, were
conceived as equally powerful rivals for the homage of mankind.
Now, ignorance is guided rather by terror than by love, or even
by self-interest; to the undisciplined mind the supernatural, the
unexpected, makes a stronger appeal than the ordinary phenomena of daily life. Of this the Church took full advantage;
the brutal unrestraint of the seigneur and the callous indifference of the degraded peasant were alike influenced by an appeal
to the awful powers of natural phenomena rather than to the
Christian ideal of loving service. "We cannot," says a learned
writer, "understand the motives and acts of our forefathers
unless we take into considera-
tion the mental condition
engendered by the consciousness of this daily and hourly
personal conflict with Satan."[1]
But the Christian theory of
the realm of Satan was not
the outcome only of practical
needs. The emergence of differences of speculative opinion
within the Christian fold—in
other words, the growth of
heresy—caused the gradual

ST. DUNSTAN AND THE DEVIL.
(Luttrell Psalter.)

formulation of the science of theology. The Church had to put
into words its views of the relations of God to man in every
detail of life. Nor did the Church's account of the matter
stop at the threshold of the grave. The speculative mind
of the independent thinker had penetrated to the life beyond
and the Church had unhesitatingly followed. Christ's kingdom
was not of this world, and those to whom He had committed
the care of that kingdom on this side of the grave would be
more likely than anyone else to know the fate that was
preparing for its friends and foes in the unseen world. The
promise to the apostles, "Whatsoever ye bind on earth shall
be bound in heaven," seemed to arm the successors of the
apostles with the requisite authority to speak with confidence
on so grave a subject.

[1] Lea, "History of the Inquisition," iii., 379.

The Temptation.

The Penalty.

The Tables Turned.

The Tempter Punished.

93   THE TEMPTATION OF A MONK (MS. Roy. 10 E. iv.).

. Theological speculation, then, combined with more practical motives to exalt the realm of Satan and the powers of darkness until they were regarded as equal in extent and influence to the kingdom of God. Thus all natural phenomena of a destructive kind—storms, famines, pestilences, and even eclipses—were regarded as manifestations of Satan's power. But these were exceptional and affected the world at large. The individual was touched through the arts of the sorcerer and the sorceress, who were the priests of devil-worship. Hence sorcery was treated with extraordinary leniency by the Church. In England the laws of some of the Anglo-Saxon kings dealt with it occasionally, but after the Norman Conquest it finds no place in the treatises of the great lawyers of the twelfth and thirteenth centuries. It was considered a matter for exorcism, not for punishment; for it was not regarded as fraud, but merely as the exercise of certain powers which their possessors only obtained by entering into an agreement with the devil and his servants. The opinions of the great minds of the thirteenth century are instructive on this point. Roger Bacon, the most enlightened writer of his age, acknowledges that much of magic is simply fraud; but he maintains that charms and spells are not useless under all circumstances, and that their efficacy depends on the aspect of the heavens under which they are made and used. Astrology was little less dangerous than magic; its denial of free will and its generally fatalistic tendency caused the orthodox Churchman to look askance at it (p. 110). Nevertheless, Roger Bacon, monk though he was, believed that the stars were the cause of human events, that the character of every man was shaped by the aspect of the heavens at his birth, and that the past and future could be read from suitably constructed astronomical tables. Thomas Aquinas, the greatest of medieval theologians, drew a distinction. Astrology was lawful for the prediction of natural events, such as drought or rain; but the denial of free will necessarily involved in the attempt to divine the future acts of men showed that any such attempt could only be undertaken at the instigation of the powers of darkness. All attempts to foretell the future came to be classed as sorcery.

In the fourteenth century arises the belief in witchcraft. "The world has probably never seen," says a writer already quoted,[1] " a society more vile than that of Europe in the fourteenth and fifteenth centuries." Hence may be traced the recrudescence of the gross superstitions of earlier ages, which Christianity had vainly endeavoured to repress. The thinly veiled belief in the dual government of the world led straight to the awful idea of compacts made with Satan. The stories, whencesoever derived, of the witches' sabbath or meeting, where every kind of sensual delight was indulged in, could not but attract a wretched peasantry sunk in ignorance and constantly on the verge of starvation. It is not astonishing that men so situated, reckless as regards the present and hopeless in view of the future, should attempt, by a transference of their allegiance to the king of the nether world, to obtain some alleviation from the miseries of their present existence. Thence arose all kinds of strange practices—unmeaning, unexplainable, profane, disgusting, and even positively obscene. It is difficult to believe that the most enlightened men of the age really regarded these practices as injurious to those against whom they were aimed. Yet there is perhaps no set of cases about which we possess more circumstantial details than about cases of witchcraft. We are tempted to think that the charges alleged in the condemnation of an offender were merely convenient pretexts advanced by the ecclesiastical judges for getting rid of some otherwise obnoxious person. But the majority of the victims were drawn from the poorest classes, out of whom nothing in the shape of bribes or forfeited goods was to be obtained. The truth is that to those accused of witchcraft torture was as a matter of course applied, and, in order to prevent continued torture, the victims confessed whatever their inquisitors desired. The confession, once made, was adhered to: for, the confessor knew that he was doomed and that a retractation would only prolong his sufferings. Hence, when his confession was read in public at his condemnation, he affirmed it. Often, too, torture and imprisonment had produced mental derangement, so, that the victims actually came to believe the things of which they were accused. Moreover, the Church taught that the reception of the sacrament of extreme unction was necessary to salvation. This was only granted to contrite and repentant sinners, and the desire to be eligible for it would induce the confessed wizard to stick to the last to the truth of his confession.

---

[1] Lea, "History of the Inquisition," iii., 642.

But this exaltation of the realm of Satan may have been partly due to less creditable motives than the exigencies of dogmatic theology and the need of finding arguments to entice barbarians into the Christian fold. The power of the Church to rescue mankind from the clutches of demons came from the authority with which its officers, the priests, were endowed. The more formidable the obstacle to be overcome, the greater must be the power of those by whose help alone it can be overcome. The instruments of priestly assistance were the ordinances of the Church and the symbols of spiritual things which her recognition had consecrated. The option of withholding the absolution or the sacraments placed in the priests' hands the keys of both worlds alike. It was easier to govern by hard and fast rules than to attempt to discover the mode of action suitable to each case. Implicit obedience was the only virtue recognised: faith became all in all. Unity was the one thing essential to the life of the Church, the one weapon in which lay her hope of successful resistance. That unity must be obtained at the sacrifice of all the humaner virtues. Those who attempt any compromise with the powers which the Church does not recognise must be stamped out as dangerous heretics. The immense emphasis laid upon unity produced two deplorable results. In the first place, a perfectly artificial and arbitrary standard of conduct was created. Right acting was entirely subordinated to correct belief, and the whole of the moral life was subjected to purely mechanical tests. Even the deepest mysteries were portrayed in material forms. Symbolical acts were not merely outward manifestations of faith and aids to the

Faith and Morals. inner workings of the heart. With the mass of worshippers the heart came to play no part in the matter: their responsibility ended with the performance of the appropriate symbolical act; such due performance was the test of a lively faith. This is illustrated by the working of the whole penitential system of the Church: the pardon of sins as undertaken by her ministers became a mere matter of arithmetical calculation. But, in the next place, the Church was not content with the censorship of outward conduct. She insisted, quite rightly, that it is not the act but the mental process that is of primary importance. But with a fatuous disregard of the sense of relation, she jumbled up wrong-doing and wrong-thinking until in her eyes wilful sin was

THE FORTERESSE DE LA FOY. (MS. Roy. 17 F. vi)

[To face p. 772.

more pardonable than earnest heresy. A man who took interest
for money, knowing that it was wrong, committed an act which
could be condoned by a penance ; whereas his belief that he had
done no wrong would brand him unmistakably as a heretic.
The priestly view of the relation between morals and faith found

ST. MICHAEL WEIGHING A SAINT AGAINST A DEVIL.
(*From a Fresco in South Leigh Church, Oxfordshire.*)

allowance for every kind of actual sin ; but difference of opinion
was only to be met by ruthless extermination.

Conceive the effect of this all-pervading atmosphere on the
life of the individual. He must duly perform certain acts
enjoined by the Church as the conditions of entrance to the
future world; he must not think any thoughts except such as
were warranted by the Church on pain of condemnation in this
world. Of course, occasional protests are not wanting against
this materialistic and unexpansive attitude. But it was the

penalty paid by Christianity for taking over the heathen world wholesale; and if it did not in any real sense Christianise the vast barbarian hordes on whom it was impressed, the strong restraining influence of an universal machinery played no inappreciable part in the process of civilising them. An essential element in the success of this work was the fact that its chief instruments were members of a caste. Christianity is by no means the only form of faith which has won much of the acceptance accorded to it in consequence of the asceticism practised by its missionaries. Among the early Christians the conversion of one member of a household to the faith must have made family life henceforth impossible in that household.

The Church and the Home.
Hence must have grown up a dangerous comparison between family life as such and the life in the Church as such. Family life was regarded as a hindrance rather than an instrument. A celibate clergy encouraged celibacy in others. Cut off from legitimate joys of family life and yet retaining their manly instincts and ideals, the Christian priesthood concentrated its affection and adoration on the Virgin Mother of the Lord. The little told us of her actual character and history left all the greater scope for imagination ; and legend gathered round her and was embodied in the commemoration and worship of the Church, until, in the minds of the devout multitude, she seemed to dispute the pre-eminence with her divine Son. The doctrine of the Immaculate Conception, first invented in the twelfth century, raised her even doctrinally almost to a level with divinity. In vain St. Bernard pointed out that if the doctrine that the Virgin was conceived without sin was necessary for the full honour of our Lord, it would seem logically necessary to postulate the same condition of birth in the persons of all her direct ancestors. The result was significant. Different saints were sometimes supposed to be guardians of different classes of worshippers, and were approached accordingly. But the Virgin was by far the most powerful of the saintly mediators, and the particular miraculous powers attributed to individual saints were, when the Virgin was in question, attributed to particular images of her. It is difficult to describe this attribution of miraculous gifts to the actual image otherwise than as idolatry of the grossest kind.

A celibate priesthood who added to the worship of the God-Man that of his Virgin Mother would scarcely be likely to be enthusiastic about matrimony.   To begin with, it was a heathen **Marriage.** ordinance.   At first the Church contented itself with sanctifying by a religious ceremony the marriage of its own members.   As it grew in power the religious ceremony became a sacrament ; and the parallel found to marriage in the union of Christ and the Church caused the ministers of that Church to define with increasing exactness the terms under which alone the matrimonial bond would receive their sanctification.   For, in the next place, the extreme laxity of family relations under the Roman Empire produced a state of society against which the whole

ST. ANTHONY IN THE DESERT.
(*Luttrell Psalter.*)

Christian conception was a standing protest.   Our own marriage service bears witness to the feelings of the Church with regard to the uses of matrimony.   " First, it was ordained for the pro-creation of children . . . . secondly, it was ordained for a remedy against sin."   It was the appointed physical means of propagat-ing the race: it was allowed by the Church for fear of something worse.   The purely animal side of the relationship was thrown out into relief by a body to whom were denied the comfort and consolation of a lawful helpmeet and of children born in wedlock. Hence the lawgivers of the Church did not hesitate to fence round the ecclesiastical sanction of matrimony with restrictions whose rigour only too plainly bore witness to the lax customs of the Roman Empire. Christ had given to His disciples little but general principles to follow out in their application; but He might be said to have gone out of His way in order to emphasise the permanence of the matrimonial bond; and His words were interpreted in all their literal strictness. Thus, divorce was entirely forbidden; while the archetype found in the matrimonial connection to Christ and His Church caused second marriages to be viewed with extreme repugnance. In the matter of divorce the civil law and the law of the Church were for a long time in antagonism; but the canon law ultimately prevailed; and in the twelfth century the laws of the State as well as of the Church forbade, under all circumstances, a dissolution of the matrimonial bond. A laudable desire to protect the sacredness of family life produced the table of degrees of affinity within which marriage was forbidden by the Church; but the dispensations freely granted by the Pope to kings and nobles for all kind of un-canonical unions seemed to teach subsequent generations that the law of social convenience was of more importance than the maintenance of an inflexible moral standard. It was in keeping with these views that while unlicensed marriage within the pro-hibited degrees was regarded as incestuous intercourse, the cohabitation of unrelated persons came in time to be atoned for by subsequent marriage, and their children born out of wedlock were even regarded as legitimate. England was the only country of Western Christendom where the legislators refused to accept this relaxation of the earlier reading of the law.

It would be untrue, then, to say that the Church discounten-anced matrimony; but a society of celibates reinforced by communities of monks and nuns, would not be likely to wax enthusiastic about its delights. The carnal pleasure would be the only side of it which they could understand; for, the joy that comes of permanent companionship was denied to them. Hence the forbidding aspect in which ecclesiastical writers often presented the alliance. St. Paul had led the way when he wrote that "he that giveth (the virgin) in marriage doeth well; but he that giveth her not in marriage doeth better." St. Jerome's tirades are well known: to him marriage was at best a vice; all that we can do is to excuse and purify it. Tertullian, in the excess of an unreasoning zeal, tells his readers that "celibacy must be chosen though the human race perish in consequence;" while St.

Augustine limits himself to comparing celibates to dazzling stars, their parents to stars in which light had been extinguished. It would be tedious to follow the opinions of writers down the ages. It is more to the purpose to inquire whether the tone of ecclesiastical authors was pitched in the same key when the Church had acquired a complete hold over the mind and conscience of Western Europe. Direct evidence is naturally scanty. Ecclesiastics, from the Pope downwards, set such an unedifying example of illicit connections with the other sex that it scarcely lay in their mouths to disparage a state of life which, compared to their own clandestine unions, was as a running stream of clear water to a muddy stagnant pool. But occasionally professional zeal is still found to overcome the shame that should have taught reticence and the importance of example. From the end of the thirteenth century comes a homily addressed to youthful nuns and bearing the suggestive title of "Heli Meidenhod" (Holy Maidenhood). In his desire to impress upon the young girls committed to his charge the superiority of the celibate life, the writer sticks at no kind of argument that may make them personally shrink from the matrimonial bond. Married life is a life of bondage; there are no compensations for its innumerable hardships. The prurient imagination of the writer seeks beforehand to rob even maternity of all its joy by dwelling on the pains and discomforts that attend it at all stages. Matrimony, says in effect the fanatical celibate, is no doubt allowable, but its necessity is much to be regretted. In the scale of candidates for heaven the married take distinctly the lowest place; "its fruit," in the words of the parable, is only "thirty-fold in heaven." Despite what the Church ordinarily taught about the holy estate of matrimony, he practically denies that it is an ordinance of God. "If thou askest," he says, "why God created such a thing to be, I answer thee, God created it never such; but Adam and Eve turned it to be such by their sin and marred our nature." Thus it is definitely a downward step, a fallen state. "Hence," he continues in another passage, "was wedlock legalised in holy Church as a bed for the sick, to sustain the unstrong," and he adds, "thus, then, the wedded sing, that through God's goodness and mercy of His grace, though they have driven downwards, they halt in wedlock." It is not altogether surprising that he exclaims, "well were it (for brides) were they on the day of their bridal borne to be buried"; for, as he announces in another passage, "all other sins are nothing but sins, but (matrimony) is sin and besides denaturalises thee." Judged from this standpoint widowhood is an escape from temptation to sin. The fruit in heaven of widowhood is sixty-fold and the widows' song is " to glorify their Lord and thank Him heartily that His power kept them chaste in purity, that they had tried the filth of the flesh and that He had granted them in this world to amend their sins." These estimates lead to the final estimate that " Maidenhood with a hundred-fold overpasses both " marriage and widowhood. It " is a virtue above all virtues and to Christ the most acceptable of all." " To sing that sweet song," says the author elsewhere, and " that heavenly music which no saints may sing but maidens only in heaven . . . the maidens' song is . . . common to them with the angels. In their circle is God Himself ; and His dear Mother, the precious maiden, is hidden in that blessed company of gleaming maidens, nor may any but they dance and sing."

It might with some truth be argued that this did not represent the ordinary teaching of the medieval Church. A century later Chaucer's " Parson's Tale " deals with the same subject. Its original author will not be accused of any undue partiality for the Church : the satirist who drew the pictures of the monk, the friar, the prioress, the summoner of the Canterbury Tales, held no brief on behalf of the ecclesiastical order and its views of life. We should expect that the " Tale " or sermon put into the mouth of his ideal ecclesiastic, the " Poure Persone of a toun," would contain the writer's own views on morals and religion. Unfortunately, critics seem to be agreed that the " Parson's Tale " does not come down to us in the precise shape in which it left the pen of Chaucer, and there has been some " cooking " at the hands of too officious ecclesiastics. It is perhaps impossible to decide now how much of the sermon as it stands is due to Chaucer, how much to the later interpolaters There are expressions in which we can trace the same tone of thought as, if not the interpolation of the actual words of, the fanatical pamphlet of a century previous. The fruit of maidenhood is still a hundredfold. In the " poor parson's " words, no less than in those of his predecessor, chastity is " the most precious life that is ": the Virgin is the spouse of Jesus Christ,

the life of angels; " she is the preising of this world, and she is
as the martyrs in egalitee," for " Virginitee bare our Lord Jesus
Crist, and virgin was himself." Again, it is quite in the spirit

AN INTERPRETATION OF THE PARABLE OF THE SOWER (MS. Arundel 44).
(Showing the greater blessedness of the single life.)

of the author of " Heli Meidenhod " that the effect of marriage is
described as a change of " deadly sinne into venial sinne betwene
hem that ben wedded," and it is enjoined that " a man should

love his wife by discretion, patiently and attemprely, and then is she as though it were his suster." A more modern, although still a strictly ecclesiastical, note is struck in the stress laid on the sacredness of the matrimonial bond. Not only is it "a ful grete sacrament" which "betokeneth the knitting together of Crist and holy chirche," but, contrary to the low view of its origin entertained by the previous writer, "it was made of God himself in Paradis, and confermed by Jesu Crist, for God wold himself be borne in mariage: and for to halowe mariage he was at a wedding." Again, we should feel nothing but appreciative acquiescence in the proof offered for the consideration which a man should observe towards his wife. God, says the writer, did not at the first creation of woman make her out of the head of Adam; "for she should not claim to gret lordshippe," nor out of the feet of Adam, "for she should not be beholden too lowe"; but He "made woman of the rib of Adam, for woman shuld be felow unto man." But despite these tributes to the merits of matrimony it is an ecclesiastical judgment that is at work, and, if we are scandalised, we should not be astonished to find that the author compares the breach of the matrimonial bond to the plundering of a church and the theft of a chalice, though, with the object of enhancing the heinousness of the sin, he allows that it is worse than either of these unpardonable ecclesiastical crimes.

Celibacy.   There is, then, no substantial difference of opinion on the subject of marriage between these two writers, who in point of time are a century and a half apart. Such actual depreciation of marriage is, however, rare; more commonly the ecclesiastical author confines his eloquence to a praise of virginity, which, in the fervour of its rhetoric, shows only too clearly that in his opinion the married have deliberately chosen the worse part. It has been suggested that Chaucer's "Parson's Tale" is an adaptation of a French treatise, "Le somme des Vices et des Vertues," composed in 1279. That treatise was perhaps first introduced to English readers in the celebrated "Ayenbite of Inwyt" (p. 125), which was finished in 1340, and is said to be a literal translation of the French original. Here a considerable space is devoted to the question of chastity in all its meanings; and while the author states, as did Chaucer after him, that "spoushod . . is a stat of greate autorité, for God hit made ine Paradis terestre," he yet compares the state of the celibate to that of the angels, identifies maidenhood with the treasure of the field which forms the subject of Christ's parable, and quotes with approval St. Jerome's exaltation of it above all other virtues.

The earlier treatises in praise of virginity must have been addressed, like modern temperance lectures, to an approving audience. They were written by ecclesiastics for ecclesiastical readers. This is also true of the violent little pamphlet on "Heli Meidenhod." But the French treatise, though the work of Friar Levens, was written for the use of Philip III. of France ;

THE SIEGE OF THE CASTELL D'AMOUR.
(Luttrell Psalter.)

the author of the "Ayenbite," an Augustinian Canon from Canterbury, addressed his countrymen in general; while, whatever may have been the position and object of Chaucer's interpolaters, the poet's desire in the original cast of the sermon must have been merely to make his parson speak in character. The views of the Church, then, were sufficiently well known. So, unfortunately, were the acts of individual Churchmen. The sanctity of family life owes much to the early Christians; nothing to the doctrines or practice of the medieval Church. A system, in which betrothal is regarded as of the same binding force as the ceremonial of marriage itself, in which divorce is impossible under all circumstances, while subsequent marriage legitimatises children born out of wedlock, lays an overwhelming stress on the outward forms of life which has been seen to be characteristic of the whole attitude of the medieval Church. But the conduct of too many ecclesiastics in their relations to the other sex seemed to teach that, provided no bond was entered into, all things were allowable. How was it possible to believe that the Church taught respect for the sanctity of family life when it was not an unknown thing for the parishioners in self-defence to compel a new incumbent to bring with him a female companion? Truly man's instinct in this case, chastened as it had been by the teaching of the early Christian Church, is sometimes stronger than the precepts of a powerful organisation.

The Effect on Morals. This belittling of earthly love had a serious effect on contemporary morals. It is to this attitude of the Church that an interesting modern writer has attributed what he calls the "love-longing," the worship of the abstract conception of love, which seems to beset polite society in the closing centuries of the Middle Ages. The tone of chivalry as conceived in the fourteenth century, rings hollow on a modern ear, but we must consider it as sufficiently serious at the time which gave it birth. Knights took all kinds of impossible vows; their intentions and acts all bore reference to the desired favour of the weaker sex. The fair lady might be the cause or she might be merely the occasion of valiant deeds; she might already be a wife or she might even be non-existent except in the imagination of the ardent warrior. From his first initiation in arms the knight was taught to consider that the mainspring of all he did was love. This love, however, when put to the test, proved to be little else than mere sensual desire: to judge from contemporary poems and romances, the first thought of every knight, on finding a lady unprotected and alone, was to do her violence; while almost invariably the general theme of the story set forth by the minstrel for the amusement of the lord was not merely love, but intrigue of the basest sort.

And if this was the moral standard of the gently nurtured classes, the bourgeois and the peasant would appear to us little better than savages. They shared with their social superiors a

---

[1] *See* Chaucer's "Knight's Tale."

keen interest in such brutal sports as bear-baiting, cock-fighting, and the excitement of the bull-ring.   But the men and
women lived completely separate lives.   Of course the men
drank ; but their wives with similar results frequented the taverns
in parties with their female "gossips."   In the deliciously skip-
ping verses of a medieval song; one such "gossip" discussing
with her fellows where the best wine is to be found, remarks :

> I knowe a drawght of mery-go-downe,
> The best it is in all thys towne;

adding characteristically,

> But yet wold I not, for my gowne,
> My husband it wyst, ye may me trust.

The language of the women, too, is represented by contemporary
writers as coarse and profane in the ex-
treme.   The sly satire of the Miracle plays
gives us in Noah's wife the picture of a
typical shrew of the bourgeois class who
is as ready with her fist as with her
tongue.   In some oft-quoted passages of
the Chester plays she is represented as
withstanding for some time the united
efforts of her husband and sons to get
her into the ark.   She refuses to leave
her "gossips". behind to be drowned, and
they even propose to go and have a last
drink together.   When Shem ultimately
brings his mother in, not perhaps altogether without some employment of force,
Noah somewhat injudiciously utters a
triumphant "Welcome, · wife, into this

A MASTERFUL WIFE.
(*Luttrell Psalter.*)

boat," to which the wife responds, "And have thou that for
thy note (nut) !"   The resounding slap which illustrates her
words draws from the long-suffering patriarch the exclamation,
"A! ha! marry, this is hot."   In the Towneley collection of
plays Noah is as violent as his wife.   When he first tells her
of coming. disaster she taunts him for being always haunted
with indefinable fears ; and his threat to stop her tongue with
a beating ends in a regular bout of fisticuffs.   Here she refuses
to enter the ark until she has finished some spinning that

she has on hand. Noah, with a general admonition to husbands
to chastise their wives' tongues "whiles they are young," takes
the whip to her; and the scrimmage that ensues is only ended

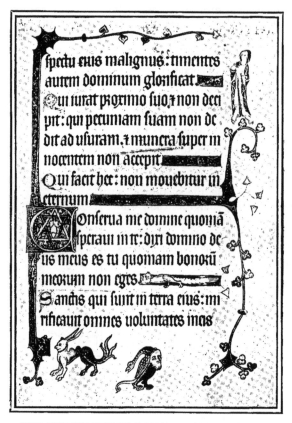

PAGE FROM THE LUTTRELL PSALTER, SHOWING GROTESQUES.

in response to the remonstrances of their children. Those for
whose amusement such scenes were interpolated lived rough
lives and fed their minds on coarse thoughts. Not that we
have outlived the attraction of such things; but at least we

GROTESQUES.
(*Luttrell Psalter and MS. Roy. 2 B. vii.*)

94

need not, perhaps, regard the equivalents among us as typical of modern life.

But it is only fair to add in conclusion that, side by side with the childishness or brutality of the popular conceptions which we have had to notice, there frequently existed a delicate sense of humour and a fine perception of the artistic value of the grotesque. That the medieval monk had a keen sympathy for the animal

BIRD MONSTER. (*Luttrell Psalter.*)

kingdom and a quick eye for its humorous aspects is attested by multitudes of illuminations as well as of legends of the saints. The edifying stories embodied in the medieval Books of Beasts probably descend in part from types furnished by the improving literature of decadent, but still ethical, Greece. The medieval monk knew his pets better, and could draw most of them with marvellous delicacy and truth. Like his fel-

RABBIT MONSTER. (*Luttrell Psalter.*)

low-artist in stone, moreover, his fancy took him far beyond such crudities as those of the popular drama. In the gargoyles and other sculptured ornaments of multitudes of churches, and in hundreds of marginal drawings[1] in MSS., there is a wealth of extravagant imagination and of subtle suggestiveness unsurpassed even among the vastly greater variety of material and opportunity afforded by our widened and crowded modern world.

[1] Frequently in Latin Psalters, presumably for the benefit of their lay owners during the chanting of the Psalms.

AUTHORITIES. 1485–1509.

General ; Contemporary.—Polydore Vergil, *Historia Anglica* (a translation published by the Camden Society), written between 1509 and 1534, and largely used by Hall, *Lancaster and York*, published 1542 ; *Works* of Bernard André, Henry VII.'s poet laureate (Rolls Series) ; the Venetian *Relation* of Francesco Capello and the London *Chronicle of the Grey Friars* (Camden Society) ; Wriothesley's *Chronicle*, Vol. I., ed. by W. D. Hamilton (Camden Society) ; the records in the Rolls Series and the State Papers, especially the volumes of extracts from the Archives at Simancas. Bacon's *Life of Henry VII.* has some of the peculiar value of a contemporary account. *Modern.*— Besides the ordinary histories (*e.g.* Bright, Green, Lingard), we have Gairdner's *Henry VII.* (Twelve Statesmen Series) and *Memorials of Henry VII.* (Rolls Series) ; Seebohm's *Oxford Reformers ;* Busch, *England under the Tudors*, 1895 ; Stubbs on Henry VII. in his *Seventeen Lectures on Medieval and Modern History.*

Religion.—Polydore Vergil and the Venetian *Relation (see* above), *The Norwich and Southwell Visitations* (Camden Society) ; Erasmus, *Colloquies ;* Lupton, *Life of Colet ;* Hook, *Lives of the Archbishops of Canterbury ;* Stubbs, *Lectures on Medieval and Modern History ;* Gasquet, *English Monasteries. See* also the authorities for the history of the Universities cited below.

Law, as in Chap. VI.—*Warfare* and *Naval Matters* as in Chap. VII.—*Architecture and Art* as in Chaps V. and VII., with the addition of Woltmann and Woermann, *History of Painting ;* Woltmann, *De Joh. Holbein ;* Walpole, *Anecdotes of Painters ;* Nichol, *Contemporaries and Successors of Holbein*, in *Archæologia*, Vol. XXXIX.

Discovery.—Hakluyt's *Voyages*, Harrisse's *Discovery of North America.*

The Universities.—More, *Epist. ad Dorpium ;* Stapleton, *Tres Thomæ :* other lives of More, Colet, Erasmus ; Maxwell Lyte, *University of Oxford ;* Seebohm, *Oxford Reformers.*

History of Printing.—Hessels, *Gutenberg : Was he the Inventor of Printing?* (London, 1882) ; A. Bernard, *De l'Origine de l'Imprimerie ;* Blades, *Life of Caxton ;* Th. de Vinne, *The Invention of Printing ;* Encycl. Brit., art. *Typography ;* Ottley, *Inquiry Concerning the Invention of Printing ;* E. Gordon Duff, *Early Printed Books.*

Scottish Literature in the Fourteenth and Fifteenth Centuries.—B. ten Brink, *Geschichte der Englischen Litteratur*, Bd. II., Th. II., 1893 ; Alois Brandl, *Mittelenglische Litteratur*, in Paul's *Grundriss der germanischen Philologie*, Bd. II., Abth. I., Lief. 6 (1892) ; H. Morley, *English Writers*, Vols. VI. and VII. : Dr. J. A. H. Murray, *The Dialect of the Southern Counties of Scotland*, Phil. Soc. Transactions, 1870–72 ; Schipper, *Englische Metrik ; Morte Arthur*, ed. E. Brock, E.E.T.S., 1875 ; Barbour, *The Bruce*, ed. Skeat, E.E.T.S., 1870, etc. : *Barbours . . . Legenden-Sammlung nebst den Fragmenten seines Trojaner-Krieges*, ed. Horstmann, Heilbronn, 1881–2 (criticised by P. Buss in *Anglia*, IX., 493 ff.) : H. Herschell, *Darstellung der Flexionslehre in John Barbour's Bruce*, Leipzig (a dissertation) : E. Köppel, "Die Fragmente von Barbour's Trojanerkreig," in *Engl. Studien*, X., 373 ff. : E. Regel, *An Inquiry into the Phonetic Peculiarities of Barbour's Bruce*, Gera, 1877 ; *Thomas of Erceldoune*, herausg. A. Brandl, Berlin, 1880 : *The Romance and Prophecies of Thomas of Erceldoune*, ed. J. A. H. Murray, E.E.T.S., 1875 ; *Sir Tristrem*, herausg. Eugen Kolbing, Heilbronn, 1882 : *Sir Tristrem*, ed. G. E. McNeill ; King James I., *The Kingis Quair*, ed Skeat ; Henry the Minstrel, *Schir William Wallace*, ed. Moir, 3 pts. (the last three pub by the Scottish Text Society, 1884–86) ; Robert Henryson, *Poems and Fables*, ed. Laing, Edin., 1865 ; Andrew of Wyntown, *Orygynale Cronykil of Scotland*, ed. D. Laing, 3 vols. (Historians of Scotland Series, 1871, etc.) ; Dunbar, *Poems*, ed. Small, introd. by Æ. Mackay (Scott. Text Soc.) : Dunbar, *Poems*, ed. Schipper, in *Denkschriften d. k. Akademie d. Wissenchaften*, Vienna, 1892 ; Schipper, *William Dunbar, sein Leben u. seine Geschichte*, Berlin, 1884 : J. Kaufmann, *Traité de la langue du Poète Écossais William Dunbar*, Inaug. Diss., Bonn, 1893 ; O. Hahn, *Zur Verbal- und Nominalflexion*, I., *bei R. Burns*, II. u. III., *bei den Schottischen Dichter (Wiss. Beilage zum Programm d. Victoriaschule)*, Berlin, 1887–9 ; Gawin Douglas, *Poetical Works*, ed.·

Small, Edin., 1802: also articles in *Dict. of Nat. Biography*, by F. Bayne, on Gawin Douglas, William Dunbar, and Henryson; by Æ. Mackay, on John Barbour and Henry the Minstrel; and by H. R. Tedder, on Thomas of Erceldoune. The "Abbotsford Series of Scottish Poets," ed. G. Eyre-Todd, is a pleasant popular edition of extracts and shorter poems from the more important authors.

History of the English Language.—Bernhard ten Brink, *Chaucer's Sprache und Verskunst* (Leipzig, 1884); A. J. Ellis, *Early English Pronunciation*, Early English Text Society, Extra Series; E. A. Freeman, *Norman Conquest*, Vol. V., Ch. xxv.; T. L. Kington-Oliphant, *Old and Middle English* and *The New English;* F. Kluge, *Geschichte der Inglischen Sprache*, in Paul's *Grundriss der Germanischen Philologie*, Bd. I., p. 780 ff. (Strassburg, 1890, etc.); Richard Morris, *The English Language* (Encyclopædia Britannica, ninth edition); L. Morsbach, *Ueber den Ursprung der neu-englischen Schriftsprache*, Heilbronn, 1888; W. W. Skeat, *Principles of English Etymology*, 2 series; Henry Sweet, *History of English Sounds*, and *A New English Grammar* (Clarendon Press, 1888 and 1892); Hermann Roemstedt, *Die engl. Schriftsprache bei Caxton* (Göttingen, 1891).

Industry and Commerce (besides the works referred to in previous chapters).—Riley, *Memorials of London Life in the Thirteenth, Fourteenth and Fifteenth Centuries;* Herbert, *History of the Livery Companies of London;* Mrs. Green's *Town Life in the Fifteenth Century;* Armstrong, *Treatise concerning the Staple and Commodities of the Realm;* Bacon, *Life of Henry VII.;* Brentano's *History and Developments of Guilds.*

Agriculture, Town Life, and Sanitary Science, as in Chap. VII.

Medieval Ideas.—Heli Meidenhod and a supplement, published by the Early English Text Society in 1866 and 1867 respectively (Nos. 18 and 23 in the series); *Babees Book* and other treatises, ed. F. T. Furnivall (E.E.T.S. also); Chaucer, *passim;* H. C. Lea, *History of the Inquisition;* Matthew Browne, *Chaucer's England.*

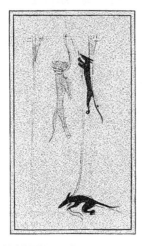

RATS HANGING A CAT (MS. Roy. 14 B. v.)

INDEX.

PRINTED BY CASSELL AND COMPANY, LIMITED, LA BELLE SAUVAGE, LONDON, E C.

Lightning Source UK Ltd.
Milton Keynes UK
UKHW021111160119
335572UK00008B/261/P